Life Science

Teacher's Edition and Resource

Book 3

interactive SCIENCE

Go to **MyScienceOnline.com** to experience science in a whole new way.

Interactive tools such as My Planet Diary connect you to the latest science happenings.

MY PLANET DIARY

- Search **Earth's Journal** for important science news from around the world.

- Use **Earth's Calendar** to find out when cool scientific events occur.

- Explore science **Links** to find even more exciting information about our planet.

- Visit **Jack's Blog** to be the first to know about what is going on in science!

PEARSON

Glenview, Illinois • Boston, Massachusetts • Chandler, Arizona • Upper Saddle River, New Jersey

Program Authors

You're an author!

As you write in this science book, your answers and personal discoveries will be recorded for you to keep, making this book unique to you. That is why you are one of the primary authors of this book.

 **In the space below, print your name, school, town, and state. Then write a short autobiography that includes your interests and accomplishments.**

YOUR NAME

SCHOOL

TOWN, STATE

AUTOBIOGRAPHY

Your Photo

Acknowledgments appear in the Program Guide, which constitutes an extension of this copyright page.

PEARSON

ISBN-13: 978-0-13-320934-1
ISBN-10: 0-13-320934-2
1 2 3 4 5 6 7 8 9 10 V052 15 14 13 12 11

ON THE COVER
Ghost Crabs
Although many crab species do use gills for gas exchange on land, gills are better suited for underwater respiration and generally pose challenges for terrestrial organisms. In crab species that spend part of their lives on land, other organs may supplement the gas-exchange function of the gills to varying degrees.

Program Authors

KATHRYN THORNTON, Ph.D.
Professor and Associate Dean, School of Engineering and Applied Science, University of Virginia, Charlottesville, Virginia
Selected by NASA in May 1984, Dr. Kathryn Thornton is a veteran of four space flights. She has logged more than 975 hours in space, including more than 21 hours of extravehicular activity. As an author on the *Scott Foresman Science* series, Dr. Thornton's enthusiasm for science has inspired teachers around the globe.

DON BUCKLEY, M.Sc.
Information and Communications Technology Director, The School at Columbia University, New York, New York
A founder of New York City Independent School Technologists (NYCIST) and long-time chair of New York Association of Independent Schools' annual IT conference, Mr. Buckley has taught students on two continents and created multimedia and Internet-based instructional systems for schools worldwide.

ZIPPORAH MILLER, M.A.Ed.
Associate Executive Director for Professional Programs and Conferences, National Science Teachers Association, Arlington, Virginia
Ms. Zipporah Miller is a former K–12 science supervisor and STEM coordinator for the Prince George's County Public School District in Maryland. She is a science education consultant who has overseen curriculum development and staff training for more than 150 district science coordinators.

MICHAEL J. PADILLA, Ph.D.
Associate Dean and Director, Eugene P. Moore School of Education, Clemson University, Clemson, South Carolina
A former middle school teacher and a leader in middle school science education, Dr. Michael Padilla has served as president of the National Science Teachers Association and as a writer of the National Science Education Standards. He is professor of science education at Clemson University.

MICHAEL E. WYSESSION, Ph.D.
Associate Professor of Earth and Planetary Science, Washington University, St. Louis, Missouri
An author on more than 50 scientific publications, Dr. Wysession was awarded the prestigious Packard Foundation Fellowship and Presidential Faculty Fellowship for his research in geophysics. Dr. Wysession is an expert on Earth's inner structure and has mapped various regions of Earth using seismic tomography. He is known internationally for his work in geoscience education and outreach.

Instructional Design Author

GRANT WIGGINS, Ed.D.
President, Authentic Education, Hopewell, New Jersey
Dr. Wiggins is a co-author of the "Understanding by Design Handbook". His approach to instructional design provides teachers with a disciplined way of thinking about curriculum design, assessment, and instruction that moves teaching from covering content to ensuring understanding.

The Association for Supervision of Curriculum Development (ASCD), publisher of the "Understanding by Design Handbook" co-authored by Grant Wiggins and registered owner of the trademark "Understanding by Design", has not authorized, approved or sponsored this work and is in no way affiliated with Pearson or its products.

Planet Diary Author

JACK HANKIN
Science/Mathematics Teacher, The Hilldale School, Daly City, California, Founder, Planet Diary Web site
Mr. Hankin is the creator and writer of Planet Diary, a science current events Web site. He is passionate about bringing science news and environmental awareness into classrooms and offers numerous Planet Diary workshops at NSTA and other events to train middle and high school teachers.

ELL Consultant

JIM CUMMINS, Ph.D.
Professor and Canada Research Chair, Curriculum, Teaching and Learning department at the University of Toronto
Dr. Cummins focuses on literacy development in multilingual schools and the role of technology in promoting student learning across the curriculum. *Interactive Science* incorporates essential research-based principles for integrating language with the teaching of academic content based on his instructional framework.

Reading Consultant

HARVEY DANIELS, Ph.D.
Professor of Secondary Education, University of New Mexico, Albuquerque, New Mexico
Dr. Daniels is an international consultant to schools, districts, and educational agencies. He has authored or coauthored 13 books on language, literacy, and education. His most recent works are *Comprehension and Collaboration: Inquiry Circles in Action* and *Subjects Matter: Every Teacher's Guide to Content-Area Reading*.

Reviewers

Contributing Writers

Edward Aguado, Ph.D.
Professor, Department of
Geography
San Diego State University
San Diego, California

Elizabeth Coolidge-Stolz, M.D.
Medical Writer
North Reading, Massachusetts

Donald L. Cronkite, Ph.D.
Professor of Biology
Hope College
Holland, Michigan

Jan Jenner, Ph.D.
Science Writer
Talladega, Alabama

Linda Cronin Jones, Ph.D.
Associate Professor of Science and
Environmental Education
University of Florida
Gainesville, Florida

T. Griffith Jones, Ph.D.
Clinical Associate Professor
of Science Education
College of Education
University of Florida
Gainesville, Florida

Andrew C. Kemp, Ph.D.
Teacher
Jefferson County Public Schools
Louisville, Kentucky

Matthew Stoneking, Ph.D.
Associate Professor of Physics
Lawrence University
Appleton, Wisconsin

R. Bruce Ward, Ed.D.
Senior Research Associate
Science Education Department
Harvard-Smithsonian Center for
Astrophysics
Cambridge, Massachusetts

Content Reviewers

Paul D. Beale, Ph.D.
Department of Physics
University of Colorado at Boulder
Boulder, Colorado

Jeff R. Bodart, Ph.D.
Professor of Physical Sciences
Chipola College
Marianna, Florida

Joy Branlund, Ph.D.
Department of Earth Science
Southwestern Illinois College
Granite City, Illinois

Marguerite Brickman, Ph.D.
Division of Biological Sciences
University of Georgia
Athens, Georgia

Bonnie J. Brunkhorst, Ph.D.
Science Education and Geological
Sciences
California State University
San Bernardino, California

Michael Castellani, Ph.D.
Department of Chemistry
Marshall University
Huntington, West Virginia

Charles C. Curtis, Ph.D.
Research Associate Professor
of Physics
University of Arizona
Tucson, Arizona

Diane I. Doser, Ph.D.
Department of Geological
Sciences
University of Texas
El Paso, Texas

Rick Duhrkopf, Ph.D.
Department of Biology
Baylor University
Waco, Texas

Alice K. Hankla, Ph.D.
The Galloway School
Atlanta, Georgia

Mark Henriksen, Ph.D.
Physics Department
University of Maryland
Baltimore, Maryland

Chad Hershock, Ph.D.
Center for Research on Learning
and Teaching
University of Michigan
Ann Arbor, Michigan

Jeremiah N. Jarrett, Ph.D.
Department of Biology
Central Connecticut State
University
New Britain, Connecticut

Scott L. Kight, Ph.D.
Department of Biology
Montclair State University
Montclair, New Jersey

Jennifer O. Liang, Ph.D.
Department of Biology
University of Minnesota–Duluth
Duluth, Minnesota

Candace Lutzow-Felling, Ph.D.
State Arboretum of Virginia &
Blanding Experimental Farm
Boyce, Virginia

Joseph F. McCullough, Ph.D.
Physics Program Chair
Cabrillo College
Aptos, California

Heather Mernitz, Ph.D.
Department of Physical Science
Alverno College
Milwaukee, Wisconsin

Sadredin C. Moosavi, Ph.D.
Department of Earth and
Environmental Sciences
Tulane University
New Orleans, Louisiana

David L. Reid, Ph.D.
Department of Biology
Blackburn College
Carlinville, Illinois

Scott M. Rochette, Ph.D.
Department of the Earth Sciences
SUNY College at Brockport
Brockport, New York

Karyn L. Rogers, Ph.D.
Department of Geological
Sciences
University of Missouri
Columbia, Missouri

Laurence Rosenhein, Ph.D.
Department of Chemistry
Indiana State University
Terre Haute, Indiana

Sara Seager, Ph.D.
Department of Planetary Sciences
and Physics
Massachusetts Institute of
Technology
Cambridge, Massachusetts

Tom Shoberg, Ph.D.
Missouri University of Science
and Technology
Rolla, Missouri

Patricia Simmons, Ph.D.
North Carolina State University
Raleigh, North Carolina

William H. Steinecker, Ph.D.
Research Scholar
Miami University
Oxford, Ohio

Paul R. Stoddard, Ph.D.
Department of Geology and
Environmental Geosciences
Northern Illinois University
DeKalb, Illinois

John R. Villarreal, Ph.D.
Department of Chemistry
The University of Texas–Pan
American
Edinburg, Texas

John R. Wagner, Ph.D.
Department of Geology
Clemson University
Clemson, South Carolina

Jerry Waldvogel, Ph.D.
Department of Biological Sciences
Clemson University
Clemson, South Carolina

Donna L. Witter, Ph.D.
Department of Geology
Kent State University
Kent, Ohio

Edward J. Zalisko, Ph.D.
Department of Biology
Blackburn College
Carlinville, Illinois

Museum of Science.

Special thanks to the Museum of
Science, Boston, Massachusetts,
and Ioannis Miaoulis, the
Museum's president and director,
for serving as content advisors for
the technology and design strand
in this program.

Teacher Reviewers

Master Teacher Board

Table of Contents

 Enter the Lab zone for hands-on inquiry.

Chapter Lab Investigation:
• Directed Inquiry: As the Stomach Churns, A breath of Fresh Air

Inquiry Warm-Ups: • Food Claims
• Observing a Heart • How Big Can You Blow Up a Balloon? • How Does Filtering a Liquid Change the Liquid?

Quick Labs: • Predicting Starch Content
• Direction of Blood Flow • Do You Know Your A-B-Os? • Modeling Respiration • Kidney Function • Perspiration

my science online.com

Go to MyScienceOnline.com to interact with this chapter's content. **Keyword: Managing Materials in the Body**

> **UNTAMED SCIENCE**
• Blood Lines

> **PLANET DIARY**
• Managing Materials in the Body

> **ART IN MOTION**
• Gas Exchange

> **INTERACTIVE ART**
• Nutrients at Work • The Heart
• The Respiratory System

> **VIRTUAL LAB**
• Up Close: Components of Blood

> **REAL-WORLD INQUIRY**
• A Digestive Journey

 Enter the Lab zone for hands-on inquiry.

Chapter Lab Investigation:
• Directed Inquiry: Ready or Not!
• Open Inquiry: Ready or Not!

Inquiry Warm-Ups: • How Simple Is a Simple Task? • What's the Signal? • What's the Big Difference? • Prenatal Growth

Quick Labs: • How Does Your Knee React? • Working Together • Making Models • Modeling Negative Feedback • Reproductive Systems • Looking at Hormone Levels • Way to Grow! • Egg-cellent Protection • Labor and Delivery

my science ONLINE

Go to MyScienceOnline.com to interact with this chapter's content.
Keyword: Controlling Body Processes

> **UNTAMED SCIENCE**
• Think Fast!

> **PLANET DIARY**
• Controlling Body Processes

> **ART IN MOTION**
• How a Nerve Impulse Travels • Stages of Prenatal Development

> **INTERACTIVE ART**
• The Nervous System • Negative Feedback in the Endocrine System • Reproductive Anatomy

> **REAL-WORLD INQUIRY**
• Sensing the World

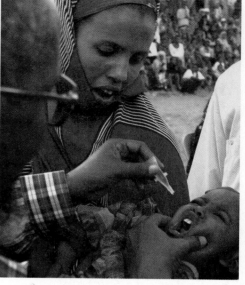

 Enter the Lab zone for hands-on inquiry.

Chapter Lab Investigation:
• Directed Inquiry: The Skin as a Barrier
• Open Inquiry: The Skin as a Barrier

Inquiry Warm-Ups: • The Agents of Disease • Which Pieces Fit Together? • How Does HIV Spread? • Types of Immunity • Causes of Death, Then and Now

Quick Labs: • How Do Pathogens Cause Disease? • How Does a Disease Spread? • Stuck Together • How Does HIV Attack? • What Will Spread HIV? • Modeling Active and Passive Immunity • What Substances Can Kill Pathogens? • What Happens When Air Flow Is Restricted? • What Does Sunlight Do to the Beads?

my science ONLINE.com

Go to MyScienceOnline.com to interact with this chapter's content.
Keyword: Fighting Disease

> **UNTAMED SCIENCE**
• Flu Detectives

> **PLANET DIARY**
• Fighting Disease

> **INTERACTIVE ART**
• Immune Response

> **ART IN MOTION**
• How Do Vaccines Work?

> **REAL-WORLD INQUIRY**
• Diagnosis Please, Doctor

> **VIRTUAL LAB**
• Up Close: Pathogens

Lab zone Enter the Lab zone for hands-on inquiry.

Chapter Lab Investigation:
• Directed Inquiry: World in a Bottle
• Open Inquiry: World in a Bottle

Inquiry Warm-Ups: • What's in the Scene?
• Populations • Can You Hide a Butterfly?
• How Communities Change

Quick Labs: • Organisms and Their Habitats
• Organizing an Ecosystem • Growing and
Shrinking • Elbow Room • Adaptations for
Survival • Competition and Predation • Type
of Symbiosis • Primary or Secondary

my science online.com

Go to MyScienceOnline.com to
interact with this chapter's content.
**Keyword: Populations and
Communities**

> **UNTAMED SCIENCE**
• Clown(fish)ing Around

> **PLANET DIARY**
• Populations and Communities

> **INTERACTIVE ART**
• Changes in Population • Animal Defense
Strategies

> **ART IN MOTION**
• Primary and Secondary Succession

> **REAL-WORLD INQUIRY**
• An Ecological Mystery

CHAPTER 16

Ecosystems and Biomes

 **Enter the Lab zone
for hands-on inquiry.**

△ **Chapter Lab Investigation:**
  • Directed Inquiry: Ecosystem Food Chains
  • Open Inquiry: Ecosystem Food Chains

△ **Inquiry Warm-Ups:** • Where Did Your
Dinner Come From? • Are You Part of a Cycle?
• How Much Rain Is That? • Where Does It
Live? • How Much Variety Is There?

△ **Quick Labs:** • Observing Decomposition
• Following Water • Carbon and Oxygen Blues
• Playing Nitrogen Cycle Roles • Inferring
Forest Climates • Dissolved Oxygen
• Modeling Keystone Species • Grocery Gene
Pool • Humans and Biodiversity

my science ONLINE.com

**Go to MyScienceOnline.com to
interact with this chapter's content.
Keyword: Ecosystems and Biomes**

▷ **UNTAMED SCIENCE**
• Give Me That Carbon!

▷ **PLANET DIARY**
• Ecosystems and Biomes

▷ **INTERACTIVE ART**
• Ocean Food Web • Water Cycle • Cycles of
Matter • Earth's Biomes

▷ **VIRTUAL LAB**
• Where's All the Food? • Life in a Coral Reef

Science™

Video Series: Chapter Adventures

Untamed Science created this captivating video series for **interactive**SCIENCE featuring a unique segment for every chapter of the program.

Featuring videos such as

Inquiry

Program Author of
Interactive Science

Associate Dean and Director of
Eugena P. Moore School of Education
Clemson University
Clemson, South Carolina

Michael J. Padilla, Ph.D.

"If students are busy doing lots of hands-on-activities, are they using inquiry skills? What is inquiry, anyway? If you are confused, you're not alone. Inquiry is the heart and soul of science education, with most of us in continuous pursuit of achieving it with our students."

What Is Inquiry?

Simply put, inquiry is thinking like a scientist —being inquisitive, asking why, and searching for answers. It's the process of taking a close examination of something in the quest for information.

Minds-on Inquiry

Students are naturally inquisitive; they want to learn, and they are always asking "Why?" They need practice and support to find answers for themselves. That's why they need experiences that are carefully scaffolded to guide them. We built that scaffolding right into this program.

Scaffolded Learning

The framework below illustrates a series of skill levels developed by educational psychologist Benjamin Bloom in the 1950s, later modified in the 1990s to reflect relevance to 21st century work. Look for the skills questions and tasks throughout the student book, scaffolded just right to provide students with the guidance and intellectual challenge they need.

Bloom's Taxonomy (adapted)

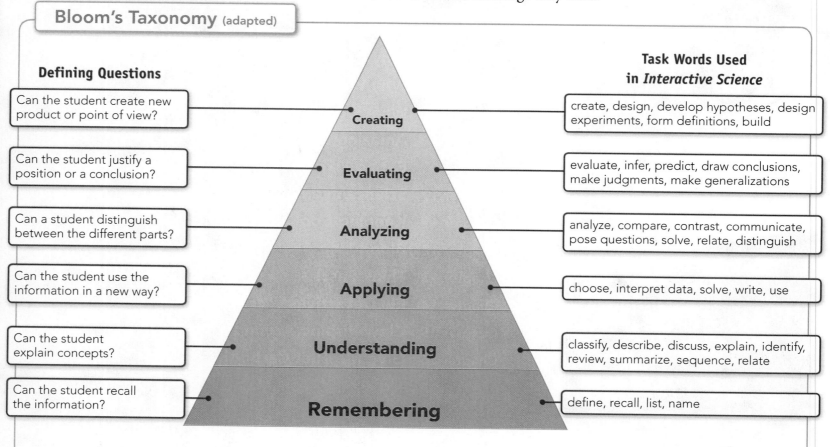

Defining Questions

Can the student create new product or point of view? — **Creating**

Can the student justify a position or a conclusion? — **Evaluating**

Can a student distinguish between the different parts? — **Analyzing**

Can the student use the information in a new way? — **Applying**

Can the student explain concepts? — **Understanding**

Can the student recall the information? — **Remembering**

Task Words Used in *Interactive Science*

create, design, develop hypotheses, design experiments, form definitions, build

evaluate, infer, predict, draw conclusions, make judgments, make generalizations

analyze, compare, contrast, communicate, pose questions, solve, relate, distinguish

choose, interpret data, solve, write, use

classify, describe, discuss, explain, identify, review, summarize, sequence, relate

define, recall, list, name

Student Interactivity

We know that students learn better when they are totally engaged in their work. That's why *Interactive Science* gets students involved in their learning every day, on every page. Because the student book is consumable, it provides students with unique opportunities to become totally engaged, whether it's marking the text, completing an illustration or a chart, summarizing relationships using Venn diagrams or other graphic devices, or recording ideas and findings about scientific concepts.

> *Apply It!* *Students combine new content understandings with their knowledge of scientific process and experimentation.*

> *Students demonstrate critical connections between text and illustration.*

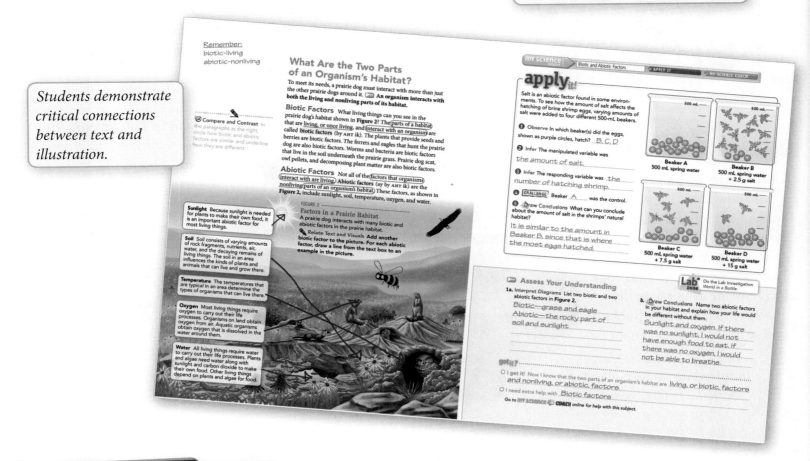

Online Labs and Simulations

For lab experiences without materials, you'll love the Online Virtual Labs. They're realistic, time efficient, and great when meeting in a laboratory is not possible. Have students use them individually, with a partner, or as a class activity to stimulate discussion or shared learning.

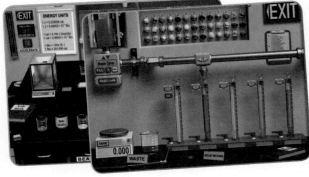

Inquiry

Teacher's Lab Resource
Life

interactive SCIENCE

- Provides in-depth labs in two forms—directed and open ended
- Offers quick labs and warm-ups for the busy teacher
- All labs available online, and editable!

PEARSON

Lab zone

Using the Labs

The yellow LabZone symbols in the student edition indicate the lab activities that support your instruction. Look for the LabZone symbol. To find your lab, look for its name in the *Teacher's Lab Resource* books or online in the teacher center.

Inquiry Warm-Ups Hands-on experience before the lesson begins

Hands-on Inquiry

We know that it is through student engagement and discovery that students really learn to think like scientists. Hands-on inquiry lab activities are built into the program; there are multiple activities per lesson.

Teacher's Lab Resource

Because there are so many labs, you will want to select which ones are best for your students and your class time. That is why the labs are organized in print as blackline masters in the *Teacher's Lab Resource.* Or access them in your teacher center at MyScienceOnline.com. There you can download and even edit the labs to more closely align them to a student's needs.

Quick Labs or Lab Investigation
Hands-on reinforcement of each lesson's key concept

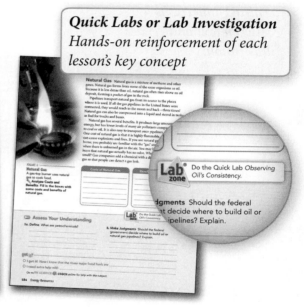

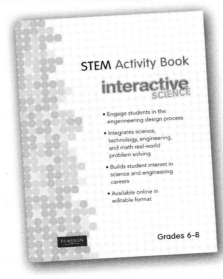

STEM Activity Book

interactive SCIENCE

- Engage students in the engineering design process
- Integrates science, technology, engineering, and math real-world problem solving
- Builds student interest in science and engineering careers
- Available online in editable format

PEARSON   Grades 6-8

STEM Activity Book

Each day, our lives are filled with more and more products and services that are the result of technology and engineering. The interconnectivity of science, technology, engineering, and mathematics is known as STEM, with each field connected to the others in important ways.

The activities in this book emphasize the interconnectivity of those fields, and use an eight-step design process designed to encourage creativity and imagination in solving design problems.

Inquiry Skill-Building Outside the Student Books

There are many forms of inquiry learning in *Interactive Science*, with lots of options to enrich your students' experiences. All components are in print or online for easy downloading.

Allow students to demonstrate their understanding of chapter concepts in longer term projects.

Provide students with opportunities to apply the science they have learned to other subject areas.

Stretch students with real-life problem solving—perfect for challenging the advanced students.

Offer students minds-on activities that incorporate the scientific method, each targeting specific science process skills.

Interactive Science—Inquiry Learning at Its Best

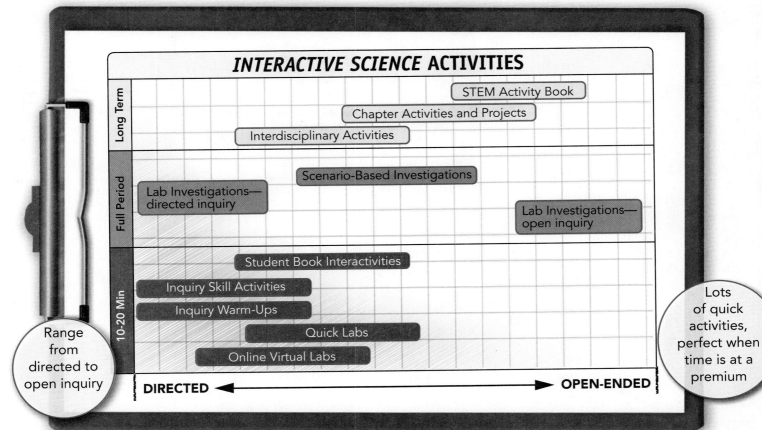

Range from directed to open inquiry

Lots of quick activities, perfect when time is at a premium

Big Ideas of Science

According to Grant Wiggins' Understanding by Design framework, students reveal their understanding most effectively when provided with complex, authentic opportunities to explain, interpret, apply, shift perspective, empathize, and self-assess. Each chapter in the student edition uses a Big Question to focus students' attention on the content of the chapter. Related Big Questions are organized under one or more Big Ideas. A Big Idea is a concept, theory, principle, or theme that helps learners make sense of a subject.

Students will explore the Big Idea before they read a chapter, writing about what they already know and what they want to know about the topic. After completing the chapter, students will return to these pages in order to record what they have learned and how their thoughts have changed during that learning process.

? BIG IDEAS OF SCIENCE

Have you ever worked on a jigsaw puzzle? Usually a puzzle has a theme that leads you to group the pieces by what they have in common. But until you put all the pieces together you can't solve the puzzle. Studying science is similar to solving a puzzle. The big ideas of science are like puzzle themes. To understand big ideas, scientists ask questions. The answers to those questions are like pieces of a puzzle. Each chapter in this book asks a big question to help you think about a big idea of science. By answering the big questions, you will get closer to understanding the big idea.

✏ **Before you read each chapter, write about what you know and what more you'd like to know.**

Grant Wiggins, coauthor of *Understanding by Design*

BIGIDEA
Living things are alike yet different.

Grasses and wildflowers look different, but they all grow in soil and need sunlight and water.

What do you already know about how all living things are alike yet different? ✏ **What more would you like to know?**

_____
_____
_____

Big Questions:

❷ How are living things alike yet different? Chapter 1

❷ How are living things other than plants and animals important to Earth? Chapter 7

❷ How do you know a plant when you see it? Chapter 8

❷ How do you know an animal when you see it? Chapter 9

✏ **After reading the chapters, write what you have learned about the Big Idea.**

_____

BIGIDEA
Living things are made of cells.

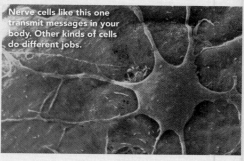

Nerve cells like this one transmit messages in your body. Other kinds of cells do different jobs.

What do you already know about what a cell does? What more would you like to know?

_____
_____
_____

Big Questions:

❷ What are cells made of? Chapter 2

❷ How do living things get energy? Chapter 3

✏ **After reading the chapters, write what you have learned about the Big Idea.**

_____
_____
_____

BIG IDEA
Genetic information passes from parents to offspring.

Once in a while, a koala joey is born with white fur instead of the usual gray fur. Even with such a striking difference, you can tell the joey is related to its mother.

What do you already know about how offspring resemble their parents? What more would you like to know?

_____

_____

_____

Big Questions:

❓ Why don't offspring always look like their parents? Chapter 4

❓ What does DNA do? Chapter 5

✏ After reading the chapters, write what you have learned about the Big Idea.

_____

_____

_____

BIG IDEA
Living things change over time.

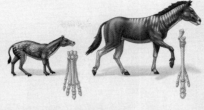

Modern horses are descended from much smaller animals with toes instead of hooves.

What do you already know about how life forms change? What more would you like to know?

_____

_____

_____

Big Question:

❓ How do life forms change over time? Chapter 6

✏ After reading the chapter, write what you have learned about the Big Idea.

_____

_____

_____

Connect to the Big Idea ❓

Have students form a group for each Big Idea and assign a notetaker and speaker for each group. Each group discusses what they already know, and then individuals write in their student editions what else they personally would like to like to know. Individuals share their items with their group as the notetaker compiles the responses and eliminates duplicates. Each group should agree on one key item they want to learn about. Finally, each group's speaker shares the group's key item with the class and the teacher compiles these items on the board. Remember to vary the roles of group notetaker and speaker to give students a variety of experiences.

EXTENSION Select one item about which students want to learn more as an extra credit project.

Connect to the Big Idea UbD

Divide the class into small groups and assign one Big Idea to each group. Each group previews the chapter(s) for the assigned Big Idea and develops an informational poster. Posters should indicate the key ideas that students expect to learn about, as well as any questions that students in the group have about the topic. Groups present their posters to the class and then display them in the classroom. Encourage students to reference the posters as they begin and work through each new chapter.

After students complete the chapter(s) for their Big Idea, they can add information to the poster to reflect on what they have learned.

BIGIDEA
Structures in living things are related to their functions.

Using its wings, a hawk flies through the air and coasts to a landing.

What do you already know about how animals move in water, on land, or in air? ✎ **What more would you like to know?**

_____
_____
_____
_____
_____

Big Question:

❓ How do animals move? Chapter 10

✎ **After reading the chapter, write what you have learned about the Big Idea.**

_____
_____
_____
_____
_____
_____
_____
_____
_____
_____
_____

BIGIDEA
Living things maintain constant conditions inside their bodies.

Like a rock climber who carefully adjusts to changing conditions on the mountain, your body adjusts to changes in your surroundings.

What do you already know about your body temperature regardless of how warm or cold it is outside? ✎ **What more would you like to know?**

_____
_____
_____

Big Questions:

❓ How does your body work? Chapter 11

❓ How do systems of the body move and manage materials? Chapter 12

❓ What systems regulate and control body processes? Chapter 13

❓ Why do you sometimes get sick? Chapter 14

✎ **After reading the chapters, write what you have learned about the Big Idea.**

_____
_____
_____
_____
_____

BIGIDEA

Living things interact with their environment.

What do you already know about how the animals and plants in your neighborhood live together?

✎ **What more would you like to know?**

_____
_____
_____
_____

Big Questions:

❓ How do living things affect one another? Chapter 15

❓ How do energy and matter move through ecosystems? Chapter 16

✎ **After reading the chapters, write what you have learned about the Big Idea.**

_____
_____
_____
_____
_____
_____
_____

These prairie dogs live in grasslands and make their homes underground. To stay alive, prairie dogs search for food and water and hide from animals that eat them.

Connect to the Big Idea ❓ UbD

Students can form small groups and choose a Big Idea to study. As each group previews the chapter(s) for the Big Idea, students should discuss and record questions they have about the key ideas in each lesson.

After each group finishes the chapter(s) for its assigned Big Idea, students work together to answer their initial questions based on what they have learned. Each group then holds a press conference. Some members of the group are scientists and the other students are reporters. The reporters should ask the group's questions and the scientists should provide answers by summarizing content from the chapters.

Managing Materials in the Body

Introduce the Big Q

Have students look at the image and read the Engaging Question and description. Ask students to explain how blood moves around their bodies. Have volunteers share their explanations. Point out that blood is flowing to all parts of our bodies continuously throughout every day and night of our lives. Ask: **What do you think causes blood to flow around your body?** *(Sample: The heart causes blood to flow.)* **Does blood move along certain pathways or does it move randomly?** *(Sample: It moves through veins and arteries.)* **What is blood made of?** *(Accept all responses.)* **What is blood's important function in the body?** *(Accept all responses.)*

Untamed Science Video

BLOOD LINES Before viewing, invite students to discuss what they know about circulation. Then play the video. Lead a class discussion and make a list of questions that this video raises. You may wish to have students view the video again after they have completed the chapter to see if their questions have been answered.

To access the online resources for this chapter, search on or navigate to *Managing Materials in the Body.*

Untamed Science Video explores the circulatory system in the setting of a hospital emergency room.

The Big Question allows students to answer the Engaging Question about blood flow.

my science online.com | Managing Materials in the Body

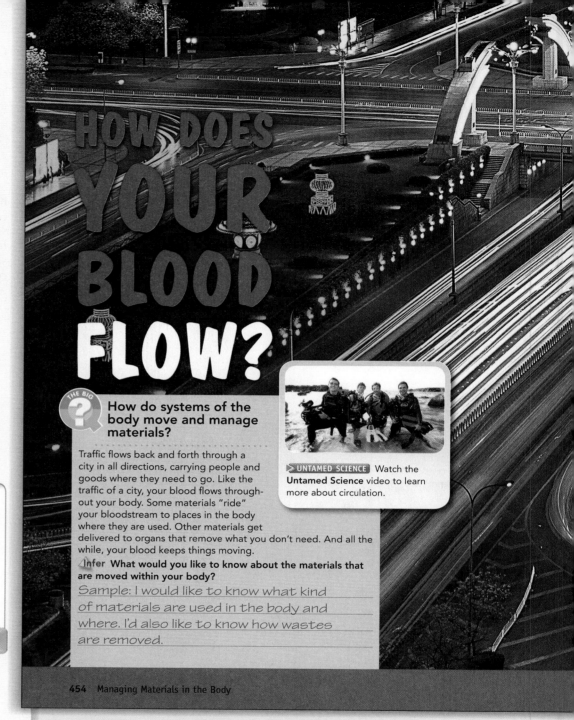

HOW DOES YOUR BLOOD FLOW?

? THE BIG **How do systems of the body move and manage materials?**

Traffic flows back and forth through a city in all directions, carrying people and goods where they need to go. Like the traffic of a city, your blood flows throughout your body. Some materials "ride" your bloodstream to places in the body where they are used. Other materials get delivered to organs that remove what you don't need. And all the while, your blood keeps things moving.

Infer What would you like to know about the materials that are moved within your body?

Sample: I would like to know what kind of materials are used in the body and where. I'd also like to know how wastes are removed.

> UNTAMED SCIENCE Watch the **Untamed Science** video to learn more about circulation.

Professional Development Note | **From the Author**

Most major cities have a public transit system. Metropolitan Washington DC's Metro consists of three major subway lines: The orange line carries passengers traveling northeast and west, the red line serves the north or northwest, and the blue line runs east and south. It's no surprise that the place where these three lines intersect, the Metro Center station, is located in the heart of the capital. It may help some students to think of the cardiovascular system as the body's transit system, transporting materials to the cells and removing waste from the cells in the same way the subway transports people.

📖 *Zipporah Miller*

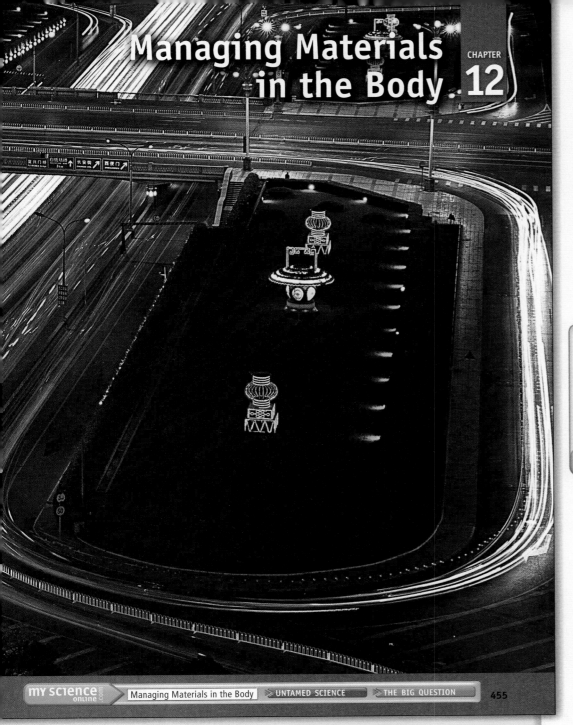

Managing Materials in the Body

CHAPTER 12

Chapter at a Glance

CHAPTER PACING: 10–14 periods or 5–7 blocks

INTRODUCE THE CHAPTER: Use the Engaging Question and the opening image to get students thinking about managing the materials in the body. Activate prior knowledge and preteach vocabulary using the Getting Started pages.

Lesson 1: Digestion

Lesson 2: The Circulatory System

Lesson 3: The Respiratory System

Lesson 4: Excretion

ASSESSMENT OPTIONS: Chapter Test, *ExamView®* Computer Test Generator, Performance Assessment, Progress Monitoring Assessments, SuccessTracker™

Preference Navigator, in the online Planning tools, allows you to customize *Interactive Science* to your own teaching style. You can also edit lesson plans by selecting the Lesson Planner option.

Digital Teacher's Edition allows you to access your Teacher's Edition and Resource online.

my science online.com

CHAPTER 12

Differentiated Instruction

L1 The Flow of Traffic Encourage students to study the photograph carefully. Invite them to say aloud words and phrases that describe or identify objects, actions, or processes that are visible in the image. Have a volunteer write students' responses on the board. Read the explanatory text to students as they continue to examine the image. Challenge them to add additional words and phrases.

L3 Transport Web Challenge students to create a three-part word web based on the three structures of the human cardiovascular system—the heart, blood vessels, and blood. Encourage students to brainstorm words and phrases that describe, explain, name, or relate to each of these important structures. Point out that students may wish to extend the activity by doing research to find additional scientific details.

455

Getting Started

Check Your Understanding

This activity assesses students' understanding of how materials circulate and are transported in the body. After students have shared their answers, point out that the materials needed by cells in the body are transported throughout the body by blood in the circulation system.

Preteach Vocabulary Skills

Invite students to look over the table. Have a volunteer read aloud the heading of the first column, and have two other volunteers read the two verbs and their definitions in that column. Then have different volunteers read aloud the heading and definitions in the second column. Ask students to identify the suffix shared by both terms. Explain that the suffix -*tion* means "the process or act of." Adding this suffix to the root word makes the word into a noun. Have volunteers read the head and the terms in the third column, and ask students to identify the suffix shared by both terms. Explain that the suffix -*atory* means "of, relating to, or connected with the thing specified." Adding this suffix to the root makes the word into an adjective. Clarify the parts of speech with students. Ask: **How do you know the terms in the first column are verbs?** *(Because verbs express actions)* **How do you know the terms in the second column are nouns?** *(Because nouns name abstract ideas)* **How do you know the terms in the third column are adjectives?** *(Because adjectives describe nouns.)*

Check Your Understanding

1. **Background** Read the paragraph below and then answer the question.

Each day, Ken **circulates** from the food pantry to senior centers around the city and then returns to the pantry. He **transports** meals and juice to the seniors and collects their empty bottles. Similarly, your blood circulates in your body. From the heart, your blood carries oxygen and **glucose** to your body cells. It picks up wastes before returning to the heart.

> To **circulate** is to move in a circle and return to the same point.
>
> To **transport** is to carry something from one place to another.
>
> **Glucose** is a sugar that is the major source of energy for the body's cells.

- What materials does your blood transport to your body cells?

  <u>Blood transports oxygen and glucose to</u>
  <u>body cells.</u>

> **MY READING WEB** If you had trouble completing the question above, visit **My Reading Web** and type in *Managing Materials in the Body*.

Vocabulary Skill

Identify Related Word Forms Learn related forms of words to increase your vocabulary. The table below lists forms of words related to key terms.

Verb	Noun	Adjective
respire, *v.* to obtain energy from the breakdown of food molecules	cellular respiration, *n.* the process by which cells obtain energy from the breakdown of food molecules	respiratory, *adj.* concerning respiration
excrete, *v.* to remove or eliminate waste	excretion, *n.* the process by which wastes are removed from the body	excretory, *adj.* concerning excretion

2. **Quick Check** Fill in the blank with the correct form of *respire*.
   - Obtaining energy from food is a <u>respiratory</u> activity.

My Reading Web offers leveled readings related to chapter content.

Vocab Flash Cards offer extra practice with the chapter vocabulary words.

Digital Lesson

- Assign the *Check Your Understanding* activity online and have students submit their work to you.
- Assign the *Vocabulary Skill* activity online and have students submit their work to you.

my science online.com ▷ | **Managing Materials in the Body** |

villi

circulatory system

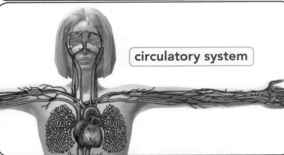
alveoli

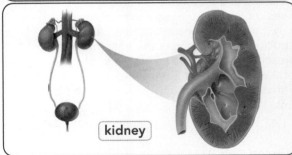
kidney

Chapter Preview

LESSON 1
- calorie • enzyme • esophagus
- peristalsis • villi
- ⟳ Reading: Chart
- △ Inquiry: Develop Hypotheses

LESSON 2
- circulatory system • heart
- atrium • ventricle • valve
- artery • aorta • capillary • vein
- hemoglobin
- ⟳ Summarize
- △ Observe

LESSON 3
- pharynx
- trachea
- cilia
- bronchi
- lungs
- alveoli
- diaphragm
- larynx
- vocal cords
- ⟳ Chart
- △ Communicate

LESSON 4
- excretion
- urea
- urine
- kidney
- ureter
- urinary bladder
- urethra
- nephron
- ⟳ Identify the Main Idea
- △ Infer

> VOCAB FLASH CARDS For extra help with vocabulary, visit **Vocab Flash Cards** and type in *Managing Materials in the Body.*

457

Preview Vocabulary Terms

Have students work individually to create a personalized glossary to organize the vocabulary terms for this chapter. Be sure to discuss and analyze each term before having students add it to their glossary. Students may choose to draw an illustration to remind them of the meaning of specific terms. As the class progresses through the chapter, have students return to their glossaries periodically to review vocabulary terms introduced in the earlier lessons. A list of Academic Vocabulary for each lesson can be found in the Support All Readers box at the start of the lesson.

L1 Have students look at the images on this page as you pronounce the vocabulary word. Have students repeat the word after you. Then read the definition. Use the sample sentence in italics to clarify the meaning of the term.

villi (*VIL eye*) Millions of tiny, finger-shaped structures that line the inner surface of the small intestine. *The villi absorb nutrient molecules from the small intestine and pass them into the blood vessels.*

circulatory system (*SUR kyuh luh TOR ee sis TUHM*) The system made up of the heart, blood vessels, and blood. *The circulatory system delivers needed substances to the body's cells.*

alveoli (*al VEE uh ly*) Compartments in the lungs that allows respiratory gases to exchange with the capillaries. *The thin walls of alveoli allow oxygen to pass into the blood stream.*

kidney (*KID nee*) One of two major organs of the excretory system. *The kidneys' main function is removing urea and other wastes from the blood.*

CHAPTER 12

ELL

Divide students into four groups and have them complete a Frayer Model diagram for one key term. It should include the definition, characteristics, an example, and a non-example of the term. Have each group teach their word to the class.

Beginning
LOW Create a drawing or symbol to support the vocabulary term. If literate, develop a definition using the native language.

HIGH Write the word on a card and introduce it to the class by pointing to it and saying it aloud.

Intermediate
LOW/HIGH Provide an example for each vocabulary term.

Advanced
LOW/HIGH Add parts of speech, pronunciation, and etymology to personal glossaries.

Digestion

 How do systems of the body move and manage materials?

Lesson Pacing: 3–4 periods or $1\frac{1}{2}$–2 blocks

🕐 **SHORT ON TIME?** To do this lesson in approximately half the time, do the Activate Prior Knowledge activity followed by a discussion of the Key Concepts to familiarize students with the lesson content. Have students do the Quick Labs. The rest of the lesson can be completed by students independently.

> **Preference Navigator,** in the online Planning tools, allows you to customize *Interactive Science* to your own teaching style. You can also edit lesson plans by selecting the Lesson Planner option.
>
> **Digital Teacher's Edition** allows you to access your Teacher's Edition and Resource materials online.

my science online.com

Lesson Vocabulary

- calorie
- enzyme
- esophagus
- peristalsis
- villi

Professional Development Note

Content Refresher

Omega-3 Fatty Acids An unsaturated fat called omega-3 fatty acid is found in all seafood, especially cold-water fish such as salmon. Lesser amounts are found in flaxseeds, soybeans, and canola oil. Research has shown that omega-3 fatty acids reduce the risk of coronary heart disease by decreasing the incidence of blood clots and irregular heartbeat, and by lowering blood pressure and triglyceride levels.

Development of some diseases depends on many factors, not just a single nutrient. For example, following a diet low in saturated fat and cholesterol can be one way to reduce the risk of heart disease. Low-fat diets rich in fruits and vegetables (which are low in fat and often contain dietary fiber, Vitamin A, or Vitamin C) may reduce the risk of some types of cancer.

LESSON OBJECTIVES

 Explain why the body needs food and what nutrients it uses.

Describe the structures and functions of the digestive system.

Blended Path
Active learning using Student Edition, Inquiry Path, and Digital Path

ENGAGE AND EXPLORE

Teach this lesson using a variety of resources. Begin by reading **My Planet Diary** as a class. Have students discuss which foods are healthy and which are less healthy. Then have students do the **Inquiry Warm-Up activity.** Students will analyze and discuss several misconceptions about food and nutrition. The **After the Inquiry Warm-Up worksheet** sets up a discussion about whether some claims about food are true or false. Have volunteers share their answers to question 4, their rewritten food claims.

EXPLAIN AND ELABORATE

Teach Key Concepts by explaining that food provides the body with energy and with materials to grow and to repair tissues. **Lead a Discussion** comparing carbohydrates, fats, and proteins as energy sources. Then **Lead a Discussion** about the role vitamins, minerals, and water play in the body.

Teach Key Concepts by explaining that the digestive system breaks down food, absorbs nutrients, and eliminates waste and discussing which organs in the digestive system fulfill these roles. **Lead a Discussion** about the mechanical and chemical digestion that takes place in the mouth. Then **Lead a Discussion** about how enzymes in saliva begin chemical digestion in the mouth by breaking down starch. The **Apply It activity** gives students an opportunity to investigate how teeth play a role in mechanical digestion. **Lead a Discussion** about the location and function of the esophagus. Use **Support the Big Q** to have students connect the chemical and mechanical digestion to how the body moves and manages materials. **Lead a Discussion** about the structure and function of the small intestine. Then **Lead a Discussion** about the structure and function of the large intestine. Hand out the **Key Concept Summaries** as a review of each part of the lesson. Students can also use the online **Vocab Flash Cards** to review key terms.

EVALUATE

Have students take the **Lesson Quiz.** For an alternate assessment, see the *ExamView®* Computer Test Generator, Progress Monitoring Assessments, or SuccessTracker™.

ⒺⓁⓁ Support

1 Content and Language
Pronounce and define aloud vocabulary terms for students. Make two sets of cards—one with the vocabulary words and the other with the definitions. Have groups play the matching game and pair each term with its definition. The winner has the most pairs of cards after all cards are claimed.

Lab zone **Inquiry Path** — Hands-on learning in the Lab zone

ENGAGE AND EXPLORE

To teach this lesson with an emphasis on inquiry, begin with the **Inquiry Warm-Up activity.** Students will analyze and discuss several misconceptions about food and nutrition. The **After the Inquiry Warm-Up worksheet** sets up a discussion about whether some claims about food are true or false. Have volunteers share their answers to question 4, their rewritten food claims.

EXPLAIN AND ELABORATE

Focus on the **Inquiry Skill** for the lesson. Remind students that developing a hypothesis means determining a possible answer to a scientific question. Use **Figure 1** to introduce students to the six types of nutrients the human body needs. Have students do the **Quick Lab** to explore making predictions about starch content.

Use **Figure 2** to introduce students to the organs of the digestive system involved in both mechanical and chemical digestion. The **Teacher Demo** provides students with a chance to see how enzymes act to break down proteins. The **Apply It activity** gives students an opportunity to identify the four types of teeth involved in mechanical digestion. Use the **Support the Big Q** to have students describe how the mechanical and chemical digestion in the digestive system moves and manages materials in the body. The **Real-World Inquiry** allows students to examine the function of organs in the digestive system and to develop hypotheses about how blockage would affect digestion. Have students do the **Quick Lab** to investigate the processes at work in the stomach. Students can use the online **Vocab Flash Cards** to review key terms.

EVALUATE

Have students take the **Lesson Quiz.** For an alternate assessment, see the *ExamView*® Computer Test Generator, Progress Monitoring Assessments, or SuccessTracker™.

Digital Path — Online learning at MY SCIENCE ONLINE.com

ENGAGE AND EXPLORE

Teach this lesson using digital resources. Begin by having students learn more and explore real-world connections to food and energy at **My Planet Diary** online. Have them access the Chapter Resources to find the **Unlock the Big Question activity.** There they can answer the questions and refine their responses as they continue through the lesson. You can re-assign the activity and have students submit their work so you can track their progress.

EXPLAIN AND ELABORATE

Students reading above, at, or below the lexile measure of this lesson can access basic content readings at their level at **My Reading Web.** Encourage students to use the online **Vocab Flash Cards** to preview key terms. Have students do the **Quick Lab** exploring how to measure the energy released from food. To give students a chance to compare and graph the number of calories burned during specific activities, assign the online **Do the Math activity** and have students submit their work to you. **Interactive Art** allows students to explore the characteristics of different nutrients. Have students complete the **Quick Lab** about predicting starch contents in different foods.

Before assigning the online **Apply It activity,** review the difference between mechanical and chemical digestion. Have students submit their work to you. Use the **Support the Big Q** to have students make connections between the function of the digestive system moves and how the body moves and manages materials. The **Real-World Inquiry** allows students to examine the function of organs in the digestive system and to develop hypotheses about how blockage would affect digestion. Before assigning the online **Do the Math activity** review how increased surface area aids absorption in the small intestine. Have students submit their work to you. Then have students do the **Quick Lab** to investigate the processes at work in the stomach. The **Key Concept Summaries** online allow students to read a summary and see an image associated with each part of the lesson. Online remediation is available at **My Science Coach.**

EVALUATE

Have students take the **Lesson Quiz.** For an alternate assessment, see the *ExamView*® Computer Test Generator, Progress Monitoring Assessments, or SuccessTracker™.

2 Frontload the Lesson

Direct students to **Figure 1.** Point out that the main function of the digestive system is to break down the food you eat into nutrients, which the body needs to carry out all its processes.

3 Comprehensible Input

Work with students to create a two-column chart listing the major organs in the digestive system and how each organ is involved in either moving or managing materials in the body.

4 Language Production

Pair or group students with varied language abilities to complete labs collaboratively for language practice. Have each student copy the completed written lab for personal reference.

5 Assess Understanding

Have students keep a content area log for this lesson using a two-column format with the headings "What I Understand" and "What I Don't Understand." Follow up so that students can move items from the "Don't Understand" to the "Understand" column.

Digestion

Establish Learning Objectives

After this lesson, students will be able to:

 Explain why the body needs food and what nutrients it uses.

 Describe the structures and functions of the digestive system.

Engage

Activate Prior Knowledge

MY PLANET DIARY Read *The Science of Food* with the class. Encourage students to think about the foods they eat every day, as well as their favorite foods. Ask: **What kinds of foods do you eat for a main course in the evenings?** *(Samples: Various meats, fish, pasta, eggs, and salads)* **Which foods do you think of as being "healthy," and which do you think of as being less "healthy"?** *(Accept all responses)*

BIG IDEAS OF SCIENCE REFERENCE LIBRARY 📖
Have students look up the following topics:
Drinking Water, Fats, Teeth, Vitamins, and Minerals.

Explore

Lab Resource: Inquiry Warm-Up 🔬

L1 **FOOD CLAIMS** Students will analyze and discuss several misconceptions about food and nutrition.

UNLOCK THE BIG ?

 Why Do You Need Food?

 What Happens in Your Digestive System?

my planet diary

CAREER

The Science of Food

You know that you need to eat food every day. But did you know that for some people studying food is their job? People called food scientists research and improve the food products you buy at the grocery store. Sometimes, they even think up new foods!

Many food scientists spend a lot of time in a lab. They use what they know about biology and chemistry to test food for nutrition, taste, and shelf life, which is how long the food will last before it spoils. If you like science and food, being a food scientist might be the job for you!

Communicate Discuss these questions with a partner. Then write your answers.

1. Why should food scientists test foods before the foods are sold?

   Sample: Scientists need to find out how long the food will last before it spoils.

2. How might food scientists improve your favorite breakfast food?

   Sample: They might make it contain less sugar so it is better for me; they might make it have a longer shelf life.

▷ PLANET DIARY Go to **Planet Diary** to learn more about food and energy.

🔬 Lab zone Do the Inquiry Warm-Up Food Claims.

458 Managing Materials in the Body

SUPPORT ALL READERS
Lexile Measure = 900L   **Lexile Word Count = 1790**

Prior Exposure to Content: May be the first time students have encountered this topic

Academic Vocabulary: *classify, infer, identify, hypothesis*

Science Vocabulary: *calorie, enzyme, esophagus, peristalsis, villi*

Concept Level: Generally appropriate for most students in this grade

Preteach With: My Planet Diary "The Science of Food" and Figure 1 activity

Go to **My Reading Web** to access leveled readings that provide a foundation for the content.

my science online.com

Vocabulary
- calorie • enzyme • esophagus
- peristalsis • villi

Skills
⟳ Reading: Chart
△ Inquiry: Develop Hypotheses

Why Do You Need Food?

All living things need food to stay alive. ⚿ **Food provides your body with materials to grow and to repair tissues. It also provides energy for everything you do.** Exercising, reading, and sleeping require energy. Even maintaining homeostasis takes energy.

Calories When food is used for energy, the amount of energy released is measured in calories. One **calorie** is the amount of energy needed to raise the temperature of one gram of water by one degree Celsius. The unit *Calorie*, with a capital C, is used to measure the energy in foods. One Calorie equals 1,000 calories. Everyone needs a certain number of Calories to meet their daily energy needs. However, the more active you are, the more Calories you need.

do the math!

The U.S. Department of Agriculture recommends that people do about 30 to 60 minutes of physical activity most days. The data table shows the Calories a 13-year-old weighing 45 kilograms burned in 30 minutes of each activity.

❶ **Graph** Use the data to draw a bar graph.

❷ **Name** Write a title for the bar graph.

❸ **CHALLENGE** Why does the type of physical activity change a person's dietary needs? Use the graph to explain your answer.

Sample: Some activities, such as soccer, burn more Calories than others, such as walking. The number of Calories a person burns changes how many Calories that person needs to eat to keep a balance in the body.

Activity	Calories Burned in 30 minutes
Soccer	275
Dancing	115
Walking	75

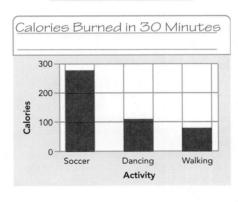

Calories Burned in 30 Minutes

459

ⒺⓁⓁ Support

1 Content and Language
Write and say the word *peristalsis*. Explain that *peri-* is a Greek prefix meaning "surrounding," and that *-stalsis* is a Greek suffix meaning "to contract." Explain that *peristalsis* refers to the involuntary contraction of the muscles around the digestive tract that pushes food through the digestive system.

2 Frontload the Lesson
Engage students in a discussion about food, including their favorite and least favorite dishes. Ask students which foods are nutritious and less nutritious.

3 Comprehensible Input
Help students make a table to compare simple and complex carbohydrates, fats, and proteins. Students should give an example of each, list the percent of daily Calories, and briefly describe how each nutrient works in the body.

Explain

Introduce Vocabulary

To help students understand that the term *calorie* is a unit of energy, explain that the word derives from the Latin word *calor*, meaning "heat." A calorie is the amount of energy needed to raise the temperature of one gram of water by one degree Celsius.

Teach Key Concepts ⚿

Explain to students that food provides the body with energy and with materials to grow and to repair tissues. The number of Calories a person requires varies from person to person. Ask: **What would happen to a living thing if it didn't have food?** *(It would die.)* **What are some ways your body uses energy?** *(Samples: walking, reading, bicycling, singing, dancing)* **What is the unit used to measure the energy value of food?** *(The Calorie)* **How are the units calorie and Calorie related?** *(One Calorie equals 1,000 calories.)* **What is the definition of calorie?** *(The amount of energy needed to raise the temperature of one gram of water by one degree Celsius)*

Elaborate

Do the Math!

If necessary, help students distinguish the data table from the bar graph. Explain that this data table and this graph express the same information in different ways. Point out that the bar graph allows you to visualize the similarities and differences among the three activities, whereas the data table lets you focus on the precise numbers of calories burned. Ask: **Where in the data table do the names of activities appear?** *(In the left column)* **Where do these names appear in the bar graph?** *(Along the horizontal axis)* **How many more calories are burned by 30 minutes of dancing than by 30 minutes of walking?** *(40)* **Which graphic aid did you use to determine the difference?** *(Data table)*

See Math *Skill and Problem-Solving Activities* for support.

My Planet Diary provides an opportunity for students to explore real-world connections to nutrient needs.

Explain

Teach With Visuals

Direct students' attention to **Figure 1**. Explain that people need six types of nutrients. In order to maintain a balanced state, people must take in a minimum amount of each type of nutrient every day. Ask: **What are the six nutrients people need?** (*Carbohydrates, fats, proteins, vitamins, minerals, and water*) **Which nutrients provide energy?** (*Carbohydrates, fats, and proteins*) **Which nutrients help in the body's chemical processes?** (*Vitamins and minerals*) **Which nutrient is the most important?** (*Water*) **Why is water the most important nutrient?** (*Because all the body's vital processes take place in water*)

Lead a Discussion

CARBOHYDRATES, FATS, AND PROTEINS Explain that carbohydrates, fats, and proteins are all energy sources, but they also play other roles in the body. Ask: **What other role do carbohydrates play in the body?** (*Carbohydrates provide raw material to make cell parts.*) **How do simple carbohydrates and complex carbohydrates differ as energy sources?** (*Simple carbohydrates provide a burst of energy; complex carbohydrates are starches that must first be broken down into sugar molecules. This makes complex carbohydrates a steady long-term source of energy.*) **How do fats and carbohydrates compare as sources of energy?** (*Fats provide more energy per gram than carbohydrates.*) **Besides providing energy, what other roles do fats play in the body?** (*Fats form part of the cell membrane; fatty tissue protects organs and insulates the body.*) **Besides providing energy, what other roles do proteins play in the body?** (*Proteins help the body with growth and tissue repair.*)

21st Century Learning 🅳🅺

CREATIVITY Have students read *Superfoods* in the **Big Ideas of Science Reference Library** and then research examples of superfoods not discussed in the reading, such as blueberries, spinach, and sweet potatoes. Ask students to create a poster that details the nutrients found in their chosen superfood and how these nutrients contribute to a healthy body. Encourage students to include on their posters several recipes that feature their chosen superfood.

What Nutrients Do You Need? Your body breaks down the food you eat into nutrients. Nutrients are the substances in food that provide the raw materials and energy the body needs to carry out all its processes. People need six types of nutrients: carbohydrates, fats, proteins, vitamins, minerals, and water.

FIGURE 1 ....
> INTERACTIVE ART   **Feeding Your Body**
The nutrients your body needs come from the foods you eat.   ✎ **Make Judgments** Why do you think it's important to eat a variety of foods every day?

Sample: Eating different kinds of food helps you get a balanced diet of nutrients that you need.

Carbohydrates

Carbohydrates (kahr boh HY drayts) are a major source of energy. They also provide raw materials to make cell parts. About 45 to 65 percent of your daily Calories should come from carbohydrates. Simple carbohydrates, called sugars, can give you a quick burst of energy. One sugar, glucose, is the major source of energy for your cells. Complex carbohydrates are made of many linked sugar molecules. Starch is a complex carbohydrate. Potatoes, rice, wheat, and corn contain starches. Your body breaks down starches into sugar molecules. In this way, starches provide a steady long-term energy source.

Fats

Like carbohydrates, fats are energy-containing nutrients. However, 1 gram of fat provides 9 Calories of energy, while 1 gram of carbohydrate provides only 4 Calories. Fats form part of the cell membrane. Fatty tissue also protects your organs and insulates your body. No more than 30 percent of your daily Calories should come from fats.

Proteins

Your body needs proteins for growth and tissue repair. Proteins also can be an energy source. About 10 to 35 percent of your daily Calorie intake should come from proteins. Proteins are made up of small, linked units called amino acids (uh MEE noh). Thousands of different proteins are built from about 20 different amino acids. Your body can make about half of the amino acids it needs. The other half must come from food. Foods from both animals and plants contain protein.

460 Managing Materials in the Body

Interactive Art allows students to explore the roles various nutrients play in the body.

Digital Lesson
• Assign the *Do the Math* activity online and have students submit their work to you.

mY SCIENCE online.com ▸ **Nutrients at Work**

Vitamins and Minerals

Unlike some nutrients, vitamins do not provide the body with raw materials and energy. Instead, vitamins act as helper molecules in your body's chemical reactions. The body can make a few vitamins, such as vitamin D, but foods are the source of most vitamins.

Nutrients that are not made by living things are called minerals. Like vitamins, minerals do not provide your body with raw materials and energy. However, your body still needs small amounts of minerals to carry out chemical processes. For example, you need calcium to build bones and teeth, and you need iron to help red blood cells function. Plant roots absorb minerals from the soil. You obtain minerals by eating plants or animals that have eaten plants.

Water

Water is the most important nutrient because all the body's vital processes take place in water. In addition, water helps regulate body temperature and remove wastes. Water accounts for about 65 percent of the average healthy person's body weight because it makes up most of the body's fluids, including blood. Under normal conditions, you need to take in about 2 liters of water every day to stay healthy.

 Do the Quick Lab
Predicting Starch Content.

🖙 Assess Your Understanding

1a. Define What does a Calorie measure?

A Calorie measures the
amount of energy in foods.

b. Draw Conclusions Why do active teenagers have high energy needs?

Individuals who are very active
burn more Calories.

c. Apply Concepts What do you think is meant by the phrase "a balanced diet"?

Sample: It means eating a mix
of foods every day that gives
you the nutrients you need.

got it?

O **I get it!** Now I know that food provides the body with *energy and the materials to grow and repair tissues.*

O **I need extra help with** *See TE note.*

Go to MY SCIENCE COACH *online for help with this subject.*

461

Differentiated Instruction

L1 Plan a Menu Based on the information in **Figure 1**, have students work in groups to create a day's menu that consists of 46–65% carbohydrates, no more than 30% fat, and 10–35% protein. Encourage students to research which foods fall into these categories. Menus should make allowances for vitamins, minerals, and water.

L3 Simple and Complex Carbohydrates Carbohydrates are made of the elements carbon (C), hydrogen (H),

and oxygen (O). Most carbohydrates contain twice as many hydrogen atoms as of carbon and oxygen atoms. Challenge students to research the chemical structure of a simple carbohydrate, such as glucose, and a complex carbohydrate, such as starch. Ask them why complex carbohydrates provide a long-lasting source of energy. *(The sugars in the long-chained complex carbohydrates are absorbed at a slower, steadier rate than the quick burst of energy provided by simple sugars.)*

Lead a Discussion

VITAMINS, MINERALS Explain that vitamins, minerals, and water do not provide energy-only carbohydrates, fats and proteins do. Ask: **Why are vitamins important to the body?** *(They act as helper molecules for the body's chemical reactions.)* **Why are minerals important to the body?** *(They help the body carry out chemical processes.)* **Why is water important to the body?** *(Water helps regulate body temperature and remove waste.)* **How do you get vitamins?** *(The body makes some vitamins, but most come from food.)* **How do you get minerals?** *(You get minerals by eating plants or animals that have eaten plants.)* **What is the main difference between vitamins and minerals?** *(Vitamins are nutrients made by living things; minerals are not made by living things; they come from the soil.)* **How much water should you drink every day?** *(About 2 liters)*

21st Century Learning

INTERPERSONAL SKILL Tell students that vitamins can be classified into two groups: fat soluble and water soluble. Invite groups of students to research vitamins. Groups should work together to classify the principle vitamins as either fat or water soluble, list foods that contain these vitamins, and explain the different ways the body handles fat and water soluble vitamins. Have groups organize their information on a chart, and display the charts around the room.

Lab Resource: Quick Lab

L1 PREDICTING STARCH CONTENT Students will conduct a starch test on food.

Evaluate ———————

Assess Your Understanding

Have students evaluate their understanding by completing the appropriate sentence.

R T I Response to Intervention

1a. If students have trouble defining what a Calorie measures, **then** have them review the definition.

b. If students have difficulty making a connection between an active lifestyle and burning calories, **then** remind them that Calories measure the energy in foods.

c. If students struggle to explain "a balanced diet," **then** discuss how to apply the concept of balance to food choices.

MY SCIENCE COACH Have students go online for help in understanding why living things need food.

461

Explain

Teach Key Concepts ▭

Explain that the three main functions of organs of the digestive system are digestion, absorption, and elimination. Ask: **What are some organs of the digestive system?** (Samples: mouth, stomach, large intestine, small intestine) **What is mechanical digestion?** (Tearing or grinding food into smaller pieces) **Where does most mechanical digestion take place?** (In the mouth and stomach) **What is chemical digestion?** (The breaking of foods into their building blocks) If students have studied chemistry, point out that mechanical digestion is a series of physical changes, while chemical digestion is a series of chemical changes in which complex molecules are broken down to make simpler ones. Ask: **What is absorption?** (The process by which nutrient molecules pass through the wall of the digestive system and move into the blood) **Where does most absorption take place?** (In the small intestine) Tell students that substances produced by the liver, pancreas, and lining of the small intestine help complete chemical digestion.

Lead a Discussion

DIGESTION BEGINS Review with students the distinctions between mechanical and chemical digestion. Have students look over **Figure 2.** Ask: **What is the function of the salivary glands?** (Producing saliva) Help students understand that saliva has several important functions. First, saliva adheres chewed particles of food into a ball that is small enough to be swallowed. Saliva also lubricates food, making it easier to swallow. Finally, saliva contains a chemical that can break down starches into sugars. **What are the functions of the tongue?** (It pushes food toward the teeth, helps mix food with saliva, and assists in swallowing.) **What is the function of the teeth?** (Teeth cut, tear, crush, and grind food.)

What Happens in Your Digestive System?

Your digestive system is about 9 meters long from beginning to end. **Figure 2** shows the structures of the digestive system. ▭ **The digestive system breaks down food, absorbs nutrients, and eliminates waste.** These functions occur one after the other in an efficient, continuous process.

Digestion The process by which your body breaks down food into small nutrient molecules is called digestion. Digestion can be mechanical or chemical. In mechanical digestion, bites of food are torn or ground into smaller pieces. This kind of digestion happens mostly in the mouth and stomach. In chemical digestion, chemicals break foods into their building blocks. Chemical digestion takes place in many parts of the digestive system. Substances made in the liver and pancreas help digestion occur.

Absorption and Elimination Absorption occurs after digestion. Absorption is the process by which nutrient molecules pass from your digestive system into your blood. Most absorption occurs in the small intestine. The large intestine eliminates materials that are not absorbed.

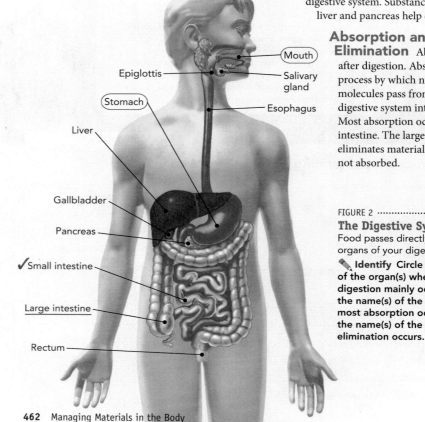

FIGURE 2 ·················
The Digestive System
Food passes directly through five organs of your digestive system.

✏ **Identify** Circle the name(s) of the organ(s) where mechanical digestion mainly occurs. Check the name(s) of the organ(s) where most absorption occurs. Underline the name(s) of the organ(s) where elimination occurs.

Mouth
Epiglottis
Salivary gland
Stomach
Esophagus
Liver
Gallbladder
Pancreas
✓ Small intestine
Large intestine
Rectum

462 Managing Materials in the Body

Digital Lesson: Assign the *Apply It* activity online and have students submit their work to you.

my science online.com | **Digestive Functions**

The Mouth Have you noticed that smelling food can be enough to start your mouth watering? This response happens because your mouth is where digestion begins. When you bite off a piece of food, both mechanical and chemical digestion begin inside your mouth. Your teeth and tongue carry out mechanical digestion. Your teeth cut, tear, crush, and grind food into small pieces. Your tongue pushes food toward your teeth.

As your teeth work, your saliva (suh LY vuh) moistens food into a slippery mass. Saliva is the fluid released by salivary glands when you eat. Saliva contains a chemical that can break down starches into sugars. This step begins the chemical digestion of your food.

The chemical in saliva that digests starch is an enzyme. An **enzyme** is a protein that speeds up chemical reactions in the body. Your body produces many different enzymes. Each enzyme has a specific chemical shape that enables it to speed up only one kind of reaction. Different enzymes are needed to complete the process of digestion. **Figure 3** shows how enzymes work.

FIGURE 3 ···
How Enzymes Work
Enzymes help break down starches, proteins, and fats.

✎ **Observe** Which molecule does not change?

The enzyme does not change.

The starch molecule binds to an enzyme that has a matching shape.

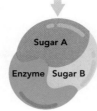
The starch molecule is broken down into two separate sugar molecules.

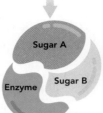
The enzyme and the sugar molecules all separate.

apply it!

You have four types of teeth. Each type has a specific function.

❶ **Name** Think about eating a carrot. Which type of teeth cuts the carrot into a bite-sized piece? *Incisors*

❷ **Identify** Which teeth at the back of your mouth crush and grind the carrot piece? *Premolars* and *Molars*

❸ **Interpret Diagrams** When people tear chicken off a bone, they use their pointed teeth called *canines.*

❹ **Summarize** Write about all the teeth people use to eat an apple.
Sample: They cut a bite-sized piece of apple with their incisors. Then they crush and grind the apple with their premolars and molars.

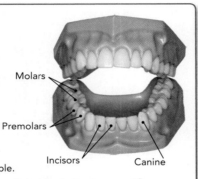
Molars
Premolars
Incisors
Canine

463

Differentiated Instruction

L1 Word Meanings Help students clarify their understanding of the concept of *mechanical digestion* by focusing their attention on the word *mechanical.* Point out that this word is related to the word *machine.* Explain that a machine is a device with some moving parts that performs work. Then help students recognize that mechanical digestion occurs when parts of the human body such as the tongue and teeth are moved.

L3 Teeth Challenge students to do research to learn more facts and details about the size, shape, number, and functions of the four types of human teeth. Encourage them to include one or more diagrams with detailed labels for all of the upper and lower teeth.

Lead a Discussion

ENZYMES Remind students that chemical digestion begins in the mouth because saliva contains an enzyme. Ask: **What is an enzyme?** *(A chemical that speeds up chemical reactions)* **What does the enzyme in saliva digest?** *(Starch)* **Can this enzyme digest proteins? Explain?** *(No; the type of enzyme found in the mouth is specialized to speed up the reaction with starch.)*

Elaborate

Teacher Demo

L3 ACTION OF ENZYMES

Materials meat tenderizer, milk, orange juice, 2 flasks or clear glasses, 2 stirrers

Time 10 minutes

Show students the container of meat tenderizer. If students do not know what it is used for, tell them that it is sprinkled on meats before cooking to make them tender. Explain that meat tenderizer contains papain, an enzyme that breaks down protein. At the beginning of class, place 2 tablespoons of milk into one flask and the same amount of orange juice in another. Add 1 tablespoon of the meat tenderizer to each flask, and stir well with separate stirrers.

Ask: **What will happen to the milk and orange juice?** *(The papain will act on the milk solution, because milk contains protein. The papain will not act on the orange juice, because orange juice does not contain protein.)*

Set aside the flasks until the end of class, and then display both flasks. The milk solution will be thick; the orange juice will be unchanged.

Ask: **What can you say about the action of digestive enzymes based on this demonstration?** *(An enzyme acts on only one type of nutrient.)*

Apply It!

L1 Before beginning the activity, review the photograph and labels carefully. If students have difficulty figuring out what the different kinds of teeth do, suggest that they think about how they bite and chew the food they eat.

Explain

Lead a Discussion

THE FUNCTION OF THE ESOPHAGUS Explain that the mouth leads to the throat, formally called the pharynx. In the pharynx, food and fluid from the mouth join air inhaled through the nose. At the back of the pharynx, the food, fluid, and air are sorted into the esophagus (food and fluid) or the windpipe (air). Explain that the epiglottis, shown in **Figure 2**, is a flap of tissue that seals off the windpipe during swallowing and prevents food from entering the lungs. Ask: **The esophagus is located between which two organs in the digestive system?** *(The mouth and the stomach)* **How does mucus in the esophagus aid digestion?** *(Mucus helps food move easily.)* Large hollow organs of the digestive system contain muscles that help the walls of these organs to move. Ask: **How do the muscles of the esophagus help food to move through the digestive system?** *(Muscles in the esophagus push food toward the stomach.)* **What is this process called?** *(Peristalsis)*

21st Century Learning

CRITICAL THINKING GRAVITY AND DIGESTION Point out that astronauts traveling in outer space are not subject to the rules of gravity. Invite students to explain how peristalsis allows astronauts to eat in space. *(Sample: Gravity doesn't affect how food travels from the mouth to the stomach. The muscles in the esophagus contract and push the food down into the stomach.)*

Support the Big Q ❓ UbD

THE FUNCTION OF THE STOMACH Ask students to think about their own perceptions about the digestive process in their bodies. Ask: **What is one way your stomach lets you know that it is empty?** *(Samples: hunger pangs; stomach "growls" or rumbles.)* Explain that these sounds are caused by peristalsis when the stomach has been empty for some time. Point out that people sometimes experience a sensation of pain, called hunger pangs, when their stomachs have been empty for a long time. Encourage students to look at **Figure 4.** Ask: **How do stomach muscles help the stomach to perform its function?** *(Layers of muscle contract to churn food and mix it with fluids.)* **What happens to food in the stomach?** *(Food is churned and mixed with fluids, including digestive juices. Proteins in the food are chemically digested. Then the food is released into the next part of the digestive system.)* Have students summarize where mechanical and chemical digestion have taken place to this point. *(Mouth—chemical and mechanical digestion; esophagus—none; stomach—chemical and mechanical digestion)*

FIGURE 4 ·······························

The Stomach
The stomach wall has three muscle layers. The microscopic view shows you the cells that line the inside of the stomach.

✎ **Answer the following questions.**

1. **Classify** What type of digestion is aided by the action of stomach muscles?

   <u>Sample: Mechanical</u>
   <u>digestion</u>

2. **Infer** How does having different layers of stomach muscles aid digestion?

   <u>Sample: The</u>
   <u>muscles can work</u>
   <u>in different ways,</u>
   <u>helping to churn</u>
   <u>the food well.</u>

To the Stomach Food moves from your mouth through your **esophagus** (ih SAHF uh gus) and then into your stomach. The stomach is a J-shaped muscular pouch where most mechanical digestion and some chemical digestion occur. Mechanical digestion occurs as layers of smooth muscle in the stomach wall contract, producing a churning motion. Chemical digestion occurs as the food mixes with digestive juice. Digestive juice is a fluid produced by cells that line the stomach. It contains the enzyme pepsin that chemically digests proteins into short chains of amino acids.

Food usually stays in your stomach for a few hours until mechanical digestion is complete. Now a thick liquid, the food enters the next part of the digestive system. That is where chemical digestion continues and absorption takes place.

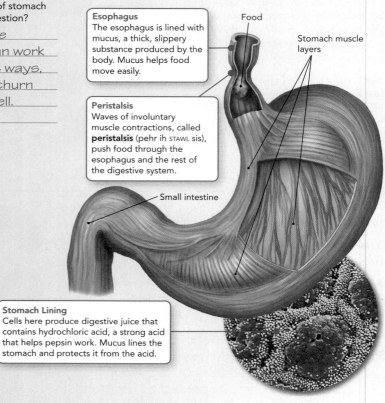

Esophagus
The esophagus is lined with mucus, a thick, slippery substance produced by the body. Mucus helps food move easily.

Food

Stomach muscle layers

Peristalsis
Waves of involuntary muscle contractions, called **peristalsis** (pehr ih STAWL sis), push food through the esophagus and the rest of the digestive system.

Small intestine

Stomach Lining
Cells here produce digestive juice that contains hydrochloric acid, a strong acid that helps pepsin work. Mucus lines the stomach and protects it from the acid.

Real-World Inquiry allows students to investigate the roles of the various organs of digestion.

my science online.com ▷ | **The Digestive System**

The Small Intestine At about 6 meters—longer than some full-sized cars—the small intestine makes up two thirds of the length of the digestive system. The small intestine is the part of the digestive system where most chemical digestion and absorption take place. Its small diameter, from 2 to 3 centimeters wide, gives the small intestine its name.

A great deal happens in the small intestine. When food reaches it, starches and proteins have been partially broken down, but fats have not been digested. 🗝 **Substances produced by the liver, pancreas, and lining of the small intestine help to complete chemical digestion.** The liver and the pancreas send their substances into the small intestine through small tubes.

FIGURE 5 ⋯⋯⋯⋯⋯⋯⋯⋯⋯⋯⋯

▶ **REAL-WORLD INQUIRY** **Organs of Digestion**

The liver, pancreas, and gallbladder aid digestion in the small intestine.

✏️ **Complete the tasks.**

1. **Identify** Fill in the missing labels.

2. △ **Develop Hypotheses** How may a blockage in the tube between the gallbladder and the small intestine affect digestion?

   Sample: Bile may
   not reach the
   small intestine,
   making digestion
   of fats harder.

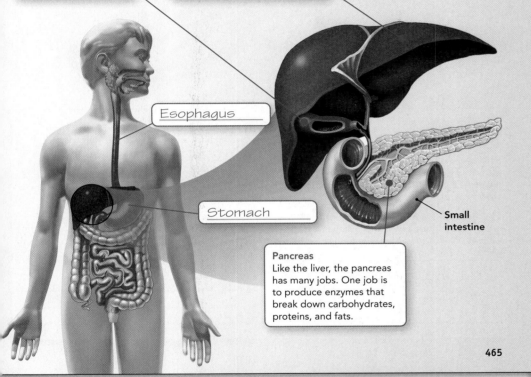

Liver
The liver has many jobs. One job is making bile for the digestive system. Bile breaks fats into smaller droplets but is not involved in chemical digestion.

Gallbladder
The gallbladder stores bile and releases it into the small intestine.

Esophagus

Stomach

Pancreas
Like the liver, the pancreas has many jobs. One job is to produce enzymes that break down carbohydrates, proteins, and fats.

Small intestine

465

Differentiated Instruction

L1 **Table of Digestive Organs** Have students draw a table with three columns labeled *Organ, Type of Digestion,* and *What Happens.* As students read this lesson, have them complete the table. Model the first row for them: mouth (*Organ*); chemical, mechanical (*Type of Digestion*); teeth cut, tear, crush, and grind food, the tongue mixes food and helps in swallowing, and enzymes in saliva break down starches (*What Happens*).

L3 **Mucus** Challenge students to use print and electronic sources to learn more about the composition of mucus, as well as its vital role in the digestive process.

Lead a Discussion

THE SMALL INTESTINE Explain that most chemical digestion and absorption take place in the small intestine. Ask: **How would you describe the shape of the small intestine?** (*The small intestine is very small and very narrow.*) **How might the shape of the small intestine aid in chemical digestion and absorption?** (*Because it is so long, it has a large surface area, which gives a lot of opportunity for absorption.*) **What is the state of food by the time it arrives in the small intestine?** (*Starches and proteins are partially broken down; fat has not been digested.*) **What does this suggest about how the body digests different types of food?** (*It takes longer for the body to digest fat than to digest starches and proteins.*)

Teach With Visuals

Direct students' attention to **Figure 5.** As you name the organs, including the esophagus and the stomach, have students find it in the illustration. Ask: **What product of the liver aids in digestion?** (*Bile*) **What is the function of bile?** (*It breaks down large fat particles into smaller fat particles.*) **What is the function of the gallbladder?** (*It stores bile.*) **What are the products of the pancreas?** (*Enzymes*) **What do these enzymes digest?** (*Proteins, carbohydrates, and fats*) Remind students that each step in digestion requires a different enzyme. For example, the pancreatic enzyme that digests protein does not affect carbohydrates or fats. If students mention that the pancreas produces insulin, tell them that insulin is not a digestive enzyme and does not enter the small intestine. The pancreas has two separate functions, to produce enzymes for digestion and to produce the hormone insulin.

△ **Develop Hypotheses** Help students understand that a hypothesis is one possible explanation or answer to a scientific question. It can be worded as an *If/then* statement.

21st Century Learning

L3 **COMMUNICATION INSULIN** Tell students that the presence of insulin causes cells in the liver and other organs to take up glucose from the blood. When insulin is absent, the body uses fat as an energy source. Diabetes is a disease in which the body cannot control the levels of insulin. Assign groups to research either Type 1 or 2 diabetes. Have students prepare an oral report on the causes, symptoms, and treatment.

Explain

Teach With Visuals

Direct students' attention to **Figure 6**. Tell students the small intestine is involved in mechanical digestion as a result of continued peristalsis, but to a lesser extent than in the mouth and stomach. Remind students most absorption takes place in the small intestine. Ask: **What does the small intestine absorb?** *(Nutrient molecules from digested foods)* **How does the structure of the small intestine aid absorption?** *(The small intestine is folded into millions of villi, making it possible to absorb more nutrients.)* **Where do nutrients go when absorbed by the small intestine?** *(Nutrients pass into the blood vessels, which deliver them to the body's cells.)*

MAKE ANALOGIES

L1 SURFACE AREA AND ABSORPTION Help students understand that increased surface area helps absorption. Contrast the greater amount of water a terrycloth hand towel can absorb with the lesser amount a smooth dish towel can absorb, even with similar dimensions. Ask: **What is different about the surfaces of these towels?** *(Sample: The hand towel has loops of thread that are raised from the surface. The dish towel is smooth and flat.)* **Which towel do you think contains more fabric?** *(The hand towel)* Point out the loops of thread increase the surface area that can hold water, much as the villi increase the surface area of the small intestine.

Elaborate

Do the Math!

Help students understand that calculating how many times greater the surface area of the small intestine is with villi rather than without it emphasizes one important function of the small intestine in digestion—absorption. Encourage students to round the decimal dimensions of the surface areas before they estimate the difference between the two decimals. Ask: **Which number will be the dividend in your equation?** *(261.80m²)* **Which will be the divisor?** *(0.57m²)*

See *Math Skill and Problem-Solving Activities* for support.

21st Century Learning

INTERPERSONAL SKILLS Have students read *Digestion* in the **Big Ideas of Science Reference Library** and then work in pairs to design a game about the digestive system. The game board should consist of a diagram of the digestive system and questions about its organs that allow players to progress through the body. After developing the game, have pairs trade games and play.

Absorption in the Small Intestine After chemical digestion takes place, the small nutrient molecules are ready for the body to absorb. The structure of the small intestine helps absorption occur. The inner surface of the small intestine is folded into millions of tiny finger-shaped structures called **villi** (VIL eye) (singular *villus*). Villi, shown in **Figure 6,** greatly increase the surface area of the small intestine. More surface area means that more nutrients can be absorbed. Nutrient molecules pass from cells on the surface of a villus into blood vessels and are then delivered to body cells.

FIGURE 6 ····················
Villi
Tiny villi line the folds of the small intestine.

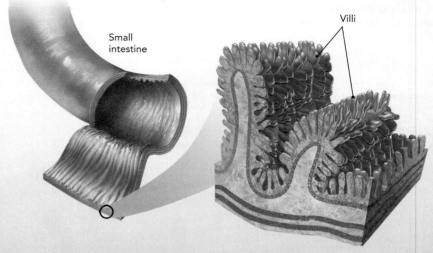

Small intestine

Villi

do the math!

If the average person's small intestine had smooth walls, its surface area would be 0.57 m². With villi, the surface area is about 250 m², about the size of a tennis court.

1 Calculate Divide to find how many times greater the surface area is with villi than it is without villi. Round your answer to the nearest whole number.

$$\frac{250 \ m^2}{0.57 \ m^2} = 438.59 = 439$$

2 Estimate In Question 1, how did you know which number to divide by to get your answer?

The surface area increases so the answer has to be larger than 250 or 0.57. Dividing by 0.57 gives a larger number.

3 CHALLENGE Some people have a wheat allergy that results in villi being destroyed. What problems might these individuals have?

Sample: They might not absorb enough nutrients to stay healthy.

Digital Lesson Assign the Do the Math activity online and have students submit their work to you.

my science online.com ▷ **The Small Intestine**

The Large Intestine By the time material reaches the end of the small intestine, most nutrients have been absorbed. The water and undigested food that is left move from the small intestine into the large intestine. The large intestine is the last section of the digestive system. As the material moves through the large intestine, water is absorbed into the bloodstream. The remaining material is readied for elimination from the body.

The large intestine is about 1.5 meters long. It contains bacteria that feed on the material passing through. These bacteria normally do not cause disease. In fact, they are helpful because they make certain vitamins, including vitamin K.

The large intestine ends in a short tube called the rectum. In the rectum waste material is compressed into solid form. This waste material is eliminated from the body through the anus, a muscular opening at the end of the rectum.

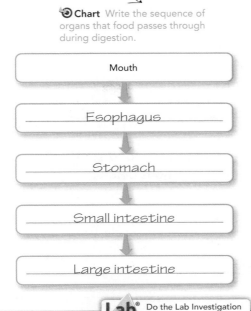

Chart Write the sequence of organs that food passes through during digestion.

Mouth

Esophagus

Stomach

Small intestine

Large intestine

Lab zone Do the Lab Investigation *As the Stomach Churns.*

🦴 **Assess Your Understanding**

2a. Define (Chemical/Mechanical) digestion occurs when enzymes break down foods into simpler substances.

b. Apply Concepts How is the stomach similar to a washing machine?

It churns food with enzymes and acid like a washing machine churns clothes with water and soap.

c. Explain How are the liver and pancreas involved in digestion?

Sample: The liver makes bile. The pancreas makes enzymes. These substances break down food.

d. Relate Cause and Effect How do villi help the small intestine carry out its function?

Villi increase the surface area for absorption.

got it?

⭕ I get it! Now I know that the digestive system works through the actions of organs that include the mouth, esophagus, stomach, small intestine, pancreas, liver, gallbladder, and large intestine.

⭕ I need extra help with See TE note.

Go to **my science COACH** online for help with this subject.

467

Explain

Lead a Discussion

THE FUNCTION OF THE LARGE INTESTINE Explain that the large intestine absorbs water and prepares the remaining material for elimination from the body. Ask: **After nutrients are absorbed, what is left in the food material as it enters the large intestine?** *(Water, bits of undigested food)* **What is left after water is absorbed into the bloodstream?** *(Bits of undigested food)* **What do the bacteria in the large intestine do?** *(Feed on the material and produce vitamins, such as vitamin K.)* **Where does material move after water is absorbed?** *(Into the rectum)* **What happens in the rectum?** *(The waste material is compressed and eliminated through the anus.)*

Chart Tell students that making a chart while reading is a good way to organize information.

Elaborate

21st Century Learning

INFORMATION LITERACY Students may have seen advertisements for yogurt products that claim to aid the digestive system. Challenge students to learn how yogurt is made, what "active cultures" means, and how the bacteria in yogurt aid the digestive system. Encourage students to evaluate the claims.

Lab Resource: Quick Lab **Lab zone**

L1 AS THE STOMACH CHURNS Students will explore how proteins are digested in the stomach.

Evaluate

Assess Your Understanding

After students answer the questions, have them evaluate their understanding by completing the appropriate sentence.

RTI Response to Intervention

2a. If students have trouble distinguishing between chemical and mechanical digestion, **then** review how *chemical* and *mechanical* apply to digestion.

b. If students struggle to compare the stomach to a washing machine, **then** discuss both the chemical and mechanical digestion that occurs in the stomach.

c. If students cannot determine the function of the liver and pancreas, **then** remind them both organs produce substances that aid digestion.

d. If students have difficulty describing the role of villi, **then** have them review Figure 5.

my science COACH Have students go online for help understanding what happens in the digestive system.

467

Differentiated Instruction

L1 Perceptions of Surface Area Give each student two pieces of blank paper of the same size. Ask them to make folds in one of the pieces and place it on top of the flat paper. Students will observe that the two pieces still have the same surface area. Have students describe how the folded paper models the villi in the small intestine. *(The villi allow for greater surface area, yet take up little space in the body.)* If students have difficulty with this concept, ask them to smooth out the folded paper and place it against the flat paper.

L3 Three Sections of the Small Intestine The small intestine can be divided into three subsections: the duodenum, the jejunum, and the ileum. Challenge students to create a diagram of the three sections of the small intestine. Diagrams should describe the function of each section.

Lab zone® **After the Inquiry Warm-Up**

Digestion

Inquiry Warm-Up, *Food Claims*

In the Inquiry Warm-Up, you investigated whether some claims about food are true or false. Using what you learned from that activity, answer the questions below.

1. **APPLY CONCEPTS** Consider the statement, "The more food you eat, the more full you feel." Write *agree* or *disagree* and give a reason.

   _____

   _____

2. **INFER** How do you think some untrue food claims got to be widely believed?

   _____

   _____

3. **PREDICT** Why might it be harmful for a person to believe an untrue food claim?

   _____

   _____

4. **APPLY CONCEPTS** Write an untrue food claim. Trade claims with a partner. Rewrite your partner's claim so that it is true.

   _____

   _____

Digestion

Why Do You Need Food?

1a. DEFINE What does a Calorie measure?

_____

b. DRAW CONCLUSIONS Why do active teenagers have high energy needs?

_____

c. APPLY CONCEPTS What do you think is meant by the phrase
"a balanced diet?"

_____

_____

got it? ....

○ **I get it!** Now I know that food provides the body with _____

_____

○ **I need extra help with** _____

_____

Assess Your Understanding

Digestion

> **What Happens in Your Digestive System?**

2a. **DEFINE** (Chemical/Mechanical) digestion occurs when enzymes break down foods into simpler substances.

b. **APPLY CONCEPTS** How is the stomach similar to a washing machine?

_____

_____

c. **EXPLAIN** How are the liver and pancreas involved in digestion?

_____

_____

d. **RELATE CAUSE AND EFFECT** How do villi help the small intestine carry out its function?

_____

_____

gotit? ···

○ **I get it!** Now I know that the digestive system works through the actions of organs that include _____

_____

○ **I need extra help with** _____

Key Concepts Summaries

Digestion

Why Do You Need Food?

All living things need food to stay alive. **Food provides your body with materials to grow and to repair tissues. It also provides energy for everything you do.** The unit *Calorie* is used to measure the energy in foods. One **calorie** is the amount of energy needed to raise the temperature of one gram of water by one degree Celsius. One Calorie equals 1,000 calories.

Your body breaks down the food you eat into nutrients. Nutrients are the substances in food that provide the raw materials and energy your body needs to carry out all its processes. People need six types of nutrients: carbohydrates, fats, proteins, vitamins, minerals, and water.

What Happens in Your Digestive System?

The digestive system breaks down food, absorbs nutrients, and eliminates waste. Digestion is the process in which the body breaks down food into nutrient molecules. In mechanical digestion, food is torn or ground into smaller pieces. In chemical digestion, foods are broken down into their building blocks.

Digestion begins in the mouth. The teeth perform mechanical digestion. Saliva, containing an **enzyme** to help break down starch, begins the process of chemical digestion.

Food moves from your mouth, through the **esophagus,** which is lined with mucus to help move food. **Peristalsis**, waves of involuntary muscle contractions, move food through the esophagus and the rest of the digestive system.

Substances produced by the liver, pancreas, and lining of the small intestine help to complete chemical digestion. The liver produces bile which helps break down fat. The pancreas produces enzymes that break down carbohydrates, proteins, and fats. In the small intestine, villi increase surface area, allowing for nutrient molecules to pass from the digestive system into the blood stream. This process is called absorption.

Water and undigested food move from the small intestine to the large intestine. The large intestine absorbs water into the bloodstream. It contains bacteria that feed on the remaining materials. These bacteria produce certain vitamins, including vitamin K. At the end of the large intestine, the rectum compresses material into solid form, which is eliminated from the body through the anus.

On a separate sheet of paper, describe what happens to a fish and rice dinner as it moves through each stage of the digestive process.

Review and Reinforce

Digestion

> ### Understanding Main Ideas
> Answer the following questions on a separate sheet of paper.

1. Identify three reasons your body needs food.
2. What are the three main functions of the digestive system?
3. How do the mouth and stomach play a role in mechanical digestion?
4. How do the liver and pancreas help complete chemical digestion?
5. How does the structure of the small intestine help absorption?
6. How does the large intestine help the body to eliminate waste?

> ### Building Vocabulary
> Match each term with its definition by writing the letter of the correct definition in the right column on the line beside the term in the left column.

7. ___ calorie

    a. a protein that speeds up chemical reactions in the body

8. ___ peristalsis

    b. the mucus-lined canal through which food passes on its way from the mouth to the stomach

9. ___ villi

    c waves of involuntary muscle contractions that move food through the digestive system

10. ___ enzyme

    d. finger-shaped structures that increase the surface area of the small intestine

11. ___ esophagus

    e. the amount of energy needed to raise the temperature of one gram of water by one degree Celsius

Enrich

Digestion

Sugar makes food taste sweet, but it also contains a lot of Calories. For this reason, some people use sugar substitutes. Read the passage below. Then use a separate sheet of paper to answer the questions that follow.

Sugar Substitutes

A *sugar substitute* is a chemical that tastes sweet but provides few or no nutrients to the body. Sugar substitutes often taste much sweeter than sugar, and some have no Calories. However, sugar substitutes are not problem-free. Some lose their sweetness over time or at high temperatures; some have an aftertaste; and some have been linked to health problems. Despite these problems, over 100 million people use sugar substitutes in the United States every year.

Saccharin (sa kur uhn), the first sugar substitute, was discovered by a scientist named Constantin Fahlberg in 1879. Saccharin has no Calories and is not digested or absorbed by the body. In 1977, a study showed that rats given saccharin had a greater risk of developing cancer. As a result, all foods containing saccharin carry labels warning that this chemical might be linked to cancer in humans.

Aspartame (AS pahr taym) is another sugar substitute. Unlike saccharin, aspartame contains amino acids, which are digested and absorbed by the body. Although the United States Food and Drug Administration (FDA) has not linked aspartame to any health problems, there is still some debate about its safety.

In 1998, the FDA approved a sugar substitute called sucralose for use in some types of foods. Sucralose is made from sugar, but it has been modified so that the body does not digest or absorb it. One advantage of sucralose is that it does not lose its sweetness at high temperatures, so it can be used in foods that are baked, such as cakes.

1. The population of the United States was about 270 million in 1998. About what percentage of the population used a sugar substitute?
2. Why do you think so many people use sugar substitutes?
3. What are some of the advantages and disadvantages of sugar substitutes?
4. Which of the three sugar substitutes described above provides the body with nutrients it can use? Explain.
5. Look at the ingredients listed on a can of diet soft drink. Does the drink contain a sugar substitute? If so, which one?

Name _____ Date _____ Class _____

Digestion

If the statement is true, write _true._ If the statement is false, change the underlined word or words to make the statement true.

1. _____ Both mechanical and chemical digestion take place in the stomach.

2. _____ Elimination is the process by which nutrient molecules pass from the digestive system into the blood.

3. _____ The peristalsis is a mucus-lined passage between the mouth and the stomach.

4. _____ The large intestine prepares undigested materials for elimination.

5. _____ Saliva contains an enzyme that breaks down fats into sugars.

Fill in the blank to complete each statement.

6. The muscles of the stomach aid in _____ digestion.

7. The unit _Calorie_ is used to measure the _____ in foods.

8. The liver produces _____ that helps break down fats.

9. The _____ produces enzymes that break down carbohydrates, fats, and proteins. .

10. The villi aid the process of absorption by increasing the _____ _____ of the small intestine.

Digestion

Answer Key

After the Inquiry Warm-Up

1. Accept all reasonable responses. Students may agree and say eating more food fills your stomach, making you feel full. Students may disagree and say eating certain foods make you feel full while others do not.

2. Accept all reasonable responses. Samples: Students may say the claims were made before it was discovered that the claims were inaccurate, or the claims were made in order to sell more of the food product.

3. It could be harmful because it could lead to unhealthy eating habits.

4. Accept all reasonable responses. Students' original food claims should be obviously untrue and their revisions should change the untrue statements to make them true.

Key Concept Summaries

In the mouth, the teeth mechanically digest fish and rice, while an enzyme in saliva breaks down the starch into sugar molecules. The fish and rice goes into the esophagus where peristalsis moves it into the stomach. The contraction of the stomach muscles continues the mechanical digestion, while the enzyme pepsin breaks down proteins into amino acids. Bile produced by the liver break down fat, while enzymes produced by the pancreas break down carbohydrates, proteins, and fats. In the small intestine, villi transfer nutrient molecules into the bloodstream. The large intestine absorbs water and bacteria feed on undigested materials. The rectum compresses remaining material to be eliminated via the anus.

Review and Reinforce

1. Your body needs food to grow, to repair tissues, and to have energy.

2. The digestive system breaks down food, absorbs nutrients, and eliminates waste.

3. The teeth rip food into smaller bits; contracting stomach muscles create a churning motion to complete mechanical digestion.

4. The liver produces bile to break down proteins; the pancreas produces enzymes that break down carbohydrates, fats, and proteins.

5. The small intestine is lined with millions of villi. With increased surface area, the villi can transfer nutrients into the bloodstream.

6. The large intestine absorbs water. Bacteria feed on the remaining materials. The rectum compresses these remaining materials for elimination.

7. e   8. c   9. d

10. a   11. b

Enrich

1. about 37% ($\frac{100}{270} \times 100$)

2. Sample: They probably are concerned about the health effects of eating too much sugar.

3. Sample: Sugar substitutes sweeten food without adding Calories. However, they provide few or no nutrients to the body and may have harmful effects on health.

4. Aspartame; it contains amino acids which are digested and absorbed by the body.

5. Accept all reasonable answers. Students will likely say yes and aspartame, as most diet soft drinks contain some form of sugar substitute.

Lesson Quiz

1. true   2. Absorption
3. esophagus   4. true
5. starches   6. mechanical
7. energy   8. bile
9. pancreas   10. surface area

The Circulatory System

Lesson Pacing: 3–4 periods or $1\frac{1}{2}$–2 blocks

🕐 **SHORT ON TIME?** To do this lesson in approximately half the time, do the Activate Prior Knowledge activity followed by a discussion of the Key Concepts to familiarize students with the lesson content. Have students do the Quick Labs. The rest of the lesson can be completed by students independently.

> **Preference Navigator,** in the online Planning tools, allows you to customize *Interactive Science* to your own teaching style. You can also edit lesson plans by selecting the Lesson Planner option.
>
> **Digital Teacher's Edition** allows you to access your Teacher's Edition and Resource materials online.

my science online.com

Lesson Vocabulary

- circulatory system • heart • atrium • ventricle
- valve • artery • aorta • capillary • vein • hemoglobin

 ## Content Refresher

Transport of Carbon Dioxide Some of the carbon dioxide produced by cells dissolves directly into the bloodstream, and some is bound to hemoglobin. However, most of the carbon dioxide carried by the blood is first converted to carbonic acid by carbonic anhydrase, an enzyme found in red blood cells. The carbonic acid readily dissolves in blood, which contains substances that act as buffers and prevent the blood from becoming dangerously acidic. In the lungs, the carbonic acid is converted back into carbon dioxide, which diffuses across the capillary walls into air in the lungs.

LESSON OBJECTIVES

- Describe the structures and functions of the cardiovascular system.
- Describe the characteristics of blood.

Blended Path
Active learning using Student Edition, Inquiry Path, and Digital Path

ENGAGE AND EXPLORE

Teach this lesson using a variety of resources. Begin by reading **My Planet Diary** as a class. Have students discuss the importance of a healthy heart. Then have students do the **Inquiry Warm-Up activity.** Students will use a stethoscope to listen to their hearts before and after exercise. The **After the Inquiry Warm-Up worksheet** sets up a discussion about your heart sounds before and after exercise. Have volunteers share their answers to question 4, telling whether the heart is a voluntary or involuntary muscle.

EXPLAIN AND ELABORATE

Teach Key Concepts by explaining that the cardiovascular system delivers blood to all parts of the body, carrying necessary substances to cells and carrying waste materials away from cells. Use **Figure 1** to emphasize the functions of the circulatory system. **Lead a Discussion** about the heart's structure and function. Use the **Support the Big Q** to establish the heart's role as the engine that moves blood throughout the body, and the blood's role of carrying materials, including oxygen and carbon dioxide. **Lead a Discussion** to introduce the three kinds of blood vessels. **Lead a Discussion** about the different structures and functions of the blood vessels. Assign the **Apply It activity** to let students observe their pulses.

Teach Key Concepts by explaining blood has four components: plasma, red blood cells, white blood cells, and platelets. Differentiate between the structures and functions of these components. **Lead a Discussion** about the role of plasma. **Lead a Discussion** about how marker molecules indicate blood type, and how blood type affects blood transfusions. **Lead a Discussion** about the positive or negative Rh factor in blood and how this affects blood transfusions. Use the **Apply It activity** to have students practice determining safe and unsafe donors for each blood type. Hand out the **Key Concept Summaries** as a review of each part of the lesson. Students can also use the online **Vocab Flash Cards** to review key terms.

EVALUATE

Have students take the **Lesson Quiz.** For an alternate assessment, see the *ExamView®* Computer Test Generator, Progress Monitoring Assessments, or SuccessTracker™.

E L L Support

1 Content and Language

Give students an index card with the vocabulary terms. Ask them to find the first time the vocabulary words are used in the chapter and to write the page number on the card. Talk about the meaning of each word and the associated illustrations in the worktext. Then give students cards with definitions and pictures of each term, and ask them to match each term with the correct definition and picture. Have them repeat this process with a partner.

Lab zone Inquiry Path
Hands-on learning in the Lab zone

ENGAGE AND EXPLORE

To teach this lesson with an emphasis on inquiry, begin with the **Inquiry Warm-Up activity.** Students will use a stethoscope to listen to their hearts before and after exercise. The **After the Inquiry Warm-Up worksheet** sets up a discussion about what your heart sounds like both before and after exercise. Have volunteers share their answers to question 4, telling whether the heart is an example of a voluntary or involuntary muscle.

EXPLAIN AND ELABORATE

Focus on the **Inquiry Skill** for the lesson. Remind students that when they observe, they are using one or more of their senses to gather information. How did students make observations in the **Inquiry Warm-Up activity?** (Sample: Feeling and hearing the pulse, counting heartbeats) **Support the Big Q** by helping students understand that the heart's function is to move blood through the parts of the heart and to different parts of the body. **Build Inquiry** to allow students to listen to their own heartbeats. Before assigning the **Apply It activity** review the units in which heart rate is measured and discuss what abnormally fast or slow heart rates might indicate. Have students do the **Quick Lab** to investigate how blood travels against the flow of gravity.

Build Inquiry by giving students the chance to view human blood under a microscope and identify, compare, and contrast red and white blood cells. Before assigning the **Apply It activity,** review Landsteiner's discovery of markers and the effect of markers on blood transfusions. Have students do the **Quick Lab** to explore blood types. Students can use the online **Vocab Flash Cards** to review key terms.

EVALUATE

Have students take the **Lesson Quiz.** For an alternate assessment, see the *ExamView*® Computer Test Generator, Progress Monitoring Assessments, or SuccessTracker™.

Digital Path
Online learning at my science online.com

ENGAGE AND EXPLORE

Teach this lesson using digital resources. Begin by having students learn more about the body's transport system and explore real-world connections to the body's transport system at **My Planet Diary** online. Have them access the Chapter Resources to find the **Unlock the Big Question activity.** There they can answer the questions and refine their responses as they continue through the lesson. You can re-assign the activity and have students submit their work so you can track their progress.

EXPLAIN AND ELABORATE

Students reading above, at, or below the lexile measure of this lesson can access basic content readings at their level at **My Reading Web.** Encourage students to use the online **Vocab Flash Cards** to preview key terms. Use the online **Interactive Art activity** to show how the human heart works. **Support the Big Q** by helping students understand that the heart's function is to move blood through the different parts of the heart and body. Discuss the units in which to measure heart rate, as well as the possible causes of an abnormally high or low heart rate. Then assign the online **Apply It activity** and have students submit their work to you. Have students do the **Quick Lab** to investigate the direction of blood flow.

The **Virtual Lab** allows students to observe the components of blood. Before assigning the online **Apply It activity,** review the discovery of marker molecules and the ramifications of this discovery on blood transfusions. Have students submit their work to you. Have students complete the **Quick Lab** to further explore blood types. The **Key Concept Summaries** online allow students to read a summary and see an image associated with each part of the lesson. Online remediation is available at **My Science Coach.**

EVALUATE

Have students take the **Lesson Quiz.** For an alternate assessment, see the *ExamView*® Computer Test Generator, Progress Monitoring Assessments, or SuccessTracker™.

2 Frontload the Lesson
Preview the lesson title and key concepts with students. Ask them to use this information to predict what they will learn about in this lesson. Be sure to have them check their predictions as they read.

3 Comprehensible Input
Have students restate the lesson objectives as questions and then write answers to the questions.

4 Language Production
Pair or group students with varied language abilities to complete labs collaboratively for language practice. Have each student copy the completed written lab for personal reference.

5 Assess Understanding
Make true or false statement using lesson content and have students indicate if they agree or disagree with a thumbs up or thumbs down gesture to check whole-class comprehension.

LESSON 12.2

The Circulatory System

Establish Learning Objectives

After this lesson, students will be able to:

🗝 Describe the structures and functions of the cardiovascular system.

🗝 Describe the characteristics of blood.

Engage

Activate Prior Knowledge

MY PLANET DIARY Read *Your Heart, Your Health* with the class. Point out that the heart completes all of these tasks without a person's conscious control, since it contains involuntary muscles. Ask: **Where in the human body is the heart located?** *(In the chest cavity slightly to the left of center)* **How does your heartbeat change when you exercise?** *(It beats faster.)* **When is your heartbeat probably at its slowest rate?** *(During sleep)*

BIG IDEAS OF SCIENCE REFERENCE LIBRARY Have students look up the following topics: Defibrillators, Heartbeat, Open-Heart Surgery.

Explore

Lab Resource: Inquiry Warm-Up

L1 **OBSERVING A HEART** Students will use a stethoscope to listen to their hearts before and after exercise.

LESSON 2

The Circulatory System

UNLOCK THE BIG Q?

🗝 **What Happens in Your Circulatory System?**

🗝 **What Does Blood Contain?**

MY PLANET DIARY

Your Heart, Your Health

Here are some fascinating facts that you may not know about your heart.

- In one year, your heart pumps enough blood to fill more than 30 competition-sized swimming pools!
- A drop of blood makes the entire trip through your body in less than a minute.
- Your heart beats about 100,000 times a day.
- Your heart pushes blood through about 100,000 kilometers of vessels. They would circle Earth more than twice!
- A child's heart is about the size of a fist. An adult's heart is about the size of two fists.

FUN FACTS

Read the following questions. Write your answers below.

1. Why is it important for a person's heart to be healthy?

   Sample: The heart needs to pump a lot of blood through the body.

2. About how many times does your heart beat in a week? In a year?

   It beats about 700,000 times in a week and 36,500,000 times in a year.

▶ **PLANET DIARY** Go to **Planet Diary** to learn more about the body's transport system.

Lab zone Do the Inquiry Warm-Up *Observing a Heart.*

What Happens in Your Circulatory System?

As shown in **Figure 1**, the circulatory system, or cardiovascular system, is made up of the heart, blood vessels, and blood. **The circulatory system delivers needed substances to cells, carries wastes away from cells, and helps regulate body temperature. In addition, blood contains cells that fight disease.**

SUPPORT ALL READERS
Lexile Measure = 880L   Lexile Word Count = 2068

Prior Exposure to Content: Most students have encountered this topic in earlier grades

Academic Vocabulary: *summarize, observe, infer, interpret, predict*

Science Vocabulary: *heart, artery, aorta, capillary, vein, atrium, ventricle*

Concept Level: Generally appropriate for most students in this grade

Preteach With: My Planet Diary "Your Heart, Your Health" and Figure 1 activity

Go to **My Reading Web** to access leveled readings that provide a foundation for the content.

my science online.com

Vocabulary

- circulatory system • heart • atrium
- ventricle • valve • artery • aorta
- capillary • vein • hemoglobin

Skills

↻ Reading: Summarize

△ Inquiry: Observe

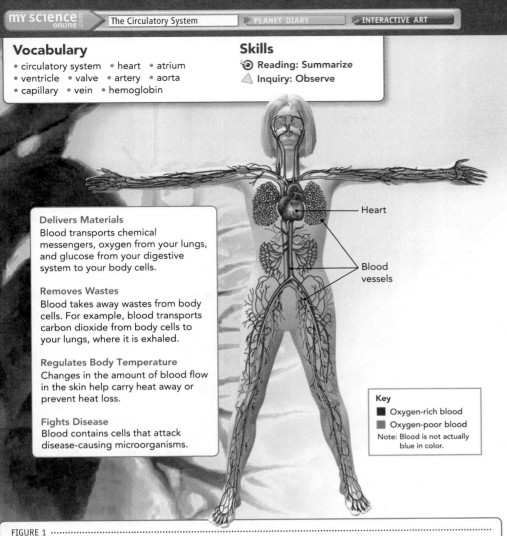

Delivers Materials
Blood transports chemical messengers, oxygen from your lungs, and glucose from your digestive system to your body cells.

Removes Wastes
Blood takes away wastes from body cells. For example, blood transports carbon dioxide from body cells to your lungs, where it is exhaled.

Regulates Body Temperature
Changes in the amount of blood flow in the skin help carry heat away or prevent heat loss.

Fights Disease
Blood contains cells that attack disease-causing microorganisms.

Heart

Blood vessels

Key
- ■ Oxygen-rich blood
- ■ Oxygen-poor blood

Note: Blood is not actually blue in color.

FIGURE 1 ·····························

The Circulatory System
Like roads that link all the parts of a town, your circulatory system links all the parts of your body.

✎ **Use the diagram to answer the questions.**

1. **Infer** What might happen if your circulatory system did not function properly?

   <u>Sample: Cells would not get the</u>
   <u>materials they need, get rid of</u>
   <u>wastes, or fight disease.</u>

2. **Pose Questions** After looking at the diagram, write a question that describes one thing you would like to learn about the circulatory system.

   <u>Sample: How does blood get</u>
   <u>from the oxygen-rich blood</u>
   <u>vessels to the oxygen-poor</u>
   <u>blood vessels?</u>

469

ⒺⓁⓁ Support

1 Content and Language
Write *artery* on the board. It comes from the Greek word *arteria,* meaning "windpipe." Tell students that ancient Greeks thought arteries were air ducts because when examining the dead, the arteries contained no blood.

2 Frontload the Lesson
Have students share their associations with *heart* and *blood,* and the words' physical and figurative meanings. Ask

what it means to "have a lot of heart" or that a certain behavior "is *in* his or her blood."

3 Comprehensible Input
Have groups make life-size diagrams of the circulatory system. Provide large sheets of paper, and have one student lie on the paper as another outlines his or her body. Use **Figure 1** as a guide.

Explain

Introduce Vocabulary

Write the word *circulatory* on the board, and explain that *-atory* is a suffix which makes the root word into an adjective. Ask students to identify the root word *circulate,* meaning "to move in a circle, circuit, or orbit." Discuss how a circle might describe the system that includes the heart, blood vessels, and blood. Also, invite students to connect the word *circuit* (the complete path of an electric current) to the circulatory system.

Cardiovascular System 🔑

Explain to students that the circulatory system delivers blood to all parts of the body, carrying necessary substances to cells and carrying waste materials away from cells. Point out that blood contains cells that fight disease, as well. Tell students that the circulatory system is also known as the cardiovascular system. Explain that *cardio* is based on a Greek word for "heart" and that *vascular* comes from a Latin word for "vessel." Ask: **Why do you think the circulatory system is also known as the cardiovascular system?** *(Help students understand that cardio is a medical prefix that comes from the Greek word for heart; vascular comes from the Latin word for vessel. Explain that the heart and the blood vessels are important organs in the circulatory system.)*

Teach With Visuals 🔑

Directs students' attention to **Figure 1.** Ask: **What are some materials that the circulatory system delivers throughout the body?** *(Chemical messengers, oxygen, glucose)* **How does the circulatory system get rid of carbon dioxide?** *(Carbon dioxide is passed from cells into the blood. Then it is carried to the lungs, where it is exhaled.)* **How does the circulatory system regulate body temperature?** *(By changing the amount of blood flow in the skin, the circulatory system carries heat away or prevents heat loss.)* **How does the circulatory system help fight disease?** *(Blood in the circulatory system carries cells that attack disease-causing microorganisms.)*

My Planet Diary provides an opportunity for students to learn more about the body's transport system.

my science online | The Circulatory System

Explain

Lead a Discussion

THE HEART'S FUNCTION Explain to students that the heart's function is to push blood through the blood vessels. Point out that the right and the left sides of the heart are the opposite of what students might expect when looking at the page. Explain that the art refers to the right and left sides of the heart, as it would be in a person. Encourage students to refer to **Figure 2** as they consider their answers to the following questions. Ask: **What are the four chambers of the heart?** *(Right atrium, right ventricle, left atrium, left ventricle)* **Which chambers contain oxygen-rich blood?** *(The left atrium and left ventricle)* **Which chambers contain oxygen-poor blood?** *(The right atrium and the right ventricle)* **Why is it so important that the body receive oxygen-rich blood?** *(All the cells in the body need oxygen.)* Have students trace the flow of blood through the heart with a pencil eraser as you describe the pattern of blood flow in both circuits through the heart. Ask: **How could having thick walls benefit the ventricles?** *(Thick walls give ventricles the muscular strength to push blood out of the heart.)*

Support the Big Q ? UbD

THE HEART AS BLOOD TRANSPORTATION HUB Point out that the heart is a kind of transportation hub for blood. Ask: **Where does blood come from before it enters the heart's left atrium?** *(The lungs)* **Since the blood came from the lungs, how would you describe this blood?** *(Full of oxygen)* **Where is this blood transported?** *(To the left ventricle and then to all parts of the body)* **Where does blood come from before it enters the heart's right atrium?** *(The body)* **Does this blood have a little or a lot of oxygen?** *(Little oxygen)* **Where is this blood transported?** *(To the right ventricle and then to the lungs)*

21st Century Learning

L3 **CRITICAL THINKING** Direct students' attention to the ventricles of the heart shown in **Figure 2.** Point out the whitish strands attached to the valves between the atria and the ventricles. Tell students that these strands, called chordae tendineae, are tendons that connect the flaps of the valves to the wall of the ventricle. Ask students to suggest the function of these tendons. *(When the ventricle contracts, blood pressure closes the valve. Without the tendons to hold the parts of the valve in place, the valve might be pushed open in the wrong direction, letting blood flow back into the atrium.)*

The Heart Without your heart, your blood would not go anywhere. As **Figure 2** shows, the **heart** is a hollow, muscular organ that pumps blood to the body through blood vessels.

The Heart's Structure The heart has a right side and left side that are completely separated by a wall of tissue called the septum. Each side has two chambers. Each upper chamber, called an **atrium** (AY tree um; plural *atria*), receives blood that comes into the heart. Each lower chamber, called a **ventricle,** pumps blood out of the heart. The pacemaker, a group of cells in the right atrium, sends out signals that regulate heart rate. These signals make the heart muscle contract.

FIGURE 2 ·······························

> **INTERACTIVE ART** **The Heart**
Your heart works 24 hours a day, resting only between beats.

✏ **Complete the activities.**

1. **Relate Text and Visuals** Find and label the septum on the diagram.
2. **CHALLENGE** Explain why the contraction of the left ventricle must be stronger than the contraction of the right ventricle.

   <u>Sample: The left ventricle must pump blood to the entire body except the lungs.</u>

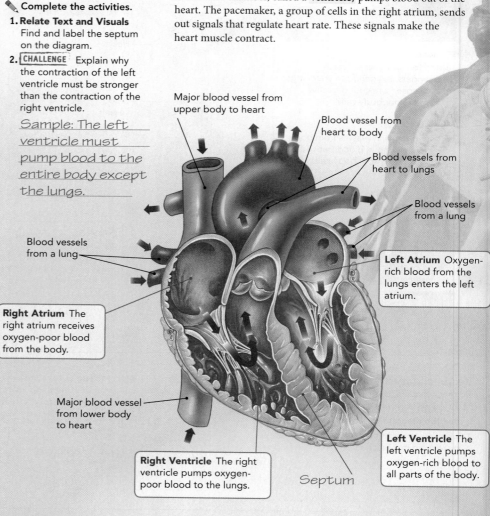

Major blood vessel from upper body to heart

Blood vessel from heart to body

Blood vessels from heart to lungs

Blood vessels from a lung

Blood vessels from a lung

Left Atrium Oxygen-rich blood from the lungs enters the left atrium.

Right Atrium The right atrium receives oxygen-poor blood from the body.

Major blood vessel from lower body to heart

Right Ventricle The right ventricle pumps oxygen-poor blood to the lungs.

Septum

Left Ventricle The left ventricle pumps oxygen-rich blood to all parts of the body.

470 Managing Materials in the Body

Interactive Art shows how the human heart works.

my science online.com ▸ **The Heart**

How the Heart Works Valves separate the atria from the ventricles. A **valve** is a flap of tissue that prevents blood from flowing backward. Valves also separate the ventricles and the large blood vessels that carry blood away from the heart.

A heartbeat sounds something like *lub-dup*. First, the heart muscle relaxes and the atria fill with blood. Next, the atria contract, squeezing blood through valves, like those in **Figure 3,** and into the ventricles. Then the ventricles contract. This contraction closes the valves between the atria and ventricles, making the *lub* sound and squeezing blood into large blood vessels. Finally, the valves between the ventricles and blood vessels snap shut, making the *dup* sound. All this happens in less than one second.

The Path of Blood Flow As you can see in **Figure 4,** the overall pattern of blood flow through the body is similar to a figure eight. The heart is at the center where the two loops cross. In the first loop, blood travels from the heart to the lungs and then back to the heart. In the second loop, blood travels from the heart throughout the body and then back to the heart.

Your body has three kinds of blood vessels: arteries, capillaries, and veins. **Arteries** carry blood away from the heart. For example, blood in the left ventricle is pumped into the **aorta** (ay AWR tuh), the largest artery in the body. From the arteries, blood flows into tiny vessels called **capillaries.** In the capillaries, substances are exchanged between the blood and body cells. From capillaries, blood flows into **veins,** which carry blood back to the heart.

FIGURE 4 ....
Blood Flow
Your heart can pump five liters of blood through the two loops each minute.

✏ Interpret Diagrams **In each box, write where the blood from the heart travels. Then tell where blood travels after it leaves each part listed below.**

Right atrium
It enters the right ventricle.

Veins from the body
It enters the right atrium.

Arteries to the lungs
It enters capillaries in the lungs.

FIGURE 3 ....
Heart Valves
Valves control the direction of blood flow through the heart.

Open Valve

Closed Valve

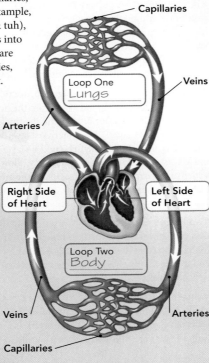

Capillaries

Loop One
Lungs

Veins

Arteries

Right Side of Heart

Left Side of Heart

Loop Two
Body

Veins

Arteries

Capillaries

471

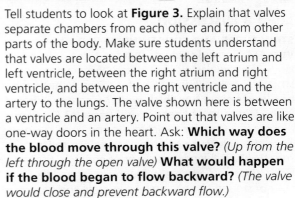

Teach With Visuals 🔑

Tell students to look at **Figure 3.** Explain that valves separate chambers from each other and from other parts of the body. Make sure students understand that valves are located between the left atrium and left ventricle, between the right atrium and right ventricle, and between the right ventricle and the artery to the lungs. The valve shown here is between a ventricle and an artery. Point out that valves are like one-way doors in the heart. Ask: **Which way does the blood move through this valve?** *(Up from the left through the open valve)* **What would happen if the blood began to flow backward?** *(The valve would close and prevent backward flow.)*

Lead a Discussion

THREE KINDS OF BLOOD VESSELS Explain that three types of blood vessels are involved in moving blood through the two loops. Ask: **What is the difference between arteries and veins?** *(Arteries carry blood away from the heart; veins carry blood to the heart.)* **What occurs in the capillaries?** *(Substances are exchanged between the blood and body cells.)*

Teach With Visuals 🔑

Tell students to look at **Figure 4.** Remind them that oxygen-rich blood is shown in red; oxygen-poor blood is in blue. Explain that while blood passes through the heart twice in completing two loops, the blood from one loop does not mix with the blood from the other loop. In the first loop, blood is moved from the heart to the lungs and back to the heart. In the second loop, blood is moved from the heart throughout the body and back to the heart. Help students locate the flow of blood to the aorta. Have students locate the blood vessels that branch off the aorta. Ask: **Why is the aorta important?** *(It is the largest artery and branches off the aorta carry blood to all parts of the body except the lungs.)* Point out that the large artery shown below the heart is the continuation of the aorta.

Elaborate ──────

Build Inquiry 🔬

L2 OBSERVE YOUR HEARTBEAT

Material stethoscope

Time 15 minutes

Explain that you can use a stethoscope to hear the sound of heart valves closing. Have students use the stethoscope to listen to their own heartbeats and then describe the sound they hear. *(After each student uses the device, use rubbing alcohol to clean the parts of the stethoscope inserted into the ears.)*

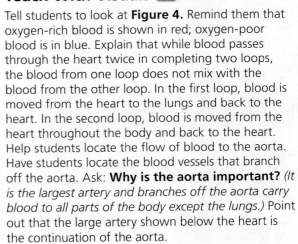

Differentiated Instruction

L1 Model a Heartbeat Give each student a beanbag or small, soft ball. Demonstrate how to squeeze the item at a steady rate to approximate 80 beats per minute. Then have students try this for a minute or two. Emphasize that the heart works continuously like this for a person's lifetime.

L3 Pacemakers Explain to students that in the case of disease or accident, an artificial pacemaker can be implanted beneath the skin and connected to the heart by wires. Tiny electrical impulses travel from the battery through the wires and make the heart contract. Have students research artificial pacemakers and present their findings in a poster or visual presentation for the class.

Explain

Lead a Discussion

STRUCTURES AND FUNCTIONS OF BLOOD VESSELS Remind students that the three different kinds of blood vessels have different functions. Their structures help support these functions. **What type of blood vessel has thick walls?** *(Arteries)* **What is the function of these blood vessels?** *(Carrying blood away from the heart to the body's cells)* **How does the structure of an artery relate to its function?** *(The innermost layer of epithelial tissue helps blood to flow freely. The muscular middle layer of smooth muscle tissue contracts and relaxes, regulating the amount of blood sent to different organs. The outer layer is connective tissue that makes the artery strong yet flexible.)* **What is the smallest type of blood vessel?** *(Capillaries)* **What happens in these thin-walled blood vessels?** *(Materials and wastes are exchanged between the body's cells and blood.)* **How does the structure of the capillaries relate to its function?** *(Capillary walls are thin so that materials can pass easily between them and the body's cells.)* **What type of blood vessel has thinner walls than artery walls?** *(Veins)* **How does the structure of veins relate to its function?** *(The thinner walls allow the veins to carry large amounts of blood from the body's cells back to the heart)*

Teach With Visuals

Tell students to look at **Figure 5.** Ask: **What is the main difference between the structure of arteries and the structures of veins?** *(Arteries are thicker than veins.)* **Why do you think this might be?** *(The extra thickness of arteries is necessary because the force of blood pumped through arteries is stronger than the force of blood flowing through veins.)*

21st Century Learning

INTERPERSONAL SKILLS Drawing Blood Vessels Have students work in pairs to draw each type of blood vessel. The drawings should include leader lines labeling any parts discussed in the text, as well as captions describing the functions of each type of vessel. Students should read the corresponding text to identify information to include in the drawings. Students can copy and expand upon the illustrations in the text or make original drawings. Encourage students to use different-colored markers or pencils to distinguish the three structures from one another.

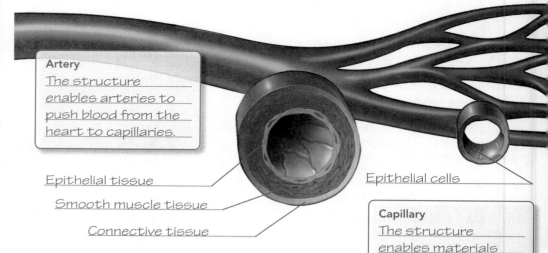

Artery
The structure enables arteries to push blood from the heart to capillaries.

Epithelial tissue

Smooth muscle tissue

Connective tissue

Epithelial cells

Capillary
The structure enables materials to be exchanged between blood and body cells.

A Closer Look at Blood Vessels Like hallways in a large building, your blood vessels run through all the tissues of your body. Although some blood vessels are as wide as your thumb, most of them are much finer than a human hair. If all the blood vessels in your body were hooked together end to end, they would stretch a distance of almost 100,000 kilometers. That's long enough to wrap around Earth twice—with a lot left over!

Arteries Arteries, shown in **Figure 5,** are thick-walled, muscular vessels. Arteries carry blood away from the heart. As they do, they split into smaller arteries. In general, the thick, elastic artery walls have three tissue layers. The innermost layer is epithelial tissue that enables blood to flow freely. The middle layer is mostly smooth muscle tissue that relaxes and contracts, allowing the artery to widen and narrow. This layer regulates the amount of blood sent to different organs. The outer layer is flexible connective tissue. These layers enable arteries to withstand the force of pumping blood.

Capillaries Blood flows from arteries into tiny capillaries. The thin capillary walls are made of a single layer of epithelial cells. Materials pass easily from the blood, through the capillary walls, and into the body cells. The waste products of cells pass in the opposite direction.

Veins Capillaries merge and form larger vessels called veins. From capillaries, blood enters veins and travels back to the heart. The walls of veins have the same tissue layers as arteries. However, the walls of veins are thinner than artery walls.

472   Managing Materials in the Body

FIGURE 5 ·······································

Blood Vessels

✎ Read the text before completing the tasks.

1. **Identify** Underline in the text what happens to blood in each kind of vessel.

2. **Interpret Diagrams** In the diagram above, label the parts of each vessel. Then write in each box how the vessel's structure enables it to function.

Professional Development Note — Teacher to Teacher

Demonstration Show students that veins have valves that prevent the backflow of blood. Press 2 fingers over the main vein on the inside of your forearm, about halfway between elbow and wrist, to temporarily stop the blood flowing up it. Massage the blood in the vein upward with your thumb. Take your thumb away, and blood should not leak back down past the valve. Take your fingers away and the vein refills from below as blood once again flows up your arm.

✐ *Mrs. Anne Rice*
Woodland Middle School
Gurnee. Illinois

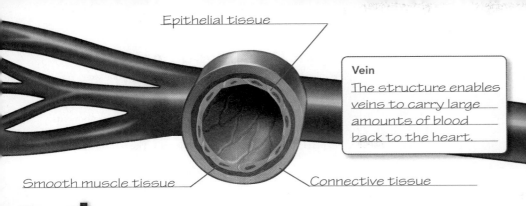

Epithelial tissue

Vein
The structure enables veins to carry large amounts of blood back to the heart.

Smooth muscle tissue   Connective tissue

apply it!

Your pulse results from the alternating relaxation and contraction of arteries as blood is forced through them. Touch the inside of your wrist and find your pulse.

1 **Observe** How does your pulse feel through your fingertips?

Sample: It feels like a lump is passing through my wrist.

2 **Observe** How many heartbeats do you count in one minute?

Sample: 65 heartbeats

 Do the Quick Lab
Direction of Blood Flow.

Assess Your Understanding

1a. Identify Blood returning from the lungs enters the heart at the (right atrium/(left atrium)/right ventricle/left ventricle).

b. Identify In which direction do arteries carry blood?

Away from the heart

c. Draw Conclusions Why is it important for your blood to complete both loops of circulation?

Sample: One loop takes oxygen into my blood and the other loop delivers oxygen to my cells.

got it?

○ **I get it!** Now I know that the circulatory system transports substances to and from cells and regulates body temperature.

○ **I need extra help with** See TE note.

Go to MY SCIENCE COACH *online for help with this subject.*

473

Differentiated Instruction

L3 Coronary Heart Disease
Challenge students to do research to learn more about the importance of coronary arteries in the context of coronary heart disease. Students might focus their research on a basic definition of this disease, which is characterized by a blockage or narrowing of the coronary artery by fatty plaques. Such a blockage causes a shortage of oxygen-rich blood

to reach the heart muscle. Effects of inadequate levels of oxygen include heart attacks and angina pectoris, both of which are potentially fatal. Encourage students to include information about a variety of ways to prevent or treat coronary heart disease, including diet changes, exercise, not smoking, medications, coronary artery bypass surgery, and balloon angioplasty.

Elaborate

Apply It!

Before they begin the activity, explain to students that heart rate is measured in beats per minute (bpm). The average heart rate for adults at rest is 60 to 100 bpm. In healthy adults, a lower heart rate at rest can indicate a healthier heart. On the other hand, an unusually high or low heart rate may be a symptom of a medical problem. Read the introductory paragraph with students. After they have completed the activity, look at the results as a class. Encourage students to identify the highest and lowest heart rates and calculate the class average. If time permits, have groups graph the class's heart rates.

Observe Explain to students that making observations means using one or more of your senses to gather information.

Lab Resource: Quick Lab

L2 DIRECTION OF BLOOD FLOW Students will explore how blood can flow against the pull of gravity.

Evaluate

Assess Your Understanding

After students have answered the questions, have them evaluate their understanding by completing the appropriate sentence.

RTI Response to Intervention

1a. If students struggle to differentiate between the four sections of the heart, **then** have them review **Figure 2.**

b. If students have trouble identifying the function of the arteries, **then** have them review the function of the three different types of blood vessels.

c. If students have difficulty drawing a conclusion about the two loops of the circulatory system, then point out that one of the main functions of the circulatory system is to deliver oxygen-rich blood to the cells.

MY SCIENCE COACH Have students go online for help in understanding what happens in the circulatory system.

Digital Lesson: Assign the *Apply It* activity online and have students submit their work to you.

MY SCIENCE online.com | **Blood Vessels**

Explain

Teach Key Concepts 🔑

Explain that blood is a complex tissue, consisting of four components: plasma, red blood cells, white blood cells, and platelets. Ask: **What is the function of red blood cells?** *(Delivery of oxygen to body cells)* **How do red blood cells perform this function?** *(The hemoglobin in red blood cells binds to oxygen molecules.)* **What do white blood cells do?** *(Recognize and alert the body to disease-causing organisms, produce chemicals to fight invading organisms, surround and kill the organisms.)* Emphasize that platelets are cell fragments. Ask: **How do platelets protect you?** *(form blood clots when a blood vessel is cut.)*

Teach With Visuals

Tell students to look at **Figure 6.** Ask: **Where is the blood vessel in this figure?** *(the thin, pink structure on the edges.)* **How does the appearance of platelets fit the fact that they are fragments of cells?** *(They are dramatically smaller than white and red blood cells.)* **In addition to color, what characteristic distinguishes red blood cells from white blood cells?** *(Sample: Size and structure—white blood cells are larger and contain nuclei.)*

Build Inquiry 🧪Lab zone

L2 OBSERVE BLOOD CELLS

Materials prepared slide of human blood (blood smear), microscope
Time 15 minutes

Have students observe human blood under a microscope. Tell them to scan for as many different-looking cells as possible. Point out that the colors they see are due to a stain that is used to make details more visible.

Ask: **Which kind of cell is most abundant?** *(Red blood cells)* **What other kinds of cells can you see?** *(White blood cells)* **How are these cells different?** *(white blood cells are larger and have nuclei, Different kinds of white blood cells have differences in the sizes and shapes of their nuclei.)*

What Does Blood Contain?

While riding your bike, you fall off and scrape your knee. Your knee stings, and blood oozes from the open wound. You go inside to clean the scrape. As you do, you wonder about what blood is.

Blood is a complex tissue. 🔑 **Blood has four components: plasma, red blood cells, white blood cells, and platelets.** About 45 percent of the volume of blood is cells. The rest is plasma.

FIGURE 6 ·······································

▶ VIRTUAL LAB **Cells in Blood**
In addition to red blood cells and white blood cells, blood contains platelets and plasma.

✏️ **Use the illustration about blood to complete the tasks.**

1. **Identify** What is the main function of hemoglobin in the blood?

   Hemoglobin carries oxygen and releases it to the body's cells.

2. **Apply Concepts** What do you think would happen to the number of white blood cells in the body when a person is fighting an infection? Explain your answer.

   The number would increase because many white blood cells would be needed to fight the infection.

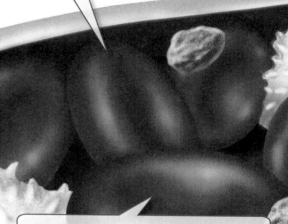

Red Blood Cells
Red blood cells take up oxygen in the lungs and deliver it to cells throughout the body. Red blood cells, like most blood cells, are produced in bone marrow. Mature red blood cells have no nuclei. Without a nucleus, a red blood cell cannot reproduce or repair itself. Mature red blood cells live only about 120 days.

Hemoglobin
A red blood cell is made mostly of **hemoglobin** (HEE muh gloh bin), a protein that contains iron and binds chemically to oxygen molecules in the lungs. Hemoglobin releases oxygen as blood travels through the capillaries. Oxygen makes red blood cells bright red. Without it, the cells are dark red. Hemoglobin also picks up some carbon dioxide produced by cells and releases it into the lungs.

474 Managing Materials in the Body

Virtual Lab allows students to observe the composition of blood.

my science online.com ▶ **Blood**

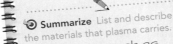
Plasma

Most materials transported in blood travel in the plasma. Plasma carries nutrients, such as glucose, fats, vitamins, and minerals. Plasma also carries chemical messengers that direct body activities, such as how your cells use glucose. In addition, plasma carries away most of the carbon dioxide and many other wastes that cell processes produce. Proteins in the plasma make it look pale yellow. Some of these proteins regulate water in the blood. Some help fight disease. Others help to form blood clots.

Summarize List and describe the materials that plasma carries.

- Nutrients such as glucose, fats, and vitamins
- Chemical messengers that direct body activities
- Waste products

White Blood Cells

Like red blood cells, white blood cells are produced in bone marrow. White blood cells are the body's disease fighters. Some white blood cells recognize disease-causing organisms, such as bacteria, and alert the body to the invasion. Other white blood cells produce chemicals to fight the invaders. Still others surround and kill the organisms. White blood cells are larger than red blood cells and contain nuclei. They may live for days, months, or even years.

Platelets

Platelets (PLAYT lits) are cell fragments that help form blood clots. When a blood vessel is cut, platelets collect and stick to the vessel at the wound. The platelets release chemicals that produce a protein called fibrin (FY brin). Fibrin weaves a net of tiny fibers across the cut. Platelets and blood cells become trapped in the net, and a blood clot forms.

475

Differentiated Instruction

L1 Red Cells vs. White Cells To help students clarify their understanding of red and white blood cells, have them create compare/contrast tables or Venn diagrams. They should include words and phrases describing the structure and function of red and white blood cells, as well as the places they are produced in the body.

L3 Research Anemia Tell students that anemia is an illness caused by a shortage of red blood cells or hemoglobin in the body. Invite students to find out more about anemia, especially reasons why some teenagers are prone to anemia (Samples: They are picky eaters, go on diets to lose weight, or become vegetarians.) Students might share their research findings in an oral presentation.

Make Analogies

L1 LIVING COMPONENTS It may help to clarify some students' understanding of the components of blood to personify red blood cells, white blood cells, and platelets. Point out that white blood cells are like a nation's soldiers, that red blood cells are like people transporting food and other valuable cargo all over the country, and that platelets are like emergency medical technicians treating injuries. Ask: **In what way are white blood cells like soldiers?** (Both fight off threats and invaders.) **How do red blood cells serve a function that is similar to people transporting valuable cargo?** (They carry oxygen, a valuable substance, to places all over the body.) **What do platelets do that resembles the work of emergency medical technicians?** (When a blood vessel is cut, they attempt to stop the bleeding by forming blood clots.)

Summarize Tell students that when they summarize, they restate the main idea of a paragraph or passage.

Lead a Discussion

THE ROLE OF PLASMA Point out that about 55 percent of the volume of blood is plasma. Plasma is not a cell. It is a water-like fluid in which red blood cells, white blood cells, and platelets are suspended. Plasma carries many materials that aid the body's cells. Ask: **What are some of the nutrients plasma carries?** (Glucose, fats, vitamins, and minerals) **How does plasma help direct the body's activities?** (By carrying chemical messengers) **How does plasma help the body eliminate waste?** (By carrying away most of the carbon dioxide and other wastes produced by cells) **How do the proteins in plasma help the body function?** (They regulate water in the blood, help fight disease, and help form blood clots.)

21st Century Learning

CREATIVITY Modeling the Components of Blood Invite students to make models of the three cell components of blood—red blood cells, white blood cells, and platelets—using colored modexling clay. Students may refer to **Figure 5** for guidance about representing the appropriate shapes, sizes, and colors of each component. After students have completed their models, have them write an information card for each one that includes the component's name and primary function.

Explain

Lead a Discussion

MARKER MOLECULES Explain to students that the presence or absence of marker molecules on the red blood cells determines a person's blood type. Point out that these marker molecules also determine which types of blood the person can safely receive in a transfusion. Encourage students to look carefully at **Figure 7.** Ask: **What type of marker molecule is on type B blood?** *(B marker)* **Why are clumping proteins in type B blood "anti-A"?** *(Clumping proteins recognize markers that are foreign or different. Because type B blood contains B markers, it recognizes A markers as "foreign" and is therefore "anti-A.")* **What would happen if a person with type B blood received type A blood?** *(The type A cells would clump together; the person would get sick and could die.)* **What difference is there between the red blood cells of a person with type A blood and the red blood cells of a person with type AB blood?** *(The red blood cells of a person with type A blood have only one kind of molecule marker—that is, a marker for type A. On the other hand, the red blood cells of a person with type AB blood has molecule markers for type A as well as molecule markers for type B.)* **What difference is there between the red blood cells of a person with type O blood and the red blood cells of people with the other three types of blood?** *(The red blood cells of a person with type O blood have no molecule markers for blood type, whereas the red blood cells of people with A, B, and AB have such molecule markers.)* **Why can a person with type B blood receive type O blood in a transfusion?** *(Type O has no markers for blood type.)*

did you know?

Transfusions for patients in hospitals and other medical facilities create a constant need for blood. In Florida, blood centers across the state collect a total of more than 1,000,000 units of blood each year. (One unit is equal to 450 mL.)

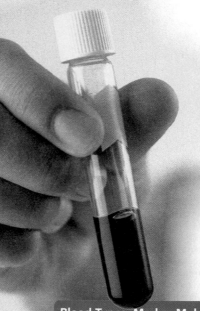

Marker Molecules and Transfusions A blood transfusion is the transfer of blood from one person to another. Most early attempts at blood transfusion failed, but no one knew why. In the early 1900s, a physician named Karl Landsteiner tried mixing blood samples from two people. Sometimes the two blood samples blended smoothly. At other times, the red blood cells clumped together. In a patient, this clumping would clog the capillaries, causing death.

Blood Types Landsteiner identified the four major types of blood: A, B, AB, and O. Blood types are determined by marker molecules on red blood cells. If your blood type is A, you have the A marker. If your blood type is B, you have the B marker. People with type AB blood have both A and B markers. People with type O blood do not have A or B markers.

Clumping proteins in your plasma recognize red blood cells with "foreign" markers that are not your type. The proteins make cells with foreign markers clump together. For example, blood type A contains anti-B clumping proteins that act against cells with B markers. Blood type O has clumping proteins for both A and B markers. In **Figure 7**, you can see all the blood type marker molecules and clumping proteins.

FIGURE 7 ....
Blood Types and Their Markers
Depending on your blood type, you may have certain marker molecules on your red blood cells and certain clumping proteins in your plasma.

✎ **Create Data Tables** In the table, label the marker molecules and then identify the clumping proteins.

Blood Types, Marker Molecules, and Clumping Proteins				
Blood Type Characteristic	**Blood Type A**	**Blood Type B**	**Blood Type AB**	**Blood Type O**
Marker Molecules on Red Blood Cells				
Clumping Proteins	anti-B	anti-A	no clumping proteins	anti-A and anti-B

Digital Lesson: Assign the *Apply It* activity online and have students submit their work to you.

my science online | **Blood**

The marker molecules on your red blood cells determine the type of blood you can safely receive in transfusions. For example, a person with type A blood can receive transfusions of type A or type O blood. But type B blood would cause clumping and would not be safe. Through a process called cross-matching, a patient's blood type is checked so that safe donor types can be determined.

Blood Type	Safe Donor(s)	Unsafe Donor(s)
A	A, O	B, AB
B	B, O	A, AB
AB	A, B, AB, O	None
O	O	A, B, AB

1 Infer Use what you know about blood types to complete the table.

2 Predict Which blood type may accept safe transfusions from any other blood type? Why?

Type AB can accept any other blood type because it has no clumping proteins.

3 CHALLENGE Which blood type is a "universal donor," that is, a blood type that can be used in transfusions to anyone? Explain your reasoning.

Type O can donate to all blood types because it does not have A or B markers.

Rh Factor Landsteiner also discovered a protein on red blood cells that he called *Rh factor*. About 85 percent of the people he tested had this protein. The rest did not. As with blood type, a marker molecule on the red blood cells determines the presence of Rh factor. An Rh-positive blood type has the Rh marker. An Rh-negative blood type does not. Clumping proteins will develop in people with Rh-negative blood if they receive Rh-positive blood. This situation may be potentially dangerous.

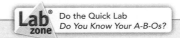 Do the Quick Lab
Do You Know Your A-B-Os?

Assess Your Understanding

2a. Identify What is plasma?

It is the liquid part of the blood.

b. Review What did Karl Landsteiner's observations lead him to discover?

Blood types and Rh factors

c. Relate Cause and Effect How might a lack of iron in a person's diet affect his or her blood?

Sample: The person might not have enough hemoglobin to make all the red blood cells needed.

got it?

○ **I get it!** Now I know that blood contains plasma, red blood cells, white blood cells, and platelets.

○ **I need extra help with** See TE note.

Go to MY SCIENCE COACH *online for help with this subject.*

477

Differentiated Instruction

L1 Karl Landsteiner Tell students that Karl Landsteiner won the Nobel Prize in Medicine in 1930 for his work on the blood groups. Invite students to research Karl Landsteiner and write a brief report on the studies that led to his discovery of the blood groups.

L3 Blood Banks Explain that the American Red Cross and America's Blood Centers control most of the blood banks in the United States. These agencies solicit citizens to donate blood that will be used in emergency transfusions. Invite students to research how blood banks work in the U.S. In their brief reports, students might choose to focus on the price of blood, on the types of procedures that require blood, or on how the need for donated blood often far outweighs the supply.

Lead a Discussion

RH FACTOR Explain that Rh factor is named after the Rhesus macaque, a monkey used by Landsteiner in his experiments with blood. Draw students' attention to a difference as well as the similarities between Rh factor and blood types. Ask: **How are both blood types and Rh factor determined?** *(by the presence or absence of markers on red blood cell molecules)* **Why is it important to match the donor's and recipient's Rh factor during a blood transfusion?** *(If the Rh factor is different, dangerous clumping proteins will develop in the recipient's blood.)* **In what important way are Rh factors and blood types different from one another?** *(Sample: There are four blood types, and two Rh factors.)* If students have previously studied genetics, they may be aware of the pattern of inheritance of A-B-O blood types. Tell them the Rh factor is also inherited, but not controlled by an allele that is part of the A-B-O inheritance pattern.

Elaborate

Apply It!

Before students begin the activity, explain that the *donor* is the blood given. Read the introductory paragraph and review the chart. The Apply It activity can be made more challenging by adding information about the Rh factor. This exercise may be done as a class discussion, an extension of the initial exercise, or for gifted students to meet the need for **differentiated instruction.**

Lab Resource: Quick Lab

L2 DO YOU KNOW YOUR A-B-OS? Students will model interactions between different blood types.

Evaluate

Assess Your Understanding

After students have answered the questions, have them evaluate their understanding by completing the appropriate sentence.

R T I Response to Intervention

2a. If students have difficulty defining plasma, **then** have them review the definition that accompanies Figure 6.

b. If students have trouble recalling Landsteiner's discovery, **then** point out he observed some bloods mixed smoothly; some clumped.

c. If students struggle to relate iron to red blood cells, **then** have them review Figure 6.

MY SCIENCE COACH Have students go online for help in understanding what blood contains.

Lab zone **After the Inquiry Warm-Up**

The Circulatory System

> **Inquiry Warm-Up, *Observing a Heart***
> In the Inquiry Warm-Up, you used a stethoscope to investigate what your heart sounds like both before and after exercise. Using what you learned from that activity, answer the questions below.

1. **PREDICT** Based on what you observed during the lab, what do you think your heart sounds like when you are sleeping? Explain.

   _____

   _____

2. **USE PRIOR KNOWLEDGE** What happens to your breathing when you exercise?

   _____

   _____

3. **DRAW CONCLUSIONS** Your heart is made up mostly of muscle tissue. How will exercise affect the heart? Explain.

   _____

   _____

   _____

4. **CLASSIFY** Is the heart an example of a voluntary or involuntary muscle? Explain.

   _____

   _____

Name _____ Date _____ Class _____

Assess Your Understanding

The Circulatory System

> ## What Happens in Your Circulatory System?

1a. **IDENTIFY** Blood returning from the lungs enters the heart at the (right atrium/left atrium/right ventricle/left ventricle).

b. **IDENTIFY** In which direction do arteries carry blood?

_____

_____

c. **DRAW CONCLUSIONS** Why is it important for your blood to complete both loops of circulation?

_____

_____

_____

got it? ....

○ **I get it!** Now I know that the circulatory system transports _____

_____

○ **I need extra help with** _____

_____

Name _____ Date _____ Class _____

The Circulatory System

What Does Blood Contain?

2a. **IDENTIFY** What is plasma?

_____

b. **REVIEW** What did Karl Landsteiner's observations lead him to discover?

_____

_____

c. **RELATE CAUSE AND EFFECT** How might a lack of iron in a person's diet affect his or her blood?

_____

_____

_____

got_{it}?··

○ **I get it!** Now I know that blood contains _____

_____

○ **I need extra help with** _____

_____

Key Concept Summaries

The Circulatory System

What Happens in Your Circulatory System?

The **circulatory system,** or cardiovascular system, is made up of the heart, blood vessels, and blood. **The circulatory system delivers needed substances to cells, carries wastes away from cells, and helps regulate body temperature. In addition, blood contains cells that fight disease.**

The **heart** is a hollow, muscular organ that pumps blood to the body through the blood vessels. Structurally, the heart has a right side and a left side. Each upper chamber, called an **atrium,** receives blood coming into the heart. Each lower chamber, called

a **ventricle,** pumps blood out of the heart. Valves separate the atria from the ventricles. A **valve** is a flap of tissue that prevents blood from flowing backward.

The circulatory system has three kinds of blood vessels. **Arteries** carry blood away from the heart. The **aorta** is the largest artery in the body. From the arteries, blood flows into tiny vessels called **capillaries,** where substances are exchanged between blood and body cells. From capillaries, blood flows into **veins,** which carry blood back to the heart.

What Does Blood Contain?

Blood has four components: plasma, red blood cells, white blood cells, and platelets. Red blood cells are made mostly of **hemoglobin.** Hemoglobin binds with oxygen in the lungs, allowing red blood cells to release oxygen to the body's cells as it travels through the capillaries. Hemoglobin also picks up carbon dioxide in the capillaries and releases it back into the lungs.

White blood cells are the body's disease fighters. Like red blood cells, white blood cells are produced in bone marrow, but white blood cells are larger than red cells and contain nuclei. Platelets are cell fragments that help form blood clots when a blood vessel is cut.

Plasma carries glucose, fats, vitamins, minerals, and chemical messengers that direct body activities. Plasma also carries away carbon dioxide and other waste.

Blood type is determined by marker molecules on red blood cells. There are four major blood types: A, B, AB, and O. In blood transfusions, plasma recognizes blood with "foreign" markers, which can result in dangerous clumping. The Rh factor is a protein in blood. Blood types are either "positive" or "negative" for the Rh factor. In transfusions, it is dangerous to mix Rh positive blood with Rh negative blood.

On a separate sheet of paper, explain how blood travels through the body and why the circulatory system is important.

Review and Reinforce

The Circulatory System

Understanding Main Ideas
Use the diagram to answer the following questions on a separate sheet of paper.

1. Draw arrows on the diagram to show the path of blood flow throughout the body.
2. What is the function of each atrium?
3. What is the function of each ventricle?
4. Which of the large blood vessels labeled *a*, *b*, *c*, and *d* are arteries and which are veins? Explain how you know.

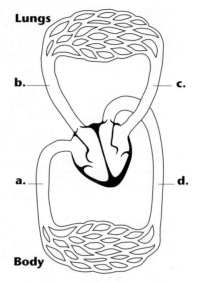

Building Vocabulary
Match each term with its definition by writing the letter of the correct definition in the right column on the line beside the term in the left column.

5. ___ circulatory system

6. ___ heart

7. ___ atrium

8. ___ ventricle

9. ___ hemoglobin

10. ___ valve

11. ___ arteries

12. ___ aorta

13. ___ capillaries

14. ___ veins

a. a protein that contains iron and binds chemically to oxygen molecules in the lungs

b. a lower chamber of the heart

c. the body's largest artery

d. the heart, blood vessels, and blood

e. blood vessels that carry blood back to the heart

f. an upper chamber of the heart

g. tiny blood vessels where substances are exchanged between the blood and body cells

h. a flap of tissue that prevents blood from flowing backward

i. a hollow, muscular organ that pumps blood throughout the body

j. blood vessels that carry blood away from the heart

Enrich

The Circulatory System

> Read the passage and study the figure. Then use a separate sheet of paper to answer the questions that follow the diagram.

Heart Murmurs

Sometimes when a doctor listens to a patient's heartbeat, he or she can hear an abnormal flow of blood through the heart. The sound of this abnormal flow is called a *heart murmur*.

Some heart murmurs are caused by blood leaking inside the heart. One type of leak occurs when there is a hole in the wall of tissue that separates the right and left sides of the heart. A hole in this wall causes blood to leak from the left side of the heart into the right side because the left side pumps with more force than the right side. The figure shows a heart with a hole between its ventricles and the direction of blood flow from its left ventricle.

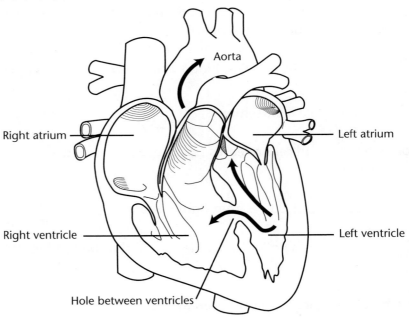

1. In what two directions does blood flow from the left ventricle of the heart in the figure?
2. How does the blood flow in this abnormal heart compare to that in a normal heart?
3. Compare the blood in the right ventricle of the heart in the figure with the blood in the right ventricle of a normal heart. (*Hint:* The wall of tissue normally prevents oxygen-rich blood from mixing with oxygen-poor blood.)
4. How might a hole between the sides of the heart affect the functioning of the circulatory system?

Lesson Quiz

The Circulatory System

If the statement is true, write *true*. If the statement is false, change the underlined word or words to make the statement true.

1. _____ White blood cells help form blood clots when a blood vessel is cut.

2. _____ Most materials, including glucose, fats, vitamins, minerals, and chemical messengers travel in the hemoglobin.

3. _____ The lower chambers, called valves, pump blood out of the heart.

4. _____ In the first loop of blood circulation, blood travels from the heart to the lungs and then back to the heart.

5. _____ From the arteries, blood flows into tiny vessels called veins.

Fill in the blank to complete each statement.

6. The hemoglobin in red blood cells releases _____ as blood travels through the capillaries.

7. Blood contains _____ that fight disease.

8. The _____ is a hollow, muscular organ that pumps blood throughout the body.

9. Red and white blood cells are both produced in _____ _____.

10. The _____ is the largest artery in the body.

The Circulatory System

Answer Key

After the Inquiry Warm-Up

1. Answers will vary. Students may predict that the heart will beat more slowly during sleep since the body is less physically active.

2. During exercise you breathing becomes faster and heavier.

3. Exercise will make the heart stronger because muscles grow stronger when they are used and exercised.

4. The heart is an example of an involuntary muscle because it is not under your conscious control.

Key Concept Summaries

Blood travels through the body in an overall pattern like a figure eight, with the heart at the center where the two loops cross. First, blood travels from the heart to the lungs, where it picks up oxygen, and back. Then blood travels from the heart throughout the body, where it delivers oxygen to the cells, and back to the heart. The circulatory system sends important substances to cells around the body, carries waste products away from cells, and fights disease.

Review and Reinforce

1. Students' should have drawn arrows showing blood being pumped out of the right ventricle along b, back to the left atrium along c, from the left atrium into the left ventricle, out of the left ventricle along d, back to the right atrium along a, and from the right atrium into the right ventricle.

2. The right atrium receives oxygen-poor blood from the body. The left atrium receives oxygen-rich blood from the lungs.

3. The right ventricle pumps the oxygen-poor blood to the lungs. The left ventricle pumps the oxygen-rich blood to all parts of the body.

4. The blood vessels labeled b and d are arteries, because they carry blood away from the heart. The blood vessels labeled a and c are veins, because they carry blood to the heart.

5. d	6. i
7. f	8. b
9. a	10. h
11. j	12. c
13. g	14. e

Enrich

1. In the heart in the figure, blood flows from the left ventricle into the aorta and into the right ventricle.

2. In a normal heart, blood only flows from the left ventricle into the aorta.

3. The blood in the right ventricle of a normal heart is oxygen-poor. The blood in the right ventricle of the abnormal heart in the figure contains a mixture of oxygen-poor and oxygen-rich blood.

4. Since oxygen-rich and oxygen-poor blood would mix, the circulatory system might not be able to deliver enough oxygen to body cells.

Lesson Quiz

1. Platelets	2. plasma
3. ventricles	4. true
5. capillaries	6. oxygen
7. white blood cells	8. heart
9. bone marrow	10. aorta

The Respiratory System

Lesson Pacing: 2–3 periods or 1–1½ blocks

🕐 **SHORT ON TIME?** To do this lesson in approximately half the time, do the Activate Prior Knowledge activity followed by a discussion of the Key Concepts to familiarize students with the lesson content. Do the Quick Labs and have students do the Interactive Art online. The rest of the lesson can be completed by students independently.

> **Preference Navigator,** in the online Planning tools, allows you to customize *Interactive Science* to your own teaching style. You can also edit lesson plans by selecting the Lesson Planner option.
>
> **Digital Teacher's Edition** allows you to access your Teacher's Edition and Resource materials online.

my science online.com

Lesson Vocabulary

- pharynx • trachea • cilia • bronchi • lungs • alveoli
- diaphragm • larynx • vocal cords

 Content Refresher

Control of Breathing To some extent, people can control their rates of breathing. However, if an individual holds his or her breath for a long time, the person would lose consciousness and the brain would take over to resume breathing. Much of the control of breathing is involuntary and is directed by breathing centers in the brain.

It is the concentration of carbon dioxide (CO_2) in the blood, rather than the concentration of oxygen (O_2), that determines the rate of breathing. In general, the higher the blood level of carbon dioxide, the more rapidly a person breathes. For example, there is an increase in the amount of carbon dioxide in blood when exercising; therefore, a person's rate of breathing increases. In contrast, the amount of carbon dioxide in the blood can fall to abnormal levels when a person hyperventilates causing the blood acidity to decline and the brain to think that it has more oxygen than it actually does. In this instance, the blood oxygen levels can decrease to treacherous levels.

LESSON OBJECTIVES

🔧 Identify the functions and structures of the respiratory system.
🔧 Explain what happens during breathing and gas exchange.

Blended Path
Active learning using Student Edition, Inquiry Path, and Digital Path

ENGAGE AND EXPLORE

Teach this lesson using a variety of resources. Begin by reading **My Planet Diary** as a class. Have students share ideas about how to perform rescue breathing. Have students do the **Inquiry Warm-Up activity.** Students will investigate factors that affect air volume exhaled in a normal breath. Discuss how students could measure air they exhale. The **After the Inquiry Warm-Up worksheet** sets up a discussion how measuring the balloon compares the volume of air exhaled with types of breaths. Have volunteers share answers to question 4 about how the balloon is similar to and different from the lungs.

EXPLAIN AND ELABORATE

Teach Key Concepts by explaining what the respiratory system takes in and what it produces as waste. Use **Figure 1** to illustrate how other body systems work with the respiratory system. **Lead a Discussion** about organs that air passes through on the way to the lungs. Have students look at **Figure 2** as you explain that the cilia sweep the mucus made by the cells in the trachea up to the pharynx. Have students trace the pathways of air from outside the body into the lungs using **Figure 3.**

Teach Key Concepts by explaining how the rib muscles and diaphragm work together to move air in and out of the lungs. **Lead a Discussion** about how the contraction and relaxation of these muscles controls the breathing process. **Lead a Discussion** about how the larynx, vocal cords, and rushing air produce sound. The **Apply It activity** lets students observe and describe how vibrations in the larynx change as pitch changes. Use the **Support the Big Q** to connect the process of gas exchange with the way the respiratory and circulatory systems work together to manage materials in the body. **Lead a Discussion** about how the surface area of alveoli facilitates gas exchange with the capillaries. Hand out the **Key Concept Summaries** as a review of each part of the lesson. Students can also use the online **Vocab Flash Cards** to review key terms.

EVALUATE

Have students take the **Lesson Quiz.** For an alternate assessment, see the *ExamView®* Computer Test Generator, Progress Monitoring Assessments, or SuccessTracker™.

E L L Support

1 Content and Language

The word *lung* comes from the German word *lunge* meaning "the light organ." Discuss why this is a fitting origin for the word *lung.*

DIFFERENTIATED INSTRUCTION KEY
L1 Struggling Students or Special Needs
L2 On-Level Students **L3** Advanced Students

LESSON PLANNER 12.3

 **Inquiry Path** Hands-on learning in the Lab zone

ENGAGE AND EXPLORE

To teach this lesson with an emphasis on inquiry, begin with the **Inquiry Warm-Up activity.** Students will see what factors affect the volume of air exhaled. Discuss how students could measure the air they exhale in a breath. Have students do the **After the Inquiry Warm-Up worksheet.** Talk about the varied amounts of air exhaled in a normal breath and the biggest breath. Have volunteers share their answers to question 4 about how lungs are similar to and different from the balloon.

EXPLAIN AND ELABORATE

Focus on the **Inquiry Skill** for the lesson. Point out that when you communicate in science you share knowledge, information, or observations in a way that can be clearly understood by others. What is the best way to communicate observations made or knowledge gained during the **Inquiry Warm-Up activity?** (Accept all reasonable responses.) Have students do the **Quick Lab** to identify the role of the nose during respiration and then share their results.

Use the **Teacher Demo** to show students how using a balloon is like the breathing process. Before assigning the **Apply It activity,** review how the larynx, vocal cords, and rushing air work together to create sound. Use the **Support the Big Q** to help students connect the process of gas exchange with the way the respiratory and circulatory systems work together to manage materials in the body. Have students do the **Lab Investigation** to further investigate the breathing process. Students can use the online **Vocab Flash Cards** to review key terms.

EVALUATE

Have students take the **Lesson Quiz.** For an alternate assessment, see the *ExamView®* Computer Test Generator, Progress Monitoring Assessments, or SuccessTracker™.

Digital Path Online learning at my science online.com

ENGAGE AND EXPLORE

Teach this lesson using digital resources. Begin by having students explore real-world connections to the respiratory system at **My Planet Diary** online. Have them access the Chapter Resources to find the **Unlock the Big Question activity.** There they can answer the questions and refine their responses as they continue through the lesson. You can re-assign the activity and have students submit their work so you can track their progress.

EXPLAIN AND ELABORATE

Students reading above, at, or below the lexile measure of this lesson can access basic content readings at their level at **My Reading Web.** Have students use the online **Vocab Flash Cards** to preview key terms. Do the **Quick Lab** to have students explore the role of the nose in respiration.

Use the online **Interactive Art** to have students explore how muscles affect the breathing process. Before assigning the online **Apply It activity,** discuss the role of the larynx, the vocal cords, and breathing in making sounds. Have students submit their work to you. Assign the online **Art in Motion activity** to give students an opportunity to explore the process of gas exchange in the lungs. Use the **Support the Big Q** to help students relate gas exchange in the alveoli to the way the respiratory and circulatory systems work together to manage materials in the body. Assign the **Lab Investigation** to have students further investigate the breathing process. The **Key Concept Summaries** online allow students to read a summary and see an image associated with each part of the lesson. Online remediation is available at **My Science Coach.**

EVALUATE

Have students take the **Lesson Quiz.** For an alternate assessment, see the *ExamView®* Computer Test Generator, Progress Monitoring Assessments, or SuccessTracker™.

2 Frontload the Lesson

Preview the lesson visuals, labels, and captions. Ask students what they know about the terms *lungs* and *vocal cords*. Explain the specific meanings these terms have in science.

3 Comprehensible Input

Have students study the visuals and their captions throughout the lesson to support the lesson's Key Concepts.

4 Language Production

Pair or group students with varied language abilities to complete labs collaboratively for language practice. Have each student copy the completed written lab for personal reference.

5 Assess Understanding

Ask students to make notes about the Key Concepts in the lesson and prepare an oral presentation of the concepts. Encourage students to use the visuals in the lesson to support their presentations.

The Respiratory System

Establish Learning Objectives

After this lesson, students will be able to:

🔑 Identify the functions and structures of the respiratory system.

🔑 Explain what happens during breathing and gas exchange.

Engage

Activate Prior Knowledge

MY PLANET DIARY Read *The Breath of Life* with the class. Remind students that air is a mixture of gases. Invite students to share their ideas about which gases are in air. Ask: **What gases make up a sample of air?** *(Students may name oxygen, carbon dioxide, and nitrogen.)* **Which gas do humans and other animals need to survive?** *(Students may indicate that living things need oxygen to survive.)*

BIG IDEAS OF SCIENCE REFERENCE LIBRARY 📖 Have students look up the following topics: Altitude, Singing, Tour de France.

Explore

Lab Resource: Inquiry Warm-Up 🔬

L1 HOW BIG CAN YOU BLOW UP A BALLOON? Students will use a balloon to investigate factors that affect the volume of air a person exhales.

LESSON 3 The Respiratory System

🔑 What Is the Role of the Respiratory System?

🔑 What Happens When You Breathe?

MY PLANET DIARY

MISCONCEPTION

The Breath of Life

Misconception: The only gas you exhale is carbon dioxide.

Actually, about 16 percent of the air you exhale is oxygen. The air you inhale is made up of about 21 percent oxygen. Your body only uses a small portion of the oxygen in each breath, so the unused portion is exhaled.

Sometimes, this exhaled oxygen can mean the difference between life and death. If a person stops breathing, he or she needs to get more oxygen quickly. A rescuer can breathe into the person's mouth to give unused oxygen to the person. This process is called rescue breathing.

Read the following question. Then write your answer below.

Why would you want to learn to perform rescue breathing?

Sample: I would want to learn it in case I need to save someone's life.

▷ PLANET DIARY Go to **Planet Diary** to learn more about the respiratory system.

🔬 **Lab zone** Do the Inquiry Warm-Up *How Big Can You Blow Up a Balloon?*

What Is the Role of the Respiratory System?

In an average day, you may breathe 20,000 times. You breathe all the time because your body cells need oxygen, which comes from the air. 🔑 **Your respiratory system moves air containing oxygen into your lungs and removes carbon dioxide and water from your body. Your lungs and the structures that lead to them make up your respiratory system.**

478 Managing Materials in the Body

SUPPORT ALL READERS

Lexile Measure = 910L   Lexile Word Count = 1357

Prior Exposure to Content: Many students may have misconceptions on this topic

Academic Vocabulary: *compare, contrast, communicate, interpret, observe, describe*

Science Vocabulary: *pharynx, larynx, trachea, cilia, bronchi, alveoli*

Concept Level: Generally appropriate for most students in this grade

Preteach With: My Planet Diary "The Breath of Life" and Figure 3 activity

Go to **My Reading Web** to access leveled readings that provide a foundation for the content.

my science online.com

Vocabulary
- pharynx • trachea • cilia • bronchi
- lungs • alveoli • diaphragm • larynx • vocal cords

Skills
- Reading: Chart
- Inquiry: Communicate

Breathing and Homeostasis Your body needs oxygen for cellular respiration. During cellular respiration, cells break down glucose, releasing energy. You use energy for activities such as reading this book or playing ball. Your body also uses energy in carrying out processes that maintain homeostasis, such as removing wastes, growing, and regulating body temperature.

Breathing gets oxygen into your body. But cellular respiration depends on body systems working together. The digestive system supplies glucose from food. And the circulatory system carries this glucose and the oxygen from the respiratory system to all the cells in the body.

FIGURE 1 ....
Systems Working Together
Body systems work together, getting the materials needed for cellular respiration to cells.

✎ **Describe System Interactions** Describe how each system provides cells with materials needed for cellular respiration. Then tell how cellular respiration helps the body maintain homeostasis.

Respiratory System
This system moves air, which contains oxygen, into the body.

Circulatory System
The blood picks up oxygen and glucose and delivers them to body cells.

Digestive System
This system provides glucose used in cellular respiration.

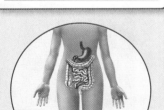

Cellular Respiration and Homeostasis
Sample: Cellular respiration supplies the energy for all life processes in the body.

479

Explain

Introduce Vocabulary
Point out that the plural form of some words ending in -*us* is -*i*. *Bronchi* is plural for *bronchus*. There are two bronchi through which air flows in and out of the lungs. *Alveoli* is plural for *alveolus*. The lungs contain many alveoli, or sacs in which oxygen moves into the blood and carbon dioxide leaves the blood.

Teach Key Concepts 🔑
Explain to students that the body must take in certain substances to survive. Point out that the body must also remove the wastes it produces. The respiratory system is one of the systems that carry out these processes. Ask: **What gas does your body need to take in?** *(Oxygen)* **What gases does the body produce as waste?** *(Carbon dioxide and water vapor)* **What body system is responsible for exchanging these gases?** *(The respiratory system)*

Teach With Visuals
Tell students to look at **Figure 1.** Explain that body systems do not work alone. Instead they interact and overlap. Ask: **How are the respiratory and digestive systems similar?** *(They both obtain substances the body needs.)* **How do the respiratory and digestive systems depend on the circulatory system?** *(The circulatory system brings materials from the respiratory and digestive systems to the cells where they are needed.)*

Address Misconceptions
L1 RESPIRATION AND BREATHING Students often confuse the two ways the term *respiration* is used. Students may have heard cellular respiration referred to simply as *respiration*, and they may also have heard of someone who stopped breathing being given *artificial respiration.* Point out that cellular respiration is a series of chemical reactions that occur within individual cells. Breathing is a physical process that involves moving air into and out of the body. Help them maintain the distinction by always referring to *breathing,* not *respiration,* when discussing the mechanics of air exchange. Ask: **How are breathing and cellular respiration related?** *(Breathing moves air into the lungs, giving the body the oxygen that cells need to carry out cellular respiration.)*

My Planet Diary provides an opportunity for students to explore real-world connections to the respiratory system.

my science online.com | The Respiratory System

ELL Support

1 Content and Language
Write the terms *trachea* and *bronchi* on the board. Draw students' attention to the *k* sound in the middle of each word. Have students pronounce each word aloud as a group. Help them recognize other similarities, such as short vowel sounds in the first syllable, and a long *e* sound at or near the end of each word.

2 Frontload the Lesson
Ask students how many times each

day they breathe in and out. Jot their responses down on the board. Urge students to estimate this number by counting the number of breaths in a minute, and multiplying that number by 1,440 (number of minutes in a day).

3 Comprehensible Input
Have pairs create a flow chart of the process of gas exchange in the lungs, using the terms *alveolus, carbon dioxide, oxygen, capillary,* and *red blood cell.*

Explain

Lead a Discussion

BREATHING STRUCTURES Explain to students that air that is inhaled must travel through several organs on its way to the lungs. Create a flowchart on the board, identifying how each organ processes air on its way to the lungs. Ask: **Into which organ does air pass after it leaves the nose on its way to the lungs?** *(It passes into the pharynx.)* **What might happen if the trachea were blocked?** *(Air would not be able to reach the lungs, and the person could suffocate.)* **How are the bronchi related to the lungs?** *(Each bronchus carries air into and out of one of the lungs.)*

Teach With Visuals

Tell students to look at **Figure 2.** Make sure students understand that the image is highly magnified so the items appear much larger than they really are. It has also been colored to make details more visible. Help students identify each of the items shown. Ask: **What to the cilia resemble?** *(Students might suggest they resemble tiny hairs or even carpet fibers.)* **What do cilia do?** *(Cilia sweep mucus containing particles out of the trachea into the throat where they can be swallowed or coughed out of the body.)*

21st Century Learning

CRITICAL THINKING Direct students' attention to **Figure 2** and ask them to think of other small particles that might get into the respiratory system. Ask: **How do the cilia and mucus help protect the body from diseases?** *(Mucus may trap bacteria or viruses that could harm the body, especially the respiratory system. The cilia move them away from the lungs.)* If students have previously studied the digestive system, ask them to identify the pathway of mucus from the trachea to the stomach. *(Trachea, pharynx, esophagus, stomach)* Point out that saliva and some secretions of the stomach contain substances that act as antibacterial agents.

did you know?

Substances in the air you breathe can affect your lungs and breathing passages. The Florida Department of Environmental Protection monitors and reports on air quality for the entire state. The reports include data about particles that can cause allergies and other pollutants that can affect human health.

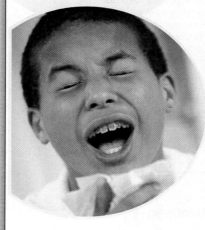

Breathing Structures When you breathe in, air and particles such as pollen and dust move through a series of structures and then into the lungs. You can see these structures— the nose, pharynx, trachea, and bronchi—on the right. These structures also warm and moisten the air you breathe.

Nose Air enters the body through the nose or the mouth. Hairs in the nose trap large particles. The air passes into spaces called nasal cavities. Some cells lining the nasal cavities produce mucus, a sticky material that moistens the air and traps more particles.

Pharynx and Trachea From the nose, air enters the **pharynx** (FAR ingks), or throat. Both the nose and the mouth connect to the pharynx. So air and food enter the pharynx. From the pharynx, air moves into the **trachea** (TRAY kee uh), or windpipe. When you swallow, a thin flap of tissue called the epiglottis covers the opening of the trachea to keep food out. Cells that line the trachea have **cilia** (SIL ee uh; singular *cilium*), tiny hairlike extensions that can move together in a sweeping motion. The cilia, like those shown in **Figure 2,** sweep the mucus made by cells in the trachea up to the pharynx. If particles irritate the trachea, you cough, sending the particles back into the air. Find the pharynx and trachea in **Figure 3.**

Bronchi and Lungs Air moves from the trachea into the left and right **bronchi** (BRAHNG ky; singular *bronchus*). These two passages take air into the lungs. The **lungs** are the main organs of the respiratory system. Inside the lungs, the bronchi branch into smaller and smaller tubes. At the end of the smallest tubes are **alveoli** (al VEE uh ly; singular *alveolus*), tiny, thin-walled sacs of lung tissue where gases can move between air and blood.

FIGURE 2 ·····
Cilia
The photo shows a microscopic view of cilia.

✏️ **Answer the questions below.**

1. **Relate Cause and Effect** How does coughing protect the respiratory system?

   It gets rid of inhaled particles.

   _____

2. **CHALLENGE** What might happen if you did not have hairs in your nose and cilia in your trachea?

   Sample: Particles in air could get into my lungs and damage them.

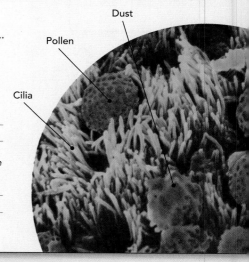

Dust

Pollen

Cilia

480 Managing Materials in the Body

FIGURE 3 ....

Structures of the Respiratory System

Particles in air are filtered out as the air moves through your respiratory system.

 Communicate In your own words, write what each part of the respiratory system does.

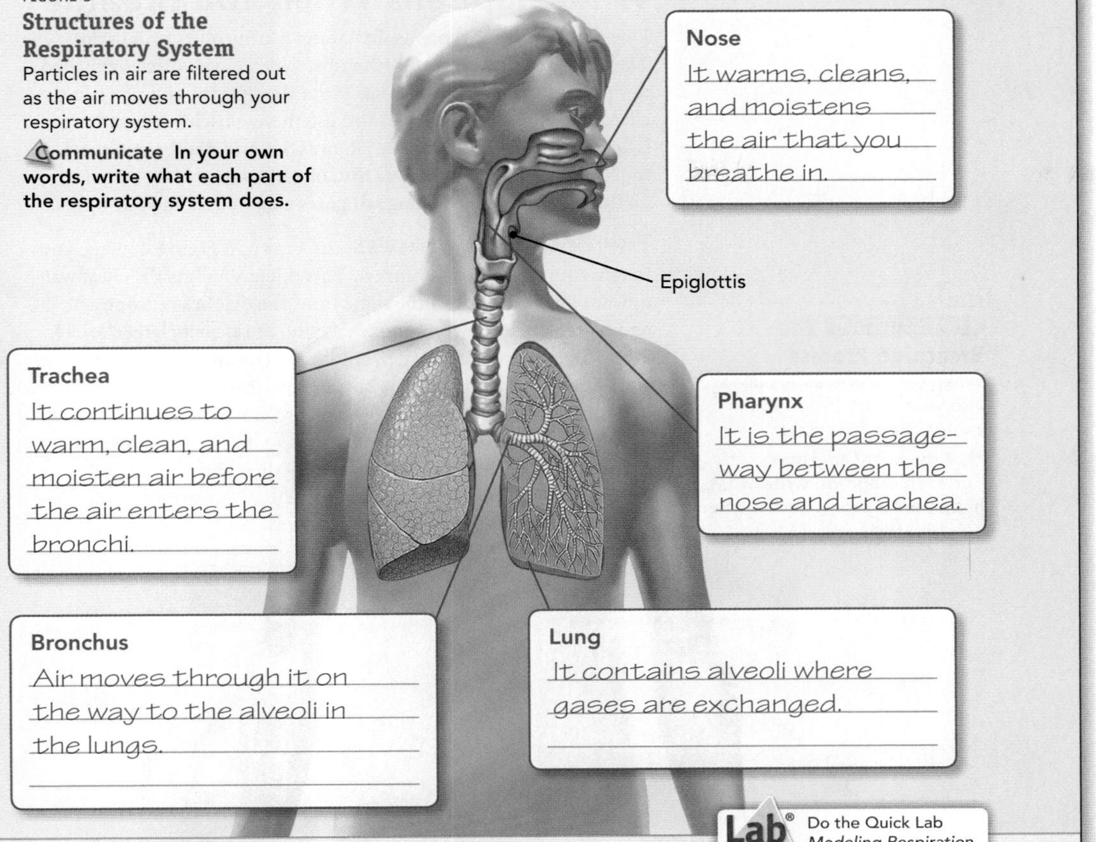

Nose
It warms, cleans, and moistens the air that you breathe in.

Epiglottis

Pharynx
It is the passageway between the nose and trachea.

Trachea
It continues to warm, clean, and moisten air before the air enters the bronchi.

Bronchus
Air moves through it on the way to the alveoli in the lungs.

Lung
It contains alveoli where gases are exchanged.

Lab zone Do the Quick Lab *Modeling Respiration.*

Assess Your Understanding

1a. Review What happens in the lungs?
In the lungs, there are alveoli, where gases move between the air and the blood.

b. Compare and Contrast How are breathing and cellular respiration different?
Breathing brings oxygen into the body; cellular respiration breaks down glucose in cells.

got it?

○ I get it! Now I know that the respiratory system takes in oxygen and removes carbon dioxide and water from the body.

○ I need extra help with See TE note.

Go to **MY SCIENCE COACH** online for help with this subject.

481

Differentiated Instruction

L1 Pathway for Air Have students write the name of each label in **Figure 3** on an index card. Have them organize the labels by the order in which air passes through the body. Suggest they write a question about each structure on the card. Have them write the answers as they read the section.

L3 Filter Air Bring in a gauze mask. Have students work together to explain the purpose of the mask and identify reasons why a person might use it. Ask students to determine why the mask must cover both the nose and the mouth.

Teach With Visuals

Direct students' attention to **Figure 3.** Help them trace the pathways of air from outside the body into the lungs. Ask: **What are the two different ways air can enter the body?** *(Through the nose or through the mouth)* **What happens when you have a cold and your nose is congested?** *(You have to breathe through your mouth.)* **Have you ever laughed or coughed while drinking a beverage? What happens?** *(Most students will have seen or experienced a beverage running out of the nose of someone who has started to laugh in the middle of swallowing. They should identify the pathway as mouth, pharynx, nose.)*

 Communicate Tell students that when they communicate, the goal is to share knowledge or information with others so that it can be understood clearly.

21st Century Learning

CRITICAL THINKING Students may have seen a person with a tube in his or her throat. Diseases, such as cancer, or infections, such as croup, may cause damage in the upper airways and block air from getting to the lungs. When an obstruction in the trachea occurs, it can reduce or stop the delivery of oxygen to the lungs. A tracheostomy can be performed to provide an airway and access to remove secretions from the lungs. A tracheostomy is an opening surgically made into the trachea for a breathing tube. Have students find out about patient care after a tracheostomy.

Elaborate

Lab Resource: Quick Lab

L2 MODELING RESPIRATION Students will identify the structures of the nose and their functions.

Evaluate

Assess Your Understanding

After students answer the questions, have them evaluate their understanding by completing the appropriate sentence.

R T I Response to Intervention

1a. If students have difficulty describing what happens in the lungs, **then** have them reread the last paragraph under the head *Breathing Structures.*

b. If students need help contrasting breathing and respiration, **then** help them define each process.

MY SCIENCE COACH Have students go online for help in understanding the role of the respiratory system.

Explain

Teach Key Concepts

Explain that breathing is controlled by muscles. Ask: **What muscles move air in and out of the lungs?** *(The muscles surrounding the ribs and the diaphragm)* **Where are the rib muscles?** *(Ribs surround the lungs and have muscles attached.)* **Where is the diaphragm?** *(The base of the lungs)*

Lead a Discussion

THE BREATHING PROCESS Explain that when you inhale, the rib muscles and diaphragm contract. When you exhale, the rib muscles and diaphragm relax. Ask: **What happens to the chest cavity when the rib muscles and diaphragm contract?** *(It becomes larger.)* **How does this affect air pressure in the lungs?** *(Pressure inside the lungs is less than it is outside the body. Air rushes into the lungs.)* **What happens to the chest cavity when the rib muscles and diaphragm relax?** *(It becomes smaller.)* **How does this affect air pressure in the lungs?** *(Pressure inside the lungs is greater than it is outside the body. Air rushes out of the lungs.)*

Elaborate

Teacher Demo

AIR PRESSURE

Material balloon **Time** 10 minutes

Blow up a balloon without tying it. Slowly open the inflated balloon and let the air escape.

Ask: **How does the pressure inside the inflated balloon compare to the pressure outside the balloon?** *(The pressure is greater inside the balloon.)* **Why does air rush out of the balloon if you open it?** *(Because the pressure in the balloon is greater than the air pressure outside the balloon)* **How is the balloon like the breathing process?** *(The inflated balloon is like the lungs after inhaling; the higher pressure forces air out of the lungs as it is forced out of the balloon.)*

What Happens When You Breathe?

Like other body movements, breathing is controlled by muscles. The lungs are surrounded by the ribs, which have muscles attached to them. At the base of the lungs is the **diaphragm** (DY uh fram), a large, dome-shaped muscle. You use these muscles to breathe.
When you breathe, your rib muscles and diaphragm work together, causing air to move into or out of your lungs. This airflow leads to the exchange of gases that occurs in your lungs.

The Breathing Process As shown in **Figure 4**, when you inhale your rib muscles contract. This tightening lifts the chest wall upward and outward. At the same time, the diaphragm contracts and flattens. These two actions make the chest cavity larger, which lowers the air pressure inside your lungs. The air pressure outside your body is now higher than the pressure inside your chest. This pressure difference causes air to rush into your lungs.

When you exhale, your rib muscles and diaphragm relax. As they relax, your chest cavity becomes smaller, making the air pressure inside your chest greater than the air pressure outside. As a result, air rushes out of your lungs.

FIGURE 4 ....

> INTERACTIVE ART The **Breathing Process**
When you inhale, air is pulled into your lungs. When you exhale, air is forced out.

✏ **Interpret Diagrams**
For each diagram, write what happens to your muscles when you breathe.

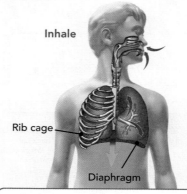

Inhale

Exhale

Rib cage

Diaphragm

Rib cage

Diaphragm

Rib Muscles
The rib muscles contract, expanding the chest cavity.

Diaphragm
The diaphragm contracts and flattens, expanding the chest cavity.

Rib Muscles
The rib muscles relax, reducing the size of the chest cavity.

Diaphragm
The diaphragm relaxes, reducing the size of the chest cavity.

482 Managing Materials in the Body

Interactive Art allows students to explore the respiratory system.

Digital Lesson: Assign the *Apply It* activity online and have students submit their work to you.

my science online.com ⟩ **Breathing**

Breathing and Speaking Did you know that the air that moves out of your lungs when you breathe also helps you to speak? Your **larynx** (LAR ingks), or voice box, is located at the top of your trachea. Two **vocal cords,** which are folds of connective tissue, stretch across the opening of the larynx. When you speak, <u>muscles make the vocal cords contract, narrowing the opening</u> <u>as air rushes through.</u> <u>Then the movement of the vocal cords</u> <u>makes air molecules vibrate, or move rapidly back and forth.</u> <u>This vibration causes a sound—your voice.</u>

 Chart In the text, underline and number the steps that help you speak. Then write these steps in the graphic organizer.

1
2
3

Sample answers

Step 1

Vocal cords contract, narrowing the opening across the larynx.

↓

Step 2

Air molecules rushing through the narrow opening vibrate.

↓

Step 3

The vibration causes a sound.

apply it!

When you sing, the sounds you make can vary in pitch. That is, you can sing low notes, high notes, and many notes in between. Press your index and middle fingers of one hand gently on the front of your throat.

❶ Observe Hum softly, and move your fingers around until you think you have located your voice box. How did humming help you find it?

The humming caused vibrations in my throat that I could feel.

❷ Describe With your fingers still in place, sing softly, switching between low notes and high notes. Describe the differences you felt.

I felt stronger vibrations and changes in shape with high notes.

❸ Develop Hypotheses How do you think the function of the vocal cords is related to these differences?

Sample: The vocal cords change shape, producing different notes.

483

Explain ────────

Lead a Discussion

SPEAKING Ask students what they do before they say a long sentence. *(Most students will say they take a deep breath.)* Point out that speaking requires a slow, controlled exhalation. Ask: **What structures are involved in producing sound?** *(Larynx and vocal cords)* **How do they make sounds?** *(Air rushing between the vocal cords makes them vibrate, which causes a sound.)*

 Chart Explain to students that a chart helps show how steps in a process fit together. By making a chart of processes, readers can help clarify their understanding.

Elaborate ────────

Apply It!

Before students begin the activity, explain that in music the term *pitch* refers to the way vibrations make a note sound high or low. Review the academic vocabulary. Ask: **What does it mean to observe?** *(It means using one or more of your senses to gather information.)* **What does it mean to describe?** *(It means to use words to give an account of something.)* **What does it mean to develop a hypothesis?** *(It means to come up with a possible scientific explanation for a question.)*

Differentiated Instruction

L1 **The Breathing Process** Ask students to slowly breathe in and out while concentrating on how their diaphragm and rib muscles are contracting and relaxing. Have students look at the structures in **Figure 4** and describe the changes that are occurring.

L3 **Deep Breathing** Athletic coaches, voice teachers, and yoga practitioners, as well as professionals working in the area of stress management promote

the benefits of slow, deep breathing from the abdomen. Have students form small groups to research the various systems of breathing techniques and exercises that are promoted. Then have students present the benefits of deep breathing to the class and demonstrate an exercise or technique that they found most helpful.

Explain

Support the Big Q ❓ UbD

GAS EXCHANGE IN THE ALVEOLI Explain to students that alveoli are like tiny balloons in the lungs. During inhalation, the alveoli fill with oxygen-filled air. That oxygen passes across the walls of the alveoli into the blood in nearby capillaries. At the same time, carbon dioxide and water pass from the blood into the alveoli. Ask: **What happens to the carbon dioxide and water that passes into the alveoli?** *(It is removed from the body during exhalation.)* **What happens to the oxygen passed from the alveoli into the blood?** *(It is carried to cells where it is needed.)* **Which part of blood carries oxygen?** *(Hemoglobin)* **How does the structure of alveoli and capillaries facilitate gas exchange?** *(Both have very thin walls, so that certain materials can pass through them easily.)* **In gas exchange, the respiratory system functions with what other system to manage materials?** *(The circulatory system)*

Address Misconceptions

EXHALED GASES Students often think that they inhale oxygen and exhale carbon dioxide because they know that this is the exchange that takes place in the lungs. Tell students that they inhale air and exhale air, and that air is a mixture of gases. There is no such thing as "a molecule of air." Ask: **What gases make up air?** *(If students have studied the atmosphere, they should recall that air is mostly nitrogen and about 21 percent oxygen, with small amounts of carbon dioxide and other gases.)* **When you inhale, which gases enter your lungs?** *(All the gases in air enter the lungs.)* **Which gas does the body take from the air in your lungs?** *(Oxygen)* **Which gas does the body add to the air in your lungs?** *(Carbon dioxide)* **How is the air you exhale different from the air you inhale?** *(It has less oxygen and more carbon dioxide and water vapor.)* Emphasize that the exhaled air still contains oxygen. Exhaled air is about 16 percent oxygen.

Gas Exchange Air's final stop in its journey through the respiratory system is an alveolus in the lungs. An alveolus has thin walls and is surrounded by many thin-walled capillaries. **Figure 5** shows some alveoli.

Because the alveoli and the capillaries have very thin walls, certain materials can pass through them easily. After air enters an alveolus, oxygen passes through the wall of the alveolus and then through the capillary wall into the blood. Similarly, carbon dioxide and water pass from the blood into the air within the alveolus. This whole process is called gas exchange.

How Gas Exchange Occurs Imagine that you are a drop of blood. You are traveling through a capillary that wraps around an alveolus. You have a lot of carbon dioxide and a little oxygen. As you move through the capillary, oxygen attaches to the hemoglobin in your red blood cells. Carbon dioxide moves into the alveolus. As you move away from the alveolus, you are rich in oxygen and poor in carbon dioxide.

FIGURE 5 ·······················

> **ART IN MOTION** **Gas Exchange**
Gases move across the thin walls of both alveoli and capillaries.

✏ **Relate Text and Visuals** Label each arrow with the gas being exchanged and describe where it is coming from and moving to.

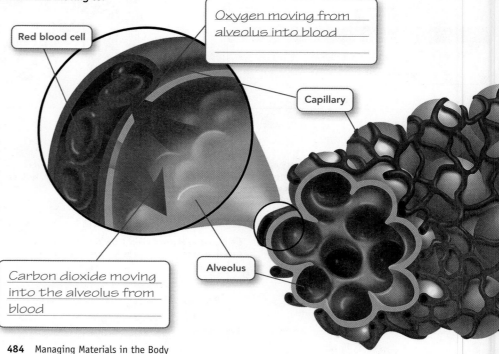

Red blood cell

Oxygen moving from alveolus into blood

Capillary

Carbon dioxide moving into the alveolus from blood

Alveolus

484   Managing Materials in the Body

Art in Motion allows students to explore the process of gas exchange in the lungs.

my science online.com Breathing

Surface Area for Gas Exchange Your lungs can absorb a large amount of oxygen because of the surface area of the alveoli. An adult's lungs have about 300 million alveoli. Together these alveoli have a surface area of about 100 meters squared (m^2)—the area of the floor in an average classroom! As a result, the alveoli provide a huge amount of surface area for exchanging gases. Therefore, healthy lungs can supply all the oxygen that a person needs—even when the person is very active.

Vocabulary Identify Related Word Forms The verb *absorb* means "to take in." Use this meaning to write a sentence using the noun *absorption*.

Sample: Paper towels take up water through absorption.

Vessel with blood rich in oxygen from lungs

Branch of bronchus

Vessel with blood rich in carbon dioxide from body

Lab zone Do the Lab Investigation *A Breath of Fresh Air.*

Assess Your Understanding

2a. Identify Where is the larynx located?

It is at the top of the trachea.

b. Explain When you inhale, why does air rush into your lungs?

The air pressure inside the chest is lower than the air pressure outside.

c. Draw Conclusions How do the alveoli enable people to be very active?

The many alveoli have a large surface area, allowing people to get all the oxygen they need.

got it?

○ **I get it!** Now I know that when I breathe, air moves into and out of my lungs and gas exchange occurs.

○ **I need extra help with** See TE note.

Go to **my science coach** *online for help with this subject.*

485

Lead a Discussion

SURFACE AREA Help students understand that the alveoli are very small. If the lungs were just single large sacs, they would have very little surface area for gas exchange. Ask: **How can the total surface of the alveoli be large if each individual alveolus is so small?** *(There are many tiny alveoli in the lungs.)* Encourage students to make connections between the way surface area works in the respiratory system and the way surface area works in the digestive system. Ask: **By increasing surface area, the alveoli in the lungs are similar to what feature in the small intestine?** *(Villi in the small intestine.)*

Make Analogies

L1 **THE IMPORTANCE OF SURFACE AREA** To understand why it is important for the lungs to have a large surface area, compare the alveoli to the counter at a fast-food restaurant. In the alveoli, oxygen and carbon dioxide are exchanged. At the restaurant, money is exchanged for food. Ask: **What would happen if the restaurant had a small counter with one person taking orders?** *(Samples: Not much food would be served; service would be slow.)* **What would happen if the restaurant had a large counter with many people taking orders?** *(Service would be faster and more food could be served.)*

Elaborate

Lab Resource: Lab Investigation

L2 **A BREATH OF FRESH AIR** Students will investigate what causes the body to inhale and exhale air.

Evaluate

Assess Your Understanding

After students answer the questions, have them evaluate their understanding by completing the appropriate sentence.

RTI Response to Intervention

2a. If students need help locating the larynx, **then** refer them to the region at the top of the trachea as depicted in Figure 3.

b. If students have difficulty relating inhalation to a difference in air pressure, **then** point out that inhaling makes the chest cavity larger, reducing the air pressure inside the body.

c. If students have trouble connecting the alveoli to accessible oxygen, **then** remind them that the alveoli increase the surface area of the lungs.

my science coach Have students go online for help in understanding what happens when you breathe.

485

Differentiated Instruction

L1 **Cause and Effect Chart** Encourage students to work in pairs to create a two-column cause-and-effect chart about breathing. Start students off by putting the sentence "The muscles of the rib cage and diaphragm contract" under *Cause.* Students should fill out the rest of the chart ending with the effect, "Carbon dioxide, water vapor, and other gases are exhaled from the lungs."

L3 **Investigate Surface Area** Ask students to examine the relationship between surface area and the measure of each side of a cube. Have students calculate out how surface area changes each time the length of each side of a cube is doubled. Tell students to present their conclusions using examples.

Lab zone **After the Inquiry Warm-Up**

The Respiratory System

Inquiry Warm-Up, *How Big Can You Blow Up a Balloon?*
In the Inquiry Warm-Up, you investigated some of the factors that affect the volume of air exhaled in a normal breath. Using what you learned from that activity, answer the questions below.

1. **DESIGN EXPERIMENTS** What experiment could you perform to measure the most air you could exhale?

   _____

   _____

2. **MEASURE** Repeat Step 1, using the biggest breath you can take. How did the circumference of the balloon compare with the average circumference you found in the experiment?

   _____

   _____

3. **DRAW CONCLUSIONS** Why is the size of the balloon a good way to measure how much air you exhale?

   _____

   _____

   _____

4. **COMPARE AND CONTRAST** How is the balloon similar to your lungs? How is it different?

   _____

   _____

   _____

Assess Your Understanding

The Respiratory System

What Is the Role of the Respiratory System?

1a. REVIEW What happens in the lungs?

_____

_____

b. COMPARE AND CONTRAST How are breathing and cellular respiration different?

_____

_____

got it? ···

○ **I get it!** Now I know that the respiratory system _____

_____

_____

○ **I need extra help with** _____

What Happens When You Breathe?

2a. IDENTIFY Where is the larynx located?

_____

b. EXPLAIN When you inhale, why does air rush into your lungs?

_____

_____

c. DRAW CONCLUSIONS How do the alveoli enable people to be very active?

_____

_____

got it? ···

○ **I get it!** Now I know that when I breathe, air _____

_____

○ **I need extra help with** _____

Key Concept Summaries

The Respiratory System

What Is the Role of the Respiratory System?

Your respiratory system moves air containing oxygen into your lungs and removes carbon dioxide and water from your body. Your lungs and the structures that lead to them make up your respiratory system. The oxygen is used by body cells during cellular respiration, in which cells break down glucose, releasing energy.

Air, containing oxygen, enters the body through the nose and then passes into the **pharynx,** or throat. It then passes into the **trachea,** or windpipe, where tiny hairlike extensions known as **cilia** sweep mucus up to the pharynx. Air then moves into the **bronchi,** which are passages to the **lungs,** the main organs of the respiratory system. The lungs consist of **alveoli,** which are tiny sacs through which gases are exchanged between the air and blood.

What Happens When You Breathe?

Breathing is controlled by rib muscles as well as a large dome-shaped muscle called the **diaphragm. When you breathe, your rib muscles and diaphragm work together, causing air to move into or out of your lungs. This airflow leads to the exchange of gases that occurs in your lungs.**

The air involved in breathing also makes speech possible. Two folds of connective tissue, known as **vocal cords,** stretch across the opening of the **larynx,** or voice box. The flow of air along with the

contraction of muscles causes the vocal cords to vibrate, thereby producing sound.

After air enters the alveolus, oxygen passes through the wall of the alveolus and then through the capillary wall into the blood. Similarly, carbon dioxide and water pass from the blood into the air in the alveolus. This whole process is called gas exchange. Gas exchange is aided by the tremendous surface area of the many alveoli in the lungs.

On a separate sheet of paper, trace the flow of an oxygen molecule from the air to the blood and explain what causes it to move.

Review and Reinforce

The Respiratory System

Understanding Main Ideas
Answer the following questions on a separate piece of paper.

1. How does respiration differ from breathing?
2. What are the two functions of the respiratory system?
3. Through what structures does air pass to get to the lungs?
4. What role do cilia play in the respiratory system?
5. What gases are exchanged in the respiratory system?
6. How do you inhale and exhale?
7. How is the sound of your voice produced?

Building Vocabulary
Label the diagram with the parts of the respiratory system.

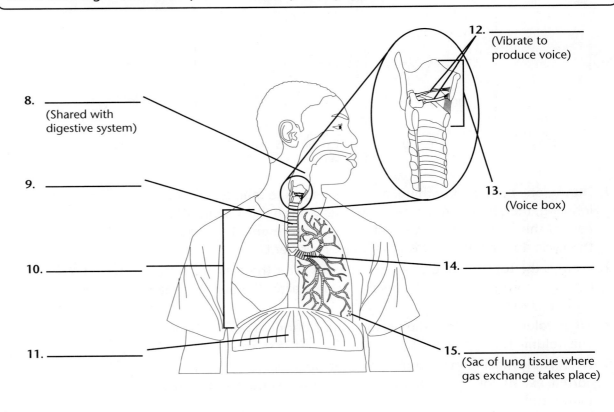

8. _____ (Shared with digestive system)

9. _____

10. _____

11. _____

12. _____ (Vibrate to produce voice)

13. _____ (Voice box)

14. _____

15. _____ (Sac of lung tissue where gas exchange takes place)

Enrich

The Respiratory System

> Read the passage and study the diagram. Then use a separate sheet of paper to answer the questions that follow.

Analyzing a Spirogram

The volume of air in the lungs increases as a person inhales and decreases as a person exhales. A *spirogram* is a graph of the volume of air in a person's lungs over time. Look at the spirogram shown below. Where the line of the graph moves upward the person is inhaling, and where the line of the graph moves downward the person is exhaling.

The first three breaths on the spirogram show normal breathing. During the fourth breath, however, the person inhaled as much air into his or her lungs as possible. The next two breaths show normal breathing again. Then, during the seventh breath, the person exhaled as much air from his or her lungs as possible.

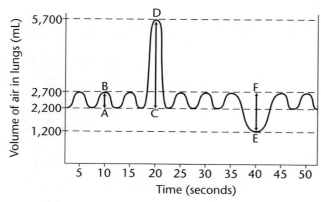

1. During one cycle of breathing, a person begins to inhale, finishes inhaling, then begins to exhale, and finally finishes exhaling. What part of this cycle does a peak on the graph represent? What part of this cycle does a low point on the graph represent?

2. What is the total volume of air in the lungs after the person inhales during a normal breath? What is the volume after the person exhales during a normal breath?

3. What volume of air does the person inhale during a normal breath? This volume is represented by the line AB on the spirogram.

4. What is the maximum volume of air that can be inhaled after a normal exhalation? This volume is represented by the line CD on the spirogram.

5. What is the maximum volume of air that can be exhaled after a normal inhalation? This volume is represented by the line EF on the spirogram.

Lesson Quiz

The Respiratory System

Fill in the blank to complete each statement.

1. Air is exchanged between blood and air in tiny sacs of lung tissue known as _____.

2. Cells that line the trachea have _____, which sweep mucus up to the pharynx.

3. Water and _____ pass from the blood into the air in an alveolus.

4. When you _____, your chest cavity becomes larger so air rushes into your body.

5. A(n) _____ is a small tube that connects arteries to veins.

If the statement is true, write *true.* **If the statement is false, change the underlined word or words to make the statement true.**

6. _____ Cellular respiration is the process through which cells release chemical energy stored in oxygen.

7. _____ Air passes from the nose into the bronchi.

8. _____ The trachea is a large, dome-shaped muscle that expands and contracts during breathing.

9. _____ The vocal cords stretch across the opening of the larynx.

10. _____ The nose produces a sticky material called mucus, which moistens the air and traps particles.

The Respiratory System

Answer Key

After the Inquiry Warm-Up

1. Sample: You could take a big breath to see how big you could make the balloon using as much air as you could exhale.

2. Answers will vary based on classroom observations, but students should notice that the balloons are bigger when they use the biggest breath they can take. They may calculate the difference between the circumferences in the different experiments.

3. Sample: The balloon captures all the air you exhale so it is a good way to contain the air and measure its volume and relative size. Without using a balloon, the air you exhale escapes and mixes into the air around you and makes it difficult to measure.

4. The balloon is similar to the lungs because they both inflate when filled with air. They are different because the lungs inflate when filled with air you inhale and the balloon inflates when filled with air you exhale.

Key Concept Summaries

When the diaphragm and rib muscles contract, the size of the chest cavity increases. This change causes air to flow into the nose. An oxygen molecule in the air will pass through the nose into the pharynx and then into the trachea. Once in the trachea, the oxygen molecule will pass into one of two bronchi, which lead into an alveolus in one of the lungs. The molecule will then pass across the wall of an alveolus and through the wall of a capillary into the blood.

Review and Reinforce

1. Respiration is the process inside cells through which glucose is broken down using oxygen to release energy. Breathing is the process in which air flows into and out of the lungs.

2. The respiratory system provides oxygen to the body and eliminates carbon dioxide and water from the body.

3. nose, pharynx, trachea, and bronchi

4. Cilia are tiny, hairlike extensions that sweep mucus, along with any particles it might contain, up out of the trachea.

5. Oxygen moves from air to the blood and carbon dioxide moves from the blood into the air.

6. Contraction and relaxation of the diaphragm and rib muscles causes inhalation and exhalation.

7. Sound is produced when air passes over the vocal cords.

8. pharynx
9. trachea
10. lung
11. diaphragm
12. vocal cords
13. larynx
14. bronchus
15. alveolus

Enrich

1. A peak represents the point where the person has just inhaled and is starting to exhale. A low point represents the point where the person has just exhaled and is starting to inhale.

2. 2,700 mL after inhalation; 2,200 mL after exhalation

3. 500 mL
4. 3,500 mL
5. 1,500 mL

Lesson Quiz

1. alveoli
2. cilia
3. carbon dioxide
4. inhale
5. capillary
6. glucose
7. pharynx
8. diaphragm
9. true
10. true

Place the outside corner, the corner away from the dotted line, in the corner of your copy machine to copy onto letter-size paper.

How do systems of the body move and manage materials?

Lesson Pacing: 2–3 periods or 1–1$\frac{1}{2}$ blocks

🕐 **SHORT ON TIME?** To do this lesson in approximately half the time, do the Activate Prior Knowledge activity followed by a discussion of the Key Concepts to familiarize students with the lesson content. Use the Explore the Big Q to help students understand how the systems of the body work together to move and manage materials. Have students do the Quick Labs. The rest of the lesson can be completed by students independently.

> **Preference Navigator,** in the online Planning tools, allows you to customize *Interactive Science* to your own teaching style. You can also edit lesson plans by selecting the Lesson Planner option.
>
> **Digital Teacher's Edition** allows you to access your Teacher's Edition and Resource materials online.

my science online.com

Lesson Vocabulary

- excretion
- urea
- urine
- kidney
- ureter
- urinary bladder
- urethra
- nephron

Content Refresher

The Formation of Urine The liquid that leaves the blood and enters the capsule in a nephron is called the *filtrate*. At first, the concentration of small molecules (such as glucose) in the filtrate is basically the same as in blood plasma. However, the concentrations of substances in plasma and urine differ greatly. Filtrate is composed of some salts, urea, glucose amino acids, and water. These differences result from selective reabsorption that occurs as the filtrate travels through the nephron. Amino acids and glucose are moved back into capillaries by active transport. After these substances are removed, water molecules follow them by osmosis. Once the filtrate moves to the collecting tubule nearly all of it has been reabsorbed. Nitrogenous wastes are not reabsorbed into the blood. Besides urea, nitrogenous wastes include creatinine, ammonia, and uric acid.

LESSON OBJECTIVES

🔑 Identify the structures and functions of the excretory system.
🔑 Explain how excretion contributes to homeostasis.

Blended Path
Active learning using Student Edition, Inquiry Path, and Digital Path

ENGAGE AND EXPLORE

Teach this lesson using a variety of resources. Begin by reading **My Planet Diary** as a class. Have students share ideas about why scientists took the time to invent a machine that can filter urine to produce water. Then have students do the **Inquiry Warm-Up activity.** Students will investigate how filtering affects a liquid. Discuss how the experiment was set up. The **After the Inquiry Warm-Up worksheet** sets up a discussion about the purpose of the filter paper. Have volunteers share their answers to question 4 about which parts of the body are represented in the model of a filter system.

EXPLAIN AND ELABORATE

Teach Key Concepts by explaining the importance of the excretory system and the body structures that are involved in the process. **Lead a Discussion** about the stages of filtration in a nephron. Use **Figure 1** to illustrate how the waste moves from the kidneys and to the urethra.

Continue to **Teach Key Concepts** by explaining that the excretory system keeps chemical levels constant by eliminating excess chemicals and retaining the ones the body needs. Have students identify which person in **Figure 3** will use the most and least amount of water. Then ask them how the body controls its use of water. **Lead a Discussion** about how organs from many systems in the body contribute to the work of the excretory system. Use the **Explore the Big Q** to have students identify the major role of specific systems in the body and describe how the different systems interact and work together. Hand out the **Key Concept Summaries** as a review of each part of the lesson. Students can also use the online **Vocab Flash Cards** to review key terms.

EVALUATE

Have students take the **Lesson Quiz.** For an alternate assessment, see the *ExamView*® Computer Test Generator, Progress Monitoring Assessments, or SuccessTracker™.

ELL Support

1 Content and Language

Explain that the term *nephron*, a single unit of the kidney, comes from the Greek word *nephros*, meaning "kidney." Write the words *epinephrine* and *nephritis* on the board and ask students to identify prefixes, suffixes, and the Greek root of both words. Explain that *-epi* is a prefix meaning "upon," *-ine* is a chemical suffix, and *-itis* is a suffix meaning "inflammation." Encourage students to use this information to suggest meanings for the two terms.

DIFFERENTIATED INSTRUCTION KEY
L1 Struggling Students or Special Needs
L2 On-Level Students **L3** Advanced Students

LESSON PLANNER 12.4

 **Inquiry Path** Hands-on learning in the Lab zone

ENGAGE AND EXPLORE

To teach this lesson with an emphasis on inquiry, begin with the **Inquiry Warm-Up activity.** Students will investigate a filtration system. Discuss the set up of the filtration system. Have students do the **After the Inquiry Warm-Up worksheet.** Talk about what was not filtered by the filtration paper. Have volunteers share their answers to question 4 about which parts of the body are represented in the filtration system.

EXPLAIN AND ELABORATE

Focus on the **Inquiry Skill** for the lesson. Point out that when you infer, you use evidence or reasoning to draw a logical explanation. What could be inferred about why certain substances passed through the filter paper in the **Inquiry Warm-Up activity?** *(The sand was too big to travel through the filter paper but the glucose was not.)* Use **Figure 2** to have students make inferences about how the kidneys work. **Build Inquiry** by diagramming the materials that enter the nephron, that are returned to the blood, and that leave the body in urine. Have students do the **Quick Lab** to model how sodium moves during urine formation and then share their results.

Use the **Explore the Big Q** to have students identify the major role of specific systems in the body and describe how the different systems interact and work together to move and manage materials. Do the **Quick Lab** to reinforce understanding of how perspiration removes excess water and regulates body temperature. Students can use the online **Vocab Flash Cards** to review key terms.

EVALUATE

Have students take the **Lesson Quiz.** For an alternate assessment, see the *ExamView®* Computer Test Generator, Progress Monitoring Assessments, or SuccessTracker™.

Digital Path Online learning at my science online.com

ENGAGE AND EXPLORE

Teach this lesson using digital resources. Begin by having students explore real-world connections to the excretory system at **My Planet Diary** online. Have them access the Chapter Resources to find the **Unlock the Big Question activity.** There they can answer the questions and refine their responses as they continue through the lesson. You can re-assign the activity and have students submit their work so you can track their progress.

EXPLAIN AND ELABORATE

Students reading above, at, or below the lexile measure of this lesson can access basic content readings at their level at **My Reading Web.** Have students use the online **Vocab Flash Cards** to preview key terms. Assign the **Do the Math activity** online and have students submit their work to you. Do the **Quick Lab** and then ask students to share their results.

Use the **Explore the Big Q** to have students identify the major role of specific systems in the body and describe how the different systems interact and work together to move and manage materials. Have students do the **Quick Lab** to investigate how perspiration removes excess water and regulates temperature. The **Key Concept Summaries** online allow students to read a summary and see an image associated with each part of the lesson. Online remediation is available at **My Science Coach.**

EVALUATE

Have students take the **Lesson Quiz.** For an alternate assessment, see the *ExamView®* Computer Test Generator, Progress Monitoring Assessments, or SuccessTracker™.

2 Frontload the Lesson
Preview the lesson visuals, labels, and captions. Ask students what they know about the words *excretion* and *urine*. Explain the specific meanings these words have in science.

3 Comprehensible Input
Have students study the visuals and captions throughout the lesson to support the lesson's Key Concepts.

4 Language Production
Pair or group students with varied language abilities to complete labs collaboratively for language practice. Have each student copy the completed written lab for personal reference.

5 Assess Understanding
Divide the class into small groups. Have each student identify a Key Concept from the lesson to discuss in his or her group. After the discussions, have students talk about the Key Concepts as a group.

Excretion

Establish Learning Objectives

After this lesson, students will be able to:

 Identify the structures and functions of the excretory system.

 Explain how excretion contributes to homeostasis.

Engage

Activate Prior Knowledge

MY PLANET DIARY Read *Useful Urine* with the class. Explain that urine is the name for liquid waste that is removed from the body. Ask: **What does it mean to purify a liquid?** *(Students may define this term as cleaning, removing contaminants, or filtering.)* **What is a filter?** *(A device that can take materials out of a substance.)* **Why do astronauts need water?** *(The human body cannot survive for very long without a source of water.)*

BIG IDEAS OF SCIENCE REFERENCE LIBRARY DK
Have students look up the following topic: Kidney Transplant.

Explore

Lab Resource: Inquiry Warm-Up Lab zone

L1 HOW DOES FILTERING A LIQUID CHANGE THE LIQUID? Students will filter different materials out of water.

LESSON

4 Excretion

 What Is the Role of the Excretory System?

 How Does Excretion Help Your Body Maintain Homeostasis?

MY PLANET DIARY

Useful Urine

You can recycle plastic, glass, and paper. Did you know that urine can be recycled, too? Some astronauts in space will see their urine turned into drinking water! NASA has developed a machine that will purify the astronauts' urine. The water that is recovered can be used for drinking, among other things.

Why do astronauts need this kind of machine? Large quantities of water are too heavy to carry into space. So the machine runs urine through a filtering system to remove waste. Then iodine is added to the filtered urine to kill any harmful bacteria. What remains is drinkable water.

FUN FACTS

Answer the questions below.

1. How else might the astronauts use the filtered urine?

   Sample: They might clean with it.

2. Do you think this system would be useful on Earth? Why or why not?

   Sample: Yes, because the system would help recycle water, which is a limited resource on Earth.

> PLANET DIARY Go to **Planet Diary** to learn more about excretion.

Lab zone® Do the Inquiry Warm-Up *How Does Filtering a Liquid Change the Liquid?*

Space shower

486 Managing Materials in the Body

SUPPORT ALL READERS

Lexile Measure = 900L   Lexile Word Count = 1069

Prior Exposure to Content: Most students have encountered this topic in earlier grades

Academic Vocabulary: *infer, summarize, calculate, relate, predict, conclusions*

Science Vocabulary: *excretion, urea, ureter, urethra kidney, nephron*

Concept Level: Generally appropriate for most students in this grade

Preteach With: My Planet Diary "Useful Urine" and Figure 1 activity

Go to **My Reading Web** to access leveled readings that provide a foundation for the content.

My science online.com

Vocabulary
- excretion • urea • urine • kidney • ureter
- urinary bladder • urethra • nephron

Skills
- 🔄 Reading: Identify the Main Idea
- △ Inquiry: Infer

What Is the Role of the Excretory System?

The human body faces a challenge similar to keeping your room clean. Just as you must clean up papers that pile up in your room, your body must remove wastes from cellular respiration and other processes. The process of removing waste is called **excretion.**

If wastes were not removed from your body, they would pile up and make you sick. 🔑 **The excretory system collects the wastes that cells produce and removes them from the body.** The system includes the kidneys, ureters, urinary bladder, urethra, lungs, skin, and liver. Two wastes that your body must eliminate every day are excess water and urea. **Urea** (yoo REE uh) is a chemical that comes from the breakdown of proteins. As you know, the lungs eliminate some water. Most remaining water is eliminated in a fluid called **urine,** which includes urea and other wastes.

do the **math!** Analyzing Data

Urine is made up of water, organic solids, and inorganic solids. The organic solids include urea and acids. The inorganic solids include salts and minerals. The solids are dissolved in the water.

1 Calculate Calculate and label on the *Normal Urine Content* graph the percentage of urine that is solids. Calculate and label on the *Solids in Normal Urine* graph the percentage of solids that is urea.

2 CHALLENGE What might a sharp decrease in the percentage of water in a person's urine indicate about the health of that person?

Sample: The person might be dehydrated
or have other medical problems.

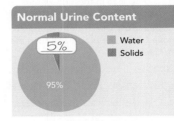

Normal Urine Content
- ■ Water
- ■ Solids

5%
95%

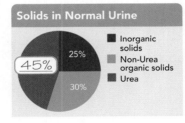

Solids in Normal Urine
- ■ Inorganic solids
- ■ Non-Urea organic solids
- ■ Urea

45%
25%
30%

ⒺⓁⓁ Support

1 Content and Language
Write *urine*, *ureters*, and *urethra* on the board, and underline the first two letters in each word. Explain that all three words derive from the same Greek word, *ouron*, meaning "urine."

2 Frontload the Lesson
Point out that during every stage of human life, from infancy to old age, people take in food and excrete waste materials. Encourage students to think

of an animal that does *not* excrete waste (*There are none*). Tell students they will learn about the body organs involved in the process of excretion.

3 Comprehensible Input
Encourage students to complete a flowchart to show the steps involved in the process of excretion. Suggest that students use *Kidneys filter urea and other wastes* as the first step in the flowchart.

Explain

Introduce Vocabulary

To help students understand the meaning of the term *excretion* in terms of the removal of wastes out of the body, explain that the prefix *ex-* means "out of."

Teach Key Concepts 🔑

Explain to students that body cells produce wastes through their normal functioning. The excretory system collects and removes these wastes.
Ask: **What would happen if wastes were not removed from your home?** (*They would pile up and eventually prevent activities in the home from taking place as normal.*) **Which would happen if wastes were not removed from the body?** (*They would build up and prevent the cells from functioning properly.*) **Which body structures are involved in excretion?** (*The kidneys, ureters, urinary bladder, urethra, lungs, skin, and liver*) **What is urea?** (*A chemical that comes from the breakdown of proteins*) **How is urea related to urine?** (*Urea is one chemical in urine.*) **What substance makes up most of the urine?** (*Water*)

Elaborate

Do the Math!

L1 Explain that a circle graph is a way to display data that represent parts of a whole. The size of each section of the circle relates to the amount of that substance. Tell students that the top graph compares the water portion of urine to the solid parts. The bottom graph shows the types of solids in the solid part of urine.

See *Math Skill and Problem-Solving Activities* for support.

My Planet Diary provides an opportunity for students to explore real-world connections to the excretory system.

Digital Lesson: Assign the *Do the Math* activity online and have students submit their work to you.

my science online | The Excretory System

Explain

Lead a Discussion

THE STAGES OF FILTRATION Remind students that the excretory system removes waste products of cellular respiration and other activities of cells. Ask: **Which organs act like filters?** *(The kidneys)* **How are they like filters?** *(They remove urea and other wastes from the blood but return materials that the body needs to the blood.)* **What is the name for the individual filter units in a kidney?** *(A nephron)* **What happens in the first stage of filtration in a nephron?** *(Both wastes and needed materials are filtered out of the blood.)* **What happens in the second stage?** *(Needed materials are returned to the blood.)* **Why is the second stage important?** *(Sample: It would be wasteful to discard useful materials, such as glucose or water.)*

Teach With Visuals

Tell students to look at **Figure 1.** Students can trace the flow of waste materials from the blood to removal from the body. Ask: **Which organs filter the blood?** *(The kidneys)* **Where do wastes go from the kidneys?** *(They travel through tubes called ureters to the urinary bladder.)* **What is the function of the urinary bladder?** *(It stores urine.)* **Where does urine go from the urinary bladder?** *(It leaves the body through a tube called the urethra.)*

21st Century Learning

CRITICAL THINKING Direct students' attention to **Figure 2** and the nephron capsule. Have students compare the size of the blood vessel leading into the capsule and the size of the blood vessel inside the capsule. Ask: **What happens to the diameter of the blood vessel inside the capsule?** *(It gets smaller.)* **How else does the blood vessel change inside the capsule?** *(It looks like a tangled knot.)* **How do you think these changes affect the blood pressure inside the small vessel?** *(They increase blood pressure.)* **How does this help the nephron function?** *(The increased pressure helps squeeze wastes out of the blood.)*

Structures That Remove Urine **Figure 1** shows the organs that remove urine from the body. Your two kidneys are the major organs of the excretory system. The **kidneys** act like filters. They remove urea and other wastes from the blood but keep materials that the body needs. These wastes are eliminated in the urine. Urine flows from the kidneys through two narrow tubes called **ureters** (yoo REE turz). The ureters carry urine to the **urinary bladder,** a muscular sac that stores urine. Urine leaves the body through a small tube called the **urethra** (yoo REE thruh).

Waste Filtration Each kidney has about one million nephrons. A **nephron** is a tiny filtering factory that removes wastes from blood and produces urine. The nephrons filter wastes in two stages. First, both wastes and needed materials are filtered out of the blood. Next, much of the needed material is returned to the blood, and the wastes are eliminated from the body. Follow this process in **Figure 2.**

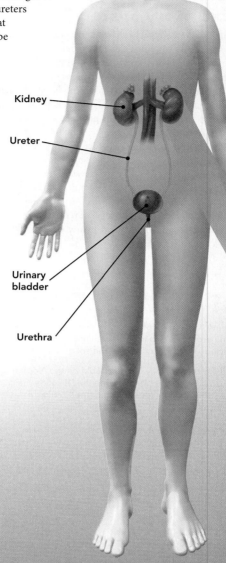

Kidney

Ureter

Urinary bladder

Urethra

FIGURE 1 ·······································
Removing Urine
Urine is produced in the kidneys and then removed from the body.

✎ **Summarize** Describe how urine is removed from the blood and then eliminated from the body.

Sample: The kidneys filter out wastes from the blood and make urine. It moves into the ureters and collects in the bladder. Urine leaves the bladder and is eliminated from the body through the urethra.

FIGURE 2 ··
How the Kidneys Work
Most of the work of the kidneys is done in the nephrons.

✏️ 🔺**Infer** In the key, write what each color represents in the diagram. Then explain below why it is important for capillaries to surround the nephron tube.

Sample: It is important because the
nephrons return needed materials to
the blood through the capillaries.

Key
■ _Capillary with_
oxygenated blood

■ _Capillary with blood_
low in oxygen

■ _Nephron tube_

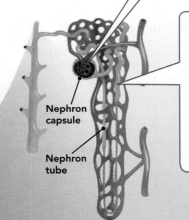

Nephron capsule

Nephron tube

Stage 1
- Blood flows into the cluster of capillaries in the thin-walled, hollow nephron capsule.
- Urea, glucose, and some water are filtered out of the blood and into the capsule.
- These materials then pass into the nephron tube.

Stage 2
- As the material flows through the nephron tube, most of the needed glucose and water move back into the blood through the capillaries.
- Most of the urea and some of the water stay in the nephron tube and become urine.

 Lab zone® Do the Quick Lab _Kidney Function._

🔖 Assess Your Understanding

1a. Name The chemical _urea_ comes from the breakdown of proteins.

b. Draw Conclusions Why is it important for a kidney to have many nephrons?
Sample: Each nephron is tiny,
and all the blood must be
filtered.

got it?

○ I get it! Now I know that the function of the excretory system is to _collect and_
remove wastes from the body.

○ I need extra help with _See TE note._

_Go to_ **my science ⬡ coach** _online for help with this subject._

489

Elaborate

🔺**Infer** Tell students that when they make an inference, they are using reasoning and prior knowledge to explain or interpret things they observe.

Build Inquiry

L1 NEPHRON FILTERS

Materials markers, paper

Time 10 minutes

Remind students that a number of materials enter the kidney, where they are filtered by the nephrons. Have students draw a diagram showing which material enter the nephron, which materials are returned to blood, and which materials leave the body in urine.

Ask: **Which materials enter the nephron?** _(Urea, water, and glucose)_ **Which materials are returned to the blood?** _(Most water and glucose along with a small amount of other materials)_ **Which materials leave the body in urine?** _(Urea and other wastes)_

Lab Resource: Quick Lab **Lab** zone®

L1 KIDNEY FUNCTION Students will model the movement of sodium during urine formation.

Evaluate

Assess Your Understanding

After students answer the questions, have them evaluate their understanding by completing the appropriate sentence.

R T I Response to Intervention

1a. If students have trouble naming the chemical, **then** ask students to make a chart showing each of the waste products eliminated from the body.

b. If students need help reaching a conclusion about the number of nephrons, **then** remind them of what they learned about the need for many alveoli in the lungs.

my science ⬡ coach Have students go online for help in understanding the role of the excretory system.

Differentiated Instruction

L3 Make a Display Have a group of students work cooperatively to investigate the causes of kidney stones, their treatment, and how the incidence of kidney stones can be reduced. Ask that group members prepare visuals to use as a display to present their findings to the class.

L1 Illustrate the System Give each student several index cards. Have them write a key term on the front of each card, and its definition on the back. Have them refer to the cards as they study **Figure 1** and **Figure 2**.

Explain

Teach Key Concepts 🔑

Explain to students that the body must maintain certain levels of substances in the blood. The process of keeping the body's internal environment stable in spite of changes in the external environment is known as *homeostasis*. The chemicals in the blood include sugars and salts, as well as water. The excretory system keeps levels constant by eliminating any extra chemicals, and retaining what the body needs. Ask: **Which organs are involved in eliminating water from the body?** *(Kidneys, lungs, and skin)* **Why is more water reabsorbed into the blood by the kidneys on a hot day?** *(Water is needed to balance the amount of water lost due to perspiration.)*

Teach With Visuals

Tell students to look at **Figure 3.** Explain that the body uses more water during some activities than others. Ask: **Why is it important to drink water before and during physical activities?** *(Students should recognize that not only does the body use water, but it also loses water through sweating.)* **How does the body control its use of water by the amount of urine it produces?** *(The body produces less urine when it needs to retain more water.)*

21st Century Learning 📖DK

INTERPERSONAL SKILLS Have students read *Kidney Transplant* in the **Big Ideas of Science Reference Library** and dramatize a television interview between a journalist and a doctor about kidney disease and organ donation. The interview should address the effects of malfunctioning kidneys on the human body and what is involved in a kidney transplant. Students can take turns playing the roles of the journalist and the doctor.

Vocabulary Identify Related Word Forms You know the noun *excretion* means "the process of removing wastes." Use this meaning to choose the correct meaning of the verb *excrete*.

- ○ relating to removing wastes
- ● to remove wastes
- ○ the state of removing wastes

How Does Excretion Help Your Body Maintain Homeostasis?

A buildup of wastes such as urea, excess water, and carbon dioxide can upset your body's balance. 🔑 **Excretion helps to maintain homeostasis by keeping the body's internal environment stable and free of harmful levels of chemicals.** The organs of excretion include the kidneys, lungs, skin, and liver.

Kidneys As the kidneys filter blood, they regulate the amount of water in your body, helping to maintain homeostasis, or internal stability. Remember that as urine is being formed, needed water passes from the nephron tubes into the blood. The amount of water that returns to the blood depends on conditions both outside and inside the body. For example, on a hot day when you have been sweating a lot and have not had much to drink, almost all the water in the nephron tubes will move back into the blood. You will excrete only a small amount of urine. On a cool day when you have drunk a lot of water, less water will move back into the blood. You will excrete a larger volume of urine. Look at **Figure 3.**

FIGURE 3 ....

Fluid Absorption
These three students have been doing different activities all day.

✏️ **Relate Text and Visuals** Which student will probably produce the least urine? Explain.

Kari is sweating and has not drunk any water, so she will produce the least urine.

Maria has been in classes all morning. She has had nothing to eat or drink.

Kari has been running sprints. She forgot to bring her water bottle.

Mike has been sitting on the bench and drinking water.

Lungs, Skin, and Liver Organs that function as part of other systems in your body also help keep you healthy by excreting wastes. For example, the lungs of the respiratory system remove carbon dioxide and some water when you exhale. The skin, part of your integumentary system, contains sweat glands that produce perspiration. Perspiration consists mostly of water, salt, and a small amount of urea.

The liver, which functions as part of the digestive system, also makes urea from the breakdown of proteins in the body. In addition, the liver breaks down other wastes into forms that can be excreted. For example, the liver breaks down old red blood cells. It even recycles some of their parts. In this way, you can think of the liver as a recycling factory.

Identify the Main Idea In your own words, write about each organ's role in excretion.

Lungs
They get rid of carbon dioxide and some water when I exhale.

Skin
Perspiration from sweat glands contains water and some urea.

Liver
It produces urea, breaks down wastes, and recycles materials.

Kidneys
They filter blood and regulate the amount of water in the body.

491

Lead a Discussion

SYSTEMS WORKING TOGETHER Explain that organs that function as part of other systems, such as the lungs, skin, and liver, also contribute to excreting wastes. Ask: **What system do the lungs belong to?** *(The respiratory system)* **How do the lungs help the body excrete waste?** *(The lungs remove carbon dioxide and water when you exhale.)* **What system does the skin belong to?** *(The integumentary system)* **How does the skin help the body excrete waste?** *(Sweat glands in the skin produce perspiration, which removes water, salt, and small amounts of urea from the body.)* **What system does the liver belong to?** *(The digestive system)* **How does the liver help the body excrete waste?** *(The liver produces urea from breaking down proteins, breaks down wastes into forms that can be excreted, and recycles materials.)*

Identify the Main Idea Explain to students that the main idea of a paragraph is the topic, central thought, or most important idea in a paragraph. Readers can identify the main idea because most of the sentences in the paragraph support, or give further details about, the main idea.

21st Century Learning

ACCOUNTABILITY Have students write ten true/false statements about the role of the excretory system, the structures of the excretory system, how the kidneys work, and what other organs in the body help the excretory system maintain homeostasis. Then have students exchange papers with a partner. Students should identify true statements and reword false statements to make them true.

Differentiated Instruction

L1 Draw a Diagram Have students prepare a poster showing a simple outline of a human body. Tell students to draw and label the lungs, skin, liver, and kidneys. Ask them to use arrows and labels to show the substances removed by each organ.

L3 Write a Paragraph Have students write a paragraph explaining how wastes are filtered in the kidneys. Ask them to begin by writing two lists—one that includes materials removed from the blood in the kidneys and one that includes materials returned to the blood.

Elaborate

Explore the Big Q ❓ UbD

Emphasize that the body's systems do not work independently. Instead, the systems work in harmony with each other to maintain homeostasis, a balanced, relatively stable internal environment. Remind students that the body's cells work best when they have this stable environment, which includes the correct water, glucose, and oxygen levels. Direct students' attention to **Figure 4.** Before students identify the main function of each system, ask: **How does the respiratory system play a role in maintaining homeostasis?** *(The respiratory system conducts gas exchange between the alveoli and the capillaries—transferring oxygen to the blood and picking up carbon dioxide and water to carry out of the body.)* **What is the primary way in which the excretory system helps maintain homeostasis?** *(The excretory system filters urea and other waste from the blood and removes them from the body in the form of urine.)* **How does the circulatory system play a role in maintaining homeostasis?** *(The blood of the circulatory system connects all the other systems. It brings oxygen from the respiratory system and nutrients from the digestive system to the cells; it sends carbon dioxide and water back through the respiratory system, and sends wastes through the digestive and excretory systems.)* **How does the digestive system play a role in maintaining homeostasis?** *(The digestive system breaks down food into nutrients that can be absorbed by the blood and removes digestive waste.)* **Which system is the most important to homeostasis?** *(Accept all well-reasoned answers. Most students should conclude that no system can function properly without the others.)*

Moving Things Along

EXPLORE THE BIG ❓

How do systems of the body move and manage materials?

FIGURE 4 ···

The systems of the body work together, helping to maintain homeostasis by changing materials and moving them to where they can be used or excreted.

✎ **Complete the following tasks.**

1. **Identify** For each system, identify its main function and tell what materials are managed or moved.

2. **Describe System Interactions** Which system is the link for moving materials among the other three systems?

   The circulatory system

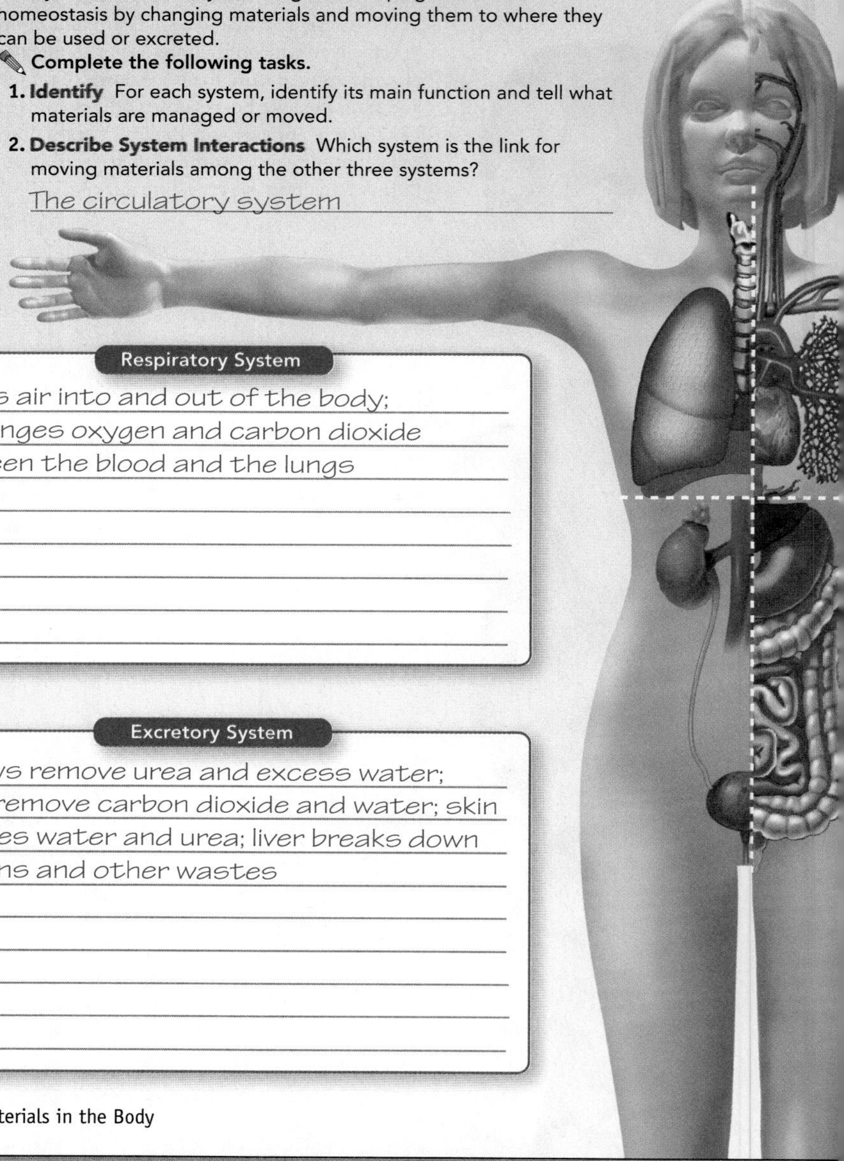

Respiratory System

Moves air into and out of the body; exchanges oxygen and carbon dioxide between the blood and the lungs

Excretory System

Kidneys remove urea and excess water; lungs remove carbon dioxide and water; skin removes water and urea; liver breaks down proteins and other wastes

Circulatory System

Circulates blood, which carries oxygen, nutrients, carbon dioxide, other wastes, and other materials through the body

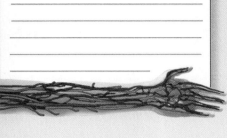

Digestive System

Breaks down food into smaller molecules, which are absorbed into the blood and then used by body cells; also removes digestive wastes

---

 Do the Quick Lab
Perspiration.

☞ Assess Your Understanding

2a. Review How does removing wastes from the body help maintain homeostasis?

The body is protected from a buildup of harmful chemicals.

b. Predict On a long bus trip, a traveler does not drink water for several hours. How will the volume of urine she produces that day compare to the volume on a day when she drinks several glasses of water? Explain.

She will produce less urine on the bus trip because most of the water in her kidneys will be reabsorbed.

c. How do systems of the body move and manage materials?

Sample: The digestive system moves food and breaks it down into simple substances. The circulatory system moves blood, which carries oxygen, carbon dioxide, and other materials. The respiratory system moves air into and out of the body. The excretory system filters the blood and removes wastes.

got it? ·······································

○ I get it! Now I know that excretion helps maintain homeostasis in my body by removing wastes and excess water.

○ I need extra help with See TE note.

Go to **my science COACH** *online for help with this subject.*

493

Lab Resource: Quick Lab

L1 **PERSPIRATION** Students will investigate how perspiration removes excess water and regulates temperature.

Evaluate ———————

Assess Your Understanding

After students answer the questions, have them evaluate their understanding by completing the appropriate sentence.

R T I Response to Intervention

2a. If students have trouble connecting waste removal with maintaining homeostasis, **then** help them recognize that cellular processes naturally produce waste and that too much waste in the body can cause sickness.

b. If students need help relating urine production to drinking water, **then** point out that the kidneys regulate the amount of water in the body and have students review **Figure 3.**

c. If students struggle to describe the way the body's systems move and manage materials, **then** review each of the body's systems independently and help students identify how each system either moves materials, manages materials, or both.

my science COACH Have students go online for help in understanding how excretion helps the body maintain homeostasis.

Differentiated Instruction

L1 **Chart the Body's Systems** Have students create a card for each of the four systems involved in moving and managing materials: the digestive system, the circulatory system, the respiratory system, and the excretory system. On the back of each card, have students identify the ways in which the system moves and manages materials in the body. Have pairs of students quiz each other by reading the backs of the cards and naming the system and/or

reading the system and describing the way that system manages and moves materials.

L2 **A Narrative of Consumption** Point out that the digestive, respiratory, circulatory, and excretory systems all play a role in processing the food we eat. Challenge students to write a paragraph tracking a piece of food through the body and to mention all four systems as they describe the path that item takes from consumption to excretion.

Lab zone® **After the Inquiry Warm-Up**

Excretion

Inquiry Warm-Up, *How Does Filtering a Liquid Change the Liquid?*
In the Inquiry Warm-Up, you investigated how filtering affects a liquid. Using what you learned from that activity, answer the questions below.

1. **COMMUNICATE** Draw the experiment set-up you used in the space below. Label your drawing.

2. **INFER** Why do you think the glucose passed through the filter while the sand did not?

_____

_____

3. **PREDICT** What do you think would have happened without the filter paper in place? Explain.

_____

_____

4. **MAKE MODELS** Assume that the experiment is a model for your body. What does each component, the liquid, the glucose, the sand, and the filter, represent?

_____

_____

Assess Your Understanding

Excretion

What Is the Role of the Excretory System?

1a. **NAME** The chemical _____ comes from the breakdown of proteins.

b. **DRAW CONCLUSIONS** Why is it important for a kidney to have many nephrons?

_____

_____

got it? ·

○ **I get it!** Now I know that the function of the excretory system is to _____

_____

○ **I need extra help with** _____

How Does Excretion Help Your Body Maintain Homeostasis?

2a. **REVIEW** How does removing wastes from the body help maintain homeostasis?

_____

_____

b. **PREDICT** On a long bus trip, a traveler does not drink water for several hours. How will the volume of urine she produces that day compare to the volume on a day when she drinks several glasses of water? Explain.

_____

c. **ANSWER** How do systems of the body move and manage materials?

_____

_____

_____

got it? ·

○ **I get it!** Now I know that excretion helps maintain homeostasis in my body by

_____

○ **I need extra help with** _____

Key Concept Summaries

Excretion

What Is the Role of the Excretory System?

Excretion is the process of removing waste. **The excretory system collects the wastes that cells produce and removes them from the body.** The system consists of the kidneys, ureters, urinary bladder, and urethra. One waste the body must eliminate is **urea,** which is a chemical that comes from the breakdown of proteins.

Urea, water, and other wastes are eliminated in a fluid called **urine.** The process through which urine is produced takes place in the **kidneys,** which are the major organs of the excretory system. **Nephrons** in the kidneys filter materials from the blood. They remove the wastes in urine and return any needed materials back to the blood. Urine then flows from the kidneys through two narrow tubes called **ureters,** which carry urine to a saclike organ known as the **urinary bladder.** Urine leaves the body through a small tube called the **urethra.**

How Does Excretion Help Your Body Maintain Homeostasis?

Excretion helps to maintain homeostasis by keeping the body's internal environment stable and free of harmful levels of chemicals. The organs of excretion include kidneys, lungs, skin, and liver. The kidneys filter blood. They regulate the amount of water in the body. The lungs and skin also remove wastes. The lungs, for example, remove carbon dioxide and some water. The skin removes some water and urea through perspiration. The liver produces urea and breaks down some wastes into forms that can be excreted.

On a separate sheet of paper, explain the importance of the excretory system in the human body.

Name _____ Date _____ Class _____

Excretion

Understanding Main Ideas
Answer the following questions in the spaces provided.

1. What is excretion?

_____

2. Compare and contrast ureters and the urethra.

_____

3. What is urea?

_____

4. What is urine?

_____

5. How do the kidneys maintain water balance in the body?

_____

_____

6. What are the two stages of filtration in the nephrons?

_____

_____

Building Vocabulary
Label the diagram with the names of the parts of the excretory system.

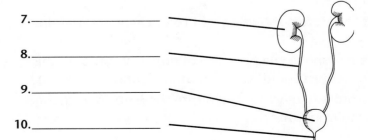

7. _____

8. _____

9. _____

10. _____

Excretion

Read the passage and study the table. Then use a separate sheet of paper to answer the questions that follow.

Urinalysis

The table below lists some common urine tests, their possible results, and what these results indicate. Testing for the presence of protein, glucose, ketones, and nitrite involves chemical analysis. These tests are usually performed by dipping into the urine a strip of paper or plastic called a dipstick. There is a specific kind of dipstick for each type of test. If the dipstick changes color, the patient has the condition being tested. Testing for the presence of red and white blood cells is performed by looking at a urine sample with a microscope. Red and white blood cells are visible when magnified if they are present.

Test	Results	Condition Indicated by Test Results
color and texture	pale to dark yellow	normal
	foamy	presence of a protein
	red or red-brown	presence of red blood cells
presence of protein	slight color change in dipstick	kidney disease
	major color change in dipstick	severe kidney disease
presence of glucose	dipstick changes color	diabetes
presence of ketones	dipstick changes color	severe diabetes
presence of nitrite	dipstick changes color	bacteria in urine
presence of red blood cells	cells visible	kidney disease
presence of white blood cells	cells visible	bacteria in urine

1. A patient's urine tests positive for glucose and ketones. What do these results indicate?

2. The dipstick test for protein shows a slight color change. What does this indicate?

3. A patient's urine test shows the presence of nitrite. What does this indicate? What other test could you perform to confirm this result?

4. Dipstick tests for protein, glucose, and nitrite show no color change. What do these results indicate?

Lesson Quiz

Excretion

Write the letter of the correct answer on the line at the left.

1. ___ What is the chemical that comes from the breakdown of proteins and must be eliminated?

    A   nephron

    B   salt

    C   water

    D   urea

2. ___ What substance is produced by sweat glands in the skin?

    A   carbon dioxide

    B   perspiration

    C   urine

    D   protein

3. ___ In which structure is blood filtered within the kidneys?

    A   nephron

    B   ureter

    C   bladder

    D   gland

4. ___ What is the process through which the body maintains stable internal conditions?

    A   gas exchange

    B   circulation

    C   homeostasis

    D   recycling

Fill in the blank to complete each statement.

5. The process of removing waste from the body is called _____.

6. Water, urea, and other wastes are eliminated in a fluid called _____.

7. Two _____ connect the kidneys to the urinary bladder.

8. Nephrons are located within the _____, which are the two main organs of the excretory system.

9. Urine flows through the _____ and out of the body.

10. The _____ makes urea and breaks down old red blood cells.

Excretion

Answer Key

After the Inquiry Warm-Up

1. Students should draw a container with a funnel inserted and indicate filter paper in the funnel. They should also show liquid being poured from one container to the other. They should label the glucose solution, sand, filter paper, funnel, and containers.

2. Sample: The sand was too big to pass through the paper, but the glucose was dissolved in the water so it could pass through.

3. The sand would have gone into the second container when I poured the liquid.

4. Sample: liquid – blood; glucose – nutrients; sand – waste; filter paper – natural filters in the body

Key Concept Summaries

Processes in cells produce wastes. If these wastes build up, the body cannot remain healthy. The excretory system removes wastes from the body. It also maintains homeostasis, which is a relatively stable internal environment.

Review and Reinforce

1. the process of removing waste from the body

2. Each of the two ureters carries urine from a kidney to the bladder. The urethra carries urine outside the body from the bladder.

3. a chemical that is a result of the breakdown of proteins

4. the watery fluid that contains urea and other wastes; produced by the kidneys

5. When the body has more water than needed, the kidneys excrete a large amount of water. When the body needs water, the kidneys produce more concentrated urine so less water is excreted.

6. First the nephrons filter both waste and needed material out of the blood. In the second stage, needed material is returned to the blood and wastes are eliminated.

7. kidney

8. ureter

9. urinary bladder

10. urethra

Enrich

1. The results indicate that the person has a severe condition of diabetes.

2. The results indicate that the person has a kidney disease.

3. Nitrite indicates bacteria in the urine. You could examine the urine under a microscope for the presence of white blood cells. A positive result would confirm the presence of bacteria.

4. The results indicate that the person does not have diabetes, kidney disease, or bacteria in the urine.

Lesson Quiz

1. D
2. B
3. A
4. C
5. excretion
6. urine
7. ureters
8. kidneys
9. urethra
10. liver

Study Guide

Review the Big Q **UbD**

Have students complete the statement at the top of the page. This Key Concept supports their understanding of the chapter's Big Question. Have students return to the chapter opener pages. What is different about how students view the image of the highway now that they have completed the chapter? Thinking about this will help them prepare for the *Apply the Big Q* activity in the Review and Assessment.

Partner Review

Have partners review definitions of vocabulary using the Study Guide to quiz each other. Students could read the Key Concept statements and leave out words for their partner to fill, or change a statement so it is false and ask their partner to correct it.

Pair Activity: Concept Map

Help pairs of students show how information in this chapter is related. Remind them that the digestive, circulatory, respiratory, and excretory systems all work together to move and manage materials in the body. Provide pairs with poster paper, markers, and index cards. Have students identify Key Concepts, key terms, details, and examples, and write each on an index card. Use the questions below to add to and organize information on the cards into a concept map on the poster. Prompt students to use phrases such as "moves materials into the body," "carries needed materials to cells," "carries waste away from cells," "breaks down food into nutrient molecules," and "processes waste" to indicate the organization of the map. The phrases should form a sentence between a set of concepts.

- What organs in what systems bring materials into the body?
- What organs in what systems transfer materials across a system?
- What organs in what systems carry waste away from cells?
- What organs in what systems break down food into nutrient molecules?
- What organs in what systems process and eliminate waste?

My Science Coach allows students to complete the *Practice Test* online.

The Big Question allows students to complete the *Apply the Big Q* activity about the functions of the body systems that work together to provide energy from an apple.

Vocab Flash Cards offer a way to review the chapter vocabulary word.

my science online.com   Managing Materials in the Body

REVIEW THE BIG **?**   Materials in the body are managed and moved by the <u>*digestive*</u>, <u>*circulatory*</u>, <u>*respiratory*</u>, and <u>*excretory*</u> systems.

LESSON 1 Digestion

🗝 Food provides your body with materials for growth and repair. It also provides energy.

🗝 The digestive system breaks down food, absorbs nutrients, and eliminates waste.

🗝 Substances produced by the liver, pancreas, and lining of the small intestine help to complete chemical digestion.

Vocabulary
- calorie   - enzyme   - esophagus
- peristalsis   - villi

LESSON 2 The Circulatory System

🗝 The circulatory system delivers substances to cells, carries wastes away, and regulates body temperature. Blood cells fight disease.

🗝 Blood has four components: plasma, red blood cells, white blood cells, and platelets.

Vocabulary
- circulatory system   - heart   - atrium   - ventricle
- valve   - artery   - aorta   - capillary   - vein
- hemoglobin

LESSON 3 The Respiratory System

🗝 Your respiratory system moves air containing oxygen into your lungs and removes carbon dioxide and water from your body. Your lungs and the structures that lead to them make up your respiratory system.

🗝 When you breathe, your rib muscles and diaphragm work together, causing air to move into or out of your lungs. This airflow leads to the exchange of gases that occurs in your lungs.

Vocabulary
- pharynx   - trachea   - cilia   - bronchi   - lungs   - alveoli
- diaphragm   - larynx   - vocal cords

LESSON 4 Excretion

🗝 The excretory system collects the wastes that cells produce and removes them from the body.

🗝 Excretion helps maintain homeostasis by keeping the body's internal environment stable and free of harmful levels of chemicals.

Vocabulary
- excretion   - urea   - urine   - kidney   - ureter
- urinary bladder   - urethra   - nephron

E L L Support

4 Language Production

Divide the class into four groups and have each group focus on the essential questions from one of the lessons. Have students discuss all they have learned that relates to the questions. Group members should take notes during the discussion. After they have answered the question, have each group organize their notes into an oral report that they deliver to the class. All group members should have a speaking role.

Beginning

LOW/HIGH Allow students to answer with drawings, single words, or short phrases.

Intermediate

LOW/HIGH Have students draft complete sentences when writing their oral reports.

Advanced

LOW/HIGH Have students assist and/or edit the work of classmates with lower language proficiency.

Review and Assessment

LESSON 1 Digestion

1. Mechanical digestion begins in the

   a. liver.   **b.** esophagus.

   (c.) mouth.   **d.** small intestine.

2. _Peristalsis_ is the involuntary contraction of muscles that pushes food forward.

3. Interpret Diagrams How do you think acid reflux, the condition illustrated in the diagram below, affects the esophagus?

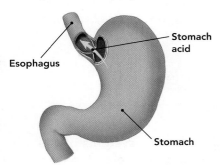

Esophagus

Stomach acid

Stomach

Sample: It causes stomach acid to burn the esophagus.

4. Apply Concepts How does the function of the digestive system contribute to homeostasis?

Sample: The digestive system makes nutrients available for growth repair, and energy.

5. [Write About It] Have you ever choked while eating? Explain what happens in a person's body when they choke. Describe some things people can do to avoid choking while eating.

See TE rubric.

LESSON 2 The Circulatory System

6. What structure regulates the direction of blood flow through the heart?

   a. ventricle   **b.** pacemaker

   (c.) valve   **d.** artery

7. The _veins_ in your body carry blood back to your heart.

8. Classify Which chambers of the heart below are the ventricles? Which chamber receives oxygen-poor blood from the body?

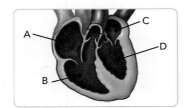

A

C

D

B

The ventricles are B and D. Oxygen-poor blood enters from the body into A.

9. Predict Is it safe for a person with blood type O+ to receive a blood transfusion from a person who has blood type A+? Explain.

No. A person with type O+ blood will make anti-A clumping proteins, so the match of Rh factor will not matter.

10. [Write About It] People who do not have enough iron in their diets sometimes develop anemia, a condition in which their blood cannot carry a normal amount of oxygen. Write a paragraph to explain why this is so.

See TE rubric.

Review and Assessment

Assess Understanding

Have students complete the answers to the Review and Assessment Questions. Have a class discussion about what students find confusing. Write Key Concepts on the board to reinforce knowledge.

RTI Response to Intervention

4. If students cannot connect the functions of the digestive system to homeostasis, **then** have them review the Key Concept detailing the three main functions of the digestive system. Point out that the digestive system breaks down food into nutrient molecules and then absorbs the nutrients for use by the cells.

9. If students cannot predict the results of the blood transfusion, **then** have them review the section on Landsteiner's discovery. Remind them that blood is only compatible if it has the same marker molecules and Rh factor.

Alternate Assessment

3D MODEL Challenge student groups or pairs to make a 3D model of the small intestine, the heart, the lungs, or the kidneys. Using a variety of materials such as clay, cardboard, paint, construction paper, tape, glue, and paper maché, students should strive to make their models illustrate how these organs work move and/or manage materials in the body.

CHAPTER 12

[Write About It] Assess student's writing using this rubric.				
SCORING RUBRIC	**SCORE 4**	**SCORE 3**	**SCORE 2**	**SCORE 1**
Explain anatomy of choking	Explains choking in good anatomical detail	Explains choking with few anatomical details	Partially explains choking	Fails to explain choking
Describe ways to avoid choking while eating	Describes several ways to avoid choking	Describes two ways to avoid choking	Describes one way to avoid choking	Fails to describe any ways to avoid choking

[Write About It] Assess student's writing using this rubric.				
SCORING RUBRIC	**SCORE 4**	**SCORE 3**	**SCORE 2**	**SCORE 1**
Explain how poor diet can lead to anemia and a lack of energy	Thoroughly explains connection between diet, anemia, and lack of energy	Explains connection between diet, anemia, and lack of energy	Poorly connects diet, anemia, and lack of energy	Fails to explain the cause or effects of anemia

Review and Assessment, Cont.

R T I Response to Intervention

14. If students cannot trace carbon dioxide from the blood to exhalation, **then** review the process of gas exchange that takes place between the alveoli in the lungs and the capillaries.

19. If students cannot recall the role of the kidneys in homeostasis, **then** have them review the kidneys' part in fluid absorption.

Apply the Big Q ❓ UbD

TRANSFER Student answers should describe the roles of the digestive and circulatory systems in providing energy to the body and describe cellular respiration. See the scoring rubric below.

Connect to the Big Idea ❓ UbD

BIG IDEA Life can be organized in a functional and structural hierarchy. Life is maintained by various physiological functions essential for growth, reproduction, and homeostasis.

L3 WRITING IN SCIENCE Ask students to write a blog entry that explains to readers how to keep the different systems of the body healthy. In their blogs, students should use what they learned about how the digestive, circulatory, respiratory, and excretory systems manage materials in the body. They should also discuss what nutrients and other materials these systems process.

CHAPTER 12 Review and Assessment

LESSON 3 The Respiratory System

11. Your voice is produced by the
a. pharynx.　　　ⓑ larynx.
c. trachea.　　　d. alveoli.

12. Clusters of air sacs in the lungs are _alveoli._

13. Classify What part of the respiratory system connects the mouth and nose?
It is the pharynx.

14. Sequence What happens to the carbon dioxide in blood when it flows through the capillaries in the alveoli?
It passes from the blood
through the thin capillary wall
and the wall of the alveolus
into the alveolus. Then it is
exhaled.

15. Compare and Contrast How do mucus and cilia work together to remove dust that enters your nose? How do they differ?
Mucus traps particles in the
nose and trachea. Cilia in the
trachea sweep the mucus into
the pharynx. Mucus traps
particles and cilia sweeps
them away.

16. **Write About It** Suppose you are a doctor with patients who are mountain climbers. Write a letter to these patients that explains how gas exchange is affected at the top of a mountain, where air pressure is lower and there is less oxygen than at lower elevations.
See TE rubric.

LESSON 4 Excretion

17. Urine leaves the body through the
a. ureters.　　　b. nephrons.
c. urinary bladder.　　ⓓ urethra.

18. Urine is stored in the _urinary bladder._

19. Relate Cause and Effect How do the kidneys help maintain homeostasis?
They adjust the amount of
water reabsorbed during
excretion to regulate the
amount of water in the body.

 How do systems of the body move and manage materials?

20. You eat an apple. Describe how the functions of your body systems working together can provide you with energy from the apple.
The digestive system breaks
down the apple into sugars.
These are absorbed into the
bloodstream. Then the cir-
culatory system carries the
sugars and oxygen from the
respiratory system to my
cells. The cells carry out cellular
respiration, releasing energy I
can use.
See TE rubric.

Write About It Assess student's writing using this rubric.

SCORING RUBRIC	SCORE 4	SCORE 3	SCORE 2	SCORE 1
Explain effect of low air pressure on breathing	Fully explains why breathing is more difficult	Adequately explains why breathing is more difficult	Partially explains why breathing is more difficult	Fails to explain why breathing is more difficult
Explain effect of low oxygen on breathing	Fully explains why low oxygen causes rapid breathing	Partially explains why low oxygen causes rapid breathing	Describes breathing as more rapid; gives no reason	Incorrectly describes effect of low oxygen on breathing

How do systems of the body move and manage materials?

SCORING RUBRIC	SCORE 4	SCORE 3	SCORE 2	SCORE 1
Describe roles of digestive and circulatory system	Fully describes roles of both systems	Adequately describes roles of both systems	Adequately describes role of one system	Fails to describe role of either system
	Fully describes cellular respiration	Adequately describes cellular respiration	Weakly describes cellular respiration	Fails to describe cellular respiration

Standardized Test Prep

Multiple Choice

Circle the letter of the best answer.

1. Which statement below correctly describes the diagram?

   A Blood Vessel A carries blood to the heart.

   Ⓑ Blood Vessel A is where a pulse can be measured.

   C Blood Vessel B is where diffusion takes place.

   D Blood Vessel B carries blood to the lungs.

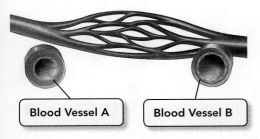

Blood Vessel A   **Blood Vessel B**

2. Which of the following nutrients provides the *most* energy for the body?

   Ⓐ fats

   B proteins

   C carbohydrates

   D vitamins

3. Which of the following parts of the digestive system is paired with its function?

   A esophagus—digests carbohydrates

   B stomach—digests fats

   Ⓒ large intestine—absorbs water

   D small intestine—begins mechanical digestion

4. Which of the following organs functions as both a respiratory organ and an excretory organ?

   A the liver

   B the skin

   C the kidneys

   Ⓓ the lungs

5. The correct sequence for the path of blood through the body is

   A heart—lungs—other body parts

   B lungs—other body parts—heart

   Ⓒ heart—lungs—heart—other body parts

   D heart—other body parts—lungs—heart

Constructed Response

Use the table below and your knowledge of science to help you answer Question 6. Write your answer on a separate sheet of paper.

Blood Types		
Blood Type	**Marker Molecules**	**Clumping Proteins**
A	A	anti-B
B	B	anti-A
AB	A and B	none
O	none	anti-A and anti-B

6. A blood bank stores donated blood for transfusions. Which blood type should a blood bank store the most of? People with which blood type will have the greatest chance of finding donated blood that will not cause clumping in a transfusion? Explain your answers. *See TE note.*

497

Standardized Test Prep

Test-Taking Skills

INTERPRETING DIAGRAMS Tell students that when they answer questions like Question 1, which includes a diagram, they should make sure that they study all parts of the diagram carefully, including illustrations and labels. Urge students to get the diagram's information clear in their minds before they analyze how the diagram relates to the question as a whole.

Constructed Response

6. The blood bank should store the most type O blood. This is the most common blood type, and people with type O cannot receive any other type. Also, type O can be given to anyone, so it is used the most. The person with the greatest chance of finding blood that will not cause clumping is someone who is type AB because their blood has no clumping proteins and will accept A, B, or O as well as AB.

Additional Assessment Resources

Chapter Test
EXAMVIEW® Assessment Suite
Performance Assessment
Progress Monitoring Assessments
SuccessTracker™

Remediate If students have trouble with...

QUESTION	SEE LESSON	STANDARDS
1	2	
2	1	
3	1	
4	3, 4	
5	2	
6	2	

Science Matters

Frontiers of Technology

Have students read *Artificial Blood.* Point out that artificial blood compounds have properties that have several advantages. They are 1) easily available, 2) long-lasting and storable; 3) processed to avoid contamination; and 4) usable for all blood types. However, as the article mentions, they do not perform all the functions that blood does.

Ask: **What kind of job does artificial blood compounds do well?** *(Sample: Artificial blood compounds are effective at carrying oxygen through the blood vessels.)* **What do artificial blood compounds still have to do in order to be a substitute for blood?** *(Sample: In order to do the same job as blood, artificial blood compounds have to carry oxygen, nutrients, hormones, cells that fight disease and infections to all parts of the body, and carry away waste products from the body's cells.)*

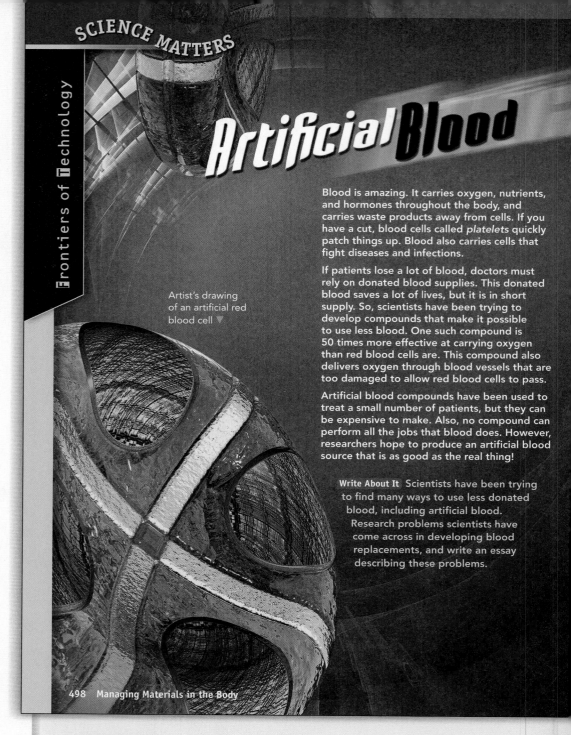

Artificial Blood

Blood is amazing. It carries oxygen, nutrients, and hormones throughout the body, and carries waste products away from cells. If you have a cut, blood cells called *platelets* quickly patch things up. Blood also carries cells that fight diseases and infections.

If patients lose a lot of blood, doctors must rely on donated blood supplies. This donated blood saves a lot of lives, but it is in short supply. So, scientists have been trying to develop compounds that make it possible to use less blood. One such compound is 50 times more effective at carrying oxygen than red blood cells are. This compound also delivers oxygen through blood vessels that are too damaged to allow red blood cells to pass.

Artificial blood compounds have been used to treat a small number of patients, but they can be expensive to make. Also, no compound can perform all the jobs that blood does. However, researchers hope to produce an artificial blood source that is as good as the real thing!

Write About It Scientists have been trying to find many ways to use less donated blood, including artificial blood. Research problems scientists have come across in developing blood replacements, and write an essay describing these problems.

Artist's drawing of an artificial red blood cell ▼

Quick Facts

The greater the body mass, the more the heart works to get blood with oxygen and nutrients to the body. The Body Mass Index (BMI) is a measurement for assessing body fat in proportion to a person's height and weight. To calculate it, multiply a person's weight in pounds by 703, divide by their height in inches, and divide again by their height in inches—that's the BMI. According to the National Center for Health Statistics: individuals with BMI values under 18.5 are underweight, values from 18.5 to 24.9 are healthy, and values over 25.0 are overweight. The American Heart Association and other health organizations have programs that encourage people to evaluate their health and to follow guidelines to get healthy. Have students form groups and research health organizations in your state. How do their programs promote health? Have groups report to the class.

Understanding Fitness Assessments

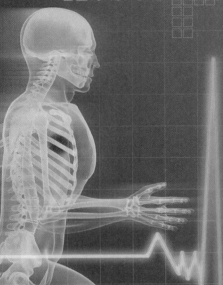

How hard does your heart work to pump blood? One tool for learning about a person's physical fitness is to measure how exercise affects his or her heart rate.

Cardiovascular appraisals measure the difference between a person's heart rate before exercise and during exercise. In simple cardiovascular fitness appraisals, participants check and record their resting heart rates. They then do some form of exercise for a set period of time. The exercises must be aerobic exercises—activities that increase the body's need for oxygen and raise the heart rate. Running, climbing stairs, or riding a bike are common aerobic exercises. After a period of time, participants stop their exercises and immediately check their heart rates again.

The graph below shows how exercise affects the heart rates of two people. Which person is more physically fit? Explain your reasoning.

Heart Rate Response to Exercise

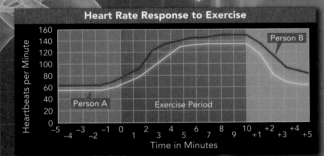

Analyze It Just how much can you tell about the fitness and activity levels of the two people in the graph? List characteristics of Person A and Person B that might have affected the results of this fitness appraisal. Design a questionnaire that would allow you to find out more about the test subjects.

499

Think Like a Scientist

Have students read *Understanding Fitness Assessments*. Point out that the graph, which shows the heart rate response to exercise, measures the heart rate as beats per minute (bpm) before, during, and after exercise. Have students examine the graph. Have them look at the following: 1) how long the exercise period is (10 minutes); 2) what the highest bpm rate is for the trained participant (about 135 bpm) and the untrained participant (about 150 bpm); and 3) how long it took each participant to get back to their normal heart rate (trained took five minutes and untrained took over five minutes).

Ask: **Which participant's heart shown on the graph is pumping more blood? How do you know?** (Sample: The untrained participant's heart is pumping more blood because the untrained participant's rate was higher at about 150 bpm.) **Why is aerobic exercise used to test cardiovascular fitness?** (Sample: Aerobic exercise raises the body's heart rate so that the beats per minute can be measured before, during, and after the aerobic activity.)

CHAPTER 13

Controlling Body Processes

Introduce the Big Q ?UbD

Have students look at the image and read the Engaging Question and description. Ask the students to infer how they might react when they are about to collide with somebody. Have volunteers share their inferences with the class. Point out that avoiding a collision can involve more than one of our senses, as well as numerous muscles and the brain. Ask: **How might these athletes be using sight to help them avoid a collision?** *(These players' eyes see other people's bodies about to crash into them.)* **How might the athletes be using other senses?** *(They might hear the sounds of other bodies getting near, and they might feel other people's bodies brushing against their own.)* **How do your muscles "know" what to do to avoid a collision?** *(Accept all responses at this time.)*

Untamed Science Video

THINK FAST! Before viewing, invite students to discuss what they know about the nervous system. Then play the video. Lead a class discussion and make a list of questions that this video raises. You may wish to have students view the video again after they have completed the chapter to see if their questions have been answered.

To access the online resources for this chapter, search on or navigate to *Controlling Body Processes*.

Untamed Science Video shows the nervous system in action during a baseball game.

The Big Question allows students to answer the Engaging Question about how the athletes' bodies sense and react to their surroundings.

my science online.com ▸ Controlling Body Processes

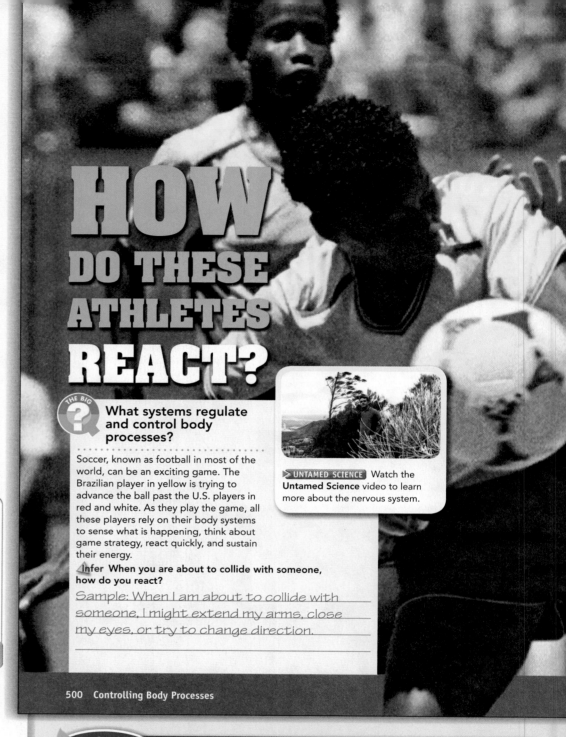

HOW DO THESE ATHLETES REACT?

What systems regulate and control body processes?

Soccer, known as football in most of the world, can be an exciting game. The Brazilian player in yellow is trying to advance the ball past the U.S. players in red and white. As they play the game, all these players rely on their body systems to sense what is happening, think about game strategy, react quickly, and sustain their energy.

Infer When you are about to collide with someone, how do you react?

Sample: When I am about to collide with someone, I might extend my arms, close my eyes, or try to change direction.

▸ **UNTAMED SCIENCE** Watch the **Untamed Science** video to learn more about the nervous system.

Professional Development Note — From the Author

A study of the human nervous system is about our bodies and how we interact with everything around us. Talking to friends, listening to music, and understanding a movie are all possible because of a well-developed nervous system. Ask students to take five to ten minutes to write down messages their senses pick up every few seconds. Then try experiments with blocking sight, hearing, or smell and have them reflect upon these experiences. There are many opportunities in this chapter for addressing students' individual needs and taking advantage of those teachable moments in the classroom.

✉ *Zipporah Miller*

Controlling Body Processes

CHAPTER 13

Chapter at a Glance

CHAPTER PACING: 9–13 periods or $4\frac{1}{2}$–$6\frac{1}{2}$ blocks

INTRODUCE THE CHAPTER: Use the Engaging Question and the opening image to get students thinking about controlling body processes. Activate prior knowledge and preteach vocabulary using the Getting Started pages.

Lesson 1: The Nervous System

Lesson 2: The Endocrine System

Lesson 3: The Male and Female Reproductive Systems

Lesson 4: Pregnancy and Birth

ASSESSMENT OPTIONS: Chapter Test, *ExamView*® Computer Test Generator, Performance Assessment, Progress Monitoring Assessments, SuccessTracker™

Preference Navigator, in the online Planning tools, allows you to customize *Interactive Science* to your own teaching style. You can also edit lesson plans by selecting the Lesson Planner option.

Digital Teacher's Edition allows you to access your Teacher's Edition and Resource online.

my science online.com

CHAPTER 13

Differentiated Instruction

L1 Bundle of Nerves Invite students to use the word *nerve* as a springboard to brainstorm a list of related words and phrases. Write these terms, such as *nervous, nerve-racking, touched a nerve, got on someone's nerves, nervous breakdown*, and *someone's got nerve*, and discuss the meanings and connotations of each one. Finally, write *nervous system* on the board and ask students to speculate about where this system can be found in the human body.

L3 A Multitude of Reactions Challenge students to brainstorm a list of specific ways in which their bodies react to surroundings. Point out that students should note reactions involving all five senses and include both causes (something in their surroundings) and effects (their reactions). You might offer an example such as *sees a red stop sign and stops.*

Getting Started

Check Your Understanding

This activity assesses students' understanding of sense organs and voluntary and involuntary actions. After students have shared their answers, point out that breathing, blinking, swallowing, and the heart's beating are all examples of involuntary actions.

Preteach Vocabulary Skills

Draw students' attention to the headings and entries of the 3-column chart. Point out that when a prefix is added to a word, the meaning of the prefix is added to or combined with the meaning of the base word. Learning the meanings of prefixes can make it easier to learn new vocabulary words. Explain to students that the prefixes *hypo-* and *re-* appear in many words. Encourage students to think of examples, such as *repeat, reinvent, redo, redesign, review, hypodermic, hypoglycemic,* and *hypoallergenic.*

Check Your Understanding

1. **Background** Read the paragraph below and then answer the question.

> Rajev wakes up gasping. Smoke enters his nose and stings his eyes. He feels the **involuntary** pounding of his heart. His **sense organs** send signals to his brain— alarms, shouts, smoke, heat, and sirens. Instantly, Rajev interprets the signals and takes **voluntary** action. He crawls to the window as the fire ladder rises below him.

> **Involuntary** action is not under a person's conscious control.
>
> **Sense organs,** such as eyes and ears, are body structures that gather information from your surroundings.
>
> **Voluntary** action is under a person's conscious control.

- Why is Rajev's crawling to the window a voluntary rather than an involuntary action?

  Sample: Rajev's crawl to the window was a conscious choice he made.

> **MY READING WEB** If you had trouble completing the question above, visit **My Reading Web** and type in *Controlling Body Processes.*

Vocabulary Skill

Prefixes A prefix is a word part that is added to the beginning of a word to change its meaning. The table below lists prefixes that will help you learn terms in this chapter.

Prefix	Meaning	Term
inter-	(between,) among	interneuron, *n.* a neuron, or nerve cell, that is between other neurons
re-	back, over again	reflex, *n.* an automatic response that occurs rapidly without conscious control

2. **Quick Check** The prefix *inter-* has more than one meaning. In the table above, circle the meaning of *inter-* that relates to the word *interneuron.*

My Reading Web offers leveled readings that offer a foundation for the chapter content.

Vocab Flash Cards offer extra practice with the chapter vocabulary words.

Digital Lesson

- Assign the *Check Your Understanding* activity online and have students submit their work to you.
- Assign the *Vocabulary Skill* activity online and have students submit their work to you.

MY SCIENCE online .com ▶ **Controlling Body Processes**

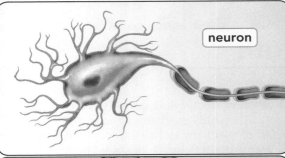

neuron

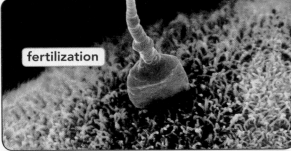

pituitary gland

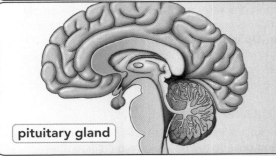

fertilization

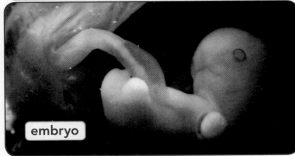

embryo

Chapter Preview

LESSON 1
- neuron • nerve impulse
- nerve • synapse
- central nervous system
- peripheral nervous system
- reflex
- 🎯 Identify Supporting Evidence
- ⚠ Infer

LESSON 2
- gland • duct • hormone
- target cell • hypothalamus
- pituitary gland
- negative feedback
- 🎯 Identify the Main Idea
- ⚠ Make Models

LESSON 3
- fertilization • egg • sperm
- zygote • testes • testosterone
- scrotum • semen • penis
- ovary • estrogen
- Fallopian tube • uterus • vagina
- menstrual cycle • menstruation
- ovulation
- 🎯 Sequence
- ⚠ Develop Hypotheses

LESSON 4
- embryo • fetus • amniotic sac
- placenta • umbilical cord
- 🎯 Compare and Contrast
- ⚠ Calculate

> VOCAB FLASH CARDS For extra help with vocabulary, visit **Vocab Flash Cards** and type in *Controlling Body Processes.*

503

CHAPTER 13

Preview Vocabulary Terms

Have students create a personalized science glossary for the vocabulary terms in this chapter. In their glossaries, students should define each term and reference the pages in the chapter that define and explain the term. Encourage students to include drawings and diagrams that help explain the meaning of the terms and concepts. A list of Academic Vocabulary for each lesson can be found in the Support All Readers box at the start of the lesson.

L1 Have students look at the images on this page as you pronounce the vocabulary word. Have students repeat the word after you. Then read the definition. Use the sample sentence in italics to clarify the meaning of the term.

neuron *(NOOR ahn)* A cell that carries information through the nervous system. *A message enters a neuron at one end and exits at the other end.*

pituitary gland *(pih TOO uh tehr ee gland)* An endocrine gland that helps to control many body activities. *The pituitary gland releases hormones during certain physical activities.*

fertilization *(fur tuh lih ZAY shun)* A process in which an egg cell and a sperm cell join. *A new human life always begins with fertilization.*

embryo *(EM bree oh)* A developing human for the eight weeks following the division of a fertilized egg into two cells. *The brain begins to develop in the embryo.*

(ELL) Support

Have students complete the Preview Vocabulary Terms activity either alone or in pairs. Before students begin creating their science glossaries, write each word and introduce it to students by pointing and saying it aloud.

Beginning
LOW Draw a picture or other visual aid for each vocabulary term in the glossary to associate the term with its definition.
HIGH Include words and phrases in the native language to help students remember specific terms they have trouble with.

Intermediate
LOW/HIGH Include English pronunciations for each term in the glossary.

Advanced
LOW/HIGH For each vocabulary term in the glossary, write a sentence that uses the term correctly.

The Nervous System

1 What systems regulate and control body processes?

Lesson Pacing: 3–4 periods or $1\frac{1}{2}$–2 blocks

🕐 **SHORT ON TIME?** To do this lesson in approximately half the time, do the Activate Prior Knowledge activity followed by a discussion of the Key Concepts to familiarize students with the lesson content. Have students do the Quick Labs. The rest of the lesson can be completed by students independently.

> **Preference Navigator,** in the online Planning tools, allows you to customize *Interactive Science* to your own teaching style. You can also edit lesson plans by selecting the Lesson Planner option.
>
> **Digital Teacher's Edition** allows you to access your Teacher's Edition and Resource materials online.

Lesson Vocabulary

- neuron • nerve impulse • nerve • synapse
- central nervous system • peripheral nervous system • reflex

Content Refresher
Professional Development Note

What Causes a Nerve Impulse? The start of a nerve impulse is related to the distribution of potassium and sodium ions inside and outside a neuron's cell membrane. A neuron's cell membrane is polarized, or electrically charged, because of a difference in charges between its inner and outer surfaces. When a neuron is not transmitting a nerve impulse, the outside of the cell has a net positive charge, and the inside has a net negative charge. This difference is due to the fact that more potassium ions (K+) leak out across the cell membrane than sodium ions (Na+) leak in, leaving the inside of the cell negatively charged with respect to the outside.

During a nerve impulse, a neuron receives enough stimulus to cause sodium ions to rush into the cell, temporarily leaving the inside of the membrane more positively charged than the outside. This reversal of charges starts the nerve impulse traveling down the axon. After the impulse passes, the original distribution of potassium and sodium ions across the membrane is restored.

LESSON OBJECTIVES

- 🔑 Identify the functions of the nervous system.
- 🔑 Describe the parts of the nervous system and how each part functions.
- 🔑 Describe how your senses work.

Blended Path
Active learning using Student Edition, Inquiry Path, and Digital Path

ENGAGE AND EXPLORE

Teach this lesson using a variety of resources. Begin by reading **My Planet Diary** as a class. Have students share ideas about situations that caused a part of their body to "fall asleep." Then have students do the **Inquiry Warm-Up activity.** Students will investigate the organs, movements, and processes involved in performing a simple task. Discuss the steps students wrote for picking up a penny. The **After the Inquiry Warm-Up worksheet** sets up a discussion about what else the body is doing while it is focused on picking up a penny. Have volunteers share their answers to question 4 about all the other things the body was doing at the same time.

EXPLAIN AND ELABORATE

Teach Key Concepts by explaining that the nervous system receives information from inside and outside the body and directs how the body responds. **Lead a Discussion** about how it allows people to react to their environment. **Support the Big Q** by identifying the stimulus and response in each given situation.

Continue to **Teach Key Concepts** by describing the structure of a neuron. Use **Figure 2** to illustrate why the structure of the dendrite matches its function. **Lead a Discussion** about what a synapse is and how it relates to nerve impulses. Use **Support the Big Q** to illustrate the activities controlled by the brain. **Lead a Discussion** about the role of the peripheral nervous system. Use **Figure 7** to illustrate the how the spinal cord sends an impulse to the motor neurons in response to a stimulus.

Teach Key Concepts by explaining that the eyes respond to the stimulus light and convert that stimulus into impulses that the brain interprets. **Lead a Discussion** about how the senses of smell and taste work together. Use **Figure 9** to show how sound waves travel to the inner ear. Hand out the **Key Concept Summaries** as a review of each part of the lesson. Students can also use the online **Vocab Flash Cards** to review key terms.

EVALUATE

Have students take the **Lesson Quiz.** For an alternate assessment, see the *ExamView®* Computer Test Generator, Progress Monitoring Assessments, or SuccessTracker™.

ELL Support

1 Content and Language
The word *synapse* contains the Greek prefix *syn-* meaning "together."

DIFFERENTIATED INSTRUCTION KEY
L1 Struggling Students or Special Needs
L2 On-Level Students **L3** Advanced Students

LESSON PLANNER 13.1

Inquiry Path
Hands-on learning in the Lab zone

ENGAGE AND EXPLORE

To teach this lesson with an emphasis on inquiry, begin with the **Inquiry Warm-Up activity.** Students will identify the many organs, movements, and processes involved in a simple task. Discuss the organs, movements, and processes involved in simply picking up a penny. Have students do the **After the Inquiry Warm-Up worksheet.** Talk about what the other parts of the body are doing while a penny is being picked up. Have volunteers share their answers to question 4 about the differences between all the steps involved in picking up a penny and all the other things the body does at the same moment.

EXPLAIN AND ELABORATE

Focus on the **Inquiry Skill** for the lesson. Point out that when you infer, you draw conclusions based on information, knowledge, and evidence. Based on the **Inquiry Warm-Up activity,** what can be inferred about the two different types of activities described in questions 2 and 3? *(The body has to think about some of the movements and processes but others are automatic.)* **Support the Big Q** by identifying the stimulus and response in each of the described situations. Before beginning the **Apply It activity** review the Key Concept statement about the functions of the nervous system. Have students share their descriptions. Do the **Lab Investigation** to develop and test hypotheses about how the time of day affects reaction time.

Have students do the **Apply It activity** and ask students to share how they sequenced the nerve functions. **Support the Big Q** to illustrate where the cerebrum, cerebellum, and brain stem are located and what their functions are. Do the **Quick Lab** to reinforce understanding of reflex actions.

Have students do the **Quick Lab** to better understand how senses work together. Students can use the online **Vocab Flash Cards** to review key terms.

EVALUATE

Have students take the **Lesson Quiz.** For an alternate assessment, see the *ExamView®* Computer Test Generator, Progress Monitoring Assessments, or SuccessTracker™.

Digital Path
Online learning at my science online.com

ENGAGE AND EXPLORE

Teach this lesson using digital resources. Begin by having students explore real-world connections to the role of the nervous system at **My Planet Diary** online. Have them access the Chapter Resources to find the **Unlock the Big Question activity.** There they can answer the questions and refine their responses as they continue through the lesson. You can re-assign the activity and have students submit their work so you can track their progress.

EXPLAIN AND ELABORATE

Students reading above, at, or below the lexile measure of this lesson can access basic content readings at their level at **My Reading Web.** Have students use the online **Vocab Flash Cards** to preview key terms. To **Support the Big Q,** ask students to identify the stimuli and responses in a set of given situations. Review the Key Concept statement about the functions of the nervous system before assigning the online **Apply It activity.** Ask volunteers to share their descriptions. Have students submit their work to you.

Have students do the online **Art in Motion activity** to see how nerve impulses travel across a synapse. Assign the **Apply It activity** and ask students to submit their work. **Support the Big Q** to illustrate the locations of the three major regions of the brain and then discuss their functions.

Have students do the online **Interactive Art activity** to explore the nervous system. The **Key Concept Summaries** online allow students to read a summary and see an image associated with each part of the lesson. Online remediation is available at **My Science Coach.**

EVALUATE

Have students take the **Lesson Quiz.** For an alternate assessment, see the *ExamView®* Computer Test Generator, Progress Monitoring Assessments, or SuccessTracker™.

2 Frontload the Lesson
Preview the lesson visuals, labels, and captions. Ask students what they know about the terms *system, reflex,* and *nerve.* Explain the specific meanings these words have in science.

3 Comprehensible Input
Have students study the visuals and their captions to support the Key Concepts of the lesson.

4 Language Production
Pair or group students with varied language abilities to complete labs collaboratively for language practice. Have each student copy the completed written lab for personal reference.

5 Assess Understanding
Have students create a portfolio of their notes and then do oral presentations of lesson content.

The Nervous System

Establish Learning Objectives

After this lesson, students will be able to:

🔑 Identify the functions of the nervous system.

🔑 Describe the parts of the nervous system and how each part functions

🔑 Describe how your senses work.

Engage

Activate Prior Knowledge

MY PLANET DIARY Read *Wake Up!* with the class. Point out that there are nerves in virtually every part of the body. Urge students to think of parts of their bodies that have "fallen asleep." Ask: **Which body parts have "fallen asleep"?** *(Samples: arms, legs, hands, feet)* **In what way was this an example of communication being interrupted in your body?** *(Samples: While the body part was "asleep," it was no longer in communication with my brain.)*

BIG IDEAS OF SCIENCE REFERENCE LIBRARY DK
Have students look up the following topics: ALS, Simulators, Sleep.

Explore

Lab Resource: Inquiry Warm-Up 🔲 Lab zone

L1 HOW SIMPLE IS A SIMPLE TASK? Students will infer and list the impulses, thoughts, movements, and processes that underlie the completion of a simple task.

LESSON

1 The Nervous System

UNLOCK THE BIG ?

🔑 **What Is the Role of the Nervous System?**

🔑 **How Do the Parts of Your Nervous System Work?**

🔑 **What Do Your Senses Do?**

MY PLANET DIARY

FUN FACTS

Wake Up!

Did you ever wake from a nap, only to find that your arm is "asleep"? What causes this "pins-and-needles" sensation? If you lie on your arm for a long period of time, too much pressure is placed on the nerves. The communication between your arm and brain no longer flows smoothly. A decrease in normal signals makes your arm feel odd. The pins-and-needles feeling actually happens when you remove the pressure from the nerves. They begin to send a normal flow of messages from your arm to your brain again. You slowly regain normal feeling in your arm. Remember to change your position often when you sit or lie down. If you don't, you'll end up having to wake up your arms and legs!

Read the following questions. Then write your answers below.

1. Why would your arm feel numb if you put too much pressure on it?

   The nerves in my arm would stop sending impulses to my brain, which would make my arm feel numb.

2. Describe a time when one of your limbs fell asleep. How did it feel?

   Sample: I crossed my legs so one was pressed against the floor. When I got up, I felt pins and needles in my leg.

▶ PLANET DIARY Go to **Planet Diary** to learn more about the nervous system.

 Lab zone
Do the Inquiry Warm-up
How Simple Is a Simple Task?

504 Controlling Body Processes

SUPPORT ALL READERS
Lexile Measure = 950L   Lexile Word Count = 2624

Prior Exposure to Content: May be the first time students have encountered this topic

Academic Vocabulary: *compare, contrast, infer*

Science Vocabulary: *nerve, nerve impulse, neuron, synapse*

Concept Level: Generally appropriate for most students in this grade

Preteach With: My Planet Diary "Wake Up!" and Figure 2 activity

Go to **My Reading Web** to access leveled readings that provide a foundation for the content.

my science online.com

Vocabulary
- neuron • nerve impulse • nerve
- synapse • central nervous system
- peripheral nervous system • reflex

Skills
- Reading: Identify Supporting Evidence
- Inquiry: Infer

What Is the Role of the Nervous System?

You can use the Internet to chat with a friend hundreds of miles away. You can also use it to gather information from anywhere in the world. Like the Internet, your nervous system is a communications network. It includes the brain, the spinal cord, and the nerves that run throughout the body. It also includes the eyes, ears, and other sense organs. **Your nervous system receives information about what is happening both inside and outside your body. It directs how your body responds to this information. In addition, your nervous system helps maintain homeostasis.** Without your nervous system, you could not move, think, or sense the world around you.

Receiving Information Your nervous system makes you aware of what is happening around you. For example, if you were at a cookout like the one shown in **Figure 1,** you would know when the wind was blowing or a fly was buzzing around your head. Your nervous system also checks conditions inside your body, such as the level of glucose in your blood and your internal body temperature.

FIGURE 1 ···
Gathering Information
The nervous system allows people to react to their environment.
✎ **Describe** List four things that your nervous system would help you notice if you were enjoying a meal with this family.

Sample: I would notice the plates,
the smell of food, the sound
of people talking, and the
temperature.

505

Explain

Introduce Vocabulary

To help students understand the term *neuron,* explain that this term is derived from the Greek word *neuron,* meaning "nerve."

Teach Key Concepts 🔑

Explain to students that the nervous system receives information and directs how the body responds to this information. The nervous system also helps maintain homeostasis in the body. Remind students that homeostasis is the process of maintaining stable internal conditions. Ask: **What kind of information does the nervous system receive?** *(Information about what is happening outside the body and what is happening inside the body)* **What parts of the body are part of the nervous system?** *(The brain, spinal cord, nerves, eyes, ears, and other sense organs)* **How is the nervous system like a communications network?** *(Sample: The nervous system receives and sends messages about what is happening in the body and in the world.)* **What information does your body receive if you touch a hot object?** *(Sample: Information about the temperature of the object touching the skin)* **What message might the nervous system send about how the body should respond to this information?** *(Sample: It might send the message to move away from the hot object.)*

Lead a Discussion

REACTIONS TO THE ENVIRONMENT Ask: **What does it mean when people say that something makes them nervous?** *(Students may say it means that they are anxious or worried about something.)* Explain that anxiety and worry are different ways in which people react to their environment. Point out that the nervous system allows people to react to their environment in a wide variety of ways.

My Planet Diary provides an opportunity for students to explore real-world connections to the role of the nervous system.

my science online | Role of the Nervous System

Explain

Support the Big Q ❓ UbD

RECEIVING AND RESPONDING TO INFORMATION Have students identify the stimulus and the response in each of the following situations: **Tasting a lemon wedge** *(Sour taste; mouth puckers)*; **Smelling vinegar** *(Sour smell; nose wrinkles)*; **Someone throwing a ball toward you** *(Speed and direction of ball; you move your hands and body into position to catch the ball.)*

Elaborate

21st Century Learning

CRITICAL THINKING Ask: **When you run, how does your breathing change?** *(You breathe faster and deeper.)* **What information does the nervous system receive, and what is its response?** *(Sample: The nervous system receives information about the muscles moving and working. The nervous system's response is to have the body breathe deeper and faster in order provide more oxygen for the muscles.)*

Apply It!

L1 Before beginning the activity, review the Key Concept statement about the functions of the nervous system. Point out that the nervous system includes sense organs such as eyes and ears.

⚠ **Infer** Remind students that when they infer, they combine evidence with their knowledge. Explain that they can use their memories and imaginations to identify the evidence in this still photograph.

Lab Resource: Lab Investigation 🔬Lab zone

L2 **READY OR NOT!** Students will develop and test hypotheses in order to draw conclusions about the effect of time of day on reaction times.

Evaluate

Assess Your Understanding

Have students evaluate their understanding by completing the appropriate sentence.

RTI Response to Intervention

If students have trouble understanding the functions of the nervous system, **then** have them review the Key Concept statement.

MY SCIENCE Ⓢ **COACH** Have students go online for help in understanding the role of the nervous system.

Responding to Information Any change or signal in the environment that an organism can recognize and react to is called a stimulus (STIM yoo lus; plural *stimuli*). For example, a buzzing fly is a stimulus. After your nervous system analyzes a stimulus, it directs a response. A response is a reaction to a stimulus. Some nervous system responses, such as swatting a fly, are voluntary, or under your control. But heart rate, breathing, sweating, and other necessary processes are involuntary responses to stimuli inside your body.

Maintaining Homeostasis The nervous system helps maintain homeostasis by directing your body to respond properly to information it receives. For example, when your blood's glucose level drops, your nervous system signals that you are hungry. So, you eat. This action maintains homeostasis by supplying your body with needed nutrients and energy.

apply it!

Soccer goalies rely on their nervous systems.

❶ **Infer** Read the headings in each box. Then describe how the goalie is doing each task.

❷ **CHALLENGE** Suppose the goalie starts sweating. What may have caused this response?

Sample: Her internal body temperature may have increased as she lunged for the ball.

Receiving Information
Sample: The goalie sees the ball moving toward her.

Maintaining Homeostasis
Sample: The goalie's nervous system adjusts her breathing and heart rates.

Responding to Information
Sample: The goalie blocks the shot.

🔬**Lab zone** Do the Lab Investigation *Ready or Not!*

📖 Assess Your Understanding

got it?

○ **I get it!** Now I know that the nervous system receives information, directs a response to it, and helps maintain homeostasis.

○ **I need extra help with** See TE note.

Go to **MY SCIENCE** Ⓢ **COACH** *online for help with this subject.*

Digital Lesson: Assign the *Apply It* activity online and have students submit their work to you.

MY SCIENCE online.com ▶ **Role of the Nervous System**

How Do the Parts of Your Nervous System Work?

Your nervous system includes your brain, spinal cord, and the nerves that connect these organs to all parts of your body. Individual cells that carry information through your nervous system are called **neurons** (NOO rahnz), or nerve cells. The message that a neuron carries is called a **nerve impulse.** These impulses may occur as either electrical or chemical signals.

Neurons 🔑 **Neurons carry nerve impulses throughout the body.** A neuron has a large cell body that contains a nucleus, threadlike extensions called dendrites, and an axon, as shown in **Figure 2.** Nerve impulses begin in a dendrite and move through the neuron's cell body to the tips of the axon. Axons and their tissue covering make up nerve fibers. Nerve fibers are often arranged in parallel bundles covered with more connective tissue. They look like uncooked spaghetti wrapped in thin plastic. A bundle of nerve fibers is called a **nerve.**

Three Kinds of Neurons Your nervous system includes three kinds of neurons. A sensory neuron picks up a stimulus and converts it into a nerve impulse. The impulse travels along sensory neurons until it reaches an interneuron usually in the brain or spinal cord. An interneuron carries a nerve impulse to another interneuron or to a motor neuron. A motor neuron sends an impulse to a muscle or gland, enabling it to respond.

FIGURE 2 ....

Structure of a Neuron

A neuron has only one axon but can have many dendrites that extend from the cell body.

✎ **Use the diagram to complete these tasks.**

1. **Interpret Diagrams** Draw a line with an arrow to show the path of a nerve impulse in the neuron.

2. **Draw Conclusions** How does having both dendrites and an axon help a neuron function?

   <u>Neurons can both receive and</u>
   <u>send impulses.</u>

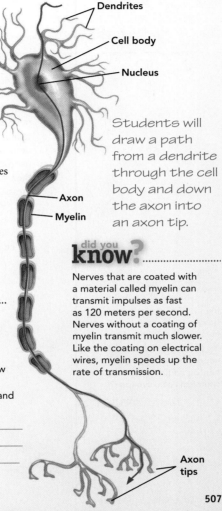

Dendrites

Cell body

Nucleus

Axon

Myelin

Axon tips

Students will draw a path from a dendrite through the cell body and down the axon into an axon tip.

did you know? ....

Nerves that are coated with a material called myelin can transmit impulses as fast as 120 meters per second. Nerves without a coating of myelin transmit much slower. Like the coating on electrical wires, myelin speeds up the rate of transmission.

507

Explain

Teach Key Concepts 🔑

Remind students that the nervous system receives and transmits messages all through the body. The neurons are the cells that carry out this function. Ask: **What is a message carried by a neuron called?** *(A nerve impulse)* **What are the three parts of a neuron?** *(A nucleus, dendrites, and an axon)* **What do axons and dendrites do?** *(Dendrites pick up impulses and bring them into the cell body. Axons carry impulses away from the cell body.)* **How many axons and axon tips are there in a neuron?** *(One axon, many axon tips)* **How many dendrites are there in a neuron?** *(There are many dendrites.)* **What is a bundle of neurons called?** *(A nerve)*

Teach With Visuals

Tell students to look at **Figure 2**. Ask: **How would you describe the structure of dendrites?** *(Sample: The structure of dendrites is like threads or fingers.)* **In what way does this structure seem well matched with the function of dendrites?** *(Sample: The structure allows dendrites to "reach out" and pick up nerve impulses from many places.)* **How are dendrites and axons different?** *(There is only one axon, but many dendrites. The axon is a sender of information and is long, while dendrites are receivers of information and are short. The axon has myelin around it and the dendrites do not.)*

Differentiated Instruction

L1 Related Terms Emphasize that *nerve cell* and *neuron* have the same meaning. However, a neuron is not the same as a *nerve* or a *nerve fiber*. As an analogy, show a piece of cable with the insulation removed and explain the differences among these three structures.

L3 What Has a Nervous System? Challenge students to do research to learn about the wide range of organisms that have a nervous system. Students should be able to explain that nervous systems can be found in vertebrates and most invertebrates from cnidarians upward. Students might include information about variations in brains and sense organs. Encourage students to present their information in an illustrated poster.

Explain

Lead a Discussion

Review the movement of an impulse within a nerve cell from dendrite to cell body to axon. Explain to students that at the axon tips, electrical signals change to a chemical form. Point out that this allows the message to cross the gap in the synapse. Ask: **What carries the impulse across the synapses?** (A chemical) **What do you think would happen if the chemical were not available?** (Sample: The nerve impulse would stop.) **Where can impulses be received?** (Other dendrites, muscles, glands)

Elaborate

21st Century Learning

L3 CRITICAL THINKING Ask students to think about what happens at the synapse. Ask: **Do you think the axon releases the chemical that crosses the synapse all the time?** (No) **When does the axon release the chemical that crosses the synapse?** (Only when an impulse reaches the axon) **What would happen if the chemical were present in the synapse all the time?** (Impulses would never go away. Your senses would overload the brain, and all parts of your body would be trying to move at the same time.)

Apply it!

L1 Before beginning the activity, review the path of a nerve impulse in a neuron.

apply it!

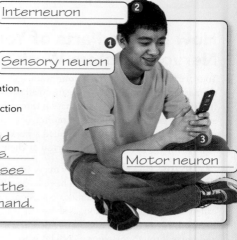

Interneuron ②

① **Sensory neuron**

Motor neuron ③

When you answer the phone, the three kinds of neurons in your body—sensory neurons, interneurons, and motor neurons must work together.

❶ **Interpret Photos** Label the type of neuron at each location.

❷ **Sequence** Describe the order in which the neurons function together to enable the boy to answer the phone.

The sensory neurons convert the sound of the phone ringing into nerve impulses. The interneurons carry the nerve impulses to your brain. The motor neurons send the nerve impulses to the muscles in your hand.

Moving Impulses Between Neurons Every day, billions of nerve impulses travel through your nervous system from neurons to other neurons or body structures. The place where a neuron transfers an impulse to another structure is called a **synapse** (SIN aps). **Figure 3** shows the gap within the synapse between the axon tip of one neuron and the dendrite of another neuron. At the axon tips, electrical signals carried through the neuron change into a chemical form. This change allows the message to cross the gap. The message then continues in electrical form through the next neuron. These changes are like answering a phone and then writing down the information you hear. The change from hearing information to writing it is like the change from electrical to chemical form.

FIGURE 3 ·······································

> **ART IN MOTION** **The Synapse**
At a synapse, chemicals leave the tip of a neuron's axon and travel across a gap to the next nerve cell.

✎ **Predict** What would happen to an impulse if a neuron could not produce chemicals at a synapse?

The impulse would not travel any farther in the body.

Chemical carrying impulse
Dendrite
Axon tip
Dendrite
Synapse
Axon tip

Art in Motion shows how nerve impulses travel across a synapse.

my science ONLINE .com | **Nerve Impulse Transport**

The Central Nervous System Like a traffic cop directing car drivers through a busy intersection, your nervous system directs your movements. It has two divisions that work together: the central nervous system and the peripheral nervous system. The **central nervous system** includes the brain and spinal cord and acts like the traffic cop. The **peripheral nervous system** includes all the nerves outside of the central nervous system, which are like the car drivers. **Figure 4** shows both systems.

 The brain is the control center of the central nervous system. The spinal cord is a thick column of nervous tissue that links the brain to the peripheral nervous system. Most impulses from the peripheral nerves travel through the spinal cord to get to the brain. The brain then directs a response, which usually travels through the spinal cord and back to peripheral nerves.

FIGURE 4 ···

The Nervous System
All information about what is happening in the outside world and inside your body travels through your nervous system.

✎ **Use the diagram and the boxes to complete these tasks.**

1. **Identify** Circle the name of each structure that is part of the central nervous system.

2. **Summarize** Explain in your own words the function of the structures in the diagram.

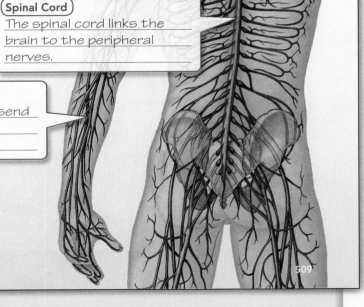

(Brain)
The brain is the control center.

(Spinal Cord)
The spinal cord links the brain to the peripheral nerves.

Peripheral Nerves
The peripheral nerves send and receive impulses.

509

Explain

Teach Key Concepts 🔑

Explain to students that the central nervous system controls the functions of the body, with the brain serving as the control center. Ask: **What other structure is part of the central nervous system?** *(The spinal cord)* **What is the function of the spinal cord?** *(It links the brain to the peripheral nervous system.)* **What structures make up the peripheral nervous system?** *(The peripheral nervous system is made up of all the nerves outside of the central nervous system.)* **How does an impulse travel from the peripheral nervous system to the brain?** *(It moves from a peripheral nerve through the spinal cord to the brain.)* **What is the path of a response to that impulse?** *(A response travels from the brain through the spinal cord to a peripheral nerve.)* Students are likely aware that information from the senses reach the brain along nerves of the peripheral nervous system. Make sure students are aware of the fact that the peripheral nervous system also includes nerves that carry messages to and from the internal organs.

Differentiated Instruction

L3 Path of a Nerve Impulse
Challenge students to create a poster-sized illustration of the path of a nerve impulse during a common activity or event. For example, students can provide textual and graphic information about the role played by sensory neurons, interneurons, and motor neurons during the action of hearing a telephone ring and picking it up to answer it. Students' diagrams might include details that show receptors in the ear picking up a stimulus from the environment (the ringing phone). The nerve impulse passes from sensory neurons to interneurons in the brain, which causes the person to realize that a phone is ringing. Then impulses travel along motor neurons to the muscles. The muscles carry out the response, and the person reaches for the telephone.

509

Explain

Support the Big Q ? UbD

FUNCTIONS OF THE BRAIN Review with students the three kinds of neurons. Ask: **Which type of neuron is found in the brain?** *(Interneuron)* Explain that the brain has three main regions that receive and process information. Have students locate these regions in **Figure 3**. Ask: **What are the activities controlled by the cerebrum?** *(Sample responses: Learning, remembering, movement, senses)* **What are the functions of the cerebellum?** *(Coordinating muscle actions and helping maintain balance)* **Which part of the brain controls involuntary actions?** *(The brain stem)*

Teach With Visuals

Tell students to look at **Figure 5**. Direct students to study the relative locations of the cerebrum, the brain stem, and the cerebellum in the illustration. Ask: **How are the structures of the cerebrum and cerebellum different?** *(The cerebrum is larger than the cerebellum, and the cerebrum's surface is creased by deeper folds.)* Point out that folds increase the surface area of the cerebrum, allowing it to fit into a small space. Invite students to close their eyes and visualize the illustration of the brain's regions as they point to their own spinal cord near the base of their skull, brain stem, cerebellum, and cerebrum.

Lead a Discussion

PROTECTING THE BRAIN Discuss with students how the brain is protected from damage. Ask: **How does the skull protect the brain?** *(It is hard, so if a person is hit in the head, the skull absorbs the blow and the brain is not harmed.)* **If you shake your head vigorously, why doesn't your brain get damaged?** *(The layers of connective tissue and the fluid within the layers fill the space between the skull and the brain, so the brain does not bounce around inside the skull.)* Point out that the layers of connective tissue and the fluid surround the spinal cord, too. Ask: **Why do you think this fluid is called cerebrospinal fluid?** *(Sample: It is named for two of the structures it protects, the cerebrum and the spinal cord.)*

◉ Identify Supporting Evidence Which structures protect the brain from injury? <u>The skull, the connective tissue, and the fluid</u>

The Brain Your brain has about 100 billion neurons, all of which are interneurons. Each of those neurons may receive up to 10,000 messages from other neurons and may send messages to about 1,000 more! Three layers of connective tissue under the skull cover the brain. Fluid fills the space between the middle layer and the innermost layer of connective tissue. The skull, the connective tissue, and the fluid all help protect the brain from injury. Three main regions of the brain are the brain stem, the cerebellum, and the cerebrum, as shown in **Figure 5**.

The Spinal Cord The brain stem connects to the spinal cord. Run your fingers down the center of your back to feel the bones of the vertebral column. The vertebral column surrounds and protects your spinal cord. Like the brain, layers of connective tissue cover the spinal cord. Also like the brain, fluid protects the spinal cord.

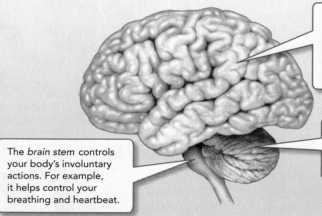

The *cerebrum* (suh REE brum) interprets input from your senses, controls movement, and carries out complex mental processes such as learning and remembering.

The *cerebellum* (sehr uh BEL um) coordinates your muscle actions and helps you keep your balance.

The *brain stem* controls your body's involuntary actions. For example, it helps control your breathing and heartbeat.

FIGURE 5

The Brain
Different regions of the brain receive and process different information.

✎ **Apply Concepts** In the chart, write examples of how you use each region of your brain.

Region	Activity
Cerebrum	Sample: I am able to see things, study, and talk to my friends.
Cerebellum	Sample: I don't fall when I walk to class, and I can balance when I ride a bike.
Brain stem	Sample: I am constantly breathing and my heart is always beating.

510 Controlling Body Processes

The Peripheral Nervous System The second division of the nervous system is the peripheral nervous system. The peripheral nervous system is a network of nerves that branches out from the central nervous system and connects it to the rest of the body. The peripheral nervous system is involved in both involuntary and voluntary actions.

The peripheral nervous system has 43 pairs of nerves. Twelve pairs begin in the brain. The other 31 pairs—the spinal nerves—begin in the spinal cord. One nerve in each pair goes to the left side of the body, and the other goes to the right. Look at the spinal nerves shown in **Figure 6.** Each spinal nerve contains axons of both sensory and motor neurons. The sensory neurons carry impulses from the body to the central nervous system. In contrast, the motor neurons carry impulses from the central nervous system to the body.

Somatic and Autonomic Systems The peripheral nervous system has two groups of nerves. They are the nerves of the somatic (soh MAT ik) nervous system and those of the autonomic (awt uh NAHM ik) nervous system. The somatic nervous system controls voluntary actions, such as using a fork. The autonomic nervous system controls involuntary actions, such as digesting food.

Vocabulary Prefixes The prefix *auto-* comes from the Greek word for "self." How can this prefix help you to remember the function of the autonomic nervous system?

It controls actions
by itself.

FIGURE 6
The Spinal Nerves
The spinal nerves leave the spinal cord through spaces between the vertebrae.

Infer On the diagram, circle the two spinal nerves that are a pair. Then explain how a spinal nerve is like a two-lane highway.

Impulses travel on a spinal
nerve in two directions—both
to and from the central
nervous system.

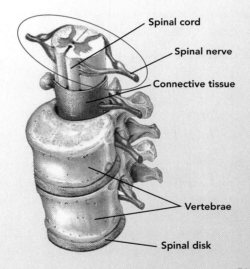

Spinal cord

Spinal nerve

Connective tissue

Vertebrae

Spinal disk

511

Lead a Discussion

PERIPHERAL NERVOUS SYSTEM Explain to students that the peripheral nervous system is involved in both involuntary and voluntary actions. Ask: **How can you describe the peripheral nervous system?** *(It is a network of nerves that branch out from the central nervous system and connect it to the rest of the body.)* Have students look back at **Figure 6** and note how the spinal nerves branch off the spinal cord. Explain that the spinal nerves in the neck and shoulder region of the spinal cord connect with peripheral nerves in the arms and hands. Spinal nerves on lower portions of the spinal cord connect with peripheral nerves in the legs. Ask: **How do impulses travel on spinal nerves?** *(Impulses travel in two directions—both to and from the central nervous system.)* **How does a spinal nerve's structure help it to function in this way?** *(It contains both sensory neurons and motor neurons.)* Emphasize that, although a nerve carries impulses in two directions, these impulses travel along different neurons. Remind students that sensory neurons carry impulses toward the central nervous system and motor neurons carry impulses away from the central nervous system. Ask: **What might you assume about a person who is in an accident and cannot feel or move his or her legs afterward?** *(The person damaged a portion of the spinal cord containing spinal nerves that connect with the muscles of legs.)*

Elaborate

Build Inquiry Lab zone

CLASSIFY SOMATIC AND AUTONOMIC FUNCTIONS

Materials none

Time 15 minutes

Brainstorm with the class examples of voluntary and involuntary actions. Divide the class into small groups. Challenge each group to think of a task a person might do that involves voluntary and involuntary actions and then to act out a skit without speaking. An example is eating a meal (after pretending to take a bite, students might point to their stomachs to show involuntary action). Have students classify each action as somatic or autonomic. Ask: **What is a situation in which all functions of the body are under autonomic control?** *(Sample: while a person is unconscious or asleep)*

Differentiated Instruction

L1 Brain Stem To help students understand the term *brain stem*, invite them to visualize a stem that they might see on a tree or plant. Explain that one of the most common definitions of *stem* is "a plant part such as a branch that grows out of the main vertical part and supports another part, such as a leaf or fruit." Have students look at the illustration of the brain stem in **Figure 5.** Encourage students to see that a brain stem is similar to a plant stem in the sense that it connects the spinal cord (a main vertical part) with the cerebrum and cerebellum (leaves or fruits).

Explain

Lead a Discussion

REFLEX ACTION Explain that a reflex action by the nervous system allows for a quick response because it does not require interpretation by the brain. Ask: **What are some examples of reflexes?** *(Samples: "Jumping" when startled, blinking, jerking a hand away from a hot object)* **What happens during most reflexes?** *(Sensory neurons detect a stimulus. They send impulses to the spinal cord. There, interneurons pass the impulses in two different directions. The impulse is sent to motor neurons, enabling a quick response. The impulse is also sent to the brain, making the person aware of what just happened.)* Emphasize that awareness comes after the response takes place.

Teach With Visuals

Tell students to look at **Figure 7.** Remind students that the brain is not part of the reflex reaction. Direct students to trace the path of the impulse in the figure from the stimulus to its response. Ask: **How does it benefit people that the spinal cord is able to send an impulse to motor neurons in response to a stimulus without involving the brain?** *(Sample: It allows people to respond more quickly to danger than if the nerve impulses traveled all the way to and from the brain.)*

Elaborate

Lab Resources: Quick Lab

L1 **HOW DOES YOUR KNEE REACT?** Students will model and observe reflex action in the knee.

Evaluate

Assess Your Understanding

After students answer the questions, have them evaluate their understanding by completing the appropriate sentence.

RTI Response to Intervention

1b. If students need help comparing and contrasting the two groups of peripheral nerves, **then** have them locate the highlighted terms and reread the section called Somatic and Autonomic Systems.

2b. If students have trouble drawing a conclusion about protection of the brain, **then** remind them of the vital functions the brain controls.

FIGURE 7 ·

> INTERACTIVE ART **A Reflex Action**
Reflexes help protect your body.

✎ **Relate Text and Visuals** On the diagram, number the steps in a reflex action.

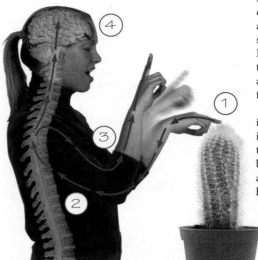

Reflexes The brain usually controls the contraction of skeletal muscles. Sometimes, however, skeletal muscles contract without involving the brain. A **reflex** is an automatic response that occurs rapidly without conscious control. For example, when your finger touches a sharp object, sensory neurons detect a pain stimulus. They send impulses to the spinal cord. Interneurons there pass those impulses directly to motor neurons. The motor neurons cause your arm muscles to contract, pulling your finger away from the sharp object like the cactus in **Figure 7.**

As the reflex action happens, other nerve impulses travel to your brain. As your brain interprets them, you feel a pain in your finger. It takes longer for the pain impulses to reach the brain and be interpreted than it does for the reflex action to occur. By the time you feel the pain, you have already jerked your hand away.

Lab zone® Do the Quick Lab *How Does Your Knee React?*

🔑 **Assess Your Understanding**

1a. Name What is another name for a nerve cell?
Neuron

b. Compare and Contrast How do the two groups of peripheral nerves differ?
The somatic system controls voluntary actions, while the autonomic system controls involuntary actions.

2a. Identify The part of the brain that helps you keep from falling is the cerebellum .

b. Draw Conclusions Why is it important for the brain to be so well protected?
Sample: The brain is the body's control center. If it is injured, many of the body's functions could be affected.

got it? ·

○ I get it! Now I know that messages are carried through the nervous system along structures that include neurons, the brain, the spinal cord, and the peripheral nervous system.

○ I need extra help with See TE note.
Go to MY SCIENCE 🔵 **COACH** *online for help with this subject.*

512 Controlling Body Processes

Interactive Art allows students to explore the nervous system.

MY SCIENCE ONLINE.COM   **Peripheral Nervous System**

What Do Your Senses Do?

Going to the movie theater can be a treat for your senses. Show times and titles flash on displays. Moviegoers chatter in line. As you walk into the theater, you can smell the popcorn. When you finally sit in your seat, you can feel the texture of the cushions on your body. You take a bite of your snack, and enjoy the show.

🔑 **Your eyes, ears, nose, mouth, and skin are specialized sense organs that enable you to get information from the outside world.** Each of these organs contains sensory neurons that send impulses to your brain. Your brain interprets them, enabling you to understand more about your environment.

How You See You would not be able to enjoy the visual experience of a movie without your sense of sight. Your eyes respond to the stimulus of light. They convert that stimulus into impulses that your brain interprets, enabling you to see.

The eye has many parts, as shown in **Figure 8.** Notice that light rays enter the eye through the pupil. Then they pass through the lens. Muscles attached to the lens adjust its shape and focus light rays on the retina. Because the lens bends light rays, it produces an upside-down image. The retina contains light-sensitive cells that produce nerve impulses. These impulses travel through the optic nerve to the brain. Your brain turns the image right-side up and combines the images from both eyes to produce a single image.

FIGURE 8 ·····················
The Eye
Light from an object produces an image on the retina.

✏️ **Develop Hypotheses** Hold your hand in front of your face. Look at it with one eye closed, then with the other. Explain why the image of your hand shifts.

Sample: I think my hand appears to move because each eye sees my hand from a different angle.

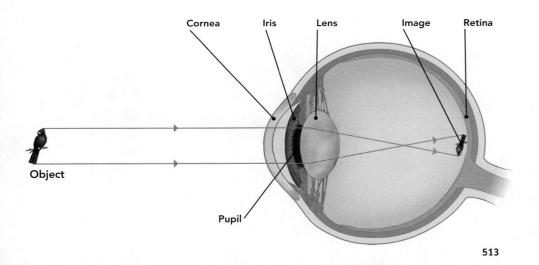

Cornea   Iris   Lens   Image   Retina

Object

Pupil

513

LESSON 13.1

Explain ——————
Teach Key Concepts

Explain to students that the five sense organs make it possible to see, hear, smell, taste, and feel. Ask: **What type of neurons are involved in helping you to understand your environment?** *(Sensory neurons)*

Lead a Discussion

HOW THE EYE WORKS Explain that your eye has many parts that must work together to produce the images you see. Ask: **What stimulus is involved in the sense of sight?** *(Light)* **How do the eyes respond to this stimulus?** *(They send impulses to the brain.)* **What role does the brain play in sight?** *(The brain interprets the impulses from the eyes as images.)* Explain that the eye functions similarly to the lens of a camera. Discuss how the lens bends light rays to focus them on photographic film or digital sensor, and how the aperture of a camera controls the amount of light. Ask: **Which parts of the eye correspond to the parts of a camera?** *(Lens of eye and lens of camera; pupil of eye and aperture of camera; retina of eye and film or sensor)* **Even though you have two eyes, why do you only see one image?** *(The brain combines the image from both eyes to produce a single image.)*

Differentiated Instruction

L1 Two Routes for Impulses Have students illustrate how the impulse for a voluntary action and the impulse for an involuntary action travel through the nervous system. Students might create two separate drawings, or they might use two different color markers or colored pencils to indicate voluntary and involuntary impulses on a single diagram. Encourage students to include a key to help the viewer understand the information in the diagram.

L3 Reflexes Students are aware of the patellar, or knee-jerk reflex, but may not know about other reflexes a doctor may use to assess the health of a patient's nervous system. For example, the Babinski's reflex is found in children less than two. If detected after this age, it is a sign of nerve damage between the spinal cord and brain (CNS damage). Encourage students to research other reflexes such as the Achilles reflex and the plantar reflex.

Explain

Teach With Visuals

TASTE AND SMELL Ask: **What happens when you hold your nose while chewing something?** (*You have a hard time tasting the food.*) Invite students to hold their noses while chewing something such as an apple slice or a jelly bean. Ask students to describe the taste. Explain to students that the sense of smell and taste work together and both depend on chemicals in food or in the air. Point out that these chemicals trigger responses in receptors in the nose and mouth.

Address Misconceptions

TASTE BUDS Many people think that the bumps that they can see on the surface of the tongue are the taste buds. Explain that these are structures called *papillae,* which can contain many taste buds.

Teach With Visuals

HOW YOU HEAR Invite students to look at **Figure 9.** Explain that the ear converts sound waves to nerve impulses just as the eye converts light waves to nerve impulses. Encourage a student volunteer to explain that sound waves are caused by vibrations. Then direct students to trace on **Figure 9** the path of a sound wave as it passes from the outer ear to the middle ear. Ask: **What happens when the sound waves reach the eardrum?** (*Sound waves make the eardrum vibrate, which in turn passes the vibrations to the bones of the middle ear.*) Ask students to locate where the auditory nerve connects to the inner ear. Point out the cochlea. Ask: **What happens to vibrations in this structure?** (*The vibrations stimulate receptor cells to send impulses to the brain through the auditory nerve.*)

21st Century Learning

CRITICAL THINKING Have students take note of the series of causes and effects that occur between the action that creates the source of a sound and its interpretation as sound in the brain. Ask: **What part of the ear do sound waves reach first?** (*The outer ear*) **How do sound waves reach the eardrum?** (*They travel down the ear canal*) **What happens when the sound waves reach the eardrum?** (*They make it vibrate.*) **What happens next?** (*The vibrations pass along to the hammer, anvil, and stirrup.*) **What happens when the vibrations reach the stirrup?** (*The vibrations are transmitted to the inner ear.*) **What happens in the cochlea?** (*The vibrations are transmitted into nerve impulses.*) **Then what happens?** (*Sensory neurons send nerve impulses to the brain.*) **What happens when the nerve impulses reach the brain?** (*The brain interprets the impulses as sound.*) Point out to students that this is the moment that we understand that we hear something.

514 Controlling Body Processes

---

did you know?

There is a type of berry that can temporarily alter your tastebuds. For about 15 to 30 minutes after eating one of these berries, everything sour tastes sweet. At a Miami, Florida hospital, researchers are studying whether this berry can help cancer patients whose chemotherapy treatments have left them with dulled taste buds.

FIGURE 9 ·······································
The Ear
Sound waves pass through the structures of the ear and are carried by nerve impulses to the brain.

✎ **Use the diagram to complete the tasks.**

1. **Identify** Circle the names of the three bones of the middle ear.

2. **Predict** What might happen if the eardrum became damaged?

   <u>Vibrations would</u>
   <u>not pass to the</u>
   <u>middle ear and</u>
   <u>beyond, so you</u>
   <u>would lose hearing.</u>

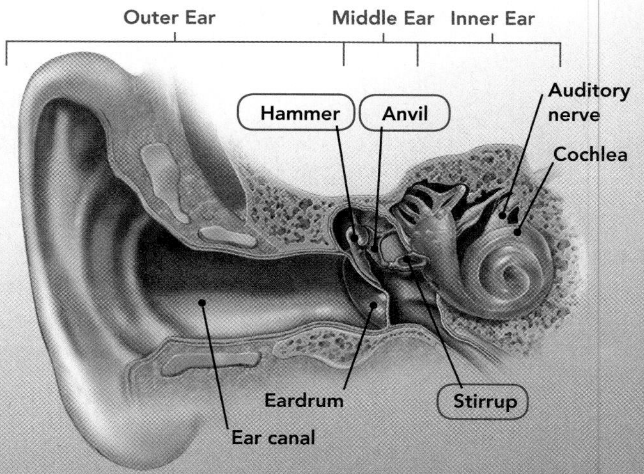

514 Controlling Body Processes

Taste and Smell The senses of taste and smell work together. Both depend on chemicals in the air or in food. The chemicals trigger responses in receptors in the nose and mouth. Nerve impulses then travel to the brain and are interpreted as smells or tastes.

The nose can distinguish at least 50 basic odors. In contrast, there are only five main taste sensations—sweet, sour, salty, bitter, and a meatlike taste called *umami*. When you eat, however, you experience a wider variety of flavors, since both smell and taste affect the flavor of food.

How You Hear When you hear your alarm clock ring, your brain tells you that it is time to get up. Most sounds are caused by the vibrations of air particles. The air particle vibrations move outward from the source of the sound, like waves moving out from a stone dropped in the water. In this way, sound is carried as waves. Ears are the sense organs that convert sound waves into nerve impulses that your brain interprets.

The three parts of the ear—outer, middle, and inner—are shown in **Figure 9.** Sound waves enter your outer ear through the ear canal. When the sound waves reach your eardrum, they cause it to vibrate. The vibrations pass to three tiny bones in your middle ear, which transmit the vibrations to your inner ear. There, sensory neurons in the cochlea convert these vibrations into nerve impulses. These impulses travel through the auditory nerve to the brain. Your brain interprets these impulses as sounds.

Outer Ear · Middle Ear · Inner Ear

Hammer · Anvil · Auditory nerve · Cochlea · Eardrum · Stirrup · Ear canal

---

Professional Development Note
Teacher to Teacher

Activity Here is a fast, inexpensive hands-on activity to engage the students. Although our skin is made up of millions of cells, our sense of touch can be fooled. To demonstrate this, we fill three flat containers with hot, cold, and warm water. We place both hands in the warm water and record what we feel. We then simultaneously place one hand in cold and one hand in hot water for 60 seconds. Finally, we put both hands back into warm water. Students are amazed at the results!

✆ *Leslie Pohley*
Largo Middle School
Largo, Florida

Touch Unlike your other senses, the sense of touch is not found in one place. It is in all areas of your skin. Your skin has different kinds of touch receptors that respond to different stimuli. All of the touch receptors are located in the dermis, or the inner layer of skin.

The receptors that respond to light touch are in the upper part of the dermis. These receptors also let you feel textures, such as smooth glass and rough sandpaper. Receptors deeper in the dermis pick up the feeling of heavy pressure. For example, if you press down hard on your desk, you will feel pressure in your fingertips.

The dermis also contains receptors that respond to temperature and pain. Pain can be one of your most important sensations because it alerts you to danger.

FIGURE 10 ·······················
Touch
Your skin lets you feel the world around you.
✎ **Classify** In the box next to each photo, describe the kind of touch receptors each person is using.

Sample: The person uses light touch receptors to feel the texture.

Sample: The person feels knee pain and uses temperature receptors for relief.

 Lab zone   Do the Quick Lab *Working Together.*

🔑 **Assess Your Understanding**

3a. Name Light-sensitive cells that produce nerve impulses are found in the <u>retina.</u>

b. Predict If a head cold interferes with your sense of smell, how do you think your sense of taste would be affected?
<u>Sample: I wouldn't be able to</u>
<u>taste as many flavors.</u>

c. Describe Describe the eardrum's function.
<u>It vibrates when sound hits it.</u>
<u>The vibrations pass to the</u>
<u>middle ear.</u>

d. Compare and Contrast How is the sense of touch different from the other senses?
<u>It's not found in one place, but</u>
<u>is in all areas of the skin.</u>

got it? ·····························

○ **I get it!** Now I know that my sense organs enable me to <u>get information from the</u>
<u>outside world.</u>

○ **I need extra help with** <u>See TE note.</u>

Go to my science 💬 coach *online for help with this subject.*

515

Differentiated Instruction

L1 Textures To help students deepen their understanding of the term *textures*, have them brainstorm two lists of words. One list should contain words that describe various textures, such as *soft* and *jagged*. The second list should contain words that name objects that have distinctive textures, such as *wool* and *steel*.

L3 Amusement Park Ride Invite students to write a description of how they feel after an especially bumpy, disorienting amusement park ride. Point out that students should explain how various sensations are related to the structure and function of the semicircular canals in the inner ear, as well as the senses of touch, sight, and hearing.

Explain

Lead a Discussion

Explain to students that the skin has different kinds of touch receptors that respond to different stimuli. Remind them that the sense of touch allows them to enjoy things in the environment, such as stroking a dog's soft fur, and the sense of touch protects them from injury, such as when they are able to detect a very hot drink that they have pressed against their lips. Explain that touch is different from the other senses in that receptors that sense touch are not located in a specific place. Ask: **What kinds of receptors are in the dermis?** *(Receptors that respond to light pressure, heavy pressure, pain, and temperature change)* Tell students that the greatest density of touch receptors is found on the fingers, toes, and face. Ask: **What might be the advantage to this?** *(Sample: These body parts are more exposed and are easier to injure. Hands perform many tasks and need to be able to distinguish different pressures.)*

➔ **Identify the Supporting Evidence** Remind students that supporting evidence offers other information or further explains the main idea.

Address Misconceptions

L1 MORE THAN JUST FINGERS Many students associate the sense of touch with their ability to feel things only with their fingers. Explain that all of the regions of the skin are sensitive to touch. Remind students that the sense of touch includes pressure, temperature, and pain.

Elaborate

Lab Resource: Quick Lab **Lab** zone

L1 WORKING TOGETHER Students examine how their senses work together.

Evaluate

Assess Your Understanding

After students answer the questions, have them evaluate their understanding by completing the appropriate sentence.

R T I Response to Intervention

3a. If students do not remember which cells in the eye are light-sensitive, **then** have them review the section *How You See.*

c. If students have problems describing the function of the eardrum, **then** have them review the path of sound waves using **Figure 9.**

Lab zone **After the Inquiry Warm-Up**

The Nervous System

Inquiry Warm-Up, *How Simple Is a Simple Task?*

In the Inquiry Warm-Up, you investigated the variety of organs, movements, and processes that are involved in performing even a very simple task. Using what you learned from that activity, answer the questions below.

1. **SEQUENCE** Think about all the organs, movements, and processes involved in simply picking up the penny. List all the steps involved in order, being sure to tell what organ, sense organ, or muscle group is performing each step. Be as detailed as possible.

   _____

   _____

   _____

   _____

2. **LIST** List all the sense organs, organs, and muscle groups involved in simply picking up the penny.

   _____

   _____

3. **USE PRIOR KNOWLEDGE** As you pick up the penny, what else is your body doing? List any other movements or processes going on in your body at the same time. Be sure to tell what organ, sense organ, or muscle group is performing each activity or process.

   _____

   _____

   _____

4. **COMPARE AND CONTRAST** Is there a difference between all the steps involved in picking up a penny and all the other things your body was doing while you picked up the penny? Explain.

   _____

   _____

Assess Your Understanding

The Nervous System

> ## What Is the Role of the Nervous System?

got_{it}**?**··

○ **I get it!** Now I know that the nervous system _____

_____

○ **I need extra help with** _____

_____

> ## How Do the Parts of Your Nervous System Work?

1a. NAME What is another name for a nerve cell?

_____

b. COMPARE AND CONTRAST How do the two groups of peripheral nerves differ?

_____

_____

_____

2a. IDENTIFY The part of the brain that helps you keep from falling is the _____

b. DRAW CONCLUSIONS Why is it important for the brain to be so well protected?

_____

_____

got_{it}**?**··

○ **I get it!** Now I know that messages are carried through the nervous system along structures that include _____

_____

_____

○ **I need extra help with** _____

_____

Assess Your Understanding

The Nervous System

What Do Your Senses Do?

3a. NAME Light sensitive cells that produce nerve impulses are found

in the _____

b. PREDICT If a head cold interferes with your sense of smell, how do you think your sense of taste would be affected?

_____

_____

c. DESCRIBE Describe the eardrum's function

_____

_____

d. COMPARE AND CONTRAST How is the sense of touch different from the other senses?

_____

_____

got₁ₜ?..got₁ₜ?

○ **I get it!** Now I know that my sense organs enable me to _____

_____

○ **I need extra help with** _____

_____

Name _____ Date _____ Class _____

The Nervous System

What Is the Role of the Nervous System?

The nervous system includes the brain, spinal cord, and nerves that run throughout the body, as well as sense organs such as the eyes and ears. **Your nervous system receives information about what is happening both inside and outside your body. It directs how your body responds to this information. In addition, your nervous system helps maintain homeostasis.** Without your nervous system, you could not move, think, or sense the world around you. Any change or signal in the environment that an organism can recognize and react to is called a stimulus. A response is a reaction to a stimulus.

How Do the Parts of Your Nervous System Work?

Individual cells that carry information through your nervous system are called **neurons,** or nerve cells. **Neurons carry nerve impulses throughout the body.** The message that a neuron carries is called a **nerve impulse.**

Nerve impulses travel as electrical signals between neurons. The place where a neuron transfers an impulse to another structure is called a synapse. A **synapse** contains a gap between the axon tip of one neuron and the dendrite of another neuron.

The **central nervous system** includes the brain and spinal cord and acts like a traffic cop. **The brain is the control center of the central nervous system.**

The spinal cord is a thick column of nervous tissue that links the brain to the peripheral nervous system.

The peripheral nervous system is a network of nerves that branch out from the central nervous system and connect it to the rest of the body. The peripheral nervous system is involved in both involuntary and voluntary actions. Sensory neurons carry impulses from the body to the central nervous system. Motor neurons carry impulses from the central nervous system to the body. A **reflex** is an automatic response that occurs rapidly without conscious control.

What Do Your Senses Do?

Your eyes, ears, nose, mouth, and skin are specialized sense organs that enable you to get information from the outside world. Your eyes respond to the stimulus of light. They convert that stimulus into impulses that your brain interprets, enabling you to see. The senses of smell and taste work together. Chemicals in food or in the air trigger responses in receptors in the nose and mouth. Nerve impulses then travel to the brain and are interpreted as smells or tastes. Ears are the sense organs that convert sound waves into nerve impulses that your brain interprets.

Your skin has different kinds of touch receptors that respond to different stimuli. Unlike the other four senses, the sense of touch is not found in one place.

On a separate sheet of paper, describe the structure of a neuron and briefly explain how nerve impulses travel from one neuron to another.

Review and Reinforce

The Nervous System

Understanding Main Ideas

Answer the following questions on a separate sheet of paper.

1. What are three main functions of the nervous system? Give an example of each.
2. What are the three kinds of neurons? How do they work together to produce a response to an environmental stimulus?
3. Explain how your brain and sensory organs get information from the outside world.
4. What are the two main parts of the peripheral nervous system? What are the two main parts of the central nervous system?

Building Vocabulary

Match each term in the left column with its definition in the right column by writing the letter of the correct definition on the line beside the term.

5. ____ central nervous system

6. ____ reflex

7. ____ neurons

8. ____ nerve impulse

9. ____ peripheral nervous system

10. ____ nerve

11. ____ synapse

a. cells that carry information through your nervous system

b. the message that a neuron carries

c. a bundle of nerve fibers

d. a system of nerves that branches out and connects it to the rest of the body

e. a system that controls the functions of the body with the brain serving as the control center

f. the place where a neuron transfers an impulse to another structure

g. an automatic response that occurs rapidly without conscious control

The Nervous System

Read the passage and study the diagram below. Then use a separate sheet of paper to answer the questions that follow.

Polygraph Test

A *polygraph*, or lie detector, test is sometimes used to help determine whether a person is telling the truth. In such a test, the subject is connected to a polygraph machine that records information about his or her body. This information includes such things as heart rate, blood pressure, breathing rate, and sweat gland activity. An examiner asks the subject questions. As the subject answers, the machine records changes in the subject's body. The examiner uses these changes to determine whether the subject has answered truthfully.

The polygraph test relies upon responses of the subject's nervous system. If the subject gives an untruthful answer, fear of being caught in a lie triggers several responses that are largely involuntary. For example fear might cause the subject's heart rate to increase or even skip a beat, and these changes would be recorded by the polygraph. However, there is disagreement among scientists about how reliable polygraphs are. Some studies indicate that lack of sleep or the use of some drugs can affect the results.

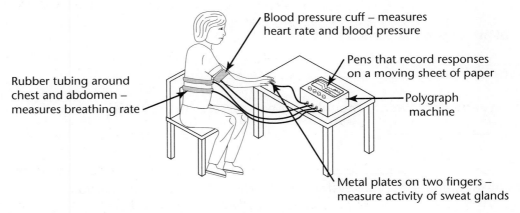

Blood pressure cuff – measures heart rate and blood pressure

Pens that record responses on a moving sheet of paper

Polygraph machine

Rubber tubing around chest and abdomen – measures breathing rate

Metal plates on two fingers – measure activity of sweat glands

1. Why do you think it is important that a polygraph measures responses that are largely involuntary instead of responses that are voluntary?

2. Sometimes subjects are given a "practice test" to record their body's response to lying. The examiner tells the subject to think of a number between 1 and 10 and answer "no" to all questions. Then the examiner asks "Is the number 1?," "Is the number 2?," and so on, until the examiner has asked the question for all the numbers from 1 to 10. Why is this a good practice test?

3. Name a voluntary response and an involuntary response of the nervous system during a polygraph test.

The Nervous System

If the statement is true, write *true*. If the statement is false, change the underlined word or words to make the statement true.

1. _____ The nervous system receives information about what is happening both inside and outside your <u>head</u>.

2. _____ <u>Nerve impulses</u> travel through your nervous system from neurons to other neurons or body structures.

3. _____ A reflex is an <u>involuntary</u> response that occurs rapidly without conscious control.

4. _____ Your eyes convert the stimulus of light into <u>impulses</u> that your brain interprets enabling you to see.

5. _____ The <u>brain stem</u> is a thick column of nervous tissue that links the brain to the peripheral nervous system.

Fill in the blank to complete each statement.

6. The senses of _____ and taste work together.

7. Cells that carry information through your nervous system are called nerve cells, or _____.

8. The _____ contains the nerves of the somatic nervous system and those of the autonomic nervous system.

9. A(n) _____ is the place where a neuron transfers an impulse to another structure.

10. The message that a neuron carries is called a(n) _____ _____.

The Nervous System

Answer Key

After the Inquiry Warm-Up

1. Answers will vary. Sample: eyes see penny, visual information is sent from eyes to brain, brain recognizes penny, brain directs arm to reach, muscles move arm, skin feels penny, brain tells fingers to pick up penny, muscles move fingers to pick up penny

2. organ: brain; sense organs: eyes, skin; muscle groups: eye muscles, arm muscles

3. Answers will vary. Sample: lungs breathing; heart pumping; esophagus swallowing saliva; ears hearing sounds; eyes blinking; back muscles keeping me sitting up; skin sensing touch of chair; nose smelling air; brain coordinating all these activities

4. Answers will vary. Sample: I thought about most of the movements involved in picking up the penny. Most of the other processes happened without me thinking about them.

Key Concept Summaries

A neuron has a large cell body that contains the nucleus, threadlike extensions called dendrites, and an axon. Nerve impulses begin in a dendrite and move through the neuron's cell body to the axon tips. When a nerve impulse reaches an axon tip, the message it carries can pass to another structure, such as another neuron or an organ.

Review and Reinforce

1. The functions are to receive information about the external environment, respond to information, and maintain homeostasis. For example, when you smell newly baked bread, you receive information. You respond by eating a slice. You maintain homeostasis by supplying your body with nutrients.

2. The three kinds of neurons are sensory neurons, interneurons, and motor neurons. Sensory neurons pick up information from the environment. Interneurons carry impulses from one neuron to another neuron. Motor neurons send impulses to activate muscles.

3. Sensory neurons in each sensory organ send impulses to the brain. The brain interprets the impulses.

4. The peripheral nervous system contains the autonomic system and somatic system. The central nervous system contains the brain and the spinal cord.

5. e
6. g
7. a
8. b
9. d
10. c
11. f

Enrich

1. Voluntary responses could be controlled by the subject. A subject who is untruthful would probably try to control these responses to hide the fact that he or she is lying.

2. This is a good practice test because the examiner knows that nine of the answers will be truthful and one will be a lie. The examiner can compare the information recorded by the polygraph for this test to information recorded for other answers given by the subject.

3. Sample: A voluntary response is speaking aloud the answer to a question. An involuntary response is an increase in sweating.

Lesson Quiz

1. body
2. true
3. true
4. true
5. spinal cord
6. smell
7. neurons
8. peripheral nervous system
9. synapse
10. nerve impulse

The Endocrine System

Lesson Pacing: 2–3 periods or 1–1$\frac{1}{2}$ blocks

🕐 **SHORT ON TIME?** To do this lesson in approximately half the time, do the Activate Prior Knowledge activity followed by a discussion of the Key Concepts to familiarize students with the lesson content. Have students do the Quick Lab. The rest of the lesson can be completed by students independently.

> **Preference Navigator,** in the online Planning tools, allows you to customize *Interactive Science* to your own teaching style. You can also edit lesson plans by selecting the Lesson Planner option.
>
> **Digital Teacher's Edition** allows you to access your Teacher's Edition and Resource materials online.

MY SCIENCE online.com

Lesson Vocabulary

- gland • duct • hormone • target cell • hypothalamus
- pituitary gland • negative feedback

 Content Refresher

Professional Development Note

Functions of the Adrenal Glands The adrenal glands, located on top of the kidneys, consist of two parts: an outer region called the adrenal cortex and an inner core called the adrenal medulla.

The adrenal cortex secretes hormones that affect metabolism, chemicals in the blood, and certain body characteristics. For example, cortisol controls the body's use of fats, proteins, and carbohydrates. Aldosterone affects salt and water balance.

The adrenal medulla helps a person cope with physical and emotional stress. For example, adrenaline and noradrenalin increase the rate of glycogen breakdown and glucose release during "fight-or-flight" situations.

LESSON OBJECTIVES

🔑 Describe how the glands of the endocrine system control body processes.

🔑 Explain how negative feedback controls hormone levels.

Blended Path
Active learning using Student Edition, Inquiry Path, and Digital Path

ENGAGE AND EXPLORE

Teach this lesson using a variety of resources. Begin by reading **My Planet Diary** as a class. Have students discuss the causes of acne. Then have students do the **Inquiry Warm-Up activity.** Students will play a game to model how the body uses nerve impulses as signals. The **After the Inquiry Warm-Up worksheet** sets up a discussion about how signals transmit information. Have volunteers share their answers to question 4, telling how the activity modeled what goes on in the human body when signals travel from one part to another.

EXPLAIN AND ELABORATE

Teach Key Concepts by explaining that the endocrine system regulates short-term and long-term activities by sending chemicals throughout the body. **Lead a Discussion** explaining that the endocrine system regulates the body's activities by sending hormones through the body in the blood. **Support the Big Q** by using **Figure 1** to identify the glands that cause the body to change over a person's lifetime. **Lead a Discussion** about how the nervous and endocrine systems cooperate, not compete, to keep the body functioning normally.

Teach Key Concepts by explaining that when the amount of a hormone in the blood reaches a certain level, the endocrine system sends signals that stop the release of that hormone. Use **Figure 4** to identify the senses the people are using. Then **Lead a Discussion** about the body systems being used by the people in **Figure 4.** **Explore the Big Q** by determining which specific glands and parts of the nervous system and endocrine system control the reactions and activities of the people in **Figure 4.** To **Answer the Big Q,** discuss which systems regulate and control body processes. Hand out the **Key Concept Summaries** as a review of each part of the lesson. Students can also use the online **Vocab Flash Cards** to review key terms.

EVALUATE

Have students take the **Lesson Quiz.** For an alternate assessment, see the *ExamView®* Computer Test Generator, Progress Monitoring Assessments, or SuccessTracker™.

ⒺⓁⓁ Support

1 Content and Language

Write the term *duct* on the board and say the word aloud. Point out that some English words have more than one meaning. Have students find the term in a dictionary. Read the definitions and have students predict which definition fits the way the word will be used in the lesson based on a preview of the illustrations in the lesson.

DIFFERENTIATED INSTRUCTION KEY
L1 Struggling Students or Special Needs
L2 On-Level Students L3 Advanced Students

Lab zone Inquiry Path
Hands-on learning in the Lab zone

Digital Path
Online learning at my science online.com

ENGAGE AND EXPLORE

To teach this lesson with an emphasis on inquiry, begin with the **Inquiry Warm-Up activity.** Students will play a game to model how the body uses nerve impulses as signals. The **After the Inquiry Warm-Up worksheet** sets up a discussion about how signals transmit information. Have volunteers share their answers to question 4 telling how the activity modeled what goes on in the human body when signals travel from one part to another.

EXPLAIN AND ELABORATE

Focus on the **Inquiry Skill** for the lesson. Remind students that making models helps people understand things they cannot observe directly. Point out that physical models take the form of drawings, diagrams, and three-dimensional structures, whereas mental models include mathematical equations and words that describe how something works. What model was used in the **Inquiry Warm-Up Activity?** (*A game was used to model how the body uses nerve impulses as signals.*) Before beginning the **Apply It activity,** review the paragraph about the special relationship between a hormone and specific target cells. **Support the Big Q** by using **Figure 1** to identify the glands that cause the body to change over a person's lifetime. Do the **Build Inquiry** to help students learn more about the functions of hormones. Have students do the **Quick Lab** making models showing how the structures of a hormone and a target cell enable the two to fit together.

Have students do the **Real-World Inquiry** to see how the endocrine and nervous systems cause people to react to their surroundings. **Explore the Big Q** by determining which specific glands and parts of the nervous system and endocrine system control the reactions and activities of the people in **Figure 4.** Have students do the **Quick Lab** to model the concept of negative feedback. To **Answer the Big Q,** discuss which systems regulate and control body processes. Students can use the online **Vocab Flash Cards** to review key terms.

EVALUATE

Have students take the **Lesson Quiz.** For an alternate assessment, see the *ExamView*® Computer Test Generator, Progress Monitoring Assessments, or SuccessTracker™.

ENGAGE AND EXPLORE

Teach this lesson using digital resources. Begin by having students explore real-world connections to endocrine system function at **My Planet Diary** online. Have them access the Chapter Resources to find the **Unlock the Big Question activity.** There they can answer the questions and refine their responses as they continue through the lesson. You can re-assign the activity and have students submit their work so you can track their progress.

EXPLAIN AND ELABORATE

Students reading above, at, or below the lexile measure of this lesson can access basic content readings at their level at **My Reading Web.** Encourage students to use the online **Vocab Flash Cards** to preview key terms. Assign the **Apply It activity** online and have students submit their work to you. **Support the Big Q** by using **Figure 1** to identify the glands that cause the body to change over a person's lifetime. Have students do the **Quick Lab** making models to show how the structures of a hormone and a target cell enable the two to fit together.

Use the **Interactive Art activity** online to show the process of negative feedback. **Explore the Big Q** by determining which specific glands and parts of the nervous system and endocrine system control the reactions and activities of the people in **Figure 4.** Have students do the **Quick Lab** to model the concept of negative feedback. To **Answer the Big Q,** discuss which systems regulate and control body processes. The **Key Concept Summaries** online allow students to read a summary and see an image associated with each part of the lesson. Online remediation is available at **My Science Coach.**

EVALUATE

Have students take the **Lesson Quiz.** For an alternate assessment, see the *ExamView*® Computer Test Generator, Progress Monitoring Assessments, or SuccessTracker™.

2 Frontload the Lesson

Direct students to **Figure 1.** Explain that the artist positioned the glands of the endocrine system on the outline of a body to show placement. Then direct their attention to **Figure 2** and read the caption aloud. Discuss what outline could be drawn around the whole illustration to show the location of the hypothalamus and the pituitary gland.

3 Comprehensible Input

Have students use a main-idea-and-details chart to explain how negative feedback works.

4 Language Production

Pair or group students with varied language abilities to complete labs collaboratively for language practice. Have each student copy the completed written lab for personal reference.

5 Assess Understanding

Make true or false statements using lesson content and have students indicate if they agree or disagree with a thumbs up or thumbs down gesture to check whole-class participation.

The Endocrine System

Establish Learning Objectives

After this lesson, students will be able to:

🔑 Describe how the glands of the endocrine system control body processes.

🔑 Explain how negative feedback controls hormone levels.

Engage ——————

Activate Prior Knowledge

MY PLANET DIARY Read *The Cause of Acne* with the class. Many students will have little trouble identifying a variety of thoughts and feelings about acne, including related terms such as *pimples, zits,* and *blackheads*. Remind them that adolescent acne is normal, as well as temporary. Ask: **What is one way to help reduce blockage of hair follicles on the skin on your face?** *(Frequent washing with soap and water)*

BIG IDEAS OF SCIENCE REFERENCE LIBRARY 📖
Have students look up the following topics: Astronauts, Hypothalamus.

Explore ——————

Lab Resource: Inquiry Warm-Up 🧪

L1 WHAT'S THE SIGNAL? Students will play a game to model how the body uses nerve impulses as signals.

LESSON

2 The Endocrine System

🔑 **How Does the Endocrine System Function?**

🔑 **What Controls Hormone Levels?**

MY PLANET DIARY

MISCONCEPTION

The Cause of Acne

Misconception: Eating oily foods can cause acne.

Scientists have not found a link between eating certain foods and acne. So, what does cause acne? Much of the blame falls on certain hormones. Your body starts to produce these hormones when you enter adolescence. They stimulate your body to produce an oily substance called sebum. When your body produces too much sebum, some hair follicles in your skin may become blocked. This blockage causes bacteria to get trapped. Because the sebum and bacteria have nowhere to go, your skin becomes inflamed. The result is acne.

Communicate Discuss the following question with a partner. Write your answer below.

How would you explain to a friend what causes acne?

Sample: I would tell my friend that during adolescence, the body starts to produce certain hormones. These hormones produce sebum, an oily substance that can block hair follicles, so bacteria get trapped. The sebum and bacteria have nowhere to go, so acne forms.

▶ **PLANET DIARY** Go to **Planet Diary** to learn more about the endocrine system.

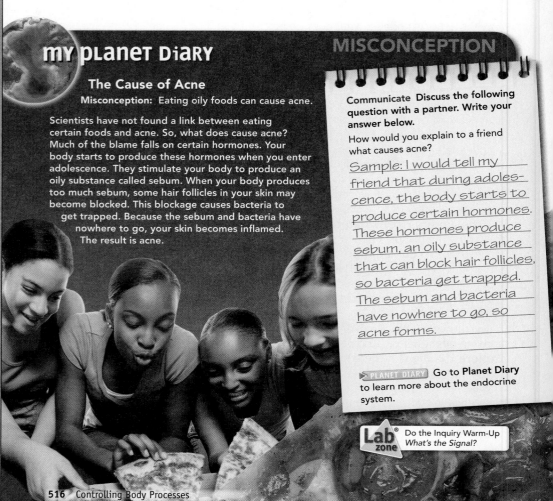

🧪 **Lab** Do the Inquiry Warm-Up *What's the Signal?*

516 Controlling Body Processes

SUPPORT ALL READERS

Lexile Measure = 970L   Lexile Word Count = 1013

Prior Exposure to Content: May be the first time students have encountered this topic

Academic Vocabulary: *identify, main idea, model*

Science Vocabulary: *gland, hormone, hypothalamus, pituitary gland*

Concept Level: Generally appropriate for most students in this grade

Preteach With: My Planet Diary "The Cause of Acne" and Figure 1 activity

Go to **My Reading Web** to access leveled readings that provide a foundation for the content.

MY SCIENCE online.com

Vocabulary
- gland • duct • hormone • target cell • hypothalamus
- pituitary gland • negative feedback

Skills
- ↻ Reading: Identify the Main Idea
- △ Inquiry: Make Models

How Does the Endocrine System Function?

Have you ever been so afraid that you heard your heart thump rapidly in your chest? When something frightens you, your body's endocrine system (EN duh krin) reacts.

Your body has two systems that regulate its activities: the nervous system and the endocrine system. The nervous system regulates most activities by sending nerve impulses throughout the body. ☞ **The endocrine system regulates short-term and long-term activities by sending chemicals throughout the body. Long-term changes include growth and development.**

The endocrine system is made up of glands. A **gland** is an organ that produces or releases a chemical. Some glands, such as those producing saliva and sweat, release their chemicals into tiny tubes, or **ducts.** The ducts deliver the chemicals to specific places in the body or to the skin's surface. However, the glands of the endocrine system do not have delivery ducts. The endocrine glands produce and release chemicals directly into the blood. Then the blood carries those chemicals throughout the body.

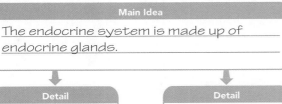

Main Idea
The endocrine system is made up of endocrine glands.

Detail	Detail
A gland makes or releases a chemical.	Endocrine glands release chemicals into the blood.

✎ ↻ **Identify the Main Idea**
In the graphic organizer, write the main idea of the third paragraph. Then write two details that support the main idea.

517

Explain

Introduce Vocabulary

To help students understand the term *hormone,* explain that the word comes from a Greek word meaning "stir up." Point out that hormones are chemicals that get "stirred up," or moved around the body in the blood.

Teach Key Concepts 🔑

Explain to students that the endocrine system regulates short-term and long-term activities by sending chemicals throughout the body. Long-term changes include growth and development. Ask: **What two systems in the human body regulate its activities?** *(Nervous system, endocrine system)* **Unlike the nervous system, which sends out nerve impulses, how does the endocrine system regulate the body's activities?** *(By sending out chemicals)* **What organs release the chemicals?** *(Glands)* Point out that the glands producing saliva and sweat are examples of exocrine glands. Ask: **What is the difference between an exocrine gland and an endocrine gland?** *(Exocrine glands release their chemicals into delivery tubes called ducts, whereas endocrine glands release their chemicals into the bloodstream.)*

↻ **Identify the Main Idea** Remind students that the main idea is the most important idea in a paragraph or section of text. Details and other information in the text support or further explain the main idea. Point out that some main ideas are stated directly, whereas others must be identified by the reader.

My Planet Diary provides an opportunity for students to explore real-world connections to endocrine system function.

my science online | Endocrine System Function

ⒺⓁⓁ Support

1 Content and Language
Write *negative feedback* on the board. *Feedback* as it relates to the endocrine system is different from verbal feedback, which is intended to assist a peer's work, and audio feedback, which adds to an original sound. *Negative feedback* stops a process.

2 Frontload the Lesson
Use **Figure 1** to show the endocrine system. Have students point to glands and say their names. Tell students they will learn how the hypothalamus and the pituitary gland work to keep the endocrine system running smoothly.

3 Comprehensible Input
Encourage groups to use different approaches to demonstrate negative feedback. Students might draw a large cycle diagram as in **Figure 3** or show the sequence using narration, physical gestures, and movement.

Explain

Lead a Discussion

PRODUCTION OF HORMONES Remind students that the nervous system regulates the body's activities by transmitting nerve impulses. Explain that the endocrine system also regulates the body's activities by sending hormones throughout the body in the blood. Ask: **What is the function of hormones?** *(They turn on, turn off, speed up, or slow down activities of the body's organs and tissues.)* Explain that the body's responses to hormones are slower and longer-lasting than its responses to nerve impulses. Ask: **What is the benefit of hormones being carried by the blood?** *(Tissues and organs far from the endocrine glands can be regulated.)* **Why do hormones affect certain cells only?** *(A hormone interacts only with specific target cells that recognize the hormone's chemical structure.)* Encourage students to recall instances when they experienced the effects of adrenaline on their body. Ask: **What would you identify as the cause of adrenaline being released into your blood?** *(Students may cite a variety of especially frightening, alarming, or surprising events.)* Explain to students that the release of adrenaline is part of the "fight-or-flight" response, during which an increased breathing rate gets oxygen into the body more quickly and an increased heart rate gets blood to the body more quickly. Ask: **How might an increased heart rate and breathing rate help a person who sees danger?** *(Sample: These adjustments give the person greater strength, energy, and speed.)* Tell students that they may feel the effects of adrenaline minutes after running or after hearing an especially loud clap of thunder.

Elaborate

Apply It!

L1 Before beginning the activity, review the paragraph about the special relationship between a hormone and specific target cells.

△ **Make Models** Explain that making models helps people understand things that they cannot observe directly. Point out that physical models take the form of drawings, diagrams, and three-dimensional structures, whereas mental models include mathematical equations and words that describe how something works.

Hormones A chemical produced by an endocrine gland is called a **hormone.** Hormones are chemical messengers that travel in the blood. Hormones turn on, turn off, speed up, or slow down the activities of organs and tissues.

Nerve impulses from the brain act quickly. In contrast, hormones usually cause a slower, longer-lasting response. For example, if you see danger, your brain interprets the information and sends an impulse to an endocrine gland. The gland releases the hormone adrenaline into your blood. Adrenaline speeds up your heart rate and breathing rate. Even a quick hormonal response such as releasing adrenaline is much slower than a nerve response.

Each hormone affects specific target cells. Target cells are cells that are specialized in a way that enables them to recognize a hormone's chemical structure. Hormones travel in the blood until they find their target cells. Read about the endocrine glands and the hormones they produce in **Figure 1** on the next page.

Key A · Lock A · Sample drawing

apply it!

Hormones interact with target cells much like keys interact with locks.

1 △**Make Models** Look at Key A and Lock A. Then draw the shapes of the keyholes for the locks that Key B and Key C will unlock.

Key B · Lock B · Sample drawing

2 Draw Conclusions How do a hormone and a target cell function like a key and a lock?

Sample: A hormone interacts only with
a specific target cell, just as a key
unlocks only a specific lock.

3 CHALLENGE What body system does the endocrine system depend on to function? Explain.

It depends on the circulatory system
because the hormones of the
endocrine glands must travel through
the bloodstream.

 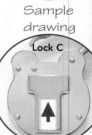

Key C · Lock C

Digital Lesson: Assign the *Apply It* activity online and have students submit their work to you.

my **science** online.com **Endocrine System Function**

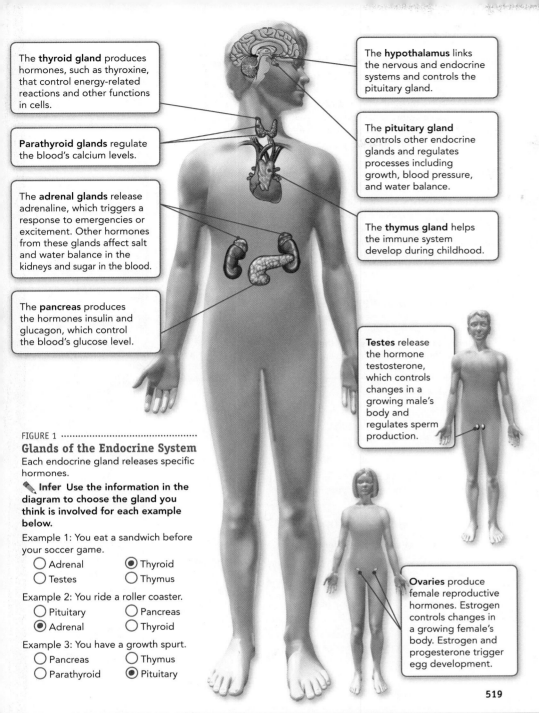

The **thyroid gland** produces hormones, such as thyroxine, that control energy-related reactions and other functions in cells.

Parathyroid glands regulate the blood's calcium levels.

The **adrenal glands** release adrenaline, which triggers a response to emergencies or excitement. Other hormones from these glands affect salt and water balance in the kidneys and sugar in the blood.

The **pancreas** produces the hormones insulin and glucagon, which control the blood's glucose level.

The **hypothalamus** links the nervous and endocrine systems and controls the pituitary gland.

The **pituitary gland** controls other endocrine glands and regulates processes including growth, blood pressure, and water balance.

The **thymus gland** helps the immune system develop during childhood.

Testes release the hormone testosterone, which controls changes in a growing male's body and regulates sperm production.

Ovaries produce female reproductive hormones. Estrogen controls changes in a growing female's body. Estrogen and progesterone trigger egg development.

FIGURE 1 ·····················

Glands of the Endocrine System
Each endocrine gland releases specific hormones.

✎ **Infer** Use the information in the diagram to choose the gland you think is involved for each example below.

Example 1: You eat a sandwich before your soccer game.
- ○ Adrenal
- ○ Testes
- ● Thyroid
- ○ Thymus

Example 2: You ride a roller coaster.
- ○ Pituitary
- ● Adrenal
- ○ Pancreas
- ○ Thyroid

Example 3: You have a growth spurt.
- ○ Pancreas
- ○ Parathyroid
- ○ Thymus
- ● Pituitary

519

Explain
Teach With Visuals

Tell students to look at **Figure 1.** Point out that the body relies on many different types of hormones throughout life. Call on volunteers to read the labels. Ask: **Which two glands control other glands?** *(Hypothalamus, pituitary)* Invite students to compare and contrast the endocrine glands of males and females. Ask: **Are all of the glands in males and females the same?** *(No)* **Which glands are found only in males?** *(Testes)* **Only in females?** *(Ovaries)*

Support the Big Q ? UbD

GLANDS AND CHANGES Direct students' attention to **Figure 1.** Have them skim the labels and underline any information that indicates how endocrine glands cause changes over a person's lifetime. Ask: **Which gland regulate and control body processes? How?** *(The pituitary gland regulates growth. The thymus gland helps the immune system develop. The testes control changes in a growing male's body. The ovaries control changes in a growing female's body.)*

Elaborate

21st Century Learning

CRITICAL THINKING Challenge students to predict the symptoms that might accompany a disorder in various endocrine glands. For example, ask: **What do you think would happen to a person whose pancreas was not functioning properly?** *(The body could not control the amount of glucose in the blood.)*

Build Inquiry Lab zone

L2 FUNCTIONS OF HORMONES

Materials poster paper, markers, note cards, up-to-date reference books or information from reliable Internet sites. Remind students to follow prescribed guidelines for Internet use.

Time 20 minutes

Tell students that in this activity they will learn more about the functions of hormones. Divide students into six groups, and assign each group one of the glands shown in **Figure 1,** except the testes, ovaries, and hypothalamus. Challenge the members of each group to find out what hormones are secreted by the gland and how those hormones affect the body. Each group should then work together to devise a way to show their findings graphically. Have groups present their posters to the class and explain the action of each gland.

Differentiated Instruction

L1 Summarize Information About Hormones Review with students the relationship between main ideas and details in a paragraph or section of text. Point out that a summary contains the most important ideas in a piece of text. Then have students reread the paragraphs on hormones and target cells and summarize each one by restating the main idea in their own words.

L3 Adrenaline in Detail Challenge students to do research on adrenaline. Urge students to gather facts about epinephrine and norepinephrine, the two related but distinct hormones that are secreted by the adrenal glands. Students could narrow the topic to, for example, "the effect of adrenaline on sports performance."

Lead a Discussion

ENDOCRINE REGULATORS

If students have previously studied the nervous system, they have seen how the brain controls many functions of the body. Tell them that the nervous and endocrine systems cooperate, not compete, to keep the body functioning normally. Ask: **How does the hypothalamus work with the nervous system?** *(The hypothalamus sends nerve messages that control sleep, hunger and other body processes.)* **How do the hypothalamus and the pituitary gland work together?** *(The hypothalamus sends nerve impulses or hormone signals to the pituitary gland, and the pituitary gland releases certain hormones in response.)*

21st Century Learning

INTERPERSONAL SKILLS Have students read *Astronauts* in the **Big Ideas of Science Reference Library** and work in pairs to find out more about the effects of microgravity on the human body. Then ask students to write and perform an interview between a reporter and an astronaut that explores what happens to the astronaut's body during space missions.

Elaborate

Lab Resource: Quick Lab

L1 **MAKING MODELS** Students will make models showing how the structures of a hormone and a target cell enable the two to fit together.

Evaluate

Assess Your Understanding

After students answer the questions, have them evaluate their understanding by completing the appropriate sentence.

RTI Response to Intervention

1a. If students have difficulty explaining the effect of adrenaline on the heart, **then** have them reread the first two paragraphs in *Hormones*.

b. If students need help explaining how the hypothalamus affects growth, **then** review with them the paragraphs explaining the relationship between the functions of the hypothalamus and the pituitary gland.

MY SCIENCE COACH Have students go online for help in understanding the functions of the endocrine system.

Regulators of the Endocrine System The nervous system and the endocrine system work together. The part of your brain that links the two systems is the **hypothalamus** (hy poh THAL uh mus). It sends out nerve messages that control sleep, hunger, and other basic body processes. It also produces hormones that control other endocrine glands and organs. You can see the hypothalamus in **Figure 2.**

Just below the hypothalamus is the pituitary gland, an endocrine gland about the size of a pea. The **pituitary gland** (pih TOO ih tehr ee) works with the hypothalamus to control many body activities. The hypothalamus sends messages to the pituitary gland to release its hormones. Some of those pituitary hormones signal other endocrine glands to produce hormones. Other pituitary hormones, such as growth hormone, control body activities directly.

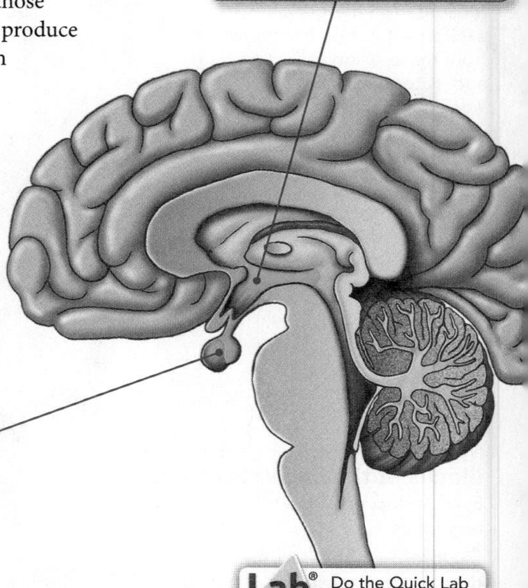

> **Hypothalamus**
> It sends out nerve messages that control basic body processes. It produces hormones that control other glands and organs.

FIGURE 2 ·····················

The Hypothalamus and Pituitary Gland
The hypothalamus and the pituitary gland are located deep within the brain.

 Identify In the boxes, describe the functions of these two endocrine glands.

> **Pituitary Gland**
> Some of its hormones signal other glands to produce hormones. Others directly control some body activities.

 Do the Quick Lab Making Models.

Assess Your Understanding

1a. Explain How does adrenaline affect the heart?
It speeds up the heart rate.

b. Relate Cause and Effect Explain how the hypothalamus affects growth.
It sends messages to the pituitary gland, which releases growth hormone.

got it?

○ **I get it!** Now I know that my endocrine system uses hormones to regulate short-term and long-term activities, growth, and development.

○ **I need extra help with** See TE note.

Go to MY SCIENCE COACH *online for help with this subject.*

What Controls Hormone Levels?

Suppose you set a thermostat at 20°C. If the room temperature falls below 20°C, the thermostat signals the furnace to turn on. When heat from the furnace warms the room to 20°C, the thermostat shuts off the furnace. In certain ways, the endocrine system works like a thermostat. It uses a process called **negative feedback** in which a system is turned off by the condition it produces.

🔑 **When the amount of a hormone in the blood reaches a certain level, the endocrine system sends signals that stop the release of that hormone.** In **Figure 3**, you can see how negative feedback regulates the level of the hormone thyroxine in the blood.

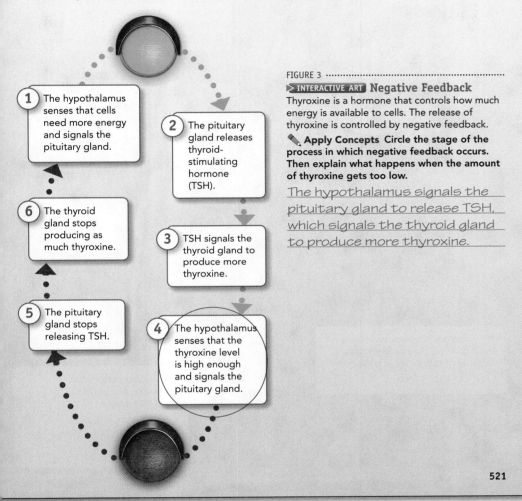

1. The hypothalamus senses that cells need more energy and signals the pituitary gland.

2. The pituitary gland releases thyroid-stimulating hormone (TSH).

3. TSH signals the thyroid gland to produce more thyroxine.

4. The hypothalamus senses that the thyroxine level is high enough and signals the pituitary gland.

5. The pituitary gland stops releasing TSH.

6. The thyroid gland stops producing as much thyroxine.

FIGURE 3 ·············
▶ **INTERACTIVE ART** **Negative Feedback**
Thyroxine is a hormone that controls how much energy is available to cells. The release of thyroxine is controlled by negative feedback.

✏️ **Apply Concepts** Circle the stage of the process in which negative feedback occurs. Then explain what happens when the amount of thyroxine gets too low.

The hypothalamus signals the pituitary gland to release TSH, which signals the thyroid gland to produce more thyroxine.

521

Explain

Teach Key Concepts 🔑

Explain to students that when the amount of a hormone in the blood reaches a certain level, the endocrine system sends signals that stop its release. Ask students what the term *feedback* means in relation to schoolwork. *(Sample: Information from a teacher or peer on how a student performed on a task and how he or she might improve the work)* Explain that the word *negative* as used in *negative feedback* does not mean undesirable; instead it indicates that an action stops rather than continues. Point out that just as the thermostat of a heating system turns on and shuts off to maintain a set temperature, the hypothalamus and pituitary gland work together to control the amount of certain hormones in the blood. Draw students' attention to the central fact that each system is turned off by the condition it produces. Ask: **What conditions turn off a home heating system?** *(Air that has reached the temperature set on the thermostat)* **What conditions turn off the production of a certain hormone?** *(Blood that contains the right level of hormones)* **If you compared the thyroid with a furnace, what would be a similarly appropriate comparison for a thermostat?** *(The hypothalamus, because it senses changes in the level of thyroxine)*

Interactive Art shows negative feedback.

my science online.com ▶ Hormone Control

Differentiated Instruction

L1 **Demonstrate the Negative Feedback Loop** Ask two student volunteers to help in this demonstration. The first student holds a small bowl of marbles and the second student holds a small empty bowl. The first student places marbles in the empty bowl until the second student says, "Stop." Have them do the demonstration again as you guide them to identify how their roles are like the feedback loop. *(The first*

student is a gland releasing a hormone. The marbles are the hormones traveling to the target cells. The second student is the organ giving a signal—telling the first student to stop—that it has enough of the hormone.)

L3 **The Endocrine System and Homeostasis** Challenge students to write short paragraphs describing how the endocrine system helps the body maintain homeostasis.

Explain

Teach with Visuals

Direct students' attention to the image of the football game. Help students better understand what is happening in the images by pointing out the opposing teams, the football field, the football, the referee, and the fans. Ask: **What do you think the players in yellow are doing?** *(Samples: Watching the player in blue, running, thinking)* **What senses are the players on the football field, the referee, and the people in the stands using?** *(Samples: sight, hearing, touch, smell, taste)*

Lead a Discussion

Have students look at the images in **Figure 4** and read the descriptions. Ask students to identify which body systems the players, referee, and fans are using in these images. *(The nervous system and endocrine system)* Some students may be wondering why the football players, referees, and fans are using the same body systems even though they are engaged in very different activities. Remind students that there are many different structures, parts, functions, and glands in the two body systems and they each control and regulate different body processes.

UNLOCK THE BIG ?

Sense and Respond

What systems regulate and control body processes?

FIGURE 4 ··

▷ REAL-WORLD INQUIRY The fans, players, and referee at this football game react to their surroundings because of their endocrine and nervous systems.

✎ Interpret Photos **Read the descriptions and identify what structures in the nervous system or endocrine system are involved.**

A player understands that his next move is to chase after the player with the ball.
Brain

This structure produces hormones that make this player's heart beat faster and his breathing rate increase.
Adrenal gland

A player can sense what is happening on the field and move in response.
Sensory and motor neurons (or peripheral nervous system)

522　Controlling Body Processes

Real-World Inquiry allows students to observe how the endocrine system and nervous system are involved in a person's reactions to sights, sounds, smells, and touch.

my scIence online.com ▷ **Endocrine System**

This structure produces hormones that help these fans get energy from the foods they eat.
Thyroid gland

This structure produces hormones that control how this young fan grows.
Pituitary gland

The referee watches and listens to the action so he can make the correct calls.
Eyes and ears (or the senses)

Lab zone — Do the Quick Lab *Modeling Negative Feedback.*

Assess Your Understanding

2a. Review Negative feedback works by turning a system (on/(off)) by the condition the system produces.

b. Predict What do you think would happen to the level of a hormone in the blood if negative feedback didn't happen?
The level of the hormone would keep rising.

c. ANSWER THE BIG Q What systems regulate and control body processes?
The nervous system and the endocrine system

got it? ....

○ I get it! Now I know that negative feedback controls hormone levels by *sending signals to stop the release of a hormone when the amount of the hormone in the blood reaches a certain level.*

○ I need extra help with *See TE note.*

Go to **MY SCIENCE COACH** online for help with this subject.

Elaborate

Explore the Big Q ? UbD

Direct students' attention to the images in **Figure 4**. Have students use what they know to identify which system in their body controls or regulates the processes described in the labels. *(The nervous system helps the player know what to do. The endocrine system controls the player's heartbeat. The nervous system helps players sense their surroundings. The digestive system helps the fans get energy from food. The endocrine system helps the young fan grow.)* Then discuss which parts of the nervous system and endocrine system are specifically involved in the reactions of the players, fans, and referees.

Lab Resource: Quick Lab Lab zone

L2 MODELING NEGATIVE FEEDBACK Students will use a balloon, straw and two bottles to model the concept of negative feedback.

Evaluate

Assess Your Understanding

Have students evaluate their understanding by completing the appropriate sentence.

Answer the Big Q ? UbD

To help students focus on the Big Q, lead a discussion about the body systems and the processes they control.

R T I Response to Intervention

2a. If students cannot explain how negative feedback works, **then** have them reread the boldface Key Concept statement and the material under the blue heading *What Controls Hormone Levels?*

b. If students have trouble predicting what would happen to the level of a hormone if negative feedback didn't happen, **then** have them review the the information in **Figure 3**.

L1 MY SCIENCE COACH Online remediation to assist students in understanding the systems that regulate and control body processes.

Differentiated Instruction

L1 Write the name of each gland of the endocrine system on separate note cards. Write the hormones released and/or the processes controlled by each gland on separate note cards. Have students match the name of the gland with the description of the gland. Then have students point to the corresponding gland in **Figure 1**.

L3 Have students find an image of people in a magazine or book. Ask them to describe what the people in the image are doing. Then challenge them to identify what structures in the nervous system and endocrine system are involved. Allow them to use **Figure 4** as a model for their descriptions.

Lab zone **After the Inquiry Warm-Up**

The Endocrine System

Inquiry Warm-Up, *What's the Signal?*

In the Inquiry Warm-Up, you investigated how signals transmit information. Using what you learned from that activity, answer the questions below.

1. **OBSERVE** Did you stop immediately when your teacher said "Freeze"? Explain.

   _____

   _____

2. **SEQUENCE** Describe what happens inside your body from the time your teacher said "Start" until the time you began to move.

   _____

   _____

3. **PREDICT** What might have happened if your teacher had said "Stay still" instead of "Start?"

   _____

   _____

4. **APPLY CONCEPTS** How does this activity model what goes on in your body when signals travel from one part to another?

   _____

   _____

   _____

Assess Your Understanding

The Endocrine System

How Does the Endocrine System Function?

1a. EXPLAIN How does adrenaline affect the heart?

_____

b. RELATE CAUSE AND EFFECT Explain how the hypothalamus affects growth.

_____

_____

got it? ···

○ **I get it!** Now I know that my endocrine system _____

_____

○ **I need extra help with** _____

_____

What Controls Hormone Levels?

2a. REVIEW Negative feedback works by turning a system **(on/off)** by the condition the system produces.

b. PREDICT What do you think would happen to the level of a hormone in the blood if negative feedback didn't happen?

_____

_____

c. ANSWER ❓ What systems regulate and control body processes?

_____

_____

got it? ···

○ **I get it!** Now I know that negative feedback controls hormone levels by

_____

_____

○ **I need extra help with** _____

_____

The Endocrine System

How Does the Endocrine System Function?

The human body has two systems that regulate its activities: the nervous system and the endocrine system. The nervous system regulates most activities by sending nerve impulses throughout the body. **The endocrine system regulates short-term and long-term activities by sending chemicals throughout the body. Long-term changes include growth and development.** The endocrine system is made up of glands. A **gland** is an organ that produces or releases a chemical. **Ducts,** or tubes, deliver the chemicals to a specific place in the body.

The chemical produced by an endocrine gland is called a **hormone.** Hormones turn on, turn off, speed up, or slow down the activities of organs and tissues. Each hormone affects specific target cells. **Target cells** are cells that are specialized in a way that enables them to recognize the hormone's chemical structure. Hormones travel in the blood until they find their target cells.

The endocrine system includes the hypothalamus, the pituitary gland, the thymus gland, the thyroid gland, parathyroid glands, adrenal glands, the pancreas, and testes and ovaries. The nervous system and the endocrine system work together, and they are linked by a part of the brain called the **hypothalamus,** which sends out nerve messages that control sleep, hunger, and other basic body processes. The **pituitary gland** is below and works with the hypothalamus to control many body activities. The hypothalamus sends messages to the pituitary gland to release its hormones. Some of those pituitary hormones signal other endocrine glands to produce hormones. Other pituitary hormones, such as the growth hormone, control body activities directly.

What Controls Hormone Levels?

Hormone levels are controlled by a process called **negative feedback,** in which a system is turned off by the condition it produces. **When the amount of a hormone in the blood reaches a certain level, the endocrine system sends signals that stop the release of that hormone.**

On a separate sheet of paper, explain the functions of the hypothalamus and the pituitary gland in relation to body activities.

The Endocrine System

Understanding Main Ideas
Answer the following questions on a separate sheet of paper.

1. What is the function of the endocrine system?
2. What are the endocrine system's messengers and how are they carried through the body?
3. What are the two ways the hypothalamus sends messages to the pituitary gland?
4. What is the general function of the pituitary gland?
5. How does a negative feedback system work to regulate the amount of thyroxine in the blood?

Building Vocabulary
Match each term in the left column with its definition in the right column by writing the letter of the correct definition on the line beside the term.

6. ___ gland

7. ___ hormone

8. ___ target cells

9. ___ hypothalamus

10. ___ pituitary gland

11. ___ negative feedback

12. ___ duct

a. the chemical product of an endocrine gland

b. an endocrine gland that works with the hypothalamus to control many body activities

c. a part of the brain that links the nervous system and the endocrine system

d. an organ that produces and releases a chemical

e. cells that are specialized in a way that enables them to recognize the hormone's chemical structure

f. a process in which the endocrine system is turned off by the condition it produces

g. tiny tubes into which chemicals are released

Enrich

The Endocrine System

The cells of your body get energy by breaking down a chemical called glucose. Read the passage below to learn about levels of glucose in the blood and study the diagram. Then use a separate sheet of paper to answer the questions that follow.

A Balancing Act

As you learned, the level of glucose in the blood is controlled by two hormones, insulin and glucagon. Most of the body's cells require insulin in order to take in glucose from the blood. When the blood level of glucose gets too high, the pancreas releases insulin. This allows the cells of the body to take in glucose, and the blood level of glucose falls back to normal.

If the level of glucose in the blood gets too low, the pancreas releases the hormone glucagon. The main target of glucagon is the liver. Glucagon causes the liver to release glucose into the blood. As a result, the blood level of glucose rises back to normal.

The graph below shows the level of glucose in a person's blood over time.

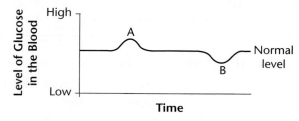

1. What hormone was released at point A? How do you know?
2. What hormone was released at point B? How do you know?
3. How do the hormones insulin and glucagon work together to regulate the level of glucose in the blood?
4. Make a cycle diagram to explain how insulin and glucagon work together to regulate the level of glucose in the blood.
5. After a meal, the blood level of glucose increases. Knowing this, do you expect the level of insulin in the blood to be higher before or after a meal?

Lesson Quiz

The Endocrine System

If the statement is true, write *true*. If the statement is false, change the underlined word or words to make the statement true.

1. _____ The <u>nervous</u> system regulates short-term and long-term activities by sending chemicals throughout the body.

2. _____ <u>Hormones</u> turn on, turn off, speed up, or slow down the activities of organs and tissues.

3. _____ The chemical product of an endocrine gland is called a(n) <u>gland</u>.

4. _____ The nervous system and the endocrine system are linked by a part of the brain called the <u>pituitary</u> gland.

5. _____ When the amount of a hormone in the blood reaches a certain level, the endocrine system sends signals that <u>stop</u> the release of that hormone.

Fill in the blank to complete each statement.

6. The endocrine glands produce and release chemicals directly into the bloodstream or into a(n) _____.

7. Long-term changes controlled by the endocrine system include _____ and development.

8. _____ cells are cells that are specialized in a way that enables them to recognize the hormone's chemical structure.

9. The _____ works with the hypothalamus to control many body activities.

10. _____ levels are controlled by a process called negative feedback.

The Endocrine System

Answer Key

After the Inquiry Warm-Up

1. Answers will vary. Students may say that they stopped immediately or that there was a short pause.

2. Sample: First, my ears heard the word "Start." Then my brain understood the message and sent a message to my legs to move. Last, my legs moved.

3. Sample: It might have taken my brain longer to understand the command was different from the one I was expecting to hear and my body may have moved on instinct.

4. Sample: Messages travel from one part of the body to another, very quickly but not instantaneously.

Key Concept Summaries

The hypothalamus sends out nerve messages that control sleep, hunger, and other basic body processes. It also produces hormones that control other endocrine glands and organs. The pituitary gland works with the hypothalamus. The hypothalamus sends messages to the pituitary gland to release its hormones. Some of those pituitary hormones signal other endocrine glands to produce hormones. Other pituitary hormones, such as the growth hormone, control body activities directly.

Review and Reinforce

1. The endocrine system controls many of the body's daily activities as well as long-term changes such as growth and development.

2. The messengers are hormones that are carried throughout the body in the blood.

3. nerve messages, hormones

4. Along with the hypothalamus, the pituitary gland works to control many body activities.

5. In a negative feedback system, the substance a system produces makes that system stop producing it. When the level of thyroxine gets high enough, the endocrine system signals the thyroid gland to stop releasing thyroxine.

6. d	**7.** a	**8.** e
9. c	**10.** b	**11.** f
12. g		

Enrich

1. Insulin was released at point A. The level of blood glucose was high at point A and fell back to normal shortly afterward.

2. Glucagon was released at point B. The level of blood glucose was low at point B and rose back to normal shortly afterward.

3. Insulin and glucagon help to keep the level of glucose in the blood constant. Insulin keeps it from getting too high, and glucagon keeps it from getting too low.

4. Students cycle diagrams should contain 6 cells and arrows pointing clockwise. Top center cell: "Blood glucose levels increase." Top right cell: "Pancreas releases insulin." Bottom right cell: "Insulin allows body cells to take in glucose." Bottom center cell: "Blood glucose levels decrease." Bottom left cell: "Pancreas releases glucagon." Top left cell: "Glucagon causes liver to release glucose into bloodstream."

5. The level of insulin is higher after a meal.

Lesson Quiz

1. endocrine	**2.** true
3. hormone	**4.** hypothalamus
5. true	**6.** duct
7. growth	**8.** Target
9. pituitary gland	**10.** Hormone

The Male and Female Reproductive Systems

Blended Path Active learning using Student Edition, Inquiry Path, and Digital Path

Lesson Pacing: 2–3 periods or 1–1$\frac{1}{2}$ blocks

🕐 **SHORT ON TIME?** To do this lesson in approximately half the time, do the Activate Prior Knowledge activity followed by a discussion of the Key Concepts to familiarize students with the lesson content. Have students do the Quick Labs. The rest of the lesson can be completed by students independently.

> **Preference Navigator,** in the online Planning tools, allows you to customize *Interactive Science* to your own teaching style. You can also edit lesson plans by selecting the Lesson Planner option.
>
> **Digital Teacher's Edition** allows you to access your Teacher's Edition and Resource materials online.

Lesson Vocabulary

- fertilization • egg • sperm • zygote • testes
- testosterone • scrotum • semen • penis • ovary
- estrogen • Fallopian tube • uterus • vagina
- menstrual cycle • menstruation • ovulation

Content Refresher
Professional Development Note

Hormones of the Menstrual Cycle Each ovary contains about 400,000 follicles, the structures in which eggs develop. During a typical menstrual cycle, one egg is released from a follicle. This process is regulated by hormones, some of which include estrogen, progesterone, follicle-stimulating hormone (FSH), and luteinizing hormone (LH). At the onset of menstruation, the low level of estrogen causes the pituitary gland to release FSH and LH. FSH stimulates follicle growth. The follicle releases estrogen, which makes the lining of the uterus thicken. Rapidly increasing levels of estrogen cause a rapid increase in the production of FSH and LH. The LH surge causes the final maturation of the follicle and release of the egg. After ovulation, LH causes the follicle to develop into a structure called the corpus luteum, which releases estrogen and progesterone. Progesterone increases the blood supply to the uterus's lining. If the egg is fertilized, it implants in the uterus. If fertilization and implantation do not occur, the corpus luteum breaks down and releases progressively less estrogen and progesterone. Decreasing levels of these hormones cause the breakdown of the lining of the uterus, and menstruation begins.

LESSON OBJECTIVES

🔑 Describe the structures and functions of the male and female reproductive systems.

🔑 Sequence the events that occur during the menstrual cycle.

ENGAGE AND EXPLORE

Teach this lesson using a variety of resources. Begin by reading **My Planet Diary** as a class. Have students discuss in vitro fertilization. Then have students do the **Inquiry Warm-Up activity.** Students will analyze, sketch, and label slides of egg cells and sperm cells. The **After the Inquiry Warm-Up worksheet** sets up a discussion about the differences between male and female reproductive cells. Have volunteers share their answers to question 4 telling which the human body produces more of, sperm cells or egg cells.

EXPLAIN AND ELABORATE

Support the Big Q by explaining that life begins from a single-cell egg and that trillions of cells result from a single fertilized egg. **Teach Key Concepts** by explaining the structures of the male reproductive system. **Lead a Discussion** using **Figure 3** to explain the structures though which sperm pass. Continue to **Teach Key Concepts** by explaining the structures of the female reproductive system.

Teach Key Concepts by explaining what happens during a menstrual cycle.

Hand out the **Key Concept Summaries** as a review of each part of the lesson. Students can also use the online **Vocab Flash Cards** to review key terms.

EVALUATE

Have students take the **Lesson Quiz.** For an alternate assessment, see the **EXAM**VIEW® Assessment Suite, Progress Monitoring Assessments, or SuccessTracker™.

ELL Support

1 Content and Language

Have students copy the vocabulary terms into a journal or personal glossary. Then ask them to find the first time the words are used in the chapter. Have them copy the definition of each vocabulary term into their journal or personal glossary.

Lab zone Inquiry Path
Hands-on learning in the Lab zone

ENGAGE AND EXPLORE

To teach this lesson with an emphasis on inquiry, begin with the **Inquiry Warm-Up activity.** Students will analyze, sketch, and label slides of egg cells and sperm cells. The **After the Inquiry Warm-Up worksheet** sets up a discussion about the differences between male and female reproductive cells. Have volunteers share their answers to question 4 telling which the human body produces more of, sperm cells or egg cells.

EXPLAIN AND ELABORATE

Focus on the **Inquiry Skill** for the lesson. Remind students that a hypothesis is one possible explanation or answer to a scientific question. Point out that a hypothesis can be worded as an *if/then* statement. Have students write a hypothesis about why the human body produces more sperm cells than egg cells as learned in the **Inquiry Warm-Up activity.** *(Answers will vary.)* **Support the Big Q** by explaining that life begins from a single-cell egg and that trillions of cells result from a single fertilized egg. Have students do the **Quick Lab** using models of egg and sperm cells to calculate the size of human sex cells.

Have students do the **Quick Lab** to model the sequence of changes in LH levels during a woman's menstrual cycle. Students can use the online **Vocab Flash Cards** to review key terms.

EVALUATE

Have students take the **Lesson Quiz.** For an alternate assessment, see the **EXAM**VIEW® Assessment Suite, Progress Monitoring Assessments, or SuccessTracker™.

Digital Path
Online learning at my science online.com

ENGAGE AND EXPLORE

Teach this lesson using digital resources. Begin by having students learn more about male and female reproductive systems and explore real-world connections to male and female reproductive systems at **My Planet Diary** online. Have them access the Chapter Resources to find the **Unlock the Big Question activity.** There they can answer the questions and refine their responses as they continue through the lesson. You can re-assign the activity and have students submit their work so you can track their progress.

EXPLAIN AND ELABORATE

Students reading above, at, or below the lexile measure of this lesson can access basic content readings at their level at **My Reading Web.** Encourage students to use the online **Vocab Flash Cards** to preview key terms. **Support the Big Q** by explaining that life begins from a single-cell egg and that trillions of cells result from a single fertilized egg. Use the **Interactive Art activity** online to show students the male reproductive system. Use the next **Interactive Art activity** online to show students the female reproductive system. Have students do the **Quick Lab** using models of egg and sperm cells to calculate the size of human sex cells.

Assign the **Do the Math activity** online and have students submit their work to you. Have students do the **Quick Lab** to model the sequence of changes in LH levels during a woman's menstrual cycle. The **Key Concept Summaries** online allow students to read a summary and see an image associated with each part of the lesson. Online remediation is available at **My Science Coach.**

EVALUATE

Have students take the **Lesson Quiz.** For an alternate assessment, see the **EXAM**VIEW® Assessment Suite, Progress Monitoring Assessments, or SuccessTracker™.

2 Frontload the Lesson

Direct students' attention to the graph in the Do the Math activity. Help them understand that the information from the table has been transferred to the graph. Name several of the points on the graph *(Day 13, Day 5, Day 25)* and have students point to the location of each point on the graph.

3 Comprehensible Input

Have students use an outline to better understand the information in this lesson. Have them use the red and blue heads to organize the information in their outlines.

4 Language Production

Pair or group students with varied language abilities to complete labs collaboratively for language practice. Have each student copy the completed written lab for personal reference.

5 Assess Understanding

Have students keep a content area log for this lesson using a two-column format with the headings "What I Understand" and "What I Don't Understand." Follow up so that students can move items from the "Don't Understand" to the "Understand" column.

The Male and Female Reproductive Systems

Establish Learning Objectives

After this lesson, students will be able to:

 Describe the structures and functions of the male and female reproductive systems.

 Sequence the events that occur during the menstrual cycle.

Engage

Activate Prior Knowledge

MY PLANET DIARY Read *In Vitro Fertilization* with the class. Explain that Steptoe and Edwards worked together for ten years before overseeing the first "test-tube baby." Their work in England led to the successful births of about 1,000 babies. Ask: **Why do you think the successful fertilization and replacement of an egg in a woman's body was so challenging?** *(Sample: Scientists needed to create conditions similar to those inside a woman's body.)*

BIG IDEAS OF SCIENCE REFERENCE LIBRARY DK
Have students look up the following topics: Menstrual Cycle, Puberty.

Explore

Lab Resource: Inquiry Warm-Up

L2 **WHAT'S THE BIG DIFFERENCE?** Students will analyze, sketch, and label slides of egg cells and sperm cells.

LESSON 3

The Male and Female Reproductive Systems

 UNLOCK THE BIG ?

What Are the Functions of the Reproductive Systems?

What Happens During the Menstrual Cycle?

my planet Diary

In Vitro Fertilization

DISCOVERY

In 1977, Dr. Patrick Steptoe and Dr. Robert Edwards had been working for years on an experimental procedure called in vitro fertilization. Their goal was to help women who could not become pregnant naturally. In vitro fertilization begins with retrieving an egg from a woman. The egg is placed in a lab dish along with a man's sperm. If the egg is successfully fertilized, it is placed back into the woman's body to grow into a baby.

Dr. Steptoe and Dr. Edwards were unsuccessful time and time again, until they met Lesley and John Brown. The doctors implanted a fertilized egg in Lesley. Nine months later, on July 25, 1978, the world's first in vitro baby was born. Her parents named her Louise Joy Brown.

Communicate Discuss the following questions with a partner. Write your answers below.

1. At what point during the in vitro fertilization process is the egg placed back into the woman's body?

   The egg is placed back into the woman's body after it has been fertilized.

2. What impact do you think in vitro fertilization has had?

   Sample: It has helped some couples who otherwise could not have children.

> PLANET DIARY Go to **Planet Diary** to learn more about the male and female reproductive systems.

Lab zone Do the Inquiry Warm-Up *What's the Big Difference?*

Louise Joy Brown
at birth

Louise Joy Brown
as an adult

524 Controlling Body Processes

SUPPORT ALL READERS

Lexile Measure = 940L   Lexile Word Count = 1323

Prior Exposure to Content: Many students may have misconceptions on this topic

Academic Vocabulary: *develop, hypothesis, sequence*

Science Vocabulary: *fertilization, zygote, testosterone, estrogen*

Concept Level: Generally appropriate for most students in this grade

Preteach With: My Planet Diary "In Vitro Fertilization" and Figure 6 activity

Go to **My Reading Web** to access leveled readings that provide a foundation for the content.

my science online.com

Vocabulary
- fertilization • egg • sperm • zygote • testes
- testosterone • scrotum • semen • penis • ovary
- estrogen • Fallopian tube • uterus • vagina
- menstrual cycle • menstruation • ovulation

Skills
- ⟳ Reading: Sequence
- △ Inquiry: Develop Hypotheses

What Are the Functions of the Reproductive Systems?

Have you noticed how a child's body changes as the child grows? Two different endocrine glands—the ovaries and the testes—release hormones that control many of these changes. They also produce the sex cells that are part of sexual reproduction.

Sexual Reproduction You were once a single cell. That cell resulted from the joining of an egg cell and a sperm cell, which is a process called **fertilization.** An **egg** is the female sex cell. The male sex cell is a **sperm.** Both cells are shown in **Figure 1.** Fertilization is part of sexual reproduction, the process by which males and females produce new individuals. Sexual reproduction involves the production of eggs by the female and sperm by the male. The egg and sperm join together during fertilization. When fertilization occurs, a fertilized egg, or **zygote,** is produced. The zygote contains all the information needed to produce a new human being.

FIGURE 1 ⋯⋯⋯⋯⋯⋯
Egg and Sperm
An egg is one of the largest cells in the body. A sperm cell is much smaller than an egg and can move.

✎ **Describe** In the table, describe each of the cells involved in fertilization.

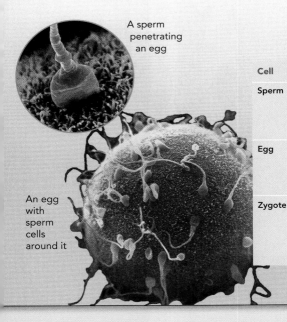

A sperm penetrating an egg

An egg with sperm cells around it

Cell	Description
Sperm	A sperm is the male sex cell. It is small and can move. It fertilizes the egg.
Egg	An egg is the female sex cell. It is a large cell. The sperm fertilizes it.
Zygote	A zygote is a fertilized egg. It has all the information needed to become a human being.

525

Explain

Introduce Vocabulary

To help students understand the terms *testosterone* and *estrogen*, encourage them to think of them as male and female versions of the same chemical product—that is, a hormone that triggers functions or characteristics specific to one gender.

Support the Big Q ❓ UbD

FERTILIZATION Have students locate a period at the end of a sentence in the text. Explain that everyone in the classroom—and in the world—began life from a single cell that was about the size of that mark of punctuation. Then point out that trillions of cells result from a single fertilized egg. Ask: **What is that single cell called?** *(A zygote)* **How does it form?** *(Through fertilization, in which an egg from a female and sperm from a male are joined)* Have students refer to **Figure 1** and read the caption. Point out that sperm are not actually blue and that scientists sometimes dye them to make them more visible. Ask: **What characteristics make eggs and sperm different?** *(The egg cell is larger than a sperm, and the sperm cell has a tail that enables it to move.)*

My Planet Diary provides an opportunity for students to explore real-world connections to the male and female reproductive systems.

my science online.com ▶ **The Reproductive Systems**

ⒺⓁⓁ Support

1 Content and Language
Write *menstruation* on the board with lines separating the word's syllables (*men/stru/a/tion*). Write and pronounce the phonetic spellings for each syllable, making sure to carefully pronounce each consonant in the second syllable.

2 Frontload the Lesson
Have volunteers write the vocabulary on the board. Under the headings *Male* and *Female,* transfer the terms *penis* and *vagina* to the appropriate columns. Students should organize the other terms into the correct columns. Note: *fertilization* could be in both columns.

3 Comprehensible Input
Have students create two cluster diagrams of organs, structures, functions, and processes of the male and female reproductive systems.

Explain

Teach Key Concepts

Explain to students that the male reproductive system produces reproductive cells and a hormone. Ask: **What are the structures of the male reproductive system?** *(The testes, scrotum, and penis.)* Explain that hundreds of coiled tubes in the testes produce sperm cells and testosterone. Ask: **What is testosterone?** *(A hormone that controls the development of adult male characteristics)* **What are examples of these characteristics?** *(Facial hair, deepening voice, broadening shoulders, the ability to produce sperm)* Explain to students that the scrotum helps the testes maintain a temperature 2°C to 3°C below normal body temperature. Ask: **What is normal body temperature?** *(37°C, or 98.6°F)* **Why is the position of the scrotum important to the development of sperm?** *(Sperm do not develop normally at 37°C.)*

Teach With Visuals

Tell students to look at **Figures 2** and **3**. Draw students' attention to the urinary bladder, the testis, and the urethra. Ask: **What two fluids leave the body through the penis?** *(Urine, semen)* **How does the body prevent urine and semen from mixing?** *(When semen passes through the urethra, muscles near the bladder contract so that no urine will mix with the semen.)*

Sperm cells

Male Reproductive System Look at the organs of the male reproductive system shown in **Figure 2.** The male reproductive system is specialized to produce sperm cells and the hormone testosterone. The structures of this system include the testes, scrotum, and penis.

The Testes The **testes** (TES teez; singular *testis*) are the organs in which sperm are produced. The testes consist of clusters of tiny, coiled tubes where sperm are formed. In addition to sperm, the testes produce testosterone. The hormone **testosterone** (tes TAHS tuh rohn) controls the development of adult male characteristics. These include facial hair, deepening of the voice, broadening of the shoulders, and the ability to produce sperm.

The testes are located in a pouch of skin called the **scrotum** (SKROH tum). The scrotum holds the testes away from the rest of the body. This distance keeps the testes about 2°C to 3°C below normal body temperature, which is 37°C. The cooler temperature is important because sperm cannot develop properly at 37°C.

FIGURE 2

> INTERACTIVE ART Structures of the Male Reproductive System

✎ Complete the tasks.

1. **Summarize** In the boxes, describe the structure and function of each organ.

2. **Calculate** Find the temperatures at which sperm develop properly.
   They develop best at 34°C to 35°C.

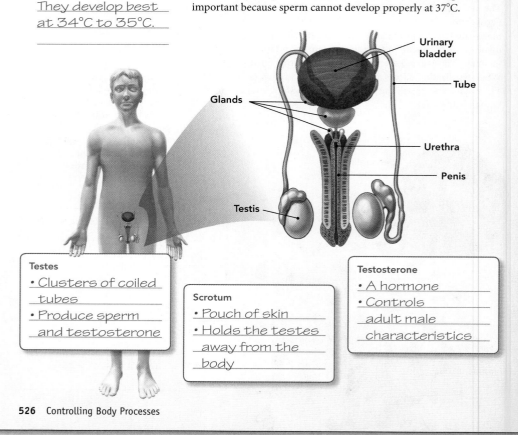

- Urinary bladder
- Tube
- Glands
- Urethra
- Penis
- Testis

Testes
- Clusters of coiled tubes
- Produce sperm and testosterone

Scrotum
- Pouch of skin
- Holds the testes away from the body

Testosterone
- A hormone
- Controls adult male characteristics

Professional Development Note **Teacher to Teacher**

Endocrine System and Reproduction One of the toughest topics to cover in middle school is human reproduction. Whether it's concern about terms or diagrams, or the snickers and giggles from students, discussions and activities related to this topic are a true challenge. The key to successful lessons can be summed up in one word—maturity. You should approach questions and comments in an honest, professional manner. If faced with a potentially "embarrassing" topic, refocus students on the science. Remind the class that "it's not sex, it's reproduction." Work collaboratively with health teachers to discuss this extremely important topic sensibly.

✆ *Rick Towle*
Noblesville Middle School
Noblesville, Indiana

Sperm The production of sperm cells begins during the teenage years. Each sperm cell has a head that contains chromosomes, and a long, whiplike tail. The chromosomes carry the information that controls inherited characteristics, such as blood type. The tail helps the sperm swim in fluid.

After forming in the testes, sperm travel through tubes in the male reproductive system. As they travel, sperm mix with fluids produced by nearby glands, as shown in **Figure 3**. This mixture of sperm cells and fluids is called **semen** (SEE mun). The fluids in semen provide an environment where sperm can swim. Semen also contains nutrients that the sperm use for energy.

Semen leaves the body through an organ called the **penis.** The semen travels through the tube in the penis called the urethra. Urine also leaves the body through the urethra. When semen passes through the urethra, however, muscles near the bladder contract. Those muscles prevent urine and semen from mixing.

🖉 **Sequence** Underline in the paragraphs the path that sperm take to leave the body. Then write the steps on the notepaper below.

FIGURE 3 ···

Sperm Production and Passage From the Body
Sperm are produced in the testes and leave the body through the urethra.

✎ **Use the diagram to complete the tasks.**

1. **Relate Text and Visuals** On the diagram, draw arrows to trace the path that sperm travel through the male reproductive system.

2. **CHALLENGE** Why do sperm need to swim?

Sample: They have to be able to travel to the female's egg cell.

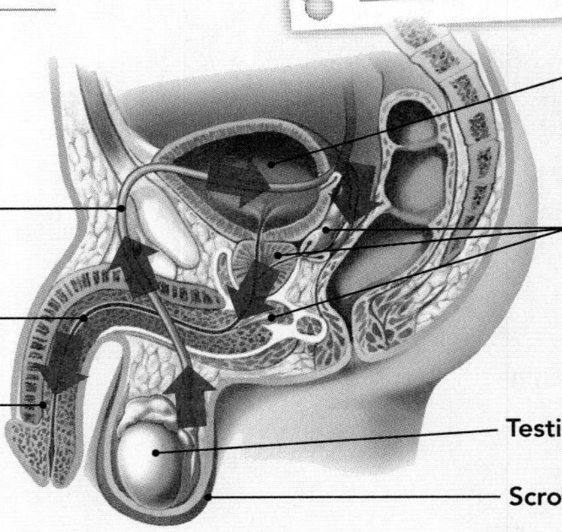

1. Sperm form in the testes.
2. They travel through tubes in the male body.
3. While moving through the tubes, sperm mix with fluids produced by glands to make semen.
4. Semen leaves the body through a tube in the penis called the urethra.

- Urinary bladder
- Tube
- Glands
- Urethra
- Penis
- Testis
- Scrotum

527

Lead a Discussion

PATHWAY FOR SPERM Direct students' attention to **Figure 3.** Help them follow the description of the structures through which sperm pass. After each structure is mentioned, students should look at the illustration and locate the structure. Make sure that students understand that the tubes, or sperm ducts, that lead out of the testes do not pass through the urinary bladder. The illustration shows the body cut in half. The sperm ducts are next to the bladder, so they are not in the same plane as the rest of the structures in the illustration. Ask: **What happens to sperm as they travel through the tubes?** (They mix with fluids produced by nearby glands.) **What is the mixture of sperm and fluids called?** (Semen)

🕙 **Sequence** Tell students that when they sequence items, they put the items in order. The order can be based on size, time, location, or another property.

Elaborate ————————

21st Century Learning

CRITICAL THINKING To help students clarify the differences between sperm and semen, point out that they cannot see sperm without a microscope. However, semen can be seen after it leaves the body. Ask: **What is the difference between sperm and semen?** (Sperm are male sex cells. Semen is a mixture of sperm and fluids.) **In what way are sperm and semen similar?** (Both are involved in sexual reproduction.)

Interactive Art shows the male reproductive system.

my science ONLINE ▸ The Reproductive Systems

Differentiated Instruction

L1 Organize Information: Reproductive Systems As students read, have them list the differences between the male and female reproductive systems in a compare-contrast table. Students should include information about sex cells, organs, and the main hormone of each system.

L3 Chromosomes Encourage students to research chromosomes in sex cells. Students should include information that defines chromosomes and their role in determining inherited characteristics such as eye color and blood type. Students should explain how every cell in the human body has 46 chromosomes, with the exception of sex cells, which have 23. During fertilization, the 23 chromosomes in a sperm join the 23 chromosomes in an egg, resulting in a zygote with 46 chromosomes.

Explain

Teach Key Concepts

Explain to students that the female reproductive system is specialized to produce eggs and to nourish a developing baby until birth. It also produces hormones including estrogen. Point out that the organs of the female reproductive system include the ovaries, Fallopian tubes, uterus, and vagina. Help students understand that the ovaries produce egg cells and that ovaries also are endocrine glands that produce estrogen, the female hormone. Ask: **In what way is the function of estrogen similar to the function of testosterone?** *(Estrogen triggers adult female physical characteristics to develop in a body; testosterone triggers adult male physical characteristics to develop in a body.)* Explain that other structures of the female reproductive system have the function of moving the egg cell for fertilization, supporting a fertilized egg, or breaking down an unfertilized egg. Ask: **What are Fallopian tubes?** *(Passageways for eggs traveling from the ovary to the uterus)* **What is a function of the uterus?** *(A place for a fertilized egg to attach itself)* **How is the function of the female reproductive system similar to and different from the function of the male reproduction system?** *(The function of the male reproduction system is to provide sperm for fertilization. The functions of the female reproduction system involve not only providing eggs for fertilization but also nourishing a developing baby until birth.)*

Make Analogies

L1 **VAGINA AS PASSAGEWAY** You may wish to enrich students' understanding of the vagina's function as a passageway involved in human reproduction. Explain that the vagina is the passageway through which a baby emerges from a woman's body during birth. Ask: **Why is the vagina also called the birth canal?** *(A canal is a passageway, and the birth canal is the passageway through which a baby passes as he or she is born.)*

---

did you know?

When the female reproductive system becomes mature, the ovaries contain about 400,000 undeveloped eggs. However, only about 450 of those eggs will actually leave the ovaries and reach the uterus during a typical woman's life.

Female Reproductive System

The female reproductive system is specialized to produce eggs and nourish a developing baby until birth. It also produces estrogen and other hormones. The organs of this system include the ovaries, Fallopian tubes, uterus, and vagina.

The Ovaries The **ovaries** (OH vuh reez) are the female reproductive structures that produce eggs. They are located slightly below the waist, one on each side of the body, as shown in **Figure 4**. Like the testes in males, the ovaries are also endocrine glands that produce hormones. One hormone, **estrogen** (ES truh jun), triggers the development of some adult female characteristics. For example, estrogen causes the hips to widen and the breasts to develop. Estrogen is also involved in the development of egg cells. Each month, one of the ovaries releases a mature egg into the nearest oviduct, or Fallopian tube. A **Fallopian tube** is the passageway an egg travels from an ovary to the uterus. Fertilization usually occurs within a Fallopian tube.

FIGURE 4 ....

> INTERACTIVE ART **Structures of the Female Reproductive System**
The word *ovary* comes from the Latin word *ova* meaning "eggs."

✎ **Summarize** In the boxes, write the functions of the ovaries and the Fallopian tubes.

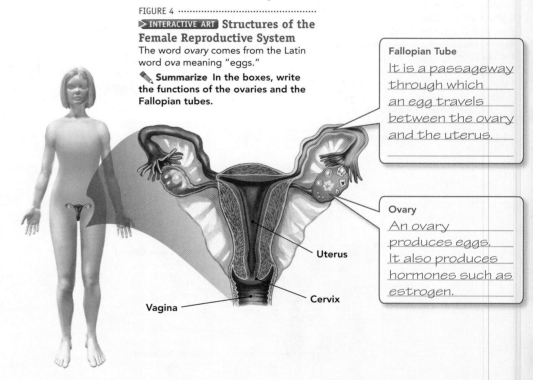

Fallopian Tube
It is a passageway through which an egg travels between the ovary and the uterus.

Ovary
An ovary produces eggs. It also produces hormones such as estrogen.

Uterus

Cervix

Vagina

Interactive Art shows the female reproductive system.

my science online.com | **The Reproductive Systems**

Egg Cells From an ovary, an egg travels through the Fallopian tube to the uterus. The **uterus** (YOO tur us) is a hollow, muscular organ. If an egg has been fertilized in the Fallopian tube, it attaches to the wall of the uterus. An unfertilized egg breaks down in the uterus. It leaves through the cervix, an opening at the base of the uterus. The egg then enters the vagina. The **vagina** (vuh JY nuh) is a muscular passageway leading to the outside of the body. The vagina, or birth canal, is the passageway through which a baby leaves its mother's body during childbirth. **Figure 5** shows the female reproductive system.

FIGURE 5 ·······················
Egg Production and Passage From the Body
Each month, an ovary produces an egg that leaves the body if it is not fertilized.

 Describe In the boxes, write the functions of the uterus and the vagina.

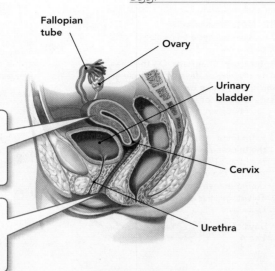

Uterus
It is where a fertilized egg becomes attached.

Vagina
It is the passageway for an egg or a baby to get to the outside of the body.

Fallopian tube
Ovary
Urinary bladder
Cervix
Urethra

·······················
Vocabulary Identify Related Word Forms When you know the meaning of a word, you can often identify and understand related words. How are the meanings of *fertilized* and *fertilization* related?

Sample: Fertilization results in a fertilized egg.

 Do the Quick Lab
Reproductive Systems.

⬅ **Assess Your Understanding**

1a. Review What is fertilization?
It is the joining of a sperm cell and an egg cell.

b. Relate Cause and Effect What changes does estrogen cause in a female's body?
Estrogen causes egg cells and breasts to develop, and the hips to widen.

got it?

○ **I get it!** Now I know that the male and female reproductive systems produce sperm cells and egg cells, which can join to produce a fertilized egg.

○ **I need extra help with** See TE note.

Go to MY SCIENCE COACH online for help with this subject.

529

Elaborate ——————————

21st Century Learning

INFORMATION LITERACY After discussing the female reproductive system, briefly review the structures of both genders' reproductive systems. Have students do research to learn more about the similarities and differences between the functions of the ovaries and the testes. They should compare hormone production and also the part of the person's life span during which sex cells are produced. Students should consider the reliability of the source of information as they do their research. If students do research on the Internet, remind them to follow prescribed guidelines for Internet use.

Lab Resource: Quick Lab

L2 REPRODUCTIVE SYSTEMS Students will use models of egg and sperm cells to calculate the size of human sex cells.

Evaluate ——————————

Assess Your Understanding

After students answer the questions, have them evaluate their understanding by completing the appropriate sentence.

R T I Response to Intervention

1a. If students have trouble defining the term *fertilization*, **then** have them locate the highlighted term and reread the definition.

b. If students have trouble identifying the effects of estrogen, **then** suggest they reread the information in the paragraph about the ovaries.

MY SCIENCE COACH Have students go online for help in understanding male and female reproductive systems.

Differentiated Instruction

L1 Visualize Vocabulary Encourage students to create a list of terms and definitions in this section. They can make flash cards with the terms on one side and the definitions on the other. Then they can work in pairs to quiz each other. Urge students to refer often to **Figure 4** and **Figure 5** to visualize the meanings of the terms.

L3 Gabriel Fallopius Challenge students to do research on the origins of the term *Fallopian tube*. Students might prepare a short written report containing information they gather about the 16th century Italian physician Gabriel Fallopius. In his work as anatomist and teacher, Fallopius made important discoveries about the human ear and the human reproductive system. He named several body parts, including the vagina, and his discovery of the tubes that connect the ovaries and uterus led to their being named for him.

Explain

Teach Key Concepts 🔑

Remind students that one of the central functions of the female reproductive system is to nourish a developing baby. Explain that during the menstrual cycle, an egg develops in an ovary and the uterus prepares for a fertilized egg. Refer students to the 28-day cycle, which is considered average, shown in **Figure 6.** Point out that the first day of a menstrual cycle is the first day of menstruation. Ask: **What is happening at the same time that the lining of the uterus is thickening?** *(An egg is maturing in the ovary.)* **At what point can the egg be fertilized?** *(During stage 4, about halfway through the cycle, for a few days after the egg is released)* **What can prevent the cycle from beginning again?** *(If the egg is fertilized, the cycle will be interrupted.)* Discuss with students the fact that each woman's menstrual cycle may be different from the average cycle of 28 days—in fact, the length of the menstrual cycle is considered normal anywhere within the range of 21 to 35 days. Moreover, the exact day when particular stages within the menstrual cycle begin and end vary among women, as well.

Address Misconceptions

L1 CONFUSING CONCEPTS AND TERMINOLOGY
Many students may confuse the terms *menstrual cycle* and *menstruation.* Explain that the menstrual cycle includes not only menstruation, but also the maturation of the egg, the thickening of the uterine lining, the release of the egg, and the breakdown of the uterine lining. Menstruation is the process by which the blood and tissue of the lining exit the body. Ask: **During which part of the menstrual cycle does menstruation take place?** *(During the first four days of the cycle)* Explain that menstruation may last longer for some women and that differences in the length of menstruation are normal.

Digital Lesson: Assign the *Do the Math* activity online and have students submit their work to you.

my scienceonline.com ▸ The Menstrual Cycle

What Happens During the Menstrual Cycle?

Usually starting sometime during a girl's teenage years, an egg develops and is released about once a month. This event is part of the **menstrual cycle** (MEN stroo ul), or the monthly cycle of changes that occurs in females. 🔑 **During the menstrual cycle, an egg develops in an ovary. At the same time, the lining of the uterus thickens in a way that prepares the uterus for a fertilized egg.** Follow the stages of the menstrual cycle in **Figure 6.**

FIGURE 6 ·······················

The Menstrual Cycle

The menstrual cycle takes about 28 days.

✎ **Interpret Diagrams** On the lines, write the day or days of the cycle in which each stage occurs. The first stage is done for you.

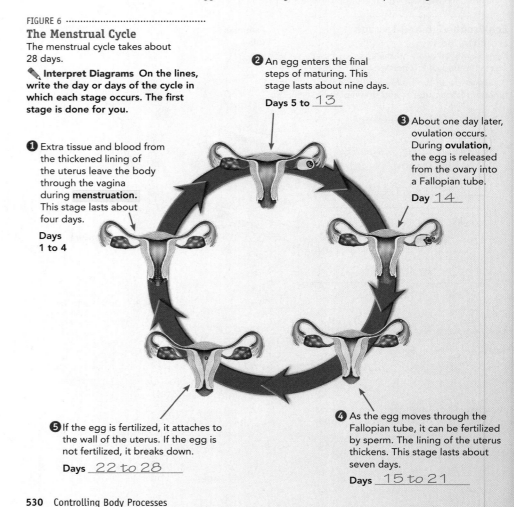

❶ Extra tissue and blood from the thickened lining of the uterus leave the body through the vagina during **menstruation.** This stage lasts about four days.

Days 1 to 4

❷ An egg enters the final steps of maturing. This stage lasts about nine days.

Days 5 to <u>13</u>

❸ About one day later, ovulation occurs. During **ovulation,** the egg is released from the ovary into a Fallopian tube.

Day <u>14</u>

❹ As the egg moves through the Fallopian tube, it can be fertilized by sperm. The lining of the uterus thickens. This stage lasts about seven days.

Days <u>15 to 21</u>

❺ If the egg is fertilized, it attaches to the wall of the uterus. If the egg is not fertilized, it breaks down.

Days <u>22 to 28</u>

530 Controlling Body Processes

do the math!

A woman's hormone levels change throughout her menstrual cycle. One such hormone is called LH.

1 Graph Use the data in the table to draw a line graph. Label the axes and write a title for the graph.

Day	1	5	9	13	17	22	25	28
Level of LH	12	13	13	70	12	12	8	10

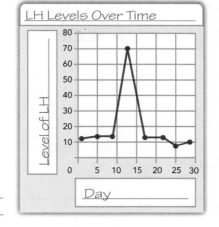

LH Levels Over Time

(y-axis: Level of LH; x-axis: Day)

2 Read Graphs On what day was the LH level the lowest? The highest?

<u>LH level was lowest on day 25 and highest on day 13.</u>

3 Develop Hypotheses How might LH level and ovulation be related?

<u>Sample: LH levels seem to increase drastically just before ovulation.</u>

 Lab zone Do the Quick Lab *Looking at Hormone Levels.*

Assess Your Understanding

2a. Identify In the menstrual cycle, what happens after ovulation occurs?

<u>The egg moves through the Fallopian tube. The lining of the uterus thickens.</u>

b. Infer What happens in the menstrual cycle if an egg is fertilized?

<u>Sample: The cycle stops until the baby is born.</u>

got it?

○ I get it! Now I know that during the menstrual cycle <u>an egg develops and the lining of the uterus thickens in a way that prepares the uterus for a fertilized egg.</u>

○ I need extra help with <u>See TE note.</u>

Go to **my science** **COACH** *online for help with this subject.*

531

Differentiated Instruction

L1 Menstruation Invite small groups to find factual information about the beginning and end of menstruation in females. Help students focus their understanding of how hormones trigger a girl's first menstruation, often between 10 and 14 years. Make sure students understand that some girls begin earlier, whereas others start later. Students should also locate information relating to the end of menstruation—

due to a drop in the production of sex hormones—in most women around the age of 50. Have students research the terms *perimenopause* and *menopause*.

L3 Interpret Health Information Ask students to use reliable sources, including their family doctors, to find out what causes painful menstrual cramps *(Chemicals called prostaglandins)* and how cramps can be treated.

Elaborate

Do the Math!

L1 Remind students that line graphs display data that show how one variable changes in relation to another variable. Point out that this line graph shows changes in LH levels (shown on the vertical axis) in relation to the days of a woman's menstrual cycle (the horizontal axis). Help students note the periods of little change—for example, days 1 through 9 and days 17 to 29—as well as the dramatic change between days 9 and 17. Help students recognize that the LH level is at its highest on day 13, just before ovulation occurs on day 14.

△ **Develop Hypotheses** Tell students that a hypothesis is one possible explanation or answer to a scientific question. Point out that a hypothesis can be worded as an *If … then …* statement.

Help students understand how analyzing the information in the table and line graph can lead them to give a possible explanation for the data about elevated LH levels during a woman's menstrual cycle.

See the *Math Skill and Problem-Solving Activities* for support.

Lab Resource: Quick Lab **Lab zone**

L2 LOOKING AT HORMONE LEVELS Students will model the sequence of changes in LH levels during a woman's menstrual cycle.

Evaluate

Assess Your Understanding

After students answer the questions, have them evaluate their understanding by completing the appropriate sentence.

RTI Response to Intervention

2a. If students have trouble identifying what happens after ovulation, **then** have them look again at **Figure 6.**

b. If students need help inferring how the menstrual cycle is affected by the fertilization of an egg, **then** remind them that fertilization represents biological "success" and that the menstrual cycle stops while the zygote develops into a baby.

my science **COACH** Have students go online for help in understanding the menstrual cycle.

Lab zone **After the Inquiry Warm-Up**

The Male and Female Reproductive Systems

> **Inquiry Warm-Up, *What's the Big Difference?***
>
> In the Inquiry Warm-Up, you investigated differences between male and female reproductive cells. Using what you learned from that activity, answer the questions below.

1. **MAKE MODELS** In the space below, draw the egg and sperm cells you observed.

2. **OBSERVE** Based on your observations, which of these cells is more likely to have the ability to move? Explain.

   _____

   _____

3. **OBSERVE** Look at the slides. Which cell are you able to see without using the microscope?

   _____

4. **INFER** During reproduction, many sperm cells attempt to combine with the same egg cell until one is successful. Based on this, which would you say the human body produces more of, sperm cells or egg cells?

   _____

Assess Your Understanding

The Male and Female Reproductive Systems

What Are the Functions of the Reproductive Systems?

1a. REVIEW What is fertilization?

_____

b. RELATE CAUSE AND EFFECT What changes does estrogen cause in a female's body?

_____

_____

got it?··

○ **I get it!** Now I know that the male and female reproductive systems _____

_____

_____

○ **I need extra help with** _____

_____

What Happens During the Menstrual Cycle?

2a. IDENTIFY In the menstrual cycle, what happens after ovulation occurs?

_____

_____

b. INFER What happens in the menstrual cycle if an egg is fertilized?

_____

got it?··

○ **I get it!** Now I know that during the menstrual cycle _____

_____

_____

○ **I need extra help with** _____

_____

Name _____ Date _____ Class _____

The Male and Female Reproductive Systems

What Are the Functions of the Reproductive Systems?

An egg cell and a sperm cell join in a process called **fertilization.** An **egg** is the female sex cell. The male sex cell is a **sperm.** Fertilization is part of sexual reproduction, the process by which males and females produce new individuals. When fertilization occurs, a fertilized egg, or **zygote** containing all the information needed to produce a human being is produced.

The male reproductive system is specialized to produce sperm cells and the hormone testosterone. The structures of this system include the testes, scrotum, and penis. The **testes** are clusters of tiny, coiled tubes where sperm are formed and testosterone is produced. The hormone **testosterone** controls the development of adult male characteristics. The testes are located in a pouch of skin called the **scrotum.** Sperm travel through tubes in the male reproductive system, mixing with fluids produced by nearby glands. This mixture of sperm cells and fluids is called **semen.** Semen leaves the body through an organ called the **penis.**

The female reproductive system is specialized to produce eggs and nourish the developing baby until birth. It also produces hormones including estrogen. The organs of this system include the ovaries, Fallopian tubes, uterus, and vagina. The **ovaries** are the female reproductive structures that produce eggs. The ovaries are also endocrine glands that produce hormones, including **estrogen,** which triggers the development of some adult female characteristics. Each month, one ovary releases a mature egg into the nearest **Fallopian tube,** a passageway from the ovary to the **uterus,** a hollow muscular organ. The baby leaves its mother's body through the **vagina,** a muscular passageway.

What Happens During the Menstrual Cycle?

An egg develops and is released about once a month in a mature woman. This event is part of the **menstrual cycle,** or the monthly cycle of changes that occurs in females. **During the menstrual cycle, an egg develops in an ovary. At the same time, the lining of the uterus thickens in a way that prepares the uterus for a fertilized egg.**

On a separate sheet of paper, summarize the functions and structures of the male and female reproductive systems.

Review and Reinforce

The Male and Female Reproductive Systems

Understanding Main Ideas
Answer the following questions on a separate sheet of paper.

1. What is the function of the male reproductive system?
2. What is the function of the female reproductive system?
3. What happens during the menstrual cycle?

Building Vocabulary
Match each term with its definition by writing the letter of the correct definition in the right column on the line beside the term in the left column.

4. ___ sperm

5. ___ zygote

6. ___ testes

7. ___ scrotum

8. ___ penis

9. ___ estrogen

10. ___ Fallopian tube

11. ___ uterus

12. ___ vagina

a. male sex cell

b. organs in which sperm are produced

c. fertilized egg

d. triggers development of female sex characteristics

e. hollow muscular organ in which developing baby grows

f. organ through which semen leaves the male body

g. a pouch of skin containing the testes

h. muscular passageway leading to the outside of the female body

i. a passageway for an egg from the ovary to the uterus

Name _____ Date _____ Class _____

The Male and Female Reproductive Systems

> Read the passage and study the diagram. Then answer the questions that follow on a separate sheet of paper.

Fertilization

In order for a sperm cell to join with an egg cell, the sperm cell must pass through two barriers that surround the egg. The outer barrier consists of a layer of cells that are released from the ovary along with the egg. The inner barrier is composed of a thick, protein-rich substance that is produced by the cells of the outer barrier. The head of a sperm cell contains chemicals that are released when it comes into contact with the cells surrounding an egg. These chemicals allow the sperm cell to tunnel through the barriers. Next the head of the sperm cell binds to the cell membrane of the egg. This binding causes a chemical change in the egg cell that prevents any more sperm cells from binding with its cell membrane. This keeps more than one sperm from fertilizing the egg.

The head of the sperm cell, which contains the cell's nucleus, is slowly pulled into the interior of the egg. A cell's nucleus contains its chromosomes. Fertilization is not complete until the nucleus of the sperm cell fuses with the nucleus of the egg cell. The process of fertilization is diagrammed below.

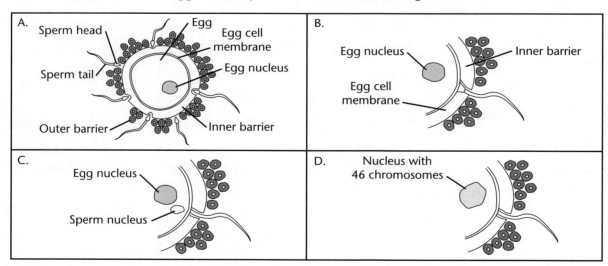

1. Write a caption for each of the figures above, explaining what is happening.
2. Why is it important that only one sperm cell fertilizes an egg cell?
3. What might happen if a woman's ovaries released several eggs at the same time instead of just one?
4. Why isn't fertilization considered to be complete until the nuclei of the two cells join together?

Lesson Quiz

The Male and Female Reproductive Systems

Fill in the blank to complete each statement.

1. The joining of an egg cell and a sperm cell is a process called _____.

2. The structures of the _____
   _____ include the testes, scrotum, and penis.

3. The mixture of sperm cells and fluids is called _____.

4. The female reproductive system is specialized to produce _____
   and the hormone estrogen, as well as to nourish the developing baby until birth.

5. During the menstrual cycle, the lining of the uterus thickens in preparation for
   a(n) _____.

If the statement is true, write _true_. If the statement is false, change the underlined word or words to make the statement true.

6. _____ The male reproductive system is specialized to produce sperm
   cells and the hormone <u>estrogen</u>.

7. _____ <u>Sexual reproduction</u> involves the production of eggs by the
   female and sperm by the male.

8. _____ The organs of the <u>female</u> reproductive system include the
   ovaries, Fallopian tubes, uterus, and vagina.

9. _____ During the menstrual cycle, an egg develops in the <u>uterus</u>.

10. _____ An egg develops and is released <u>about once a month</u> in a
    mature woman.

The Male and Female Reproductive Systems

Answer Key

After the Inquiry Warm-Up

1. Students' drawings should show the egg cell as very large in relation to the sperm cell and should show the head, middle piece, and tail of the sperm cell.

2. sperm cell: Answers will vary. Students will likely say that the sperm cells can use their tail sections to propel themselves.

3. egg cell

4. sperm cells

Key Concept Summaries

The function of the male reproductive system is the production of sperm cells and the hormone testosterone. The structures of this system include the testes, scrotum, and penis. The function of the female reproductive system is the production of eggs, the nourishment of a developing baby until birth, and the production of the hormone estrogen. Its structures include the ovaries, Fallopian tubes, uterus, and vagina.

Review and Reinforce

1. the production of sperm and the hormone testosterone

2. the production of eggs and the hormone estrogen, and the nourishment of a baby until birth

3. During the menstrual cycle, an egg develops, and the uterus prepares for the arrival of a fertilized egg. If the egg is not fertilized, the egg and the lining of the uterus are shed during menstruation. The extra blood and tissue leave the body through the vagina.

4. a   5. c

6. b   7. g

8. f   9. d

10. i   11. e

12. h

Enrich

1. A. The head of the sperm cell releases chemicals that allow it to pass through the outer barrier surrounding the egg cell. The sperm cell enters the inner barrier. B. The head of the sperm cell binds to the cell membrane of the egg. C. The head of the sperm is pulled into the egg's cytoplasm. D. The nuclei of the egg and sperm unite.

2. If more than one sperm fertilized the egg, the resulting zygote would have more than the normal number of 46 chromosomes.

3. More than one egg could be fertilized.

4. Only when the nuclei join together does the cell have a full set of chromosomes that contain all of the information needed to produce a new human being.

Lesson Quiz

1. fertilization   2. male reproductive system

3. semen   4. eggs

5. fertilized egg   6. testosterone

7. true   8. true

9. ovary   10. true

Place the outside corner, the corner away from the dotted line, in the corner of your copy machine to copy onto letter-size paper.

Pregnancy and Birth

LESSON

4 **What systems regulate and control body processes?**

Lesson Pacing: 1–2 periods or $\frac{1}{2}$–1 block

🕐 **SHORT ON TIME?** To do this lesson in approximately half the time, do the Activate Prior Knowledge activity followed by a discussion of the Key Concepts to familiarize students with the lesson content. Have students do the Quick Labs. The rest of the lesson can be completed by students independently.

> **Preference Navigator,** in the online Planning tools, allows you to customize *Interactive Science* to your own teaching style. You can also edit lesson plans by selecting the Lesson Planner option.
>
> **Digital Teacher's Edition** allows you to access your Teacher's Edition and Resource materials online.

Lesson Vocabulary

- embryo
- fetus
- amniotic sac
- placenta
- umbilical cord

Content Refresher

Professional Development Note

Early Embryonic Development Successive cell divisions of the zygote (fertilized egg) eventually produce a hollow structure called a blastocyst, which implants in the wall of the uterus. During gastrulation, the next stage of development, the embryo differentiates into three layers. The outermost layer is the ectoderm; the innermost layer is the endoderm; and the middle layer is the mesoderm.

As development proceeds to produce a recognizable embryo, the ectoderm contributes to formation of the skin and nervous system. The mesoderm is the origin of the muscular and skeletal systems, the circulatory system, and other internal organs and structures. The endoderm provides the cells that line the organs of the gastrointestinal system and many of the digestive organs themselves.

LESSON OBJECTIVES

🔑 List the stages of human development that occur before birth.

🔑 Explain how the developing embryo is protected and nourished.

🔑 Describe what happens during childbirth.

Blended Path
Active learning using Student Edition, Inquiry Path, and Digital Path

ENGAGE AND EXPLORE

Teach this lesson using a variety of resources. Begin by reading **My Planet Diary** as a class. Have students discuss why a woman should see an obstetrician when she is pregnant. Then have students do the **Inquiry Warm-Up activity.** Students will model the rate of growth of a human fetus. The **After the Inquiry Warm-Up worksheet** sets up a discussion about the growth rate of the human fetus. Have volunteers share their answers to question 4 giving their interpretations of the data on the graphs showing a fetus's growth in length and mass.

EXPLAIN AND ELABORATE

Teach Key Concepts by explaining the stages of the development of a fetus. **Support the Big Q** by helping students distinguish a zygote, an embryo, and a fetus.

Teach Key Concepts by explaining that the membranes and structures that form in the uterus during pregnancy protect and nourish the developing baby.

Teach Key Concepts by explaining the three stages in the birth of a baby: labor, delivery, and afterbirth.

Hand out the **Key Concept Summaries** as a review of each part of the lesson. Students can also use the online **Vocab Flash Cards** to review key terms.

EVALUATE

Have students take the **Lesson Quiz.** For an alternate assessment, see the **EXAM**VIEW® Assessment Suite, Progress Monitoring Assessments, or SuccessTracker™.

ELL Support

1 Content and Language
Pronounce and define each of the vocabulary terms. Have students write a sentence using the terms *embryo* and *fetus* that explains their relationship to each other. (*An embryo develops into a fetus.*) Repeat with *amniotic sac, placenta,* and *umbilical cord.*

DIFFERENTIATED INSTRUCTION KEY
L1 Struggling Students or Special Needs
L2 On-Level Students **L3** Advanced Students

LESSON PLANNER 13.4

Lab zone Inquiry Path
Hands-on learning in the Lab zone

Digital Path
Online learning at **my science online**.com

ENGAGE AND EXPLORE

To teach this lesson with an emphasis on inquiry, begin with the **Inquiry Warm-Up activity.** Students will model the rate of growth of a human fetus. The **After the Inquiry Warm-Up worksheet** sets up a discussion about the growth rate of the human fetus. Have volunteers share their answers to question 4 giving their interpretations of the data on the graphs showing a fetus's growth in length and mass.

EXPLAIN AND ELABORATE

Focus on the **Inquiry Skill** for the lesson. Remind students that it is vital to calculate accurately in order to find the correct answer to a problem. What calculation could be used in the **Inquiry Warm-Up activity?** *(Sample: A calculation that measures how the fetus grows twice as much during the second half of pregnancy as it did during the first half of pregnancy)* **Support the Big Q** by helping students distinguish a zygote, an embryo, and a fetus.

Have students do the **Quick Lab** to model the function of the amniotic sac in protecting a developing baby.

Do the **Build Inquiry** having students research facts about twins. Have students do the **Quick Lab** to model how a mother's cervix must dilate to allow the fetus to pass through during delivery. Students can use the online **Vocab Flash Cards** to review key terms.

EVALUATE

Have students take the **Lesson Quiz.** For an alternate assessment, see the **EXAM**VIEW® Assessment Suite, Progress Monitoring Assessments, or SuccessTracker™.

ENGAGE AND EXPLORE

Teach this lesson using digital resources. Begin by having students explore real-world connections to pregnancy and birth at **My Planet Diary** online. Have them access the Chapter Resources to find the **Unlock the Big Question activity.** There they can answer the questions and refine their responses as they continue through the lesson. You can re-assign the activity and have students submit their work so you can track their progress.

EXPLAIN AND ELABORATE

Students reading above, at, or below the lexile measure of this lesson can access basic content readings at their level at **My Reading Web.** Encourage students to use the online **Vocab Flash Cards** to preview key terms. **Support the Big Q** by helping students distinguish a zygote, an embryo, and a fetus. Use the **Art in Motion activity** online to show students the stages of prenatal development.

Assign the **Do the Math activity** online and have students submit their work to you. Have students do the **Quick Lab** to model the function of the amniotic sac in protecting a developing baby.

Have students do the **Quick Lab** to model how a mother's cervix must dilate to allow the fetus to pass through during delivery. The **Key Concept Summaries** online allow students to read a summary and see an image associated with each part of the lesson. Online remediation is available at **My Science Coach.**

EVALUATE

Have students take the **Lesson Quiz.** For an alternate assessment, see the **EXAM**VIEW® Assessment Suite, Progress Monitoring Assessments, or SuccessTracker™.

2 Frontload the Lesson
Have students survey the visuals in the lesson. Then have them write questions they have about the lesson based on their surveys. After students read the lesson, have them answer the questions they wrote at the start of the lesson.

3 Comprehensible Input
Have the students rewrite the lesson objectives as questions. Then ask them to write answers to the questions. Challenge them to use each of the vocabulary terms for the lesson in their answers.

4 Language Production
Pair or group students with varied language abilities to complete labs collaboratively for language practice. Have each student copy the completed written lab for personal reference.

5 Assess Understanding
Divide the class into small groups. Have each student identify a key concept from the lesson to discuss in his or her group. After the discussions, have students talk about the Key Concepts as a group.

Pregnancy and Birth

Establish Learning Objectives

After this lesson, students will be able to:

🔑 List the stages of human development that occur before birth.

🔑 Explain how the developing embryo is protected and nourished.

🔑 Describe what happens during childbirth.

Engage

Activate Prior Knowledge

MY PLANET DIARY Read *Obstetrician* with the class. Explain that an obstetrician's job is not done after a baby is born. Post-natal care of the mother is as important as care for the newborn infant. Ask: **Given that pediatricians are physicians who specialize in children's health, how do you think an obstetrician's focus shifts after the birth of a baby?** *(Before birth, an obstetrician focuses on the baby and the mother, and after birth that focus shifts to the mother.)*

BIG IDEAS OF SCIENCE REFERENCE LIBRARY 📖
Have students look up the following topics: Pregnancy, Twins.

Explore

Lab Resource: Inquiry Warm-Up 🧪

L2 **PRENATAL GROWTH** Students will model the rate of growth of a human fetus.

Pregnancy and Birth

🔑 **What Happens Before Birth?**

🔑 **How Is the Embryo Protected and Nourished?**

🔑 **What Happens During Childbirth?**

my planet diary

Obstetrician

Some doctors specialize in caring for women during pregnancy. These doctors are called obstetricians. Obstetricians care for pregnant women, deliver babies, and make sure the mothers and new babies are healthy in the days that follow childbirth.

If you are interested in becoming an obstetrician, plan on spending at least ten years in school and training after you graduate high school. During this time you will learn how to care for mothers during pregnancy, childbirth, and after delivery. You will also learn about the serious conditions that babies may be born with. This career can be rewarding, even though it takes a lot of time and effort to get there.

CAREER

Answer the questions below.

1. What are two responsibilities of an obstetrician?

   Sample: They care for pregnant women and deliver babies.

2. Why do you think a woman should see an obstetrician when she is pregnant?

   Sample: Obstetricians are experts at treating pregnant women.

> **PLANET DIARY** Go to **Planet Diary** to learn more about pregnancy and birth.

 Lab Do the Inquiry Warm-Up *Prenatal Growth*.

What Happens Before Birth?

When sperm are deposited into the vagina, they swim into and through the uterus and enter the Fallopian tubes. An egg can be fertilized in the Fallopian tubes during the first few days after ovulation. If a sperm fertilizes an egg, pregnancy can occur. The fertilized egg is called a zygote. 🔑 **Before birth, the zygote develops first into an embryo and then into a fetus.**

SUPPORT ALL READERS
Lexile Measure = 890L   Lexile Word Count = 1005

Prior Exposure to Content: Many students may have misconceptions on this topic

Academic Vocabulary: *calculate, compare, contrast*

Science Vocabulary: *embryo, fetus, amniotic sac, placenta, umbilical cord*

Concept Level: Generally appropriate for most students in this grade

Preteach With: My Planet Diary "Obstetrician" and Figure 2 activity

Go to **My Reading Web** to access leveled readings that provide a foundation for the content.

my science online.com

Vocabulary
- embryo • fetus • amniotic sac
- placenta • umbilical cord

Skills
- Reading: Compare and Contrast
- Inquiry: Calculate

Zygote and Embryo After fertilization, the zygote divides into two cells. These cells continue to divide as they travel toward the uterus. They form a hollow ball of more than one hundred cells by the time they reach the uterus. The ball attaches to the lining of the uterus. From the two-cell stage through the eighth week, a developing human is called an **embryo** (EM bree oh).

Fetus From the end of the eighth week until birth, a developing human is called a **fetus** (FEE tus). The internal organs that began to form in the embryo, such as the brain, continue to develop and start to function. The eyes, ears, and nose also develop, as you can see in **Figure 1**. The heart becomes large enough that a doctor can use a tool to hear it beat. The fetus begins to move and kick.

FIGURE 1 ....

 **Development of the Fetus**
An embryo develops into a fetus. Note: These photos do not show the actual sizes.

✎ Interpret Photos In each box, describe the body parts of the embryo and fetus that you can see.

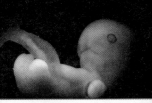

6-Week Embryo
Sample: It has the beginnings of eyes, arms, and legs.

24-Week Fetus
Sample: It has eyelids, a nose, a mouth, fingers, and toes.

Lab zone® Do the Quick Lab *Way to Grow!*

🔒 **Assess Your Understanding**

got it? ....

○ I get it! Now I know that before birth _humans grow from a zygote to an embryo and then to a fetus._

○ I need extra help with _See TE note._

Go to MY SCIENCE COACH online for help with this subject.

533

---

1 Content and Language
Write *umbilical cord* on the board. Explain that a *cord* is a long, slender, flexible material that may connect two things. Point out an *umbilical cord* connects a mother and her fetus. *Umbilical* is the adjective of the word *umbilicus,* which is Latin for "navel."

2 Frontload the Lesson
Ask students how much time elapses between the egg fertilization and the birth of a baby. Explain that a typical pregnancy lasts nine months.

3 Comprehensible Input
Urge students to create graphic devices that relate topics in the lesson. Students can make a timeline from fertilization to afterbirth, a flow chart of labor and delivery, or a T-chart with names and functions of structures that protect and nourish an embryo.

Explain

Introduce Vocabulary
To understand the term *amniotic sac,* focus on the spelling of *sac.* The word *sac* refers to a pouch that is part of an animal or plant and contains a fluid.

Teach Key Concepts 🗝
Review the path the zygote takes from the Fallopian tubes to the uterus. Ask: **What happens to the zygote as it travels toward the uterus?** *(Its cells divide many times and form a hollow ball of more than one hundred cells, becoming an embryo.)* **How long is this stage?** *(From the two-cell stage until the eighth week.)* **How long is the next development stage and what is the developing human called during this period?** *(From the end of the eighth week until birth, a fetus)*

Support the Big Q ❓ UbD
ZYGOTE, EMBRYO, FETUS Help students understand details that distinguish a zygote, embryo, and fetus. Ask: **How many cells form the zygote?** *(One)* **What begins to form in the embryo?** *(Internal organs such as the brain)* **What development occurs for the fetus?** *(The brain, the eyes, ears, and nose develop; the heart beats; the fetus begins to move.)*

Elaborate

Lab Resource: Quick Lab
L2 WAY TO GROW! Students will use a balance to model the average mass of a developing baby.

Evaluate

Assess Your Understanding
Have students evaluate their understanding by completing the appropriate sentence.

RTI Response to Intervention
If students need help identifying what happens to a developing human before birth, **then** have them review the paragraphs above.

MY SCIENCE COACH Have students go online for help in understanding a developing human.

My Planet Diary provides an opportunity for students to explore real-world connections to pregnancy and birth.

Art in Motion shows prenatal development.

my science online | Development Before Birth

Explain

Teach Key Concepts 🔑

Explain to students that the membranes and structures that form in the uterus during pregnancy protect and nourish the developing baby. Refer students to **Figure 2,** and ask them to locate the amniotic sac. Ask: **What is the function of the amniotic sac?** *(To cushion and protect the embryo)* Explain that the figure includes an enlargement that shows details of the placenta. Ask: **Is the embryo connected directly to a part of the mother's reproductive system?** *(No; it is connected to the placenta.)* Point out that separate blood vessels carry wastes from and nutrients to the developing baby. Ask: **What structure contains these blood vessels?** *(The umbilical cord)* **Why is it so important for a pregnant woman to keep herself healthy, for example, by following a healthy diet?** *(The developing baby relies completely on its mother for all its protection and nourishment.)*

🔄 **Compare and Contrast** Remind students that when they compare and contrast, they examine the similarities and differences between things.

Elaborate

21st Century Learning

CRITICAL THINKING Remind students that diffusion is a process in which particles move from an area of high concentration to an area of low concentration. Because the embryo's blood has a higher concentration of carbon dioxide than the mother's blood does, the carbon dioxide diffuses from the embryo to the mother. Point out that one example of a nutrient in the mother's blood is glucose. Challenge a volunteer to describe the relative concentrations of glucose in the mother's blood and in the embryo's blood that cause this nutrient to diffuse from the mother to the embryo.

21st Century Learning

INTERPERSONAL SKILLS As students read this lesson, tell them to think about the sequence of events in prenatal development. Students should look for key words such as *first, next, then,* and *finally.* At the end of the lesson, ask students to identify the major events involved in the human life cycle. Have students work in pairs to create a flowchart using boxes to represent the sequence of events. Have students fill in each box with one event.

How Is the Embryo Protected and Nourished?

Soon after the embryo attaches to the uterus, new membranes and structures form. 🔑 **The membranes and structures that form in the uterus during pregnancy protect and nourish the developing baby.**

Membranes **Figure 2** shows the two membranes that form during development. The **amniotic sac** (am NEE aht ik) <u>surrounds the embryo and is filled with fluid. The fluid cushions and protects the embryo and later the fetus.</u>

Another membrane helps form the **placenta** (pluh SEN tuh), which <u>links the embryo and the mother.</u> In the placenta, the embryo's blood vessels are next to the mother's blood vessels. Their blood does not mix, but <u>substances are exchanged</u> from one bloodstream to the other. The embryo's carbon dioxide and other wastes diffuse to the mother. Nutrients and oxygen diffuse from the mother to the embryo. In addition, drugs, alcohol, and chemicals in tobacco can diffuse from the mother to the embryo and cause it harm. Some effects on the development of the child are immediate. Others may not appear for many years.

✏️ **Compare and Contrast**
In the paragraphs, underline how the amniotic sac and placenta are different. Then write how they are alike below.

<u>Both are formed from</u>
<u>membranes.</u>

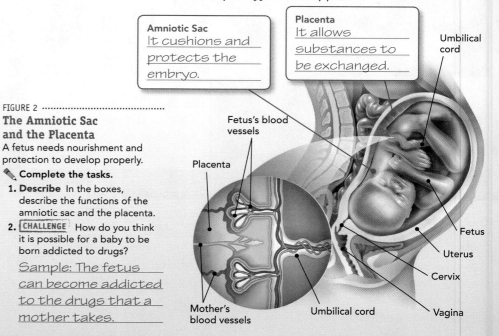

Amniotic Sac
<u>It cushions and</u>
<u>protects the</u>
<u>embryo.</u>

Placenta
<u>It allows</u>
<u>substances to</u>
<u>be exchanged.</u>

Umbilical cord

Fetus's blood vessels

Placenta

Fetus

Uterus

Cervix

Vagina

Mother's blood vessels

Umbilical cord

FIGURE 2 ·····················

The Amniotic Sac and the Placenta
A fetus needs nourishment and protection to develop properly.

✏️ **Complete the tasks.**

1. **Describe** In the boxes, describe the functions of the amniotic sac and the placenta.

2. **CHALLENGE** How do you think it is possible for a baby to be born addicted to drugs?
   <u>Sample: The fetus</u>
   <u>can become addicted</u>
   <u>to the drugs that a</u>
   <u>mother takes.</u>

534 Controlling Body Processes

Digital Lesson: Assign the *Do the Math* activity online and have students submit their work to you.

my science online.com ▶ **Protection and Nourishment**

Structures

A ropelike structure, called the **umbilical cord,** begins to form between the embryo and the placenta. It contains blood vessels from the embryo that link the embryo to the placenta.

Umbilical cord

do the math!

A pregnancy is often divided into three stages called trimesters. Each trimester is three months.

① Interpret Tables How much mass does a developing fetus gain during each trimester?

First Trimester _It gains 26 grams._

Second Trimester _It gains 614 grams. (640 – 26)_

Third Trimester _It gains 2,560 grams. (3,200 – 640)_

② ▲ Calculate To find the percentage mass increase in a trimester, divide the mass gained in the trimester by the mass at the start of the trimester. Then multiply by 100. The percentage mass increase for the second trimester is as follows: (614 ÷ 26) x 100 = about 2,361 percent.

Find the percentage mass increase for the third trimester.

_(2560 ÷ 640) x 100 = 400%_

Change in Mass of a Developing Baby	
Month of Pregnancy	Mass (grams)
1	0.02
2	2
3	26
4	150
5	460
6	640
7	1,500
8	2,300
9	3,200

Lab zone Do the Quick Lab *Egg-cellent Protection.*

🔑 Assess Your Understanding

1a. Explain What substances pass from the embryo or fetus to the mother?

The embryo or fetus passes carbon dioxide and wastes to the mother.

b. Relate Cause and Effect Why is it dangerous for a pregnant woman to drink alcohol?

Alcohol can pass through the placenta to the embryo or fetus and cause it harm.

got it? ·······················

○ **I get it!** Now I know that an embryo or fetus is protected and nourished by _membranes and structures that form during development._

○ **I need extra help with** _See TE note._

Go to my science ⬤ COACH *online for help with this subject.*

535

Do the Math!

L1 Remind students that data tables present a great deal of information in a clear, orderly way. Urge students to look at the table's title, as well as the labels of each vertical column and the numerals that form the table's nine rows. Ask: **Which rows make up the first trimester of a pregnancy?** *(The first three rows)* **Which rows make up the second trimester?** *(Rows 4, 5, and 6)* **Which rows make up the third trimester?** *(Rows 7, 8, and 9)*

▲ **Calculate** Help students understand that it is vital to calculate accurately in order to find the percent that the baby's mass increases in a trimester.

See the *Math Skill and Problem-Solving Activities* for support.

Lab Resource: Quick Lab

L2 **EGG-CELLENT PROTECTION** Students will model the function of the amniotic sac in protecting a developing baby.

Evaluate

Assess Your Understanding

After students answer the questions, have them evaluate their understanding by completing the appropriate sentence.

R T I Response to Intervention

1a. If students have trouble identifying what substances pass from the embryo to the mother, **then** have them review the second paragraph under the heading *Membranes.*

b. If students need help explaining the danger of a pregnant woman drinking alcohol, **then** remind students that drugs, alcohol, and chemicals can be transferred to the developing baby through the placenta.

my science ⬤ COACH Have students go online for help in understanding how an embryo is protected and nourished.

Differentiated Instruction

L1 **Pregnancy Timeline** Suggest that a small group of students create a timeline to show the span of a nine-month pregnancy. Encourage students to annotate the timeline with typical events during the development of the embryo and fetus, such as the formation of the amniotic sac and placenta, the growth and functioning of certain organs, increases in mass, and so on. Students can display their completed timelines in the classroom for reference as study of the chapter continues.

L3 **Identification of Gender** Have students do research to learn how and when during a pregnancy that an obstetrician can determine whether a developing baby is male or female.

Explain

Teach Key Concepts

Explain to students that the birth of a baby takes place in three stages: labor, delivery, and afterbirth. Ask: **What is the desired result of labor?** *(The cervix opening enough to allow the baby to fit through)* **What causes the baby to be pushed out of the mother's body?** *(Muscle contractions)* **What happens during delivery?** *(The mother pushes the baby out of the uterus through the cervix and vagina.)* **What is afterbirth?** *(The stage of childbirth in which the placenta and empty amniotic sac are pushed out of the uterus by muscle contractions)* **Why do you think a baby's body organs are fully developed before birth under normal circumstances?** *(Sample: The baby must be able to breathe and take in food on its own immediately after birth.)* **When is the baby no longer directly dependent on the mother?** *(After delivery, the baby is no longer in the uterus and the umbilical cord is cut. The baby can live on its own without the direct connection to the mother.)*

Teach With Visuals

Tell students to look at **Figure 4.** Point out that there are differences between identical twins and fraternal twins. Ask: **How many sperm cells and how many egg cells are needed to form identical twins?** *(One sperm cell and one egg cell)* **How are two embryos formed from one egg cell?** *(The cell splits in two.)* Point out that the two resulting cells have the same chromosomes. Ask: **When fraternal twins are formed, how many sperm cells and how many egg cells are needed to form the eggs?** *(Two sperm cells and two egg cells)* Explain that in the case of fraternal twins, the chromosomes each zygote receives are different from one another. Tell students that an increasing number of multiple births are the result of treatments for fertility, including in-vitro fertilization and drugs that cause the ovaries to release several mature eggs at once.

Address Misconceptions

L1 RELATIVE LENGTHS OF STAGES OF CHILDBIRTH
Some students may have indistinct ideas about the three distinct stages of childbirth. For example, students may be under the mistaken impression that the "pushing" stage when the mother actually delivers the baby constitutes the longest part of childbirth. Make sure that students understand that in most cases, the duration of labor far exceeds the duration of delivery and of afterbirth. Ask: **In normal circumstances, which is the longest stage of childbirth, and which is the shortest stage of childbirth?** *(Usually labor is the longest and afterbirth is the shortest stage of childbirth.)*

What Happens During Childbirth?

After about nine months of development inside a uterus, a baby is ready to be born. **The birth of a baby takes place in three stages: labor, delivery, and afterbirth.**

Labor Labor is the first stage of birth. Strong muscle contractions of the uterus cause the cervix to open. Eventually, the opening is large enough for the baby to fit through. Labor may last from about two hours to more than 20 hours.

Delivery and Afterbirth The second stage of birth is called delivery. During a normal delivery the baby is pushed out of the uterus through the vagina. The head usually comes out first. Delivery can last several minutes to an hour or so. Shortly after delivery, the umbilical cord is cut about five centimeters from the baby's abdomen, as you can see in **Figure 3**. Seven to ten days later, the rest of the umbilical cord, which is now dried, falls off. It leaves a scar called the navel, or bellybutton.

Soon after delivery, muscles in the uterus contract, pushing the placenta and empty amniotic sac out through the vagina. This last stage, called afterbirth, usually takes less than an hour.

FIGURE 3 ·······································
Birth
Contractions in the uterus signal the start of labor.

✎ **Sequence** In the boxes below, describe the events in each stage of birth.

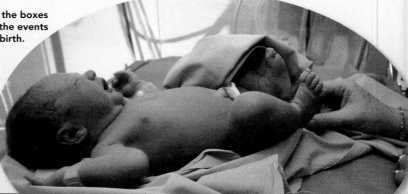

Labor	Delivery	Afterbirth
Contractions cause the cervix to open.	The baby is pushed out of the mother's body.	The placenta and amniotic sac are pushed out of the mother's body

Birth and the Baby During birth, pressure caused by the muscle contractions briefly decreases the baby's oxygen supply. In response, the baby's endocrine system releases adrenaline, which increases the baby's heart rate. Seconds after delivery, the baby cries and begins breathing. The newborn's heart rate then slows down.

Multiple Births The delivery of more than one baby from a single pregnancy is called a multiple birth. Twin births are the most common multiple births. There are two types of twins: identical and fraternal. **Figure 4** shows how both types develop.

FIGURE 4 ····································
Multiple Births
Other multiple births, such as triplets, can also be fraternal or identical.

✏️ **Interpret Diagrams** Explain on the notebook paper why fraternal twins can be different sexes and identical twins cannot.

Identical Twins
A sperm fertilizes a single egg.

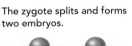

The zygote splits and forms two embryos.

Fraternal Twins
Two sperm fertilize two eggs.

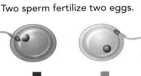

Each zygote forms an embryo.

Identical twins form from the same egg and sperm, so they must be the same sex. Fraternal twins develop from two different eggs that were fertilized by different sperm. So their sex can be different.

Lab zone® Do the Quick Lab *Labor and Delivery.*

🔑 **Assess Your Understanding**

2a. Name During labor, contractions cause the _cervix_ to open.

b. Apply Concepts Why must a baby start breathing right after birth?

It no longer gets oxygen from its mother.

got it?

○ I get it! Now I know that childbirth involves _labor, delivery, and afterbirth._

○ I need extra help with _See TE note._

Go to **my science** ⑤ **COACH** online for help with this subject.

537

Elaborate ──────────

Build Inquiry Lab zone

L2 FACTS ABOUT TWINS

Materials up-to-date reference books or reliable Internet resources, index cards

Time 25 minutes

Brainstorm a list of students' ideas about twins, and write them on the board. Give each student an index card. Ask students to write one question about twins that they would like to have answered. Examples may include: **How often are conjoined twins born? Are there any differences between identical twins? Do twins run in families?** Have students work together in small groups to find the answers to their questions. Groups can present their findings to the whole class. Have students prepare a "Facts About Twins" bulletin board display, or exhibit their findings in a hallway for other students to see.

Lab Resource: Quick Lab Lab zone

L1 LABOR AND DELIVERY Students will model how a mother's cervix must dilate to allow the fetus to pass through during delivery.

Evaluate ──────────

Assess Your Understanding

After students answer the questions, have them evaluate their understanding by completing the appropriate sentence.

RTI Response to Intervention

2a. If students have trouble identifying the cervix, **then** ask them to reread the paragraph under the heading *Labor.*

b. If students need help explaining the need for a baby to start breathing right after birth, **then** urge them to contrast the baby's source of oxygen before birth with its needs after birth.

my science ⑤ **COACH** Have students go online for help in understanding childbirth.

Differentiated Instruction

L1 Science Glossary To enrich students' understanding of childbirth, discuss with them the multiple meanings of the words *labor* and *delivery.*

L3 Oral Histories About Childbirth Challenge students to prepare a series of questions to ask one or more adult females they know well. Encourage students to draft some questions that have to do with a person's memories and impressions of the overall experience of childbirth, as well as some other questions intended to elicit specific information about labor, delivery, and the first moments of the newborn baby's life. Remind students that a mother's experience of childbirth is intense and personal, and some women may choose not to describe their experiences in detail. Invite students to relate each person's childbirth story in a short nonfiction narrative.

Lab zone   **After the Inquiry Warm-Up**

Pregnancy and Birth

Inquiry Warm-Up, *Prenatal Growth*

In the Inquiry Warm-Up, you investigated the growth rate of the human fetus. Using what you learned from that activity, answer the questions below.

1. **CALCULATE** Using the length measurements, how much growth occurs in the first 20 weeks? In the second 20 weeks? In the period in which the fetus grows more, how many times greater is the fetus's growth?

   _____

   _____

2. **GRAPH** Using the length measurements, create a graph of the fetus's development, with length on the *y*-axis and time on the *x*-axis.

3. **GRAPH** Using the mass measurements, create a graph of the fetus's development, with mass on the *y*-axis and time on the *x*-axis.

4. **INTERPRET DATA** Describe the shape of each graph. What do these graphs indicate about a fetus's development?

   _____

   _____

Assess Your Understanding

Pregnancy and Birth

What Happens Before Birth?

got it? ···

○ **I get it!** Now I know that before birth _____

_____

○ **I need extra help with** _____

_____

How Is the Embryo Protected and Nourished?

1a. **EXPLAIN** What substances pass from the embryo or fetus to the
mother?

_____

_____

b. **RELATE CAUSE AND EFFECT** Why is it dangerous for a pregnant woman
to drink alcohol?

_____

_____

got it? ···

○ **I get it!** Now I know that an embryo or fetus is protected and nourished by _____

_____

○ **I need extra help with** _____

_____

Pregnancy and Birth

What Happens During Childbirth?

2a. **NAME** During labor, contractions cause the _____ to open.

b. **APPLY CONCEPTS** Why must a baby start breathing right after birth?

_____

got_{it?}···

○ **I get it!** Now I know that childbirth involves _____

_____

○ **I need extra help with** _____

_____

Place the outside corner, the corner away from the dotted line, in the corner of your copy machine to copy onto letter-size paper.

Key Concept Summaries

Pregnancy and Birth

What Happens Before Birth?

If a sperm fertilizes an egg, pregnancy can occur. The fertilized egg is called a zygote. **Before birth, the zygote develops first into an embryo and then into a fetus.** After fertilization, the zygote divides into two cells. These cells continue to divide, eventually forming a hollow ball of over one hundred cells that attaches to the wall of the uterus. From the two-cell stage through its eighth week, a developing human is called an **embryo.** From the end of the eighth week until birth, a developing human is called a **fetus.** Internal organs that began to form in the embryo, such as the brain, develop and start to function; the eyes, ears, and nose develop; the heart grows; and the fetus begins to move and kick.

How Is the Embryo Protected and Nourished?

After the embryo attaches to the uterus, new membranes and structures form. **The membranes and structures that form in the uterus during pregnancy protect and nourish the developing baby.** The **amniotic sac** surrounds the embryo and is filled with fluid that cushions and protects the developing baby. Another membrane helps to form the **placenta,** which links the embryo and the mother. In the placenta, the embryo's blood vessels are next to the mother's blood vessels, and substances are exchanged from one bloodstream to the other. A ropelike structure, called the **umbilical cord,** begins to form between the embryo and the placenta.

What Happens During Childbirth?

After about nine months of development inside a uterus, a baby is ready to be born. **The birth of a baby takes place in three stages: labor, delivery, and afterbirth.** During labor, strong muscle contractions cause the cervix to open enough for the baby to emerge. During normal delivery, the baby is pushed out of the uterus through the vagina. Shortly, the umbilical cord is clamped and cut, leaving a scar called the navel. During the last stage of childbirth, muscle contractions of the uterus push the placenta and empty amniotic sac—the afterbirth—out of the uterus through the vagina. Seconds after delivery, the baby cries and begins breathing. The delivery of more than one baby from a single pregnancy is called a multiple birth. Twin births are the most common multiple births.

On a separate sheet of paper, give a summary of the development of a human being from zygote to the period just before childbirth.

Review and Reinforce

Pregnancy and Birth

Understanding Main Ideas
Answer the following questions on a separate sheet of paper.

1. What is the term for a fertilized egg?
2. What is the name of the first stage of birth, and what happens during this stage?
3. What is the name of the second stage of birth, and what happens during this stage?
4. What is the name of the third stage of birth, and what happens during this stage?
5. How is the development of identical twins and fraternal twins different?

Building Vocabulary
Match each term with its definition by writing the letter of the correct definition in the right column on the line beside the term in the left column.

6. ___ embryo

7. ___ fetus

8. ___ amniotic sac

9. ___ placenta

10. ___ umbilical cord

a. a developing human between the eighth week and birth

b. a ropelike structure that connects the embryo and placenta

c. a fluid-filled structure that surrounds the embryo and protects the developing baby

d. a developing human between the two-cell stage and its eighth week

e. a membrane containing blood vessels that links the embryo and the mother and allows the exchange of substances between them

Enrich

Pregnancy and Birth

> When more than one fetus is carried to term in a single pregnancy, a multiple birth occurs. The most common multiple birth is that of twins. Read the passage below. Then answer the questions that follow on a separate sheet of paper.

Twins! Double the Fun!

Twins can be identical or fraternal. It is thought that genetics may influence the birth of fraternal twins. Factors that influence these births are the number of eggs a woman releases at one time, a woman's age at pregnancy (over 35 or 40), and fertilization treatments. When two different eggs are fertilized by two different sperm, fraternal twins result. Fraternal twins are more common than identical twins. About two-thirds of the twins born are fraternal.

The birth of identical twins is usually not considered to be genetic. Identical twins develop when a single egg splits. Depending on when the split occurs, the twins develop one or two placentas. If the twins share a placenta, they are identical. If not, they are fraternal. Identical twins share a placenta, are the same sex, and have the same blood type.

Sometimes it can be confusing to determine whether twins are fraternal or identical. DNA tests can answer the question. Looks alone cannot answer the question.

1. What are the two types of twins? How do they differ?
2. A boy twin and a girl twin are born. How can you tell if they are identical or fraternal?
3. Two girl twins are born. How can you tell if they are identical or fraternal?
4. At a Twins Convention, there were 450 pairs of twins. How many were likely to be fraternal?

Lesson Quiz

Pregnancy and Birth

If the statement is true, write *true*. If the statement is false, change the underlined word or words to make the statement true.

1. _____ An egg can be fertilized by a sperm <u>during</u> ovulation.

2. _____ In the <u>placenta</u>, substances are exchanged between the embryo's bloodstream to the mother's bloodstream.

3. _____ The last stage of childbirth is <u>delivery</u>.

4. _____ During normal delivery, the baby is pushed out of the mother's body through the <u>uterus</u>.

5. _____ <u>One or two minutes</u> after delivery, the baby cries and begins breathing.

Fill in the blank to complete each statement.

6. Before birth, the _____ develops first into an embryo and then into a fetus.

7. The membranes and structures that form in the _____ during pregnancy protect and nourish the developing baby.

8. From the end of the eighth week until birth, a developing human is called a(n) _____.

9. The delivery of more than one baby from a single pregnancy is called a(n) _____.

10. Identical and _____ are the two types of twins.

Pregnancy and Birth

Answer Key

After the Inquiry Warm-Up

1. 15 cm; 33 cm; more than 2 times as much

2. Students graphs should curve up and to the right with points plotted at (12, 8), (20, 15), (28, 38), (36, 41), and (40, 48).

3. Students graphs should curve up and to the right. All mass should be converted to the same units to make graphing easier. If students used grams, the points should be plotted approximately at (12, 21), (20, 255), (28, 1000), (36, 2800), and (40, 3400). If students used kilograms, the points should be plotted approximately at (12, 0.02), (20, 0.25), (28, 1), (36, 2.8), and (40, 3.4).

4. Both graphs curve up and to the right. This indicates that the fetus develops more rapidly in the second half of pregnancy.

Key Concept Summaries

The cells in a zygote divide and form a hollow ball of over one hundred cells that attaches to the wall of the uterus. During the first eight weeks after fertilization, a developing human is called an embryo, and its internal organs begin to form. After the eighth week until birth, a developing human is called a fetus, and organs develop and start to function, and the fetus begins to move and kick. The amniotic sac and placenta grow in the mother's body to protect and nourish the developing baby until childbirth.

Review and Reinforce

1. zygote

2. During labor, muscle contractions of the uterus cause the cervix to enlarge so that the baby can fit through the opening.

3. During delivery, the baby is pushed completely out of the uterus, through the vagina, and out of the body.

4. During afterbirth, contractions push the placenta and other membranes out of the uterus through the vagina.

5. Identical twins are formed from a single zygote. Fraternal twins are formed when two different eggs are fertilized by two different sperm.

6. d
7. a
8. c
9. e
10. b

Enrich

1. fraternal, identical; Identical twins share a placenta, the same sex, and the same blood type. Fraternal twins have their own placentas, may or may not be the same sex, and do not need to have the same blood type.

2. Easily, since they do not share the same sex they are fraternal.

3. Since they share the same sex, it is more difficult to determine. A DNA test can give a definite answer.

4. Since two-thirds of twins in general are fraternal, a good estimate is $\frac{2}{3} \times 450 = 300$. About 300 pairs should be fraternal.

Lesson Quiz

1. after
2. true
3. afterbirth
4. vagina
5. Seconds
6. zygote
7. uterus
8. fetus
9. multiple birth
10. fraternal

Study Guide

Review the Big Q UbD

Have students complete the statement at the top of the page. These Key Concepts support their understanding of the chapter's Big Question. Have students return to the chapter opener pages. What is different about how students view the images of athletes reacting now that they have completed the chapter? Thinking about this will help them prepare for the *Apply the Big Q* activity in the Review and Assessment.

Partner Review

Have partners review definitions of vocabulary terms by using the Study Guide to quiz each other. Students could read the Key Concept statements and leave out words for their partner to fill in, or change a statement so that it is false and then ask their partner to correct it.

Class Activity: Concept Map

Have students develop a concept map to show how the information in this chapter is related. Encourage students to brainstorm together to identify Key Concepts, vocabulary, definitions, examples, and important details from each of the four lessons. Suggest that students write pieces of information on self-sticking notes and attach them on poster board, paper, or the board at random. Point out that students can use these notes as they develop a concept map that starts at the top with the chapter's Key Concepts. Ask students to use the following questions to help them organize the information on their sticky notes:

• How does the endocrine system function?
• What controls hormone levels?
• How does the reproductive system work?
• What happens during the menstrual cycle?
• What happens before birth?
• How is the embryo protected and nourished?
• What happens during childbirth?
• What changes occur from infancy to adulthood?

My Science Coach allows students to complete the *Practice Test* online.

The Big Question allows students to complete the *Apply the Big Q* activity about the changes that occur in a human body over a lifetime.

Vocab Flash Cards offer a way to review the chapter vocabulary words.

my science online.com ▸ **Endocrine System & Reproduction**

---

13 Study Guide

REVIEW THE BIG ?

My <u>nervous</u> and <u>endocrine</u> systems help regulate and control my body processes.

LESSON 1 The Nervous System

🔑 Your nervous system receives information about what is happening both inside and outside your body. It directs how your body responds to this information and helps maintain homeostasis.

🔑 Neurons carry nerve impulses throughout the body. The brain is the control center of the central nervous system. The spinal cord links the brain to the peripheral nervous system.

🔑 Your eyes, ears, nose, mouth, and skin are specialized sense organs that enable you to get information from the outside world.

Vocabulary
• neuron • nerve impulse • nerve • synapse • central nervous system
• peripheral nervous system • reflex

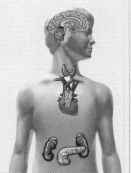

LESSON 2 The Endocrine System

🔑 The endocrine system regulates short-term and long-term activities by sending chemicals throughout the body. Long-term changes include growth and development.

🔑 When the amount of a hormone in the blood reaches a certain level, the endocrine system sends signals that stop the release of that hormone.

Vocabulary
• gland • duct • hormone • target cell • hypothalamus
• pituitary gland • negative feedback

LESSON 3 The Male and Female Reproductive Systems

🔑 The male reproductive system produces sperm and testosterone. The female reproductive system produces eggs and estrogen. It also nourishes a developing baby until birth.

Vocabulary
• fertilization • egg • sperm • zygote
• testes • testosterone • scrotum • semen
• penis • ovary • estrogen • Fallopian tube
• uterus • vagina • menstrual cycle
• menstruation • ovulation

LESSON 4 Pregnancy and Birth

🔑 Before birth, the zygote develops first into an embryo and then into a fetus.

🔑 The membranes and structures that form in the uterus during pregnancy protect and nourish the developing baby.

🔑 The birth of a baby takes place in three stages: labor, delivery, and afterbirth.

Vocabulary
• embryo • fetus • amniotic sac
• placenta • umbilical cord

ELL Support

4 Language Production

Divide the students into four groups. Each group will present an oral report that summarizes the information in one of the four lessons. Each group's report should incorporate the Key Concepts for the lesson, use relevant vocabulary terms, and rely on visual aids. Have students verbalize their understanding of the lesson before they begin to write their reports.

Beginning

LOW/HIGH Allow students to work on the visual aids for the oral report. Encourage them to label and caption.

Intermediate

LOW/HIGH Have students present the oral reports to the class.

Advanced

LOW/HIGH Have students act as recorders for their groups when planning the reports.

Review and Assessment

LESSON 1 The Nervous System

1. Which structure links the brain and the peripheral nervous system?

a. the cerebrum   b. the cerebellum

c. the cochlea   **d.** the spinal cord

2. The senses of _taste_ and _smell_ depend on chemicals in the air and food. The sense of _sight_ depends on the stimulus of light. The sense of _hearing_ depends on the stimulus of sound. The sense of _touch_ is found in all areas of your skin.

3. Make Generalizations How does the nervous system help maintain homeostasis?

It directs your body to respond properly to the information it receives.

4. Draw Conclusions What is the result if the spinal cord is cut?

Sample: Impulses cannot pass through the axons in the spinal cord.

5. Apply Concepts As a man walks barefoot along the beach, he steps on a sharp shell. His foot automatically jerks upward, even before he feels pain. What process is this an example of? How does it help protect the man?

It is an example of a reflex. The reflex action quickly protects the man from doing any more harm to himself.

6. [Write About It] The cerebrum, the cerebellum, and the brain stem are regions of the brain that carry out specific functions. Write a brief job description for each of these regions of the brain.

See TE rubric.

LESSON 2 The Endocrine System

7. The structure that links the nervous system and the endocrine system is the

a. thyroid gland.   b. umbilical cord.

c. target cell.   **d.** hypothalamus.

8. _Target cells_ recognize a hormone's chemical structure.

9. Make Generalizations What is the endocrine system's role?

The endocrine system produces hormones that regulate many body activities and changes such as growth.

10. Infer Study the diagram below. Then suggest how the hormones glucagon and insulin might work together to maintain homeostasis in a healthy person.

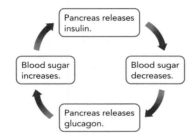

Sample: These hormones regulate the body's blood sugar level. Glucagon increases the blood sugar level, and insulin decreases the blood sugar level.

539

Review and Assessment

Assess Understanding

Have students complete the answers to the Review and Assessment questions. Have a class discussion about what students find confusing. Write Key Concepts on the board to reinforce knowledge.

RTI Response to Intervention

3. If students have difficulty explaining the role of the nervous system in maintaining homeostasis, **then** have them recall what happens when their blood glucose level drops.

10. If students have trouble explaining how glucagon and insulin might maintain homeostasis, **then** have students review the concept of negative feedback under the blue heading _What Controls Hormone Levels?_

Alternate Assessment

L1 DESIGN A GAME Have students work in pairs or small groups to design a game about the human life cycle. Students can design a board game that requires players to answer trivia questions in order to advance. Remind students to create rules, spinners, game pieces, and questions for their games. The questions for the game should include vocabulary terms and Key Concepts from the chapter. Students can exchange games with or play their own game against other groups or pairs.

CHAPTER 13

| Write About It | Assess student's writing using this rubric. |

SCORING RUBRIC	SCORE 4	SCORE 3	SCORE 2	SCORE 1
Write job descriptions of three parts of brain	Skillfully uses job description format	Uses job description format	Uses job description format but not consistently	Does not use job description format
Identify the function of each part of the brain	Accurately explains function of all parts	Accurately explains functions of two of parts	Accurately explains function of one part	Fails to explain function of any parts

RTI Response to Intervention

14. If students need help recalling details of the menstrual cycle, **then** encourage them to study the details shown in **Figure 6.**

19. If students need help sequencing the stages of development, **then** encourage them to review the images in **Figure 1.**

Apply the Big Q ? UbD

TRANSFER Students should be able to demonstrate understanding of changes that occur in the human body over a lifetime by answering this question. See the scoring rubric below.

Do the Math!

16. Ovulation will occur on the 7th day of a 21-day cycle and on the 21st day of a 35-day cycle.

Connect to the Big Idea ? UbD

BIG IDEA Life can be organized in a functional and structural hierarchy. Life is maintained by various physiological functions essential for growth, reproduction, and homeostasis.

If all chapters have been completed, send students to the Big Questions pages at the end of the unit.

L3 WRITING IN SCIENCE Ask students to write an article for a science magazine that explains to readers how the human body changes over a lifetime.

LESSON 3 The Male and Female Reproductive Systems

11. The release of an egg from an ovary is called
- **a.** ovulation.
- **b.** menstruation.
- **c.** fertilization.
- **d.** negative feedback.

12. A mixture of sperm and fluids is called
semen.

13. Draw Conclusions What is the role of the fluids in semen?
Fluids give sperm nutrients and an environment to swim in.

14. Relate Cause and Effect What changes occur in the uterus during the menstrual cycle?
The lining of the uterus thickens as the egg moves through a Fallopian tube. If the egg is fertilized, it attaches to the uterus. If not, the egg and lining break down.

15. Compare and Contrast In what ways are the functions of the ovaries and the testes similar? How do their functions differ?
Both produce sex cells and hormones. Testes produce sperm and testosterone, while ovaries produce eggs, estrogen, and other hormones.

16. math! The average menstrual cycle is 28 days in length. But it can vary from 21 to 35 days. Ovulation usually occurs 14 days before the end of the cycle. On what day will ovulation occur after the start of a 21-day cycle? A 35-day cycle?

See TE note.

540 Controlling Body Processes

LESSON 4 Pregnancy and Birth

17. The membrane that protects and cushions the embryo is called the
- **a.** umbilical cord.
- **b.** scrotum
- **c.** amniotic sac.
- **d.** ovary.

18. The _umbilical cord_ contains blood vessels from the embryo that link the embryo and the placenta.

19. Sequence What three stages of development does a fertilized egg go through before birth?
The three stages are zygote, embryo, and fetus.

20. Compare and Contrast Fraternal twins develop from (a single egg,(two eggs)). Identical twins develop from (a single egg/two eggs).

 What systems regulate and control body processes?

21. The body goes through many changes during adolescence. Suppose a tumor in the pituitary gland causes the gland to function incorrectly. How might a person's development during adolescence be affected? Explain.
Sample: The pituitary gland produces hormones, including growth hormones, that cause girls and boys to look more like adults. If the pituitary gland were not functioning correctly, an adolescent might not grow taller or develop the physical characteristics of an adult.
See TE rubric.

What systems regulate and control body processes?

SCORING RUBRIC	SCORE 4	SCORE 3	SCORE 2	SCORE 1
Use of details about pituitary gland's function and its relation to adolescence	Thoroughly explains effect of pituitary gland's malfunction on adolescent development	Explains effect of pituitary gland's malfunction on adolescent development, though without much detail	Partially explains effect of pituitary gland's malfunction on adolescent development	Does not explain effect of pituitary gland's malfunction on adolescent development

Standardized Test Prep

Multiple Choice

Circle the letter of the best answer.

1. What is the function of the part labeled A on the neuron shown below?

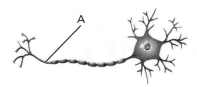

A It carries the nerve impulse toward the cell body.

B It protects the neuron from damage.

C It carries the nerve impulse away from the cell body.

D It picks up stimuli from the environment.

2. You are riding your bike when a small child suddenly darts out in front of you. Which of your endocrine glands is most likely to release a hormone in response to this situation?

A pituitary gland

B adrenal gland

C thyroid gland

D parathyroid gland

3. A change that occurs in girls during puberty is

A their skin wrinkles.

B egg production begins.

C muscle strength decreases.

D ovulation and menstruation begins.

4. A woman gives birth to twins who developed from a single fertilized egg that split early in development. Which of the following is a reasonable prediction that you can make about the twins?

A They will be the same sex.

B They will have similar interests.

C They will not look alike.

D They will have different inherited traits.

5. During pregnancy, which structure permits diffusion of substances from the mother to the fetus?

A zygote

B placenta

C uterus

D fallopian tubes

Constructed Response

Use the diagram below and your knowledge of science to help you answer Question 6. Write your answer on a separate sheet of paper.

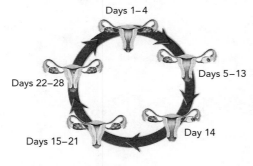

6. Describe what happens during each of the five stages of the menstrual cycle.
See TE note.

Standardized Test Prep

Test-Taking Skills

INTERPRETING DIAGRAMS Point out that when students encounter questions that include a diagram, they should be sure to study all parts of the diagram carefully, including details of the graphic image as well as any labels. Remind students that it is vital for them to grasp the nature of the information presented in the diagram before they analyze how the diagram relates to the test question as a whole.

Constructed Response

6. Sample: First, during days 1–4 the extra tissue and blood from the thickened lining of the uterus leave the body through the vagina. This is called menstruation. During days 5–13, an egg in the ovary enters the final steps of maturing. On day 14, the egg is released from the ovary into a Fallopian tube. The release of an egg is called ovulation. On days 15–21, the egg moves through the Fallopian tube. It can be fertilized if sperm are present. The lining of the uterus becomes thick. Finally, around days 22–28 if the egg is not fertilized, it breaks down and enters the uterus. Then the cycle repeats.

Additional Assessment Resources

Chapter Test
EXAMVIEW® Assessment Suite
Performance Assessment
Progress Monitoring Assessments
SuccessTracker™

ELL Support

5 Assess Understanding

Have ELLs complete the Alternate Assessment. Provide guidelines on the information it must cover and a rubric for assessment. You may wish to have them complete the activity in small groups of varying language proficiencies.

Beginning

LOW/HIGH Allow students extra time to complete their presentations.

Intermediate

LOW/HIGH Allow students to refer to their books or notes when working on their presentations.

Advanced

LOW/HIGH Challenge students to use vocabulary terms from the lesson in their presentations. In addition, students can act as coaches within their groups to help less proficient students.

Remediate If students have trouble with...

QUESTION	SEE LESSON	STANDARDS
1	1	
2	2	
3	3	
4	4	
5	4	
6	3	

Science Matters

Everyday Science

Have students read *Seeing is Believing ...Sometimes.* Point out that optical illusions cover many categories such as distortion of shapes, colors, pictures, sizes, distances, geometrics, and senses. Some optical illusions occur from the image itself, some depend on voluntary eye movement to produce an optical illusion effect, and some rely on the eye to focus on a particular point of the image. In all cases, the brain fills in a gap in the information it receives.

Ask: **How do researchers explain certain types of optical illusions?** (*In the lag of time that it takes for visual information to become a visual image in the brain, the brain predicts the image that will occur in about one tenth of a second.*) **What does the brain do when the predicted image does not match reality?** (*Sample: The brain registers a false image—an optical illusion.*) **What is a sample of an illusion of motion?** (*Television and movies are a series of images that play rapidly fooling the eye that the subjects are moving.*)

SEEING IS BELIEVING ... SOMETIMES

▲ What do you see? What does someone else see? Can you see the faces and the vase at the same time?

Your eyes are constantly checking out the world around you and sending visual information to your brain. Signals from the optic nerves take about one tenth of a second to become a visual image in the brain. Researchers think this lag causes the brain to predict images that will occur one tenth of a second in the future, filling in the gaps. This lag may explain why you see certain types of optical illusions.

Many optical illusions rely on the fact that the brain easily perceives patterns. Scientists think that when there is a gap in a pattern, the brain tries to predict what fills the gap. When these predictions don't match reality, you may end up seeing a false image. You probably experience an optical illusion every day without even noticing it. Television and movies are actually a series of images that are played rapidly, creating the illusion of motion.

Is the figure above an image of a vase or of two people facing each other? You can't see both images at the same time, because your brain gets fooled by thinking there's only one possible background. You can see both images at different times by shifting your attention.

Research It Research more about optical illusions. Then present three of your favorite optical illusions to your class and explain how each one works.

542 Controlling Body Processes

Quick Facts

Sure, celebrities look cool in designer shades, but some sunglasses do more than just make a statement. Polarized sunglasses are specialized eyewear designed to reduce the optical distortion of glare from surfaces such as water, snow, and glass. Optical distortion is a type of optical illusion. When sunlight reflects off horizontal surfaces and the eye catches it at a similar angle, glare occurs from the light off the water or road surface. Normally light passes directly through the eye, where optic nerves send the signals, and the brain processes the visual information. Glare distorts how the eyes see objects and makes them harder for the brain to distinguish. Have students research the optical distortion of glare. Have them test polarizing sunglasses or polarizing sheets in different positions to see if they can cut road or water glare on a sunny day. Have them write a one-page report on their findings.

FETAL SURGERY

Michael Skinner had surgery at a very young age. How young? He was the first patient ever to undergo fetal surgery—an operation on a developing fetus.

In 1981, Michael's mother was pregnant with twins. Although one twin was developing normally, doctors noticed that Michael had a serious condition that affected his development. After consulting with medical ethicists who helped them consider the risks, Michael's parents and doctors decided to risk surgery on the fetus. Surgeons used a long needle to reach the fetus inside the mother's uterus and to deliver the treatment Michael needed. The risk paid off, and the surgery was a success!

Hospitals in the United States now perform two types of fetal surgery. In some cases, surgeons use a needle, as they did with Michael Skinner's mother, to deliver treatment. Sometimes, surgeons are able to insert tiny cameras and surgical instruments through a small incision in the uterus. The cameras allow doctors to view the fetus on a computer monitor. These procedures are much less invasive than surgeries in which the uterus is opened. Therefore, they greatly reduce the risks to the mother and the developing fetus.

For other problems, surgeons may need to open the mother's uterus and operate on the fetus directly. At the end of surgery, the surgeon closes the uterus. The fetus is allowed to develop normally inside the mother.

Think About It List three questions you have about fetal surgery. Research to find the answers, and write one or two paragraphs to answer each question.

543

Frontiers of Technology

Have students read *Fetal Surgery.* Point out that open fetal surgery is not commonly performed. In the United States, only an estimated 600 candidates are considered each year. Using small incisions in fetal surgery has become a more useful option for some, because it is less invasive to the mother and the fetus. Explain that the less invasive a procedure is, less healthy tissue is damaged during the procedure. Meaning there's less risk of infection or other complications resulting from the surgery, such as scarring.

Ask: **What are the two types of fetal surgeries performed in U.S. hospitals?** *(Sample: One type of fetal surgery involves making a small incision in the mother's uterus for needles, cameras, and surgical instruments to perform procedures. The other type of surgery involves opening the mother's uterus, operating directly on the fetus, and closing the uterus upon completion.)* **What is an advantage of using small incisions to perform fetal surgery?** *(Sample: Using a small incision for surgery is a less invasive option than open fetal surgery and greatly reduces the risks to the mother and fetus.)*

Fighting Disease

Introduce the Big Q ? UbD

Have students look at the image and read the Engaging Question and description. Ask students to infer what steps they can take to prevent themselves or someone else from getting a disease. Have student volunteers share their inferences with the rest of the class. Point out that preventing disease can involve doing something such as taking a vaccine, whereas other times it can involve *not* doing something, such as not using products that are known to cause disease. Ask: **How is the vaccine being given to the girl in the photo?** *(Liquid is being put in her mouth.)* **What opinion does the girl appear to have about getting the vaccine?** *(She seems to dislike the process.)* **What makes this unpleasant experience worthwhile?** *(The vaccine will protect the girl from a very serious disease.)*

Untamed Science Video

FLU DETECTIVES Before viewing, invite students to discuss what they know about how the human body fights diseases. Then play the video. Lead a class discussion and make a list of questions that this video raises. You may wish to have students view the video again after they have completed the chapter to see if their questions have been answered.

To access the online resources for this chapter, search on or navigate to *Fighting Disease.*

Untamed Science Video shows flu prevention tracking.

The Big Question allows students to answer the Engaging Question about why people sometimes get sick.

my science online.com ⟩ Fighting Disease

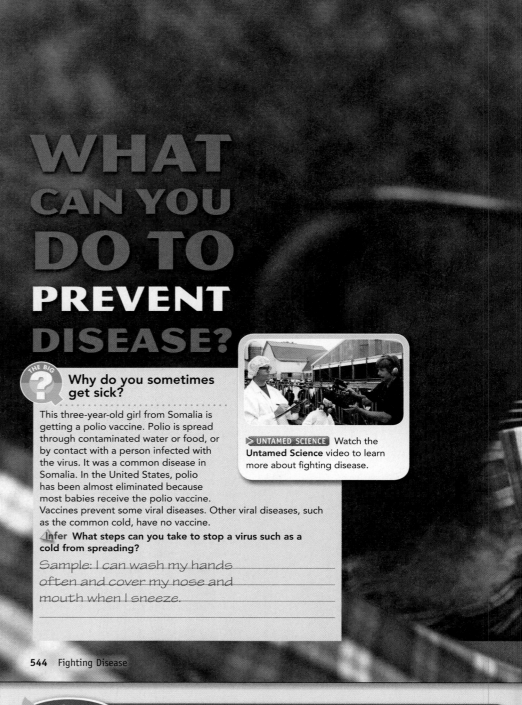

WHAT CAN YOU DO TO PREVENT DISEASE?

? Why do you sometimes get sick?

This three-year-old girl from Somalia is getting a polio vaccine. Polio is spread through contaminated water or food, or by contact with a person infected with the virus. It was a common disease in Somalia. In the United States, polio has been almost eliminated because most babies receive the polio vaccine. Vaccines prevent some viral diseases. Other viral diseases, such as the common cold, have no vaccine.

Infer What steps can you take to stop a virus such as a cold from spreading?

Sample: I can wash my hands often and cover my nose and mouth when I sneeze.

> **UNTAMED SCIENCE** Watch the **Untamed Science** video to learn more about fighting disease.

Professional Development Note **From the Author**

I spent most of a recent holiday sick with a cold. After about 12 days, I went to see my doctor. I knew that if I had a viral infection, no antibiotic would cure me. Here are some questions the doctor asked to determine whether my illness was viral or bacterial. *How long have you been ill? What are your symptoms? What medicines are you taking? What color is your mucus?* He took my temperature, checked my breathing, and asked me to cough. Because he detected a fever and a "chesty" cough, and I had had symptoms for 12 days, I ended up getting an antibiotic. It made me feel good, knowing about the overuse of antibiotics, that he screened me so well before prescribing.

✎ *Michael Padilla*

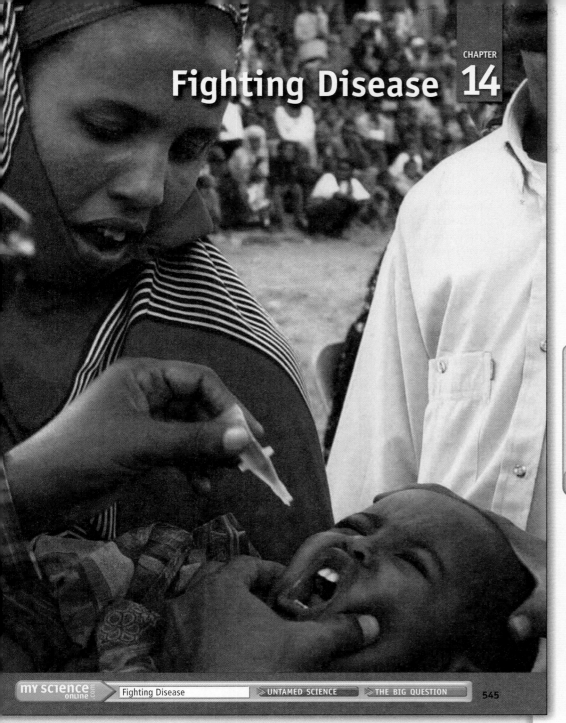

Fighting Disease

Chapter at a Glance

CHAPTER PACING: 9–14 periods or $5\frac{1}{2}$–7 blocks

INTRODUCE THE CHAPTER: Use the Engaging Question and the opening image to get students thinking about fighting disease. Activate prior knowledge and preteach vocabulary using the Getting Started pages.

Lesson 1: Infectious Disease

Lesson 2: The Body's Defenses

Lesson 3: HIV and AIDS

Lesson 4: Infectious Disease and Your Health

Lesson 5: Noninfectious Disease

ASSESSMENT OPTIONS: Chapter Test, **EXAM**VIEW® Assessment Suite, Performance Assessment, Progress Monitoring Assessments, SuccessTracker™

Preference Navigator, in the online Planning tools, allows you to customize *Interactive Science* to your own teaching style. You can also edit lesson plans by selecting the Lesson Planner option.

Digital Teacher's Edition allows you to access your Teacher's Edition and Resource online.

MY SCIENCE online.com

Fighting Disease | UNTAMED SCIENCE | THE BIG QUESTION | 545

Differentiated Instruction

L1 Under the Weather Invite students to brainstorm a list of words and phrases they associate with disease and fighting disease. List terms on the board. Encourage students to look for ways to arrange terms in logical groupings such as "symptoms," "diseases," "medicines," and "causes of sickness."

L3 Diseases in History Challenge students to do research to find basic information about a variety of diseases that have been notable during the last several centuries. Encourage students to use reference books and online sources to gather data about diseases such as tuberculosis, influenza, bubonic plague, yellow fever, AIDS, hemophilia, cholera, and smallpox. Remind students to follow prescribed guidelines for Internet use.

Getting Started

Check Your Understanding

This activity assesses students' understanding of the nature and causes of infections. After students have shared their answers, point out that scientists' understanding of and ability to treat infections has advanced dramatically during the last few centuries.

Preteach Vocabulary Skills

Explain to students that many English words with Latin origins have meanings related to disease and medicine. Learning Latin word origins can make it easier to learn new vocabulary words. Also point out that often several related words—such as *toxin, toxic,* and *toxicology*—have similar meanings because they have origins in the same Latin word. Explain that for many careers in the health care field, knowledge of Latin word origins is important since many medical terms have Latin roots. Students considering a career in health care sometimes decide to study Latin in high school.

CHAPTER
14 Getting Started

Check Your Understanding

1. **Background** Read the paragraph below and then answer the question.

> Camila steps on a nail that punctures her foot. She knows that **bacteria** can cause a disease called tetanus in a wound that is **contaminated**. Fortunately, Camila just received a shot to prevent tetanus. However, to help stop **infection**, she soaks her foot in warm soapy water.

Bacteria are single-celled organisms that lack a nucleus.

An object that is **contaminated** has become unclean and could possibly infect the body.

Infection is the process in which disease-causing microorganisms invade the body and then multiply.

- How can a wound lead to an infection?

  Sample: Bacteria can enter the body through the wound and then multiply inside the body, causing infection.

> **MY READING WEB** If you had trouble completing the question above, visit **My Reading Web** and type in *Fighting Disease.*

Vocabulary Skill

Latin Word Origins Some terms in this chapter contain word parts with Latin origins. The table below lists some of the Latin words from which these terms come.

Latin Word	Meaning	Key Term
toxicum	(poison)	toxin, *n.* a poison produced by bacteria that damages cells
tumere	a swelling	tumor, *n.* an abnormal mass of tissue that results from uncontrolled division of cells

2. **Quick Check** In the table above, circle the meaning of the Latin word *toxicum.* The meaning may help you remember the term *toxin.*

My Reading Web offers leveled readings that provide a foundation for the chapter content.

Vocab Flash Cards offer extra practice with the chapter vocabulary words.

Digital Lesson
- Assign the *Check Your Understanding* activity online and have students submit their work to you.
- Assign the *Vocabulary Skill* activity online and have students submit their work to you.

my science online.com | **Fighting Disease**

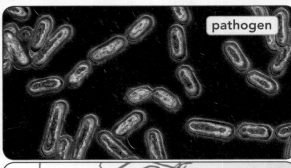

pathogen

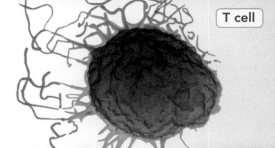

T cell

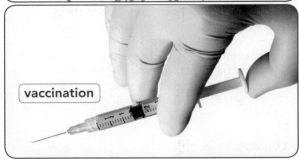

vaccination

allergen

Chapter Preview

LESSON 1
- microorganism • pathogen
- infectious disease • toxin
- 🔄 **Identify the Main Idea**
- △ **Develop Hypotheses**

LESSON 2
- inflammatory response
- phagocyte • immune response
- lymphocyte • T cell • antigen
- B cell • antibody
- 🔄 **Compare and Contrast**
- △ **Make Models**

LESSON 3
- AIDS • HIV
- 🔄 **Sequence**
- △ **Graph**

LESSON 4
- immunity • active immunity
- vaccination • vaccine
- passive immunity • antibiotic
- antibiotic resistance
- 🔄 **Relate Cause and Effect**
- △ **Interpret Data**

LESSON 5
- noninfectious disease • allergy
- allergen • histamine • asthma
- insulin • diabetes • tumor
- carcinogen
- 🔄 **Summarize**
- △ **Draw Conclusions**

> **VOCAB FLASH CARDS** For extra help with vocabulary, visit **Vocab Flash Cards** and type in **Fighting Disease.**

547

Preview Vocabulary Terms

Have students create a three-column chart to rate their knowledge of the vocabulary terms before they read the chapter. In the first column of the chart, students should list the terms for the chapter. In the second column, students should identify whether they can define and use the word, whether they have heard or seen the word before, or whether they do not know the word. As the class progresses through the chapter, have students write definitions for each term in the last column of the chart. A list of Academic Vocabulary for each lesson can be found in the Support All Readers box at the start of the lesson.

L1 Have students look at the images on this page as you pronounce the vocabulary word. Have students repeat the word after you. Then read the definition. Use the sample sentence in italics to clarify the meaning of the term.

pathogens *(PATH uh jenz)* Organisms that cause disease. *This group of pathogens can be seen with a microscope.*

T cell *(TEE sel)* A lymphocyte that identifies pathogens and distinguishes one pathogen from another. *A T cell has the ability to recognize marker molecules on a pathogen.*

vaccination *(vak suh NAY shun)* The process by which harmless antigens are introduced into a person's body to produce active immunity. *Getting a vaccination can prevent a disease from occurring.*

allergen *(AL ur jen)* Any substance that causes an allergy. *Seasonal plants produce allergens that affect many people.*

E L L Support

Have students work in small groups to complete their charts cooperatively for the Preview Vocabulary Terms activity. Read aloud and review the vocabulary terms before students begin their charts.

Beginning
LOW Complete the chart using the vocabulary terms in students' native language.

HIGH Write a definition for each known vocabulary term in the native language.

Intermediate
LOW/HIGH Discuss the definitions for known vocabulary terms in cooperative groups.

Advanced
LOW/HIGH Write a sentence using each of the vocabulary terms that is known.

Infectious Disease

1

Why do you sometimes get sick?

Lesson Pacing: 1–2 periods or $\frac{1}{2}$–1 block

🕐 **SHORT ON TIME?** To do this lesson in approximately half the time, do the Activate Prior Knowledge activity followed by a discussion of the Key Concepts to familiarize students with the lesson content. Have students do the Quick Labs. The rest of the lesson can be completed by students independently.

> **Preference Navigator,** in the online Planning tools, allows you to customize *Interactive Science* to your own teaching style. You can also edit lesson plans by selecting the Lesson Planner option.
>
> **Digital Teacher's Edition** allows you to access your Teacher's Edition and Resource materials online.

my science online.com

Lesson Vocabulary

- microorganism
- pathogen
- infectious disease
- toxin

Content Refresher

Koch's Postulates In 1890 Robert Koch developed guidelines for determining whether a specific microorganism causes a disease. Later research has shown these criteria to have their limitations. Koch's original postulates are summarized below.

1. If a microorganism is suspected of causing a disease, it should be found in the body of each organism that has the disease.

2. The microorganism must be isolated from the body of an organism with the disease and then grown in the laboratory in a pure culture, i.e., a culture that contains no other types of microorganisms.

3. When microorganisms from the pure culture are placed in the body of a healthy organism, e.g., a laboratory animal, they should cause the same disease that was found in the original host organism.

4. The suspected organisms must then be isolated from the second host. It should be the same kind of microorganism as the original pathogen.

LESSON OBJECTIVES

🔑 Describe the relationship between pathogens and infectious disease.

🔑 Identify pathogens that cause infectious diseases in humans and how they spread.

Blended Path
Active learning using Student Edition, Inquiry Path, and Digital Path

ENGAGE AND EXPLORE

Teach this lesson using a variety of resources. Begin by reading **My Planet Diary** as a class. Have students share ideas about why it is important to get a flu vaccine every year. Then have students do the **Inquiry Warm-Up activity.** Students will test for the presence of microbes in the classroom. Discuss the items in the classroom that were tested for microbes. The **After the Inquiry Warm-Up worksheet** sets up a discussion about the characteristics of the areas tested that when swabbed had the least and greatest amounts of microbe growth. Have volunteers share their answers to question 4 about the factors that may contribute to heavy microbe growth in an area.

EXPLAIN AND ELABORATE

Teach Key Concepts by explaining the term *pasteurized* and how it relates to the germs that cause diseases. **Teach Key Concepts** by explaining how Robert Koch's work built on and expanded Pasteur and Lister's work on the germ theory. Use **Figure 1** to illustrate Lister's method for killing microorganisms that caused infections that often followed surgery. **Support the Big Q** by discussing how the discovery of pathogens has changed the face of infectious diseases. Use **Figure 2** to describe how Koch followed the scientific method in his research of pathogens.

Continue to **Teach Key Concepts** by identifying the four major types of human pathogens and how they cause illnesses. Use the images in **Figure 3** to compare and contrast the size and characteristics of pathogens. **Lead a Discussion** about which pathogens cause which types of diseases. Then have students practice the inquiry skill in the **Apply It activity.** Hand out the **Key Concept Summaries** as a review of each part of the lesson. Students can also use the online **Vocab Flash Cards** to review key terms.

EVALUATE

Have students take the **Lesson Quiz.** For an alternate assessment, see the **EXAM**VIEW® Assessment Suite, Progress Monitoring Assessments, or SuccessTracker™.

ELL Support

1 Content and Language

The word *pathogen* is formed from the word parts *patho* and *-gen*. The word *patho* comes from the Greek word *pathos* meaning suffering. The word part *-gen* means "the cause of." Therefore, a *pathogen* is the cause of a disease.

Inquiry Path
Hands-on learning in the Lab zone

ENGAGE AND EXPLORE

To teach this lesson with an emphasis on inquiry, begin with the **Inquiry Warm-Up activity.** Students will investigate microbes around the classroom. Discuss why it is important to only touch each sterile swab to the specific area. Have students do the **After the Inquiry Warm-Up worksheet.** Talk about the characteristics and uses of the area with the greatest amount of growth and the least amount of growth. Have volunteers share their answers to question 4 about the factors might that promote heavy microbe growth in an area.

EXPLAIN AND ELABORATE

Focus on the **Inquiry Skill** for the lesson. Point out that when you develop a hypothesis, you state a possible explanation for a set of observations or an answer to a scientific question. What hypothesis could be developed based on the **Inquiry Warm-Up activity?** *(Most microbes grew in areas that are warm, damp, attract a lot of human traffic, and are not regularly cleaned or disinfected.)* Use the **Support the Big Q** to emphasize the breakthrough discovery about pathogens made by Koch. Have students do the **Quick Lab** to see how pathogens cause diseases and then share their results.

Review the section with the heading *Soil, Food, and Water* before beginning the **Apply It activity.** Ask volunteers to share the hypotheses they developed. Do the **Quick Lab** to reinforce understanding of how diseases are spread. Students can use the online **Vocab Flash Cards** to review key terms.

EVALUATE

Have students take the **Lesson Quiz.** For an alternate assessment, see the **EXAM**VIEW® Assessment Suite, Progress Monitoring Assessments, or SuccessTracker™.

Digital Path
Online learning at **my science online**.com

ENGAGE AND EXPLORE

Teach this lesson using digital resources. Begin by having students explore real-world connections to infectious diseases at **My Planet Diary** online. Have them access the Chapter Resources to find the **Unlock the Big Question activity.** There they can answer the questions and refine their responses as they continue through the lesson. You can re-assign the activity and have students submit their work so you can track their progress.

EXPLAIN AND ELABORATE

Students reading above, at, or below the lexile measure of this lesson can access basic content readings at their level at **My Reading Web.** Have students use the online **Vocab Flash Cards** to preview key terms. To **Support the Big Q** discuss why Koch's discovery about pathogens was important to understanding infectious diseases. Do the **Quick Lab** and then ask students to share their results.

Have students do the online **Virtual Lab** to explore disease-causing viruses and organisms at different scales. Review the section titled *Soil, Food, and Water* before assigning the online **Apply It activity.** Ask volunteers to share their hypotheses. Have students submit their work to you. Do the **Quick Lab** to simulate the spread of a disease. The **Key Concept Summaries** online allow students to read a summary and see an image associated with each part of the lesson. Online remediation is available at **My Science Coach.**

EVALUATE

Have students take the **Lesson Quiz.** For an alternate assessment, see the **EXAM**VIEW® Assessment Suite, Progress Monitoring Assessments, or SuccessTracker™.

2 Frontload the Lesson
Preview the lesson visuals, labels, and captions. Ask students what they know about the words *pathogen* and *toxin.* Explain the specific meanings these words have in science.

3 Comprehensible Input
Have students study the visuals and their captions to support the Key Concepts of the lesson.

4 Language Production
Pair or group students with varied language abilities to complete labs collaboratively for language practice. Have each student copy the completed written lab for personal reference.

5 Assess Understanding
Make true or false statements using lesson content and have students indicate if they agree or disagree with a thumbs up or thumbs down gesture to check whole-class comprehension.

LESSON 14.1

Infectious Disease

Establish Learning Objectives

After this lesson, students will be able to:

🔑 Describe the relationship between pathogens and infectious disease.

🔑 Identify pathogens that cause infectious diseases in humans and how they spread.

Engage ————————

Activate Prior Knowledge

MY PLANET DIARY Read *Fight the Flu* with the class. Explain that the influenza vaccine uses inactivated versions of the viruses. These are used so that the vaccine does not cause the disease. Exposure to the killed strains causes the body to make antibodies against them. Then the body is better prepared to fight live viruses. Ask: **Have you ever had a flu shot? Did getting the flu shot prevent you from having the flu that year?** *(Most students will likely say yes.)*

BIG IDEAS OF SCIENCE REFERENCE LIBRARY 📖 Have students look up the following topics: Mold, Pandemic, Rats.

Explore ————————

Lab Resource: Inquiry Warm-Up 🧪

L2 **THE AGENTS OF DISEASE** Students will test common objects in the classroom for the presence of microbes.

---

1 Infectious Disease

🔑 How Do Pathogens Cause Disease?

🔑 What Pathogens Cause Infectious Disease and How Are They Spread?

MY PLANET DIARY

Fight the Flu

Misconception: You cannot catch the flu if you have gotten a flu shot.

The flu vaccine decreases your chances of catching the flu, but it does not protect you 100 percent. However, if you get the shot and still end up catching the flu, your symptoms probably will be milder than if you had not gotten vaccinated.

There are many strains of the flu virus. Each year, scientists choose the strains that they think will appear in the United States. Then a vaccine is made that contains those strains. The vaccine is given to people across the country. However, getting a flu shot will not protect you against any strain that is not in the vaccine.

 Do the Inquiry Warm-Up *The Agents of Disease.*

MISCONCEPTION

Read the following questions. Write your answers below.

1. What is one challenge that scientists face when making the flu vaccine?

   Sample: They have to choose which strains will appear that year.

2. Does a person need to get a flu shot every year? Why or why not?

   Yes; the flu strains in the vaccine vary from year to year.

> PLANET DIARY Go to **Planet Diary** to learn more about infectious diseases.

548 Fighting Disease

SUPPORT ALL READERS
Lexile Measure = 950L   **Lexile Word Count = 1466**

Prior Exposure to Content: Many students may have misconceptions on this topic

Academic Vocabulary: *develop, hypothesis, identify, main idea*

Science Vocabulary: *microorganism, pathogen, infectious disease, toxin*

Concept Level: Generally appropriate for most students in this grade

Preteach With: My Planet Diary "Fight the Flu" and Figure 3 activity

Go to **My Reading Web** to access leveled readings that provide a foundation for the content.

my science online.com

Vocabulary
- microorganism • pathogen
- infectious disease • toxin

Skills
- ⟳ Reading: Identify the Main Idea
- △ Inquiry: Develop Hypotheses

How Do Pathogens Cause Disease?

In ancient times, people had different ideas about what caused disease. They thought that things such as evil spirits or swamp air caused disease. In fact, they sometimes cut holes in the skulls of sick people to let the evil spirits out. The ancient Greeks thought that disease resulted from an imbalance of four body fluids: blood, phlegm (flem) or mucus, black bile, and yellow bile.

Louis Pasteur and Microorganisms It was not until the 1860s that a French scientist named Louis Pasteur discovered the cause of some diseases. After investigating what causes foods to spoil, Pasteur concluded that **microorganisms,** living things too small to see without a microscope, were the cause. Pasteur thought that microorganisms might be causing disease in animals and people, too. So he investigated a disease attacking silkworms at the time. Pasteur found microorganisms inside silkworms with the disease. He was able to show that these organisms caused the disease. Pasteur's work led to an understanding of what causes most infectious diseases—microorganisms.

✎ ⟳ **Identify the Main Idea**
In the graphic organizer, write the main idea of the first paragraph. Then write three details that support the main idea.

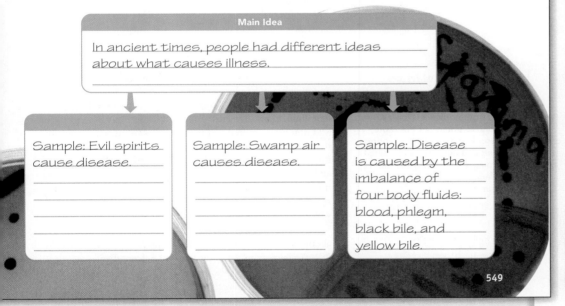

Main Idea

In ancient times, people had different ideas about what causes illness.

Sample: Evil spirits cause disease.

Sample: Swamp air causes disease.

Sample: Disease is caused by the imbalance of four body fluids: blood, phlegm, black bile, and yellow bile.

549

Explain

Introduce Vocabulary

To help students understand the term *microorganisms,* explain that the word combines the word *organisms* ("living things") with the prefix *micro-* ("small"). Point out that this compound word contains two successive o's and that each o is pronounced separately, as if there were a hyphen between them.

Lead a Discussion

GERM THEORY OF DISEASE Students may find the ancient notions about disease amusing. But when Pasteur first suggested that tiny living things caused disease, it was not immediately accepted. Ask: **What food-related word do you know that is related to Pasteur?** *(Pasteurization)* **What products are pasteurized?** *(Milk and cream)* **What does pasteurizing do to food?** *(Samples: kill germs; keep milk from spoiling)*

21st Century Learning

COMMUNICATION Invite students to brainstorm a list of familiar diseases. Then divide the diseases into two groups: diseases that students think can be spread from person to person and diseases that students think cannot be spread that way. Revisit students' responses after they have begun to study this section of the lesson.

⟳ **Identify the Main Idea** Explain that the main idea is the most important or biggest idea in a paragraph or section of text. Point out that some main ideas are stated directly, whereas readers may have to identify other main ideas by themselves.

My Planet Diary provides an opportunity for students to explore real-world connections to infectious diseases.

my science online | Pathogens and Disease

ⒺⓁⓁ Support

1 Content and Language
Write the term *microorganisms* on the board and draw a vertical line between the two o's. Explain that this word contains the Greek prefix *micro-,* meaning "small." Point out that *microorganisms* are organisms that are too small to be seen with the naked eye.

2 Frontload the Lesson
Ask student volunteers to name illnesses or diseases with which they are familiar.

Encourage students to speculate on the cause or causes of any of these illnesses.

3 Comprehensible Input
Invite students to create a cause-and-effect diagram relating to pathogens. Some students might choose to show how pathogens cause infectious disease, and others might show several ways in which infectious diseases are spread.

Explain

Teach Key Concepts 🔑

Explain to students that in cases of infectious disease, pathogens are in the body causing harm. Ask: **How do pathogens differ from other organisms?** *(They cause disease.)* **How do pathogens make you sick?** *(They damage large numbers of cells.)* Explain to students that one scientist's work often builds on the earlier work of another scientist. Point out that, even after the idea of microorganisms as causes of disease was accepted, some scientists did not think that each disease was caused by a specific microorganism. Pasteur and Lister were not concerned with specific organisms, but the development and use of the germ theory in general. Robert Koch's work built on and expanded what Pasteur and Lister had learned. Ask: **What can you infer about scientists' current research on infectious diseases?** *(Sample: Scientists are trying to move forward using present-day conclusions, assumptions, and understandings.)* **What advantages do scientists working today have over Koch?** *(Samples: They have more modern equipment; they have a larger base of knowledge to start from.)*

Teach With Visuals

Point out that the first image in **Figure 1** illustrates some details mentioned in the text's descriptions of Joseph Lister's surgical procedures. Tell students to look at **Figure 1**. Ask: **What is the significance of the substance being sprayed on the patient's body?** *(It is carbolic acid, a chemical that kills microorganisms.)* **What is the significance of the towels or bandages being placed on the patient's body?** *(They have been dipped in carbolic acid and are placed around the patient's wound.)* **Why do you think the towel is being held over the patient's face?** *(Sample: The carbolic acid is a harsh chemical and they did not want to get it in the patient's eyes or allow the patient to inhale it.)*

Support the Big Q ❓ UbD

THE DISCOVERY OF PATHOGENS Remind students that the discovery of pathogens was relatively recent. Explain that in the United States in 1900, the three leading causes of death were pneumonia, tuberculosis, and intestinal infections—all of which were caused by pathogens. Today, infectious diseases rank far behind two noninfectious diseases, cancers and heart disease, as the leading causes of death. Ask: **How might scientists identify the pathogen that causes a specific disease?** *(Sample: They determine whether the pathogen is present in every person or animal that has the disease.)* Tell students that Koch's procedure is still followed in the research of infectious diseases.

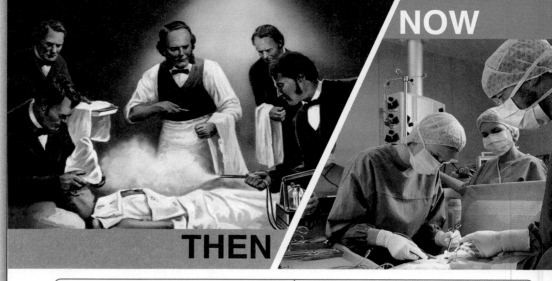

NOW

THEN

Then	Now
Sample: They do not wear masks or gloves. They wear street clothes, and they use spray disinfectant.	Sample: They use masks and gloves, wear special clothes, and use many specialized instruments.

FIGURE 1 ·······································

Preventing Infection

A clean environment reduces the chance of infection after surgery.

✏️ **Communicate** Observe the pictures above. In the table, describe the operating rooms then and now. Then in a small group, discuss how technology affects surgery today. Write your ideas below.

Sample: Technology has made better ways to clean and sterilize surgical tools.

550 Fighting Disease

Joseph Lister Pasteur's work influenced a British surgeon named Joseph Lister. Before the twentieth century, surgery was risky because most surgeons operated with dirty instruments and did not wash their hands. The sheets on hospital beds were rarely washed between patients. Even if people lived through an operation, many died later from an infection.

Lister hypothesized that microorganisms cause the infections that often followed surgery. He planned an experiment to test his hypothesis. Before performing operations, he washed his hands and surgical instruments with carbolic acid, a chemical that kills microorganisms. He also sprayed the patients with the acid, as shown in **Figure 1**. After the surgeries, he covered the patients' wounds with bandages dipped in carbolic acid.

Lister's results were dramatic. Before he used his new methods, about 45 percent of his surgical patients died from infection. With Lister's new techniques, only about 15 percent died.

Robert Koch In the 1870s and 1880s, the German physician Robert Koch showed that a specific microorganism causes each disease. For example, the microorganism that causes strep throat cannot cause chickenpox or other diseases. Look at **Figure 2** to see how Koch identified the microorganism for a disease called anthrax.

Organisms that cause disease are called **pathogens.** A disease caused by a pathogen is an **infectious disease.** 🔑 **When you have an infectious disease, pathogens are in your body causing harm.** Pathogens damage large numbers of individual cells, which makes you sick.

FIGURE 2 ·····
Koch's Experiment
Koch followed the scientific method in his research of pathogens.

✏️ **Draw Conclusions** How would Koch's conclusion have been different if Mouse B's blood had not contained the pathogen found in Mouse A's blood?

<u>He could not have</u>
<u>concluded that the</u>
<u>pathogen in Mouse A's</u>
<u>blood caused anthrax.</u>

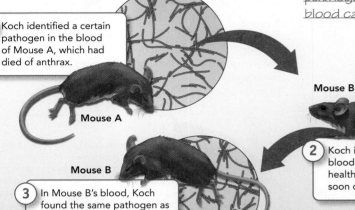

1. Koch identified a certain pathogen in the blood of Mouse A, which had died of anthrax.

Mouse A

Mouse B

2. Koch injected Mouse A's blood into Mouse B, a healthy mouse. Mouse B soon developed anthrax.

Mouse B

3. In Mouse B's blood, Koch found the same pathogen as the one in Mouse A's blood.

Lab zone Do the Quick Lab *How Do Pathogens Cause Disease?*

🔑 **Assess Your Understanding**

1a. Define What is an infectious disease?
<u>It is a disease caused by a</u>
<u>pathogen.</u>

b. Make Generalizations How did Pasteur's work affect Lister's work?
<u>Lister killed microorganisms,</u>
<u>which Pasteur discovered</u>
<u>cause infection.</u>

got it?

○ **I get it!** Now I know that pathogens cause disease by <u>getting inside the body</u> <u>and causing harm by damaging</u> <u>cells.</u>

○ **I need extra help with** <u>See TE note.</u>

Go to **MY SCIENCE COACH** online for help with this subject.

551

Differentiated Instruction

L3 Anthrax Challenge students to do research to learn more about the disease anthrax. Encourage students to include information on the disease's cause (a spore-forming bacterium, *Bacillus anthracis*), type (an acute infectious disease), and the fact that it most commonly occurs in cattle, goats, sheep, and other herbivores. Students might

also wish to note how anthrax can be transmitted, its symptoms, as well as details about vaccines and treatments. If students do their research on the Internet, remind them to follow prescribed guidelines for Internet use. Have students focus on the symptoms of and type of bacteria that causes anthrax.

Teach With Visuals

Tell students to look at **Figure 2.** Lead them through a discussion of the steps that Koch followed. Step 1 is similar to what Pasteur did. Koch observed a microorganism that came from a sick animal. Step 2 is what makes Koch's work so important. Ask: **What hypothesis would lead from finding a microorganism to injecting it into the healthy mouse?** *(Sample: This microorganism is the pathogen that causes anthrax.)* **Does what you see in Step 3 support this hypothesis? Explain.** *(Sample: Yes; the mouse died and the same microorganism was found in its blood.)* **Why was it important to test the blood of the second mouse?** *(Sample: The fact that the mouse died indicated that the mouse got anthrax from the injection, but the presence of the same pathogen proved that the injected pathogen was the cause.)*

Elaborate

21st Century Learning

CREATIVITY Ask students to think about conditions in hospitals during Lister's time. It was a lot easier to leave the sheets on the bed between patients than to wash sheets and soak them with carbolic acid. Challenge students to write a speech that Lister might have given to fellow surgeons, urging them to adopt his new practices. You may wish to have students deliver their speeches to the class.

Lab Resource: Quick Lab

L2 HOW DO PATHOGENS CAUSE DISEASE?
Students will observe prepared slides of pathogens under a microscope.

Evaluate

Assess Your Understanding

After students answer the questions, have them evaluate their understanding by completing the appropriate sentence.

RTI Response to Intervention

1a. If students have trouble explaining an infectious disease, **then** have them reread the definition and the Key Concept statement.

b. If students need help explaining the effect of the scientists' work, **then** have them review the section *Joseph Lister.*

MY SCIENCE COACH Have students go online for help in understanding pathogens.

Explain

Teach Key Concepts 🔑

Explain to students that bacteria, viruses, fungi, and protists are the four major types of human pathogens. They can be spread through contact with a sick person or other living things or an object in the environment. Point out to students that most microorganisms are harmless. However, some can make you sick. Ask: **What are two ways that bacteria cause illness?** *(They can damage body cells directly, and they can produce toxins that damage cells.)* **How do viruses cause illness?** *(They reproduce inside living cells, damaging or destroying them in the process.)* **How do viruses differ from the other three types of pathogens?** *(Sample: Viruses are not living, whereas bacteria, fungi, and protists are living microorganisms.)* **Why is it unlikely that a fungus would grow on the skin of a person's arm?** *(Fungi grow best in warm, dark, moist areas of the body, not on areas that are dry and exposed to light.)*

Teach With Visuals

Tell students to look at **Figure 3.** Explain that the photographs on these pages show images of pathogens that have been taken with a light microscope or an electron microscope. Tell students that pathogens such as bacteria are not necessarily multicolored organisms. Color is often added to micrographs to make details visible. Ask: **How does the image of the virus differ from the images of the other three pathogens?** *(Sample: It has the appearance of a single dense mass, whereas the other three pathogens show more variation in the shapes and composition of their structures.)* Point out that the images shown in **Figure 3** are not to scale. The tetanus bacteria are actually more than a hundred times larger than the adenovirus, even though they appear smaller on this page. Ask: **What would the virus in Figure 3 look like if it were shown at the same scale as the bacteria?** *(Sample: like a tiny dot)*

What Pathogens Cause Infectious Disease and How Are They Spread?

You share Earth with many kinds of organisms. Most of these organisms are harmless, but some can make you sick. Some diseases are caused by multicelled animals, such as worms. However, most pathogens can be seen only with a microscope.

Types of Pathogens 🔑 **The four major types of human pathogens are bacteria, viruses, fungi, and protists. They can be spread through contact with a sick person, other living things, or an object in the environment.** You can see some examples of pathogens in **Figure 3.**

Bacteria Bacteria are one-celled microorganisms. They cause many diseases, including ear infections, food poisoning, tetanus, and strep throat. Some bacteria damage body cells directly. Other bacteria, such as those that cause tetanus, damage cells indirectly by producing a poison, or **toxin.**

FIGURE 3 ⋯⋯⋯⋯⋯⋯⋯⋯

▶ VIRTUAL LAB **Pathogens**
Microscopic organisms cause many common diseases.

✏ **Compare and Contrast** In the table on the next page, use information in the text to write notes about pathogens. Then fill in the circle below to indicate which type of pathogen produces toxins.

○ viruses
● bacteria
○ protists
○ fungi

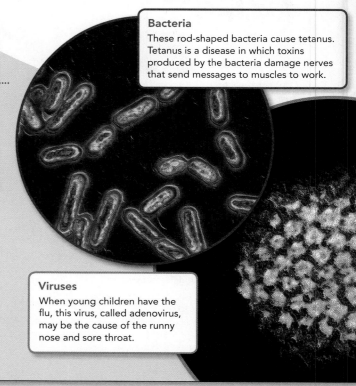

Bacteria
These rod-shaped bacteria cause tetanus. Tetanus is a disease in which toxins produced by the bacteria damage nerves that send messages to muscles to work.

Viruses
When young children have the flu, this virus, called adenovirus, may be the cause of the runny nose and sore throat.

Virtual Lab allows students to explore disease-causing viruses and organisms at different scales.

my science online.com ▶ **Types of Pathogens**

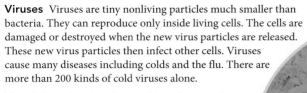
Viruses Viruses are tiny nonliving particles much smaller than bacteria. They can reproduce only inside living cells. The cells are damaged or destroyed when the new virus particles are released. These new virus particles then infect other cells. Viruses cause many diseases including colds and the flu. There are more than 200 kinds of cold viruses alone.

Fungi Some fungi, such as molds and yeasts, also cause infectious diseases. Fungi that cause disease may be one-celled or multicelled living things. Fungi grow best in warm, dark, moist areas of the body. Athlete's foot and ringworm are two fungal diseases.

Protists Most protists are one-celled microorganisms and some can cause disease. They are larger than bacteria but still tiny. One type of protist causes the disease malaria, which is common in tropical areas. African sleeping sickness and hiker's disease are other diseases caused by protists.

Protists
This microorganism is called *Giardia* (jee AHR dee uh). People who drink from streams or lakes with this protist can get an intestinal disease called hiker's disease.

Fungi
This fungus causes a skin infection called athlete's foot.

Pathogen	Size	Characteristics	Type of Disease
Bacteria	One-celled microorganisms	Damage cells directly or indirectly with toxins	Sample: strep throat, ear infections, tetanus
Viruses	Smaller than bacteria	Reproduce in cells, destroying them; nonliving	Sample: flu, colds
Fungi	One-celled or multicelled living things	Grow in warm, dark areas of the body	Sample: athlete's foot, ringworm
Protists	One-celled microorganisms larger than bacteria	Cause diseases common in tropical areas	Sample: malaria, giardia

553

Lead a Discussion

DISEASES FROM PATHOGENS Remind students that each pathogen causes a specific disease. Sometimes different pathogens cause symptoms that are so similar that they appear to be the same disease. For example, there is a form of pneumonia caused by a virus and a form of pneumonia caused by a bacterium. Ask: **What other diseases are caused by viruses?** *(Common cold, flu)* **What are some diseases caused by bacteria?** *(Ear infections, food poisoning, strep throat)* **What are some diseases caused by protists?** *(Malaria, African sleeping sickness, hiker's disease)* Students may ask if hiker's disease is the same disease that people get from drinking the water in foreign countries. Tell them that the most common version of "traveler's diarrhea" is caused by a bacterium, *Escherichia coli,* although it can also be caused by other pathogens, including a type of amoeba.

Elaborate

21st Century Learning

CRITICAL THINKING Remind students that colds and the flu are caused by viruses. Ask: **Why do you think there is no vaccine to prevent the common cold?** *(Sample: Because the cold is caused by so many different viruses, one vaccine could not protect against all of them.)*

Differentiated Instruction

L1 Science Terms Students may need help recognizing and understanding the differences among the related words *fungus, fungi,* and *fungal.* First, explain that *fungi* is the plural form of *fungus.* Then help students understand that *fungal* is the adjective form used in expressions such as *fungal disease.*

L3 Four Sicknesses from Four Pathogens Challenge students to do research on an illness caused by each of the four types of pathogens. Encourage students to prepare an oral report on the four illnesses, but caution them to avoid delving too deeply into research on any one sickness. For example, students might find out basic facts about each illness, including the specific pathogens that cause it, symptoms, complications, method of transmission, and any vaccines available to treat it. Suggest students use a chart to gather information about each illness.

Explain

21st Century Learning

CRITICAL THINKING Tell students that environmental changes can affect how frequently some infectious diseases occur. Explain, for example, that in the southwestern U.S. in 1993, heavy snows and rainfall resulted in abundant plant growth. This increase in available food led to a growing population of deer mice. The mice carried a pathogen called *hantavirus* that could be transmitted to humans. Point out that with ten times more mice than usual, the likelihood increased that humans would come into contact with mice. Though hantavirus infection in humans was not new, the number of people infected was more than might otherwise have been expected. Ask: **Why do you think a disease that is transmitted by mosquitoes might occur more frequently when rainfall is higher than usual?** *(Sample: More rain causes more water to accumulate, and mosquitoes breed in water.)*

Address Misconceptions

L1 **THE SPREAD OF PATHOGENS** Some students may be confused by the wide variety of ways that diseases are spread. Point out that pathogens that cause some diseases are spread in very specific ways, while pathogens that cause other diseases, such as the common cold or the flu can be spread in many different ways. This may be a good time to introduce the idea that there is a basic difference between infectious diseases and noninfectious diseases. You may wish to point out that a noninfectious disease, such as cancer or diabetes, cannot be spread via towels, keyboards, kissing, or water. Ask: **Can you get the flu from an inanimate object?** *(If a person infected with the flu touches an inanimate object such as a towel, keyboard, telephone, or doorknob, another person can get the flu by using one of those objects.)*

Elaborate

Apply It!

L1 Before beginning the activity, review the material on the spread of pathogens in the paragraph about *Soil, Food, and Water.*

▲ **Develop Hypotheses** Remind students that a hypothesis is a possible explanation for a set of observations or an answer to a scientific question. Point out that students should apply to their study of the map what they already know about the way cholera is spread.

Pathogens are spread through contaminated water.

✎ **Apply Concepts** If you have a cold, what can you do to prevent spreading it?

Sample: I can avoid contact with others, and wash my hands often.

How Pathogens Are Spread Pathogens can infect you in several ways. They can spread through contact with an infected person; through soil, food, or water; and through a contaminated object or an infected animal.

Infected People Pathogens often pass from one person to another through direct physical contact, such as kissing and shaking hands. For example, if you kiss someone with an open cold sore, the virus that causes cold sores can get into your body. Pathogens spread indirectly, too. For example, when a person with a cold sneezes, pathogens shoot into the air. People who inhale these pathogens may catch the cold.

Soil, Food, and Water Some pathogens occur naturally in the environment. For example, the bacteria that cause botulism, a severe form of food poisoning, live in soil. These bacteria can produce toxins in foods that have been improperly canned. Other pathogens contaminate food and water and sicken people who eat the food or drink the water. Cholera and dysentery, deadly diseases that cause severe diarrhea, are spread through contaminated food or water.

apply it!

Cholera is a deadly disease caused by bacteria in drinking water. This map shows the locations of cholera cases in the 1854 cholera epidemic in London, England, and the city's water pumps.

❶ ✎ **Develop Hypotheses** Which pump was probably the source of the contaminated water? What evidence do you have?

Sample: Pump 5 was probably the source because most of the cholera victims surround it.

❷ **Pose Questions** Suppose a doctor at the time learned that two more people had died of cholera. What two questions would the doctor most likely have asked?

Sample: Where did the victims live? Which pump did they use?

Cholera Cases, London, 1854

⦂ Cholera victims
◯ Water pump

Oxford Street
Broad Street
Golden Square
Regent Street

① ④ ② ③ ⑤ ⑥ ⑦ ⑧ ⑨

Professional Development Note — Teacher to Teacher

Fighting Disease In the mid 1800s, less than 150 years ago, the leading theory of disease transmission was called *miasma theory.* It stated that diseases were caused by pollution or a noxious form of "bad air." In 1854 Dr. John Snow demonstrated that a cholera outbreak was caused by contaminated water in certain city wells. He mapped the cases of cholera and noticed that they clustered around certain wells. By shutting down the wells he stopped the spread. He is credited with founding the science of epidemiology. Since then we have been able to control the most common communicable diseases.

✉ *Joel Palmer, Ed.D.*
Mesquite ISD
Mesquite, Texas

Contaminated Objects Some pathogens can survive for a time outside a person's body. People can contact pathogens by using objects, such as towels or keyboards, that an infected person touched. Colds and flu can be spread in this way. Tetanus bacteria can enter the body if a contaminated nail or other object punctures the skin.

Infected Animals If an animal that is infected with certain pathogens bites a person, the pathogens can pass to the person. For example, people get rabies, a serious disease of the nervous system, from the bite of an infected animal, such as a dog or raccoon. In tropical regions, mosquito bites transfer the malaria protist to people. Deer ticks, as shown in **Figure 4,** live mostly in the northeastern and upper mideastern United States. The bites of some deer ticks spread Lyme disease. If left untreated, Lyme disease can damage joints and cause many other health problems.

FIGURE 4 ·····························
Deer Ticks and Lyme Disease
To prevent Lyme disease, wear a long-sleeved shirt and tuck your pants into your socks if you plan to walk where ticks may live.

✏️ **Infer** Explain how a deer tick could infect you without your realizing it.

Sample: A deer tick is
so tiny that I might
not see or feel it.

_____

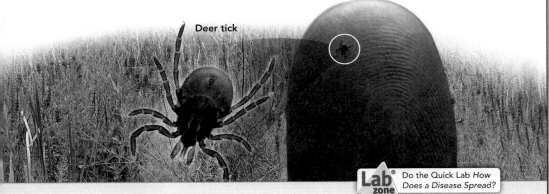

Deer tick

 Do the Quick Lab *How Does a Disease Spread?*

🔑 Assess Your Understanding

2a. Identify Name four types of pathogens that cause disease in humans.

They are bacteria, viruses,
fungi, and protists.

b. CHALLENGE How could people make bacteria-contaminated water safe to drink in order to prevent illness?

Sample: People could boil the
water to kill the bacteria.

_____

_____

got it?

○ I get it! Now I know that disease-causing pathogens include bacteria, viruses, fungi, and protists , and they are spread by infected people; soil, food, and water; contaminated objects; and infected animals.

_____

○ I need extra help with See TE note.

Go to **MY SCIENCE 🎯 COACH** online for help with this subject.

555

Lab zone **After the Inquiry Warm-Up**

Infectious Disease

Inquiry Warm-Up, *The Agents of Disease*

In the Inquiry Warm-Up, you investigated where microbes that might cause disease can be found in your classroom. Using what you learned from that activity, answer the questions below.

1. **ANALYZE SOURCES OF ERROR** Why did the procedure for the lab warn you to be careful not to touch each sterile swab to anything other than the target area?

   _____

   _____

   _____

2. **DESCRIBE** Consider the target area that, when swabbed, led to the least microbe growth in the Petri dish. Describe the physical characteristics of the area, as well as the activities that take place in it.

   _____

   _____

   _____

3. **DESCRIBE** Consider the target area that, when swabbed, led to the most microbe growth in the Petri dish. Describe the physical characteristics of the area, as well as the activities that take place in it.

   _____

   _____

   _____

4. **DEVELOP HYPOTHESES** Consider your responses to Questions 2 and 3. What are some factors that you think may promote heavy microbe growth in an area?

   _____

   _____

   _____

Assess Your Understanding

Infectious Disease

How Do Pathogens Cause Disease?

1a. DEFINE What is an infectious disease?

_____

b. EXPLAIN How did Pasteur's work affect Lister's work?

_____
_____

got it?···

○ **I get it!** Now I know that pathogens cause disease by _____
_____
_____

○ **I need extra help with** _____
_____

What Pathogens Cause Infectious Disease and How Are They Spread?

2a. IDENTIFY Name four types of pathogens that cause disease in humans.

_____
_____

b. CHALLENGE How could people make bacteria-contaminated water safe to drink in order to prevent illness?

_____
_____

got it?···

○ **I get it!** Now I know that disease-causing pathogens include _____
_____, and

they are spread by_____
_____
_____

○ **I need extra help with** _____

Infectious Disease

How Do Pathogens Cause Disease?

In ancient times, people had various beliefs about what caused disease. In the 1860s, the French scientist Louis Pasteur concluded that **microorganisms,** living things too small to see with a microscope, were the cause of most infectious diseases. A physician named Joseph Lister applied Pasteur's work to surgery, washing his hands and instruments and treating patients' post-surgical wounds with carbolic acid. Lister's methods dramatically reduced the percentage of patients who died from infection after surgery.

In the 1870s and 1880s, Robert Koch refined Pasteur's conclusions by showing that a specific microorganism causes each disease. An organism that causes disease is called a **pathogen.** A disease caused by a pathogen is an **infectious disease. When you have an infectious disease, pathogens are in your body causing harm.** Pathogens damage large numbers of individual cells, which makes you sick.

What Pathogens Cause Infectious Disease and How Are They Spread?

Most of the organisms on Earth are harmless, but some cause disease. Most pathogens can be seen only with a microscope. **The four major types of human pathogens are bacteria, viruses, fungi, and protists. They can be spread through contact with a sick person or object in the environment, including other living things.**

Bacteria are one-celled microorganisms that can damage body cells directly or indirectly by producing a poison, or **toxin.** Viruses are nonliving particles that damage body cells by reproducing inside them. Fungi are one-celled or multicelled organisms that grow in warm, dark, moist areas. Protists are one-celled organisms that can cause diseases such as malaria and hiker's disease.

On a separate sheet of paper, define the terms *pathogen* and *infectious disease* and explain how they relate to one another. Also, identify the four major types of human pathogens.

Infectious Disease

Understanding Main Ideas
Fill in the blank to complete each statement.

1. Diseases such as colds can be spread by indirectly when infected people

   _____.

2. A person catching the flu after using utensils that a sick person
   used previously is an example of pathogens spreading through

   _____.

3. A disease such as _____ is likely to have as its source a
   bite from an infected animal.

4. Contact with a pathogen that lives naturally in the soil, water, or

   food can causes a disease such as _____.

Answer the following question in the space provided.

5. What are the four major groups of human pathogens?

   _____

   _____

Building Vocabulary
Match each term with its definition by writing the letter of the correct definition in the
right column on the line beside the term in the left column.

6. ___ microorganisms

7. ___ pathogens

8. ___ infectious disease

9. ___ toxin

a. a disease caused by a pathogen

b. a poison

c. living things too small to see without a microscope

d. organisms that cause disease

Infectious Disease

> Read the passage and study the diagram. Then answer the questions that follow on a separate sheet of paper.

Stopping Malaria

Malaria is an infectious disease caused by the protist *Plasmodium*. This pathogen is transmitted from one person to another by the bite of the female *Anopheles* mosquito. The disease infects more than 150 million people a year and kills between 1.5 and 3.0 million people. Although malaria is treatable, it occurs in parts of the world where effective treatments are largely unavailable. For this reason, the battle against the spread of malaria has focused on prevention. The diagram below provides information about the spread of malaria and the life cycle of the *Anopheles* mosquito.

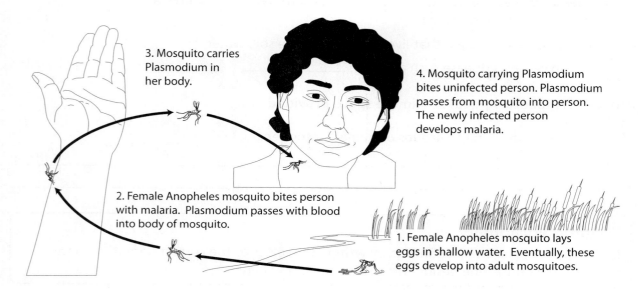

3. Mosquito carries Plasmodium in her body.

4. Mosquito carrying Plasmodium bites uninfected person. Plasmodium passes from mosquito into person. The newly infected person develops malaria.

2. Female Anopheles mosquito bites person with malaria. Plasmodium passes with blood into body of mosquito.

1. Female Anopheles mosquito lays eggs in shallow water. Eventually, these eggs develop into adult mosquitoes.

1. Diseases can be spread in four basic ways. In which of these ways is malaria spread?
2. Where does the female *Anopheles* mosquito lay eggs?
3. How does *Plasmodium* get into the body of a female *Anopheles* mosquito?
4. How does a person get malaria?
5. Sometimes shallow pools and swamps in an area are drained to help prevent the spread of malaria. Use the diagram to explain why this strategy is effective.
6. What are other ways to prevent the spread of malaria?

Lesson Quiz

Infectious Disease

If the statement is true, write *true*. If the statement is false, change the underlined word or words to make the statement true.

1. _____ Viruses are <u>living</u> particles that damage body cells by reproducing inside them.

2. _____ When you have an infectious disease, <u>toxins</u> are in your body causing harm.

3. _____ Human pathogens <u>cannot be</u> spread through contact with a sick person or object in the environment, including other living things.

4. _____ <u>Most</u> pathogens can be seen only with a microscope.

5. _____ Fungi are one-celled or multicelled organisms that grow in warm, dark, <u>moist</u> areas.

Fill in the blank to complete each statement.

6. In the 1860s, the French scientist Louis Pasteur concluded that _____ were the cause of most infectious diseases.

7. Joseph Lister's methods dramatically reduced the percentage of patients who died from infection after _____.

8. The four major types of human pathogens are bacteria, _____, fungi, and protists.

9. A disease caused by a pathogen is a(n) _____.

10. _____ are one-celled organisms that can cause diseases such as malaria.

Infectious Disease

Answer Key

After the Inquiry Warm-Up

1. If the sterile swab touched anything else it might have picked up microbes outside the target area, so any growth in the Petri dish would not accurately reflect the amount or kind of microbes located in the target area.

2. Answers will vary.

3. Answers will vary.

4. Answers will vary. Students may suggest that warmth, dampness, a lot of human traffic and contact, and/or a lack of regular cleaning and disinfection promote heavy microbe growth.

Key Concept Summaries

A pathogen is an organism that causes disease. The four major types of human pathogens are bacteria, viruses, fungi, and protists. An infectious disease is a disease caused by a pathogen.

Review and Reinforce

1. Sample: sneeze, cough

2. contaminated objects

3. Samples responses: rabies, Lyme disease

4. Sample responses: botulism, cholera, dysentery

5. The four major types of human pathogens are bacteria, viruses, fungi, and protists.

6. c   7. d

8. a   9. b

Enrich

1. through an infected animal

2. She lays eggs only in shallow water.

3. She bites a person who has malaria.

4. A person gets malaria by being bitten by a female *Anopheles* mosquito that has bitten a person with malaria.

5. This would eliminate Step 1 in the process. The result would be fewer mosquitoes to carry the malaria protist *Plasmodium*.

6. Answers will vary. Samples: Control the mosquitoes with insecticides. Prevent *Anopheles* mosquitoes from biting people through the use of insect repellent and screens. Cure everyone with malaria so no more *Plasmodium* can enter a mosquito's body.

Lesson Quiz

1. nonliving   2. pathogens

3. can be   4. true

5. true   6. microorganisms

7. surgery   8. viruses

9. infectious disease   10. Protists

Place the outside corner, the corner away from the dotted line, in the corner of your copy machine to copy onto letter-size paper.

The Body's Defenses

 Why do you sometimes get sick?

Lesson Pacing: 2–3 periods or 1–1½ blocks

🕐 **SHORT ON TIME?** To do this lesson in approximately half the time, do the Activate Prior Knowledge activity followed by a discussion of the Key Concepts to familiarize students with the lesson content. Have students do the Quick Lab. The rest of the lesson can be completed by students independently.

> **Preference Navigator,** in the online Planning tools, allows you to customize *Interactive Science* to your own teaching style. You can also edit lesson plans by selecting the Lesson Planner option.
>
> **Digital Teacher's Edition** allows you to access your Teacher's Edition and Resource materials online.

my science online.com

Lesson Vocabulary

- inflammatory response
- phagocyte
- immune response
- lymphocyte
- T cell
- antigen
- B cell
- antibody

Professional Development Note ## Content Refresher

T Cells and B Cells The first time the immune system encounters and reacts to an antigen, a primary immune response occurs. Subsequent infections of the body with the same pathogen—and, therefore, the same antigen—produce a secondary immune response. During a primary response, after activation by a T cell, most B cells produce antibodies. A few B cells, however, are activated to reproduce rather than to produce antibodies. These B cells remain in the circulatory system for a long time, perhaps years, and are called *memory B cells*. If these memory B cells encounter the same antigen again, a secondary immune response occurs. During the secondary response, the B cells produce antibodies very quickly, so quickly the pathogen may never get well established in the body.

There are helper T cells, killer T cells, and suppressor T cells. When helper T cells are activated by an antigen, they strongly stimulate B cells and killer T cells and also stimulate suppressor T cells. The gradually increasing activity of suppressor T cells shuts off the immune response when it is no longer needed. Some helper T cells become memory T cells and can help trigger a secondary immune response if the pathogen attacks again.

LESSON OBJECTIVES

 Explain how the body's first line of defense guards against pathogens.

Describe how the inflammatory response and the immune response function.

Blended Path
Active learning using Student Edition, Inquiry Path, and Digital Path

ENGAGE AND EXPLORE

Teach this lesson using a variety of resources. Begin by reading **My Planet Diary** as a class. Have students share ideas about places where they have encountered other people's saliva. Then have students do the **Inquiry Warm-Up activity.** Students will investigate antigens and antibodies using a model. Discuss how the paper changed when it was torn in two. The **After the Inquiry Warm-Up worksheet** sets up a discussion about the importance of the shapes of the cells in the body. Have volunteers share their answers to question 4 about whether a young child or an adult would have more infections.

EXPLAIN AND ELABORATE

Teach Key Concepts by explaining how the skin functions as a barrier to pathogens. **Lead a Discussion** about how people can avoid catching an infectious disease.

Continue to **Teach Key Concepts** by explaining the body's second line of defense—the inflammatory response. **Lead a Discussion** about how inflammation helps fight pathogens. **Support the Big Q** by discussing how a fever helps destroy some pathogens. **Lead a Discussion** about the lymphocytes. Use **Figure 4** to illustrate how T cells function. **Lead a Discussion** about the function of B cells. **Figure 5** illustrates how B cells fit on specific antigens. Before beginning the **Apply It activity,** review the section about *The Immune Response.* Then have students share how they described the steps of the immune response. Hand out the **Key Concept Summaries** as a review of each part of the lesson. Students can also use the online **Vocab Flash Cards** to review key terms.

EVALUATE

Have students take the **Lesson Quiz.** For an alternate assessment, see the **EXAM**VIEW® Assessment Suite, Progress Monitoring Assessments, or SuccessTracker™.

ELL Support

1 Content and Language

Write the words *lymphocyte* and *phagocyte* on the board. Underline the word part *-cyte* which means "cell." Remind students that *phagocytes* and *lymphocytes* are different types of white blood cells

DIFFERENTIATED INSTRUCTION KEY
L1 Struggling Students or Special Needs
L2 On-Level Students **L3** Advanced Students

LESSON PLANNER 14.2

 **Inquiry Path** Hands-on learning in the Lab zone

ENGAGE AND EXPLORE

To teach this lesson with an emphasis on inquiry, begin with the **Inquiry Warm-Up activity.** Students will model the specificity of antigens and antibodies. Discuss how the paper changed when it was torn. Have students do the **After the Inquiry Warm-Up worksheet.** Talk about how defender and pathogen cells recognize and attack other body cells. Have volunteers share their answers to question 4 about whether an adult or a young child be more likely to have more infections.

EXPLAIN AND ELABORATE

Focus on the **Inquiry Skill** for the lesson. Point out that when you make a model, you represent a situation or object in order to more directly observe it. What models were made in the **Inquiry Warm-Up activity?** *(Antigens and antibodies)* Do the **Teacher Demo** to show students that bacteria are everywhere. Assign the **Lab Investigation** to help students understand how the skin works as a barrier.

Support the Big Q by explaining why a fever is an effect of an infection. To **Build Inquiry** have students perform skits to dramatize the immune response. Review the section about *The Immune Response* before beginning the **Apply It activity.** Ask volunteers to share how they described the immune response against the bacteria that caused strep throat. Have students do the **Quick Lab** to model how an antibody keeps a pathogen from entering a cell. Students can use the online **Vocab Flash Cards** to review key terms.

EVALUATE

Have students take the **Lesson Quiz.** For an alternate assessment, see the **EXAM**VIEW® Assessment Suite, Progress Monitoring Assessments, or SuccessTracker™.

Digital Path Online learning at MY SCIENCE ONLINE.com

ENGAGE AND EXPLORE

Teach this lesson using digital resources. Begin by having students explore real-world connections to the body's defenses at **My Planet Diary** online. Have them access the Chapter Resources to find the **Unlock the Big Question activity.** There they can answer the questions and refine their responses as they continue through the lesson. You can re-assign the activity and have students submit their work so you can track their progress.

EXPLAIN AND ELABORATE

Students reading above, at, or below the lexile measure of this lesson can access basic content readings at their level at **My Reading Web.** Have students use the online **Vocab Flash Cards** to preview key terms.

Support the Big Q by explaining how a fever helps fight off an infection. Have students do the online **Interactive Art** to show the body's response to pathogens. Review *The Immune Response* section before assigning the online **Apply It activity.** Ask volunteers to share the steps of the immune response against the bacteria that caused strep throat. Have students submit their work to you. Do the **Quick Lab** and then ask students to share their results. The **Key Concept Summaries** online allow students to read a summary and see an image associated with each part of the lesson. Online remediation is available at **My Science Coach.**

EVALUATE

Have students take the **Lesson Quiz.** For an alternate assessment, see the **EXAM**VIEW® Assessment Suite, Progress Monitoring Assessments, or SuccessTracker™.

2 Frontload the Lesson

Preview the lesson visuals, labels, and captions. Ask students what they know about the terms *inflammatory response* and *immune response.* Explain the specific meanings these words have in science.

3 Comprehensible Input

Have students study the visuals and their captions to support the Key Concepts of the lesson.

4 Language Production

Pair or group students with varied language abilities to complete labs collaboratively for language practice. Have each student copy the completed written lab for personal reference.

5 Assess Understanding

Have students keep a content area log for this lesson using a two-column format with the headings "What I Understand" and "What I Don't Understand." Follow up so that students can move items from the "Don't Understand" to the "Understand" column.

The Body's Defenses

Establish Learning Objectives

After this lesson, students will be able to:

🗝 Explain how the body's first line of defense guards against pathogens.

🗝 Describe how the inflammatory response and the immune response function.

Engage

Activate Prior Knowledge

MY PLANET DIARY Read *The Kissing Disease* with the class. Explain that the disease is caused by the Epstein-Barr virus. Point out that if young children contract this virus, their bodies become protected against mononucleosis. Ask: **Is mononucleosis an infectious disease?** *(Yes)* **How do you know?** *(Sample: It is spread to noninfected people through saliva.)*

BIG IDEAS OF SCIENCE REFERENCE LIBRARY 📖
Have students look up the following topics: Common Cold, Rheumatoid Arthritis.

Explore

Lab Resource: Inquiry Warm-Up

L1 **WHICH PIECES FIT TOGETHER?** Students will model the specificity of antigens and antibodies.

The Body's Defenses

 UNLOCK THE BIG ?

🗝 **What Is the Body's First Line of Defense?**

🗝 **What Are the Inflammatory and Immune Responses?**

MY PLANET DIARY

FUN FACTS

The Kissing Disease

Have you ever heard of mononucleosis? Also known as mono, or the kissing disease, mononucleosis is most common among older teenagers and people in their twenties. It got its nickname because the disease can be spread through kissing. But, be careful. Because mono is passed through saliva, it can also be spread by sharing cups, forks, straws, and other utensils. Some common symptoms of mono are fever, sore throat, swollen glands, and fatigue. If you display these symptoms, you might want to pay your doctor a visit, even if you haven't kissed anyone!

Read the following questions. Write your answers below.

1. How can mononucleosis be spread?

   It can be spread by kissing and by using objects that may have come in contact with another's saliva.

2. What can you do to lower your chances of catching mono?

   Sample: I will not use anyone else's eating utensils.

▶ PLANET DIARY Go to **Planet Diary** to learn more about the body's defenses.

Lab zone Do the Inquiry Warm-Up *Which Pieces Fit Together?*

SUPPORT ALL READERS
Lexile Measure = 990L   Lexile Word Count = 1192

Prior Exposure to Content: May be the first time students have encountered this topic

Academic Vocabulary: *compare, contrast, model*

Science Vocabulary: *phagocyte, lymphocyte, T cell, antigen, antibody*

Concept Level: Generally appropriate for most students in this grade

Preteach With: My Planet Diary "The Kissing Disease" and Figure 2 activity

Go to **My Reading Web** to access leveled readings that provide a foundation for the content.

my science online.com ▶

Vocabulary
- inflammatory response • phagocyte
- immune response • lymphocyte • T cell
- antigen • B cell • antibody

Skills
- ⟳ Reading: Compare and Contrast
- △ Inquiry: Make Models

What Is the Body's First Line of Defense?

You have probably battled invaders in video games. Video games have fantasy battles, but on and in your body, real battles against invading pathogens happen all the time. You are hardly ever aware of these battles because the body's disease-fighting system has lines of defense that effectively eliminate pathogens before they can harm your cells. ⚷ **In the first line of defense, the surface of your skin, breathing passages, mouth, and stomach function as barriers to pathogens. These barriers trap and kill most pathogens with which you come into contact.**

Skin Your skin is an effective barrier to pathogens, as you can see in **Figure 1.** Pathogens on the skin are exposed to destructive chemicals in oil and sweat. Even if these chemicals do not kill them, the pathogens may fall off with dead skin cells. Most pathogens get through the skin only when it is cut. However, blood clots at a cut. Then a scab forms over the cut. So pathogens have little time to enter the body this way.

FIGURE 1 ....

Skin as a Barrier
The dots are groups of bacteria. The bacteria were on the skin of a person's hand.

✏ **Use the photo to complete the tasks.**

1. **Identify** In each box, write one of the skin's defenses against pathogens.

2. [CHALLENGE] Why would you want a cut to bleed some?

   Sample: So the blood clots and forms a scab.

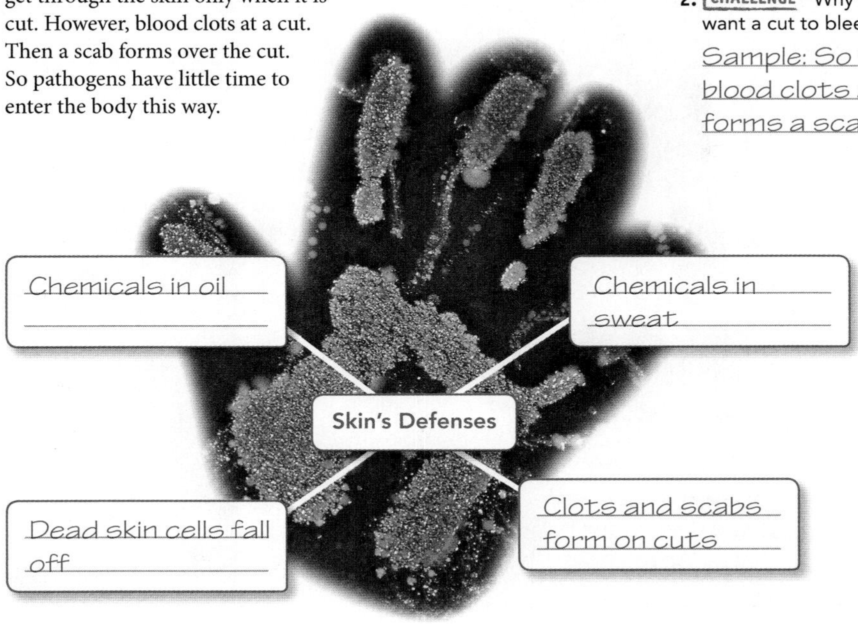

Chemicals in oil

Chemicals in sweat

Skin's Defenses

Dead skin cells fall off

Clots and scabs form on cuts

557

Explain

Introduce Vocabulary

To help students understand the term *antibody*, point out the prefix *anti-*, which means "against." Tell students that an antibody fights against bodies, or organisms that can cause diseases.

Teach Key Concepts ⚷

Explain to students that the body's first line of defense consists of barriers that trap and kill most pathogens with which people come into contact. Ask: **What structures make up this first line of defense?** *(The surface of the skin, breathing passages, the mouth, and the stomach)* **How does your skin function as a barrier?** *(It covers the body and keeps pathogens from entering. It also produces destructive chemicals in oil and sweat.)* **What happens to protect the body in the event of a cut?** *(The blood clots and a scab forms, blocking the entry for pathogens after a short time.)* **Is getting a scab on a cut a "good thing" or a "bad thing"?** *(A scab is a natural, positive part of the healing process.)* Explain that the blood forms a clot at the site of the cut, which prevents further bleeding. Point out that a scab is the dried clot. Make sure students understand that a scab is a natural part of the healing process and that a scab may take several hours to a few days to form over a cut.

Lead a Discussion

RESISTANCE TO INFECTIOUS DISEASES Tell students that people can adopt behaviors that help the body's lines of defense. Ask: **What are some things people can do to avoid becoming ill with an infectious disease?** *(Samples: Getting enough rest, eating healthy foods, avoiding objects contaminated by an infected persons, washing hands, getting vaccinated)*

My Planet Diary provides an opportunity for students to explore real-world connections to the body's defenses.

my science online.com ▷ Skin as a Barrier

ⒺⓁⓁ Support

1 Content and Language
Have students read the title of the first section of this lesson. Point out that the term *line of defense*, derives from battle soldiers forming a line.

2 Frontload the Lesson
Ask students to identify and describe forms of inflammation in body tissues. Urge them to recall getting a splinter, cut, or bruise. Tell students that they will learn about the body's efforts to fight infection and disease.

3 Comprehensible Input
Remind students that many body organs and structures fight pathogens. Have them work in pairs or small groups to prepare physical demonstrations of these actions. Ask some students to portray pathogens as other students enact organs, structures, and substances.

Elaborate

Make Analogies

L1 **SWEEP OUT THE PATHOGENS** To help students focus their understanding on one aspect of the first line of defense, compare the function of coughing and sneezing to the act of sweeping dirt out the door of a house. Remind students that structures in the nose, pharynx, trachea, and bronchi trap pathogens from the air. Explain that the act of coughing or sneezing forces these pathogens back out of the body. Ask: **How does sneezing and coughing when you have a cold demonstrate that your body is fighting off disease?** *(It is your body's response to the presence of pathogens in breathing passages.)*

Teacher Demo

L1 **BACTERIA ARE EVERYWHERE**

Materials disposable petri dish with nutrient agar, sterile cotton ball, tape

Time 10 minutes for setup, 5 minutes each day over several days

Explain that normally harmless bacteria are present on the skin. Rub your palm with the cotton ball, and then brush the cotton over the agar. Tape the dish closed, and place it upside down in a warm place (not over 37°C). Each day for several days, allow students to examine the dish with the cover closed. *(The agar should be covered with dots.)* Explain that each dot is a colony that contains millions of bacteria. *CAUTION: Do not allow students to open the dishes. Follow local regulations for disposal of live materials.*

Ask: **Why can you see the bacteria?** *(Because the bacteria multiplied on the agar, and now there are millions of them.)* **Why is hand-washing important even if you are not ill?** *(You can pick up pathogens from the environment.)*

Lab Resource: Lab Investigation

L2 **THE SKIN AS A BARRIER** Students will use apples to demonstrate the skin as a barrier.

Evaluate

Assess Your Understanding

Have students evaluate their understanding by completing the appropriate sentence.

RTI Response to Intervention

If students need help identifying the body's first lines of defense, **then** direct their attention to the Key Concept statements.

my science COACH Have students go online for help in understanding the body's defenses.

Breathing Passages Your breathing passages defend you from many pathogens you inhale. The nose, pharynx, trachea, and bronchi have hairs, mucus, and cilia, all of which trap pathogens from the air. In addition, you sneeze and cough when pathogens irritate your breathing passages. Sneezing and coughing force pathogens out of your body.

Mouth and Stomach Even if foods are handled safely, they still contain potential pathogens. Most of these pathogens are destroyed in your mouth or stomach. Saliva in your mouth contains destructive chemicals, and your stomach produces acid. **Figure 2** shows three of your body's barriers to pathogens.

FIGURE 2 ·······················

Barriers to Pathogens
Your breathing passages, mouth, and stomach are part of your first line of defense against pathogens.

✎ **Summarize** In each box, write how the barrier protects the body from pathogens.

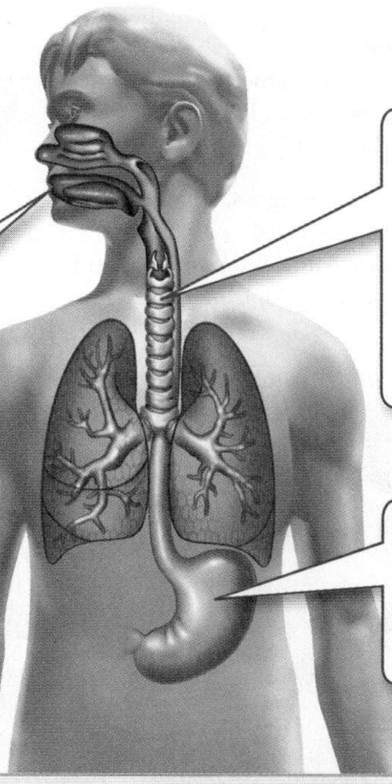

Mouth
Chemicals in saliva kill pathogens.

Breathing Passages
Hairs, mucus, and cilia trap pathogens. Sneezing and coughing force pathogens out of the body.

Stomach
Acid in the stomach kills pathogens.

 Do the Lab Investigation *The Skin as a Barrier.*

🔑 Assess Your Understanding

got it? ···································

○ **I get it!** Now I know that the body's first lines of defense are the surfaces of the skin, breathing passages, mouth, and stomach.

○ **I need extra help with** See TE note.

Go to **my science COACH** online for help with this subject.

What Are the Inflammatory and Immune Responses?

Sometimes the first line of defense fails, and pathogens get into your body. Fortunately, your body has a second and third line of defense—the inflammatory response and the immune response.

 In the inflammatory response, fluid and white blood cells leak from blood vessels and fight pathogens in nearby tissues. In the immune response, certain immune cells in the blood and tissues react to each kind of pathogen with a defense targeted specifically at the pathogen.

Inflammatory Response Have you ever scraped your knee? When body cells are damaged, they release chemicals that trigger the **inflammatory response,** which is your body's second line of defense. The inflammatory response is the same regardless of the pathogen, so it is a general defense. This response involves white blood cells, inflammation, and sometimes fever.

Vocabulary Latin Word Origins The Latin word *inflammare* means "to set on fire." How does the Latin meaning relate to the word *inflammation*?

Sample: An inflamma-
tion is a red, warm,
swollen place.

Compare and Contrast Use the first paragraph of the text to list how the inflammatory and immune responses are alike and different in the Venn diagram.

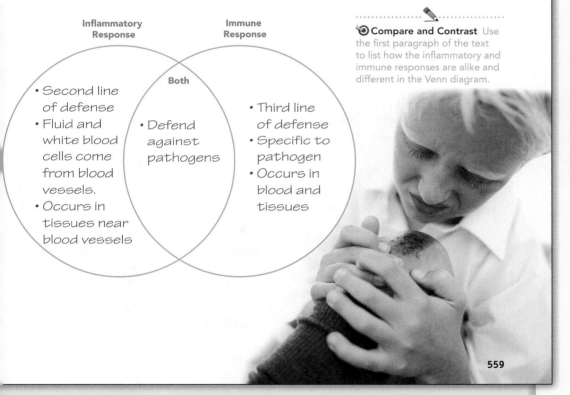

Inflammatory Response
- Second line of defense
- Fluid and white blood cells come from blood vessels.
- Occurs in tissues near blood vessels

Both
- Defend against pathogens

Immune Response
- Third line of defense
- Specific to pathogen
- Occurs in blood and tissues

559

Explain

Teach Key Concepts 🔑

Explain to students that the second line of defense is the inflammatory response and that the third line of defense is the immune response. Point out that the inflammatory response involves white blood cells, inflammation, and sometimes fever. Then explain that the immune response involves particular cells in the blood and tissues reacting to each type of pathogen with a defense targeted specifically at that pathogen. Ask: **Why is the body's second line of defense necessary?** (*Sometimes the first line of defense fails.*) **What is the inflammatory response?** (*Fluid and white blood cells leak from blood vessels and fight pathogens in nearby tissues.*) **Why is the inflammatory response considered a "general" defense?** (*The response is the same regardless of the type of pathogen in the body.*) Have students imagine waking up and not feeling well. Ask: **Why does taking your body's temperature with a thermometer help determine whether or not you are sick?** (*A fever indicates the presence of an infectious disease, and it indicates that the body's first line of defense is engaged in fighting it.*) **How is the immune response different from the inflammatory response?** (*In the immune response, cells react to each kind of pathogen with a specific defense.*)

Compare and Contrast Explain to students that when they compare and contrast, they examine the similarities and differences between things.

Differentiated Instruction

L1 Draw First Line of Defense Have students sketch an outline of a body, then indicate and label the parts of the body that are involved in the first line of defense. Ask students to write brief sentences in their own words describing how each component of the first line of defense protects against pathogens.

L3 Digestive Defenses Challenge students to do research to find information about how the digestive system defends against pathogens. Students can research the antibacterial properties of saliva and stomach secretions.

Explain

Lead a Discussion

THE SECOND LINE OF DEFENSE Ask one or more student volunteers to explain the function of phagocytes to the rest of the class *(Phagocytes engulf pathogens and break them down.)* Ask: **How does inflammation help fight pathogens?** *(The process of inflammation involves the widening of blood vessels, which increases the flow of blood and therefore the number of white cells to the affected area.)* **What are some signs of inflammation?** *The area may become red and swollen. It may feel warmer than usual.* Point out that inflammation is typically a local response to a local infection.

Support the Big Q ? UbD

FEVER Because fever is a symptom of an infection, students often think of the fever as a cause, rather than an effect. Ask: **What causes a fever?** *(Chemicals released during the inflammatory response)* **Why is a fever helpful?** *(Some pathogens cannot survive at a temperature higher than normal body temperature.)*

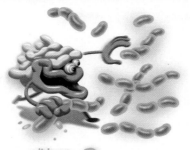

did you know? ....

Your red bone marrow produces about 1 billion new white blood cells every day. Some of them are on patrol in your body right now, looking for pathogens and destroying them.

White Blood Cells Most white blood cells are disease fighters. However, each type of white blood cell has a particular function. The type of white blood cell involved in the inflammatory response is the phagocyte. A **phagocyte** (FAG uh syt) is a white blood cell that engulfs pathogens and destroys them by breaking them down.

Inflammation The inflammatory response is shown in **Figure 3**. During this response, capillaries widen in the area with pathogens. This enlargement increases blood flow to the area. Fluid and phagocytes leak out of the enlarged capillaries, and the affected area becomes red and swollen. In fact, if you touch the area, it will feel slightly warmer than usual. The phagocytes engulf the pathogens and destroy them.

Fever Chemicals produced during the inflammatory response sometimes cause a fever. Although a fever makes you feel bad, it helps your body fight the infection. Some pathogens do not grow or reproduce well at higher temperatures.

FIGURE 3 ....

The Inflammatory Response
Inflammation is a sign your phagocytes are working.

✎ **Sequence** In the text above, underline the steps in the inflammatory response. In the boxes below, describe what is happening in each diagram.

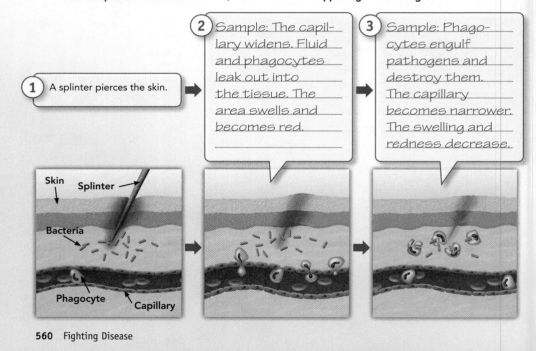

1 A splinter pierces the skin.

2 Sample: The capillary widens. Fluid and phagocytes leak out into the tissue. The area swells and becomes red.

3 Sample: Phagocytes engulf pathogens and destroy them. The capillary becomes narrower. The swelling and redness decrease.

Skin Splinter

Bacteria

Phagocyte Capillary

560 Fighting Disease

Immune Response If an infection from a pathogen is severe enough, it triggers the body's third line of defense—the **immune response.** The immune response is controlled by the immune system. The cells of the immune system can distinguish between different kinds of pathogens. They react to invaders with a defense targeted against that pathogen.

The white blood cells that distinguish between different kinds of pathogens are called **lymphocytes** (LIM fuh syts). Your body has two major kinds of lymphocytes: T cells and B cells.

T Cells A **T cell** is a lymphocyte that identifies pathogens and distinguishes one pathogen from another. Each kind of T cell recognizes a different kind of pathogen. What T cells actually recognize are a pathogen's marker molecules, which are called antigens. **Antigens** are molecules that the immune system recognizes either as part of your body or as coming from outside your body. Each different pathogen has its own antigen, with its own chemical structure. Look at **Figure 4** to see how T cells function.

T cell

FIGURE 4 ·······························
T Cell Function
Healthy people have tens of millions of T cells in their blood.

✎ **Describe** What two roles does a T cell play after it divides?

Some T cells attack cells damaged by pathogens. Others activate B cells.

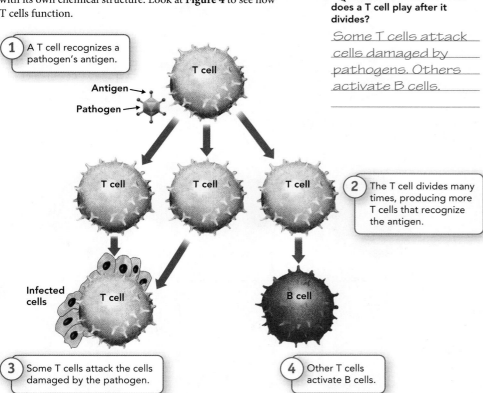

1 A T cell recognizes a pathogen's antigen.

Antigen →
Pathogen →

T cell

T cell   T cell   T cell

2 The T cell divides many times, producing more T cells that recognize the antigen.

Infected cells   T cell

B cell

3 Some T cells attack the cells damaged by the pathogen.

4 Other T cells activate B cells.

561

Lead a Discussion

T CELLS Point out that that there are several kinds of white blood cells. Phagocytes are one kind of white blood cell and lymphocytes are another. Ask: **How are lymphocytes different from phagocytes?** *(Phagocytes can attack many kinds of pathogens. Each lymphocyte identifies and targets specific pathogens.)* **What are the two major kinds of lymphocytes?** *(T cells and B cells)* **What is the major function of T cells?** *(To identify pathogens and distinguish one kind from another)* **How do T cells recognize pathogens?** *(By the antigens that are found on each pathogen)* **What is an antigen?** *(A molecule that the body's immune system can recognize as part of the body or coming from outside the body)*

Teach With Visuals

Tell students to look at **Figure 4.** Have student volunteers read aloud each step in the figure and then identify the steps performed by T cells. Ask: **What begins the immune response?** *(T cells recognize a pathogen's antigen.)* **How do T cells first respond to the presence of the antigen?** *(They divide many times and produce more T cells that recognize the antigen.)* **What do the T cells do next?** *(They attack damaged cells and activate B cells.)* Make sure students understand that attacking the body's own cells gets rid of damaged cells and also kills any viruses that are inside the cells. Explain to students that the mumps is a viral infection that affects salivary glands. Ask: **Which body cells would T cells attack if you had the mumps?** *(Cells in salivary glands)*

Differentiated Instruction

L1 **Model Phagocytes** Demonstrate the action of phagocytes by grasping a small object completely in your hand. Explain to students that phagocytes surround a pathogen, and then break it down with chemicals. Provide students with lumps of clay and buttons, and ask them to model the action of phagocytes. *(Students should wrap clay completely around each button.)*

L1 **Science Term** Encourage pairs of students to use dictionaries to learn about the etymology of the word *phagocyte.* Students should be able to find information that clarifies the meanings of *phag* ("eat") and *kytos* ("cell"). Have students explain how this helps them understand what a phagocyte does. If necessary, help students see that phagocytes take in pathogens the way a person takes in food.

Explain

Lead a Discussion

B CELLS Remind students that the two major kinds of lymphocytes are T cells and B cells. Ask: **What is the major function of B cells?** *(To produce antibodies that help destroy pathogens)* Tell students that some B cells develop into memory cells that circulate through the body indefinitely. If a person is exposed to the same pathogen, the memory cells will become active and trigger rapid production of antibodies, which allows the body to attack the pathogen before infection occurs.

Teach With Visuals

Tell students to look at **Figure 5.** Have students identify the function performed by B cells. *(B cells produce antibodies.)* **What detail in the B cell on the left helps you draw an antigen with the correct shape?** *(The shape of the opening at the end of the antibody)* **How would you describe that opening?** *(Rectangular)* **How is this opening different from those on the center and right B cells?** *(The opening on the center B cell is triangular, and the opening on the right B cell is circular.)*

△ **Make Models** Explain that making models helps people understand things that they cannot observe directly. Point out that physical models take the form of drawings, diagrams, and three-dimensional structures, whereas mental models include mathematical equations and words.

Elaborate

Build Inquiry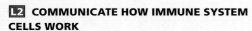

L2 COMMUNICATE HOW IMMUNE SYSTEM CELLS WORK

Materials tape, paper

Time 30 minutes

Ask students to name key terms related to the immune system. Place students in small groups of four or five, and have them create skits that dramatize the immune response. Group tasks can include research, writing, acting, and narrating. Suggest that students identify their roles within the immune response by using paper signs. Roles should include pathogens, T cells, B cells, antigens, antibodies, and phagocytes.

Invite students to think of a time when they had a cold or a sore throat.

Ask: **At what point might you have known that your immune system was "winning the fight"?** *(When I started to feel better)*

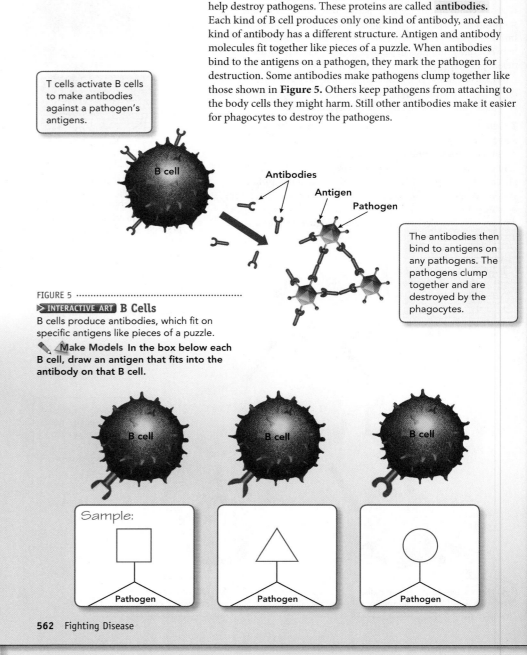

B Cells The lymphocytes called **B cells** produce proteins that help destroy pathogens. These proteins are called **antibodies.** Each kind of B cell produces only one kind of antibody, and each kind of antibody has a different structure. Antigen and antibody molecules fit together like pieces of a puzzle. When antibodies bind to the antigens on a pathogen, they mark the pathogen for destruction. Some antibodies make pathogens clump together like those shown in **Figure 5.** Others keep pathogens from attaching to the body cells they might harm. Still other antibodies make it easier for phagocytes to destroy the pathogens.

T cells activate B cells to make antibodies against a pathogen's antigens.

The antibodies then bind to antigens on any pathogens. The pathogens clump together and are destroyed by the phagocytes.

FIGURE 5 ·········
▶ **INTERACTIVE ART** **B Cells**
B cells produce antibodies, which fit on specific antigens like pieces of a puzzle.

✎ **Make Models** In the box below each B cell, draw an antigen that fits into the antibody on that B cell.

Sample:

Pathogen   Pathogen   Pathogen

562 Fighting Disease

Interactive Art shows the body's responses to pathogens.

Digital Lesson: Assign the *Apply It* activity online and have students submit their work to you.

my science online.com   **Responses to Pathogens**

apply it!

Certain bacteria cause strep throat. Your T cells and B cells work together to combat the infection.

❶ **Identify** Number each step in the immune response.

❷ **Sequence** Describe each step of the immune response against the bacteria that causes strep throat.

1. A T cell identifies the bacteria that cause strep.

2. The T cell divides, making more T cells.

3. Some T cells attack the infected throat cells damaged by the bacteria.

4. Some T cells activate B cells.

5. B cells make antibodies against the bacteria antigens.

6. The antibodies attach to the bacteria antigens. Bacteria clump together and are destroyed.

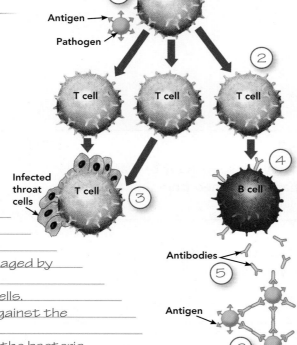

T cell

Antigen
Pathogen

① T cell

T cell ② T cell

Infected throat cells

T cell ③

④ B cell

Antibodies

⑤

Antigen

⑥

Lab zone
Do the Quick Lab
Stuck Together.

Assess Your Understanding

1a. Name Identify the key cells that are part of the immune response.

They are T cells and B cells.

b. Explain How does the inflammatory response defend against pathogens?

It enables phagocytes to leak from blood vessels and fight pathogens in nearby tissues.

got it?

○ I get it! Now I know the inflammatory and immune responses are the body's second and third lines of defense against pathogens.

○ I need extra help with See TE note.

Go to **MY SCIENCE COACH** *online for help with this subject.*

563

Apply It!

L1 Before beginning the activity, review the four paragraphs in the section *The Immune Response.* Ask: **How does the T cell identify the bacteria that cause strep?** *(It "reads" or recognizes the antigens on the pathogen.)* **On what structure are antibodies made?** *(B cells)* **How would you describe the important relationship between an antigen and an antibody in the immune response?** *(Sample: Antibodies fit onto antigens much as puzzle pieces fit together.)*

21st Century Learning

CREATIVITY Have students read *Common Cold* in the **Big Ideas of Science Reference Library.** Ask them to use the information in the reading to write a song or poem that describes how it feels to suffer through the common cold and how the body works to fight the virus. Students can present their finished work to the class.

Lab Resource: Quick Lab

L2 STUCK TOGETHER Students will model one way an antibody keeps a pathogen from entering a cell.

Evaluate

Assess Your Understanding

After students answer the questions, have them evaluate their understanding by completing the appropriate sentence.

RTI Response to Intervention

1a. If students have trouble identifying key cells in the immune response, **then** help them review the material on T cells and B cells.

b. If students need help explaining how the inflammatory response defends against pathogens, **then** encourage them to look again at **Figure 4** and **Figure 5.**

MY SCIENCE COACH Have students go online for help in understanding the inflammatory and immune responses.

Differentiated Instruction

L1 T Cells and B Cells Read the passages on T cells and B cells aloud as students follow along with you. Stop periodically to help students find supporting visuals in **Figure 4** and **Figure 5.** When you have read both passages, ask students to summarize the immune response in their own words.

L3 Describe the Lymphatic System Ask students to identify the organs and tissues that make up the immune system (such as lymph nodes, spleen, and bone marrow) and their functions. Encourage students to make informational posters to use as they present their findings orally to the rest of the class.

563

563

Name _____ Date _____ Class _____

The Body's Defenses

Inquiry Warm-Up, *Which Pieces Fit Together?*
In the Inquiry Warm-Up, you used a model to investigate how some body cells are able to stop pathogens from getting people sick. Using what you learned from that activity, answer the questions below.

1. **SOLVE PROBLEMS** When you tear a piece of paper in two, you change its size. What else about the paper is changed when you tear it in two along a jagged edge?

   _____

   _____

2. **INFER** Consider the model used in the lab and your answer to Question 1. How do you think a specific defender cell in your body recognizes a specific pathogen?

   _____

   _____

3. **APPLY CONCEPTS** The factor that enables a defender cell in the body to recognize a pathogen is the same factor that enables that pathogen to attack other body cells. What factor enables a pathogen to attack other body cells?

   _____

4. **INFER** In the lab you were asked whether an adult or a young child would have more types of defender cells. Based on your answer, would an adult or a young child be likely to have more infections? Explain.

   _____

   _____

Name _____ Date _____ Class _____

Assess Your Understanding

The Body's Defenses

What Is the Body's First Line of Defense?

got it? ....

○ **I get it!** Now I know that the body's first line of defense is _____
_____

○ **I need extra help with** _____
_____

What Are the Inflammatory and Immune Responses?

1a. NAME Identify the key cells that are part of the immune response.
_____

b. EXPLAIN How does the inflammatory response defend against pathogens?
_____
_____

got it? ....

○ **I get it!** Now I know the inflammatory and immune responses are the body's _____
_____
_____

○ **I need extra help with** _____
_____

The Body's Defenses

What Is the Body's First Line of Defense?

The body has a disease-fighting system to eliminate pathogens before they can harm your cells. **In the first line of defense, the surface of your skin, breathing passages, mouth, and stomach function as barriers to pathogens. These barriers trap and kill most pathogens with which you come into contact.**

The skin blocks pathogens with destructive chemicals in oil and sweat, the shedding of dead skin cells, and blood clotting and scabbing. The nose, pharynx, trachea, and bronchi trap pathogens from the air, and coughing and sneezing force pathogens out of your body. Most potential pathogens in food are destroyed by saliva in the mouth and acid in the stomach.

What Are the Inflammatory and Immune Responses?

In the inflammatory response, fluid and white blood cells leak from blood vessels and fight pathogens in nearby tissues. In the immune response, certain immune cells in the blood and tissues react to each kind of pathogen with a defense targeted specifically at the pathogen.

Cells damaged by pathogens release chemicals that trigger the body's second line of defense, the **inflammatory response,** which is a general response of white blood cells, inflammation, and sometimes fever. Each type of white blood cell has a certain function. A **phagocyte** is a white blood cell that engulfs and destroys pathogens by breaking them down during the inflammatory response. Chemicals produced at this time sometimes cause a fever, which helps fight the infection.

A severe infection triggers the body's third line of defense—the **immune response.** White blood cells that can distinguish kinds of pathogens are called **lymphocytes.** A **T cell** is a lymphocyte that identifies pathogens and distinguishes one pathogen from another. Each kind of T cell identifies **antigens,** molecules that the immune system recognizes either as part of your body or as coming from outside your body. Lymphocytes called **B cells** produce proteins called **antibodies** that help destroy pathogens. When antibodies bind to the antigens on a pathogen, they mark the pathogen for destruction.

On a separate sheet of paper, explain how the body employs three lines of defense against disease.

Review and Reinforce

The Body's Defenses

Understanding Main Ideas
Answer the following questions on a separate sheet of paper

1. What is the body's first line of defense?
2. What is the body's second line of defense?
3. What is the body's third line of defense?

Building Vocabulary
Fill in the blank to complete each statement.

4. Cells that identify pathogens and distinguish one from another are called

   _____.

5. Cells that produce antibodies that help destroy pathogens are called

   _____.

6. Marker molecules on a pathogen that the immune system recognizes as part of your

   body or coming from outside your body are called _____.

7. A(n) _____ is a white blood cell that engulfs and destroys pathogens
   by breaking them down.

8. During the _____, capillaries widen in the area
   affected by pathogens.

9. In the _____, the body reacts to each kind of
   pathogen with a defense targeted specifically for that pathogen.

10. Proteins that help destroy a pathogen by binding onto its antigens are called

    _____.

11. The type of white blood cells that can distinguish between different kinds of

    pathogens are called _____.

Name _____ Date _____ Class _____

The Body's Defenses

Read the passage and study the graph. Then answer the questions that follow on a separate sheet of paper.

Inflammation: Clue to Infection

Hepatitis is a disease that is caused by a virus that infects the liver. The graph below shows the fever pattern in a person with hepatitis. Symptoms last a minimum of several weeks. (Remember that normal body temperature is 37°C.)

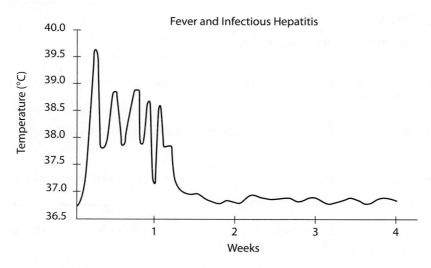

1. What was the person's body temperature before the first fever spike during the first week?

2. During the first week of infection, about what was the person's highest temperature?

3. During the first week of infection, what was the greatest change in the person's body temperature?

4. Describe how this person's temperature changed during the course of the disease.

5. If you were a doctor and suspected your patient had infectious hepatitis, would you rule out the disease if the patient had a near-normal temperature? Explain.

Place the outside corner, the corner away from the dotted line, in the corner of your copy machine to copy onto letter-size paper.

Lesson Quiz

The Body's Defenses

Fill in the blank to complete each statement.

1. The body has a disease-fighting system to eliminate _____ before they can harm your cells.

2. In the _____ response, fluid and white blood cells leak from blood vessels and fight pathogens in nearby tissues.

3. _____ are molecules that the immune system recognizes either as part of your body or as coming from outside your body.

4. In the _____ response, certain cells in the blood and tissues react to each kind of pathogen with a defense targeted specifically at the pathogen.

5. T cells and B cells are the two major types of _____.

If the statement is true, write *true*. If the statement is false, change the underlined word or words to make the statement true.

6. _____ If an infection is severe enough, it triggers the body's third line of defense, the <u>immune</u> response.

7. _____ Most potential pathogens in food are <u>produced</u> by saliva in the mouth and acid in the stomach.

8. _____ In the <u>second</u> line of defense, the surface of your skin, breathing passages, mouth, and stomach function as barriers to pathogens.

9. _____ The <u>inflammatory</u> response is a general response of white blood cells, inflammation, and sometimes fever.

10. _____ When cells are damaged, they release chemicals that trigger the inflammatory response, the body's <u>first</u> line of defense.

The Body's Defenses

Answer Key

After the Inquiry Warm-Up

1. When you tear a piece of paper in two along a jagged edge, you change its shape.

2. A specific defender cell recognizes a specific pathogen by its shape.

3. its shape

4. A young child would be likely to have more infections than an adult because a young child has fewer types of defender cells.

Key Concept Summaries

In the first line of defense, the body uses barriers—the skin, breathing passages, mouth, and stomach—to keep pathogens out of the body. If this fails, the second line of defense is the inflammatory response, during which fluid and white blood cells fight pathogens in nearby tissues. The body's third line of defense is the immune response, in which certain cells in the blood and tissues react with defenses targeted to particular pathogens.

Review and Reinforce

1. The body's first line of defense is barriers to pathogens in the skin, breathing passages, the mouth, and stomach.

2. The body's second line of defense is the inflammatory response of fluid and white blood cells.

3. The body's third line of defense is the immune response.

4. T cells

5. B cells

6. antigens

7. phagocyte

8. inflammatory response

9. immune response

10. antibodies

11. lymphocytes

Enrich

1. about 36.7°C

2. about 39.6°C

3. about 3°C (39.6°C–36.7°C)

4. Sample: During the first week there are a number of fever spikes, each followed by a drop of about 1 to 1.5°C. Starting in the second week, temperatures do not fluctuate greatly and hover around normal.

5. Sample: No. Somewhere toward the end of the first week, a patient with infectious hepatitis might have a near-normal temperature. In addition, if the doctor saw the patient during the second to fourth weeks, a near-normal temperature would be expected even though the patient still had infectious hepatitis.

Lesson Quiz

1. pathogens
2. inflammatory
3. Antigens
4. immune
5. lymphocytes
6. true
7. destroyed
8. first
9. true
10. second

Place the outside corner, the corner away from the dotted line, in the corner of your copy machine to copy onto letter-size paper.

Lesson Pacing: 1–2 periods or $\frac{1}{2}$–1 block

🕐 **SHORT ON TIME?** To do this lesson in approximately half the time, do the Activate Prior Knowledge activity followed by a discussion of the Key Concepts to familiarize students with the lesson content. Have students do the Quick Labs. The rest of the lesson can be completed by students independently.

Preference Navigator, in the online Planning tools, allows you to customize *Interactive Science* to your own teaching style. You can also edit lesson plans by selecting the Lesson Planner option.

Digital Teacher's Edition allows you to access your Teacher's Edition and Resource materials online.

my science online.com

Lesson Vocabulary

- AIDS
- HIV

 Content Refresher

Professional Development Note

T Cells, AIDS, and Antibiotics Although human immunodeficiency virus (HIV) can infect all T cells, the virus has a very high affinity for the antigens of helper T cells. Infected helper T cells are much less efficient when activated, and over time, they die. This loss of T-cell function, in addition to infection of other immune-system cells such as macrophages, accounts for the vulnerability of people with AIDS to pathogens that are too weak to cause disease in healthy people. Development of these disorders, called *opportunistic infections,* is one sign that a person with HIV infection may have developed the disease AIDS.

One type of drug used to treat some cases of AIDS is antibiotics. Antibiotics do not affect the virus, but do help to combat secondary infections. Some antibiotics kill bacteria, whereas others inhibit their growth. Antibiotic resistance occurs when bacteria change in some way that reduces or eliminates the effectiveness of drugs, chemicals, or other agents designed to cure or prevent infections. The bacteria survive and continue to multiply, causing more harm. This is the reason a person should take a full course of antibiotics; bacteria that survive from an incomplete treatment may be resistant to the antibiotic that was used.

LESSON OBJECTIVES

🔑 Identify how HIV affects the body.

🔑 Describe how HIV infection spreads and how it is treated.

Blended Path   Active learning using Student Edition, Inquiry Path, and Digital Path

ENGAGE AND EXPLORE

Teach this lesson using a variety of resources. Begin by reading **My Planet Diary** as a class. Have students share ideas about other symbols or projects that show support for people around the world. Then have students do the **Inquiry Warm-Up activity.** Students will investigate how HIV spreads through a population. Discuss whether you could tell if someone had black chips in their cup when you began sharing. The **After the Inquiry Warm-Up worksheet** sets up a discussion about how to avoid getting a black chip. Have volunteers share their answers to question 4 about how the number of students with black chips, at the end of the activity, would differ between the two scenarios.

EXPLAIN AND ELABORATE

Teach Key Concepts by explaining that HIV is the only virus known to attack the human immune system directly and destroy T cells. **Support the Big Q** by discussing the effects of HIV.

Continue to **Teach Key Concepts** by explaining how HIV can be spread from one person to another. Hand out the **Key Concept Summaries** as a review of each part of the lesson. Students can also use the online **Vocab Flash Cards** to review key terms.

EVALUATE

Have students take the **Lesson Quiz.** For an alternate assessment, see the **EXAM**VIEW® Assessment Suite, Progress Monitoring Assessments, or SuccessTracker™.

E L L Support

1 Content and Language

The word *epidemic* comes from the Greek word *epidēmía,* which means "prevalence of disease."

DIFFERENTIATED INSTRUCTION KEY
L1 Struggling Students or Special Needs
L2 On-Level Students **L3** Advanced Students

LESSON PLANNER 14.3

Inquiry Path Hands-on learning in the Lab zone

ENGAGE AND EXPLORE

To teach this lesson with an emphasis on inquiry, begin with the **Inquiry Warm-Up activity.** Students will investigate how HIV is spread. Discuss whether you could tell if a person you were sharing with had a black chip. Have students do the **After the Inquiry Warm-Up worksheet.** Talk about how you could prevent yourself from getting a black chip. Have volunteers share their answers to question 4 about whether more or less people would have black chips at the end of the original activity or at the end of the activity described in question 4.

EXPLAIN AND ELABORATE

Focus on the **Inquiry Skill** for the lesson. Point out that when you graph, you chart a relationship between at least two pieces of data. What could be graphed from the **Inquiry Warm-Up activity?** *(The number of people who had black chips at the end of the original activity)* **Support the Big Q** by discussing the effects of HIV. Have students do the **Quick Lab** to model how HIV attacks the immune system.

Have students do the **Quick Lab** to explore how HIV is and is not spread. Students can use the online **Vocab Flash Cards** to review key terms.

EVALUATE

Have students take the **Lesson Quiz.** For an alternate assessment, see the **EXAM**VIEW® Assessment Suite, Progress Monitoring Assessments, or SuccessTracker™.

Digital Path Online learning at my science online.com

ENGAGE AND EXPLORE

Teach this lesson using digital resources. Begin by having students explore real-world connections to HIV and AIDS at **My Planet Diary** online. Have them access the Chapter Resources to find the **Unlock the Big Question activity.** There they can answer the questions and refine their responses as they continue through the lesson. You can re-assign the activity and have students submit their work so you can track their progress.

EXPLAIN AND ELABORATE

Students reading above, at, or below the lexile measure of this lesson can access basic content readings at their level at **My Reading Web.** Have students use the online **Vocab Flash Cards** to preview key terms. Assign the **Do the Math activity** online and have students submit their work to you. **Support the Big Q** by identifying the effects of HIV. Do the **Quick Lab** and then ask students to share their models.

Do the **Quick Lab** to reinforce understanding of how HIV is and is not spread. The **Key Concept Summaries** online allow students to read a summary and see an image associated with each part of the lesson. Online remediation is available at **My Science Coach.**

EVALUATE

Have students take the **Lesson Quiz.** For an alternate assessment, see the **EXAM**VIEW® Assessment Suite, Progress Monitoring Assessments, or SuccessTracker™.

2 Frontload the Lesson
Preview the lesson visuals, labels, and captions. Ask students what they know about the terms *virus, T cell,* and *immune system.* Explain the specific meanings these words have in science.

3 Comprehensible Input
Have students diagram a flowchart that shows what HIV is, how it is spread, and how it turns into AIDS.

4 Language Production
Pair or group students with varied language abilities to complete labs collaboratively for language practice. Have each student copy the completed written lab for personal reference.

5 Assess Understanding
Have students create a portfolio of their notes and then do oral presentations of lesson content.

Lexile Measure = 890L

LESSON 14.3

HIV and AIDS

Establish Learning Objectives

After this lesson, students will be able to:

🔑 Identify how HIV affects the body.

🔑 Describe how HIV infection spreads and how it is treated.

Engage

Activate Prior Knowledge

MY PLANET DIARY Read *The NAMES Project Foundation—AIDS Memorial Quilt* with the class. Point out that the virus that causes this disease was spreading in the United States during the 1970s and early 1980s before it was finally discovered. Ask: **What does the AIDS Memorial Quilt indicate about the spread of this disease?** *(AIDS has spread to countries all over the world.)*

BIG IDEAS OF SCIENCE REFERENCE LIBRARY 📖
Have students look up the following topic: HIV/AIDS.

Explore

Lab Resource: Inquiry Warm-Up

L1 HOW DOES HIV SPREAD? Students will model one of the ways in which HIV spreads through a population.

LESSON

3 HIV and AIDS

🔓 UNLOCK THE BIG ❓

🔑 How Does HIV Affect the Body?

🔑 How Is HIV Spread and Treated?

my planet diary

PROFILE

The NAMES Project Foundation— AIDS Memorial Quilt

Headquarters: Atlanta, Georgia

How do you cope with loss? Some who have lost loved ones to AIDS express their feelings by making panels to add to the AIDS Memorial Quilt. Begun in 1987 in San Francisco, the NAMES Project Foundation takes care of the quilt. The quilt is made up of more than 47,000 individual panels from countries all around the world. The panels help people honor those whom they have lost to the tragic disease. The large number of panels sadly illustrates that AIDS has taken so many lives. Yet, the quilt is a symbol of unity that supports continuing research to find a cure for this devastating disease.

Communicate Discuss the following questions with a partner. Write your answers below.

1. The quilt is made up of panels from around the world. What does this tell you about AIDS?

   Sample: AIDS is a worldwide problem.

2. Why do you think scientists are important in the fight against AIDS?

   Scientists perform research and experiments to find a cure for AIDS.

▶ **PLANET DIARY** Go to **Planet Diary** to learn more about HIV and AIDS.

Lab zone — Do the Inquiry Warm-Up *How Does HIV Spread?*

564 Fighting Disease

SUPPORT ALL READERS

Lexile Measure = 890L   Lexile Word Count = 762

Prior Exposure to Content: May be the first time students have encountered this topic

Academic Vocabulary: *graph, sequence*

Science Vocabulary: *AIDS, HIV*

Concept Level: Generally appropriate for most students in this grade

Preteach With: My Planet Diary "NAMES" and Figure 1 activity

Go to **My Reading Web** to access leveled readings that provide a foundation for the content.

my science online.com

Vocabulary
- AIDS
- HIV

Skills
- Reading: Sequence
- Inquiry: Graph

How Does HIV Affect the Body?

Our immune system protects us well. So we usually do not even realize that our body has been attacked by a pathogen. But what happens when our immune system itself is sick?

Acquired immunodeficiency syndrome, or **AIDS,** is a disease caused by a virus that attacks the immune system. The virus that causes AIDS is called the human immunodeficiency virus, or **HIV.** **HIV is the only kind of virus known to attack the human immune system directly and destroy T cells.** Once inside the body, HIV enters T cells and reproduces. People can be infected with HIV—that is, have the virus living in their T cells—for many years before they become sick.

In 1981, the first case of AIDS was reported in the United States. Nearly one million Americans may now be infected with HIV. Many of these people—one in four—do not realize yet that they are infected. However, the disease is not found only in the United States. It is a worldwide epidemic.

do the math!

The table shows the number of men, women, and children under age 15 worldwide living with HIV in 2007.

1. **Graph** Use the data in the table to make a bar graph. Then write a title for the graph.

2. **Interpret Data** What do you notice about the number of men and women living with HIV in 2007?

   About the same number of men and women are living with HIV.

3. **Draw Conclusions** What conclusion can you make about the populations the virus affects?

   Sample: The virus affects men and women equally. It also affects many children.

Populations Living With HIV in 2007

Population	Number of People
Men	15.3 million
Women	15.5 million
Children under age 15	2 million

People Living With HIV in 2007

[Bar graph: Number of People Living With HIV (millions) on y-axis (0–20), Population on x-axis with bars for Men (~15), Women (~16), Children under age 15 (~2)]

565

Explain

Introduce Vocabulary

To help students understand the terms *AIDS* and *HIV*, point out that both are acronyms. Explain that acronyms are words that are formed from the first letters, or first syllables, of two or more words. Write the terms *acquired immunodeficiency syndrome* and *human immunodeficiency virus* on the board. Then have students circle the four letters *a, I, d,* and *s* in the first term and the three letters *h, I,* and *v* in the second term.

Teach Key Concepts

Explain to students that HIV is the only kind of virus known to attack the human immune system directly and destroy T cells. Review with students the functions of T cells. Ask: **Which body cells does HIV target?** *(T cells)* **What disease does HIV cause?** *(AIDS)* **How long does it take AIDS to develop in the body of a person with HIV?** *(It can take many years.)*

Elaborate

Do the Math!

L1 Explain that the statistics in the table represent people who have contracted HIV. Point out that students will need to transfer the data in the table into the graph.

Graph Remind students that bar graphs show comparisons and contrasts between categories. Explain that their graph will use three bars on the horizontal axis to compare and contrast three segments of the population who are living with HIV. Have students locate the label of the *y*-axis to learn that the graph's unit of measurement is millions of people. Explain that the values that fall between the horizontal lines of a graph can be approximated by determining the increments between lines and then estimating the percentage of that increment that the value takes up.

See the *Math Skill and Problem-Solving Activities* for support.

My Planet Diary provides an opportunity for students to explore real-world connections to HIV and AIDS.

Digital Lesson: Assign the *Do the Math* activity online and have students submit their work to you.

(E)(L)(L) Support

1 Content and Language
Write the terms *AIDS* and *HIV* on the board. Ask students to identify one way in which these terms look different from other words. *(They contain only capital letters.)* Explain that acronyms such as these are sometimes pronounced as words, while others are spoken as letters.

2 Frontload the Lesson
Invite students to reflect on when they first became aware of the terms *HIV* and *AIDS*. Explain that though the two terms are related, they identify two distinct things. Encourage student volunteers to explain the difference between them.

3 Comprehensible Input
Have students create a cause-and-effect diagram that shows a single effect and several potential causes. Encourage students to describe various causes in detail.

Explain

Support the Big Q ❓UbD

EFFECTS OF HIV Explain that AIDS is a disease of the immune system. Ask: **What is one of the symptoms of AIDS?** *(The body becomes less able to fight disease.)* **What is the cause of this symptom?** *(The destruction of T cells by HIV)* Make sure students understand that people with AIDS can get many other additional diseases, including pneumonia and tuberculosis, with a variety of symptoms. Ask: **Why do you think these other diseases that occur in AIDS patients are called "opportunistic infections?"** *(Sample: The pathogens take advantage of the opportunity afforded them by the patient's weakened immune system.)*

⟳ **Sequence** Explain that when students sequence items, they put the items in order. The order can be based on position, time, size, or another characteristic.

Elaborate

Lab Resource: Quick Lab 🔬

L2 HOW DOES HIV ATTACK? Students will make a model of the steps of HIV attacking the immune system.

Evaluate

Assess Your Understanding

Have students evaluate their understanding by completing the appropriate sentence.

🟥🟥🟥 Response to Intervention

If students have trouble identifying the effect of HIV on the body, **then** help students clarify the cause-and-effect relationship between HIV and AIDS, and have students reread the paragraph about *Infections*.

MY SCIENCE 🅢 COACH Have students go online for help in understanding how HIV affects the body.

⟳ **Sequence** Complete the steps that happen after a person is infected with HIV and develops AIDS.

Step 1 A person is infected.

Step 2

The person may get flulike symptoms after about one month.

Step 3

After time—up to 10 years—the person loses the ability to fight disease.

Step 4

The person gets diseases that healthy people do not normally get.

Step 5

The person's immune system fails, and they die.

HIV and AIDS When people first become infected with HIV, they often have no symptoms. A month or so later, they may seem to have the flu, but it goes away. Although they may not have symptoms at first, people can still spread the virus.

It may take ten years or more for severe symptoms to appear. However, in time, HIV begins to destroy the T cells it has infected. As the virus destroys T cells like the one shown in **Figure 1**, the body begins to lose its ability to fight disease. This is a symptom of the disease called AIDS.

Infections People with AIDS start to get diseases that healthy people do not get normally. Development of these infections is one symptom of the disease AIDS. Most people infected with HIV eventually develop the symptoms of AIDS. Many survive attack after attack of infections. Yet, in time, their immune systems fail, and they die.

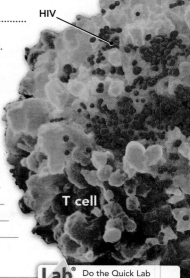

FIGURE 1 ···
HIV
HIV reproduces inside T cells. It then bursts out to attack other T cells.

✏️ **CHALLENGE** Use what you see in the photo to explain why HIV destroys an immune system.

Sample: So many viruses attack a T cell that it is destroyed and weakens immunity.

HIV

T cell

🔬 Lab zone Do the Quick Lab *How Does HIV Attack?*

🔑 Assess Your Understanding

got it? ···

○ **I get it!** Now I know that HIV affects the body by *attacking the immune system directly and destroying T cells.*

○ **I need extra help with** *See TE note.*

Go to **MY SCIENCE 🅢 COACH** *online for help with this subject.*

How Is HIV Spread and Treated?

Like all other viruses, HIV can reproduce only inside cells. However, the virus can survive for a short time outside the human body in fluids. These fluids include blood and the fluids that the male and female reproductive systems produce.

HIV can spread from one person to another if body fluids from an infected person come in contact with body fluids of an uninfected person. Sexual contact is one way this transfer happens. HIV may also pass from an infected woman to her baby during pregnancy or childbirth, or through breast milk. Infected blood can also spread HIV. For example, drug users who share needles can pass HIV. Since 1985, all donated blood in the United States has been tested for HIV.

At this time, there is no cure for AIDS. However, combinations of drugs that fight the virus in different ways can delay the development of AIDS and extend life expectancy. See **Figure 2** for information about young people living with AIDS.

FIGURE 2 ··

Young People and AIDS

The graph shows how advances in HIV treatments enabled more people to live with AIDS.

✎ **Read Graphs** Using the graph, estimate how many 13- to 24-year-olds were living with AIDS in 2007.

Sample: I estimate more than 9,000 young people were living with AIDS because the number increased every year from 2002.

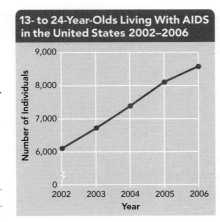

13- to 24-Year-Olds Living With AIDS in the United States 2002–2006

(Graph: Number of Individuals vs Year, 2002–2006)

Lab zone — Do the Quick Lab
What Will Spread HIV?

Assess Your Understanding

1a. Review Where does HIV reproduce in people?

HIV reproduces in T cells.

b. Summarize How is AIDS treated?

Combinations of drugs fight the virus in different ways.

got it? ·······················

O **I get it!** Now I know that HIV can spread _through the contact of body fluids from an infected person with the body fluids of an uninfected person._

O **I need extra help with** _See TE note._

Go to my science ⑤ **COACH** *online for help with this subject.*

567

Differentiated Instruction

L1 How HIV Is Not Spread Invite students to make collages that illustrate a wide variety of ways that HIV is *not* spread. Students might wish to include images that show people infected with HIV and people not infected with HIV involved in activities such as hugging, shaking hands, using a sink or shower, bumping into one another while playing sports, and sharing common objects such as pencils, books, music players, or articles of clothing.

L3 AIDS Statistics Challenge students to do research to gather statistics that show the changing number of people with AIDS in the U.S. and worldwide since 1980. Encourage students to include an effective graphic device, such as a line graph or a 3-column chart with horizontal rows for years, to convey this information. Publish students' work on a classroom or school bulletin board or wall.

Explain

Teach Key Concepts 🔑

Explain that HIV can spread from one person to another if body fluids from an infected person contact body fluids of an uninfected person. Make sure that students understand that these fluids include blood as well as the fluids produced by the reproductive systems. Ask students to identify the following as ways HIV can or cannot be spread: **Sexual contact?** *(Yes)* **From an infected woman to her unborn child?** *(Yes)* **From an infected woman to her newborn baby?** *(Yes)* **Eating food prepared by a person with HIV?** *(No)* **Breathing the same air as someone with HIV?** *(No)* **Using a pencil after a person with HIV has handled it?** *(No)* **Using a needle that a person with HIV used to take drugs?** *(Yes)* **What are ways that people can reduce the risk of infection with HIV?** *(Sample: Avoid sexual contact and illegal drug use.)*

Elaborate

21st Century Learning

CRITICAL THINKING: Infer Tell students that people with AIDS are able to live longer because better drug treatments have been developed in recent years. Ask: **Does this fact relate in any way to the data shown in Figure 2? How?** *(Sample: The simple, meaning of the data is that increasing numbers of 13- to 24-year olds are living with AIDS. Though this could be due partly to increasing numbers of people contracting AIDS, it may also be due partly to the fact that more people with AIDS are living longer.)*

Lab Resource: Quick Lab 🔬

L1 WHAT WILL SPREAD HIV? Students will explore ways in which HIV is and is not spread.

Evaluate

Assess Your Understanding

After students answer the questions, have them evaluate their understanding by completing the appropriate sentence.

R T I Response to Intervention

1a. If students need help identifying where HIV reproduces, **then** suggest they look at **Figure 1.**

b. If students have trouble explaining how AIDS is treated, **then** have them reread the last paragraph.

my science ⑤ **COACH** Have students go online for help in understanding how HIV is spread and treated.

Lab®
zone **After the Inquiry Warm-Up**

HIV and AIDS

Inquiry Warm-Up, *How Does HIV Spread?*

In the Inquiry Warm-Up, you used a model to investigate one of the ways in which HIV spreads through a population. Using what you learned from that activity, answer the questions below.

1. **OBSERVE** Think about when you shared chips with another student for the first time in Step 3. Could you tell by looking at the student or the student's cup whether the cup had any black chips in it?

   _____

2. **PREDICT** Suppose your class performed the activity again. This time you stand off to one side and do not pair up with any other students. If you had no black chips in your cup to start, would you pick up any black chips during the activity? Explain.

   _____

   _____

3. **PREDICT** Suppose your class performed the activity again. This time you pair up with different students but you do not share chips with any of them. If you had no black chips in your cup to start, would you pick up any black chips during the activity? Explain.

   _____

   _____

4. **PREDICT** Suppose your class performed the activity again. This time everyone pairs up with different students but half the students never share chips with anyone else. How do you think the number of students with black chips at the end of the activity would compare to the number of students with black chips at the end of the original activity?

   _____

   _____

   _____

Name _____ Date _____ Class _____

HIV and AIDS

> **How Does HIV Affect the Body?**

got it? ⋯⋯⋯⋯⋯⋯⋯⋯⋯⋯⋯⋯⋯⋯⋯⋯⋯⋯⋯⋯⋯⋯⋯⋯⋯⋯⋯

○ **I get it!** Now I know that HIV affects the body by _____

_____

○ **I need extra help with** _____

_____

> **How Is HIV Spread and Treated?**

1a. REVIEW Where does HIV reproduce in people?

_____

b. SUMMARIZE How is AIDS treated?

_____

_____

got it? ⋯⋯⋯⋯⋯⋯⋯⋯⋯⋯⋯⋯⋯⋯⋯⋯⋯⋯⋯⋯⋯⋯⋯⋯⋯⋯⋯

○ **I get it!** Now I know that HIV can spread _____

_____

_____

○ **I need extra help with** _____

_____

Name _____ Date _____ Class _____

HIV and AIDS

How Does HIV Affect the Body?

Acquired immunodeficiency syndrome, or **AIDS,** is a disease caused by a virus that attacks the immune system. The virus that causes AIDS is called the human immunodeficiency virus, or **HIV. HIV is the only kind of virus known to attack the human immune system directly or destroy T cells.**

Once inside the body, HIV enters T cells and reproduces. People can have the virus living in their T cells for many years before they become sick. Since the first case of AIDS in the United States was reported in 1981, many people around the world have been infected with HIV. Today nearly one million Americans may be infected with the virus.

How Is HIV Spread and Treated?

Though HIV reproduces in cells only, the virus can survive briefly outside the human body in fluids including blood and the fluids that the male and female reproductive systems produce. **HIV can spread from one person to another if body fluids from an infected person contact body fluids of an uninfected person.**

Sexual contact is one way this transfer occurs. HIV may pass from an infected woman to her baby during pregnancy or childbirth, as well as through breast milk after the baby's birth. Infected blood can also spread HIV. Drug users who share needles can pass HIV in this way. All blood that is donated to blood banks and hospitals in the United States is tested for HIV, and no infected blood is used in transfusions. A cure for AIDS has not been discovered. Combinations of drugs can fight HIV in different ways. These kind of treatments can delay the development of HIV into AIDS and extend the life of people with HIV.

On a separate sheet of paper, explain the difference between HIV and AIDS.

Review and Reinforce

HIV and AIDS

Understanding Main Ideas

Answer the following questions in the spaces provided. Use a separate sheet of paper if you need more room.

1. What causes acquired immune deficiency syndrome, or AIDS?

   _____

   _____

2. What does HIV do after it enters the body?

   _____

   _____

3. What damage does HIV cause to the body?

   _____

   _____

4. What are three ways that HIV can be spread and three ways in which it cannot be spread?

   _____

   _____

Building Vocabulary

Write a definition for each of these terms on the lines below. Be sure to include what each term stands for.

5. AIDS

   _____

   _____

6. HIV

   _____

   _____

HIV and AIDS

> Read the passage and study the table. Then use a separate sheet of paper to answer the questions that follow.

Treatment But No Cure

Although the first AIDS cases were identified in 1981, there still is no cure. Today we have effective treatments, but that was not always the case. When the first anti-HIV drug, zidovuvine (ZDV), was approved in 1987, it dramatically reduced the amount of HIV in patients' blood. Sadly, its effect was brief. Within two years, the amount of virus returned to pre-treatment levels. The next four drugs approved also had short-lived benefits. The problem was that all five drugs targeted HIV at the same single point in its life cycle. HIV attaches to certain molecules on a T cell. It then fuses, or binds, itself to the cell membrane and releases its genetic material into the cell. An enzyme called *reverse transcriptase* copies HIV's genetic material onto a strand of DNA. A second enzyme, *integrase*, inserts this HIV DNA into the cell's own DNA, causing the cell to make HIV proteins. A third enzyme, *protease*, assembles these HIV proteins into copies of the virus.

The breakthrough in HIV treatment came in 1995. Saquinavir, the first drug in a second class of anti-HIV drugs called *protease inhibitors*, was approved. By giving patients drugs from both classes, doctors were finally able to lower HIV levels for long periods of time. This multidrug approach is known as *highly active antiretroviral therapy (HAART)*. By the end of 2009, anti-HIV drugs in five different classes had become available. The drugs in each class *inhibit*, or interfere with, a particular step in HIV's life cycle.

Classes of Anti-HIV Drugs (Approved Through 2009)		
Class of Drug	**Date**	**How It Works**
Nucleoside reverse transcriptase inhibitors	1987	Causes faulty copies of HIV's genetic material to be made
Protease inhibitors	1995	Interferes with assembly of new HIV particles
Non-nucleoside reverse transcriptase inhibitors	1996	Interferes with copying of HIV's genetic material
Fusion/Entry inhibitors	2003	Prevents HIV from attaching to cell membrane
Integrase inhibitors	2007	Prevents insertion of HIV DNA into cell DNA

Researchers now think that, on average, people with HIV who are on HAART may expect to live for 35 years after diagnosis. But these powerful drugs often have serious side effects including headache, difficulty sleeping, nausea, diarrhea, high blood pressure, high cholesterol, and kidney damage.

1. After AIDS was first identified, how many years was it until an effective therapy in the form of HAART became available?
2. How does HAART work?
3. Which class of anti-HIV drug targets the virus before it enters cells?

Lesson Quiz

HIV and AIDS

If the statement is true, write *true*. If the statement is false, change the underlined word or words to make the statement true.

1. _____ People can have HIV living in their T cells for <u>many years</u> before they become sick.

2. _____ Infected blood <u>cannot</u> spread HIV.

3. _____ HIV is <u>one of several viruses</u> known to attack the human immune system directly or destroy T cells.

4. _____ HIV <u>can survive briefly</u> outside the human body in fluids including blood and the fluids that the male and female reproductive systems produce.

5. _____ HIV can spread from one person to another if <u>body fluids</u> from an infected person contact body fluids of an uninfected person.

Fill in the blank to complete each statement.

6. _____ is a disease caused by a virus that attacks the immune system.

7. AIDS is caused by _____.

8. Once inside the body, HIV enters _____ and reproduces.

9. Drug users who share _____ can spread HIV.

10. Combinations of _____ can fight HIV in different ways.

HIV and AIDS

Answer Key

After the Inquiry Warm-Up

1. no

2. No, I would not pick up any black chips because I would not share chips with anyone else.

3. No, I would not pick up any black chips because I would not share chips with anyone else.

4. If half of the students in class never exchanged chips with other students, fewer students would have black chips at the end of the activity than had black chips at the end of the original activity.

Key Concept Summaries

AIDS, or acquired immunodeficiency syndrome, is a disease caused by a virus that attacks the immune system. HIV, or human immunodeficiency virus, is not a disease—it is the virus that causes the disease AIDS.

Review and Reinforce

1. AIDS is caused by a virus, HIV, that attacks the immune system.

2. It enters T cells, where it reproduces.

3. HIV damages the body's immune system, so that eventually the body has trouble fighting diseases.

4. Samples: HIV can be spread through sexual contact with an infected person, by sharing needles with an infected person, through a mother's blood to her unborn baby and through her breast milk to a baby. HIV cannot be spread through casual contact between people's bodies, such as hugging, shaking hands, or brushing or bumping each other, and it cannot be spread through sharing objects such as pencils, compact disks, books, or money.

5. AIDS, which stands for acquired immunodeficiency syndrome, is a disease caused by a virus that attacks the immune system.

6. HIV, which stands for human immunodeficiency virus, is a virus that attacks the immune system and causes AIDS.

Enrich

1. 14 years

2. HAART combines anti-HIV drugs from two or more classes to target the virus at multiple steps in its life cycle.

3. fusion/entry inhibitors

Lesson Quiz

1. true

2. can

3. the only kind of virus

4. true

5. true

6. AIDS

7. the human immunodeficiency virus, or HIV

8. T cells

9. needles

10. drugs

Place the outside corner, the corner away from the dotted line, in the corner of your copy machine to copy onto letter-size paper.

Infectious Disease and Your Health

Lesson Pacing: 2–3 periods or 1–1½ blocks

🕐 **SHORT ON TIME?** To do this lesson in approximately half the time, do the Activate Prior Knowledge activity followed by a discussion of the Key Concepts to familiarize students with the lesson content. Have students do the Quick Labs. The rest of the lesson can be completed by students independently.

Preference Navigator, in the online Planning tools, allows you to customize *Interactive Science* to your own teaching style. You can also edit lesson plans by selecting the Lesson Planner option.

Digital Teacher's Edition allows you to access your Teacher's Edition and Resource materials online.

my science online .com

Lesson Vocabulary

- immunity • active immunity • vaccination • vaccine
- passive immunity • antibiotic • antibiotic resistance

 ## Content Refresher

The Type II Diabetes Epidemic In the United States, about 24 million people have been diagnosed with diabetes, which is the sixth leading cause of death. 90 to 95% of the diagnosed cases of diabetes are Type II.

The increase in Type II diabetes is due largely to the increase in obesity and sedentary lifestyle. Extra fat tissue can make the body resistant to the action of insulin and lead to insulin resistance, a condition in which muscle, fat, and liver cells fail to use insulin effectively. This condition usually precedes the onset of Type II diabetes. Lack of exercise further reduces muscles' ability to use insulin. As insulin resistance develops, the pancreas tries to compensate by producing more insulin. Eventually, the pancreas cannot keep up as cells become more resistant. Some people with insulin resistance have high levels of both glucose and insulin in the blood at the same time. People who have insulin resistance can reduce their risk of developing diabetes by losing weight and increasing physical activity.

LESSON OBJECTIVES

🔑 Distinguish between kinds of immunity and tell how immunity is acquired.

🔑 Describe methods for treating and preventing infectious diseases.

Blended Path
Active learning using Student Edition, Inquiry Path, and Digital Path

ENGAGE AND EXPLORE

Teach this lesson using a variety of resources. Begin by reading **My Planet Diary** as a class. Have students share ideas about what they know about chickenpox. Then have students do the **Inquiry Warm-Up activity.** Students will examine types of immunity. Discuss the cases that were examples of active immunity. The **After the Inquiry Warm-Up worksheet** sets up a discussion about what causes active versus passive immunity. Have volunteers share their answers to question 4 about any theories about injections and immunity based on question 3.

EXPLAIN AND ELABORATE

Teach Key Concepts by explaining active and passive immunity in relation to the chickenpox. **Lead a Discussion** about why active immunity is so important. **Support the Big Q** by comparing and contrasting the similarities and differences between getting a disease and getting a vaccine against a disease. Use **Figure 2** to illustrate how a vaccine activates the immune response. **Lead a Discussion** about how a person acquires passive immunity both artificially and naturally.

Continue to **Teach Key Concepts** by explaining how bacterial diseases can be treated, why viruses cannot be treated, and how both diseases can be prevented. Then have students practice the inquiry skill in the **Apply It activity. Lead a Discussion** about how you can prevent the spread of both bacterial and viral diseases. Hand out the **Key Concept Summaries** as a review of each part of the lesson. Students can also use the online **Vocab Flash Cards** to review key terms.

EVALUATE

Have students take the **Lesson Quiz.** For an alternate assessment, see the **EXAM**VIEW® Assessment Suite, Progress Monitoring Assessments, or SuccessTracker™.

ⒺⓁⓁ Support

1 Content and Language
Remind students that the prefix *anti-* means "against." Explain that an *antibiotic* fights against bacteria causing a disease in the body.

DIFFERENTIATED INSTRUCTION KEY
L1 Struggling Students or Special Needs
L2 On-Level Students **L3** Advanced Students

LESSON PLANNER 14.4

Lab zone Inquiry Path
Hands-on learning in the Lab zone

Digital Path
Online learning at my science online.com

ENGAGE AND EXPLORE

To teach this lesson with an emphasis on inquiry, begin with the **Inquiry Warm-Up activity.** Students will investigate active and passive immunity. Discuss the examples of active immunity that were observed. Have students do the **After the Inquiry Warm-Up worksheet.** Talk about how you can differentiate between active and passive immunity. Have volunteers share their answers to question 4 about how their responses to question 3 helped them to develop theories about injections and immunity.

EXPLAIN AND ELABORATE

Focus on the **Inquiry Skill** for the lesson. Point out that when you interpret data, you compare and contrast information while looking for patterns. What pattern could be seen in the data about injections and immunity from the **Inquiry Warm-Up activity?** *(Injections can cause passive and active immunity.)* **Support the Big Q** by discussing the similarities and differences between getting a disease and getting a vaccine against a disease. Have students do the **Quick Lab** to model active and passive immunity and then share their results.

Review the title and the labels in the table before beginning the **Apply It activity.** Ask volunteers to share their interpretations of the data. Do the **Quick Lab** to determine what products can kill pathogens and then have students share the results. Students can use the online **Vocab Flash Cards** to review key terms.

EVALUATE

Have students take the **Lesson Quiz.** For an alternate assessment, see the **EXAM**VIEW® Assessment Suite, Progress Monitoring Assessments, or SuccessTracker™.

ENGAGE AND EXPLORE

Teach this lesson using digital resources. Begin by having students explore real-world connections to how infectious diseases affect your health at **My Planet Diary** online. Have them access the Chapter Resources to find the **Unlock the Big Question activity.** There they can answer the questions and refine their responses as they continue through the lesson. You can re-assign the activity and have students submit their work so you can track their progress.

EXPLAIN AND ELABORATE

Students reading above, at, or below the lexile measure of this lesson can access basic content readings at their level at **My Reading Web.** Have students use the online **Vocab Flash Cards** to preview key terms. Use the **Support the Big Q** to illustrate similarities and differences between getting a disease and getting a vaccine against a disease. Have students do the **Art in Motion activity** to see the process of active immunity through vaccination. Do the **Quick Lab** and then ask students to share their results.

Review the title and labels for the table before assigning the online **Apply It activity.** Ask volunteers to share their interpretations of the data. Have students submit their work to you. Have students do the **Quick Lab** to explore what products can kill pathogens. The **Key Concept Summaries** online allow students to read a summary and see an image associated with each part of the lesson. Online remediation is available at **My Science Coach.**

EVALUATE

Have students take the **Lesson Quiz.** For an alternate assessment, see the **EXAM**VIEW® Assessment Suite, Progress Monitoring Assessments, or SuccessTracker™.

2 Frontload the Lesson
Preview the lesson visuals, labels, and captions. Ask students what they know about the words *vaccination* and *antibiotic.* Explain the specific meanings these words have in science.

3 Comprehensible Input
Have students study the visuals and their captions in **Figure 1** and **Figure 3** to support the Key Concepts of the lesson.

4 Language Production
Pair or group students with varied language abilities to complete labs collaboratively for language practice. Have each student copy the completed written lab for personal reference.

5 Assess Understanding
Divide the class into small groups. Have each student identify a Key Concept from the lesson to discuss in his or her group. After the discussions, have students talk about the Key Concepts as a group.

Infectious Disease and Your Health

Establish Learning Objectives

After this lesson, students will be able to:

🔑 Distinguish between kinds of immunity and tell how immunity is acquired.

🔑 Describe methods for treating and preventing infectious diseases.

Engage

Activate Prior Knowledge

MY PLANET DIARY Read *Chickenpox Vaccine* with the class. Explain that chicken pox causes numerous small blisters to break out over the skin. The disease usually occurs in children between two and six years old. Ask: **Why would a party for small children spread a disease like chickenpox?** *(Sample: Small children are likely to be in close contact with each other and are careless about what they touch and how they cough.)*

BIG IDEAS OF SCIENCE REFERENCE LIBRARY 📖
Have students look up the following topics: Malaria, Sleep, Vaccines.

Explore

Lab Resource: Inquiry Warm-Up 🔺Lab zone

L1 TYPES OF IMMUNITY Students will examine case studies and determine whether people have acquired active or passive immunity.

LESSON 4
Infectious Disease and Your Health

🔑 How Can You Become Immune?

🔑 How Can Infectious Diseases Be Treated and Prevented?

 UNLOCK THE BIG ?

my planet Diary   DISCOVERY

Chickenpox Vaccine

Before the chickenpox vaccine was developed, more than 4 million Americans were infected with the chickenpox virus every year. Parents planned chickenpox parties to spread the disease. Parents wanted to expose their children to chickenpox early in life because children are less likely to get seriously ill from chickenpox than adults.

The development of a chickenpox vaccine in 1995 has made chickenpox parties mostly a thing of the past. Now, anyone over one year old can get the vaccine. The vaccine has reduced the likelihood of getting chickenpox to just 10 to 30 percent. Since the vaccine is somewhat new, more research is being done to determine if the vaccine can last through adulthood.

Write your answers to the questions below.

1. What was the purpose of chickenpox parties?

   Sample: Parents wanted their young children to catch chickenpox so they wouldn't run the risk of catching it as adults.

2. Why do you think there is a 10 to 30 percent chance of chickenpox with the vaccine?

   Sample: The vaccine is not 100 percent effective on all people.

▶ PLANET DIARY Go to **Planet Diary** to learn more about how infectious diseases affect your health.

🔺Lab zone Do the Inquiry Warm-Up *Types of Immunity.*

568 Fighting Disease

SUPPORT ALL READERS
Lexile Measure = 940L   Lexile Word Count = 1012

Prior Exposure to Content: May be the first time students have encountered this topic

Academic Vocabulary: *cause, data, effect, interpret, relate*

Science Vocabulary: *immunity, vaccination, antibiotic*

Concept Level: Generally appropriate for most students in this grade

Preteach With: My Planet Diary "Chickenpox Vaccine" and Figure 1 activity

Go to **My Reading Web** to access leveled readings that provide a foundation for the content.

my science online.com

Vocabulary
- immunity • active immunity • vaccination • vaccine
- passive immunity • antibiotic • antibiotic resistance

Skills
- ⟳ Reading: Relate Cause and Effect
- △ Inquiry: Interpret Data

How Can You Become Immune?

People get diseases. However, they get some diseases only once. This is because people develop immunity to some diseases once they recover from them. **Immunity** is the body's ability to destroy pathogens before they can cause disease. Immunity can be active or passive. 🔑 **You acquire active immunity when your own immune system produces antibodies against a pathogen in your body. You acquire passive immunity when the antibodies come from a source outside your body.**

Active Immunity People who have had chickenpox were once invaded by the chickenpox virus. In response, their immune systems produced antibodies. The next time the chickenpox virus invades their bodies, their immune systems will produce antibodies quickly. So they will not become sick with chickenpox again. This reaction is called **active immunity** because the body has produced the antibodies that fight pathogens. Active immunity can result from either getting the disease or being vaccinated. It often lasts for many years. Sometimes it lasts for life.

⟳ **Relate Cause and Effect**
Complete the graphic organizer with the effects of contracting the chickenpox virus.

Cause	Effect
Contract chickenpox virus the first time.	Sickness; immune system produces antibodies.

Cause	Effect
Contract chickenpox virus the second time.	No sickness; antibodies produced much faster.

569

(E)(L)(L) Support

1 Content and Language
Explain that the terms *vaccine* and *vaccination* come from the Latin word *vacca*, meaning "cow." Tell students that the virus that sickens cows with the disease cowpox can be given to humans to protect them against the disease smallpox. The smallpox vaccine was the first successful vaccine developed.

2 Frontload the Lesson
Encourage student volunteers to share notable experiences with and perceptions of infectious diseases. Tell students they will learn about two types of infectious disease.

3 Comprehensible Input
Have students create a Venn diagram to compare and contrast bacterial diseases and viral diseases. Encourage students to include information relating to the causes, characteristics, treatments, and prevention of each type of disease.

Explain

Introduce Vocabulary

Students are probably aware of vaccines and vaccination from first-hand experience as well as from news stories in print or on television. Explain that a vaccine is the substance and vaccination is the process of introducing the vaccine into the body.

Teach Key Concepts 🔑

Explain to students that there are two kinds of immunity, active immunity and passive immunity. Ask: **How do you acquire active immunity?** *(Your own immune system produces antibodies against a pathogen in your body.)* **How do you acquire passive immunity?** *(You receive antibodies from a source outside your body.)* Survey students to determine those who have had chickenpox, those who have had the chickenpox vaccine, and those who have had neither. Ask: **Which students have active immunity to chickenpox?** *(Those who already had the disease and those who were vaccinated)* **Which students will most likely never experience chickenpox in the future?** *(Those who already had the disease and those who were vaccinated)* Encourage students to discuss why people get immunizations. Ask them to list diseases for which they think vaccines do and do not exist.

⟳ **Relate Cause and Effect** Explain that a cause makes something happen. An effect is what happens. Point out to students that by recognizing that one event causes another, they are relating cause and effect.

Lead a Discussion

ACTIVE IMMUNITY Point out to students that an active immunity is the result of exposure to an antigen. Remind students of the actions of B cells in response to an infection. Some B cells and T cells live a long time in the body and retain the ability to produce antibodies. This is the result of an active immunity. Ask: **Why is active immunity so important?** *(If the antibodies can be made faster, the pathogen is killed before you can get sick from it.)*

My Planet Diary provides an opportunity for students to explore real-world connections to how infectious diseases affect their health.

Explain

Support the Big Q ❓UbD

HOW ACTIVE IMMUNITY IS ACQUIRED Remind students that the immune response is the human body's third line of defense against disease. Ask: **What is similar about getting a disease and getting a vaccine against a disease?** *(In both cases, B cells are stimulated to produce antibodies.)* **What is different?** *(A person who gets a disease is infected by pathogens that have not been weakened or killed. The person may become ill with the disease. A person who receives a vaccine receives killed or weakened pathogens.)* Remind students that the common cold is caused by more than 200 viruses. Tell them that on average, preschoolers have 9 colds per year and kindergartners have 12. Ask: **Why do you think this is true?** *(Kindergartners are in a school that is new to them, and are exposed to more different people who may carry more different pathogens.)* **Older students and adults have fewer colds. Why do you think this is true?** *(Sample: People develop immunity to each type of cold virus when they are infected with it. Over time, people develop immunity to a wide variety of cold viruses.)*

Teach With Visuals

Tell students to look at **Figure 2**. Ask: **At the time a person is about to get a vaccination for a certain disease, do they have that disease?** *(No)* **Why don't the pathogens in the vaccine make the person sick with the disease?** *(The pathogens are dead or weak.)* **How many of the pathogens are destroyed by antibodies?** *(All of them)* **What action, not shown in Figure 2, happens after the pathogens are destroyed?** *(The immune system produces new cells that "remember" the pathogens just destroyed.)*

Lead a Discussion

PASSIVE IMMUNITY Review the difference between the meanings of the terms *active* ("full of action") and *passive* ("acted upon"). Ask: **How does a person acquire passive immunity naturally?** *(A baby receives antibodies passed from the mother to the baby during pregnancy.)* **How does a person acquire passive immunity artificially?** *(The person is given antibodies from another source.)* Tell students that a mother's breast milk plays an important role in providing a child with passive immunity. Explain that it is the sustained presence of the antibodies from breast milk that provides a more long-term passive immunity that the infant needs, as opposed to the passive immunity that results from the antibodies passed from the mother's blood to the baby's blood during pregnancy.

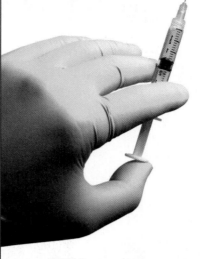

The Immune Response The immune system produces active immunity as part of the immune response. Recall that during the immune response, T cells and B cells help destroy pathogens. After the person recovers, some T cells and B cells keep the "memory" of the pathogen's antigen. If that kind of pathogen invades again, these memory cells recognize the antigen. They start the immune response so quickly that the person often does not get sick.

Vaccination Vaccination is another way of gaining immunity, as shown in **Figure 1**. **Vaccination** (vac suh NAY shun), or immunization, is the process by which harmless antigens are put into a person's body to produce active immunity. Vaccinations are given by injection, by mouth, or through a nasal spray.

The substance used in a vaccination is a vaccine. A **vaccine** (vak SEEN) usually consists of weakened or killed pathogens that trigger the immune response into action. The T cells and B cells still recognize and respond to the antigens of these weakened or killed pathogens and destroy them. So when you receive a vaccination, you usually do not get sick. However, after destroying these pathogens, your immune system responds by producing memory cells and active immunity to the disease.

FIGURE 1 ....

> **ART IN MOTION** **Vaccination**
A vaccine activates the immune response.

✎ **Interpret Diagrams** In the empty boxes, describe what is happening in each diagram.

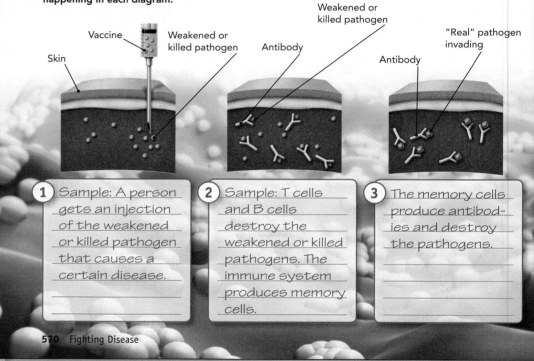

1. Sample: A person gets an injection of the weakened or killed pathogen that causes a certain disease.

2. Sample: T cells and B cells destroy the weakened or killed pathogens. The immune system produces memory cells.

3. The memory cells produce antibodies and destroy the pathogens.

570 Fighting Disease

Art in Motion shows the process of active immunity through vaccination.

my science online.com ▸ Immunity

Passive Immunity Some diseases, such as rabies, are uncommon. So people rarely receive vaccinations against them. However, someone who is bitten by an animal with rabies is usually given injections containing antibodies to the rabies antigen. This type of protection is called passive immunity. **Passive immunity** results when antibodies are given to a person. Unlike active immunity, passive immunity usually lasts no more than a few months.

A baby acquires passive immunity to some diseases before birth. This immunity results from antibodies that are passed from the mother's blood into the baby's blood during pregnancy. After birth, these antibodies protect the baby for about six months.

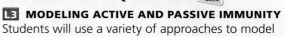

FIGURE 2 ....
Immune Responses
Your body can destroy pathogens in two different ways.

 Compare and Contrast Use the Venn diagram to compare and contrast active immunity and passive immunity.

Active Immunity

Sample:
• Body makes antibodies.
• Memory cells recognize antigens.
• Long lasting

Both

Sample:
• Can prevent diseases
• Can involve injections

Passive Immunity

Sample:
• Antibodies come from outside the body.
• Lasts a short time

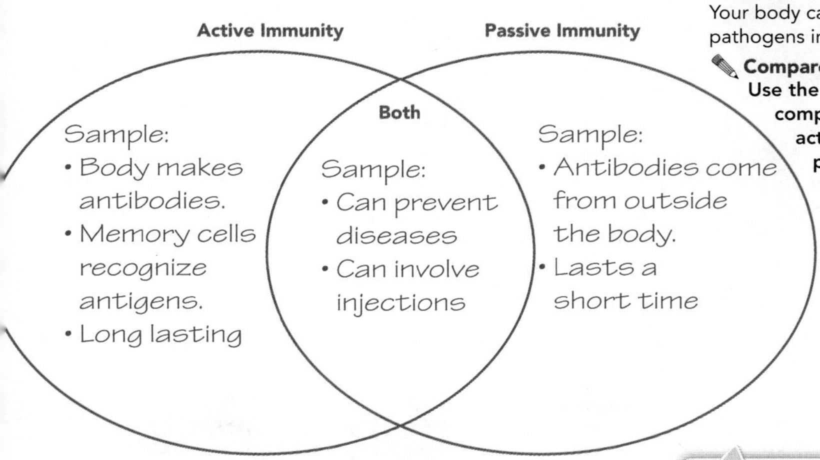

Lab zone — Do the Quick Lab *Modeling Active and Passive Immunity.*

Assess Your Understanding

1a. Explain What are two ways that you could acquire active immunity?

<u>You could get a disease that</u>
<u>produces an immune response,</u>
<u>and you could be vaccinated.</u>

b. Develop Hypotheses Why does passive immunity usually not last for long?

<u>Sample: It will not last because</u>
<u>it does not produce memory</u>
<u>cells.</u>

got it? ....

○ **I get it!** Now I know that I can become immune by <u>acquiring active or passive</u>
<u>immunity.</u>

○ **I need extra help with** <u>See TE note.</u>

Go to my science 🔊 **coach** *online for help with this subject.*

571

Elaborate ─────────────

21st Century Learning

CRITICAL THINKING Point out that some vaccines are administered to give a person active immunity, and other vaccines are administered to give a person passive immunity. Ask: **What is the difference between vaccines that give active immunity and vaccines that give passive immunity?** *(Vaccines that give active immunity contain pathogens; vaccines that give passive immunity contain antibodies to fight pathogens that may already have been introduced into the body.)*

Lab Resource: Quick Lab 🔬

L3 MODELING ACTIVE AND PASSIVE IMMUNITY Students will use a variety of approaches to model the difference between the body's response to pathogens in active immunity and passive immunity.

Evaluate ─────────────

Assess Your Understanding

After students answer the questions, have them evaluate their understanding by completing the appropriate sentence.

RTI Response to Intervention

1a. If students cannot explain two ways to acquire active immunity, **then** suggest they review the two subsections under *Active Immunity.*

b. If students need help determining why passive immunity usually does not last for long, **then** review with students how the immune system produces memory cells after vaccination for active immunity.

my science 🔊 **coach** Have students go online for help in understanding immunity.

Differentiated Instruction

L1 Vaccination Help students clarify their understanding of the series of events that occur after vaccination. Explain each step in **Figure 2** as you point to the labels. Then ask questions that encourage students to focus on each event in the sequence.

L3 Table of Common Vaccinations Challenge students to research vaccines recommended for children from birth to age 18. Have them make a table of the vaccines and the diseases they prevent. Instruct them to include information about which vaccines require boosters. If students do their research on the Internet, remind then to follow prescribed guidelines for Internet use.

Explain

Teach Key Concepts 🔑

Explain to students that bacterial diseases can be treated with specific medicines, yet viral diseases have no known cure. Ask: **How are some bacterial diseases treated?** (Antibiotics) **Where do antibiotics come from?** (Some antibiotics are produced naturally by fungi and by bacteria; other antibiotics are produced artificially in factories.) **What is the principle behind an antibiotic's effectiveness in treating a disease?** (Sample: An antibiotic kills bacteria without harming the body's cells.) **What situation can arise that makes antibiotics ineffective?** (Some bacteria have become resistant to antibiotics.) Explain to students that neither antibiotics nor any other medicine can treat a viral disease. Point out that viruses are not living, and scientists have not yet discovered a way of destroying viruses. Ask: **What is the effect of medicines given to people suffering from viral diseases?** (These medicines reduce the effects of symptoms, though they do not treat the viruses themselves.) Discuss with students the various actions people can take to prevent getting sick from a viral disease or a bacterial disease.

Elaborate

Apply It!

L1 Before beginning the activity, encourage students to look at the title of the table and the labels of all four columns. Invite a student volunteer to explain concisely that this table presents information about the estimated number of TB cases in seven countries in three specific years.

⚠ **Interpret Data** Remind students that when they interpret data, they look for patterns as they compare and contrast statistics.

How Can Infectious Diseases Be Treated and Prevented?

Bacteria and viruses can cause infectious diseases that require treatment. 🔑 **Bacterial diseases can be treated with specific medications. Viral diseases have no known cure. Both types of diseases can be prevented.**

Bacterial Diseases If you get a bacterial disease, you may be given an antibiotic. An **antibiotic** (an tih by AHT ik) is a chemical that kills bacteria or slows their growth without harming body cells. Antibiotics are made naturally by some bacteria and fungi. They also are made in factories. Some antibiotics, such as amoxicillin, cause the cell walls of certain bacteria to burst.

Over time, many bacteria can become resistant to antibiotics. **Antibiotic resistance** results when some bacteria are able to withstand the effects of an antibiotic. For example, in the 1940s, the use of antibiotics caused the number of tuberculosis cases to drop significantly. Yet, a few tuberculosis bacteria resisted the antibiotics. As resistant bacteria survive and reproduce, the number of resistant bacteria increases. As a result, the number of tuberculosis cases worldwide has increased over the last 20 years.

Rod-shaped bacteria that cause tuberculosis

apply it!

Tuberculosis (TB) is a bacterial disease that affects the lungs. The data table shows the estimated number of new TB cases in 1997, 2002, and 2007.

❶ ⚠ **Interpret Data** Which country has the greatest problem with TB? Explain how you know.

Sample: South Africa has the greatest problem. It has the most TB cases each year and the number of cases increased the most from 1997 to 2007.

❷ **CHALLENGE** Why are the data presented as the number of new cases per 100,000 people?

Sample: The populations of countries differ, so this way of showing data lets you see where the problem is serious.

Estimated TB Cases per 100,000 Population			
Country	1997	2002	2007
Brazil	67	57	48
China	109	103	98
India	168	168	168
Mexico	39	28	20
Russia	94	108	110
South Africa	360	780	948
United States	7	5	4

572 Fighting Disease

Digital Lesson: Assign the *Apply It* activity online and have students submit their work to you.

my science online.com ▸ **Bacterial and Viral Diseases**

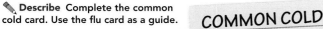

Viral Diseases Medicines you take when you have a cold or the flu do not kill the viruses because the viruses are nonliving. But, medicines can reduce your symptoms so you feel better. Always follow the medicine's directions. Medicine can sometimes hide symptoms that should send you to see a doctor.

To recover from a bacterial or viral disease, get plenty of rest and drink fluids. If you do not feel better in a short time, see a doctor.

Prevention There are ways to prevent getting sick from microorganisms. You can avoid contact with infected people and wash your hands often. You can also eat a balanced diet and exercise to stay healthy. To prevent some diseases, such as the flu, you can get a vaccine. However, you cannot get a vaccine for cold viruses.

FIGURE 3
Colds and the Flu
✎ **Describe** Complete the common cold card. Use the flu card as a guide.

INFLUENZA (Flu)

Symptoms: High fever; sore throat; headache; cough

How It Spreads: Contact with contaminated people or objects; inhaling droplets

Treatment: Bed rest; fluids

Prevention: Vaccine (mainly for the high-risk ill, elderly, and young)

Sample answers

COMMON COLD

Symptoms: Headache; body ache; loss of appetite

How It Spreads: Contact with an infected person or contaminated objects

Treatment: Take medication for symptoms; drink fluids; rest

Prevention: Avoid contact with infected people; eat healthful food

 Lab zone Do the Quick Lab What Substances Can Kill Pathogens?

 Assess Your Understanding

2a. Review What is the best treatment for viral diseases?

Drink fluids, rest, and take med-
icine to treat the symptoms.

b. Infer Explain why antibiotics are ineffective against viral diseases.

Sample: Viruses are not alive
and are not cells.

got it?

○ **I get it!** Now I know that if I get sick, I can treat _bacterial diseases with antibiotics_
and prevent _diseases in many ways._

○ **I need extra help with** _See TE note._

Go to **MY SCIENCE COACH** *online for help with this subject.*

573

Differentiated Instruction

L1 Antibiotics and Antibodies
Explain that while *antibiotics* can kill several types of bacteria; *antibodies* respond only to the antigens of a particular pathogen. Antibiotics do not work against viruses; antibodies do. Have students list the differences between antibiotics and antibodies in a 2-column chart.

L3 Smallpox Challenge students to do research on the history of smallpox.

Students might use reference books and online sources to gather information including the disease's first recorded appearance (during the Roman Empire) and the first attempts to develop vaccines to fight it in the 1800s. In 1967, the World Health Organization launched a worldwide vaccination campaign against smallpox. The world's last known natural case of smallpox occurred in 1977. The disease was declared officially eradicated in 1980.

Explain

Lead a Discussion

DISEASE PREVENTION Remind students that many diseases, both bacterial and viral, can be prevented. Ask: **How do people prevent specific diseases, such as chicken pox?** (*By getting vaccinated against the disease.*) **What can you do to avoid catching a disease for which there is no vaccine?** (*Avoid contact with infected people, wash your hands often.*) **What can you do to keep yourself healthy so that you do not get too sick if you do catch a disease?** (*Eat a balanced diet, get enough sleep, and exercise to stay healthy.*) Make sure students understand that antibiotics are not used as a preventive measure. They do not confer immunity, and they do not remain in the body long enough to be helpful "just in case" a disease is caught. Although the discussion in the students' worktext focuses on avoiding getting a disease, take time to discuss things students can do to avoid giving a disease to someone else. Staying home to avoid infecting others, being careful about how they sneeze and cough, and washing their hands before touching anything others might touch are among the ways an infected person can avoid passing on the pathogens.

Lab Resource: Quick Lab

L2 WHAT SUBSTANCES CAN KILL PATHOGENS? Students will design an experiment to explore products that can kill pathogens.

Evaluate

Assess Your Understanding

After students answer the questions, have them evaluate their understanding by completing the appropriate sentence.

RTI Response to Intervention

2a. If students have trouble identifying the best treatment for viral diseases, **then** have them review the information in *Viral Diseases*.

b. If students need help explaining why antibiotics are ineffective against viral diseases, **then** point out that the action of antibiotics—killing living bacteria—is useless against nonliving things such as viruses.

MY SCIENCE COACH Have students go online for help in understanding bacterial and viral diseases.

573

Lab zone ® After the Inquiry Warm-Up

Infectious Disease and Your Health

Inquiry Warm-Up, *Types of Immunity*

In the Inquiry Warm-Up, you discussed five case studies and determined whether the people involved had acquired active or passive immunity. Using what you learned from that activity, answer the questions below.

1. **OBSERVE** For which diseases did the case studies involve a person who actually became infected and developed an illness? Were these examples of active or passive immunity?

   _____

2. **INFER** What theory might you develop based on your observations in Question 1?

   _____

   _____

3. **OBSERVE** For which diseases did the case studies involve an injection? Were these examples of active or passive immunity?

   _____

4. **INFER** Do your observations in Question 3 lead you to develop any theories about injections and immunity? Explain.

   _____

   _____

   _____

Name _____ Date _____ Class _____

Infectious Disease and Your Health

How Can You Become Immune?

1a. **EXPLAIN** What are two ways that you could acquire active immunity?

_____

_____

b. **DEVELOP HYPOTHESES** Why does passive immunity usually not last for long?

_____

_____

got it?..

○ **I get it!** Now I know that I can become immune by _____

_____

○ **I need extra help with** _____

_____

How Can Infectious Diseases Be Treated and Prevented?

2a. **REVIEW** What is the best treatment for viral diseases?

_____

_____

b. **INFER** Explain why antibiotics are ineffective against viral diseases.

_____

_____

got it?..

○ **I get it!** Now I know that I can treat _____

_____ and prevent _____

○ **I need extra help with** _____

_____

Key Concept Summaries

Infectious Disease and Your Health

How Can You Become Immune?

Immunity is the body's ability to destroy pathogens before they can cause disease. Immunity can be active or passive. **You acquire immunity when your own immune system produces antibodies against a pathogen in your body. You acquire passive immunity when the antibodies come from a source outside your body.**

When people get sick with a pathogen their immune systems produce antibodies. After the person recovers from such a disease, some of their T cells and B cells keep the "memory" of the pathogen's antigen. The next time the same pathogen invades their bodies, their immune systems produce antibodies quickly to avoid them becoming sick with the same pathogen again. This reaction is called **active immunity** because the body has produced the antibodies that fight pathogens.

Vaccination, or immunization, is the process by which harmless antigens are introduced into a person's body to produce active immunity. The substance in a vaccination, a **vaccine,** usually consists of weakened or killed pathogens that trigger the immune response into action.

Passive immunity results when antibodies are given to a person. Usually passive immunity lasts only a few months. Babies acquire passive immunity to some diseases before birth and are protected during the first six months after they are born.

How Can Infectious Diseases Be Treated and Prevented?

Bacteria and viruses cause diseases that require treatment. **Bacterial diseases can be treated with specific medications. Viral diseases have no known cure. Both types of diseases can be prevented.**

An **antibiotic** is a chemical that can kill bacteria without harming body cells. Antibiotics are made naturally by bacteria and fungi, as well as artificially by human beings. **Antibiotic resistance** results when some bacteria are able to survive in the presence of an antibiotic. Getting rest and drinking a lot of fluids are ways of treating viral diseases. Prevention of viral diseases and bacterial diseases requires avoiding contact with infected persons, washing your hands often, eating a balanced diet, and exercising.

On a separate sheet of paper, explain how bacterial diseases and viral diseases are alike and different.

Place the outside corner, the corner away from the dotted line, in the corner of your copy machine to copy onto letter-size paper.

Infectious Disease and Your Health

Understanding Main Ideas
Complete the table below by stating whether each characteristic applies to passive immunity, active immunity, or both.

Type of Immunity	Characteristic
1.	lasts only a few months
2.	can last for a lifetime
3.	may be gained by coming down with a disease
4.	passes from a pregnant mother to her unborn child
5.	can be acquired through vaccination

Answer the following questions on a separate sheet of paper.

6. Explain two ways in which immunity is produced.

7. Why might you treat a bacterial infection but not a viral disease with an antibiotic?

Building Vocabulary
Match each term with its definition by writing the letter of the correct definition in the right column on the line beside the term in the left column.

8. ___ immunity

9. ___ active immunity

10. ___ vaccination

11. ___ vaccine

12. ___ passive immunity

13. ___ antibiotic

14. ___ antibiotic resistance

a. the process by which harmless antigens are introduced into a person's body to produce active immunity

b. the temporary immunity gained from introducing antibodies from another source into a person's own body

c. a circumstance in which some bacteria are able to survive in the presence of an antibiotic

d. the immunity gained when a person's own immune system produces antibodies in response to a pathogen

e. a chemical that can kill bacteria without harming body cells

f. the body's ability to destroy pathogens before they can cause disease

g. the substance used in a vaccination

Infectious Disease and Your Health

> Read the passage and study the graphs. Then answer the questions that follow on a separate sheet of paper.

Testing a Vaccine

Vaccines have been developed to protect people and animals against many infectious diseases. Years ago, the only way to discover whether a vaccine worked against a certain disease was to expose a group of people or animals who were vaccinated to the pathogen that caused the disease. This was dangerous, of course, because if the vaccine didn't work, the people or animals might get the disease.

Today, many vaccines are made using only part of the pathogen. When injected, this part—called the antigen—stimulates the body to form antibodies. Using lab techniques, scientists can measure the concentration of antibodies. Later, the antigen can be injected again and the concentration of antibodies measured once more.

When a vaccine is made, scientists first make several variations of it. Then they test the variations to determine which is the best one. The graphs below show possible results of test of two variations of a vaccine.

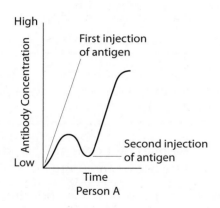

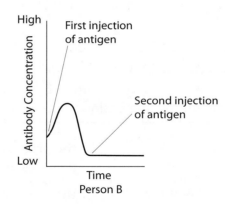

1. Do tests involve active or passive immunity? Explain.
2. In both cases, what happened to the person's antibody level after the vaccine was first injected?
3. Which person had most likely already been exposed to the pathogen? Explain.
4. Which version of the vaccine seemed to be more effective? Explain.

Lesson Quiz

Infectious Disease and Your Health

Fill in the blank to complete each statement.

1. You acquire _____ when your own immune system produces antibodies against a pathogen in your body.

2. Babies acquire _____ immunity to some diseases before birth and are protected during the first six months after they are born.

3. _____ diseases can be treated with specific medications.

4. Immunization, also known as _____, is the process by which harmless antigens are introduced into a person's body to produce active immunity.

5. _____ are made naturally by bacteria and fungi, as well as artificially by human beings.

If the statement is true, write *true*. If the statement is false, change the underlined word or words to make the statement true.

6. _____ Resistance is the body's ability to destroy pathogens before they can cause disease.

7. _____ You acquire passive immunity when the antibodies come from a source outside your body.

8. _____ Both bacterial diseases and viral diseases can be prevented.

9. _____ Bacterial diseases have no known cure.

10. _____ In the reaction called active immunity, the body produces the antibodies that fight pathogens.

Place the outside corner, the corner away from the dotted line, in the corner of your copy machine to copy onto letter-size paper.

Infectious Disease and Your Health

Answer Key

After the Inquiry Warm-Up

1. smallpox, chicken pox; active immunity

2. When a person becomes infected with a pathogen and becomes ill, he or she develops active immunity to that pathogen.

3. smallpox, rabies, polio; Smallpox and polio involved active immunity; rabies involved passive immunity.

4. No, some injections led to active immunity, while another injection led to passive immunity. Whether a person receives an injection does not seem to determine whether active or passive immunity is conferred.

Key Concept Summaries

Both bacterial diseases and viral diseases need treatment. Bacterial diseases can be treated with specific medicines, such as antibiotics. However, in the case of most viral diseases, only the symptoms can be treated with medicines. The treatment for a viral disease such as the flu is rest and the drinking of fluids. Both bacterial and viral diseases can be prevented.

Review and Reinforce

1. passive

2. active

3. active

4. passive

5. active or passive

6. Sample: One way is by coming down with a disease. The body produces antigens that protect against catching that disease again. Another way is by getting vaccinated. The body responds to the vaccination by producing antibodies and memory cells that protect against getting that particular disease.

7. Sample: An antibiotic could be used to treat a bacterial infection because it kills the living bacteria. An antibiotic is useless in treating a viral infection because it does not affect nonliving things such as viruses.

8. f
9. d
10. a
11. g
12. b
13. e
14. c

Enrich

1. active immunity; Active immunity involves your own body producing antibodies against a pathogen. Passive immunity involves introducing antibodies from another source into a person's body.

2. The concentration of antibodies increased.

3. Person B; This person had a concentration of antibodies to the pathogen before being vaccinated.

4. The vaccine given to Person A. When the person was exposed to the antigen a second time, a large number of antibodies were rapidly produced. This would keep the person from getting the disease.

Lesson Quiz

1. immunity
2. passive
3. Bacterial
4. vaccination
5. Antibiotics
6. Immunity
7. true
8. true
9. Viral
10. true

Place the outside corner, the corner away from the dotted line, in the corner of your copy machine to copy onto letter-size paper.

Lesson Pacing: 2–3 periods or 1–1½ blocks

🕐 **SHORT ON TIME?** To do this lesson in approximately half the time, do the Activate Prior Knowledge activity followed by a discussion of the Key Concepts to familiarize students with the lesson content. Use the Explore the Big Q to help students understand why they sometimes get sick. Do the Quick Labs and have students do the Real-World Inquiry online. The rest of the lesson can be completed by students independently.

Preference Navigator, in the online Planning tools, allows you to customize *Interactive Science* to your own teaching style. You can also edit lesson plans by selecting the Lesson Planner option.

Digital Teacher's Edition allows you to access your Teacher's Edition and Resource materials online.

my science online.com

Lesson Vocabulary

- noninfectious disease
- allergy
- allergen
- histamine
- asthma
- insulin
- diabetes
- tumor
- carcinogen

Content Refresher

Risk Factors for Cancer In cancer, many factors typically work together to cause the disease. Some cancers, such as breast and colon cancers, have a genetic link, but scientists think environment and behavior play a greater role as possible causes of cancer.

Over half of all cancers can be attributed to environmental factors, such as cigarette smoking and excessive exposure to ultraviolet light. Environmental pollution, pesticides, and asbestos account for less than 10 percent of cancer cases. People who have direct contact with carcinogenic agents in the workplace are at the highest risk for cancer. Occupational exposure to vinyl chloride, for example, is limited by federal law.

Dietary factors have received much attention as risks for cancer. Obesity is associated with increased cancer risk. An increase of bile acids in the intestine, which results from a high-fat diet, can also promote colon cancer.

LESSON OBJECTIVES

☞ Describe how allergies, diabetes, and asthma affect the body.
☞ Define cancer and explain how it may be treated.

Blended Path
Active learning using Student Edition, Inquiry Path, and Digital Path

ENGAGE AND EXPLORE

Teach this lesson using a variety of resources. Begin by reading **My Planet Diary** as a class. Have students share ideas about what they know about how asthma is treated. Then have students do the **Inquiry Warm-Up activity.** Students will investigate what caused deaths then and now. Discuss the leading cause of deaths in 1900 and how it ranks today. The **After the Inquiry Warm-Up worksheet** sets up a discussion about how the death rates from infectious and noninfectious diseases have changed. Have volunteers share their answers to question 4 about why the total number of deaths, from the top ten causes today, is different from the total number in 1900.

EXPLAIN AND ELABORATE

Teach Key Concepts by identifying noninfectious chronic diseases. **Lead a Discussion** about diseases that are not caused by pathogens. **Lead a Discussion** about what causes allergies and how the body responds to these invaders. Before beginning the **Apply It activity,** review the nature of allergens and histamines. Then ask students to share their responses. **Lead a Discussion** about the various causes of asthma. Use **Figure 1** to illustrate how the airways are affected by asthma. **Lead a Discussion** about how diabetes affects the body.

Continue to **Teach Key Concepts** by explaining that cancer is a disease in which cells multiply uncontrollably destroying healthy tissues. **Lead a Discussion** about how students can avoid or protect themselves from carcinogens that can cause cancer. **Lead a Discussion** about the different types of cancer. **Explore the Big Q** by discussing the boy's symptoms and trying to determine if he has an infectious or noninfectious disease or sickness. To help students **Answer the Big Q** discuss why people sometimes get sick. Hand out the **Key Concept Summaries** as a review of each part of the lesson. Students can also use the online **Vocab Flash Cards** to review key terms.

EVALUATE

Have students take the **Lesson Quiz.** For an alternate assessment, see the **EXAM**VIEW® Assessment Suite, Progress Monitoring Assessments, or SuccessTracker™.

ELL Support

1 Content and Language
The word *noninfectious* contains the prefix *non-* meaning "not." A *noninfectious disease* is not cause by pathogens.

DIFFERENTIATED INSTRUCTION KEY
L1 Struggling Students or Special Needs
L2 On-Level Students **L3** Advanced Students

LESSON PLANNER 14.5

Lab zone **Inquiry Path** Hands-on learning in the Lab zone

ENGAGE AND EXPLORE

To teach this lesson with an emphasis on inquiry, begin with the **Inquiry Warm-Up activity.** Students will investigate how the causes of death have changed over time. Discuss the types of diseases that caused deaths in 1900. Have students do the **After the Inquiry Warm-Up worksheet.** Talk about how the death rates from infectious and noninfectious disease have changed. Have volunteers share their answers to question 4 about why the number of today's deaths, from the top ten causes in each column, is different from the number in 1900.

EXPLAIN AND ELABORATE

Focus on the **Inquiry Skill** for the lesson. Point out that when you draw conclusions, you sum up what you have learned from an experiment or question. Based on the **Inquiry Warm-Up activity,** what conclusion could be drawn about the total number of deaths from the top ten causes in each column when comparing today's numbers to those of 1900? *(Fewer people per 100,000 die from the top ten causes today than did in 1900.)* Review the nature of allergens and histamines before beginning the **Apply It activity.** Ask volunteers to describe what caused Suzy's rash and how a doctor might relieve it. Do the **Build Inquiry activity** to reinforce understanding of how the body responds to an allergen versus a pathogen. Have students do the **Quick Lab** to explore the effects of asthma and then share their results.

Have students do the **Real-World Inquiry** to diagnose and treat patients with viral infections, bacterial infections, and allergies. **Explore the Big Q** by using the symptoms to try to identify if the boy has an infectious or noninfectious disease. Do the **Quick Lab** to explore the effects of sunshine on ultraviolet-sensitive beads. Have students **Answer the Big Q** and then share their responses. Students can use the online **Vocab Flash Cards** to review key terms.

EVALUATE

Have students take the **Lesson Quiz.** For an alternate assessment, see the **EXAM**VIEW® Assessment Suite, Progress Monitoring Assessments, or SuccessTracker™.

Digital Path Online learning at my science online.com

ENGAGE AND EXPLORE

Teach this lesson using digital resources. Begin by having students explore real-world connections to noninfectious diseases at **My Planet Diary** online. Have them access the Chapter Resources to find the **Unlock the Big Question activity.** There they can answer the questions and refine their responses as they continue through the lesson. You can re-assign the activity and have students submit their work so you can track their progress.

EXPLAIN AND ELABORATE

Students reading above, at, or below the lexile measure of this lesson can access basic content readings at their level at **My Reading Web.** Have students use the online **Vocab Flash Cards** to preview key terms. Review the nature of allergens and histamines before assigning the **Apply It activity.** Do the **Quick Lab** and then ask students to share their results.

Assign the **Do the Math activity** online and have students submit their work to you. Assign the online **Real-World Inquiry** to allow students to diagnose and treat patients with viral infections, bacterial infections, and allergies. To **Explore the Big Q,** have students investigate the boy's symptoms to determine if he has an infectious or noninfectious disease. Do the **Quick Lab** and then ask students to share their results. To **Answer the Big Q,** discuss why people sometimes get sick. The **Key Concept Summaries** online allow students to read a summary and see an image associated with each part of the lesson. Online remediation is available at **My Science Coach.**

EVALUATE

Have students take the **Lesson Quiz.** For an alternate assessment, see the **EXAM**VIEW® Assessment Suite, Progress Monitoring Assessments, or SuccessTracker™.

2 Frontload the Lesson

Preview the lesson visuals, labels, and captions. Ask students what they know about the terms *allergy, asthma,* and *diabetes.* Explain the specific meanings these words have in science.

3 Comprehensible Input

Have students study the visuals and their captions to support the Key Concepts of the lesson.

4 Language Production

Pair or group students with varied language abilities to complete labs collaboratively for language practice. Have each student copy the completed written lab for personal reference.

5 Assess Understanding

Have students create a portfolio of their notes and then do oral presentations of lesson content.

LESSON 14.5

Noninfectious Disease

Establish Learning Objectives

After this lesson, students will be able to:

🔑 Describe how allergies, diabetes, and asthma affect the body.

🔑 Define cancer and explain how it may be treated.

Engage

Activate Prior Knowledge

MY PLANET DIARY Read *Athletes with Asthma* with the class. Point out that asthma can be dangerous if untreated and that athletes should consult a doctor to find out about appropriate treatment that will allow their safe participation in sports. Ask: **Which important body function does asthma affect?** *(Breathing)* **What do successful athletes with asthma have in common?** *(Sample: They keep their asthma under control.)*

BIG IDEAS OF SCIENCE REFERENCE LIBRARY Have students look up the following topics: Allergies, Cancer Treatment.

Explore

Lab Resource: Inquiry Warm-Up 🧪

L2 CAUSES OF DEATH, THEN AND NOW Students will investigate how death rates from infectious and noninfectious diseases have changed.

---

5 Noninfectious Disease

🔑 How Do Allergies, Asthma, and Diabetes Affect the Body?

🔑 What Is Cancer and How Can It Be Treated?

Inhaler used to control asthma

MY PLANET DIARY

Athletes With Asthma

Asthma is a disease that causes shortness of breath and wheezing or coughing. You may think people who have asthma cannot excel in sports. But asthma does not have to stop anyone from succeeding. Here are some facts about asthma and athletics.

• One out of six athletes in the 1996 Summer Olympics had a history of asthma. Thirty percent of them won a medal.

• 22 percent of the athletes in the 1998 Winter Olympics suffered from asthma.

• Jerome Bettis (NFL football player), Jackie Joyner-Kersee (Olympic track and field medalist), Hakeem Olajuwon (NBA basketball player), and Amy VanDyken (Olympic swimmer) all live with asthma.

SCIENCE STATS

Answer the following questions.

1. Why might people think that someone with asthma cannot play sports?

   Sample: They may think someone with asthma cannot get enough oxygen when playing sports.

2. What would you tell a friend who has asthma and wants to join the swim team?

   Sample: See a doctor to get help controlling the asthma.

▶ PLANET DIARY Go to Planet Diary to learn more about noninfectious disease.

🧪 Do the Inquiry Warm-Up *Causes of Death, Then and Now*

SUPPORT ALL READERS

Lexile Measure = 940L   Lexile Word Count = 1394

Prior Exposure to Content: May be the first time students have encountered this topic

Academic Vocabulary: *conclusion, summarize*

Science Vocabulary: *noninfectious disease, allergy, asthma, carcinogen*

Concept Level: Generally appropriate for most students in this grade

Preteach With: My Planet Diary "Athletes With Asthma" and Figure 1 activity

Go to **My Reading Web** to access leveled readings that provide a foundation for the content.

my science online.com

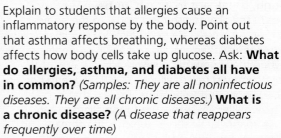

Vocabulary
- noninfectious disease
- allergy
- allergen
- histamine
- asthma
- insulin
- diabetes
- tumor
- carcinogen

Skills
- **Reading:** Summarize
- **Inquiry:** Draw Conclusions

How Do Allergies, Asthma, and Diabetes Affect the Body?

Americans are living longer than ever before. A person who was born in 2000 can expect to live about 77 years. In contrast, a person who was born in 1950 could expect to live only about 68 years, and a person born in 1900 only about 50 years.

Progress against infectious disease is one reason why life spans have increased. However, as most infectious diseases have become less common, noninfectious diseases have grown more common. **Noninfectious diseases** are diseases that are not caused by pathogens. Unlike infectious diseases, noninfectious diseases cannot be transmitted from person to person. Two noninfectious diseases, cardiovascular disease and cancer, are the first and second leading causes of death from disease in the United States. Allergies, asthma, and diabetes are other noninfectious diseases. While not often fatal, these diseases are chronic. That is, they reappear frequently over time. **Allergies cause an inflammatory response by the body. Asthma affects breathing, while diabetes affects how body cells take up glucose.**

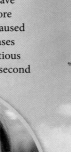

Summarize Use your own words to summarize the information about diseases on this page.

Sample: People in the United States are living longer today than long ago. Infectious diseases are down, but noninfectious diseases are up. You cannot catch a noninfectious disease such as cancer, cardio-vascular disease, or allergies from another person.

575

Explain

Introduce Vocabulary

To help students understand the terms *allergen* and *carcinogens*, point out that both words contain the Greek word part *-gen-*, meaning "producer." Explain that an allergen is something that produces or causes an allergy and that a carcinogen is something that produces or causes cancer.

Teach Key Concepts 🔑

Explain to students that allergies cause an inflammatory response by the body. Point out that asthma affects breathing, whereas diabetes affects how body cells take up glucose. Ask: **What do allergies, asthma, and diabetes all have in common?** (*Samples: They are all noninfectious diseases. They are all chronic diseases.*) **What is a chronic disease?** (*A disease that reappears frequently over time*)

Summarize Explain that a summary is a short statement that presents the main ideas and most important points in a text. Point out that summarizing helps you distinguish main ideas from the information that supports those ideas.

Lead a Discussion

DISEASES THAT ARE NOT SPREAD Ask students to brainstorm a list of diseases that are not caused by pathogens. Record their responses on the board. As they study this lesson, students can update the list to add items not already listed and remove diseases that they learn are caused by pathogens.

My Planet Diary provides an opportunity for students to explore real-world connections to noninfectious diseases.

ELL Support

1 Content and Language
Write the term *histamine* on the board. Most people are more familiar with the word *antihistamine*. Point out that *histamine* is a chemical that causes sneezing, watery eyes, and a rash.

2 Frontload the Lesson
Ask how many students in the class have ever been diagnosed with allergies or asthma. Invite volunteers to describe for their classmates the symptoms and how they can relieve them.

3 Comprehensible Input
Have students work in pairs to model the contrast between a normal airway and an airway affected with asthma, as shown in **Figure 1**. Students can use cardboard cylinders from rolls of paper towels to represent the airways. Urge students to experiment to find an especially effective way to model the mucus in an asthmatic airway.

575

Explain

Lead a Discussion

THE CAUSE OF ALLERGIES Remind students that the immune system recognizes foreign invaders and makes antibodies to them. Ask: **What are some invaders that cause an allergic response?** *(Samples: Pollen, dust, molds, some foods, pet dander, some medicines)* **What is the term for these invaders?** *(Allergens)* **What happens in this situation to make a person's body sneeze, cough, break out in a rash, or have watery eyes?** *(The allergen sends a signal to the body's cells, and the cells release histamine. This chemical causes the allergic symptoms.)* Ask if students or anyone they know has a severe allergy. Two of the more common severe allergic reactions are to bee or wasp venom and to peanuts. Explain that in cases of severe allergies, exposure to the allergen can cause anaphylactic shock, which is life-threatening. Symptoms include swelling of the tongue and/or airway, decreased blood pressure, dizziness, fainting, and heart failure. If not treated promptly, anaphylactic shock can be fatal.

21st Century Learning

CRITICAL THINKING Help students focus each step of causes and effects that underlie an allergic reaction. Ask: **How can avoiding an allergen decrease allergic symptoms?** *(If the body's cells do not encounter an allergen, they do not get signals to release the chemical histamine.)*

Elaborate

Apply It!

L1 Before the activity, review the nature of allergens and histamines. Ask: **In this scenario, where are the allergens located?** *(In strawberries)* **How does the allergen "communicate" with the body?** *(It enters the body, in this case through the mouth, and signals the body's cells of its presence.)* **How does the body react to such signals?** *(It produces histamine.)* **What does this chemical cause to happen?** *(Symptoms of an allergic reaction such as sneezing or itching)*

21st Century Learning

INFORMATION LITERACY Have students read *Allergies* in the **Big Ideas of Science Reference Library.** Assign different allergy treatments for each student to research. Treatments include homeopathic medicines, over-the-counter medication, and allergy shots. Students should explore how treatment prevents or lessens allergy symptoms and how effective the treatment is. Students can summarize their findings in a presentation.

576 Fighting Disease

Observe Name two foods that many people are allergic to.

Sample: People are allergic to strawberries and to peanuts.

Allergies People who sneeze a lot in the spring may not have a cold. Instead, they may be showing a symptom of an allergy. An **allergy** is a reaction caused when the immune system is overly sensitive to a foreign substance—something not normally found in the body.

Any substance that causes an allergy is an **allergen.** Allergens include pollen, dust, molds, some foods, pet dander (dandruff), and even some medicines. Unfortunately, the bodies of many people react to one or more allergens.

Allergens may get into your body when you inhale them, eat them in food, or touch them. Allergens signal cells in the body to release a substance called histamine. **Histamine** (HIS tuh meen) is a chemical that is responsible for the symptoms of an allergy, such as a rash, sneezing, and watery eyes. Drugs that interfere with the action of histamine, called antihistamines, may lessen this reaction. However, if you have an allergy, the best way to prevent allergy symptoms is to try to avoid the substance to which you are allergic.

apply it!

Suzy ate some strawberries. A short time later, she broke out in a rash.

❶ **Identify** What might have caused Suzy's rash?

Sample: Suzy may be allergic to strawberries.

❷ **Sequence** Explain how eating strawberries can cause a rash.

Sample: After Suzy digested the strawberries, the allergen entered her blood and signaled certain cells to produce histamines. Histamines can cause an allergic rash.

❸ **Predict** What might a doctor prescribe to relieve Suzy's rash?

Sample: An antihistamine could help. She should probably avoid strawberries in the future.

576 Fighting Disease

Digital Lesson: Assign the *Apply It* activity online and have students submit their work to you.

my science online

Allergies, Asthma, & Diabetes

Asthma Some allergic reactions can cause a condition called asthma. **Asthma** (AZ muh) is a disease in which the airways in the lungs narrow significantly. This narrowing causes wheezing, coughing, and shortness of breath. Other factors that may trigger asthma attacks include stress and heavy exercise. Tobacco smoke, air pollution, strong odors, and respiratory infections can also trigger an attack. More than 20 million Americans have asthma.

Figure 1 shows a normal airway and an airway affected by asthma. During an asthma attack, the muscles around the airways tighten, narrowing the airways. At the same time, the inner walls of the airways become irritated, red, swollen, and warm. They produce mucus. The mucus clogs the airways and makes breathing even more difficult.

Someone who is having an asthma attack needs medicines, such as an inhaler, to open the airways and reduce swelling. A severe attack may require emergency care. An asthma attack can be fatal.

FIGURE 1 ....
Airways With and Without Asthma
Asthma is a common condition among young people.

✎ **Relate Text and Visuals** Look at the diagram of a normal airway. Then in each box of the second diagram, describe what happens in an airway affected by asthma.

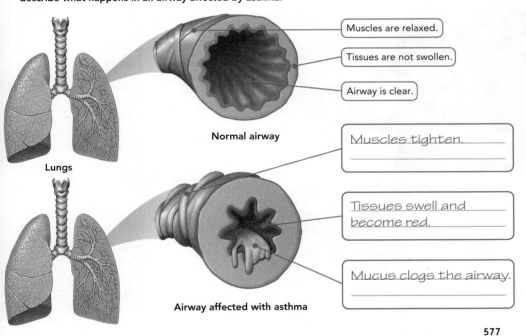

Lungs

Muscles are relaxed.

Tissues are not swollen.

Airway is clear.

Normal airway

Muscles tighten.

Tissues swell and become red.

Mucus clogs the airway.

Airway affected with asthma

577

Explain
Lead a Discussion

CAUSES OF ASTHMA Explain that asthma is a disorder in which the lungs' airways narrow significantly. Point out that asthma has more than one cause. Ask: **How can asthma be related to an allergic reaction?** *(Some allergic reactions can bring on an asthma attack.)* **What are other causes of asthma?** *(Stress, heavy exercise, tobacco smoke, strong odors, air pollution, respiratory infections)* Help students understand that each of these events or substances has the same effect—narrowing the air passages in the lungs.

Teach With Visuals

Tell students to look at **Figure 1.** Ask: **How do these illustrations convey the seriousness of an asthma attack?** *(In an asthma attack, a person's ability to breathe is reduced dramatically.)* If students have difficulty seeing the importance of the narrow airway, ask them to imagine the difference between trying to inhale a lungful of air through a section of garden hose or through a narrow straw. Another useful analogy is to compare air having trouble getting through a clogged airway to blood having trouble passing through a vessel when plaque has built up on its walls.

Elaborate
Build Inquiry **Lab zone**

L2 **MODEL ACTION OF IMMUNE CELLS**
Materials none

Time 20 minutes

Point out that allergens are normally harmless. Have students diagram what happens when a pathogen invades the body and what happens when an allergen invades the body. Ask students to label their drawings and write captions describing what happens at each stage.

Ask: **Why does your immune system react to these substances if they are not pathogens?** *(Your immune system recognizes them as foreign.)*

Differentiated Instruction

L1 **Organization of Information**
Students may have difficulty organizing the information in this section. Model a concept map for one disease, showing its causes, symptoms, and treatments. Then, encourage students to create similar concept maps for another disease in this section.

L3 **Food Sensitivities** Not all food sensitivities are allergies. Invite interested students to do research to find out about food sensitivities or intolerances, such as lactose intolerance.

Explain

Lead a Discussion

HOW DIABETES AFFECTS THE BODY Review the functions of insulin. Explain that although a person with diabetes may eat a healthy diet, glucose from the food does not enter the cells. Ask: **What are the symptoms of diabetes, and what causes these symptoms?** *(Symptoms such as weight loss, weakness, hunger, frequent urination, and thirst are caused by high levels of glucose in the blood but a lack of glucose in cells.)* Point out that in the cases of some people with Type II diabetes, the body cells do not respond normally to insulin, or the pancreas stops producing sufficient insulin. Ask: **What are the range of treatments for Type II diabetes?** *(Exercise, diet, weight control, insulin injections)*

Elaborate

Lab Resource: Quick Lab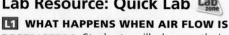

L1 WHAT HAPPENS WHEN AIR FLOW IS RESTRICTED? Students will observe their own breathing patterns in restricted circumstances to explore the effects of asthma.

Evaluate

Assess Your Understanding

After students answer the questions, have them evaluate their understanding by completing the appropriate sentence.

RTI Response to Intervention

1a. If students have difficulty identifying asthma, **then** ask them to review **Figure 1** carefully.

b. If students need help explaining the effect of Type I diabetes on insulin levels, **then** have them reread the information about insulin and about Type I diabetes in the section "Diabetes."

MY SCIENCE COACH Have students go online for help in understanding allergies, asthma, and diabetes.

FIGURE 2
Glucose Testing
The student is using a device called a glucometer to measure the amount of glucose in his blood.

Summarize Write notes in the table about Type I and Type II diabetes.

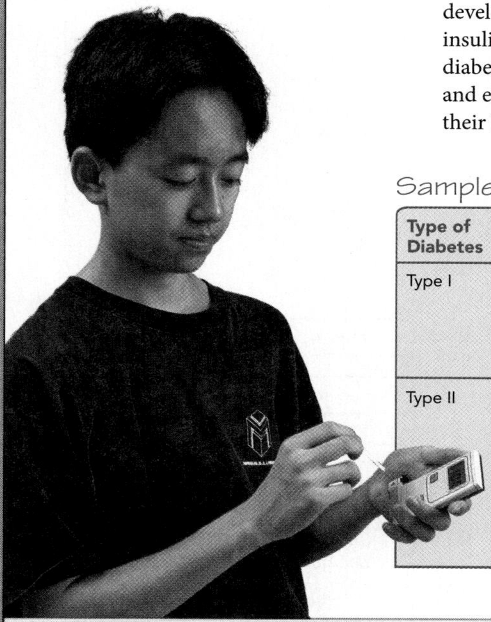

Diabetes One function of the pancreas is to produce insulin. **Insulin** (IN suh lin) is a substance that enables body cells to take glucose from the blood and use it for energy. In the condition called **diabetes** (dy uh BEE teez), either the pancreas produces too little insulin or body cells do not use insulin properly. People with diabetes, or diabetics, have high levels of glucose in their blood but not enough of it in their body cells. If untreated, diabetics may lose weight and feel weak and hungry. They also may urinate often and feel thirsty.

Diabetes has two main forms. Type I diabetes often begins in childhood. The pancreas produces little or no insulin. People with this condition need insulin injections. Type II diabetes usually develops in adults. Either body cells stop responding normally to insulin or the pancreas stops making enough insulin. Some Type II diabetics can control their symptoms through diet, weight control, and exercise instead of insulin injections. All diabetics must check their blood frequently, as shown in **Figure 2**.

Sample:

Type of Diabetes	Cause	Symptoms	Treatment
Type I	Pancreas makes little or no insulin.	Weakness, hunger, thirst	Insulin injections
Type II	Pancreas makes too little insulin or cells can't use insulin.	Weakness, hunger, thirst	Diet, exercise

Lab zone Do the Quick Lab *What Happens When Air Flow Is Restricted?*

Assess Your Understanding

1a. Name Asthma _____ is a disorder in which airways of the lungs narrow significantly.

b. Relate Cause and Effect How are insulin levels affected in Type I diabetes?
The pancreas produces little or no insulin.

got it?

○ I get it! Now I know that allergies, asthma, and diabetes affect inflammation, breathing, and glucose level.

○ I need extra help with See TE note.

Go to MY SCIENCE COACH *online for help with this subject.*

What Is Cancer and How Can It Be Treated?

Usually, the body produces new cells at about the same rate that other cells die. **However, cancer is a disease in which cells multiply uncontrollably, over and over, destroying healthy tissue. Treatments include surgery, radiation, and drugs.**

How Cancer Develops As cells divide over and over, they often form abnormal masses of cells called **tumors.** Not all tumors are cancerous. Cancerous tumors invade and destroy the healthy tissue around them. Eventually, cells from a tumor may break away from the tumor and enter the blood or lymph vessels. The blood or lymph carries the cancer cells to other parts of the body, where they may form new tumors. Unless stopped by treatment, cancer progresses through the body.

Causes of Cancer Different factors may work together to cause cancer. Inherited characteristics make some people more likely to develop certain cancers. For example, daughters of mothers who had breast cancer have an increased chance of developing breast cancer themselves. Factors in the environment, called **carcinogens** (kahr SIN uh junz), can also cause cancer. The tar in cigarette smoke is a carcinogen.

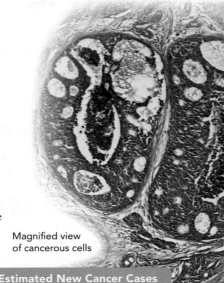

Magnified view of cancerous cells

do the math!

This data table shows the estimated number of new cases of different cancers in the United States in 1981 and 2007.

1 Interpret Tables Which type of cancer has increased the most from 1981 to 2007 in men? In women?

Men _Prostate cancer_

Women _Breast cancer_

2 Draw Conclusions Explain why the number of new cancer cases might increase as tests to detect cancer improve.

Sample: The increase
happens because the
improved tests identify
cancer that may not have
been diagnosed before.

Estimated New Cancer Cases

Type of Cancer	New Cases (1981)	New Cases (2007)
Men		
Prostate	70,000	218,890
Lung	88,000	114,760
Colon and Rectum	58,000	79,130
Oral Cavity and Pharynx	18,400	24,180
Women		
Breast	110,000	178,480
Lung	34,000	98,620
Colon and Rectum	62,000	74,630
Uterus	54,000	50,230

579

Explain

Teach Key Concepts

Explain to students that cancer is a disease in which cells multiply uncontrollably, destroying healthy tissue. Point out that cancer cells are not foreign; rather, they are the body's own cells. Ask: **What body structure does cancer involve?** (Cells) **What does this tell you about where cancer can appear in the body?** (Cancer can appear in a wide variety of places.) **What is a tumor?** (A mass of cancer cells) **How do different factors work together to cause cancer?** (Some people may be more likely to develop certain cancers. Exposure to carcinogens may increase the risk.) **How is cancer treated?** (Surgery, radiation, and drugs)

Elaborate

21st Century Learning

CRITICAL THINKING Invite students to apply their prior knowledge about the structures and functions of cells. Ask: **Which part of a cell does a carcinogen most likely damage to make the cell divide uncontrollably?** (The nucleus, which is the cell's control center and which contains information that determines the cell's characteristics)

Do the Math!

L1 Remind students that data tables are useful for presenting information in an orderly format. Have students begin by looking at the table's title before analyzing the three columns. Then students can identify the types of cancer—and their two groupings—shown in rows on the table's left side. Help students understand that this table presents information about cases of six types of cancer that affected men and women in 1981 and in 2007.

Draw Conclusions Explain that a conclusion is a statement that sums up what is learned from a question. Help students understand that drawing conclusions often leads to new questions and revisions. Point out that students' conclusions can be drawn from analysis of the number of new cases in 1981 and 2007, combined with their inferences about possible effects of improved methods of detecting cancer.

See the *Math Skill and Problem-Solving Activities* for support.

Digital Lesson: Assign the *Do the Math* activity online and have students submit their work to you.

Differentiated Instruction

L3 Health Effects of Industrial Environments Challenge interested students to research how health conditions were affected by the Industrial Revolution in the U.S., England, Scotland, and other places during the 1800s. Students may include information relating to the soot generated by coal fires burning in the chimneys of factories and homes, as well as the effects of industrial pollution on water and land. Students can share their research with the class.

Explain

Lead a Discussion

CANCER PREVENTION Tell students that skin cancer is the most common form of cancer in the United States today. Ask: **To prevent skin cancer, is it necessary to stay out of sunlight?** *(People do not need to stay out of sunlight, but they should protect their skin with clothing or sunscreen when they spend time in sunlight.)* Point out that the use of tobacco products is another common source of cancer. Encourage students to have a discussion about strategies they can use to avoid cigarettes and other tobacco products.

Lead a Discussion

TYPES OF CANCER Ask students to name different types of cancers they have heard of. Give a brief description of the difference between solid tumors, such as breast cancer, and blood cancers, such as leukemia.

Address Misconceptions

L1 **THE CAUSES OF CANCER** Many students may believe that chemicals cause the majority of cancers and that, therefore, the prevention of cancer is beyond their control. Tell students that except for chemicals in tobacco, chemicals represent a small proportion of all causes of cancer. Have students use reliable print or online sources—such as the American Cancer Society and the Center for Disease Control—to research a variety of causes of cancer. If students do their research on the Internet, remind them to follow prescribed guidelines for Internet use.

Cancer Treatment Surgery, radiation, and drugs are used to treat cancer. If cancer is detected before it has spread, doctors may remove tumors with surgery. After surgery, radiation or drugs may be used to kill remaining cancer cells.

Radiation treatment uses high-energy waves to kill cancer cells. When these waves are aimed at tumors, the intense energy damages and kills cancer cells. Drug therapy is the use of chemicals to destroy cancer cells. It is often called chemotherapy. However, many of these chemicals can destroy some normal cells, too. Both radiation and chemotherapy can have side effects, such as nausea and hair loss.

Cancer Prevention People can reduce their risk of cancer by avoiding carcinogens, such as those in tobacco and sunlight. A low-fat diet that includes plenty of fruits and vegetables can help prevent cancers of the digestive system.

Also, people can get regular checkups to increase their chance of surviving cancer. The earlier cancer is detected, the more likely it can be treated successfully. In **Figure 3,** you can see a blackened spot on skin. This spot is a skin cancer called melanoma. Exposing unprotected skin to sunlight too often contributes to the development of skin cancer. It is especially important to avoid sunburns, which damage skin cells.

FIGURE 3 ·······························

Melanoma
Melanoma is the most serious skin cancer. It can affect many other organs in your body if not treated quickly.

✎ On the notebook paper, write answers to the questions below.

1. **Explain** What can you do to prevent skin cancer?
2. **CHALLENGE** What steps might a doctor take to treat melanoma?

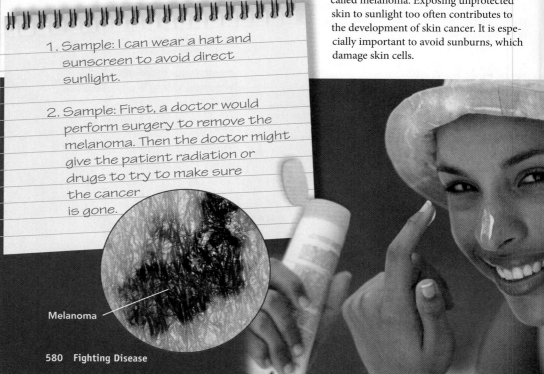

1. Sample: I can wear a hat and sunscreen to avoid direct sunlight.

2. Sample: First, a doctor would perform surgery to remove the melanoma. Then the doctor might give the patient radiation or drugs to try to make sure the cancer is gone.

Melanoma

580 Fighting Disease

Real-World Inquiry allows students to diagnose and treat patients with viral infections, bacterial infections, and allergies.

my science online.com   > Cancer

INVISIBLE INVADERS

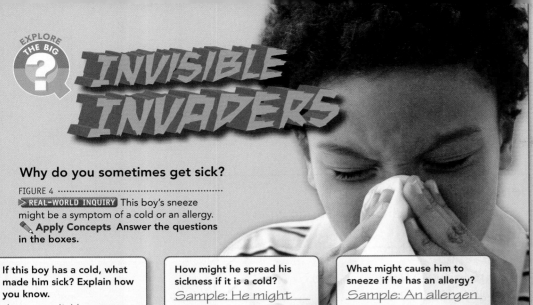

Why do you sometimes get sick?

FIGURE 4 ·······················
> REAL-WORLD INQUIRY This boy's sneeze might be a symptom of a cold or an allergy.
✎ Apply Concepts Answer the questions in the boxes.

If this boy has a cold, what made him sick? Explain how you know.
A virus did because viruses cause colds.

How might he spread his sickness if it is a cold?
Sample: He might sneeze, cough, or leave pathogens on a keyboard or towel.

What might cause him to sneeze if he has an allergy?
Sample: An allergen such as dust may have entered his body and caused the release of histamines that make him sneeze.

Lab zone Do the Quick Lab What Does Sunlight Do to the Beads?

🖉 Assess Your Understanding

2a. Review What is a tumor?
It is an abnormal tissue mass.

b. Relate Cause and Effect How do cancerous tumors harm the body?
They invade and destroy the healthy tissue around them.

c. ANSWER ? THE BIG Why do you sometimes get sick?
Sometimes your body's lines of defense cannot get rid of pathogens it is exposed to.

got it? ·······················

○ I get it! Now I know that cancer is a disease that causes cells to multiply uncontrollably. It can be treated with surgery, radiation, or drugs.

○ I need extra help with See TE note.

Go to MY SCIENCE COACH *online for help with this subject.*

581

Differentiated Instruction

L1 Normal Cells and Cancer Cells
Urge students to illustrate a normal cell and a cancerous cell. Have students reread the Key Concept statement and explanatory material. Then have them examine photographs or diagrams of a normal and a cancer cell. Invite students to make illustrations based on these images and the text. Students should add simple labels.

L3 Radiation and Chemotherapy
Challenge students to do research about these two treatments for cancer. Urge students to look for information that illuminates benefits and potential drawbacks of each treatment, as well as details that link each with certain types or locations of cancer in the body. Students might present some of their findings in graphic form, such as diagrams or charts.

Elaborate

Explore the Big Q ? UbD

Direct students' attention to the image of the boy holding a handkerchief to his nose and mouth. Invite students to note details—his closed eyes, the positioning of the handkerchief—that indicate that he is sneezing. Ask: **Is this boy's sickness infectious or noninfectious?** *(It's impossible to tell from the evidence in the photo. If he has a cold, it is infectious; if he has an allergy, it is not infectious.)* **What is the difference between a symptom and a sickness?** *(Sample: Sickness is another word for a disease or medical condition, such as a cold or cancer or diabetes. A symptom is a physical reaction—such as a runny nose, swollen tissue, or weakness—that occurs as a result of a disease or condition.)*

Lab Resource: Quick Lab

L1 WHAT DOES SUNLIGHT DO TO THE BEADS? Students will observe and make hypotheses about the effect of sunshine on ultraviolet-sensitive beads.

Evaluate

Assess Your Understanding

After students answer the questions, have them evaluate their understanding by completing the appropriate sentence.

Answer the Big Q ? UbD

To help students focus on the Big Question, lead a class discussion about why people sometimes get sick.

RTI Response to Intervention

2a.,b. If students have trouble explaining what a tumor is and how cancerous tumors harm the body, **then** have them reread the definition and explanations in the section *How Cancer Develops.*

c. If students have trouble explaining why they get sick, **then** review with them the kinds of diseases people get and the kinds of pathogens and environmental factors that cause diseases.

MY SCIENCE COACH Have students go online for help in understanding cancer and treatments for cancer.

Lab zone **After the Inquiry Warm-Up**

Noninfectious Disease

Inquiry Warm-Up, *Causes of Death, Then and Now*

In the Inquiry Warm-Up, you investigated causes of death in 1900 and today. Using what you learned from that activity, answer the questions below.

1. **INTERPRET DATA** What was the leading cause of death in 1900? How does its position on the list of modern causes of death compare? Why do you think that is?

   _____

   _____

2. **INTERPRET DATA** What is the leading cause of death today? How does its position on the list of 1900 causes of death compare? Why do you think that is?

   _____

   _____

3. **COMPARE AND CONTRAST** What kind of diseases were the top three causes of death in 1900? What kind are the top three causes of death now? Write an explanation.

   _____

   _____

   _____

4. **DRAW CONCLUSIONS** Compare the total number of deaths from the top ten causes in each column, most of which are diseases in both columns. Explain why you think today's number is different from the number in 1900.

   _____

   _____

   _____

Name _____ Date _____ Class _____

Assess Your Understanding

Noninfectious Disease

How Do Allergies, Asthma, and Diabetes Affect the Body?

1a. **NAME** _____ is a disorder in which airways of the lungs narrow significantly.

b. **RELATE CAUSE AND EFFECT** How are insulin levels affected in Type I diabetes?

_____

got it? ....

○ **I get it!** Now I know that allergies, asthma, and diabetes affect _____

_____

○ **I need extra help with** _____

_____

What Is Cancer and How Can It Be Treated?

2a. **REVIEW** What is a tumor?

_____

b. **RELATE CAUSE AND EFFECT** How do cancerous tumors harm the body?

_____

_____

c. **ANSWER** Why do you sometimes get sick?

_____

_____

got it? ....

○ **I get it!** Now I know that cancer is _____

_____

_____

○ **I need extra help with** _____

_____

Noninfectious Disease

How Do Allergies, Asthma, and Diabetes Affect the Body?

Noninfectious diseases are diseases that are not caused by pathogens and that cannot be transmitted from person to person. Two noninfectious diseases, cardiovascular disease and cancer, are the leading causes of death from disease in the U.S. Allergies, asthma, and diabetes are other noninfectious diseases. **Allergies cause an inflammatory response by the body. Asthma affects breathing, while diabetes affects how body cells take up glucose.**

An **allergy** is a disorder in which the immune system is overly sensitive to a foreign substance. Any substance that causes an allergy is an **allergen.** **Histamine** is a chemical that brings on the symptoms of an allergy, such as a rash, sneezing, and watery eyes.

Asthma is a disorder in which the airways in the lungs narrow significantly, causing wheezing, coughing, and shortness of breath. Other factors that may trigger asthma are stress, heavy exercise, tobacco smoke, air pollution, strong odors, and respiratory infections.

Insulin is a substance that enables body cells to take glucose from the blood and use it for energy. In the condition called **diabetes,** the pancreas produces too little insulin or body cells do not use insulin properly. There are two types of diabetes, and all diabetics must check their blood frequently to stay healthy.

What Is Cancer and How Can It Be Treated?

Cancer is a disease in which cells multiply uncontrollably, over and over, destroying healthy tissue. Treatments include surgery, radiation, and drugs. As cells divide over and over, they often form abnormal tissue masses called **tumors.** Cancerous tumors invade and destroy the healthy tissue around them. Cells from a tumor can enter the blood or lymph vessels, and get carried to other parts of the body, where they may form new tumors.

Cancer can be caused by inherited characteristics or environmental factors, called **carcinogens.** Cancer is treated with surgery, radiation, and drugs. People can reduce their risk of cancer by avoiding carcinogens, eating a low-fat diet with fruits and vegetables, and having regular checkups.

On a separate sheet of paper, identify and briefly describe four major noninfectious diseases.

Review and Reinforce

Noninfectious Disease

Understanding Main Ideas

Answer the following questions on a separate sheet of paper.

1. What is an allergy?
2. What is the difference between Type I and Type II diabetes?
3. What is asthma?
4. What is cancer, and why is it dangerous?
5. What are two factors that make a person more likely to develop cancer?
6. What are three methods used to treat cancer?
7. Should you be worried about getting diabetes or cancer from a friend who has one of those diseases? Explain.

Building Vocabulary

Match each term with its definition by writing the letter of the correct definition in the right column on the line beside the term in the left column.

8. ___ noninfectious diseases

9. ___ allergy

10. ___ allergen

11. ___ histamine

12. ___ asthma

13. ___ insulin

14. ___ diabetes

15. ___ tumors

16. ___ carcinogens

a. a substance that enables body cells to take glucose from the blood and use it for energy

b. substances in the environment that cause cancer

c. a chemical that is responsible for the symptoms of an allergy

d. a disorder in which the immune system is overly sensitive to a foreign substance

e. abnormal tissue masses

f. diseases that are not caused by pathogens

g. any substance that causes an allergy

h. a condition in which people have high levels of glucose in their blood but not enough of it in their cells

i. a disorder in which the airways in the lungs narrow significantly

Noninfectious Disease

> Read the passage and study the graph. Then answer the questions that follow on a separate sheet of paper.

Reducing the Danger from Sunlight

Medical scientists estimate that more than one million Americans will get skin cancer this year. About 10,000 people will die of the disease. Yet many of these cases and deaths could be prevented if people reduced their exposure to sunlight. That's because sunlight contains ultraviolet light that can cause cancer. The likelihood that you get skin cancer is directly related to your total exposure to the sun in your lifetime.

The strength of sunlight varies. Sunlight is strongest between 10 A.M. and 3 P.M. It is stronger during the summer than the winter, on a sunny day than on a cloudy one, and at high elevations or closer to the equator. If you are around snow, water, and sand, you will be exposed to more ultraviolet light, because sunlight reflects off these objects.

Sunscreen helps protect against sunlight by blocking the ultraviolet light in sunlight from reaching skin cells. Sunscreen products are rated according to their sun protection factor, or SPF. The higher the SPF, the better the sunscreen protects against ultraviolet radiation. Using the SPF, you can estimate your exposure to ultraviolet radiation, relative to not using any sunscreen.

The graph shows the effect of sunscreen with different SPF ratings for a person who would get a sunburn after 30 minutes without sunscreen midday.

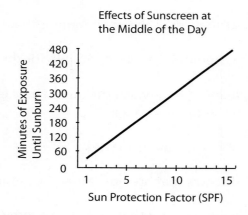

Effects of Sunscreen at the Middle of the Day

1. Based on the graph, if a person were to use a sunscreen with an SPF of 5, how long might it take the person to get a sunburn?

2. If a person were spending the day at the beach, would sunscreen with an SPF of 10 be a good choice to prevent sunburn? Explain.

3. What factors not mentioned above can affect the amount of sunlight and ultraviolet radiation that reaches a person's skin?

Lesson Quiz

Noninfectious Disease

If the statement is true, write *true*. If the statement is false, change the underlined word or words to make the statement true.

1. _____ In recent decades, infectious diseases have grown <u>less</u> common.

2. _____ Cancer cells multiply <u>uncontrollably</u>, destroying healthy tissue.

3. _____ Allergies, asthma, and diabetes are <u>infectious</u> diseases.

4. _____ <u>Histamine</u> enables body cells to take glucose from the blood and use it for energy.

5. _____ <u>Not all</u> tumors are cancerous.

Fill in the blank to complete each statement.

6. _____ cause an inflammatory response by the body.

7. Cancer can be caused by inherited characteristics or _____ in the environment.

8. _____ is a disorder in which the airways in the lungs narrow significantly.

9. In the condition called _____, the pancreas produces too little insulin or body cells do not use insulin properly.

10. Treatments for _____ include surgery, radiation, and drugs.

Noninfectious Disease

Answer Key

After the Inquiry Warm-Up

1. pneumonia, influenza; It is lower on today's list because scientists learned how to treat it.

2. heart disease; It is lower on the 1900 list because lifestyles in the United States have changed to increase the risk of heart disease.

3. 1900 – infectious diseases; today – noninfectious diseases; Many cures for infectious disease have been found.

4. Fewer people per 100,000 die from the top ten causes today than did in 1900. This is likely because advances in treatment since 1900 mean fewer people are dying from diseases.

Key Concept Summaries

Allergies cause an inflammatory response by the body because the immune system is overly sensitive to a foreign substance. Asthma is a disorder in which the airways in the lungs narrow significantly, causing wheezing, coughing, and shortness of breath. Diabetes is a condition in which the pancreas produces too little insulin or body cells do not use insulin properly. Cancer is a disease in which cells multiply uncontrollably, over and over, destroying healthy tissue.

Review and Reinforce

1. a disorder in which the immune system is overly sensitive to a foreign substance

2. In Type I diabetes, the pancreas produces little or no insulin, and people with this type of diabetes need insulin injections. Type I usually begins in childhood. In Type II diabetes, which usually begins in adulthood, the pancreas does not make enough insulin or body cells do not respond normally to insulin.

3. Asthma is a disorder in which the airways in the lungs narrow significantly.

4. Cancer is a disease in which cells multiply uncontrollably. It is dangerous because the multiplying cells destroy healthy tissues.

5. Some people are more likely to develop cancer if their relatives developed it. Also, exposure to carcinogens makes a person more susceptible.

6. surgery, drugs, radiation

7. No, because they are noninfectious diseases.

8. f
9. d
10. g
11. c
12. i
13. a
14. h
15. e
16. b

Enrich

1. 150 minutes, or 2 hours and 30 minutes

2. No; The person might be able to stay out 5 hours without getting a sunburn, but he or she might be outdoors longer than that. In addition, sunlight would also be reflecting off the sand and water.

3. Answers will vary. Samples: Lower ozone levels may be increasing the amount of sunlight reaching Earth's surface; clothing and hats; sunscreen may rub off or wash off in water.

Lesson Quiz

1. true
2. true
3. noninfectious
4. Insulin
5. true
6. Allergies
7. carcinogens
8. Asthma
9. diabetes
10. cancer

Place the outside corner, the corner away from the dotted line, in the corner of your copy machine to copy onto letter-size paper.

Study Guide

Review the Big Q UbD

Have students complete the statement at the top of the page. These Key Concepts support their understanding of the chapter's Big Question. Have students return to the chapter opener pages. What is different about how students view the image of the girl getting a polio vaccine now that they have completed the chapter? Thinking about this will help them prepare for the *Apply the Big Q* activity in the Review and Assessment.

Partner Review

Have partners review definitions of vocabulary terms by using the Study Guide to quiz each other. Students could read Key Concept statements and leave out words for their partner to fill in, or change a statement so that it is false and ask for corrections.

Class Activity: Concept Map

Have students work in four groups. Group one might focus on infectious diseases; group two on the body's three lines of defense; group three on immunity, as well as the treatment and prevention and group four on noninfectious diseases. Invite students in each group to brainstorm to identify Key Concepts, vocabulary, definitions, examples, and important details from a lesson. Encourage students to write information on sticky notes and to attach them on poster board or the board. Groups can use these notes to develop a concept map that begins at the top with the lesson's Key Concept statements. Bring the four groups together and discuss how the concept maps relate to one another. Ask students to use the following questions to help them organize the information.

- How do pathogens cause disease?
- What pathogens cause infectious disease?
- What is the body's first line of defense?
- What are inflammatory and immune responses?
- How can you become immune?
- How can bacterial and viral diseases be treated?
- How do allergies, asthma, and diabetes affect you?
- What is cancer and how can it be treated?

My Science Coach allows students to complete the *Practice Test* online.

The Big Question allows students to complete the *Apply the Big Q* activity about how we get sick.

Vocab Flash Cards offer a way to review the chapter vocabulary words.

my science online.com > Fighting Disease

---

14 Study Guide

REVIEW THE BIG ?

A _pathogen_ in my body may cause an _infectious_ disease. I can also get sick from a _noninfectious_ disease.

LESSON 1 Infectious Disease

🔑 When you have an infectious disease, pathogens are in your body causing harm.

🔑 The four major types of human pathogens are bacteria, viruses, fungi, and protists. They can be spread through contact with a sick person, other living things, or an object in the environment.

Vocabulary
- microorganism
- pathogen
- infectious disease
- toxin

LESSON 2 The Body's Defenses

🔑 The first line of defense is your outer coverings, which trap and kill most pathogens.

🔑 In the inflammatory response, fluid and white blood cells fight pathogens in nearby tissues. In the immune response, cells in the blood and tissues target each kind of pathogen.

Vocabulary
- inflammatory response
- phagocyte
- immune response
- lymphocyte
- T cell
- antigen
- B cell
- antibody

LESSON 3 HIV and AIDS

🔑 HIV is the only kind of virus known to attack the human immune system directly and destroy T cells.

🔑 HIV can spread from one person to another if body fluids from an infected person come in contact with body fluids of an uninfected person.

Vocabulary
- AIDS
- HIV

LESSON 4 Infectious Disease and Your Health

🔑 You acquire active immunity when your own immune system produces antibodies. You acquire passive immunity when the antibodies come from a source outside your body.

🔑 Bacterial diseases can be treated with medications. Viral diseases have no known cure.

Vocabulary
- immunity
- active immunity
- vaccination
- vaccine
- passive immunity
- antibiotic
- antibiotic resistance

LESSON 5 Noninfectious Disease

🔑 Allergies cause an inflammatory response by the body. Asthma affects breathing, while diabetes affects how body cells take up glucose.

🔑 Cancer is a disease in which cells multiply uncontrollably, destroying healthy tissue. Treatments include surgery, radiation, and drugs.

Vocabulary
- noninfectious disease
- allergy
- allergen
- histamine
- asthma
- insulin
- diabetes
- tumor
- carcinogen

ELL Support

4 Language Production

Divide the class into five groups and do a Gallery Walk to review. Post five large sheets of paper with the essential questions from each lesson at the top of each. Position each group at one poster. Have them write down all they have learned that responds to the questions. Then have them rotate to add information until all groups have worked with all posters.

Beginning
LOW/HIGH Allow students to answer with drawings, words, or short phrases.

Intermediate
LOW/HIGH Have students draft sentences to answer the questions.

Advanced
LOW/HIGH Have students assist and/or edit the work of classmates with lower language proficiency.

Review and Assessment

LESSON 1 Infectious Disease

1. Organisms that cause disease are called
   - a. histamines.
   - **b.** pathogens.
   - c. phagocytes.
   - d. toxins.

2. _Microorganisms_ are living things too small to see with a microscope that cause most infectious diseases.

3. **Classify** What are the four ways in which a person can become infected with a pathogen?

   A pathogen can infect a person through contact with an infected person; soil, food, or water; a contaminated object; or an infected animal.

4. **Compare and Contrast** Describe how bacteria and viruses are alike and different in terms of how they cause disease.

   Sample: Both damage cells. Bacteria damage cells directly or by producing toxins. Viruses reproduce inside cells.

5. **Apply Concepts** Can you catch a cold by sitting in a chilly draft? Explain.

   No. Viruses, not drafts, cause colds.

6. **Write About It** Write a short speech that Joseph Lister might have delivered to other surgeons to convince them to use his surgical techniques. In the speech, Lister should explain why his techniques were so successful.

   See TE rubric.

LESSON 2 The Body's Defenses

7. Proteins produced by B cells are called
   - a. phagocytes.
   - b. T cells.
   - **c.** antibodies.
   - d. pathogens.

8. _Phagocytes_ engulf pathogens and destroy them.

9. **Communicate** How does the body make it difficult for a pathogen to reach a part of the body where it can cause disease?

   The body has barriers to keep pathogens out. The skin, breathing passages, the mouth, and the stomach trap and kill most pathogens.

10. **Interpret Diagrams** In the diagram below, identify each labeled structure and its role in the immune response.

    Structure A: B cell, produces antibodies;
    Structure B: antibody, recognizes and binds to pathogens;
    Structure C: antigen, structure on pathogen recognized by an antibody

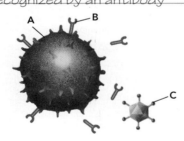

583

Review and Assessment

Assess Understanding

Have students complete the answers to the Review and Assessment questions. Have a class discussion about what students find confusing. Write Key Concepts on the board to reinforce knowledge.

R T I Response to Intervention

3. If students cannot identify how people can become infected with a pathogen, **then** have them reread the information for the red heading *How Pathogens Are Spread*.

9. If students have trouble explaining why it is difficult for pathogens to gain access to certain parts of the body, **then** ask them to identify the body's first line of defense.

Alternate Assessment

L3 MULTIMEDIA PRESENTATION Have students work in small groups to create a multimedia presentation that addresses what they have learned in this chapter about fighting disease. Have students brainstorm to identify Key Concepts, vocabulary, details, and examples to include in their presentations, as well appropriate visual aids, props, and videos.

Write About It Assess student's writing using this rubric.

SCORING RUBRIC	SCORE 4	SCORE 3	SCORE 2	SCORE 1
Prepare a persuasive speech to explain why techniques were successful	Writes a focused speech to intended audience using persuasive techniques and including many details	Writes a somewhat focused speech to intended audience using persuasive techniques and including some details	Writes a speech with unclear audience or purpose and including few details	Does not write a persuasive speech to intended audience

Review and Assessment, Cont.

RTI Response to Intervention

12. **If** students need help with explaining how HIV is spread, **then** have them reread the second Key Concept statement in the lesson.

15. **If** students have trouble identifying antibiotics as chemicals that kill bacteria without harming body cells, **then** urge students to recall that antibiotics are often prescribed by doctors to kill infections.

18. **If** students cannot identify the term for a substance that causes an allergy, **then** remind them that the Greek word part *-gen-* means "producer."

Apply the Big Q ? UbD

TRANSFER Students should be able to demonstrate understanding of how people get sick by answering this question. See the scoring rubric below.

Connect to the Big Idea ? UbD

BIG IDEA: Living things maintain constant conditions inside their bodies.

Send students back to the Big Ideas of Science at the beginning of their student edition. Have them read what they wrote about living things' keeping conditions inside their bodies constant before they started the chapter. Lead a class discussion about how their thoughts have changed. If all chapters have been completed, have students fill in the bottom section for the Big Idea.

L3 **WRITING IN SCIENCE** Have students write an article that explains to readers why we sometimes get sick, how our bodies fight infectious disease, and how noninfectious disease affects the body.

CHAPTER 14 Review and Assessment

LESSON 3 HIV and AIDS

11. HIV attacks the human immune system and destroys

    a. B cells.
    b. antigens.
    c. antibodies.
    (d.) T cells.

12. HIV spreads from an infected person to an uninfected person through the contact of
<u>body fluids.</u>

13. **Relate Cause and Effect** How does the destruction of T cells interfere with the body's ability to fight disease?
<u>The body loses its ability to</u>
<u>mount a response aimed at</u>
<u>specific pathogens.</u>

LESSON 4 Infectious Disease and Your Health

14. Which of the following produce active immunity without causing illness?

    (a.) vaccines
    b. antibody injections
    c. antibiotics
    d. phagocytes

15. <u>Antibiotics</u> are chemicals that can kill bacteria without harming body cells.

16. **Infer** Describe one way that a person can acquire active immunity and passive immunity.
<u>Sample: A person can acquire</u>
<u>active immunity from a vaccine.</u>
<u>An unborn baby can acquire</u>
<u>passive immunity from</u>
<u>antibodies in its mother's</u>
<u>blood.</u>

LESSON 5 Noninfectious Disease

17. Abnormal tissue masses are called

    a. allergies.
    b. cancer.
    c. diabetes.
    (d.) tumors.

18. An <u>allergen</u> is any substance that causes an allergy.

19. **Write About It** For some people, dander of a cat causes an allergic reaction. On a separate paper, describe how a person's body responds when exposed to this allergen. How can they lessen the reaction?
See TE rubric.

APPLY THE BIG ? Why do you sometimes get sick?

20. Strep throat is an example of an infectious disease, while asthma is an example of a noninfectious disease. Compare and contrast what causes these diseases and how your body protects you from them.
<u>Sample: Pathogens cause strep</u>
<u>throat. Asthma is a disease</u>
<u>in which the lungs' airways</u>
<u>narrow. My body's first line of</u>
<u>defense and inflammatory and</u>
<u>immune responses protect me</u>
<u>from strep throat. It does not</u>
<u>protect me from asthma.</u>
<u>See TE rubric.</u>

 Write About It Assess student's writing using this rubric.

SCORING RUBRIC	SCORE 4	SCORE 3	SCORE 2	SCORE 1
Describe the body's allergic response and how it can be lessened	Describes the body's allergic reaction in detail, and explains in detail two ways that an allergic reaction can be lessened	Describes the body's allergic reaction and explains two ways that an allergic reaction can be lessened, with few details	Gives a general description of the body's allergic reaction and mentions a way that an allergic reaction can be lessened	Does not describe the body's response to allergen and does not explain how an allergic reaction can be lessened

? Why do you sometimes get sick?
Assess student's response using this rubric.

SCORING RUBRIC	SCORE 4	SCORE 3	SCORE 2	SCORE 1
Compare and contrast causes of the diseases and explain how the human body protects itself	Compares and contrasts the causes of both diseases, clearly and describes of how the human body offers protection from each disease	Compares and contrasts the causes of both diseases, with some inaccuracies, describes how the body protects itself	Compares and contrasts the causes of both incompletely, partially describes how body protects itself	Does not compare and contrast causes of the two diseases. Does not explain how the human body offers protection

Standardized Test Prep

Multiple Choice

Circle the letter of the best answer.

1. SARS is a respiratory disease caused by a virus. Use the data table to decide which statement below is true.

SARS Cases (Nov. 2002–July 2003)		
Country	No. of Cases	No. of Deaths
Canada	251	43
China, mainland	5,327	349
China, Taiwan	346	37
Singapore	238	33
United States	29	0

  A Most of the people who got SARS died.

  Ⓑ Most SARS cases were in mainland China.

  C Most SARS cases were in North America.

  D Most SARS cases were in Singapore.

2. All of the following are the body's defenses against pathogens *except*

  A a physical barrier such as the skin.

  B the inflammatory response.

  C the immune response.

  Ⓓ attacks by red blood cells.

3. Abnormal masses of cells that can lead to cancer are called

  A vaccines

  B phagocytes

  Ⓒ tumors

  D antibodies

4. Which of these diseases occurs when the airways in the lungs narrow significantly during an allergic reaction?

  Ⓐ asthma

  B diabetes

  C AIDS

  D melanoma

5. Which of the following is paired correctly?

  Ⓐ rabies: infectious disease

  B diabetes: infectious disease

  C AIDS: noninfectious disease

  D allergy: infectious disease

Constructed Response

Use the graph below and your knowledge of science to help you answer Question 6. Write your answer on a separate sheet of paper.

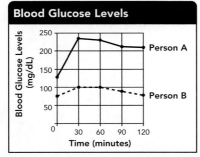

6. In a glucose tolerance test, a doctor gives a patient a sugar drink and measures the blood glucose level over time. The graph above shows two people's test results. Which person may have diabetes? Explain your answer.

See TE note.

Standardized Test Prep

Test-Taking Skills

INTERPRETING DATA TABLES Point out that when students encounter questions like Question 1, which includes a data table, they should be sure to study all parts of the table carefully, including title, labels, and numbers. Remind students that it is vital for them to grasp the nature of the information presented in the data table before they analyze how the table relates to the test question as a whole.

Constructed Response

6. Sample: Person A may have diabetes because the blood glucose level remained high two hours after drinking the sugar drink. Though people with diabetes have high levels of glucose in their blood, they do not have enough glucose in their body cells because their pancreas is producing too little insulin or their body cells are not using insulin properly. Insulin enables body cells to take glucose from the blood and use it for energy. Person B's blood seems to have taken glucose from the blood, whereas Person A's blood has not.

Additional Assessment Resources

Chapter Test
EXAMVIEW® Assessment Suite
Performance Assessment
Progress Monitoring Assessments
SuccessTracker™

ⒺⓁⓁ Support

5 Assess Understanding

Have ELLs complete the Alternate Assessment. Provide guidelines on the information it must cover, and a rubric for assessment. You may wish to have them complete the activity in small groups of varying language proficiencies.

Beginning

LOW/HIGH Suggest students work on the visual aids and props for the presentations.

Intermediate

LOW/HIGH Allow students to refer to their books or notes when delivering their presentations.

Advanced

LOW/HIGH Suggest that students assume roles that will challenge them the most. If a student is a more proficient writer than speaker, encourage him or her to be the group speaker.

Remediate If students have trouble with...

QUESTION	SEE LESSON	STANDARDS
1	1	
2	2	
3	4, 5	
4	5	
5	1, 3, 5	
6	5	

Science Matters

Museum of Science

Have students read *Making H₂O A-OK*. Point out that the grayish powder in a water-purifying packet is potent with chemicals. As mentioned in the article, adding the powder to water results in clear, clean, and safe drinking water. Costs are low for this type of water purification and a few companies have even provided free packets to some countries when hit by unexpected water emergencies. Because of the size and convenience of the packets, they can easily be used in remote locations and in emergency situations.

Ask: **How do the water powder packets described in the article purify dirty, polluted water?** *(Sample: The powder is made up of bleach, which kills bacteria and viruses, and iron sulfate, which binds solids, such as metals and parasites to form clumps that can be filtered through a cotton cloth.)* **What are some advantages of the water purifying packets?** *(Sample: Costs are low and because of the size and convenience of the packets, they can easily be used in remote locations and in emergency situations.)* **How many water purifying packets would it take to clean 10 gallons of water?** *(Sample: 4 packets)*

Making H2O A-OK

What runs, but never walks? *Water!* Even though water is all around us, over 1 billion people across the world can only dream of having clean drinking water. Every day, about 4,000 children die from water-related diseases because they drink unsafe water. But now, a packet of powder the size of a ketchup packet at a cafeteria can stop this from happening.

Scientists have created a powder that can purify dirty, polluted water in 30 minutes. Just one small packet of the stuff can clean 2.5 gallons of water! The powder is made up of bleach and iron sulfate. The bleach kills bacteria and viruses. The iron sulfate causes solids in the water, such as metals like lead, to bind together in clumps. These clumps can be filtered out using a cotton cloth.

With helpful technology like this, more kids will be able to have safe and clean drinking water.

Write About It Natural disaster victims, such as those who survive a hurricane or a flood, often have a hard time getting clean drinking water. Write a letter to a rescue agency, such as the Red Cross, explaining the importance of having clean drinking water and what they can do to purify the water.

Museum of Science.

586 Fighting Disease

Quick Facts

The Ready Campaign is a Federal Emergency Management Agency (FEMA) program that encourages Americans to prepare for emergencies such as natural disasters and violent strikes. The Ready Campaign goal is to get citizens involved in the preparedness of the nation. The Ready.gov website, advises taking a few simple steps to get started. The first step is to prepare an emergency kit of basic supplies. Step two is to make a plan that all family members can follow. Step three is to learn about the types of emergencies that could occur in the immediate region and how to respond to them.

Have students form small groups and find out more about FEMA's Ready America campaign, including how to prepare a kit, make a plan, and be informed. Have each group prepare a brochure about emergency preparedness and share them in class.

Colwell's Gift

Cholera is an infection of the intestines that is spread by drinking water or eating food contaminated with cholera bacteria. It causes diarrhea, vomiting, and cramps. When cholera strikes, approximately one victim in 20 can become seriously ill, and may die within hours. Because most places in the United States have safe drinking water, we don't see a lot of cholera here. But in many developing countries, cholera is still common.

For a long time, scientists could not predict cholera epidemics. Outbreaks happened suddenly, with no warning. And after the epidemic, scientists could not detect the cholera bacteria in the water. So, where did the bacteria go, and how did they reappear so suddenly?

Rita Colwell suspected that the cholera bacteria were present in the water in an inactive state between outbreaks. She thought that the bacteria became active when the water temperature rose.

After many years, Colwell proved her hypothesis. Using new methods, scientists were able to detect the inactive cholera bacteria in water where they had not previously been able to detect cholera. Satellite data also confirmed that cholera outbreaks occur when ocean temperatures rise. Warmer water causes cholera bacteria to multiply. Now, scientists use this information to help prevent future cholera outbreaks.

Illustrate It Rita Colwell developed a simple cloth filter to help prevent the spread of cholera. Research the life cycle of cholera bacteria. Prepare an information card that uses diagrams to explain how Colwell's filter helps to stop the spread of bacteria.

587

Science and History

Have students read *Colwell's Gift.* Point out that Rita Colwell's simple cloth filter method is an inexpensive and effective way to filter water. Rita Colwell developed this method using sari cloth, which is a readily available fabric used for women's clothing in the Indian subcontinent. Often the filter is made from an older cloth rather than newer one because the space between the fibers in an old cloth is closer after repeated washings. The cloth used to filter water is folded to make four or eight layers. The folded cloth is placed over the container used to collect water. When water is poured into the container, it passes through the cloth, which traps particles, and plankton that carry cholera bacteria. After filtering water, the cloth is rinsed and dried in the sun for a couple of hours.

In some places in the world, disinfectants for unsafe water and fuel for boiling water are difficult to get. The cloth filter becomes a valuable method for reducing the occurrences of cholera.

Ask: **How does the simple cloth filter method work to reduce cholera?** (Sample: The cloth is folded to make four or eight layers that are placed over a container to collect the water. The cloth traps the plankton that carry cholera bacteria in the water.) **What did Rita Colwell think triggered cholera outbreaks?** (Sample: Rita Colwell suspected that cholera was already present in the water, but it became active when the water temperature rose, greatly increasing the amount of cholera bacteria in the water.)

CHAPTER 15

Populations and Communities

Introduce the Big Q

Have students look at the image and read the Engaging Question and description. Ask them to write a hypothesis for how the sea anemone might benefit from having the clownfish nearby. Have volunteers read their hypotheses out loud. Point out that living things interact with one another in many ways. Tell students they will learn more about how living things affect one another in this chapter. Ask: **Which people in your community help others who live there?** *(Firefighters save people from fires, police keep everyone safe from criminals)* **Can anyone think of something or someone that may hurt the community?** *(A thief, the flu)* **Are there ways to protect yourself from these dangers?** *(Locking doors, getting a flu shot)*

Untamed Science Video

CLOWN(FISH)ING AROUND Before viewing, invite students to suggest some ways in which organisms interact. Then play the video. Lead a class discussion and make a list of questions that this video raises. You may wish to have students view the video again after they have completed the chapter to see if their questions have been answered.

To access the online resources for this chapter, search or navigate to *Populations and Communities.*

Untamed Science Video shows interactions between organisms.

The Big Question allows students to answer the Engaging Question about how the sea anemone benefits from its interaction with the clownfish.

MY SCIENCE online.com ▶ **Populations and Communities**

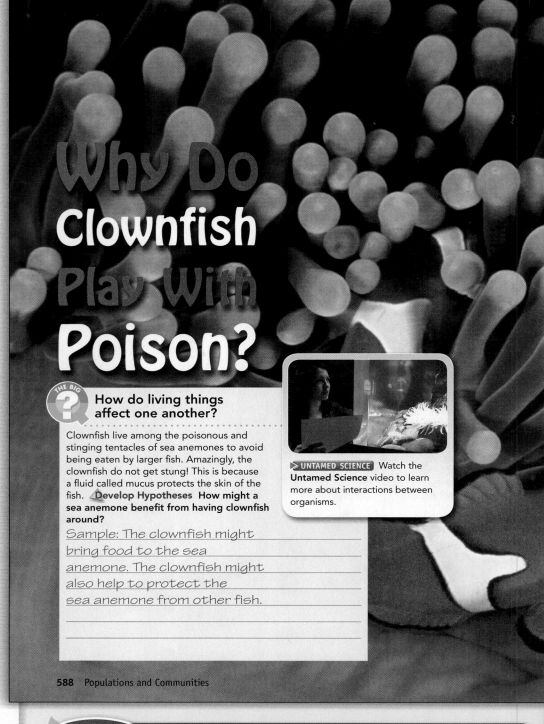

Why Do Clownfish Play With Poison?

How do living things affect one another?

Clownfish live among the poisonous and stinging tentacles of sea anemones to avoid being eaten by larger fish. Amazingly, the clownfish do not get stung! This is because a fluid called mucus protects the skin of the fish. **Develop Hypotheses How might a sea anemone benefit from having clownfish around?**

Sample: The clownfish might bring food to the sea anemone. The clownfish might also help to protect the sea anemone from other fish.

▶ **UNTAMED SCIENCE** Watch the **Untamed Science** video to learn more about interactions between organisms.

588 Populations and Communities

Professional Development Note **From the Author**

I have a pecan tree in my backyard very near my porch. On a recent winter day I noticed a series of holes in the trunk that were evenly drilled around the entire trunk, from top to bottom. It looked like someone had measured and taken a drill to make them. When I looked this up on the Internet, I found I had a tree that was well appreciated by a Yellow-Bellied Sapsucker. You may think this is a fictitious bird created by a comedian for a joke, but it is really a type of woodpecker. This bird drills the hole to create a sap well and then returns to trees that produce large amounts to lick its meals. Learning this made me think about all the unique niches animals and plants fill in our world. What an amazing place!

✏ *Michael Padilla*

588 Populations and Communities

Populations and Communities

CHAPTER 15

my science online.com | Populations and Communities | UNTAMED SCIENCE | THE BIG QUESTION   589

Chapter at a Glance

CHAPTER PACING: 8–12 periods or 4–6 blocks

INTRODUCE THE CHAPTER: Engage students with the Engaging Question and the opening image. Activate prior knowledge and preteach vocabulary using the Getting Started pages.

Lesson 1: Living Things and the Environment

Lesson 2: Populations

Lesson 3: Interactions Among Living Things

Lesson 4: Changes in Communities

ASSESSMENT OPTIONS: Chapter Test, **EXAM**VIEW® Assessment Suite, Performance Assessment, Progress Monitoring Assessments, SuccessTracker™

Preference Navigator, in the online Planning tools, allows you to customize *Interactive Science* to your own teaching style. You can also edit lesson plans by selecting the Lesson Planner option.

Digital Teacher's Edition allows you to access your Teacher's Edition and Resource materials online.

my science online.com

Differentiated Instruction

L1 **Sea Anemones** Make sure that students understand that the sea anemone is an animal, not a plant. Students who have seen jellyfish may be surprised at the short tentacles of the anemone. Tell students that jellyfish and anemones are related, and that stinging tentacles are a characteristic of this group of animals. To give students some sense of the size of the organisms

shown, point out that the photograph is enlarged. A clownfish is usually about 8 cm long.

L3 **Clownfish** Have students research the clownfish to find out more about its habitat, life cycle, and behavior, giving special attention to the relationship between the clownfish and the sea anemone. Students can present their findings to the class.

Getting Started

Check Your Understanding

This activity assesses students' understanding of what living things get from their environment. After students have shared their answers, point out that precipitation provides the water that all living things need to carry out their life processes. The atmosphere provides carbon dioxide required by plants. The composition of the soil in an area influences what kinds of plants can grow there.

Preteach Vocabulary Skills

Explain to students that many English words come from Latin, the language originally spoken in Ancient Rome. Learning the meaning of Latin roots can make it easier to learn new vocabulary words. Also point out the definition of *immigration*. Have students note that the prefix *im-* is similar in meaning to the word *in*. This may help them remember that immigration is movement into a population.

---

15 Getting Started

Check Your Understanding

1. **Background** Read the paragraph below and then answer the question.

> Raquel planted a garden in a sunny area near her home. First, she loosened the **soil**, so the plant roots could easily grow. If days passed with no **precipitation,** she watered the plants. That was all she had to do—the rest of what the plants needed came from the **atmosphere!**

Soil is made up of rock fragments, water, air, and decaying plant and animal matter.

Rain, hail, sleet, and snow are all types of **precipitation.**

Earth's **atmosphere** contains oxygen, carbon dioxide, nitrogen, and other gases.

- How do soil, precipitation, and the atmosphere help a plant grow?

  Sample: Plants get minerals from the soil, water from precipitation, and gases (carbon dioxide and oxygen) from the atmosphere.

> **MY READING WEB** If you had trouble completing the question above, visit **My Reading Web** and type in **Populations and Communities.**

Vocabulary Skill

Latin Word Origins Some key terms in this chapter contain word parts with Latin origins. The table below lists two of the Latin words that key terms come from.

Latin Word	Meaning of Latin Word	Example
aptare	to fit	adaptation, *n.* a characteristic that allows an organism to live successfully in its environment
migrare	to move	immigration, *n.* movement into a population

2. **Quick Check** The terms *immigration* and *emigration* both come from the Latin word *migrare*. Circle the meaning of *migrare* in the table above.

My Reading Web offers leveled readings related to chapter content.

Vocab Flash Cards offer extra practice with the chapter vocabulary words.

Digital Lesson

- Assign the *Check Your Understanding* activity online and have students submit their work to you.
- Assign the *Vocabulary Skill* activity online and have students submit their work to you.

MY SCIENCE online.com | **Populations and Communities** |

organism

immigration

adaptation

predation

Chapter Preview

LESSON 1
- organism • habitat
- biotic factor • abiotic factor
- species • population
- community • ecosystem
- ecology
- ↻ Compare and Contrast
- △ Draw Conclusions

LESSON 2
- birth rate • death rate
- immigration • emigration
- population density
- limiting factor
- carrying capacity
- ↻ Relate Cause and Effect
- △ Infer

LESSON 3
- natural selection • adaptation
- niche • competition • predation
- predator • prey • symbiosis
- mutualism • commensalism
- parasitism • parasite • host
- ↻ Relate Text and Visuals
- △ Classify

LESSON 4
- succession • primary succession
- pioneer species
- secondary succession
- ↻ Compare and Contrast
- △ Observe

> VOCAB FLASH CARDS For extra help with vocabulary, visit **Vocab Flash Cards** and type in *Populations and Communities.*

591

Preview Vocabulary Terms

Have students work together to create a word wall to display the vocabulary terms for the chapter. Be sure to discuss and analyze each term before posting it on the wall. As the class progresses through the chapter, the words can be sorted and categorized in different ways. A list of Academic Vocabulary for each lesson can be found in the Support All Readers box at the start of the lesson.

L1 Have students look at the images on this page as you pronounce the vocabulary word. Have students repeat the word after you. Then read the definition. Use the sample sentence in italics to clarify the meaning of the term.

organism *(awr guh NIZ um)* A living thing. *The prairie dog in the image is an example of an organism.*

immigration *(im uh GRAY shun)* Moving into a population. *These white-tailed deer are on their way from one place to another in a process known as immigration.*

adaptation *(ad ap TAY shun)* The behaviors and physical characteristics that allow organisms to live successfully in their environments. *An adaptation helpful to the survival of this animal, the pangolin, is its ability to roll up into an armored ball when threatened.*

predation *(pree DAY shun)* An interaction in which one organism kills another for food or nutrients. *The predation method used by this plant, a sundew, is to snag its food with its sticky bulbs.*

CHAPTER 15

Living Things and the Environment

How do living things affect one another?

Lesson Pacing: 2–3 periods or 1–1½ blocks

🕐 **SHORT ON TIME?** To do this lesson in approximately half the time, do the Activate Prior Knowledge activity followed by a discussion of the Key Concepts to familiarize students with the lesson content. Use the Explore the Big Q to help students understand how living things affect one another. Have students do the Quick Labs and the Real-World Inquiry online. The rest of the lesson can be completed by students independently.

> **Preference Navigator,** in the online Planning tools, allows you to customize *Interactive Science* to your own teaching style. You can also edit lesson plans by selecting the Lesson Planner option.
>
> **Digital Teacher's Edition** allows you to access your Teacher's Edition and Resource online.

Lesson Vocabulary

- organism
- habitat
- biotic factor
- abiotic factor
- species
- population
- community
- ecosystem
- ecology

Content Refresher

Professional Development Note

Carbon Dioxide Carbon dioxide is an abiotic factor that all plants and some algae require to carry out photosynthesis. Chlorophyll, the green pigment in plants and some algae, absorbs energy from sunlight. The organism uses this energy to combine carbon dioxide and water in a chemical reaction that produces sugars, including glucose. The sugars provide energy for sustaining the organism's life processes. Other organisms obtain this energy when they eat plants or algae. The energy is released during cellular respiration when glucose is broken down into carbon dioxide and water.

Biosphere All of Earth's communities are part of a higher level of organization, the biosphere. The levels of organization that make up the biosphere interact with each other. But they also interact in various ways with Earth's other "spheres." These include the atmosphere, the hydrosphere, and the lithosphere.

LESSON OBJECTIVES

🔧 Identify the needs that must be met by an organism's surroundings.

🔧 Identify biotic and abiotic parts of a habitat.

🔧 Describe the levels of organization within an ecosystem.

Blended Path
Active learning using Student Edition, Inquiry Path, and Digital Path

ENGAGE AND EXPLORE

To teach this lesson using a variety of resources, begin by reading **My Planet Diary** as a class. Have students share ideas about the mouse lemur population and identify what they know about habitats. Then do the **Inquiry Warm-Up activity.** Students will identify living and nonliving things in magazine pictures. Discuss the connections different students chose and how they decided to test the living thing's dependence. The **After the Inquiry Warm-Up worksheet** sets up a discussion about how living things also depend on other living things. Have volunteers share their answers to number 4 about the effect of different seasons.

EXPLAIN AND ELABORATE

Teach Key Concepts by explaining the term *habitat* and having students answer questions about what a habitat provides.

Continue to **Teach Key Concepts** by explaining the difference between biotic and abiotic factors. Ask students to compare and contrast living and nonliving things in their own environment. Use **Figure 2** to illustrate biotic and abiotic factors in the prairie dog's habitat. Then have students practice the lesson's inquiry skill in the **Apply It activity.** In the chapter **Lab Investigation activity,** students will build a terrarium and observe the interactions between the biotic and abiotic parts of the closed ecosystem.

Using a park ecosystem as an example, **Teach Key Concepts** by asking students to identify the levels of organization from smallest to largest. Use the **Explore the Big Question activity** to illustrate the levels of an ecosystem. Students can do the **Real-World Inquiry** online to experiment with the effects of changing certain factors of a population in a habitat. Discuss student responses to the **Answer the Big Question activity.** Hand out the **Key Concept Summaries** as a review of each part of the lesson. Students can also use the online **Vocab Flash Cards** to review key terms.

EVALUATE

Have students take the **Lesson Quiz.** For an alternate assessment, see the **EXAM**VIEW® Assessment Suite, Progress Monitoring Assessments, or SuccessTracker™.

ⒺⓁⓁ Support

1 Content and Language

Compare the words *organism/organize*, *abiotic/biotic*, and *ecosystem/ecology*, featured in the lesson vocabulary. Explain what the word parts signal: *organ-* to arrange into systems; *a-* not; *bio-* living; *eco-* relating to the environment.

Lab zone Inquiry Path
Hands-on learning in the Lab zone

Digital Path
Online learning at **my science online**.com

ENGAGE AND EXPLORE

To teach this lesson with an emphasis on inquiry, begin with the **Inquiry Warm-Up activity.** Students identify living and nonliving things in magazine pictures. Lead a discussion about the connections different students chose and how they decided to test the living thing's dependence. Have students do the **After the Inquiry Warm-Up worksheet.** Talk about how living things also depend on other living things. Have volunteers share their answers to number 4 about the effect of different seasons.

EXPLAIN AND ELABORATE

Focus on the **Inquiry Skill** for the lesson. Point out that when you draw a conclusion, you make a statement summing up what you have learned from an experiment. What conclusion can be drawn from the **Inquiry Warm-Up activity?** *(All living things depend on other living things and non-living things in their habitat to survive.)* Have students do the first **Quick Lab** and then share their results. How do their inferences differ? Have volunteers suggest why that may be.

Do the **Teacher Demo** and classify the various materials under the headings BIOTIC and ABIOTIC on the board. Review *control, manipulated variable*, and *responding variable* before beginning the **Apply It activity.** Ask volunteers to share their conclusions. Have students do the **Lab Investigation.** In this investigation, students build a terrarium and observe the interactions between the biotic and abiotic parts of the closed ecosystem. You may elect to have them do the Open Inquiry version.

Use the **Explore the Big Q activity** to illustrate the levels of an ecosystem. Students can do the **Real-World Inquiry** online to experiment with the effects of changing certain factors of a population in a habitat. Do the **Quick Lab** to reinforce understanding of ecosystems. Discuss student responses to the **Answer the Big Q activity** in the student edition. Students can use the online **Vocab Flash Cards** to review key terms.

EVALUATE

Have students take the **Lesson Quiz.** For an alternate assessment, see the **EXAM**VIEW® Assessment Suite, Progress Monitoring Assessments, or SuccessTracker™.

ENGAGE AND EXPLORE

To teach this lesson using digital resources, begin by having students explore the real-world connections to living things and their environment at **My Planet Diary** online. Have them access the Chapter Resources to find the **Unlock the Big Question activity.** There they can answer the questions and refine their responses as they continue through the lesson. You can re-assign the activity and have students submit their work so you can track their progress.

EXPLAIN AND ELABORATE

Students reading above, at, or below the lexile measure of this lesson can access basic content readings at their level at **My Reading Web.** Have students use the online **Vocab Flash Cards** to preview key terms. Do the **Quick Lab** and then ask students to share their results. How do their inferences differ? Have volunteers suggest why that may be.

Review *control, manipulated variable*, and *responding variable* before assigning the online **Apply It activity.** Ask volunteers to share their conclusions and have all students submit their work to you. Do the **Teacher Demo** and classify the various materials under the headings BIOTIC and ABIOTIC on the board.

Assign the online **Real-World Inquiry** ahead of time. In this activity, students have an opportunity to experiment with the effects of changing certain factors of a population in a habitat. Have them answer the questions and submit their work. Discuss student responses to the online **Answer the Big Q.** The **Key Concept Summary** online allows students to read a summary and see an image associated with each part of the lesson. Online remediation is available at **My Science Coach.**

EVALUATE

Have students take the **Lesson Quiz.** For an alternate assessment, see the **EXAM**VIEW® Assessment Suite, Progress Monitoring Assessments, or SuccessTracker™.

2 Frontload the Lesson
Preview the lesson visuals, labels, and captions. Ask students what they know about the words *population* and *community*. Explain the specific meanings these words have in science.

3 Comprehensible Input
Have students study the visuals and their captions in **Figures 2** and **3** to support the key concepts of the lesson.

4 Language Production
Pair or group students with varied language abilities to complete labs collaboratively for language practice. Have each student copy the completed written lab for personal reference.

5 Assess Understanding
Make true or false statements using lesson content and have students indicate if they agree or disagree with a thumbs up or thumbs down gesture to check whole-class comprehension.

Living Things and the Environment

Establish Learning Objectives

After this lesson, students will be able to:

🔑 Identify the needs that must be met by an organism's surroundings.

🔑 Identify biotic and abiotic parts of a habitat.

🔑 Describe the levels of organization within an ecosystem.

Engage

Activate Prior Knowledge

MY PLANET DIARY Read *Love Song* with the class. Point out that mouse lemurs live only on the island of Madagascar, off the eastern coast of Africa. Ask: **Why do you think mouse lemurs live only on this island?** *(It has the food they like to eat.)* **Different organisms live in different places, or habitats. What is your habitat?** *(My home; my room)* **What about that place makes it uniquely yours?** *(It has my stuff in it. It is comfortable for me. My family is there.)*

BIG IDEAS OF SCIENCE REFERENCE LIBRARY 📖 Have students look up the following topics: Amazon River, Colorado Plateau, Deep Sea Vents, Supercooling Frogs.

Explore

Lab Resource: Inquiry Warm-Up 🧪

L1 WHAT'S IN THE SCENE Students will identify parts of a habitat.

LESSON
1

Living Things and the Environment

🔓 **UNLOCK THE BIG ❓**

🔑 **What Does an Organism Get From Its Environment?**

🔑 **What Are the Two Parts of an Organism's Habitat?**

🔑 **How Is an Ecosystem Organized?**

my planet diary

DISCOVERY

Love Song

The gray, golden brown, and Goodman's mouse lemurs are some of the world's smallest primates. These three lemurs look similar. Looking so similar makes it difficult for the lemurs to find members of their own kind or species during mating season. However, it seems that the lemurs can identify their own species by song. Scientists recorded the mating calls of the three species of lemurs. They discovered that the lemurs reacted more to the calls from their own species. This allows the lemurs to pick the right mate, even at night.

Communicate Answer these questions. Discuss your answers with a partner.

1. If you were looking for your sneakers among several pairs that looked just like yours, what characteristics would make it easier for you to find them?
   Size, smell, scuff marks, wear pattern

2. What do you think would happen if a lemur mated with a different kind of lemur?
   They would not be able to have offspring.

▷ **PLANET DIARY** Go to **Planet Diary** to learn more about habitats.

Golden brown mouse lemur

Goodman's mouse lemur

Gray mouse lemur

🧪 **Lab zone** Do the Inquiry Warm-Up *What's in the Scene?*

SUPPORT ALL READERS

Lexile Measure = 960L   **Lexile Word Count = 992**

Prior Exposure to Content: Most students have encountered this topic in earlier grades

Academic Vocabulary: *compare, contrast, describe*

Science Vocabulary: *abiotic factor, biotic factor*

Concept Level: Generally appropriate for most students in this grade

Preteach With: My Planet Diary "Love Song" and Figure 1 activity

Go to **My Reading Web** to access leveled readings that provide a foundation for the content.

my science online.com

Vocabulary
- organism • habitat • biotic factor • abiotic factor
- species • population • community • ecosystem
- ecology

Skills
- ↻ Reading: Compare and Contrast
- △ Inquiry: Draw Conclusions

What Does an Organism Get From Its Environment?

If you were to visit Alaska, you might see a bald eagle fly by. A bald eagle is one type of **organism,** or living thing. Different types of organisms live in different types of surroundings, or environments. ⚷ **An organism gets food, water, shelter, and other things it needs to live, grow, and reproduce from its environment.** An environment that provides the things a specific organism needs to live, grow, and reproduce is called its **habitat.**

In a forest habitat, mushrooms grow in the damp soil and wood-peckers build nests in tree trunks. Organisms live in different habitats because they have different requirements for survival and reproduction. Some organisms live on a prairie, with its flat terrain, tall grasses, and low rainfall amounts. A prairie dog, like the one shown in **Figure 1,** obtains the food and shelter it needs from a prairie habitat. It could not survive on this rocky ocean shore. Likewise, the prairie would not meet the needs of a sea star.

FIGURE 1 ············
What's Wrong With This Picture?
Most people would never expect to see a prairie dog at the beach.
✎ **List** Give three reasons why this prairie dog would not survive in this habitat.

Sample: There is no grass to eat; it is too wet; there is no grass to hide from predators.

 Lab zone Do the Quick Lab *Organisms and Their Habitats.*

⚷ **Assess Your Understanding**

got it? ·················

○ **I get it!** Now I know that an organism's environment provides food, water, and shelter for the organism to live, grow, and reproduce.

○ **I need extra help with** See TE note.

Go to **my science ⬡ COACH** *online for help with this subject.*

593

ⒺⓁⓁ Support

1 Content and Language
Ask students to restate the objectives in their own words. Have pairs complete and use flash cards with key vocabulary terms on one side, and a definition, visual, and sentence with the word on the other. Allow students with limited English to use their native languages for support.

2 Frontload the Lesson
Have students name an organism they see often (a specific plant or animal) and list the things found in that organism's environment. Explain how some are living and others not.

3 Comprehensible Input
Explain the Explore the Big Q image and caption, restating information as needed. Have students complete the Apply Concepts activity, allowing them to draw or write according to their language proficiency level.

Explain ————————

Introduce Vocabulary
To help students understand the term *habitat,* tell them that in Latin the word means "it inhabits." *Inhabit* means "lives in, resides, occupies."

Teach Key Concepts ⚷
Explain to students that organisms get the vital things they need to survive from their habitat. A habitat is an environment that is home to a particular organism. Ask: **Are all parts of the forest where organisms live the same?** *(No)* **How do they differ?** *(Some parts get more sunlight than other; some organisms live on the ground, others in the treetops.)* **Why do you find different kinds of organisms in different habitats?** *(Each kind of organism has specific needs. Different habitats provide different things.)*

Elaborate ————————

21st Century Learning ⬡ DK
CRITICAL THINKING Have students read *Deep Sea Vents* in the **Big Ideas of Science Reference Library.** Deep sea vents, also known as smokers, can be black, grey, white, or clear. Have students research one or more of these types and create a short multimedia presentation in which they answer these questions: What minerals cause the difference in color? What organisms live in this habitat?

Lab Resource: Quick Lab
L1 ORGANISMS AND THEIR HABITATS Students will infer what an animal's habitat is like.

Evaluate ————————

Assess Your Understanding
Have students evaluate their understanding by completing the appropriate sentence.

RTI Response to Intervention
If students have trouble identifying what a habitat provides, **then** remind them that the basic needs of food, water, and shelter are the same for human beings.

my science ⬡ COACH Have students go online for help in understanding habitats.

My Planet Diary provides an opportunity for students to explore real-world connections to living things and their environments.

my science online | Habitat

Explain

LESSON 15.1

Teach Key Concepts 🔑

Explain to students that there are living and nonliving parts to their surroundings. They need both parts in order to survive. Ask: **What are some living things in or near your home?** *(Family, dog, cat, some foods, squirrels, birds, plants)* **What are some nonliving things in or near your home?** *(Furniture, clothing, toys, car, roads)* Point out to students that biotic factors include things that were once living or came from living things. Dead plants and animals are biotic factors, as are waste products. If students do not know the word *scat*, tell them that it is a term for animal droppings. Owl pellets are another waste product. Most of the indigestible parts of animals that an owl eats are regurgitated as pellets.

🔁 **Compare and Contrast** Explain that comparing and contrasting shows how ideas, facts and events are similar and different. The results of the comparison can be important.

Teach With Visuals

Tell students to look at **Figure 2.** Make sure students understand the meaning of decaying remains and aquatic. Help students identify the ferret, eagle, and owl in the prairie dog's habitat. (Ferret, eagle, owl) Point out that the prairie dog's habitat is also the ferret's habitat. Ask: **How do the prairie dog and ferret interact?** *(The ferret hunts the prairie dog.)* **What kind of factor in the ferret's habitat is the prairie dog?** *(Biotic)*

21st Century Learning

INFORMATION LITERACY Help students classify factors in an organism's environment. Ask: **What are the two kinds of factors in an organism's environment?** *(Biotic and abiotic)* **What factors in Figure 2 are biotic?** *(Prairie dogs, ferrets, eagle, owl, grass, flowers)* **What factors are abiotic?** *(Abiotic factors that can be seen are water and soil.)* **What factors cannot be seen?** *(Sunlight, temperature, oxygen)*

What Are the Two Parts of an Organism's Habitat?

To meet its needs, a prairie dog must interact with more than just the other prairie dogs around it. 🔑 **An organism interacts with both the living and nonliving parts of its habitat.**

Biotic Factors What living things can you see in the prairie dog's habitat shown in **Figure 2**? The parts of a habitat that are living, or once living, and interact with an organism are called **biotic factors** (by AHT ik). The plants that provide seeds and berries are biotic factors. The ferrets and eagles that hunt the prairie dog are also biotic factors. Worms and bacteria are biotic factors that live in the soil underneath the prairie grass. Prairie dog scat, owl pellets, and decomposing plant matter are also biotic factors.

Abiotic Factors Not all of the factors that organisms interact with are living. **Abiotic factors** (ay by AHT ik) are the nonliving parts of an organism's habitat. These factors, as shown in **Figure 2**, include sunlight, soil, temperature, oxygen, and water.

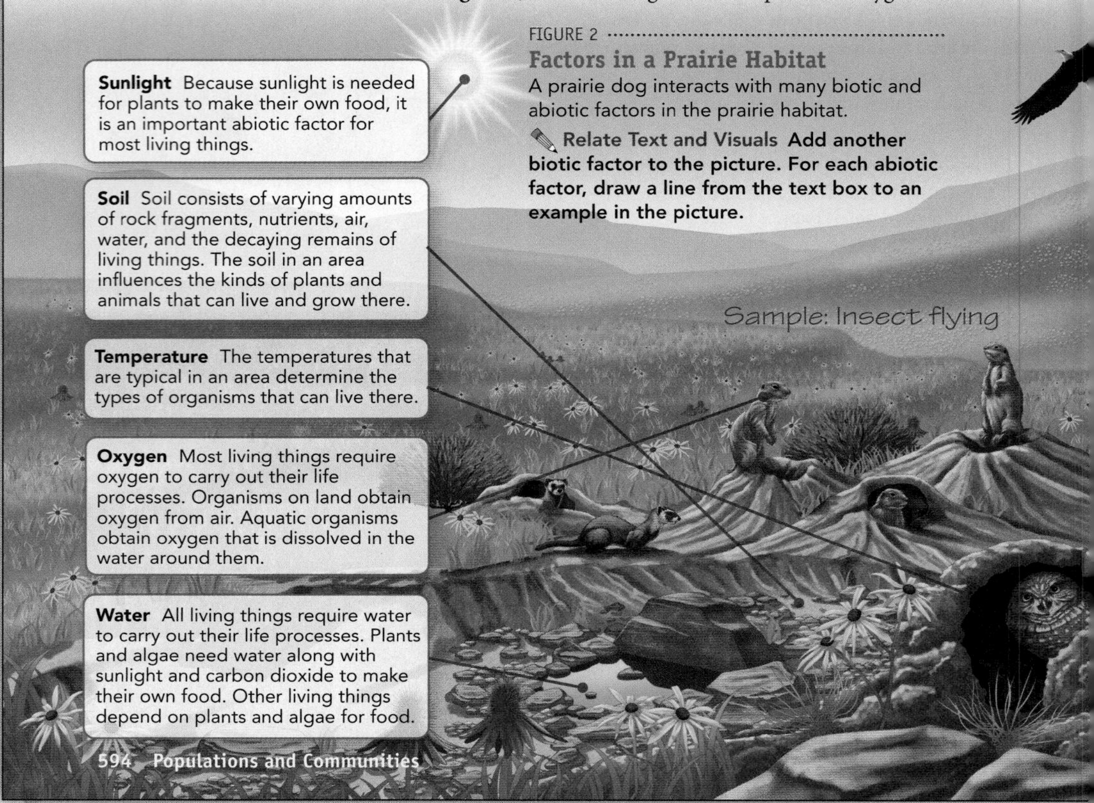

✏️ **Compare and Contrast** In the paragraphs at the right, circle how biotic and abiotic factors are similar and underline how they are different.

FIGURE 2
Factors in a Prairie Habitat
A prairie dog interacts with many biotic and abiotic factors in the prairie habitat.

✏️ **Relate Text and Visuals** Add another biotic factor to the picture. For each abiotic factor, draw a line from the text box to an example in the picture.

Sample: Insect flying

Sunlight Because sunlight is needed for plants to make their own food, it is an important abiotic factor for most living things.

Soil Soil consists of varying amounts of rock fragments, nutrients, air, water, and the decaying remains of living things. The soil in an area influences the kinds of plants and animals that can live and grow there.

Temperature The temperatures that are typical in an area determine the types of organisms that can live there.

Oxygen Most living things require oxygen to carry out their life processes. Organisms on land obtain oxygen from air. Aquatic organisms obtain oxygen that is dissolved in the water around them.

Water All living things require water to carry out their life processes. Plants and algae need water along with sunlight and carbon dioxide to make their own food. Other living things depend on plants and algae for food.

594 Populations and Communities

Digital Lesson: Assign the *Apply It* activity online and have student submit their work to you.

my science online.com · **Biotic and Abiotic Factors**

apply it!

Salt is an abiotic factor found in some environments. To see how the amount of salt affects the hatching of brine shrimp eggs, varying amounts of salt were added to four different 500-mL beakers.

1 **Observe** In which beaker(s) did the eggs, shown as purple circles, hatch? <u>B, C, D</u>

2 **Infer** The manipulated variable was <u>the amount of salt.</u>

3 **Infer** The responding variable was <u>the number of hatching shrimp.</u>

4 **CHALLENGE** Beaker <u>A</u> was the control.

5 **Draw Conclusions** What can you conclude about the amount of salt in the shrimps' natural habitat?
<u>It is similar to the amount in Beaker B, since that is where the most eggs hatched.</u>

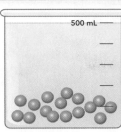
Beaker A
500 mL spring water

Beaker B
500 mL spring water
+ 2.5 g salt

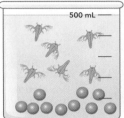
Beaker C
500 mL spring water
+ 7.5 g salt

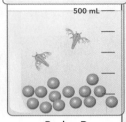
Beaker D
500 mL spring water
+ 15 g salt

 Lab zone Do the Lab Investigation *World in a Bottle.*

🔑 Assess Your Understanding

1a. Interpret Diagrams List two biotic and two abiotic factors in **Figure 2**.
<u>Sample: Biotic—grass and eagle</u>
<u>Sample: Abiotic—the rocky part of soil and sunlight</u>

b. 🔺**Draw Conclusions** Name two abiotic factors in your habitat and explain how your life would be different without them.
<u>Sample: Sunlight and oxygen. If there was no sunlight, I would not have enough food to eat. If there was no oxygen, I would not be able to breathe.</u>

got it? ....

○ **I get it!** Now I know that the two parts of an organism's habitat are <u>living, or biotic, factors and nonliving, or abiotic, factors.</u>

○ **I need extra help with** <u>See TE note.</u>

Go to my science 🔵 coach *online for help with this subject.*

595

Differentiated Instruction

L1 Identify Biotic and Abiotic Factors Have students describe the environment where they live. Encourage them to make a list of features, including the climate, physical features, and organisms native to the area. Have students review their lists with the class.

L3 Life Without Oxygen Most organisms need oxygen to carry out their life processes. Some organisms are able to live without oxygen, and some must live without oxygen. Have students research anaerobic bacteria to find examples of bacteria that live without oxygen and learn what happens to these bacteria when oxygen is present.

L1 Words in Context Explain that the meaning of an unfamiliar word can often be determined by examining the words and phrases surrounding it. Have students examine the text surrounding the word *aquatic*. Point out the word *water* in the sentence. They can get the meaning of *aquatic* from the context.

Elaborate ────────

Teacher Demo 🔺Lab zone

L1 OBSERVING SOIL COMPONENTS

Materials soil sample, jar with screw-in lid, water

Time 10 minutes

Place about 200 mL of soil in a jar. Add water up to about 3 cm from the top. Screw on the lid tightly and shake the jar. Allow the contents to settle for a few minutes. Then allow students to observe the contents without shaking or opening the jar.

Ask: **What materials can you identify in the soil?** *(Small particles of rock, bits of plants, small invertebrates)* **Which materials are abiotic factors?** *(Particles of rock)* **Which materials are biotic factors?** *(Plant materials, invertebrates)*

Apply It!

L2 Review *control, manipulated variable*, and *responding variable* before beginning the activity.

🔺 **Draw Conclusions** If students have trouble coming up with a conclusion, point out that the best environment for brine shrimp is the one in which the greatest number of them was produced. Help students understand that a conclusion is not necessarily the end of a scientific investigation: A conclusion may lead right into another experiment.

Lab Resource: Lab Investigation 🔺Lab zone

L2 WORLD IN A BOTTLE Students will explore the interactions of biotic and abiotic factors in a closed system.

Evaluate ────────

Assess Your Understanding

After students answer the questions, have them evaluate their understanding by completing the appropriate sentence.

R T I Response to Intervention

1a. If students need help listing biotic and abiotic factors, **then** have them review the definitions of each type of factor.

b. If students have trouble explaining the importance of biotic and abiotic factors, **then** remind them that human beings need water for all vital body functions.

my science 🔵 coach Have students go online for help in understanding biotic and abiotic factors.

595

Explain

Teach Key Concepts 🔑

Explain to students the progression from smallest to largest levels of organization of an ecosystem. Ask: **Using a park as an ecosystem, what is one squirrel considered to be?** *(An individual)* **What is the name given to a group of squirrels living in the park?** *(A population)* **If you add the birds, chimpmunks, ants, and butterflies that live in the park, what is the group of organisms called?** *(A community)* **Now add the nonliving parts, such as water in a pond and oxygen in the air. What do you call this area now?** *(An ecosystem)* If possible, this exercise could be done outside or looking out a window. Have a volunteer select an animal or plant that is visible and build the ecosystem from there.

Lead a Discussion

DEFINE A POPULATION Review with students the definition of *population*. *(All the members of a species living in a particular area)* Ask: **If a grassland community includes grass, grasshoppers, field mice, and red-tailed hawks, what level of an ecosystem to the red-tailed hawks represent?** *(Population)* **Do all members of this species live in the same grassland?** *(No)* **If a forest contains birch, maple, and pine trees, do these trees make up a population? Explain.** *(No. They are a community because they are different species.)*

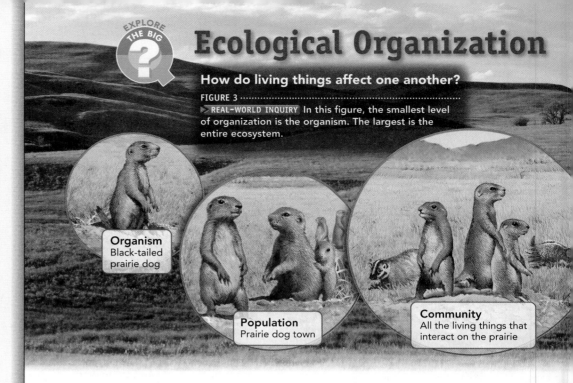

Ecological Organization

How do living things affect one another?

FIGURE 3 ....

▶ **REAL-WORLD INQUIRY** In this figure, the smallest level of organization is the organism. The largest is the entire ecosystem.

Organism
Black-tailed prairie dog

Population
Prairie dog town

Community
All the living things that interact on the prairie

How Is an Ecosystem Organized?

Most organisms do not live all alone in their habitat. Instead, organisms live together in populations and communities that interact with abiotic factors in their ecosystems.

Organisms Black-tailed prairie dogs that live in prairie dog towns on the Nebraska plains are all members of one species. A **species** (SPEE sheez) is a group of organisms that can mate with each other and produce offspring that can also mate and reproduce.

Populations All the members of one species living in a particular area are referred to as a **population.** The prairie dogs in the Nebraska town are one example of a population.

Communities A particular area contains more than one species of organism. The prairie, for instance, includes prairie dogs, hawks, snakes, and grasses. All the different populations that live together in an area make up a **community.**

Real-World Inquiry allows students to determine what factors may be affecting a population within its habitat.

my science ONLINE.com ▸ Ecosystems

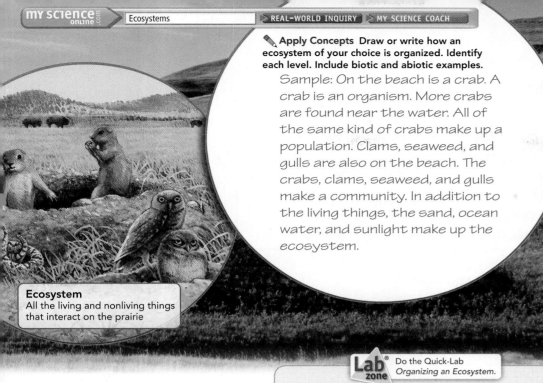

Ecosystem
All the living and nonliving things that interact on the prairie

✏️ **Apply Concepts** Draw or write how an ecosystem of your choice is organized. Identify each level. Include biotic and abiotic examples.

Sample: On the beach is a crab. A crab is an organism. More crabs are found near the water. All of the same kind of crabs make up a population. Clams, seaweed, and gulls are also on the beach. The crabs, clams, seaweed, and gulls make a community. In addition to the living things, the sand, ocean water, and sunlight make up the ecosystem.

Ecosystems The community of organisms that live in a particular area, along with their non-living environment, make up an **ecosystem.** A prairie is just one of the many different ecosystems found on Earth. Other ecosystems are deserts, oceans, ponds, and forests.

Figure 3 shows the levels of organization in a prairie ecosystem. 🔑 **The smallest level of organization is a single organism, which belongs to a population that includes other members of its species. The population belongs to a community of different species. The community and abiotic factors together form an ecosystem.**

Because the populations in an ecosystem interact with one another, any change affects all the different populations that live there. The study of how organisms interact with each other and with their environment is called **ecology.**

Lab zone ® Do the Quick-Lab *Organizing an Ecosystem.*

🔑 **Assess Your Understanding**

2a. Classify All of the different kinds of organisms in a forest are a (community/ population).

b. 🅰️NSWER How do living things affect one another?

Sample: Living things live together and interact with one another.

got it? ·······················

○ I get it! Now I know that ecosystems are organized into organisms, populations, and communities.

○ I need extra help with See TE note.

Go to **my science** 💬 **COACH** *online for help with this subject.*

597

Elaborate

Explore the Big Q ❓ UbD

Direct students' attention to the images of the prairie ecosystem. Help students identify the badger, prairie chicken, owls, snake, and bison in the images. Ask: **What is the smallest level of organization?** *(Organism)* **With what other animals is the prairie dog interacting in the second circle?** *(Other prairie dogs)* **What other animals are part of the community shown in the third circle?** *(A badger and a prairie chicken)* **What other living things are part of the community shown in the third circle?** *(Grasses)* **What abiotic factor is visible in the fourth circle?** *(Soil)*

Lab Resource: Quick Lab

L1 ORGANIZING AN ECOSYSTEM Students will explore the four levels of an ecosystem: organism, population, community, and ecosystem.

Evaluate

Assess Your Understanding

After students answer the questions, have them evaluate their understanding by completing the appropriate sentence.

Answer the Big Q ❓ UbD

To help students focus on the Big Question, lead a class discussion about the ways living things interact with each other.

R T I Response to Intervention

2a. If students have trouble distinguishing between population and community, **then** have them review the definitions and give another example of each using a different animal.

b. If students need help describing how living things affect one another, **then** have them list examples of interactions at each level of organization: member of a species mates with another member; pair lives in the population; members of the population are eaten by other animals in the community.

my science 💬 **COACH** Have students go online for help in understanding the organization of an ecosystem.

Differentiated Instruction

L3 Compare Habitats Have students describe their own habitat and make a list of its biotic and abiotic factors. Then tell the students to explain how these factors differ from those of organisms living in natural habitats.

L1 Multiple Meanings Students likely have seen the word *population* used to mean the number of people living in a particular state or country. In science, *population* means a group of individuals of the same species, not necessarily humans. In common use, *community* also refers to a group of people. In sciences, *community* includes more than one species.

L3 Other Ecosystems Ask students who have lived in, or traveled to, other ecosystems to share their experiences with the class.

Lab zone **After the Inquiry Warm-Up**

Living Things and the Environment

Inquiry Warm-Up, *What's in the Scene*?

In the Inquiry Warm-Up, you investigated living things and nonliving things in an environment. Using what you learned from that activity, answer the questions below.

1. **OBSERVE** What nonliving things could you observe in the picture?

_____

_____

2. **INFER** What nonliving things do you know of that are found in most environments but could not be observed in the picture?

_____

_____

3. **OBSERVE** Give an example of a living thing in the picture that is needed by another living thing in the picture. Explain why it is needed.

_____

_____

4. **PREDICT** How would the scene look different in another season? How might this affect the living things in this environment?

_____

_____

_____

_____

Assess Your Understanding

Living Things and the Environment

What Does an Organism Get From Its Environment?

got_it? ···

○ **I get it!** Now I know that an organism's environment provides _____
_____
_____
_____

○ **I need extra help with** _____
_____

What Are the Two Parts of an Organism's Habitat?

1a. **INTERPRET DIAGRAMS** List two biotic and two abiotic factors in Figure 2.

BIOTIC   **ABIOTIC**

_____   _____

_____   _____

b. **DRAW CONCLUSIONS** Name two biotic factors in your habitat and explain you your life would be different without them.

FACTOR   **AFFECT**

_____   _____

_____   _____

got_it? ···

○ **I get it!** Now I know that the two parts of an organism's habitat are _____
_____

○ **I need extra help with** _____
_____

Assess Your Understanding

Living Things and the Environment

How Is an Ecosystem Organized?

2a. **CLASSIFY** All of the different kinds of organisms in a forest are a (community/population).

b. **ANSWER** 🄰 How do living things affect one another?

got it? ··

○ **I get it!** Now I know that ecosystems are organized into _____

_____

_____

○ **I need extra help with** _____

_____

Key Concept Summaries

Living Things and the Environment

What Does an Organism Get From Its Environment?

A living thing, or **organism**, needs certain things to live, grow, and reproduce. An organism gets food, water, shelter, and other things that it needs from its environment.

An environment that provides the things a specific organism needs to live, grow, and reproduce is called its **habitat**. A prairie dog gets food, shelter, and other things from a prairie habitat that has flat land, tall grasses, and little rainfall. A rocky ocean shore habitat would not provide what a prairie dog needs to survive.

What Are the Two Parts of an Organism's Habitat?

Biotic factors are the living, or once living, parts of a habitat. In the prairie dog's habitat, plants that provide food and decomposing plants are biotic factors. Ferrets and eagles that hunt the prairie dog are also biotic factors. Worms and bacteria that live in the soil are biotic factors too.

Abiotic factors are the nonliving parts of a habitat. Water, sunlight, oxygen, temperature, and soil are all abiotic factors in a prairie dog's habitat.

How Is an Ecosystem Organized?

A **species** is a group of organisms that can mate with each other and produce offspring that can also mate and reproduce. The black-tailed prairie dogs of the Nebraska plains are all members of one species. A **population** refers to all the members of one species living in a particular area. All of the prairie dogs in a prairie dog town are a population.

All of the different populations that live together in an environment are a **community**. For example, a prairie includes prairie dogs, hawks, grasses, snakes, and many other organisms. An **ecosystem** is made up of the community of organisms that live in a particular area, as well the nonliving surroundings.

On a separate sheet of paper, list the four levels of an ecosystem from smallest to largest and give an example of each.

Living Things and the Environment

> **Understanding Main Ideas**
> Answer the following questions in the spaces provided.

1. What is ecology?

_____

_____

2. Name four abiotic factors found in a prairie ecosystem.

_____

_____

3. Name three populations found in a prairie ecosystem.

_____

Complete the table to show the levels of organization in an ecosystem. Start with the smallest unit.

4.

5.

6.

7.

> **Building Vocabulary**
> Fill in the blank to complete each statement.

8. An environment that provides the things a specific organism needs to live, grow, and reproduce is its _____.

9. All the living and nonliving things that interact in a particular area make up a(n) _____.

10. The parts of an organism's environment that are living or once living, and interact with the organism are _____.

11. All the different populations that live together in an area make up a(n) _____.

Name _____ Date _____ Class _____

Living Things and the Environment

> The drawing below shows an ecosystem. Study the drawing and then answer the questions that follow.

1. Name the biotic factors in this ecosystem.

_____

_____

2. Name the abiotic factors in the ecosystem.

_____

_____

3. Identify the specific habitat of each animal shown.

bear _____

blue jay _____

squirrel _____

fish _____

lizard _____

dragonfly _____

frog _____

Name _____ Date _____ Class _____

Living Things and the Environment

Write the letter of the correct answer on the line at the left.

1. ___ Which of the following lives in a prairie ecosystem?

    A   grass

    B   mushroom

    C   oak tree

    D   woodpecker

2. ___ Which of the following is a biotic factor?

    A   temperature

    B   sunlight

    C   bacteria

    D   water

3. ___ Which of the following lists the levels of an ecosystem in order from largest to smallest?

    A   population, organism, community, ecosystem

    B   ecosystem, community, organism, population

    C   organism, community, population, ecosystem

    D   ecosystem, community, population, organism

4. ___ An organism gets food, water, shelter, and other things it needs to live, grow, and reproduce from its

    A   population

    B   habitat

    C   abiotic factors

    D   species

If the statement is true, write _true_. If the statement is false, change the underlined word or words to make the statement true.

5. _____ The nonliving things that interact with an organism are called <u>biotic factors</u>.

6. _____ The study of how living things interact with each other and their environment is called <u>ecology</u>.

7. _____ A group of organisms that can mate with each other and produce offspring that can also mate and reproduce is called a <u>species</u>.

8. _____ <u>Oxygen</u> is an abiotic factor in the environment that is important for plants to make their own food.

9. _____ All the organisms that live in a particular area and their nonliving surroundings make up an <u>ecosystem</u>.

10. _____ All the members of one <u>community</u> living in a particular area make up a population.

Living Things and the Environment

Answer Key

After the Inquiry Warm-Up

1. Sample: water, soil, buildings or roads; students may list light if the sun is visible in the picture.

2. Sample: air, light

3. Students will likely identify one animal that eats another or an animal that eats a plant shown in the picture.

4. Accept all reasonable predictions. Sample: In the winter the water would be frozen and there would be fewer plants to eat. Animals might move to warmer areas to survive.

Key Concept Summaries

Sample:

Organism: one white pine tree

Population: all the white pine trees in a particular forest

Community: all the trees and animals in that forest

Ecosystem: the community in the forest and the nonliving factors, such as soil, water, and air

Review and Reinforce

1. Ecology is the study of how living things interact with each other and with their environment.

2. Accept four of the following: sunlight, soil, temperature, oxygen, water.

3. Accept three of the following: prairie dog, grass, owl, snake, eagle, ferret.

4. organism
5. population
6. community
7. ecosystem
8. habitat
9. ecosystem
10. biotic factors
11. community

Enrich

1. trees, bushes, bear, blue jay, squirrel, fish, lizard, dragonfly, flowering plant, grass, frog, water lilies, cattails (also bacteria and fungi, which are not visible)

2. soil, rocks, water, sunlight, air oxygen, temperature

3. Bear: the forest and grassy land

   Blue jay: trees, air, and ground

   Squirrel: trees and the ground around them

   Fish: the deeper water in the stream

   Lizard: dry land and rocks

   Dragonfly: the plants around the stream and the air

   Frog: the stream and the land close to the edge of the stream

Lesson Quiz

1. A
2. C
3. D
4. B
5. abiotic factors
6. true
7. true
8. sunlight
9. true
10. species

Populations

 How do living things affect one another?

Lesson Pacing: 2–3 periods or 1–1½ blocks

🕐 **SHORT ON TIME?** To do this lesson in approximately half the time, do the Activate Prior Knowledge activity followed by a discussion of the Key Concepts to familiarize students with the lesson content. Have students do the Quick Labs. The rest of the lesson can be completed by students independently.

> **Preference Navigator,** in the online Planning tools, allows you to customize *Interactive Science* to your own teaching style. You can also edit lesson plans by selecting the Lesson Planner option.
>
> **Digital Teacher's Edition** allows you to access your Teacher's Edition and Resource materials online.

my science online.com

Lesson Vocabulary

- birth rate • death rate • immigration • emigration
- population density • limiting factor • carrying capacity

 Content Refresher

Professional Development Note

Competitive Exclusion The Gause principle, also known as the principle of competitive exclusion, was named for G. F. Gause, a Soviet biologist. Gause was the first to suggest that species cannot coexist for long if they occupy the same niche. Gause developed his ideas by studying two similar species of *Paramecium*. When he grew populations of the two species separately, both grew rapidly and then leveled off at a population size that could be supported by available resources in the growing medium. However, when Gause grew the two species together, one species (*P. aurelia*) survived and the other species (*P. caudatum*) died out. Gause concluded that the surviving species had a competitive advantage in obtaining food and other resources. His work was later confirmed by other studies.

LESSON OBJECTIVES

🔧 Explain the causes of changes in population size.
🔧 Identify factors that limit population growth.

Blended Path
Active learning using Student Edition, Inquiry Path, and Digital Path

ENGAGE AND EXPLORE

To teach this lesson using a variety of resources, begin by reading **My Planet Diary** as a class. Have students share ideas and thoughts about this method of prairie dog population control. Then have students do the **Inquiry Warm-Up activity.** Students will use the process of estimation. Discuss the methods of estimation that different students chose and the accuracy of those methods. The **After the Inquiry Warm-Up worksheet** sets up a discussion about estimation of a population. Have volunteers share their answers to number 4 about the estimation of a tree population.

EXPLAIN AND ELABORATE

Teach Key Concepts by explaining the terms *birth rate, death rate, immigration, emigration,* and *population density* and having students answer questions about how these affect population size. **Lead a Discussion** explaining to students the processes of *immigration* and *emigration*. Use **Figure 2** to graphically demonstrate changes in a rabbit population. Then have students practice the inquiry skill in the **Apply It activity.**

Continue to **Teach Key Concepts** by explaining that environmental factors can limit population size. Ask students to name four limiting factors that affect population growth by relating cause and effect. Use the **Support the Big Q** to review *biotic* and *abiotic factors* and how they relate to population size. Then have students complete the **Apply It activity.**

Hand out the **Key Concept Summaries** as a review of each part of the lesson. Students can also use the online **Vocab Flash Cards** to review key terms.

EVALUATE

Have students take the **Lesson Quiz.** For an alternate assessment, see the **EXAM**VIEW® Assessment Suite, Progress Monitoring Assessments, or SuccessTracker™.

E L L Support

1 Content and Language

Compare the words *immigration* and *emigration* in the vocabulary. Students will learn in their textbook the root *migrate* "to move" and the prefixes *im-* in and *e-* out. Explain that the *-ation* means a process. *Immigration* is the process of moving into and *emigration* is the process of moving out of.

DIFFERENTIATED INSTRUCTION KEY
L1 Struggling Students or Special Needs
L2 On-Level Students **L3** Advanced Students

LESSON PLANNER 15.2

Lab zone Inquiry Path
Hands-on learning in the Lab zone

Digital Path
Online learning at my science online.com

ENGAGE AND EXPLORE

To teach this lesson with an emphasis on inquiry, begin with the **Inquiry Warm-Up activity.** Students will use the process of estimation. Lead a discussion about the methods of estimation different students chose and the accuracy of those methods. Have students do the **After the Inquiry Warm-Up worksheet.** Talk about estimation of a population. Have volunteers share their answers to number 4 about estimation of a tree population.

EXPLAIN AND ELABORATE

Focus on the inquiry skill for the lesson. Point out that when you infer, you draw a conclusion by reasoning. What conclusion can be drawn about estimation in the **Inquiry Warm-Up activity?** *(Accurate estimation of a sample can give a close calculation of population size.)*

Build Inquiry so students understand *birth rate* and *death rate.* Have students do the first **Quick Lab** to reinforce changes in population size and then share their results. Review *population density* and *carrying capacity* before beginning the **Apply It activity.** Ask volunteers to share what they know about limiting factors.

Use the **Support the Big Q** to review *biotic* and *abiotic factors* and how they relate to population size. Then have students complete the **Apply It activity.** Have students do the remaining **Quick Lab** to reinforce understanding of space as a limiting factor. Students can use the online **Vocab Flash Cards** to review key terms.

EVALUATE

Have students take the **Lesson Quiz.** For an alternate assessment, see the **EXAM**VIEW® Assessment Suite, Progress Monitoring Assessments, or SuccessTracker™.

ENGAGE AND EXPLORE

To teach this lesson using digital resources, begin by having students explore prairie dog population control at **My Planet Diary** online. Have them access the Chapter Resources to find the **Unlock the Big Question activity.** There they can answer the questions and refine their responses as they continue through the lesson. You can re-assign the activity and have students submit their work so you can track their progress.

EXPLAIN AND ELABORATE

Students reading above, at, or below the lexile measure of this lesson can access basic content readings at their level at **My Reading Web.** Have students use the online **Vocab Flash Cards** to preview key terms. Do the **Quick Labs** and then ask students to share their results.

Assign the **Do the Math activity** online and have students submit their work to you. Review *population density* and *limiting factors* before assigning the **Apply It activity.** Ask volunteers to share what they know about limiting factors.

Use the **Support the Big Q** to review *biotic* and *abiotic factors* and how they relate to population size. Then have students complete the **Apply It activity.**

The **Key Concept Summaries** online allow students to read a summary and see an image associated with each part of the lesson. Online remediation is available at **My Science Coach.**

EVALUATE

Have students take the **Lesson Quiz.** For an alternate assessment, see the **EXAM**VIEW® Assessment Suite, Progress Monitoring Assessments, or SuccessTracker™.

2 Frontload the Lesson
Preview the lesson visuals, labels, and captions. Ask students what they know about the words *population density* and *limiting factors.* Explain the specific meanings these words have in science.

3 Comprehensible Input
Have students study the visuals and their captions to support the key concepts of the lesson.

4 Language Production
Pair or group students with varied language abilities to complete labs collaboratively for language practice. Have each student copy the completed written lab for personal reference.

5 Assess Understanding
Make true or false statements using lesson content and have students indicate if they agree or disagree with a thumbs up or thumbs down gesture to check whole-class comprehension.

LESSON 15.2

Populations

Establish Learning Objectives

After this lesson, students will be able to:

🔑 Describe how populations change in size.

🔑 Identify the factors that limit population growth.

Engage

Activate Prior Knowledge

MY PLANET DIARY Read *Prairie Dog Picker-Upper* with the class. Point out that prairie dog populations can be very large, with some colonies including millions of individuals and covering hundreds of acres. Students may find this passage upsetting. In fact, this program is controversial, in part because prairie dogs are threatened in some areas. Farmers see prairie dogs as threats, but they are an important biotic factor in the prairie ecosystem.

BIG IDEAS OF SCIENCE REFERENCE LIBRARY 📖
Have students look up the following topics: Bats, GPS Tracking.

Explore

Lab Resource: Inquiry Warm-Up 🧪

L1 POPULATIONS Students will explore ways to estimate the size of a population.

---

2 Populations

🔑 How Do Populations Change in Size?

🔑 What Factors Limit Population Growth?

MY PLANET DIARY   TECHNOLOGY

Prairie Dog Picker-Upper

Did you know that vacuum cleaners do more than just clean carpets? Across the Great Plains, farmers are using specially designed vacuum cleaners to help them remove black-tailed prairie dogs from the farm land. Prairie dogs can eat crops, cause soil erosion, and endanger cattle and farm machinery. The prairie dog vacuum uses a 4-in. plastic hose to suck prairie dogs out of the ground at 483 km/h! The prairie dogs end up in a padded tank, usually unharmed. They are then relocated or donated to the U.S. Fish and Wildlife Service to be fed to endangered eagles, hawks, and black-footed ferrets.

Prairie dogs

Communicate Discuss these questions with a group of classmates. Write your answers below.

1. If all of the prairie dogs were removed, how do you think the prairie ecosystem would be affected?
   Sample: The organisms that depend on the prairie dogs for food could starve.

2. Should prairie dogs be used as food for endangered species? Explain.
   Sample: No, one type of organism is not more important than another type of organism.

> **PLANET DIARY** Go to **Planet Diary** to learn more about populations.

🧪 Do the Inquiry Warm-Up *Populations*.

How Do Populations Change in Size?

Ecologists are scientists who study biotic and abiotic factors of an ecosystem and the interactions between them. Some ecologists study populations and monitor the sizes of populations over time.
🔑 **Populations can change in size when new members join the population or when members leave the population.**

SUPPORT ALL READERS
Lexile Measure = 960L   Lexile Word Count = 1485

Prior Exposure to Content: May be the first time students have encountered this topic

Academic Vocabulary: *cause, effect, infer*

Science Vocabulary: *carrying capacity, limiting factor*

Concept Level: May be difficult for students who struggle with math

Preteach With: My Planet Diary "Prairie Dog Picker-Upper" and the *Do the Math* activity

Go to **My Reading Web** to access leveled readings that provide a foundation for the content.

LESSON 15.2

Vocabulary
- birth rate
- death rate
- immigration
- emigration
- population density
- limiting factor
- carrying capacity

Skills
- ⦿ Reading: Relate Cause and Effect
- △ Inquiry: Infer

Births and Deaths The most common way in which new individuals join a population is by being born into it. If more individuals are born into a population than die in any period of time, a population can grow. So when the **birth rate,** the number of births per 1,000 individuals for a given time period, is greater than its **death rate,** the number of deaths per 1,000 individuals for a given time period, the population may increase. The main way that individuals leave a population is by dying. If the birth rate is the same as the death rate, then the population may stay the same. In situations where the death rate is higher than the birth rate, then the population may decrease.

do the math!

Depending on the size and age of the female, an American Alligator can lay between 10 and 50 eggs per year.

❶ **Graph** Using the data table and colored pencils, create a double bar graph showing alligator births and deaths for four years.

❷ Label the x-axis and y-axis.

❸ Write a title for the graph.

❹ Fill in the graph using the colors shown.

❺ **Develop Hypotheses** What factors might explain the number of births and deaths in Year 3?

<u>Sample: Food may have</u>
<u>been more abundant and</u>
<u>there may have been</u>
<u>construction near the</u>
<u>alligators' habitat.</u>

Data Table

Year	Births	Deaths
1	32	8
2	28	13
3	47	21
4	33	16

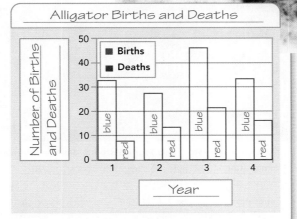

Alligator Births and Deaths

■ Births
■ Deaths

Number of Births and Deaths (y-axis: 0, 10, 20, 30, 40, 50)
Year (x-axis: 1, 2, 3, 4)

599

Explain

Introduce Vocabulary
To help students understand the terms *immigration* and *emigration*, point out the root word *migrate*, meaning "to move to a new place."

Teach Key Concepts 🔑
Explain to students that populations change in size when new members join the population or when members leave the population. Tell students that populations increase or decrease all the time. In some cases, the changes are small. In other cases, the changes are large. Ask: **What kinds of events can cause a population to increase?** *(Birth of new individuals or individuals moving into the population)* **What could cause a population to decrease?** *(More individuals die than are born; more individuals move out of the population than move into it.)* **What might cause a population to decrease rapidly?** *(A natural disaster or a disease epidemic)*

Elaborate

Do the Math!

L1 Point out that a graph makes it possible to see trends in data. If students have trouble drawing a double-bar graph, suggest that they graph all the birth data first, then draw the bars for death data next to each blue (birth) bar. Ask: **Look at the bars for Year 1. How is the number of deaths compared to the number of births different from other years?** *(Year 1 has the fewest deaths compared to number of births.)*
See *Math Skill and Problem-Solving Activities* for support.

My Planet Diary provides an opportunity for students to explore real-world connections to populations.

Digital Lesson: Assign the *Do the Math* activity online and have students submit their work to you.

my science online.com | Population Size

1 Content and Language
Write the words *immigration* and *emigration* on the board and circle *migration* in each. Explain that migration means "traveling from one place to another." Have volunteers demonstrate these terms by walking in and out of the room.

2 Frontload the Lesson
Help students understand the ideas of birth rate and death rate. Explain that a rate tells how often something happens in a period of time.

3 Comprehensible Input
Before students read the Apply It passage on pandas, review the meaning of *endangered*. Ask students what *danger* means, and what it means to be *in danger*. Point out that endangered species are in danger of completely dying out.

Explain

Lead a Discussion

EMIGRATION AND IMMIGRATION Explain to students that *immigration* occurs when an individual moves into a population. *Emigration* occurs when an individual leaves a population. Ask: **What might cause individuals to immigrate?** *(Possible answers might include an abundant food supply.)* **Why might individuals emigrate?** *(Students might suggest decrease in food supply, drought, or habitat loss.)* **Why might scientists want to monitor the size of a population?** *(If the population gets too large, it could lead to starvation of some individuals or damage to the environment. If the population gets too small, it could be endangered.)*

21st Century Learning

CRITICAL THINKING Have students read the caption for **Figure 1.** Point out the words *due to* in the first sentence. Explain to students that this indicates a cause. Over-hunting is the cause. Ask: **What is the effect of over-hunting?** *(Population decreased so much that the deer were almost extinct in Iowa.)* **What is the cause and the effect described in the second sentence?** *(Immigration from other states is the cause. Reestablishment of the population is the effect.)*

Vocabulary Latin Word Origins
Both the terms *immigration* ("moving into a population") and *emigration* ("moving out of a population") come from the Latin word *migrare* ("to move"). What do you think the prefixes *im–* and *e–* mean?

Sample: _im–_ means "in" and _e–_ means "out."

The Population Statement When the birth rate in a population is greater than the death rate, the population will generally increase. This can be written as a mathematical statement using the "is greater than" sign:

> If birth rate > death rate, population size increases.

However, if the death rate in a population is greater than the birth rate, the population size will generally decrease. This can also be written as a mathematical statement:

> If death rate > birth rate, population size decreases.

Immigration and Emigration The size of a population also can change when individuals move into or out of the population. **Immigration** (im ih GRAY shun) means moving into a population. **Emigration** (em ih GRAY shun) means leaving a population. For instance, if food is scarce, some members of an antelope herd may wander off in search of better grassland. If they become permanently separated from the original herd, they will no longer be part of that population.

FIGURE 1 ······

Immigration

In 1898, white-tailed deer were almost extinct in Iowa due to over-hunting. The deer population was reestablished as animals from Minnesota, Wisconsin, and Missouri immigrated into Iowa.

✎ **Apply Concepts** Using your classroom, describe an example of each of the following.

Immigration: Sample: A new student, Sally, was added to my English class. She had moved from Denver when her dad was transferred for work.

Emigration: Sample: Jordan had his schedule changed the first week of school and was moved into a different science class.

600 Populations and Communities

Interactive Art demonstrates how populations change over time.

my science ONLINE.com ▸ **Population Size**

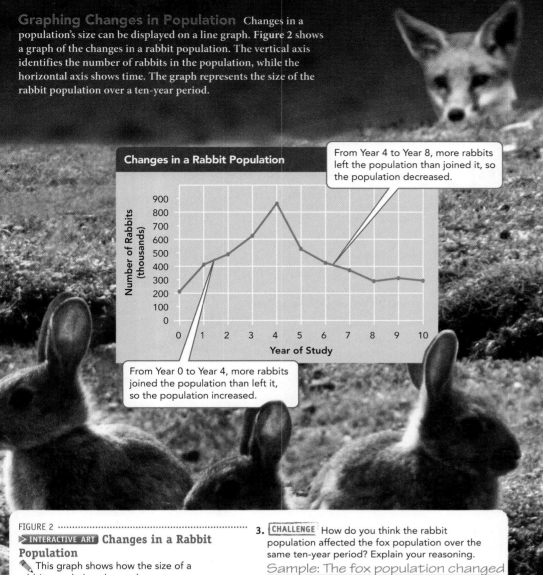

Graphing Changes in Population

Changes in a population's size can be displayed on a line graph. **Figure 2** shows a graph of the changes in a rabbit population. The vertical axis identifies the number of rabbits in the population, while the horizontal axis shows time. The graph represents the size of the rabbit population over a ten-year period.

Changes in a Rabbit Population

From Year 4 to Year 8, more rabbits left the population than joined it, so the population decreased.

From Year 0 to Year 4, more rabbits joined the population than left it, so the population increased.

FIGURE 2 ·······

> **INTERACTIVE ART** **Changes in a Rabbit Population**

✎ This graph shows how the size of a rabbit population changed over ten years.

1. **Interpret Data** In Year ___4___, the rabbit population reached its highest point.

2. **Read Graphs** What was the size of the rabbit population in that year? About 850,000

3. **CHALLENGE** How do you think the rabbit population affected the fox population over the same ten-year period? Explain your reasoning.

Sample: The fox population changed in relation to its food (rabbits). As the number of rabbits increased, so did the number of foxes. When the number of rabbits decreased, so did the number of foxes.

601

Elaborate

Build Inquiry 🔬

L3 CALCULATING GROWTH RATE

Materials none

Time 5 minutes

Review with students the definitions of *birth rate* and *death rate*. Tell students that growth rate is the difference between birth rate and death rate.

$$growth\ rate = birth\ rate - death\ rate$$
$$g = b - d$$

Ask: **Suppose 1,600 snow geese were born the same year that 1,200 died. What would be the growth rate for that year?** *(1,600 − 1,200 = 400, so the growth rate is 400.)* **What does a negative growth rate mean?** *(There were more deaths than births.)* Look back at the *Do the Math* activity. **What are the growth rates for each year?** *(Year 1, 24; Year 2, 15; Year 3, 25; Year 4, 17)*

21st Century Learning

INTERPERSONAL SKILLS Have students read *GPS Tracking* in the **Big Ideas of Science Reference Library** and share ideas with a partner about the pros and cons of placing tracking devices on animals.

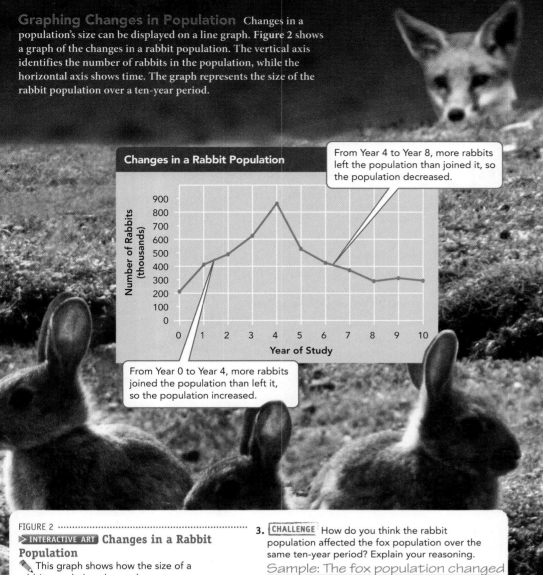

Differentiated Instruction

L1 Inequalities Help students review the use of the "is greater than" sign (>) in mathematical statements. Point out that the smaller value appears on the side of the symbol that forms the point. The larger value is on the side of the symbol with the wider, open end. If students still have difficulty with the concept, tell them to think of the sign as an alligator that always wants to eat the larger amount.

L3 Growth Rate of a Population Challenge advanced students to figure out how to use the data in **Figure 2** to find growth rates of the rabbit population. Make sure students can explain their reasoning. *(The increase or decrease in population from one year to the next is the growth rate for that year.)*

Elaborate

Apply It!

L1 Review the concept of population density before beginning the activity.

⚠ **Infer** Make sure students understand that one piece of information, the total number of flamingos, is changing, while the other piece of information, the size of the pond, is not.

Lab Resource: Quick Lab

L2 **GROWING AND SHRINKING** Students will explore the use of graphs to show changes in a population.

Evaluate

Assess Your Understanding

After students answer the questions, have them evaluate their understanding by completing the appropriate sentence.

RTI Response to Intervention

1a. If students have trouble identifying the ways populations change, **then** have them review information on births, deaths, immigration, and emigration.

b. If students need help with calculating changes in populations, **then** suggest that they write the problem as two equations, one for the births and a second one for the deaths.

MY SCIENCE **COACH** Have students go online for help in understanding how populations change.

Population Density Sometimes an ecologist needs to know more than just the total size of a population. In many situations, it is helpful to know the **population density**—the number of individuals in an area of a specific size. Population density can be written as an equation:

$$\text{Population density} = \frac{\text{Number of individuals}}{\text{Unit area}}$$

For example, suppose you counted 20 butterflies in a garden measuring 10 square meters. The population density would be 20 butterflies per 10 square meters, or 2 butterflies per square meter.

apply it!

In the pond on the top, there are 10 flamingos in 8 square meters. The population density is 1.25 flamingos per square meter.

❶ **Calculate** What is the population density of the flamingos in the pond on the bottom?

About 2.5 flamingos/m²

❷ **Infer** If 14 more flamingos landed in the pond on the bottom, what would the population density be then?

4.25 flamingos/m²

❸ **CHALLENGE** What do you think would happen if the population density of flamingos in the pond on the bottom became too great?

Sample: There would not be enough
food or space for all of the flamingos
to survive.

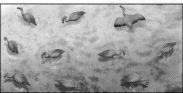

← 2 meters →
← 4 meters →
← 2 meters →

Lab Do the Quick Lab
Growing and Shrinking.

🔑 Assess Your Understanding

1a. Review Two ways to join a population are _birth_ and _immigration_.
Two ways to leave a population are _death_ and _emigration_.

b. Calculate Suppose a population of 8 wolves has produced 20 young in a year. If 7 wolves have died, how many wolves are in the population now? (Assume no wolves have moved into or out of the population for other reasons.)

_21_

got it? ....

○ **I get it!** Now I know that population size changes due to _birth and immigration and_ _death and emigration._

○ **I need extra help with** _See TE note._

Go to **MY SCIENCE** **COACH** online for help with this subject.

Digital Lesson: Assign the *Apply It* activity online and have students submit their work to you.

MY SCIENCE online.com | **Population Size**

What Factors Limit Population Growth?

When the living conditions in an area are good, a population will generally grow. But eventually some environmental factor will cause the population to stop growing. A **limiting factor** is an environmental factor that causes a population to stop growing or decrease in size. 🔑 **Some limiting factors for populations are weather conditions, space, food, and water.**

Climate Changes in climate conditions, such as temperature and the amount of rainfall, can limit population growth. A cold spring season can kill the young of many species of organisms, including birds and mammals. Unusual events like floods, hurricanes, and the tornado shown in **Figure 3**, can also have long-lasting effects on population size.

FIGURE 3 ·······················

Weather as a Limiting Factor
A tornado or flood can destroy nests and burrows.

✎ **Identify** Name two types of natural disasters that you think can also limit population growth.

<u>Sample: Volcanic eruptions</u>
<u>and droughts</u>

Tornado funnel
touching ground

✎ **Relate Cause and Effect** As you read about the four factors that can limit populations, fill in the graphic organizer below.

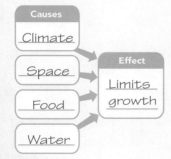

Causes
- Climate
- Space
- Food
- Water

Effect
- Limits growth

Explain ──────────────

Teach Key Concepts 🔑

Explain to students that limiting factors are factors that influence a population and affect its size. Ask: **What are some limiting factors for populations?** *(Weather conditions, space, food, and water.)* Explain to students that frost occurs when solid surfaces cool to below a point at which water vapor in the surrounding air will condense. Ask students if they have ever seen dew. Point out to them that frost can be considered frozen dew. Ask: **How might an unusually severe frost affect populations?** *(It might be too cold for some animals to stay warm enough to survive. The frost might kill some plants.)* Point out that limiting factors are different for different species. For example, a rain-forest plant requires much more water than a cactus does. A trout requires higher oxygen levels in a stream than a catfish does. For some microorganisms, oxygen is not a limiting factor at all because the organisms do not need oxygen to survive.

↻ **Relate Cause and Effect** Explain that cause-and-effect relationships shows how ideas, facts, and events are related to one another.

Support the Big Q ❓ UbD

LIMITING FACTORS OF POPULATIONS Review with students the biotic and abiotic factors that might be found in an organism's habitat. Ask: **If all the needs of a population are met, what is likely to happen to the population?** *(It will increase.)* **Can a population continue to increase indefinitely? Explain.** *(No. Eventually it will run out of something it needs.)* **Is food a limiting factor for plants? Explain.** *(No. Plants make their own food.)* **What factors do limit the size of a plant population?** *(The amount of sunlight, the amount of carbon dioxide in the air, the amount of water available, the amounts of nutrients in the soil)*

Differentiated Instruction

L1 Practice Calculations For students who need extra help with the *Apply It* activity, help them understand that the calculations involve two steps. First, they need to calculate the area of the pond. Then they can calculate the population density. Use this example: a lawn has 144 dandelions in an area that is 12 m long and 6 m wide. The area of the lawn is 72 m². Dividing 144 by 72 produces an answer of 2 dandelions/m². You may wish to allow students to use calculators.

L1 Population Density Before students go on to read about factors that limit population growth, make sure that they understand the concept of population density. Draw two circles of the same size on the board. Draw a few small triangles in one circle and about twice as many in the other circle. Ask students to identify the circle that has the greater population density of triangles and to explain their thinking.

Elaborate

21st Century Learning

CRITICAL THINKING Explain to students that being able to compete successfully for space is important to plants because they cannot move to a new place if their habitat becomes crowded. The roots of the sorghum plant produce a chemical that suppresses the growth of other species of plants. This chemical is called sorgolene. Ask: **How might sorgolene be useful for gardeners?** *(It might be used as a weed killer.)*

Make Analogies

L1 CARRYING CAPACITY To help students understand the concept of carrying capacity, compare an ecosystem to a container, such as a storage case for CDs. Ask: **What limits the number of CDs that you can keep in a storage case?** *(The size of the case)* **What would happen if you tried to put extra CDs into the storage case?** *(Some of the CDs might break.)* **How is this like a limiting factor that determines the carrying capacity of an ecosystem?** *(Space is a limiting factor that determines how many individuals can survive in an ecosystem. If there are too many individuals in an ecosystem, some of them will not survive.)*

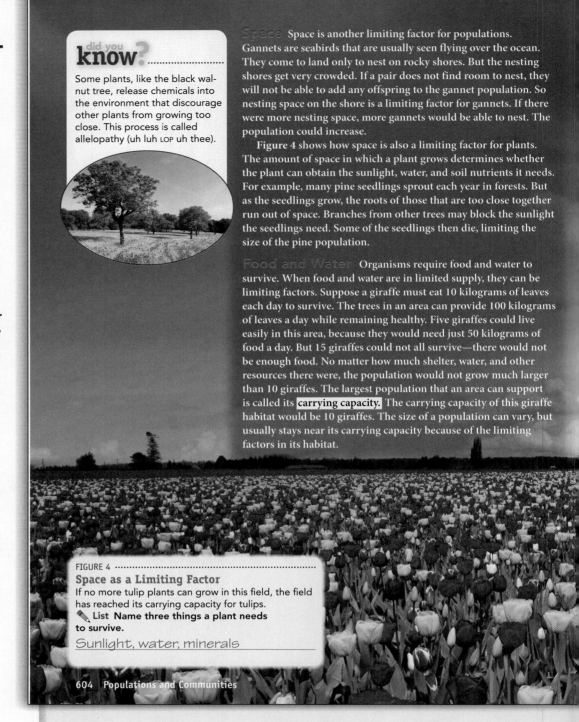

did you know?

Some plants, like the black walnut tree, release chemicals into the environment that discourage other plants from growing too close. This process is called allelopathy (uh luh LOP uh thee).

Space Space is another limiting factor for populations. Gannets are seabirds that are usually seen flying over the ocean. They come to land only to nest on rocky shores. But the nesting shores get very crowded. If a pair does not find room to nest, they will not be able to add any offspring to the gannet population. So nesting space on the shore is a limiting factor for gannets. If there were more nesting space, more gannets would be able to nest. The population could increase.

Figure 4 shows how space is also a limiting factor for plants. The amount of space in which a plant grows determines whether the plant can obtain the sunlight, water, and soil nutrients it needs. For example, many pine seedlings sprout each year in forests. But as the seedlings grow, the roots of those that are too close together run out of space. Branches from other trees may block the sunlight the seedlings need. Some of the seedlings then die, limiting the size of the pine population.

Food and Water Organisms require food and water to survive. When food and water are in limited supply, they can be limiting factors. Suppose a giraffe must eat 10 kilograms of leaves each day to survive. The trees in an area can provide 100 kilograms of leaves a day while remaining healthy. Five giraffes could live easily in this area, because they would need just 50 kilograms of food a day. But 15 giraffes could not all survive—there would not be enough food. No matter how much shelter, water, and other resources there were, the population would not grow much larger than 10 giraffes. The largest population that an area can support is called its carrying capacity. The carrying capacity of this giraffe habitat would be 10 giraffes. The size of a population can vary, but usually stays near its carrying capacity because of the limiting factors in its habitat.

FIGURE 4

Space as a Limiting Factor
If no more tulip plants can grow in this field, the field has reached its carrying capacity for tulips.
✎ **List** Name three things a plant needs to survive.

Sunlight, water, minerals

604 Populations and Communities

Digital Lesson: Assign the *Apply It* activity online and have students submit their work to you.

MY SCIENCE online.com ⟩ **Limiting Factors**

apply it!

Giant pandas live in the mountains of south central China. Most (99 percent) of the pandas' diet is made up of the bamboo plant. Bamboo is not nutrient rich. Pandas spend 55 percent of their day eating between 9 and 38 kilograms of bamboo. Getting enough bamboo to eat can be a challenge. Farming and the timber industry have destroyed the pandas' habitat and bamboo forests. In addition, when a bamboo plant flowers, the plant dies and does not regrow for several years. It is difficult for scientists to know exactly how many giant pandas exist in the wild. The best estimate is that there are about 1,600 of them. Due to the small population size, this species is classified as endangered.

✎ **Communicate** Write a letter to the editor that describes how food and space may be limiting factors for the giant panda species. Add a headline to your letter.

Sample headline: Pandas in Peril!
Sample: Dear Editor, I am concerned that pandas are endangered due to a lack of space and food. Pandas depend on bamboo to survive. When the bamboo plants die off or are destroyed, there may not be enough food to feed many pandas. Habitat destruction has also limited the space the pandas have to reproduce. If the pandas cannot reproduce, then there is no hope of increasing the panda population.

 Do the Quick Lab
Elbow Room.

Assess Your Understanding

2a. Summarize When the climate changes or there is not enough 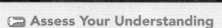space or food or water, a population can (begin/**stop**) growing in size.

b. Relate Cause and Effect Choose a limiting factor and describe the factor's effect on population growth.
Sample: When there is not enough food, some organisms may die.

got it?

○ I get it! Now I know that populations can be limited when there is climate change, not enough space, or not enough food and water.

○ I need extra help with See TE note.

Go to MY SCIENCE ⬥ COACH *online for help with this subject.*

605

Elaborate

Apply It!

[L1] Remind students that an effective letter begins with a topic statement that indicates the writer's main concern before beginning the activity.

Lab Resource: Quick Lab 🔬

[L1] **ELBOW ROOM** Students will explore space as a limiting factor.

Evaluate

Assess Your Understanding

After students answer the questions, have them evaluate their understanding by completing the appropriate sentence.

RTI Response to Intervention

2a. If students have trouble identifying limiting factors, **then** have them think about the things an organism needs to survive.

b. If students need help with relating limiting factors to population growth, **then** have them choose a factor and ask themselves what would happen to the population if there were too little of that factor.

MY SCIENCE ⬥ COACH Have students go online for help in understanding the factors that limit population growth.

Differentiated Instruction

[L3] **Space for Plants** Have interested students look at garden catalogs or gardening books to find instructions for spacing plants in a garden. Explain to students that each plant must have adequate room to grow. Provide students with graph paper to plan the proper spacing of plants in a garden.

[L1] **Classroom Density** If your classroom has movable desks and chairs, seat one student alone at a desk or table. Then seat a second student at the same desk or table. Seat a third, then a fourth, then a fifth. Each time you add a student, ask the seated students to try to write in their notebooks. Students should see that, as more people sit at a table, the workspace becomes more crowded until nobody has enough space to work. Based on their experience, students should estimate the carrying capacity of a desk or table.

Name ______________________ Date __________ Class __________

Lab zone® After the Inquiry Warm-Up

Populations

Inquiry Warm-Up, *Populations*

In the Inquiry Warm-Up, you investigated the process of estimation. Using what you learned from that activity, answer the questions below.

1. **ESTIMATE** What method did you use to estimate the size of the population?

____

____

2. **EVALUATE** What are possible sources of inaccuracy or error in your method?

____

____

3. **INTERPRET DATA** What must be true of the beans if an estimate is to give reasonable results?

____

____

4. **PREDICT** How do you think a scientist might estimate the size of a population of trees?

____

____

____

____

Place the outside corner, the corner away from the dotted line, in the corner of your copy machine to copy onto letter-size paper.

Assess Your Understanding

Populations

How Do Populations Change in Size?

1a. **REVIEW** Two ways to join a population are _____

and _____. Two ways to leave a population are

_____ and _____.

b. **CALCULATE** Suppose a population of 8 wolves has produced 20 young
in a year. If 7 wolves have died, how many wolves are in the population now? (Assume no wolves have moved into or out of the population for other reasons.)

_____

got it? ··

○ **I get it!** Now I know that population size changes due to _____

_____

○ **I need extra help with** _____

_____

What Factors Limit Population Growth?

2a. **SUMMARIZE** When the climate changes or there is not

enough _____ or _____ or

_____, a population can (begin/stop) growing in size.

b. **RELATE CAUSE AND EFFECT** Choose a limiting factor and describe the
factor's effect on population growth.

got it? ··

○ **I get it!** Now I know that populations can be limited when _____

_____

_____

○ **I need extra help with** _____

_____

_____

Populations

How do Populations Change in Size?

Populations change in size when new members are born into it or when members die. The **birth rate** counts number of births in a population over a certain amount of time. The **death rate** counts the number of deaths over a certain amount of time.

When the birth rate is greater than the death rate, the population will generally increase. The population will generally decrease when the death rate is greater than the birth rate. For example, the white-tailed deer population in Iowa decreased due to over-hunting.

The population can also change when individuals move into or out of the population. **Immigration** means moving into a population and **emigration** means leaving a population. Ecologists can graph how a population changes over time. The **population density** is a measure of all of the individuals in one area at one time.

What Factors Limit Population Growth?

A **limiting factor** is something in the environment that keeps a population from growing or makes a population smaller. Some limiting factors are weather conditions, space, food, and water.

Climate changes and unusual weather events, such as tornados, can limit population growth. The amount of available space can limit population growth.

For example, a plant needs to grow in a large enough space to obtain the things it needs to survive. Food and water are also often limiting factors because they are in limited supply.

Limiting factors determine an area's carrying capacity. **Carrying capacity** is the largest population that an area can support.

On a separate sheet of paper, explain two ways a population increases and two ways it decreases.

Populations

Understanding Main Ideas
Answer the following questions on a separate sheet of paper.

1. A vegetable garden is 12 meters long by 7 meters wide. It is home to 168 mice. What is the population density of the mice?
2. What are two ways that the size of a population can increase? What are two ways that the size of a population can decrease?
3. Identify three limiting factors that can prevent a population from increasing. Explain how each factor limits a population's size.

The line graph below shows how the size of the squirrel population in a city park changed over time. Use the line graph to answer questions 4–6.

4. Over which time period(s) did the squirrel population increase?
5. Over which time period(s) did the squirrel population decrease?
6. In which year did the population reach its lowest point? What was the size of the population that year?

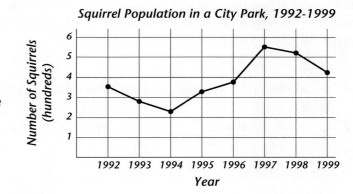

Squirrel Population in a City Park, 1992-1999

Building Vocabulary
Fill in the blank to complete each statement.

7. Moving into a population is called _____.
8. Moving out of a population is called _____.
9. The largest _____ an area can support is called the carrying capacity.
10. The number of individuals that die in a population in a certain time period is the _____.

Enrich

Populations

> Read the passage below. Then complete the table and answer the questions that follow the passage.

Population Growth

Suppose that the organisms in a population have unlimited food, water, space, and other resources. Also suppose that the organisms are not killed by other organisms or by disease. With no limits on its growth, the population would increase at its highest possible rate.

Bacteria are microscopic, single-celled organisms that are often used to study population growth. Most bacteria reproduce by splitting in half. Under ideal conditions, bacteria can divide about every 30 minutes. In the first half hour, one bacterium produces two bacteria. In the second half hour, the two bacteria split to produce four bacteria. In the third half hour, the four bacteria split to produce eight bacteria. Every 30 minutes, the population doubles!

Time (hours)	Number of Bacteria
0	1
0.5	2
1.0	4
1.5	8
2.0	
2.5	
3.0	
3.5	
4.0	
4.5	
5.0	
5.5	
6.0	
7.5	
8.0	
8.5	
9.0	
9.5	
10.0	

1. On a sheet of graph paper, graph the data in your completed table.

2. Describe the shape of the graph, and explain what it shows about the bacteria population.

   _____

   _____

3. Does the graph show what usually happens in real life? Why or why not?

   _____

   _____

   _____

Lesson Quiz

Populations

If the statement is true, write *true*. If the statement is false, change the underlined word or words to make the statement true.

1. _____ The size of a population increases if the number of individuals added to the population is <u>equal to</u> the number of individuals leaving the population.

2. _____ Immigration means moving <u>out of</u> a population.

3. _____ Three coyotes per square kilometer is an example of <u>population density</u>.

4. _____ If foxes arrive in an area and catch and eat a large number of rabbits, the foxes are causing an increase in the <u>birth rate</u> of the rabbit population.

5. _____ Sunlight can be a limiting factor for populations of <u>plants</u>.

Fill in the blank to complete each statement.

6. Water and food are examples of _____ for populations.

7. If an area has all the wolves that it can support, the wolf population has reached its _____.

8. A population can decrease due to deaths or _____.

9. If animals cannot find enough places to build nests, it is because _____ is a limiting factor for the population.

10. A flood that covers and meadow and drowns animals and a late frost that kills young plants are examples of how _____ can affect the size of a population.

Populations

Answer Key

After the Inquiry Warm-Up

1. Answers may vary. Sample: I filled a small beaker with beans and counted the beans. Then I transferred the beans from one jar to the other, one beaker at a time. I kept track of the number of beakers of beans and multiplied that by the number of beans in one beaker.

2. Answers may vary. Sample: I may not have filled the beaker to the same height each time. I may have jostled the beaker, causing the beans to settle, giving an inaccurate measure on the transfers.

3. The beans must all be the same size.

4. Answers may vary. Sample: The scientist could count all the trees in a small measured area, such as 100 square meters, then measure the entire area. Multiple the entire area by the number of trees/100 square meters.

Key Concept Summaries

A population increases when new organisms are born. Immigration, the moving of organisms into a population, also increases the population. Deaths decrease population. Emigration, the moving of organisms away from a population, decreases the population.

Review and Reinforce

1. 168 mice/(12 m × 7 m) = 2 mice per square meter

2. A population can increase due to births or immigration. A population can decrease due to deaths or emigration.

3. Food: If food is limited, the population will not increase beyond the number that the food supply can support. Space: Without enough space, organisms may not be able to reproduce or ay not get enough of the things that they need to survive, such as water, sunlight, and nutrients. Weather: Both normal seasonal changes in temperature or rainfall and severe weather conditions can kill many members of a population.

4. 1994–1997

5. 1992–1994 and 1997–1999

6. 1994; about 225 squirrels

7. immigration

8. population

9. emigration

10. death rate

Enrich

After 10 hours, there will be 262,144 bacteria.

1. The graph should show time (0 to 10 hours) on the x-axis and number of bacteria (in thousands, from 0 to 1,000) on the y-axis. The curve is nearly flat until 7 hours, when it begins to climb. Steepest slope is between 9 and 10 hours.

2. The curve goes up at a steep angle at the end, showing that the population is increasing rapidly.

3. The graph does not show what usually happens because limiting factors, such as lack of space or food, usually prevent such rapid growth of a population.

Lesson Quiz

1. greater than

2. into

3. true

4. death rate

5. true

6. limiting factors

7. carrying capacity

8. emigration

9. space

10. weather

Place the outside corner, the corner away from the dotted line, in the corner of your copy machine to copy onto letter-size paper.

Teacher Notes

Interactions Among Living Things

How do living things affect each other?

Lesson Pacing: 2–3 periods or 1–1½ blocks

🕐 **SHORT ON TIME?** To do this lesson in approximately half the time, do the Activate Prior Knowledge activity followed by a discussion of the Key Concepts to familiarize students with the lesson content. Have students do the Quick Labs. The rest of the lesson can be completed by students independently.

Preference Navigator, in the online Planning tools, allows you to customize *Interactive Science* to your own teaching style. You can also edit lesson plans by selecting the Lesson Planner option.

Digital Teacher's Edition allows you to access your *Teacher's Edition and Resource* materials online.

my science online.com

Lesson Vocabulary

- natural selection
- adaptation
- niche
- competition
- predation
- predator
- prey
- symbiosis
- mutalism
- commensalism
- parasitism
- parasite
- host

Content Refresher

Professional Development Note

Wolf and Moose Populations When a population grows beyond the carrying capacity of its habitat, a population crash may occur. Moose came to Isle Royale around 1900, by swimming from the mainland. By 1935 the moose population increased to about 3,000, due to a lack of predators. As a result, the supply of food became exhausted, and 90% of the moose starved. After this crash, the moose population increased again until 1948 and then declined sharply once more because of lack of food. Wolves arrived around 1950, and the moose and wolf populations have cycled up and down since then. In the early 1980s, the Isle Royale wolf population declined sharply. Biologists hypothesize that extreme genetic uniformity is one reason for the decline. Populations that lack genetic variability often have low reproductive success and are susceptible to disease.

LESSON OBJECTIVES

- 🔑 Explain how adaptations help an organism survive.
- 🔑 Describe competition and predation.
- 🔑 Identify the three types of symbiosis.

Blended Path
Active learning using Student Edition, Inquiry Path, and Digital Path

ENGAGE AND EXPLORE

To teach this lesson using a variety of resources, begin by reading **My Planet Diary** as a class. Have students share ideas about predators such as trap-jaw ants. Then have students do the **Inquiry Warm-Up activity.** Students will learn how coloring can help camouflage an animal. The **After the Inquiry Warm-Up worksheet** sets up a discussion about successful and unsuccessful camouflaging. Have volunteers share their answers to number 4 about how the results of the lab might differ with real butterflies.

EXPLAIN AND ELABORATE

Teach Key Concepts by explaining that are the behaviors and physical characteristics that allow organisms to live successfully in their environments. **Lead a Discussion** about natural selection based on **Figure 1.** Then have students do the **Apply It activity.**

Continue to **Teach Key Concepts** by explaining the two major types of interaction among organisms. Ask students to name them and tell how they differ. Use the **Support the Big Q** to illustrate how limited resources affect competition. Use **Figure 2** to illustrate how three bird species have adaptations that allow them to feed from different parts of the same tree. Use **Figures 3** and **4** to help students visualize predators and prey and predator adaptations in animals and plants.

Hand out the **Key Concept Summaries** as a review of each part of the lesson. Students can also use the online **Vocab Flash Cards** to review key terms.

EVALUATE

Have students take the **Lesson Quiz.** For an alternate assessment, see the **EXAM**VIEW® Assessment Suite, Progress Monitoring Assessments, or SuccessTracker™.

ⒺⓁⓁ Support

1 Content and Language

Introduce the term camouflage. Students may be familiar with the term because of clothing or family in the military. Explain that this is also an adaptation that helps an organism survive in a habitat.

DIFFERENTIATED INSTRUCTION KEY
L1 Struggling Students or Special Needs
L2 On-Level Students **L3** Advanced Students

LESSON PLANNER 15.3

 **Inquiry Path** Hands-on learning in the Lab zone

ENGAGE AND EXPLORE

To teach this lesson with an emphasis on inquiry, begin with the **Inquiry Warm-Up activity.** Students will learn how coloring can help camouflage an animal. Discuss the coloring different students have observed and how the coloring helped hide an organism. Have students do the **After the Inquiry Warm-Up worksheet.** Talk about camouflaging efforts. Have volunteers share their answers to number 4 about how real butterflies differ from the lab results.

EXPLAIN AND ELABORATE

Focus on the **Inquiry Skill** for the lesson. Point out that when you classify, you assign something to a category. How could you classify the butterflies in the **Inquiry Warm-Up activity?** *(Those that were hidden, those that were not)* Have students do the **Quick Lab.** Review the meanings of *niche* and *adaptations* before assigning the **Apply It activity.** Ask volunteers to share their answers.

Continue to **Teach Key Concepts.** Use the **Support the Big Q** to illustrate how limited resources affect competition. Use **Build Inquiry** to introduce students to a plant that is a predator to an animal, a fairly unusual occurrence and **Figure 5 Interactive Art** to rate prey adaptation.

Do the **Quick Lab** to reinforce understanding of competition and predation. Continue to **Teach Key Concepts** by explaining the three types of symbiosis. Use **Figure 6** to explore mutalism with students and **Figure 7** to explore parasitism. **Lead a Discussion** about parasites students may be familiar with. Review the inquiry skill before assigning the **Apply It activity.** Have students complete the **Quick Lab** to identify types of symbiosis. Students can use the online **Vocab Flash Cards** to review key terms.

EVALUATE

Have students take the **Lesson Quiz.** For an alternate assessment, see the **EXAM**VIEW® Assessment Suite, Progress Monitoring Assessments, or SuccessTracker™.

Digital Path Online learning at my science online.com

ENGAGE AND EXPLORE

To teach this lesson using digital resources, begin by having students explore predators, such as trap-jaw ants, at **My Planet Diary** online. Have them access the Chapter Resources to find the **Unlock the Big Question activity.** There they can answer the questions and refine their responses as they continue through the lesson. You can re-assign the activity and have students submit their work so you can track their progress.

EXPLAIN AND ELABORATE

Students reading above, at, or below the lexile measure of this lesson can access basic content readings at their level at **My Reading Web.** Encourage students to use the online **Vocab Flash Cards** to preview key terms. Review *niche* and *adaptation* before assigning the online **Apply It activity.** Ask volunteers to share their sample answers and have them submit their work to you.

Continue to **Teach Key Concepts** by discussing the two interactions: competition and predation. Have students **Support the Big Q** by noting that there are limited resources in an ecosystem.

The **Key Concept Summaries** online allow students to read a summary and see an image associated with each part of the lesson. Online remediation is available at **My Science Coach.**

EVALUATE

Have students take the **Lesson Quiz.** For an alternate assessment, see the **EXAM**VIEW® Assessment Suite, Progress Monitoring Assessments, or SuccessTracker™.

2 Frontload the Lesson
Preview the lesson questions that appear in blue heads. Ask students if there are any words they do not understand. Explain the specific meanings these words have in science.

3 Comprehensible Input
Have students help make a chart that briefly shows the differences in the three types of symbiosis.

4 Language Production
Pair or group students with varied language abilities to complete oral summaries collaboratively for language practice. Have each group share its summary with the class.

5 Assess Understanding
Have students keep a content area log for this lesson using a two-column format with the headings "What I Understand" and "What I Don't Understand." Follow up so that students can move items from the "Don't Understand" to the "Understand" column.

LESSON 15.3

Interactions Among Living Things

Establish Learning Objectives

After this lesson, students will be able to:

 Explain how adaptations help an organism survive.

 Describe competition and predation.

 Identify the three types of symbiosis.

Engage

Activate Prior Knowledge

MY PLANET DIARY Read *Predator Power* with the class. Point out that the ants use their jaws either to capture prey or propel themselves. Tell students that large numbers of trap-jaw ants have been observed jumping up and down when the nest is threatened. Ask: **How might this action help them protect the nest?** (*The sudden action might confuse an animal that was going to attack the nest.*)

BIG IDEAS OF SCIENCE REFERENCE LIBRARY Have students look up the following topics: Bush Baby, Butterflies, Camouflage, Patterns in Nature, Sharks, Vultures.

Explore

Lab Resource: Inquiry Warm-Up

L1 **CAN YOU HIDE A BUTTERFLY?** Students will explore how an organism's coloring can help it survive.

LESSON 3 Interactions Among Living Things

 How Do Adaptations Help an Organism Survive?

 What Are Competition and Predation?

 What Are the Three Types of Symbiosis?

MY PLANET DIARY

Predator Power

What predator can close its jaws the fastest? You might think it is a lion or a shark, but you would be wrong. It is the trap-jaw ant that has the fastest strike in the animal kingdom. The trap-jaw ant closes its mouth around its prey in 0.13 milliseconds at speeds of 35 to 64 meters per second! The force created when its jaw snaps shut also helps the ant escape danger by either jumping up to 8.3 centimeters high or 39.6 centimeters sideways.

A trap-jaw ant stalks its prey.

FUN FACT

Communicate Answer the questions below. Discuss your answers with a partner.

1. How does the trap-jaw ant's adaptation help it avoid becoming the prey of another organism?
   The ant can jump away from predators if they try to attack.

2. What are some adaptations that other predators have to capture prey?
   Sample: speed, sharp teeth and claws, good eyesight

> **PLANET DIARY** Go to **Planet Diary** to learn more about predators.

Lab Do the Inquiry Warm-Up *Can You Hide a Butterfly?*

How Do Adaptations Help an Organism Survive?

As day breaks, a sound comes from a nest tucked in the branch of a saguaro cactus. Two young red-tailed hawks are preparing to fly. Farther down the stem, a tiny elf owl peeks out of its nest in a small hole. A rattlesnake slithers around the base of the saguaro, looking for breakfast. Spying a shrew, the snake strikes it with needle-like fangs. The shrew dies instantly.

606 Populations and Communities

SUPPORT ALL READERS
Lexile Measure = 950L   Lexile Word Count = 1982

Prior Exposure to Content: Many students may have misconceptions on this topic

Academic Vocabulary: *classify, interpret, resources*

Science Vocabulary: *natural selection, adaptation, competition*

Concept Level: May be difficult for students who struggle with abstract ideas

Preteach With: My Planet Diary "Predator Power" and Figure 1 activity

Go to **My Reading Web** to access leveled readings that provide a foundation for the content.

my science online.com

Vocabulary
- natural selection • adaptation • niche • competition
- predation • predator • prey • symbiosis • mutualism
- commensalism • parasitism • parasite • host

Skills
⟳ Reading: Relate Text and Visuals
△ Inquiry: Classify

Figure 1 shows some organisms that live in, on, and around the saguaro cactus. Each organism has unique characteristics. These characteristics affect the individual's ability to survive and reproduce in its environment.

Natural Selection A characteristic that makes an individual better suited to a specific environment may eventually become common in that species through a process called **natural selection.** Natural selection works like this: Individuals whose unique characteristics are well-suited for an environment tend to survive and produce more offspring. Offspring that inherit these characteristics also live to reproduce. In this way, natural selection results in **adaptations,** the behaviors and physical characteristics that allow organisms to live successfully in their environments. For example, the arctic hare has fur that turns from gray to white in the winter which helps camouflage the hare against the snow.

Individuals with characteristics poorly suited to a particular environment are less likely to survive and reproduce. Over time, poorly suited characteristics may disappear from the species. If a species cannot adapt to changes in its environment, the entire species can disappear from Earth and become extinct.

FIGURE 1 ·······················
Saguaro Community
✎ Describe Circle two examples of how organisms interact in this scene. Describe each one.

<u>Sample: The wasps have built a hive under a branch of the cactus. The red-tailed hawk has built a nest between branches of the cactus.</u>

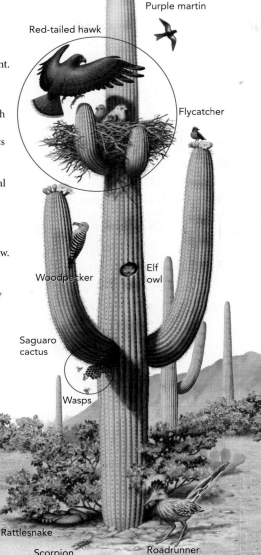

Purple martin
Red-tailed hawk
Flycatcher
Woodpecker
Elf owl
Saguaro cactus
Wasps
Gila monster
Rattlesnake
Scorpion
Roadrunner

607

Explain
Introduce Vocabulary
Students may be surprised to see the word *host* as a vocabulary term. Point out that in common use, a host welcomes guests. In parasitism, the "guest" is not welcome.

Lead a Discussion
NATURAL SELECTION Review the process of natural selection. Make sure that students understand that individuals in a population may vary in many ways. Have students locate the roadrunner shown in **Figure 1.** Tell them that this bird eats other animals, such as scorpions, snakes, lizards, rodents, and birds. Ask: **What makes these animals difficult to catch?** *(They can move quickly.)* **How do the long legs of a roadrunner help it get food?** *(They help it run fast after other animals.)* **If a population of roadrunners had some birds that could run faster than others, which birds would be more likely to survive?** *(The ones that run faster)* **What would you expect the next generation of roadrunners to be like?** *(They would be fast runners.)*

Address Misconceptions
L1 CHANGES WITHIN SPECIES Remind students that an organism does not change its traits to fit the environment. Describe a population of mice that have either gray or brown fur. Brown mice are more common because they escape predators more successfully. Then new predators that hunt by sound move in. Ask: **What traits might now determine how easily a mouse is caught?** *(How quietly or how quickly a mouse moves)* **Will any mice develop these traits because of the predators?** *(No.)* **How might the population of mice change?** *(The mice that make the most noise will likely be caught and eaten. The mice that are quiet will likely survive and produce offspring that are quiet.)*

My Planet Diary provides an opportunity for students to explore real-world connections to adaptations.

1 Content and Language
Have students read the caption for **Figure 6.** If students are confused by the use of the word *cruise*, explain to them that the use of *cruise* is that the bird gets a ride on the impala. The word *snack* in the caption means that the bird gets its food.

2 Frontload the Lesson
Use **Figure 1** to help students understand adaptations. Point to an organism and ask how that organism lives. Ask what body parts it has that enable it to do these tasks, and how they help the organism survive.

3 Comprehensible Input
Have each student make a two-column chart. Tell them to choose an organism from **Figure 1.** In the first column of the chart they should list the organism's adaptations. In the second column they should tell how each adaptation helps the organism survive.

LESSON 15.3

Explain

Teach Key Concepts

Explain to students that each organism has adaptations that help it occupy a particular niche. Ask: **What are adaptations?** *(Behaviors and physical characteristics that allow organisms to live successfully in their environments)* **How does natural selection result in adaptations being common in a population?** *(Individuals that have an adaptation are more likely to survive and reproduce. They pass the adaptation on to their offspring. Individuals that lack the adaptation are less likely to survive and reproduce, so the next generation will have fewer individuals that lack the adaptation.)*

Elaborate

Apply It!

L1 Review *biotic* and *abiotic* factors with students before beginning the activity.

Lab Resource: Quick Lab

L2 **ADAPTATIONS FOR SURVIVAL** Students will model a variety of adaptations for feeding.

Evaluate

Assess Your Understanding

After students answer the questions, have them evaluate their understanding by completing the appropriate sentence.

RTI Response to Intervention

1a. If students cannot define *adaptation,* **then** have them look back through the section for the highlighted term and reread the definition.

b. If students have trouble listing examples of adaptations, **then** have them look back at **Figure 1** and think about how a snake uses its fangs.

MY SCIENCE COACH Have students go online for help in understanding adaptations.

Niche The organisms in the saguaro community have adaptations that result in specific roles. The role of an organism in its habitat is called its **niche.** A niche includes what type of food the organism eats, how it obtains this food, and what other organisms eat it. A niche also includes when and how the organism reproduces and the physical conditions it requires to survive. Some organisms, like the birds in **Figure 2,** share the same habitat but have very specific niches that allow them to live together. **Every organism has a variety of adaptations that are suited to its specific living conditions and help it survive.**

apply it!

Organisms occupy many niches in an environment like the one in this picture.

❶ **Identify** List two abiotic factors in the picture.
<u>Sample: Sunlight and water</u>

❷ **Interpret Diagrams** Describe the niche of the squirrel in the picture.
<u>Sample: The squirrel eats nuts</u>
<u>and seeds in the daytime.</u>

❸ **Make Generalizations** What adaptations might the squirrel have that make it able to live in this environment?
<u>Sample: A squirrel has sharp</u>
<u>teeth to open seeds and nuts.</u>

Lab zone Do the Quick Lab *Adaptations for Survival.*

Assess Your Understanding

1a. Define Adaptations are the <u>behaviors</u> and <u>physical</u> characteristics that allow organisms to live successfully in their environments.

b. Explain How are a snake's sharp fangs an adaptation that help it survive in the saguaro community?
<u>The sharp fangs help the snake</u>
<u>bite and poison its prey.</u>

got it?

○ **I get it!** Now I know that adaptations are <u>characteristics that suit an organism</u> <u>for specific environments and help it survive.</u>

○ I need extra help with <u>See TE note.</u>

Go to **MY SCIENCE COACH** online for help with this subject.

Digital Lesson: Assign the *Apply It* activity online and have students submit their work to you.

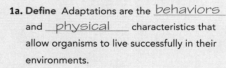 **Adaptation and Niche**

What Are Competition and Predation?

During a typical day in the saguaro community, a range of inter-actions takes place among organisms. 🔑 **Two major types of interactions among organisms are competition and predation.**

Competition Different species can share the same habitat and food requirements. For example, the flycatcher and the elf owl both live on the saguaro and eat insects. However, these two species do not occupy exactly the same niche. The flycatcher is active during the day, while the owl is active mostly at night. If two species occupy the same niche, one of the species might eventually die off. The reason for this is **competition.** The struggle between organisms to survive as they attempt to use the same limited resources is called competition. For example, weeds in a garden compete with vegetable crops for soil nutrients, water, and sunlight.

In any ecosystem, there are limited amounts of food, water, and shelter. Organisms that share the same habitat often have adaptations that enable them to reduce competition. For example, the three species of warblers in **Figure 2** specialize in feeding only in a certain part of the spruce tree.

Cape May Warbler
This species feeds at the tips of branches near the top of the tree.

Bay-Breasted Warbler
This species feeds in the middle part of the tree.

Yellow-Rumped Warbler
This species feeds in the lower part of the tree and at the bases of the middle branches.

FIGURE 2 ....
Niche and Competition
✎ Each of these warbler species occupies a very specific location in its habitat. By feeding on insects in different areas of the tree, the birds avoid compet-ing for food and are able to live together.

1. **Predict** What could happen if these warbler species fed in the same location on the tree?
   One warbler would get more food and the other species might not survive.

2. **List** For what resources do the tree and the grass compete?
   Sunlight, water, minerals, space

609

Explain

Teach Key Concepts 🔑

Explain to students that organisms interact in one of two ways, competition or predation. Ask: **Why might two individuals compete with each other?** *(Possible answer: They might compete for food, shelter, or water.)* **Why might two organisms interact through predation?** *(One of the organisms is food for the other.)*

Support the Big Q ❓ UbD

LIMITED RESOURCES Remind students that in any ecosystem, there is a limited amount of some resources. Ask: **What happens when more than one species requires the same limited resources?** *(Competition)* **How does avoiding competition benefit species like the birds shown in Figure 2?** *(They don't waste energy chasing each other away from food as they would if they were competing for food.)*

Make Analogies

L1 NOT IN COMPETITION Point out to students that a niche is very specific. Although all three birds eat insects, the fact that they hunt in different places keeps them out of competition with each other. Ask: **How are people who work shifts at different times of day avoiding competition?** *(The person who wants to work at night is not competing for a job with the person who wants to work during the day.)* **How might organisms avoid competition by working different "shifts"?** *(Some organisms are active at night and sleep during the day, while other organisms are active during the day, and sleep at night. They do not feed at the same time.)*

LESSON 15.3

Differentiated Instruction

L1 Niche vs. Habitat Organisms are often said to "occupy a niche." This may lead students to think a niche is a place to live. Remind them that an organism's place to live is its habitat. The organism's niche is *how* it lives, not *where* it lives. It may help students remember the difference if they think of a niche as the organism's occupation, or job.

L1 Competition To help students better understand the concept of competition, use a Venn diagram to compare and contrast the scientific meaning of competition with the more general sports-related meaning. Help students understand that the winner of a competition is the person (or team) with the best skills and abilities.

Explain

Teach With Visuals

Tell students to look at **Figure 4.** Point out that with the touch of their toxic tentacles, some jellyfish can catch and kill fish. Ask: **How is the jellyfish like the sundew?** *(They both are predators.)*
How is predation by a jellyfish different from predation by a sundew? *(The jellyfish can swim, so it can interact with prey more easily. The sundew cannot move, so it has to wait for an insect to come to it.)*

Address Misconceptions

L1 TO PREY OR NOT TO PREY? Some students may think predation is only bad for the prey. Point out to them that predation can be used to control overgrown populations, as a method of pest reduction, or to keep the prey species healthy. Ask: **How can predation keep the prey species healthy?** *(By preferentially killing the weak/sick members, leaving stronger and healthier members alive to reproduce)*

FIGURE 3 ·····················
Predation
This tiger shark and this albatross are involved in a predator-prey interaction.

✎ **Interpret Photos**
Label the predator and the prey in the photo.

Prey

Predator

Predation In **Figure 3**, a tiger shark bursts through the water to seize an albatross in its powerful jaws. An interaction in which one organism kills another for food or nutrients is called **predation.** The organism that does the killing is the **predator.** The organism that is killed is the **prey.** Even though they do not kill their prey, organisms like cows and giraffes are also considered predators because they eat plants.

Predation can have a major effect on a prey population size. Recall that when the death rate exceeds the birth rate in a population, the population size can decrease. So, if there are too many predators in an area, the result is often a decrease in the size of the prey population. But a decrease in the number of prey results in less food for their predators. Without adequate food, the predator population can decline. Generally, populations of predators and their prey rise and fall in related cycles.

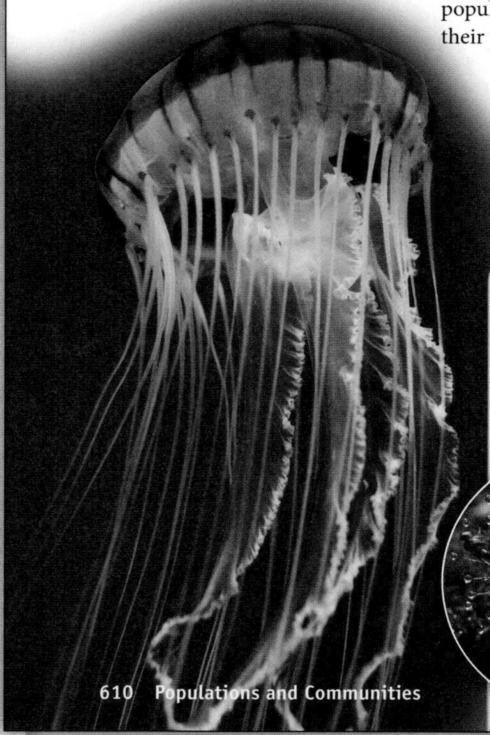

FIGURE 4 ·····················
Predator Adaptations
A jellyfish's tentacles contain a poisonous substance that paralyzes tiny water animals. The sundew is a plant that is covered with sticky bulbs on stalks. When a fly lands on a bulb, it remains snared in the sticky goo while the plant digests it.

✎ **Make Models** Imagine an ideal predator to prey upon a porcupine. Draw or describe your predator below and label its adaptations.

Sample: The predator would have long, sharp claws and thick fur to protect itself from the sharp porcupine quills.

610   Populations and Communities

Professional Development Note   **Teacher to Teacher**

Adaptations A common misconception students have when discussing adaptations is the belief that an individual organism *deliberately* chooses to change if its surrounding environment changes. To address this misconception I choose activities in which organisms become extinct. Placing black, white, and newspaper cutouts of moths on newspaper gives students a visual of how camouflage can affect an organism's ability to evade predators. Moving the cutouts to solid black or white paper shows students that, when a habitat changes, individual organisms are not able to choose at will to change their behaviors and structures.

✐ *Emily Compton*
Park Forest Middle School
Baton Rouge, LA

Predator Adaptations Predators, such as those in **Figure 4**, have adaptations that help them catch and kill their prey. A cheetah can run very fast for a short time, enabling it to catch its prey. Some predators, such as owls and bats, have adaptations that enable them to hunt at night when their prey, small mammals and insects, are active.

Prey Adaptations How do organisms avoid being killed by effective predators? The smelly spray of a skunk and the sharp quills of a porcupine help keep predators at a distance. As you can see in **Figure 5**, organisms have many kinds of adaptations that help them avoid becoming prey.

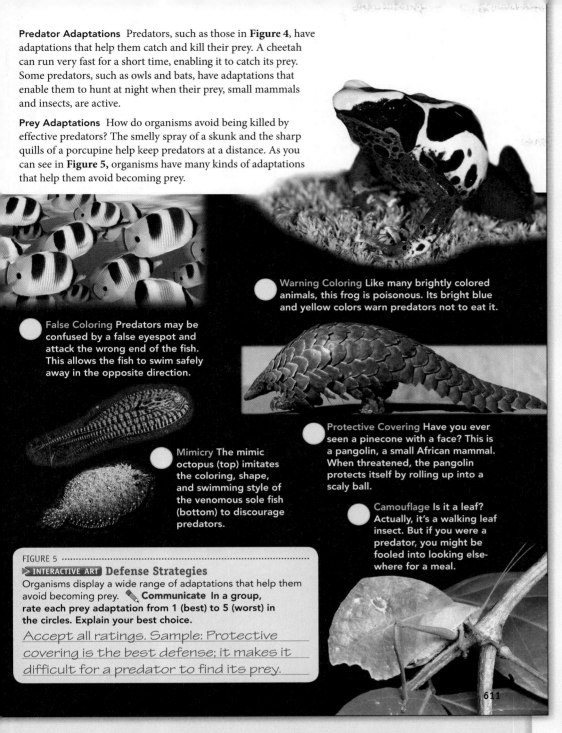

Warning Coloring Like many brightly colored animals, this frog is poisonous. Its bright blue and yellow colors warn predators not to eat it.

False Coloring Predators may be confused by a false eyespot and attack the wrong end of the fish. This allows the fish to swim safely away in the opposite direction.

Mimicry The mimic octopus (top) imitates the coloring, shape, and swimming style of the venomous sole fish (bottom) to discourage predators.

Protective Covering Have you ever seen a pinecone with a face? This is a pangolin, a small African mammal. When threatened, the pangolin protects itself by rolling up into a scaly ball.

Camouflage Is it a leaf? Actually, it's a walking leaf insect. But if you were a predator, you might be fooled into looking elsewhere for a meal.

FIGURE 5 ....

> **INTERACTIVE ART** Defense Strategies

Organisms display a wide range of adaptations that help them avoid becoming prey. ✎ **Communicate** In a group, rate each prey adaptation from 1 (best) to 5 (worst) in the circles. Explain your best choice.

Accept all ratings. Sample: Protective
covering is the best defense; it makes it
difficult for a predator to find its prey.

611

Elaborate

Build Inquiry

L2 OBSERVE AN INSECT-EATING PLANT

Materials sundew or Venus's fly-trap, cooked ground beef, tweezers

Time 5 minutes a day for several days

Have students take turns feeding the plant small pieces of the ground beef from time to time. Students should use the tweezers to place a small piece of meat on a trap. (**CAUTION:** _Remind students to wash their hands afterward._)

Ask: **What did you observe after you fed meat to the plant?** _(The leaves closed, trapping the meat inside.)_ **What did you notice when the leaves opened again?** _(The meat was gone.)_ **How does this adaptation enable carnivorous plants to live in areas of poor soil?** _(The plants get nutrients from the insects they consume.)_ Make sure that students understand that the plant is not getting energy from the food, as an animal would. It is only getting nutrients to help the plant make its own food.

Teach With Visuals

Tell students to look at **Figure 5**. Ask: **Which end of the brightly colored fish is the front?** _(Students may say it is the yellow end, but that is the false coloring. The pointed blue end is the front.)_ **What other animal do you know of that can roll up into a ball to protect itself?** _(Students may mention the armadillo or an isopod, also called a sow bug)_ **What are some other kinds of defensive adaptations of plants and animals?** _(Accept all reasonable answers. Possible answers: thorns on a rose bush, spines on a porcupine, the foul-smelling liquid a skunk sprays.)_

Interactive Art allows students to categorize images of different defense strategies.

my science online | Competition and Predation

Differentiated Instruction

L1 **Classify Roles** Give students examples of predator-prey pairs, such as lion-zebra, snake-mouse, and fox-rabbit. Ask students to identify the predator and prey in each pair and encourage them to use a graphic organizer of their choice to record the information.

L3 **Radar in Animals** Some predators have unusual adaptations that help them hunt. For example, bats use a form of radar called _echolocation_ to find flying insects. Invite students to research how bats are adapted for hunting as they fly in the dark.

Elaborate

Do the Math!

L1 Tell students that a line graph is a good way to show changes over time. Plotting two sets of data on one grid makes it easy to compare the data and identify trends. Have students look at high and low points of the wolf population. Ask: **What happens to the moose population in the few years following these points?** *(A spike in wolf population is followed by a decrease in moose population. A dip in wolf population is followed by an increase in moose population.)* **What is the lowest moose population recorded? What is the highest moose population recorded?** *(Lowest is about 400. Highest is about 2,400)* **What is the lowest wolf population recorded? What is the highest wolf population recorded?** *(Lowest is about 14. Highest is about 50.)* See *Math Skills and Problem-Solving Activities* for support.

Lab Resource: Quick Lab

L2 **COMPETITION AND PREDATION** Students will simulate competition for available food.

Evaluate

Assess Your Understanding

After students answer the questions, have them evaluate their understanding by completing the appropriate sentence.

RTI Response to Intervention

2a. If students have trouble with classifying interactions, **then** have them reread the Key Concept statement on the first page of this section.

b. If students cannot define *competition,* **then** have them scan for the highlighted term in the text and reread the definition.

c. If students need help with identifying adaptations, **then** have them look back at **Figure 5** and summarize the information.

MY SCIENCE COACH Have students go online for help in understanding competition and predation.

---

do the math!

Predator-Prey Interactions

On Isle Royale, an island in Lake Superior, the populations of wolves (the predator) and moose (the prey) rise and fall in cycles. Use the graph to answer the questions.

1 **Read Graphs** What variable is plotted on the horizontal axis? What two variables are plotted on the vertical axis?

Year; number of wolves and moose

2 **Interpret Data** How did the moose population change between 2002 and 2007? What happened to the wolf population from 2003 through 2006?

The moose population decreased; the wolf population increased.

3 **Draw Conclusions** How might the change in moose population have led to the change in the wolf population?

As the moose increased, more food was available to the wolf population, and it increased.

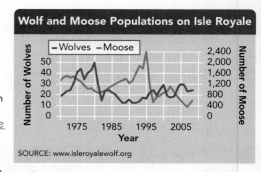

Wolf and Moose Populations on Isle Royale

SOURCE: www.isleroyalewolf.org

4 **Explain** What adaptations does a wolf have that make it a successful predator?

Sharp claws and teeth, good sense of smell and eyesight, speed

5 **Predict** How might disease in the wolf population one year affect the moose population the next year?

Disease would cause a decrease in the wolf population, so fewer moose would be eaten and the population would increase.

Lab zone Do the Quick Lab *Competition and Predation.*

🦴 Assess Your Understanding

2a. Review Two main ways in which organisms interact are ___*competition*___ and ___*predation*___.

b. Describe Give an example of competition. Explain your answer.

Sample: Weeds and crops compete for resources such as water.

c. Apply Concepts Owls often prey on mice. What adaptations do you think the mice have that help them avoid becoming prey?

Sample: The color of the mice provides camouflage, and their small size helps them hide.

got it?

○ I get it! Now I know that competition and predation *are two major types of interactions between organisms.*

○ I need extra help with *See TE note.*

Go to **MY SCIENCE COACH** *online for help with this subject.*

612 Populations and Communities

Digital Lesson: Assign the *Do the Math* activity online and have students submit their work to you.

MY SCIENCE online.com | **Competition and Predation**

What Are the Three Types of Symbiosis?

In addition to competition and predation, symbiosis is a third type of interaction among organisms. **Symbiosis** (sim bee OH sis) is any relationship in which two species live closely together and at least one of the species benefits. 🔑 **The three main types of symbiotic relationships are mutualism, commensalism, and parasitism.**

Mutualism In some relationships, two species may depend on one another. This is true for some species of acacia trees and stinging ants in South America. The stinging ants nest only in the acacia tree, whose thorns discourage the ants' predators. The tree also provides the ants' only food. The ants, in turn, attack other animals that approach the tree and clear competing plants away from the base of the tree. This relationship is an example of **mutualism** (MYOO choo uh liz um). A relationship in which both species benefit is called mutualism. Other examples of mutualism can be seen in **Figure 6.**

FIGURE 6 ·······················
Mutualism
✎ An oxpecker rides and snacks aboard an impala. The oxpecker eat ticks living on the impala's ears. This interaction is an example of mutualism because both organisms benefit.

1. Infer How does the oxpecker benefit?
The oxpecker gets food.

2. Infer How does the impala benefit?
The impala gets rid of ticks.

3. CHALLENGE Explain how the relationship between the hummingbird and the flower is an example of mutualism.
The hummingbird benefits by getting food, and the flower benefits by getting pollinated.

613

Explain ─────────────

Teach Key Concepts 🔑

Explain to students that symbiosis is a general term for relationships in which two species live closely together. There are three types of symbiosis, defined by which species benefits and which, if any, is harmed. Ask: **Which of the species in mutualism benefit?** *(Both)* **How many species benefit in commensalism?** *(One)* **What happens to the other species?** *(It is neither harmed nor helped.)* **Which of the species benefits in parasitism?** *(Parasite)* **Which of the species is harmed?** *(Host)*

Teach With Visuals

Tell students to look at **Figure 6.** Ask: **What kind of food does the hummingbird get from the flower?** *(Nectar)* Students are probably most aware of the role of bees as pollinators. Point out that some birds and bats are also important pollinators

Differentiated Instruction

L3 Predator-Prey Interactions
Another factor in the fluctuations of the moose population on Isle Royale is available food, especially in the winter. Have students research this limiting factor and how it affects the moose population. Students can report their findings to the rest of the class in a presentation.

L1 Types of Symbiosis To help students distinguish among the three different types of symbiosis, have them create a chart for each type that lists pairs of species as examples. Students should identify how each species either benefits or is harmed in the relationship. Encourage students to illustrate their charts with photographs or other images of the species used as examples.

Explain

Lead a Discussion

PARASITES Ask students to name some examples of parasites. *(Students may mention ticks, tapeworms, or leeches.)* Ask: **How does a tick harm its host?** *(The tick takes blood from the host. The host may get an infection at the site of the bite. Some ticks carry diseases, such as Lyme disease.)* **How does a tapeworm harm its host?** *(The tapeworm consumes some of the host's food, which can cause the host to become weak.)*

Teach With Visuals

Tell students to look at **Figure 7.** Ask: **How is the cowbird different from the other parasites shown in Figure 7?** *(The cowbird does not live in direct contact with the host.)* Point out to students that this kind of parasitism, called brood parasitism or nest parasitism, is unusual. Most parasites live in direct contact with the host.

Relate Text and Visuals Explain that the text and visuals each provide important information that the student must synthesize.

21st Century Learning

COMMUNICATION Help students infer the effect of ticks on a moose population. Tell students that the moose tick is a parasite that lives on the blood of the moose. A tick does not consume much blood, but a moose may have as many as 80,000 ticks feeding on it. Too many ticks can weaken the moose, making it vulnerable to wolves and also to diseases. Unusually warm summers in the years 2001 though 2005 favored large tick populations. Have students look back at the graph of wolf and moose populations in the *Do the Math* activity. Ask: **What, if any, effect did the large number of parasites have on the moose population?** *(They did affect the moose population. The moose population dropped steadily over those years, even though the wolf population was not unusually large.)*

Relate Text and Visuals List the names of the parasites and the hosts in **Figure 7**.

Parasites	Hosts
Cowbird	Yellow warblers
Fish lice	Fish
Dwarf mistletoe	Tree

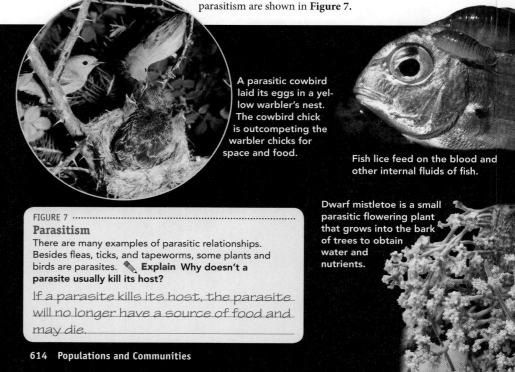

Commensalism Have you ever seen a bird build a nest in a tree? The bird gets a place to live while the tree is unharmed. This relationship is an example of commensalism. **Commensalism** (kuh MEN suh liz um) is a relationship in which one species benefits and the other species is neither helped nor harmed. In nature, commensalism is not very common because two species are usually either helped or harmed a little by any interaction.

Parasitism Many family pets get treated with medication to prevent tick and flea bites. Without treatment, pets can suffer from severe health problems as a result of these bites. A relationship that involves one organism living with, on, or inside another organism and harming it is called **parasitism** (PA ruh sit iz um). The organism that benefits is called a **parasite.** The organism it lives on or in is called a **host.** The parasite is usually smaller than the host. In a parasitic relationship, the parasite benefits while the host is harmed. Unlike a predator, a parasite does not usually kill the organism it feeds on. If the host dies, the parasite could lose its source of food or shelter.

Some parasites, like fleas and ticks, have adaptations that enable them to attach to their host and feed on its blood. Other examples of parasitism are shown in **Figure 7.**

A parasitic cowbird laid its eggs in a yellow warbler's nest. The cowbird chick is outcompeting the warbler chicks for space and food.

Fish lice feed on the blood and other internal fluids of fish.

Dwarf mistletoe is a small parasitic flowering plant that grows into the bark of trees to obtain water and nutrients.

FIGURE 7
Parasitism
There are many examples of parasitic relationships. Besides fleas, ticks, and tapeworms, some plants and birds are parasites. **Explain** Why doesn't a parasite usually kill its host?

If a parasite kills its host, the parasite will no longer have a source of food and may die.

Digital Lesson: Assign the *Apply It* activity online and have students submit their work to you.

my science online.com | Symbiosis |

apply it!

⚠️ **Classify** Each photograph on the right represents a different type of symbiosis. Classify each interaction as mutualism, commensalism, or parasitism. Explain your answers.

Interaction 1: A remora fish attaches itself to the underside of a shark without harming the shark, and eats leftover bits of food from the shark's meals.

Interaction 2: A vampire bat drinks the blood of horses.

Interaction 3: A bee pollinates a flower.

❶ Interaction 1
Commensalism; the remora benefits and the shark is unaffected.

❷ Interaction 2
Parasitism; the bat benefits and the horse is harmed.

❸ Interaction 3
Mutualism; the bee gets food and the flower is able to reproduce.

Interaction 1

Interaction 2

Interaction 3

 Lab zone Do the Quick Lab
Type of Symbiosis.

🔑 Assess Your Understanding

3a. Identify The three types of symbiosis are
mutualism , commensalism ,
and parasitism .

b. ⚠️ **Classify** Microscopic mites live at the base of human eyelashes, where they feed on tiny bits of dead skin. What type of symbiosis could this be? Explain your answer.
Commensalism, because the mites benefit by getting food and humans are unaffected

c. Compare and Contrast Name each type of symbiosis and explain how the two species are affected.
Mutualism—both species benefit; commensalism—one species benefits the other is unaffected; parasitism—one species benefits and the other is harmed.

got it? ....

○ **I get it!** Now I know that the three types of symbiosis differ in how each organism in the relationship is affected.

○ **I need extra help with** See TE note.

Go to MY SCIENCE 🖱 COACH *online for help with this subject.*

615

Elaborate

Apply It!

L1 Review the kinds of symbiosis and decide which one is a win-win situation (*Mutualism*), which is a win-lose situation (*Parasitism*), and which is a win-neutral situation (*Commensalism*) before beginning the activity.

⚠️ **Classify** Have students review the three kinds of symbiosis, and think of them as categories into which the descriptions should fit. Ask: **Which animal shown is a parasite?** (*The vampire bat*)

Lab Resource: Quick Lab [Lab zone]

L1 **TYPES OF SYMBIOSIS** Students will identify and compare symbiotic relationships.

Evaluate

Assess Your Understanding

After students answer the questions, have them evaluate their understanding by completing the appropriate sentence.

R T I Response to Intervention

3. If students have trouble identifying the different kinds of symbiosis, **then** have them review the section, locate the highlighted terms, and reread the definitions.

MY SCIENCE 🖱 COACH Have students go online for help in understanding symbiosis.

Differentiated Instruction

L3 **Cowbirds** The cowbird is a nest parasite, laying its eggs in the nest of another species of bird, such as a warbler or a sparrow. Have students research the cowbird to learn more about this behavior.

L1 **Symbiosis** Help struggling students use mathematical symbols to summarize the three kinds of symbiosis. Use a plus sign for an organism that is helped, a minus sign for an organism that is harmed, and a zero for an organism that is neither helped nor harmed. Mutualism is +/+. Parasitism is +/−. Commensalism is +/0.

Interactions Among Living Things

Inquiry Warm-Up, *Can You Hide a Butterfly?*

In the Inquiry Warm-Up, you investigated how coloring can help an animal hide from an enemy. Using what you learned from that activity, answer the questions below.

1. **OBSERVE** Was your butterfly found or missed? If there were other butterflies that looked like yours, were they found or missed? Suggest a reason for any difference.

   _____

   _____

2. **EVALUATE** Was any particular surface a better place for butterflies to hide than others? If so, explain why.

   _____

   _____

   _____

3. **OBSERVE** Was there anything about the way the person who looked for the butterflies that made some butterflies more likely to remain hidden?

   _____

   _____

   _____

4. **PREDICT** If these were real butterflies, what might cause some of the butterflies to be found, even if their colors matched the environment?

   _____

   _____

Assess Your Understanding

Interactions Among Living Things

How Do Adaptations Help an Organism Survive?

1a. **DEFINE** Adaptations are the _____ and

_____ characteristics that allow organisms to live successfully in their environments.

b. **EXPLAIN** How are a snake's sharp fangs an adaptation that help it survive in the saguaro community?

got it? ··

○ **I get it!** Now I know that adaptations are _____

_____

_____

○ **I need extra help with** _____

_____

What Are Competition and Predation?

2a. **REVIEW** Two main ways in which organisms interact are

_____ and _____.

b. **DESCRIBE** Give an example of competition. Explain your answer.

_____

_____

c. **APPLY CONCEPTS** Owls often prey on mice. What adaptations do you think the mice have that help them avoid becoming prey?

_____

_____

got it? ··

○ **I get it!** Now I know that competition and predation _____

_____

○ **I need extra help with** _____

_____

Assess Your Understanding

Interactions Among Living Things

What Are the Three Types of Symbiosis?

3a. IDENTIFY The three types of symbiosis are _____,

_____, and _____.

b. CLASSIFY Microscopic mites lie at the base of human eyelashes, where they feed on tiny bits of dead skin. What type of symbiosis could this be? Explain your answer.

_____

_____

c. COMPARE AND CONTRAST Name each type of symbiosis and explain how the two species are affected.

_____

_____

_____

gotit? ···

○ **I get it!** Now I know that the three types of symbiosis differ in _____

_____

_____

○ **I need extra help with** _____

_____

Key Concept Summaries

Interactions Among Living Things

How Do Adaptations Help an Organism Survive?

Individuals with characteristics that are best suited for their environment tend to survive and pass on these characteristics to their offspring through a process called **natural selection**. The behaviors and characteristics that allow organisms to live successfully in their environments are called **adaptations**. Individuals with characteristics that are poorly suited for their environment are less likely to survive and reproduce.

An organism has a role, or **niche**, in its habitat. A niche includes the type of food the organism eats and how it gets this food. A niche also includes when and how the organism reproduces and the physical conditions that it needs to survive. Each organism has unique characteristics that affect the organism's ability to survive and reproduce in its environment. For example, many organisms live in and around the saguaro cactus.

What Are Competition and Predation?

Two major types of interactions among organisms are competition and predation. **Competition** is the struggle between organisms to survive as they attempt to occupy the same niche and use the same limited resources. Organisms that share the same habitat often have adaptations that reduce competition. For example, three types of birds can each get food from different parts of the same tree.

An interaction is which one organism kills another for food or nutrients is called **predation**. The **predator**

species kills the **prey** species. Predators have adaptations that help them catch prey. Organisms have adaptations that help them avoid becoming prey.

Predators can affect population size. If there are too many predators in an area, the number of prey will decrease. As a result, there is less food for predators and the predator population will go down too.

What Are the Three Types of Symbiosis?

The three main types of symbiotic relationships are mutualism, commensalisms, and parasitism. **Mutualism** is a relationship in which both species benefit. When an oxpecker eats ticks living on the impala's ear, both organisms benefit. **Commensalism** is a relationship in which one species benefits and

the other species is not affected, such as a bird's nest in a tree. **Parasitism** is a relationship in which one organism benefits and the other organism is harmed. The organism that benefits is called a **parasite**. The organism that is harmed is called the **host**. Fish lice are parasites that feed on the blood of a host fish.

On a separate sheet of paper, compare and contrast parasitism and mutualism.

Review and Reinforce

Interactions Among Living Things

Understanding Main Ideas
Answer the following questions on a separate sheet of paper.

1. How does natural selection result in adaptations in a species?
2. What is an organism's niche?
3. How do adaptations help an organism to reduce competition for food and other resources?

The line graph below shows how the populations of lynx and snowshoe hares has changed over time. Use the line graph to answer questions 4–6.

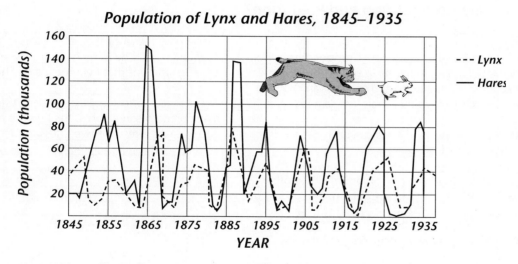

Population of Lynx and Hares, 1845–1935

4. When the hare population increased, what happened to the lynx population. Why?
5. How do you think an increase in the lynx population affected the hare population? Why?
6. What other factors could have caused a decrease in the hare population?

Building Vocabulary
On a separate sheet of paper, write a definition for each of these terms.

7. predator
8. competition
9. symbiosis

Enrich

Interactions Among Living Things

Read the passage and look at the graph below it. Then use a separate sheet of paper to answer the questions that follow the graph.

Analyzing Interactions Among Organisms

In 1997, a community decided to get rid of the population of rattlesnakes in the area. The graph below shows what happened to the populations of rattlesnakes, birds, and rodents. The rodents included animals such as mice, rats, and prairie dogs.

Populations of Rodents, Birds, and Rattlesnakes

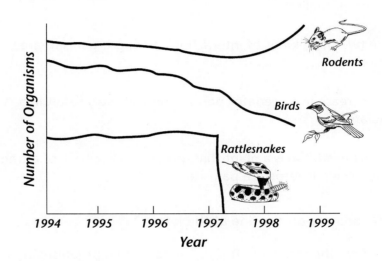

1. Did the bird populations appear to benefit from the elimination of the rattlesnakes? How do you know?
2. Did the rodent populations appear to benefit from the elimination of the rattlesnakes? How do you know?
3. What was the main source of food for the rattlesnakes? How can you tell?
4. Why do you think the bird populations decreased sharply after the rattlesnakes were eliminated?
5. Do you think it was a good idea for the community to eliminate the rattlesnake population? Explain your answer.

Name _____ Date _____ Class _____

Lesson Quiz

Interactions Among Living Things

If the statement is true, write *true*. If the statement is false, change the underlined word or words to make the statement true.

1. _____ In <u>natural selection</u>, individuals whose unique characteristics are well-suited for an environment tend to survive and produce more offspring.

2. _____ Adaptations are behaviors and <u>social</u> characteristics that allow organisms to live successfully in their environments.

3. _____ A grackle and a sparrow try to eat from the same ear of corn in a field. This is an example of <u>mutualism</u>.

4. _____ The two main kinds of interactions among organisms are competition and <u>adaptation</u>.

5. _____ An increase in a predator population will likely result in a <u>decrease</u> in the prey population.

6. _____ Dwarf mistletoe is a plant that grows into the bark of a tree to obtain water and nutrients. The mistletoe is a <u>parasite</u>.

Write the letter of the correct answer on the line at the left.

7. ___ When a snake kills a shrew, the shrew is the

   A host

   B prey

   C predator

   D parasite

8. ___ The role of an organism in its habitat is its

   A host

   B prey

   C niche

   D adaptation

9. ___ An example of an adaptation that helps a prey species avoid being caught is

   A claws

   B mimicry

   C sharp teeth

   D poisonous stingers

10. ___ A relationship in which two species live closely together and both benefit is

   A mutualism

   B predation

   C parasitism

   D commensalism

Interactions Among Living Things

Answer Key

After the Inquiry Warm-Up

1. Certain colors or patterns were better for keeping butterflies hidden.

2. Differences between horizontal and vertical surfaces may be affected by the angle of sunlight or the overhead lights.

3. Students may note that the searcher didn't look up at high places or down at low ones.

4. Sample: Their motion might give then away, or they might be found by an animal that searched by smell rather than sight.

Key Concept Summaries

Both are kinds of symbiosis. In mutualism, both organisms benefit from the relationship. In parasitism, only one organism benefits. The other is harmed.

Review and Reinforce

1. Organisms with characteristics that are well suited to their environment survive to reproduce and pass those characteristics along to their offspring. The offspring also survive and reproduce.

2. An organism's niche is its role in its habitat, what it eats and how it obtains its food.

3. Organisms' adaptations enable them to specialize in obtaining food, shelter, and other ecosystems resources so that they do not compete directly with other species.

4. The lynx increase, too, because they had more food.

5. The hares decreased because there were more lynx to prey on them.

6. lack of food or shelter; disease; predation by other predators

7. A predator is an organism that kills another organism for food.

8. Competition is the struggle between organisms to survive as they attempt to use the same resources.

9. Symbiosis is a relationship in which two species live closely together and at least one of the species benefits.

Enrich

1. No; their numbers decreased.

2. Yes; their numbers increased.

3. Rodents; when the rattlesnake population was killed off, the rodents increased.

4. Rodents may have been eating the birds' eggs and young or some of the same foods the birds were eating. When the rattlesnakes were killed, the rodents increased and the birds suffered more predation and/or competition.

5. The increasing numbers of rodents will present a problem for the community—perhaps even more of a problem than the population of rattlesnakes did.

Lesson Quiz

1. true	2. physical	3. competition
4. predation	5. true	6. true
7. B	8. C	9. B
10. A		

LESSON

4

How do living things affect one another?

Lesson Pacing: 1–2 periods or $\frac{1}{2}$–1 block

🕐 **SHORT ON TIME?** To do this lesson in approximately half the time, do the Activate Prior Knowledge activity followed by a discussion of the Key Concept to familiarize students with the lesson content. Have students do the Quick Lab. The rest of the lesson can be completed by students independently.

Preference Navigator, in the online Planning tools, allows you to customize *Interactive Science* to your own teaching style. You can also edit lesson plans by selecting the Lesson Planner option.

Digital Teacher's Edition allows you to access your *Teacher's Edition and Resource* materials online.

my science online.com

Lesson Vocabulary

- succession
- primary succession
- pioneer species
- secondary succession

 Content Refresher

Lichens Lichens are an example of one type of symbiotic relationship—mutualism. In this type of association, both organisms depend on each other and cannot live independently. In the lichen, one organism, the alga, carries out photosynthesis and produces the food that the other organisgm, the fungus, requires. The fungus absorbs vital nutrients and water for the process. Lichens can grow in most habitats, especially those unsuitable for plant growth. Because of this, they are pioneer species in succession. Their activities prepare the soil for the mosses and other small plants that follow in succession. Lichens are very sensitive to sulfur dioxide, which makes them good indicators of pollution and acid rain. Because they can tolerate and accumulate metals, they can be an indicator of industrial pollution. Lichens are also used in traditional dyes, in herbal medicines, and as human and animal food.

LESSON OBJECTIVE

🗝 Explain the difference between primary and secondary succession.

ENGAGE AND EXPLORE

To teach this lesson using a variety of resources, begin by reading **My Planet Diary** as a class. Have students share ideas any experience they may have had or knowledge of prescribed fires. Then have students do the **Inquiry Warm-Up activity.** Students will investigate the order in which organisms move into a community. The **After the Inquiry Warm-Up worksheet** sets up a discussion about kinds of plants and animals living in the area. Have volunteers share their answers to number 4 about abiotic factors that will determine which species will survive.

EXPLAIN AND ELABORATE

Teach Key Concepts by explaining the terms *primary* and *secondary succession*. Relate *pioneer species* to *primary succession*. Continue to **Teach Key Concepts** by explaining that secondary succession takes place after an area with an established ecosystem has been disturbed. Use the **Support the Big Q** to help students understand the stages of secondary succession. Ask students to use **Figures 1** and **2** to explain the difference between primary and secondary succession. Students can then practice the target skill in the **Apply It activity.**

Hand out the **Key Concept Summaries** as a review of each part of the lesson. Students can also use the online **Vocab Flash Cards** to review key terms.

EVALUATE

Have students take the **Lesson Quiz.** For an alternate assessment, see the **EXAM**VIEW® Assessment Suite, Progress Monitoring Assessments, or SuccessTracker™.

ELL Support

1 Content and Language

Compare the words *primary succession* and *secondary succession* in the vocabulary. Students may recognize the words *primary* and *secondary* from terms as *primary school* and *secondary school*. Point out that students in *primary school* may have little knowledge to build on much like an area undergoing *primary succession* with respect to organisms. Students in *secondary school* should have an established background of knowledge much like an established ecosystem in *secondary succession*.

DIFFERENTIATED INSTRUCTION KEY
L1 Struggling Students or Special Needs
L2 On-Level Students **L3** Advanced Students

LESSON PLANNER 15.4

 **Inquiry Path** Hands-on learning in the Lab zone

ENGAGE AND EXPLORE

To teach this lesson with an emphasis on inquiry, begin with the **Inquiry Warm-Up activity.** Students will investigate organisms moving into an ecosystem and the order in which they move in. Discuss pioneers in primary succession. Have students do the **After the Inquiry Warm-Up worksheet.** Have volunteers share their answers to number 4 about abiotic factors that determine which species are likely to survive.

EXPLAIN AND ELABORATE

Focus on the **Inquiry Skill** for the lesson. Point out that when you observe, you watch carefully or inspect. Review primary and secondary succession before assigning the **Apply It activity.** Ask students to share answers that are not reflected in the annotations. Have students do the **Quick Lab** and then share their observations of evidence of succession on or near their school grounds. Students can use the online **Vocab Flash Cards** to review key terms.

EVALUATE

Have students take the **Lesson Quiz.** For an alternate assessment, see the **EXAM**VIEW® Assessment Suite, Progress Monitoring Assessments, or SuccessTracker™.

Digital Path Online learning at MY SCIENCE ONLINE.com

ENGAGE AND EXPLORE

To teach this lesson using digital resources, begin by having students explore succession at **My Planet Diary** online. Have them access the Chapter Resources to find the **Unlock the Big Question activity.** There they can answer the questions and refine their responses as they continue through the lesson. You can re-assign the activity and have students submit their work so you can track their progress.

EXPLAIN AND ELABORATE

Students reading above, at, or below the lexile measure of this lesson can access basic content readings at their level at **My Reading Web.** Have students do the online **Art in Motion** activities associated with **Figures 1** and **2.** Encourage students to use the online **Vocab Flash Cards** to preview key terms.

Review *primary* and *secondary succession* before assigning the online **Apply It activity.** Ask volunteers for additional possible causes.

The **Key Concept Summaries** online allow students to read a summary and see an image associated with each part of the lesson. Online remediation is available at **My Science Coach.**

EVALUATE

Have students take the **Lesson Quiz.** For an alternate assessment, see the **EXAM**VIEW® Assessment Suite, Progress Monitoring Assessments, or SuccessTracker™.

2 Frontload the Lesson

Preview the lesson visuals, labels, and captions. In **Figure 1** be sure students understand that they must order or sequence the stages of primary succession and in **Figure 2** write titles for the stages of secondary succession.

3 Comprehensible Input

Have students study the visuals and their captions in **Figures 1** and **2** to support the key concepts of the lesson. Have students role-play pioneers in a primary succession.

4 Language Production

Pair or group students with varied language abilities to complete the sequencing and titling in **Figures 1** and **2.** Have each pair or group write a paragraph on primary or secondary succession.

5 Assess Understanding

Make statements about succession. Have students indicate if the statement applies to primary or secondary succession by holding up one hand for primary and two for secondary to check whole-class comprehension.

Lexile Measure = 1020L

Changes in Communities

Establish Learning Objective

After this lesson, students will be able to:

🔑 Explain the difference between primary and secondary succession.

Engage ─────────

Activate Prior Knowledge

MY PLANET DIARY Read *Fighting Fire With Fire* with the class. Explain that a fire is one of several ways that a community can be changed. Point out that a prescribed fire is set on a day with little wind and when conditions will help the firefighters control the burn. A prescribed fire would never be set during a very dry season. Ask: **How is a wildfire different from a prescribed fire?** *(A prescribed fire is carefully planned and controlled, and a wildfire is not.)*

BIG IDEAS OF SCIENCE REFERENCE LIBRARY 📖 Have students look up the following topic: Renewal.

Explore ─────────

Lab Resource: Inquiry Warm-Up 🔬

L1 HOW COMMUNITIES CHANGE Students will observe examples of succession.

UNLOCK THE BIG **?**

🔑 **How Do Primary and Secondary Succession Differ?**

MY PLANET DIARY

Fighting Fire With Fire

Wildfires are often reported in the national news. The images associated with these reports show how damaging these fires can be to property and to some ecosystems. What you may not know is that fire can actually help fight wildfires! Controlled burns, or prescribed burns, are fires that are purposely and carefully set by professional foresters. Prescribed burns are used to remove materials such as dead, dry branches and leaves that can fuel wildfires. A wildfire that occurs in an area that has previously been burned would cause less damage and be easier for firefighters to control.

This forester is carefully igniting a controlled burn.

MISCONCEPTION

Communicate Discuss these questions with a classmate. Write your answers below.

1. Why should only professional foresters set prescribed fires?

   Sample: Professional foresters know how to set fires and keep them controlled.

2. What do you think could be some other benefits to using prescribed burns in an ecosystem?

   Sample: They help to control insects, increase nutrients in the soil, and improve habitats.

▶ **PLANET DIARY** Go to **Planet Diary** to learn more about succession.

 Lab zone Do the Inquiry Warm-Up *How Communities Change.*

How Do Primary and Secondary Succession Differ?

Fires, floods, volcanoes, hurricanes, and other natural disasters can change communities very quickly. But even without disasters, communities change. The series of predictable changes that occur in a community over time is called **succession**.

616 Populations and Communities

SUPPORT ALL READERS

Lexile Measure = 1020L   Lexile Word Count = 686

Prior Exposure to Content: May be the first time students have encountered this topic

Academic Vocabulary: *compare, contrast, observe*

Science Vocabulary: *primary succession, secondary succession*

Concept Level: Generally appropriate for most students in this grade

Preteach With: My Planet Diary "Fighting Fire With Fire" and Figure 1 activity

Go to **My Reading Web** to access leveled readings that provide a foundation for the content.

my science online.com

Vocabulary
- succession
- primary succession
- pioneer species
- secondary succession

Skills
- Reading: Compare and Contrast
- Inquiry: Observe

Primary Succession When a new island is formed by the eruption of an undersea volcano or an area of rock is uncovered by a melting sheet of ice, no living things are present. Over time, living things will inhabit these areas. **Primary succession** is the series of changes that occurs in an area where no soil or organisms exist.

Figure 1 shows how an area might change following a volcanic eruption. Just like the pioneers that first settled new frontiers, the first species to populate an area are called **pioneer species.** They are often carried to the area by wind or water. Typical pioneer species are mosses and lichens. Lichens are fungi and algae growing in a symbiotic relationship. As pioneer species grow, they help break up the rocks. When the organisms die, they provide nutrients that enrich the thin layer of soil that is forming on the rocks.

As plant seeds land in the new soil, they begin to grow. The specific plants that grow depend on the climate of the area. For example, in a cool, northern area, early seedlings might include alder and cottonwood trees. Eventually, succession may lead to a community of organisms that does not change unless the ecosystem is disturbed. Reaching this mature community can take centuries.

FIGURE 1 ....

▶ ART IN MOTION **Primary Succession**

Primary succession occurs in an area where no soil and no organisms exist.

✎ **Sequence** In the circles, number the stage of primary succession to show the correct order of events.

③ **Soil Creation**
As pioneer species grow and die, soil forms. Some plants grow in this new soil.

② **Pioneer Species**
The first species to grow are pioneer species such as mosses and lichens.

① **Volcanic Eruption**
Shortly after a volcanic eruption, there is no soil, only ash and rock.

④ **Fertile Soil and Maturing Plants**
As more plants die, they decompose and make the soil more fertile. New plants grow and existing plants mature in the fertile soil.

617

Explain

Introduce Vocabulary
To help students understand the term *pioneer species*, explain that these are the first organisms to live in a new area. Remind them that pioneers were the first settlers to move to the western prairies.

Teach Key Concepts 🔑
Explain to students that the changes occurring in an area without any soil or organisms are called *primary succession.* Pioneer species are the first organisms to populate such an area. Ask: **What are the pioneer species in succession in Figure 1?** *(Lichens and mosses)* **How might these species arrive at the area?** *(They might be carried by wind or water)* **What pattern is there in the kinds of plants that move in as succession continues?** *(Larger and larger plants move into the area over time.)*

My Planet Diary provides an opportunity for students to explore real-world connections to changes in communities.

Art in Motion shows primary succession in motion and animates the block diagrams.

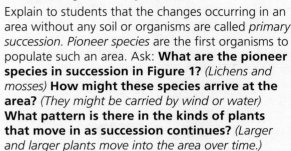

my science online | Succession

(E L L) Support

1 Content and Language
Explain that *primary* means first. Then point out that primary succession is the *first* life to enter a new place.

2 Frontload the Lesson
Have students scan the section heads and visuals and then predict what this lesson will be about. Have students confirm their predictions after reading the lesson.

3 Comprehensible Input
Help students compare and contrast the information in the lesson by having them complete a Venn diagram. One circle should contain information about primary succession and the other circle should contain information about secondary succession. The overlapping section should contain information on how the processes are similar.

Explain

Teach Key Concepts 🔑

Explain to students that secondary succession, in contrast to primary succession, is a disturbance that occurs in a place with an established ecosystem. Ask: **How does secondary succession differ from primary succession?** *(Secondary succession occurs in an area where an ecosystem has been disturbed but soil and some organisms still exist. Primary succession occurs where there is no soil and there are no organisms present.)* **What kind of succession would occur in an area that has been damaged by floods? Explain.** *(It would be secondary succession because it is likely that soil and some organisms would be left behind after the flood.)*

Support the Big Q ❓ UbD

SECONDARY SUCCESSION Help students understand that secondary succession takes place after an area has been disturbed, and tends to return the area to the kind of ecosystem that was present before the disturbance. Tell students to look at **Figure 2.** Ask: **What is the first stage in this example of succession?** *(An abandoned field)* **What do you think the area looked like before the field was abandoned?** *(It was probably plowed for farming.)* **Before the field was cleared for farming, what did the area probably look like?** *(It was likely covered with trees.)* **What was the source of the trees seen in the later stage?** *(Remaining trees near the farm were the source of seeds of the trees.)*

FIGURE 2 ··
> ART IN MOTION **Secondary Succession**
Secondary succession occurs following a disturbance to an ecosystem, such as clearing a forest for farmland.
✎ **Describe** Write a brief title that describes what happens at each of the four stages of secondary succession.

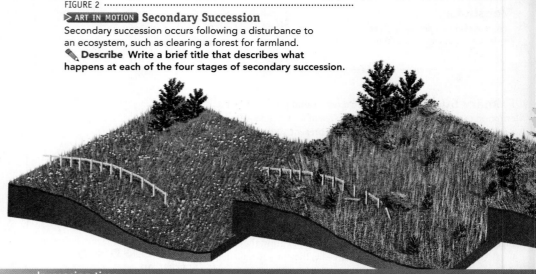

Increasing time

Title: Sample: Abandoned Field
Grasses and wildflowers have taken over this abandoned field.

Title: Sample: Tree Growth Begins
After a few years, pine seedlings and other trees replace some of the grasses and wildflowers.

apply it!

⟳ **Compare and Contrast** Based on your reading, complete the table below.

Factors in Succession	Primary Succession	Secondary Succession
Possible Cause	Volcanic eruption	Fire
Type of Area	No soil or organisms exist.	Soil and organisms exist, but have been disturbed.
Existing Ecosystem?	No	Yes

618 Populations and Communities

Secondary Succession In October 2007, huge wildfires raged across Southern California. The changes following the California fires are an example of secondary succession. **Secondary succession** is the series of changes that occurs in an area where the ecosystem has been disturbed, but where soil and organisms still exist. Natural disturbances that have this effect include fires, hurricanes, and tornadoes. Human activities, such as farming, logging, or mining, may also disturb an ecosystem and cause secondary succession to begin.

🔑 **Unlike primary succession, secondary succession occurs in a place where an ecosystem currently exists.** Secondary succession usually occurs more rapidly than primary succession because soil already exists and seeds from some plants remain in the soil. You can follow the process of succession in an abandoned field in **Figure 2.** After a century, a forest develops. This forest community may remain for a long time.

Art in Motion shows secondary succession in motion and animates the block diagrams.

Digital Lesson: Assign the *Apply It* activity online and have students submit their work to you.

MY SCIENCE online.com ▸ **Succession**

Title: Sample: A Forest Develops

As tree growth continues, the trees begin to crowd out the grasses and wildflowers.

Title: Sample: Mature Community

Eventually, a forest of mostly oak, hickory, and some pine dominates the landscape.

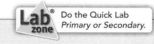 Do the Quick Lab
Primary or Secondary.

Assess Your Understanding

1a. Define Pioneer species are the ___first___ species to populate an area.

b. Observe Is grass poking through a sidewalk crack primary or secondary succession? Why?
Secondary; before the sidewalk, soil was present and an ecosystem existed there.

c. CHALLENGE Why are the changes during succession predictable?
Plants and animals that will grow in an area are determined by climate conditions that are not affected by disasters.

got it?

○ **I get it!** Now I know that primary and secondary succession differ in whether an ecosystem exists, and the rate at which succession occurs.

○ **I need extra help with** See TE note.

Go to my science COACH *online for help with this subject.*

619

Elaborate

Apply It!

L1 Review the differences between primary succession and secondary succession before beginning the activity.

 Compare and Contrast Point out that this table contrasts the two kinds of succession. To contrast is to show differences between two things. To compare is to show how two things are similar.

Lab Resource: Quick Lab

L1 **PRIMARY OR SECONDARY** Students will observe evidence of succession on or near their school grounds.

Evaluate

Assess Your Understanding

After students answer the questions, have them evaluate their understanding by completing the appropriate sentence.

RTI Response to Intervention

1a. If students cannot describe what a pioneer species is, **then** have them review **Figure 1** and reread the labels.

b. If students have trouble distinguishing between primary and secondary succession, **then** have them locate and reread the Key Concept statement for the lesson.

c. If students need help with explaining why succession is predictable, **then** discuss the climate conditions that can be inferred from **Figure 2** and help them see that the climate has not changed.

MY SCIENCE COACH Have students go online for help in understanding succession.

Differentiated Instruction

L3 **Local Succession** Encourage students to talk to friends or relatives who have lived in your area for a long time. Students should ask about natural areas and how they have changed. Students can take notes from the conversation and then tell the class what they learned. If students cannot find friends or relatives who know such information, suggest they visit the local library to learn more about the area's history.

L1 **Interpret Diagrams** Ask students to compare the pictures of the first stage in **Figures 1** and **2.** Help them see that **Figure 1** begins with an area that has no soil and no organisms, but in **Figure 2** the first picture has plants already living there. Help students relate these differences to those between primary succession and secondary succession. Have students create their own diagrams to show primary and secondary succession based on the lesson.

Lab zone **After the Inquiry Warm-Up**

Changes in Communities

> **Inquiry Warm-Up, *How Communities Change***
> In the Inquiry Warm-Up, you investigated the order in which organisms move into an area. Using what you learned from that activity, answer the questions below.

1. **OBSERVE** What trend do you see in the kinds of plants that you can see in the drawings?

   _____

   _____

2. **PREDICT** When do you think animals will be found living in the area?

   _____

   _____

3. **EXPLAIN** How does soil form after a volcanic eruption that leaves only ash and rock?

   _____

   _____

4. **INFER** What are some abiotic factors that will determine which of the species that arrive in the area will survive?

   _____

   _____

   _____

Assess Your Understanding

Changes in Communities

How Do Primary and Secondary Succession Differ?

1a. DEFINE During succession, pioneer species are the

_____ species to populate an area. They are carried to

an area by _____ and _____.

b. OBSERVE Grass poking through a crack in a sidewalk is an example of succession. Is it primary or secondary succession?

_____

_____

c. CHALLENGE Why are the changes during succession predictable?

_____

_____

gotit**?** ....

○ **I get it!** Now I know that primary and secondary succession differ in _____

_____

_____

○ **I need extra help with** _____

_____

_____

Key Concept Summaries

Changes in Communities

How Do Primary and Secondary Succession Differ?

The series of predictable changes that occur in a community over time is called succession. **Primary succession** happens where there is no soil or organisms in the environment. For example, primary succession may occur following a volcanic eruption.

Pioneer species, such as lichen, are the first organisms to populate the environment. Other plants can grow in the soil that pioneers help make. Eventually, a community of organisms develops.

Secondary succession occurs in an area where the ecosystem has been disturbed but soil and organisms remain, such as after forest is cleared. Secondary succession usually happens faster than primary succession because some soil and plant seeds remain after the disturbance.

On a separate sheet of paper, compare and contrast primary succession and secondary succession.

Review and Reinforce

Changes in Communities

Understanding Main Ideas
Answer the following questions on a separate sheet of paper.

1. What organisms are usually the pioneer species in anew area? How do these organisms prepare the area for other species?

2. The illustration below shows succession in an abandoned field. How did the plant populations in the community change over time?

$\begin{array}{cccccc} 1 & 2\text{--}4 & 5\text{--}15 & 25\text{--}50 & 150 \end{array}$

Years After Field Was Abandoned

Building Vocabulary
Identify each of the following as an example of primary succession or secondary succession. Write your answers in the spaces provided.

3. An old house was torn down. Small weeds and grasses grew in the vacant lot. Over the next few years, bushes and tree seedlings began to grow.

_____

4. An undersea volcano erupted and formed a small island. Mosses and lichens began to grow on the bare volcanic rock.

_____

Enrich

Changes in Communities

You have learned that over many years, the process of succession can transform an abandoned field into a forest. Succession can also transform a pond into a forest. How can an aquatic ecosystem change into a land ecosystem? Examine the sequence of changes shown in the figures below. Then answer the questions on a separate sheet of paper.

From Pond to Forest

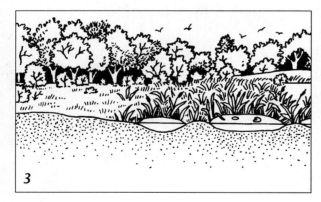

1. What type of succession is shown in this example? Explain your answer.
2. Name two pond populations that could not survive in a forest ecosystem.
3. Name two forest populations that could not survive in a pond ecosystem.
4. Describe how the ecosystem changed from Figure 1 to Figure 4.

Lesson Quiz

Changes in Communities

Fill in the blank to complete each statement.

1. Pioneer species break down rocks, forming the beginning of _____.

2. Two examples of pioneer species are _____ and lichens.

3. A lichen is a symbiotic combination of _____ and algae.

4. A forest fire is followed by _____ succession.

5. The series of changes that occur in an area where no soil or organisms exist is called _____ succession.

If the statement is true, write *true*. If the statement is false, change the underlined word or words to make the statement true.

6. _____ After a long time, a mature community is established and this community does not change unless it is <u>disturbed</u>.

7. _____ The first species to populate an area are called <u>primary</u> species.

8. _____ Unlike primary succession, secondary succession occurs in a place where an <u>ecosystem</u> currently exists.

9. _____ Secondary succession is usually <u>slower</u> than primary succession.

10. _____ Natural disturbances that lead to succession include fires, hurricanes, and <u>tornadoes</u>.

Changes in Communities

Answer Key

After the Inquiry Warm-Up

1. As time goes by, larger and larger plants are seen in the area.

2. Animals will be able to live in the area when there is available food and enough plant growth or soil development to provide shelter.

3. Soil forms from the mosses and lichens that grow and die on the ash and rock. Some plants can grow in the soil as the soil becomes fertile.

4. temperature, available water, amount of sunlight (length of day)

Key Concept Summaries

In both primary succession and secondary succession, new organisms move into an area and replace organisms that lived there before. In primary succession, the land is bare before new organisms move in. In secondary succession, the area has been disturbed, but some organisms are already there when new ones move in.

Review and Reinforce

1. Mosses and lichens are usually the pioneer species. As they grow on bare rock, they help break up the rocks to start forming soil. When they die, they provide nutrients that enrich the thin layer of soil that is forming, allowing plant seeds to grow.

2. First small weeds few, then larger weeds and pine seedlings. As the pines grew, a pine forest developed. Then seedlings of deciduous trees began to grow. Finally, a forest of mature deciduous trees replaced the pine trees.

3. secondary succession

4. primary succession

Enrich

1. secondary succession, because it occurs in a place where there already is an ecosystem

2. Sample: turtles, fish, water lilies

3. Sample: pal trees, rabbits, deer

4. In Figure 1, the pond was fairly deep. Water plants grew in the shallow water close to shore, and marsh plants grew at the edge of the pond. Fish and other aquatic organisms lived in and around the pond. In Figure 2, the pond and become shallower, but fish could still live in it. Aquatic plants grew farther out from the shore, and a wider band of marsh plants grew at the pond's edge. In Figure 3, the pond has filled in to the point where only small marshy areas are left. Some of the plants are the same, but no fish live there. In Figure 4, the marshy areas have completely filled in, and there's a meadow where the pond was. The forest has grown into the meadow.

Lesson Quiz

1. soil
2. mosses
3. fungi
4. secondary
5. primary
6. true
7. pioneer
8. true
9. faster
10. true

Place the outside corner, the corner away from the dotted line, in the corner of your copy machine to copy onto letter-size paper.

619H

Place the outside corner, the corner away from the dotted line, in the corner of your copy machine to copy onto letter-size paper.

Study Guide

Review the Big Q UbD

Have students complete the statement at the top of the page. These Key Concepts support their understanding of the chapter's Big Question. Have students return to the chapter opener question. What is different about how students view the image of the clownfish and sea anemone now that they have completed the chapter? Thinking about this will help them prepare for the *Apply the Big Q* activity in the Review and Assessment.

Partner Review

Have partners review definitions of vocabulary terms by using the Study Guide to quiz each other. Students could read the Key Concept statements and leave out words for their partner to fill in, or change a statement so that it is false and then ask their partner to correct it.

Class Activity: Concept Map

Have students develop a concept map to show how the information in this chapter is related. Have students brainstorm to identify the key concepts, vocabulary, details, and examples, then write each one on a self-sticking note and attach it at random on chart paper or on the board. Explain that the concept map will begin at the top with Key Concepts. Ask students to use the following questions to help them organize the information on the notes:

- What does an organism get from its habitat?
- What is the difference between a population and a community?
- What are some ways in which populations can be changed?
- Why are adaptations important?
- What is a symbiotic relationship?

My Science Coach allows students to complete the *Practice Test* online.

The Big Question allows students to complete the *Apply the Big Q* activity about how living things affect one another.

Vocab Flash Cards offer a way to review the chapter vocabulary words.

my science online.com | **Populations and Communities**

---

15 Study Guide

Living things interact in many ways, including competition and _predation_, as well as through symbiotic relationships such as mutualism, commensalism, and _parasitism_.

LESSON 1 Living Things and the Environment

🔑 An organism gets the things it needs to live, grow, and reproduce from its environment.

🔑 Biotic and abiotic factors make up a habitat.

🔑 The levels of organization in an ecosystem are organism, population, and community.

Vocabulary
- organism • habitat • biotic factor
- abiotic factor • species • population
- community • ecosystem • ecology

LESSON 2 Populations

🔑 Populations can change in size when new members join the population or when members leave the population.

🔑 Some limiting factors for populations are weather conditions, space, food, and water.

Vocabulary
- birth rate • death rate • immigration
- emigration • population density
- limiting factor • carrying capacity

LESSON 3 Interactions Among Living Things

🔑 Every organism has a variety of adaptations that are suited to its specific living conditions to help it survive.

🔑 Two major types of interactions among organisms are competition and predation.

🔑 The three main types of symbiotic relationships are mutualism, commensalism, and parasitism.

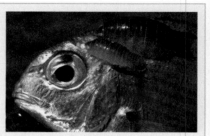

Vocabulary
- natural selection • adaptation • niche • competition
- predation • predator • prey • symbiosis • mutualism
- commensalism • parasitism • parasite • host

LESSON 4 Changes in Communities

🔑 Unlike primary succession, secondary succession occurs in a place where an ecosystem currently exists.

Vocabulary
- succession
- primary succession
- pioneer species
- secondary succession

ELL Support

4 Language Production

Divide the class into four groups and do a Gallery Walk to review each lesson. Post four large sheets of paper or poster board with the essential questions from each lesson at the top of each sheet. Position each group at one poster. Have them write down all they have learned that responds to the questions. Then have them rotate to the next poster to add information until all groups have worked with all posters.

Beginning

LOW/HIGH Allow students to answer with drawings, single words, or short phrases.

Intermediate

LOW/HIGH Have students draft sentences to answer the questions.

Advanced

LOW/HIGH Have students assist and/or edit the work of classmates with lower language proficiency.

Review and Assessment

LESSON 1 Living Things and the Environment

1. A prairie dog, a hawk, and a snake are all members of the same

  a. niche.   **(b.)** community.

  c. species.   **d.** population.

2. Grass is an example of a(n) <u>biotic factor</u> in a habitat.

3. Sequence Put these levels in order from the smallest to the largest: population, organism, ecosystem, community.

  <u>organism, population,</u>
  <u>community, ecosystem</u>

4. Apply Concepts Name two biotic and two abiotic factors you might find in a forest ecosystem.

  <u>Sample: Biotic—trees, birds;</u>
  <u>abiotic—sunlight, water</u>

5. Draw Conclusions In 1815, Mount Tambora, a volcano in Indonesia, erupted. So much volcanic ash and dust filled the atmosphere that 1816 is referred to as the "Year Without a Summer." How might a volcanic eruption affect the abiotic factors in an organism's habitat?

  <u>Sample: The ash and dust</u>
  <u>from a volcanic eruption could</u>
  <u>block out sunlight. As a result,</u>
  <u>temperatures would drop. The</u>
  <u>air, water, and soil in a habitat</u>
  <u>could also be polluted.</u>

6. [Write About It] Write at least one paragraph describing your habitat. Describe how you get the food, water, and shelter you need from your habitat. How does this habitat meet your needs in ways that another would not?
  See TE rubric.

LESSON 2 Populations

7. All of the following are limiting factors for populations except

  a. space.   **b.** food.

  (c.) time.   **d.** weather.

8. <u>Emigration</u> occurs when individuals leave a population.

Use the data table to answer the questions below. Ecologists monitoring a deer population collect data during a 30-year study.

Year	0	5	10	15	20	25	30
Population (thousands)	15	30	65	100	40	25	10

9. Graph Use the data to make a line graph.

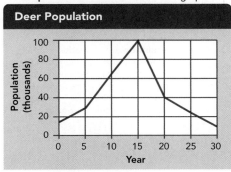

10. Interpret Data In which year was the deer population the highest? The lowest?
  <u>Year 15; Year 30</u>

11. Develop Hypotheses In Year 16 of the study, this region experienced a severe winter. How might this have affected the deer population?
  <u>The severe winter may have</u>
  <u>killed weak or injured deer. A</u>
  <u>food shortage may have also</u>
  <u>weakened or killed the deer.</u>

621

Review and Assessment

Assess Understanding

Have students complete the answers to the Review and Assessment questions. Have a class discussion about what students find confusing. Write Key Concepts on the board to reinforce knowledge.

R T I Response to Intervention

3. If students have trouble describing the organization of an ecosystem, **then** have them use the mnemonic *Only People Can Eat* to remember the progression from Organism to Population to Community to Ecosystem.

8. If students need help contrasting immigration and emigration, **then** point out that, like *emigrate*, the word exit begins with the letter e. Individuals that are emigrating are exiting, or leaving, the population.

Alternate Assessment

L3 DESIGN A GAME Have students design and produce a game that uses the chapter content. Students should be sure to use all the Key Concepts and vocabulary in the game and to address the Big Question. For example, an ecosystem board game could include game pieces that represent the populations in a community. Spaces on the board and cards drawn from a pile would instruct players to adapt or interact, or impose a condition (such as a drought) on a population. The class can then use the game as a way to review the chapter material.

CHAPTER 15

[Write About It] Assess student's writing using this rubric.

SCORING RUBRIC	SCORE 4	SCORE 3	SCORE 2	SCORE 1
Getting food, water, and shelter from habitat	Student describes sources of all items in detail.	Student describes sources of all items.	Student describes some sources of items.	Student does not describe sources of items.
How habitat is different from others	Student clearly identifies ways in which the habitat differs from others.	Student identifies ways in which the habitat differs from others.	Student incompletely identifies ways in which the habitat differs from others.	Student does not identify ways in which the habitat differs from others.

Review and Assessment, Cont.

RTI Response to Intervention

12. If students need help classifying interactions between species, **then** review with them the definitions of parasitism, mutualism, and commensalism. Invite students to give examples of each.

19. If students have trouble distinguishing primary and secondary succession, **then** review with them the definitions for both types of succession and have them provide examples of each.

Apply the Big Q ? UbD

TRANSFER Students should be able to demonstrate understanding of the relationships between living things by answering this question. See the scoring rubric below.

Connect to the Big Idea

BIG IDEA Living things interact with the environment.

Send students back to the Big Ideas of Science pages at the beginning of their student edition. Have them read what they wrote about how living things interact before they started the chapter. Lead a class discussion about how their thoughts have changed. If all chapters have been completed, have them fill in the bottom section for the Big Idea.

L3 WRITING IN SCIENCE Ask students to write a blog entry about the ways in which living things affect one another and how this demonstrates that living things interact with their environment.

---

15 Review and Assessment

LESSON 3 Interactions Among Living Things

12. In which type of interaction do both species benefit?

  a. predation   **(b.)** mutualism

  c. commensalism   **d.** parasitism

13. A parasite lives on or inside its <u>host</u>.

14. Relate Cause and Effect Name two prey adaptations. How does each adaptation protect the organism?
<u>Sample: Camouflage—An</u>
<u>organism blends in with its</u>
<u>surroundings, making it difficult</u>
<u>to see. Warning coloration—</u>
<u>Bright colors warn predators</u>
<u>not to eat the organism.</u>

15. Make Generalizations Competition for resources in an area is usually more intense within a single species than between two different species. Suggest an explanation for this observation. (*Hint:* Consider how niches help organisms avoid competition.)
<u>Organisms within a species share</u>
<u>the same niche, which intensifies</u>
<u>competition for limited resources.</u>
<u>Different species may share</u>
<u>parts of a habitat but may not</u>
<u>compete for all of the resources.</u>

16. **Write About It** Some scientists think that the relationship between clownfish and sea anemones is an example of commensalism. Other scientists think that the relationship is mutualism. If this relationship is actually mutualism, how might both the clownfish and sea anemone benefit?
See TE rubric.

LESSON 4 Changes in Communities

17. The series of predictable changes that occur in a community over time is called

  a. natural selection   **b.** ecology

  c. commensalism   **(d.)** succession

18. <u>Pioneer species</u> are the first species to populate an area.

19. Classify Lichens and mosses have just begun to grow on the rocky area shown below. What type of succession is occurring? Explain.
<u>Primary succession; there is no</u>
<u>soil present and only pioneer</u>
<u>organisms are shown.</u>

APPLY THE BIG Q ? How do living things affect one another?

20. Humans interact with their environment on a daily basis. These interactions can have both positive and negative effects. Using at least four vocabulary terms from this chapter, describe a human interaction and the effect it has on the environment.
<u>Sample: When humans clear</u>
<u>land for construction, they</u>
<u>may destroy habitats. Oil and</u>
<u>gasoline from vehicles may get</u>
<u>into the ecosystem as abiotic</u>
<u>factors. Organisms may have</u>
<u>to emigrate to new habitats to</u>
<u>survive.</u>
<u>See TE rubric.</u>

Write About It — Assess student's writing using this rubric.

SCORING RUBRIC	SCORE 4	SCORE 3	SCORE 2	SCORE 1
Ways in which clownfish benefits	Student identifies benefits to clownfish in detail.	Student identifies benefits to clownfish.	Student identifies some benefits to clownfish.	Student does not identify benefits to clownfish.
Ways in which sea anemone benefits	Student identifies benefits to sea anemone in detail.	Student identifies benefits to sea anemone.	Student identifies some benefits to sea anemone.	Student does not identify benefits to sea anemone.

? How do living things affect one another?
Assess student's response using this rubric.

SCORING RUBRIC	SCORE 4	SCORE 3	SCORE 2	SCORE 1
Interaction of humans and the environment	Student chooses an appropriate example.	Student chooses an appropriate example.	Student chooses an unlikely or inappropriate example.	Student does not identify an example.
Impact of the interaction on the environment	Student describes the impact accurately and in detail.	Student describes the impact accurately.	Student describes the impact incompletely.	Student does not describe the impact.

Standardized Test Prep

Multiple Choice

Circle the letter of the best answer.

1. Symbiotic relationships include mutualism, commensalism, and parasitism. Which of the images below shows mutualism?

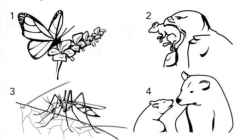

- (A) Image 1
- B Image 2
- C Image 3
- D Image 4

2. In general, which of the following is a true statement about population size?

- A If birth rate < death rate, population size increases.
- B If death rate < birth rate, population size decreases.
- (C) If birth rate > death rate, population size increases.
- D If death rate > birth rate, population size increases.

3. Ecosystems have different levels of organization. A group of similar organisms makes up a <u>population</u>, which, along with other types of organisms, makes up a(n) <u>community</u>.

- A species, population
- B habitat, ecosystem
- (C) population, community
- D population, habitat

4. Three different bird species all live in the same trees in an area, but competition between the birds rarely occurs. Which of the following is a likely explanation for this lack of competition?

- (A) The three species occupy different niches.
- B The three species eat the same food.
- C The three species have a limited supply of food.
- D The three species live in the same part of the trees.

5. Which of the following is a typical pioneer species?

- A grass
- (B) lichen
- C pine trees
- D soil

Constructed Response

Use the diagram below and your knowledge of science to help you answer Question 6. Write your answer on a separate piece of paper.

6. An organism interacts with both the biotic and abiotic factors in its habitat. List three biotic factors and three abiotic factors shown in the drawing above.
See TE note.

Standardized Test Prep

Test-Taking Skills

INTERPRETING IMAGES Tell students that when they answer questions like Question 1, where the choices are images, they should make sure they know what concept the image should represent. Students should keep that concept in mind as they look over the choices. In Question 1, choices **B** and **C** can be eliminated because an organism is being harmed. Choice **D** can be eliminated because it shows a parent and its offspring, not an example of symbiosis. Choice **A** shows mutualism, a symbiotic relationship in which both organisms benefit.

Constructed Response

6. Sample: Biotic—duck, plants, soil organisms (e.g. worm); Abiotic—sunlight, water, rock particles

Additional Assessment Resources

Chapter Test
EXAMVIEW® Assessment Suite
Performance Assessment
Progress Monitoring Assessments
SuccessTracker™

ⒺⓁⓁ Support

5 Assess Understanding
Have ELLs complete the Alternate Assessment. Provide guidelines on the information that it must cover, and a rubric for assessment.

Beginning
LOW Create the visual parts of the game, such as the game pieces and playing board.

HIGH Provide simple labels as needed.

Intermediate
LOW/HIGH Provide more extended language for parts of the game that require it, such as cards that are to be drawn by players that give simple instructions.

Advanced
LOW/HIGH Write the instructions for the game.

Remediate If students have trouble with...

QUESTION	SEE LESSON	STANDARDS
1	1, 3	
2	2	
3	1	
4	3	
5	4	
6	1, 3	

Science Matters

Careers

Have students read *Succession Ecologist*. Point out that ecology is a large field of study, and that ecologists specialize in smaller fields, such as succession ecology. Because some field work had been done in the forest that was destroyed, ecologists had data from before the eruption. This gave the ecologists a good idea of the community that existed before the eruption and helped them in their studies of the recovery.

Mount St. Helens is located in southwestern Washington. Help students locate the volcano on a map of the United States. To help students visualize the area of forest that was destroyed, find out the area of your community and tell students how many times that area would fit into 500 square kilometers. The area of forest that was destroyed is now Mount St. Helens National Volcanic Monument. You may wish to go to the website of the United States Forest Service to find images and information about the eruption and recovery.

Ask: **What are some other examples of natural and human-caused damage that a succession ecologist might study?** *(Sample: forest fires, landslides, floods, abandoned mines).* **How might information learned on Mount St. Helens be useful to ecologists helping areas recover from human-caused changes?** *(Sample: Ecologists might learn which plants grow best in a disturbed area.)*

SUCCESSION ECOLOGIST

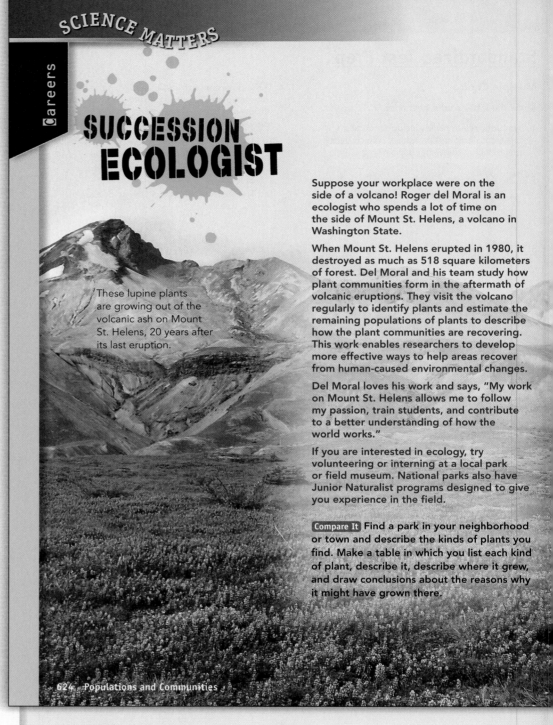

These lupine plants are growing out of the volcanic ash on Mount St. Helens, 20 years after its last eruption.

Suppose your workplace were on the side of a volcano! Roger del Moral is an ecologist who spends a lot of time on the side of Mount St. Helens, a volcano in Washington State.

When Mount St. Helens erupted in 1980, it destroyed as much as 518 square kilometers of forest. Del Moral and his team study how plant communities form in the aftermath of volcanic eruptions. They visit the volcano regularly to identify plants and estimate the remaining populations of plants to describe how the plant communities are recovering. This work enables researchers to develop more effective ways to help areas recover from human-caused environmental changes.

Del Moral loves his work and says, "My work on Mount St. Helens allows me to follow my passion, train students, and contribute to a better understanding of how the world works."

If you are interested in ecology, try volunteering or interning at a local park or field museum. National parks also have Junior Naturalist programs designed to give you experience in the field.

Compare It Find a park in your neighborhood or town and describe the kinds of plants you find. Make a table in which you list each kind of plant, describe it, describe where it grew, and draw conclusions about the reasons why it might have grown there.

Quick Facts

When the volcano erupted, the north side of the mountain exploded. Hot gases and pieces of rock blowing sideways moved at speeds varying from 360 to 1080 kilometers per hour. The force of this moving material blew trees over or broke them into pieces. The damage was not restricted to the side of Mount St. Helens. The blast was strong enough to damage trees on the sides of other mountains several kilometers away.

Have students find images of the damages to Mount St. Helen from the volcano eruption and current images of its recovery. Have students create a before-and-after recovery poster of Mount St. Helen.

BINOCULAR BOOT CAMP

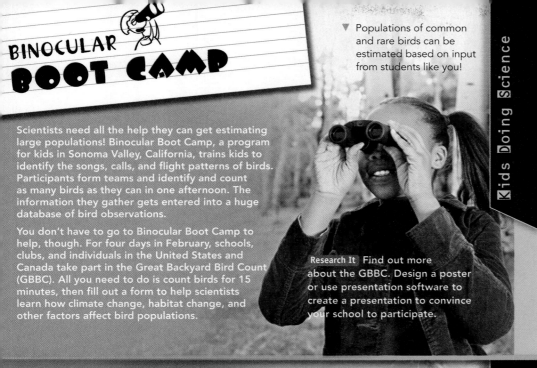

▼ Populations of common and rare birds can be estimated based on input from students like you!

Scientists need all the help they can get estimating large populations! Binocular Boot Camp, a program for kids in Sonoma Valley, California, trains kids to identify the songs, calls, and flight patterns of birds. Participants form teams and identify and count as many birds as they can in one afternoon. The information they gather gets entered into a huge database of bird observations.

You don't have to go to Binocular Boot Camp to help, though. For four days in February, schools, clubs, and individuals in the United States and Canada take part in the Great Backyard Bird Count (GBBC). All you need to do is count birds for 15 minutes, then fill out a form to help scientists learn how climate change, habitat change, and other factors affect bird populations.

Research It Find out more about the GBBC. Design a poster or use presentation software to create a presentation to convince your school to participate.

Bird Radio

How accurate are estimates of bird populations? Scientists at North Carolina State University wondered whether background noise affects scientists' ability to count bird populations. They used Bird Radio to find out.

Bird Radio won't be on the top 40—unless birds get a vote. It plays bird songs to simulate a wild bird population. Researchers adjusted background noise and the number of different bird songs. They learned that this affected people's ability to estimate the number of "birds" singing on Bird Radio. Even slight increases in background noise reduced the accuracy of population counts by up to 40 percent! Scientists are using these data to develop better ways to estimate bird populations.

Test It Create a log sheet for population estimates. The next time you are in a room with other people, close your eyes and try to estimate the number of people in the room. Then count them. Was your estimate close? What factors affected it? Try this experiment in five different settings and record what happens each time.

625

Kids Doing Science

Have students read *Binocular Boot Camp*. Ask students if they know anyone who has a birdfeeder. Invite students with some knowledge of birds and bird watching to share experiences with the class. If someone you know is a "birder," invite him or her to the class to talk about the Great Backyard Bird Count. If nature guides are available, show students some birds that are common in your area and point out the details that are used to identify birds.

Students may be able to get information about the bird count from local nature clubs or nature centers. If students do research on the Internet, suggest that they use *great backyard bird count* rather than *GBBC* as their search term.

Ask: **What could students' backyard bird count tell scientists?** *(Students will likely say that their bird counts could tell scientists what kind of birds and how many birds live in their area at a certain time of year.)* **Why might it be useful for scientists to do another Great Backyard Bird Count at another time of year?** *(Sample: Birds migrate and different kinds or different numbers of birds may be living in their area at different times of the year.)*

Think Like a Scientist

Have students read *Bird Radio*. Point out that each species of bird makes distinctive sounds. Birds that are closely related often have similar calls, or sounds, which make it difficult to distinguish between them. Some birds, such as crows and blue jays, have calls that are easy to identify. If recordings of bird calls are available at your library, you may wish to play some for the class. Some bird identification books include recorded bird calls.

Ask: **How well can you tell your friends apart by their voices?** *(Students will likely say that they can identify good friends by voice right away.)* **How well can you identify a voice when you are outdoors and there are noises from traffic and other sources? How well can you identify a voice when you are in a room where many people are talking, such as the lunchroom at school?** *(Students will likely say that background noise makes it more difficult to identify a voice.)*

Ecosystems and Biomes

Introduce the Big Q UbD

Have students look at the image and read the Engaging Question and description. Ask them to write a hypothesis about where living things get their food. Point out that all living things require food for energy to carry out life processes. Some living things produce their own food, such as plants, while others must feed on other living things. Ask: **Where do you get energy to work or play?** *(Sample: Food)* **Where does a cow or chicken or fish get energy?** *(Grass, grain, plants, other fish)* **Where does an apple tree get energy?** *(The sun)*

Untamed Science Video

GIVE ME THAT CARBON! Before viewing, invite students to suggest ways in which matter might move from one organism to another in an ecosystem. Then play the video. Lead a class discussion and make a list of questions that this video raises. You may wish to have students view the video again after they have completed the chapter to see if their questions have been answered.

To access the online resources for this chapter, search on or navigate to *Ecosystems and Biomes.*

Untamed Science Video shows how carbon moves through an ecosystem.

The Big Question allows students to answer the Engaging Question about the different ways organisms get their food.

my science online.com ▶ **Ecosystems and Biomes**

WHERE DOES FOOD COME FROM?

THE BIG ?

How do energy and matter move through ecosystems?

Flying around hunting for food, this barn owl spots a mouse for dinner. But what did the mouse eat? Perhaps it nibbled on seeds or a caterpillar. Then you might ask, where did the seeds and caterpillar get their food?

Develop Hypotheses Where do living things get their food?

Sample: Some living things can make their own food using sunlight. Other living things get their food from eating other plants and animals.

▶ **UNTAMED SCIENCE** Watch the **Untamed Science** video to learn more about ecosystems and biomes.

Professional Development Note **From the Author**

I have lived in several countries: Kenya, Italy, Nigeria and the United States. Each country has different organisms that are adapted to the climate and other conditions in the area. For example, there is a dry and a rainy season in Kenya where zebras, gazelles, lions, and flat-topped acacia trees live. The annual rainfall is 50 to 100 centimeters and the area is mostly a grassland biome called a savanna. In contrast, Maryland has a deciduous forest biome. The trees, such as flowering dogwood, sweet gum, and white oak—the Maryland state tree—are adapted to the changes in seasons. The leaves that grow in spring and summer are shed before the cold winter begins.

✎ *Zipporah Miller*

Ecosystems and Biomes

CHAPTER 16

Chapter at a Glance

CHAPTER PACING: 8–13 periods or 4–6$\frac{1}{2}$ blocks

INTRODUCE THE CHAPTER: Use the Engaging Question and the opening image to get students thinking. Activate prior knowledge and preteach vocabulary using the Getting Started pages.

Lesson 1: Energy Flow in Ecosystems

Lesson 2: Cycles of Matter

Lesson 3: Biomes

Lesson 4: Aquatic Ecosystems

Lesson 5: Biodiversity

ASSESSMENT OPTIONS: Chapter Test, **EXAM**VIEW® Assessment Suite, Performance Assessment, Progress Monitoring Assessments, SuccessTracker™

Preference Navigator, in the online Planning tools, allows you to customize *Interactive Science* to your own teaching style. You can also edit lesson plans by selecting the Lesson Planner option.

Digital Teacher's Edition allows you to access your Teacher's Edition and Resource online.

my science online.com

Differentiated Instruction

L1 Use Visuals Help students understand that the photograph is an extreme close-up action shot taken at night. Ask them to infer what happened moments before this image was taken, as well as to predict what will happen next. *(Moments before, the owl seized the rodent and took flight. Shortly the owl will kill and eat the rodent.)*

L3 Report on Owls Invite students to share facts they know about owls. Encourage interested students to research and report to the class about what owls eat. *(Students may mention that owls are nocturnal birds of prey that live in various places around the world. Owls feed on rodents, frogs, insects, and small birds.)*

Getting Started

Check Your Understanding

This activity assesses students' understanding of living and nonliving things in an ecosystem. After students have shared their answers, point out that things that once were living, such as leaves that have fallen off a tree, are considered biotic factors, even though they are no longer living.

Preteach Vocabulary Skills

Explain to students that many words can be modified by the addition of a prefix. Learning the meaning of prefixes can make it easier to learn new vocabulary words. Point out that students probably already know some of these prefixes, especially *inter-*, which makes up part of the words *internet*, *international*, and *interact*.

---

16 Getting Started

Check Your Understanding

1. **Background** Read the paragraph below and then answer the question.

> One morning, Han walks to the park and sits by the pond. He has just studied **ecosystems** in class, and now, looking at the pond, he realizes he sees things in a new way. He notices a turtle sunning itself on a rock, and knows that the sun and rock are **abiotic factors**, while the turtle, and other living things, are **biotic factors**.

> The community of organisms that live in a particular area, along with their nonliving environment, make up an **ecosystem.**
>
> **Abiotic factors** are the nonliving parts of an organism's habitat.
>
> **Biotic factors** are the living parts of an organism's habitat.

- Name one more biotic factor and one more abiotic factor that Han might see at the pond.

  Sample: biotic, plants; abiotic, water

> MY READING WEB If you had trouble answering the question above, visit **My Reading Web** and type in *Ecosystems and Biomes*.

Vocabulary Skill

Prefixes Some words can be divided into parts. A root is the part of the word that carries the basic meaning. A prefix is a word part that is placed in front of the root to change the word's meaning. The prefixes below will help you understand some vocabulary in this chapter.

Prefix	Meaning	Example
bio-	life	biodiversity, *n.* the number of different species in an area
inter-	between	intertidal, *adj.* ocean zone between the highest high-tide line and the lowest low-tide line

2. **Quick Check** Circle the prefix in each boldface word below.
- There was an **(inter)mission** between the acts of the play.
- The **(bio)sphere** is the area where life exists.

My Reading Web offers leveled readings related to chapter content.

Vocab Flash Cards offer extra practice with the chapter vocabulary words.

Digital Lesson

- Assign the *Check Your Understanding* activity online and have students submit their work to you.
- Assign the *Vocabulary Skill* activity online and have students submit their work to you.

MY SCIENCE online.com | **Ecosystems and Biomes**

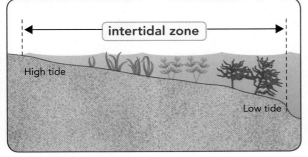

Chapter Preview

LESSON 1
- producer • consumer
- herbivore • carnivore • omnivore
- scavenger • decomposer
- food chain • food web
- energy pyramid
- ⟳ Relate Text and Visuals
- △ Classify

LESSON 2
- evaporation • condensation
- precipitation • nitrogen fixation
- ⟳ Sequence
- △ Infer

LESSON 3
- biome • climate • desert
- rain forest • emergent layer
- canopy • understory • grassland
- savanna • deciduous tree
- boreal forest • coniferous tree
- tundra • permafrost
- ⟳ Compare and Contrast
- △ Draw Conclusions

LESSON 4
- estuary
- intertidal zone
- neritic zone
- ⟳ Outline
- △ Communicate

LESSON 5
- biodiversity • keystone species
- gene • extinction
- endangered species
- threatened species
- habitat destruction
- habitat fragmentation • poaching
- captive breeding
- ⟳ Compare and Contrast
- △ Infer

> **VOCAB FLASH CARDS** For extra help with vocabulary, visit **Vocab Flash Cards** and type in *Ecosystems and Biomes.*

629

Preview Vocabulary Terms

Have students create a three-column chart to rate their knowledge of the vocabulary terms before they read the chapter. In the first column of the chart, students should list the terms for the chapter. In the second column, students should identify whether they can define and use the word, whether they have heard or seen the word before, or whether they do not know the word. As the class progresses through the chapter, have students write definitions for each term in the last column of the chart.

L1 Have students look at the images on this page as you pronounce each vocabulary word. Have students repeat the word after you. Then read the definition. Use the sample sentence in italics to clarify the meaning of the term.

consumer *(kun SOO mur)* An organism that obtains energy by feeding on other organisms. *A fox is a consumer of organisms such as berries, birds, mice, and insects.*

precipitation *(prih sip ih TAY shun)* Rain, snow, sleet, or hail that falls to Earth from clouds. *The precipitation took the form of rain and drenched the foothills.*

desert *(DEZ urt)* An area that receives less than 25 centimeters of rain per year. *The desert is home to plants such as cactus and various grasses.*

intertidal zone *(in tur TYD ul zohn)* The area on shore between the highest high-tide line and the lowest low-tide line. *An intertidal zone can stretch hundreds of meters and contains a variety of plant growth.*

CHAPTER 16

Energy Flow and Ecosystems

1 **How do energy and matter move through ecosystems?**

Lesson Pacing: 1–2 periods or $\frac{1}{2}$–1 block

🕐 **SHORT ON TIME?** To do this lesson in approximately half the time, do the Activate Prior Knowledge activity followed by a discussion of the Key Concepts to familiarize students with the lesson content. Have students do the Quick Lab. The rest of the lesson can be completed by students independently.

> **Preference Navigator,** in the online Planning tools, allows you to customize Interactive Science to your own teaching style. You can also edit lesson plans by selecting the Lesson Planner option.
>
> **Digital Teacher's Edition** allows you to access your Teacher's Edition and Resource materials online.

my science online.com

Lesson Vocabulary

- producer
- consumer
- herbivore
- carnivore
- omnivore
- scavenger
- decomposer
- food chain
- food web
- energy pyramid

Content Refresher

Professional Development Note

Moving Through Energy Pyramids Energy in an ecosystem moves in only one direction, from the bottom (producers) to the top (top-level consumers) of an energy pyramid. Only about 10 percent of the energy in an energy pyramid is transferred from one level to the next. In a food web, energy may not be transferred to the next level for two reasons. First, some energy is given off as heat. Second, not all organisms in one level are eaten by those in the next level. As a result, some energy is not transferred at all. And even those organisms that are consumed might contain parts that cannot be digested—bones, beaks, shells, and so on—which further reduces the total amount of energy that can be transferred.

LESSON OBJECTIVES

 Name and describe energy roles that organisms play in an ecosystem.

 Explain how energy moves through an ecosystem.

Blended Path
Active learning using Student Edition, Inquiry Path, and Digital Path

ENGAGE AND EXPLORE

Teach this lesson using a variety of resources. Begin by reading **My Planet Diary** as a class. Have students share ideas about wild animals that live in their region and what they eat. Then have students do the **Inquiry Warm-Up activity.** Students will classify their own food and food sources. Discuss the categories different students chose and how they classified their food sources. The **After the Inquiry Warm-Up worksheet** sets up a discussion about common food sources. Have volunteers share their answers to number 4 about which foods come from multiple sources.

EXPLAIN AND ELABORATE

Discuss the terms *producer, composer, and decomposer*. **Teach Key Concepts** by explaining that ecosystem roles are based primarily on the way organisms obtain their energy. Ask students to name three energy roles in an ecosystem and tell how an organism fills one of these roles. Use the **Support the Big Q** to illustrate how decomposers get energy and the role of decomposers in an ecosystem. Use **Figure 2** to illustrate the roles of the different animals listed in the chart.

Using food chains and food webs, **Teach Key Concepts** by asking students how energy can be obtained and how it changes as it moves within a pyramid. Then have students practice the inquiry skill in the **Apply It activity.** In the chapter **Lab Investigation activity,** students will observe food chains in a local ecosystem. Hand out the **Key Concept Summaries** as a review of each part of the lesson. Students can also use the online **Vocab Flash Cards** to review key terms.

EVALUATE

Have students take the **Lesson Quiz.** For an alternate assessment, see the **EXAM**VIEW® Assessment Suite, Progress Monitoring Assessments, or SuccessTracker™.

ⒺⓁⓁ Support

1 Content and Language

Compare the words *herbivore, carnivore,* and *omnivore* in the vocabulary. Explain what the word parts signal. The root *-vore* means to devour. The word parts *herbi-, carni-,* and *omni-* tells what the organism devours: *herbi*—vegetable matter, *carni*—meat, and *omni*—all.

Inquiry Path
Hands-on learning in the Lab zone

ENGAGE AND EXPLORE

To teach this lesson with an emphasis on inquiry, begin with the **Inquiry Warm-Up activity.** Students will classify food sources. Discuss the categories different students chose and how they classified food sources. Have students do the **After the Inquiry Warm-Up worksheet.** Talk about common food sources. Have volunteers share their answers to number 4 about which foods come from multiple sources.

EXPLAIN AND ELABORATE

Focus on the **Inquiry Skill** for the lesson. Point out that when you classify, you assign something to a category. What conclusion can be drawn from the categories in the **Inquiry Warm-Up activity?** *(Food sources can be grouped into categories based on the type of organism they come from.)* Have students do the **Quick Lab** to reinforce understanding of decomposition and then share their results.

Review *producer, consumer,* and *decomposer* before beginning the **Apply It activity.** Ask volunteers to share their categories. Have students do the **Lab Investigation activity.** In this investigation, students will observe food chains in a local ecosystem. Students can use the online **Vocab Flash Cards** to review key terms.

EVALUATE

Have students take the **Lesson Quiz.** For an alternate assessment, see the **EXAM**VIEW® Assessment Suite, Progress Monitoring Assessments, or SuccessTracker™.

Digital Path
Online learning at my science online.com

ENGAGE AND EXPLORE

Teach this lesson using digital resources. Begin by having students explore wild animals and what they eat at **My Planet Diary** online. Have them access the Chapter Resources to find the **Unlock the Big Question activity.** There they can answer the questions and refine their responses as they continue through the lesson. You can re-assign the activity and have students submit their work so you can track their progress.

EXPLAIN AND ELABORATE

Students reading above, at, or below the lexile measure of this lesson can access basic content readings at their level at **My Reading Web.** Encourage students to use the online **Vocab Flash Cards** to preview key terms. Have students do the **Quick Lab** and then share their results. What are their observations of decomposition?

Review *producer, consumer,* and *decomposer* before assigning the online **Apply It activity.** Ask volunteers to share their categories. Have students submit their work to you. Have students do the online **Interactive Art activity** to interpret food chains in a food web. Students can then do the online **Virtual Lab** to see how energy moves within a food pyramid. Assign the **Do the Math activity** online and have students submit their work to you. The **Key Concept Summaries** online allow students to read a summary and see an image associated with each part of the lesson. Online remediation is available at **My Science Coach.**

EVALUATE

Have students take the **Lesson Quiz.** For an alternate assessment, see the **EXAM**VIEW® Assessment Suite, Progress Monitoring Assessments, or SuccessTracker™.

2 Frontload the Lesson
Preview the lesson visuals, labels, and captions. Ask students what they know about the words *producer, consumer,* and *decomposer.* Explain the specific meanings these words have in science.

3 Comprehensible Input
Have students study the visuals and their captions in **Figure 2** and **Figure 4** to support the key concepts of the lesson.

4 Language Production
Pair or group students with varied language abilities to complete labs collaboratively for language practice. Have each copy the completed written lab for personal reference.

5 Assess Understanding
Have students create and illustrate their own food pyramids and cut each level as strips. Pair students to share and reassemble their food pyramids to demonstrate comprehension.

LESSON 16.1

Energy Flow in Ecosystems

Establish Learning Objectives

After this lesson, students will be able to:

🗝 Name and describe energy roles that organisms play in an ecosystem.

🗝 Explain how energy moves through an ecosystem.

Engage ———————

Activate Prior Knowledge

MY PLANET DIARY Read *I'll Have the Fish* with the class. Invite students to name wild animals that live in their region. Urge students to think about how each animal may fit into an ecosystem. Ask: **What birds live in the area?** *(Students may indicate one or many bird species.)* **What do you think any of these birds eats?** *(Students may indicate small mammals, insects, or worms.)*

BIG IDEAS OF SCIENCE REFERENCE LIBRARY 📖 Have students look up the following topics: Sushi, Upwelling.

Explore ———————

Lab Resource: Inquiry Warm-Up 🔬

L1 **WHERE DID YOUR DINNER COME FROM?**
Students will classify food sources.

LESSON

1 Energy Flow in Ecosystems

UNLOCK THE BIG ?

🗝 **What Are the Energy Roles in an Ecosystem?**

🗝 **How Does Energy Move Through an Ecosystem?**

MY PLANET DiARY

DISCOVERY

I'll Have the Fish

Scientists have noticed something fishy going on with the wolves in British Columbia, Canada. During autumn, the wolves ignore their typical food of deer and moose and feast on salmon instead. Salmon are very nutritious and lack the big horns and hoofs that can injure or kill wolves. Plus, there are plenty of fish in a small area, making them easier to find and catch.

Many animals, including the wolves, depend upon the salmon's annual mating trip upstream. Losing this important food source to overfishing would hurt the populations of bears, wolves, birds, and many other animals.

Communicate Discuss these questions with a classmate. Write your answers below.

1. What are two reasons the wolves may eat fish in autumn instead of deer or moose?
   Sample: Fish are easier to find and don't hurt the wolves.

2. What effect could overfishing salmon have on an ecosystem?
   Sample: A lack of salmon could decrease the number of predators. With fewer predators, the number of salmon could increase.

▶ PLANET DIARY Go to **Planet Diary** to learn more about food webs.

Lab zone Do the Inquiry Warm-Up *Where Did Your Dinner Come From?*

630 Ecosystems and Biomes

SUPPORT ALL READERS
Lexile Measure = 990L   Lexile Word Count = 1497

Prior Exposure to Content: May be the first time students have encountered this topic

Academic Vocabulary: *apply, classify, describe, identify*

Science Vocabulary: *producer, consumer, decomposer*

Concept Level: Many students may have misconceptions on this topic

Preteach With: My Planet Diary "I'll Have the Fish" and Figure 2 activity

Go to **My Reading Web** to access leveled readings that provide a foundation for the content.

my science online

Vocabulary

- producer • consumer • herbivore • carnivore
- omnivore • scavenger • decomposer • food chain
- food web • energy pyramid

Skills

- ➲ Reading: Relate Text and Visuals
- ◢ Inquiry: Classify

What Are the Energy Roles in an Ecosystem?

Do you play an instrument in your school band? If so, you know that each instrument has a role in a piece of music. Similar to instruments in a band, each organism has a role in the movement of energy through its ecosystem.

An organism's energy role is determined by how it obtains food and how it interacts with other organisms. 🔑 **Each of the organisms in an ecosystem fills the energy role of producer, consumer, or decomposer.**

Producers Energy enters most ecosystems as sunlight. Some organisms, like the plants and algae shown in **Figure 1,** and some types of bacteria, capture the energy of sunlight and store it as food energy. These organisms use the sun's energy to turn water and carbon dioxide into food molecules in a process called photosynthesis.

An organism that can make its own food is a **producer.** Producers are the source of all the food in an ecosystem. In a few ecosystems, producers obtain energy from a source other than sunlight. One such ecosystem is found in rocks deep beneath the ground. Certain bacteria in this ecosystem produce their own food using the energy in hydrogen sulfide, a gas that is present in their environment.

Tape grass and water milfoil

FIGURE 1 ....
Producers
Producers are organisms that can make their own food.
✎ **Identify** Complete the shopping list below to identify the producers that are part of your diet.

- ◯ wheat
- ◯ corn
- ◯ banana
- ◯ Sample: lettuce
- ◯ Sample: orange
- ◯ Sample: rice
- ◯ Sample: apple
- ◯
- ◯

631

Explain

Introduce Vocabulary

To help students understand the terms *herbivore, carnivore,* and *omnivore,* point out that the root *-vore-* is related to the Latin word *vorare,* meaning "to devour or eat."

Teach Key Concepts 🔑

Explain to students that ecosystem roles are based primarily on the way organisms obtain energy. Remind students that every organism must obtain energy from some source and that organisms interact with other organisms within an ecosystem. Ask: **What are the names of the three energy roles in an ecosystem?** (*Producer, consumer, decomposer*) **What is a producer?** (*An organism that makes its own food*) **How do most producers make their own food?** (*Through photosynthesis*) **What is the source of energy for photosynthesis?** (*The sun*)

My Planet Diary provides an opportunity for students to explore real-world connections to energy roles in an ecosystem.

ⒺⓁⓁ Support

1 Content and Language

Students will be introduced to a number of terms that look similar but can be differentiated by the prefixes (*eco-, bio-, herbi-, carni-, omni-*) and suffixes (*-ation, -er*) that are used.

2 Frontload the Lesson

Write the words *food* and *energy* on the board, and then have students complete a picture walk of the lesson. As they scan the pictures, ask them to identify the ways in which food is shown, and how this relates to energy.

3 Comprehensible Input

Ask students what is the name of the section in a local grocery store where one finds fruits and vegetables? (*Produce section*) Ask students to reason why this is the name of this area of the store.

Explain

Teach With Visuals

Have students do the detective work. As they study **Figure 2,** they should keep their eyes open for clues. Ask: **Which animal or animals might have eaten the chicken?** (Wolf, bear) **Which animal or animals might have eaten the vegetables on the ground?** (Bear, rabbit) **Which animals might have eaten food from inside the tent?** (The wolf might have eaten the beef jerky, and the rabbit might have eaten the apples.) **What animal might have eaten the strawberries?** (Bear) **How did you figure out these answers?** (Sample: In most cases, I used the chart, looked at the illustration, and used the process of elimination.)

Support the Big Q ❓ UbD

DECOMPOSERS Remind students that each organism in an ecosystem fills a specific energy role. Producers, such as oak trees, make their own food. Consumers, such as caterpillars and bluebirds, feed on other organisms. Ask: **Where do decomposers get energy?** (From the materials they break down.) **What role do decomposers play in the movement of matter through an ecosystem?** (Decomposers break down wastes and dead organisms and recycle these materials.)

21st Century Learning

INTERPERSONAL SKILLS Have students read the text about producers, consumers, and decomposers with a partner. One partner reads a paragraph aloud, and then the other partner summarizes the paragraph's main idea. Have partners switch roles until they have finished the section.

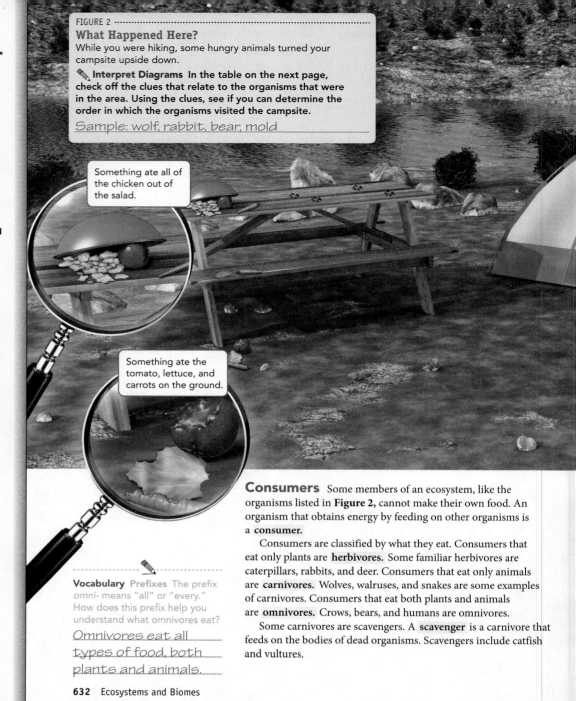

FIGURE 2

What Happened Here?
While you were hiking, some hungry animals turned your campsite upside down.

✎ **Interpret Diagrams** In the table on the next page, check off the clues that relate to the organisms that were in the area. Using the clues, see if you can determine the order in which the organisms visited the campsite.

Sample: wolf, rabbit, bear, mold

Something ate all of the chicken out of the salad.

Something ate the tomato, lettuce, and carrots on the ground.

✎ **Vocabulary** Prefixes The prefix *omni-* means "all" or "every." How does this prefix help you understand what omnivores eat?

Omnivores eat all types of food, both plants and animals.

Consumers Some members of an ecosystem, like the organisms listed in **Figure 2,** cannot make their own food. An organism that obtains energy by feeding on other organisms is a **consumer.**

Consumers are classified by what they eat. Consumers that eat only plants are **herbivores.** Some familiar herbivores are caterpillars, rabbits, and deer. Consumers that eat only animals are **carnivores.** Wolves, walruses, and snakes are some examples of carnivores. Consumers that eat both plants and animals are **omnivores.** Crows, bears, and humans are omnivores.

Some carnivores are scavengers. A **scavenger** is a carnivore that feeds on the bodies of dead organisms. Scavengers include catfish and vultures.

632 Ecosystems and Biomes

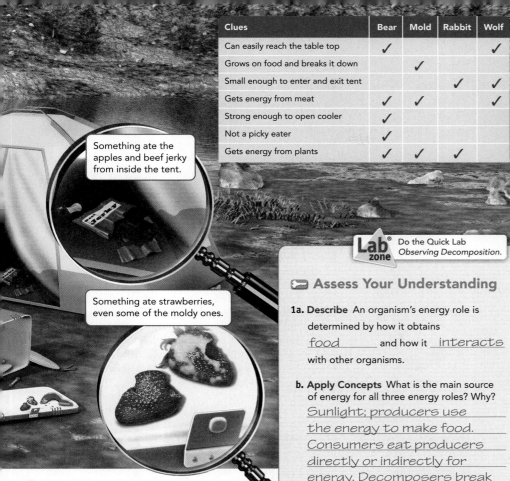

Clues	Bear	Mold	Rabbit	Wolf
Can easily reach the table top	✓			✓
Grows on food and breaks it down		✓		
Small enough to enter and exit tent			✓	✓
Gets energy from meat	✓	✓		✓
Strong enough to open cooler	✓			
Not a picky eater	✓			
Gets energy from plants	✓	✓	✓	

Something ate the apples and beef jerky from inside the tent.

Something ate strawberries, even some of the moldy ones.

Decomposers If an ecosystem had only producers and consumers, the raw materials of life, such as carbon and nitrogen, would stay locked up in wastes and the bodies of dead organisms. However, there are organisms in ecosystems that prevent this from happening. **Decomposers** break down biotic wastes and dead organisms and return the raw materials to the ecosystem.

You can think of decomposers as nature's recyclers. While obtaining energy for their own needs, decomposers return simple molecules to the environment. These molecules can be used again by other organisms. Mushrooms, bacteria, and mold are common decomposers.

Lab zone Do the Quick Lab *Observing Decomposition.*

Assess Your Understanding

1a. Describe An organism's energy role is determined by how it obtains __food__ and how it __interacts__ with other organisms.

b. Apply Concepts What is the main source of energy for all three energy roles? Why? __Sunlight; producers use the energy to make food. Consumers eat producers directly or indirectly for energy. Decomposers break down dead producers and consumers to get energy.__

got it?

○ **I get it!** Now I know that the energy roles in an ecosystem are __producers, consumers, and decomposers.__

○ **I need extra help with** __See TE note.__

Go to **MY SCIENCE** ⓢ **COACH** *online for help with this subject.*

633

Elaborate
Make Analogies

L1 CONSUMERS AND PRODUCERS To help students understand the scientific definitions of the terms *consumer* and *producer*, compare energy roles to the manufacturing process. Ask: **What does a shoe manufacturer produce?** *(Shoes)* **How does a shoe manufacturer resemble a producer in an ecosystem?** *(Sample: Both produce something using raw materials.)* **What does a shopper purchase, or "consume," in a shoe store?** *(The item produced by the manufacturer, shoes)* **How does this interaction resemble the actions of a consumer in an ecosystem?** *(Sample: Both consume something that was produced elsewhere or outside itself.)*

Lab Resource: Quick Lab

L1 OBSERVING DECOMPOSITION Students will observe how materials decay in a compost pile.

Evaluate
Assess Your Understanding

After students answer the questions, have them evaluate their understanding by completing the appropriate sentence.

RTI Response to Intervention

1a. If students have trouble describing an energy role, **then** review with them the two characteristics that determine an organism's energy role.

b. If students need help identifying the energy source, **then** call on volunteers to give examples of organisms and their energy sources. Help students trace the energy source back to the sun.

MY SCIENCE ⓢ **COACH** Have students go online for help in understanding energy roles in ecosystems.

Differentiated Instruction

L1 Concept Map Have students make a concept map of the three energy roles that organisms can fill in an ecosystem. Their maps should include an explanation of how producers, consumers, and decomposers get energy. Have students compare their concept maps when they have finished. Then ask them to make statements that describe the relationship between the roles.

L3 Observe a Local Habitat Invite students to observe a local habitat, such as their yard or the school grounds. Students should try to identify and describe at least one producer *(for example, grass or trees)*, one consumer *(worms, birds)*, and one decomposer *(mushrooms)* that they observe in this habitat. Have students present their findings orally supported with photographs, drawings, or other visual aids.

Explain

Teach Key Concepts 🔑

Explain to students that energy can be transferred from one organism to another in an ecosystem. Ask: **What happens to energy as one organism eats another in an ecosystem?** *(Energy moves through the ecosystem.)* **What is a food chain?** *(A series of events in which one organism eats another and obtains energy)* **How are food chains and a food web related?** *(A food web is made up of many overlapping food chains in the same environment.)*

Address Misconceptions

ENERGY FOR DARK ECOSYSTEMS Point out to students that producers can make their own food through photosynthesis or through chemosynthesis. Explain that not all ecosystems require light as an energy source. Help students understand that ecosystems surrounding deep-sea vents are too far below the water's surface to receive sunlight. In this ecosystem, bacteria living near the vents make food by using energy from chemicals in the water. Ask: **How is this ecosystem similar to the one based on photosynthesis?** *(Like plants, bacteria are producers in the food web.)* You may want to explain to students that deep-sea vents are just one ecosystem in which bacteria obtain energy from chemicals. Encourage interested students to research chemosynthesis to find out more about these bacteria.

How Does Energy Move Through an Ecosystem?

As you have read, energy enters most ecosystems as sunlight and is converted into food by producers. This energy is transferred to the organisms that eat the producers, and then to other organisms that feed on the consumers. 🔑 **Energy moves through an ecosystem when one organism eats another.** This movement of energy can be shown as food chains, food webs, and energy pyramids.

Food Chains One way to show how energy moves in an ecosystem is with a food chain. A **food chain** is a series of events in which one organism eats another and obtains energy. You can follow one example of a food chain in **Figure 3**.

Food Webs A food chain shows only one possible path along which energy can move through an ecosystem. Most producers and consumers are part of many food chains. A more realistic way to show the flow of energy through an ecosystem is with a food web. As shown in **Figure 4**, a **food web** consists of many overlapping food chains in an ecosystem.

Organisms may play more than one role in an ecosystem. Look at the crayfish in **Figure 4**. A crayfish is an omnivore that is a first-level consumer when it eats plants. But when a crayfish eats a snail, it is a second-level consumer.

Just as food chains overlap and connect, food webs interconnect as well. A gull might eat a fish at the ocean, but it might also eat a mouse at a landfill. The gull, then, is part of two food webs—an ocean food web and a land food web. All the world's food webs interconnect in what can be thought of as a global food web.

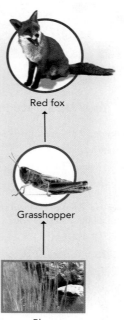
Red fox

Grasshopper

Plants

FIGURE 3 ·····················
Food Chain
In this food chain, you can see how energy moves from plants, to a grasshopper, to the fox. The arrows show how energy moves up the food chain, from one organism to the next.

apply it!

Classify Using what you have learned about food chains, draw or describe a food chain from your local ecosystem. Show at least three organisms in your food chain. Name each organism and label it as a producer, consumer, or decomposer.

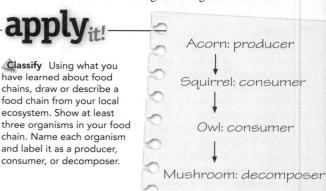
Acorn: producer
↓
Squirrel: consumer
↓
Owl: consumer
↓
Mushroom: decomposer

Interactive Art allows students to see the connections between organisms in a food web.

Digital Lesson: Assign the *Apply It* activity online and have students submit their work to you.

my science online.com   **Energy Flow in Ecosystems**

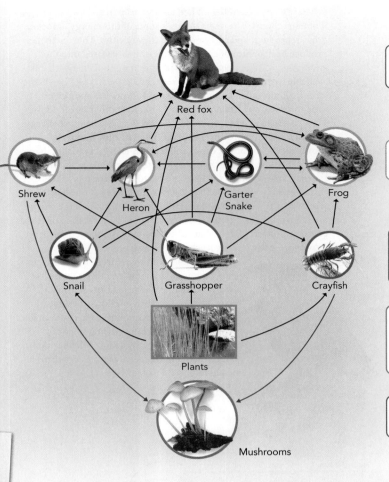

Third-level consumers eat the second-level consumers.

Red fox

Second-level consumers eat the first-level consumers.

Shrew

Heron

Garter Snake

Frog

First-level consumers are organisms that feed directly on the producers.

Snail

Grasshopper

Crayfish

Producers form the base of the food web. The first organism in a food chain is always a producer.

Plants

Decomposers consume the wastes and remains of other organisms.

Mushrooms

FIGURE 4 ·······················

► **INTERACTIVE ART** **Food Web**

A food web consists of many interconnected food chains.

✎ **Complete the tasks.**

1. **Interpret Diagrams** Pick two organisms from the food web. Draw arrows connecting them to the decomposers.

2. 🔁 **Relate Text and Visuals** How can the fox be both a second-level and third-level consumer?

If the fox eats a first-level
consumer, then the fox is a
second-level consumer. If
the fox eats a second-level
consumer, then the fox is a
third-level consumer.

635

Teach With Visuals

Tell students to look at **Figure 4.** Remind students that a food web includes several food chains. Ask: **What are the producers in this food web?** *(Plants such as grasses)* **What are the first-level consumers?** *(Snail, grasshopper, crayfish)* **What are the second-level consumers?** *(Shrew, heron, garter snake, frog, red fox)* **What is the third-level consumer?** *(Red fox)* **What is the decomposer?** *(Mushrooms)*

🔁 **Relate Text and Visuals** Explain to students that they should pay attention to how the text and visuals work together to communicate information. In **Figure 4,** the text and the visuals each provide information that the other does not: The text explains what first-level, second-level, and third-level consumers are, while the visuals show that the fox eats both first-level and second-level consumers.

Elaborate ——————

Apply It!

L1 Review how energy moves through an ecosystem and review the terms *producer, consumer,* and *decomposer* before beginning the activity.

△ **Classify** Remind students that classifying involves organizing information based on a set of chosen characteristics. If students have difficulty classifying each organism as a producer, consumer, or decomposer, have them study the relationships among organisms in the food chain shown in **Figure 3.**

Differentiated Instruction

L1 **Demonstrate Omnivores' Relationships in a Food Web** Have pairs of students take turns tracing two arrows on the food web in **Figure 4** to show how a red fox and a crayfish can be both a first-level consumer and a second-level consumer. Have students show how a shrew can be both a second-level consumer and a third-level consumer. Remind students that the arrows show the direction of energy flow, from food to the organism that eats it.

L3 **Identify the Food Chains** Challenge students to analyze **Figure 4** in order to identify all of the distinct food chains that make up the food web in the illustration. Students can create a series of drawings to show each food chain in isolation from the others in the web.

Explain

Teach Key Concepts 🔑

Explain to students that an organism obtains energy when it eats or produces its own food. When it moves, grows, reproduces, and does other activities, it produces heat and releases that heat into the environment. This release of heat causes less energy to be available to the next consumer. Ask: **In an energy pyramid, where is the most energy available?** *(At the producer level)* **How does the amount of energy change as energy moves up the pyramid?** *(Each level on the pyramid has less energy available than the level below it.)* **How do producers obtain energy?** *(From sunlight)*

🔄 **Relate Text and Visuals** Remind students that relating the text and visuals involves understanding how the text pertains to the visuals in the diagram.

21st Century Learning

CRITICAL THINKING Solidify students' understanding of the calculations shown in the energy pyramid in **Figure 5** by explaining the steps they would take to find the products. They should enter into the calculator the number shown in parentheses next to the label *Producers*. Then they can press the multiply sign and enter the number 0.1 (one-tenth) to find the product 100 kcal. This number represents the amount of energy available to the next consumer in the energy pyramid. Have them repeat this process for each level in the diagram.

Elaborate

Build Inquiry 🧪

L2 IDENTIFY AVAILABLE ENERGY

Materials index cards

Time 10 minutes

Relate the shape of an energy pyramid to the diminishing amount of energy available, moving from bottom to top. Have one student draw an empty pyramid on the board. Have another student divide it into four horizontal sections. Provide index cards with these labels: *Most Energy Available, Least Energy Available, Producers, Consumers, Top Consumer*, and the like. Have students attach their labels to the pyramid on the board.

Ask: **Which section will include the producers?** *(Level 1)* **Which section includes the top consumer?** *(Level 4)* **Which sections include the consumers?** *(Levels 2, 3, and 4)* Have students consider which section represents the most available energy, as well as the least available energy.

Ask: **Which section supports the fewest organisms?** *(Level 4)*

✏️
🔄 **Relate Text and Visuals**
Look at the energy pyramid. Why is a pyramid the best shape to show how energy moves through an ecosystem?

<u>A pyramid decreases</u>
<u>in size from the</u>
<u>bottom to the top, in</u>
<u>the same way that</u>
<u>the available food</u>
<u>energy decreases</u>
<u>from one level to the</u>
<u>next.</u>

FIGURE 5 ·····················
▶ **VIRTUAL LAB** Energy Pyramid
This energy pyramid diagram shows the energy available at each level of a food web and how it is calculated. Energy is measured in kilocalories, or kcal.

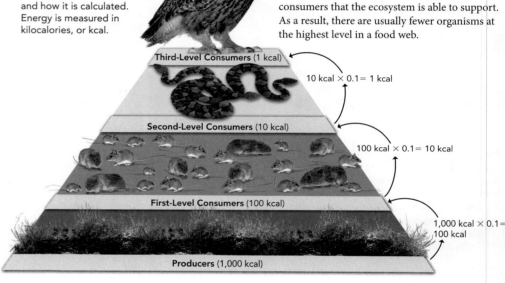

Third-Level Consumers (1 kcal)

Second-Level Consumers (10 kcal)

First-Level Consumers (100 kcal)

Producers (1,000 kcal)

10 kcal × 0.1 = 1 kcal

100 kcal × 0.1 = 10 kcal

1,000 kcal × 0.1 = 100 kcal

Energy Pyramids When an organism in an ecosystem eats, it obtains energy. The organism uses some of this energy to move, grow, reproduce, and carry out other life activities. These activities produce heat, a form of energy, which is then released into the environment. When heat is released, the amount of energy that is available to the next consumer is reduced.

A diagram called an **energy pyramid** shows the amount of energy that moves from one feeding level to another in a food web. You can see an energy pyramid in **Figure 5**. 🔑 **The most energy is available at the producer level of the pyramid. As energy moves up the pyramid, each level has less energy available than the level below.** An energy pyramid gets its name from the shape of the diagram—wider at the base and narrower at the top.

In general, only about 10 percent of the energy at one level of a food web is transferred to the next higher level. Most of the energy at each level is converted to heat. Since about 90 percent of the food energy is converted to heat at each step, there is not enough energy to support many feeding levels in an ecosystem.

The organisms at higher feeding levels of an energy pyramid do not necessarily require less energy to live than the organisms at lower levels. Because so much energy is converted to heat at each level, the amount of energy available at the producer level limits the number of consumers that the ecosystem is able to support. As a result, there are usually fewer organisms at the highest level in a food web.

Virtual Lab allows students to track the energy and biomass of a biome.

Digital Lesson: Assign the *Do the Math* activity online and have students submit their work to you.

my science online.com ▶ | **Energy Flow in Ecosystems**

do the math!

Energy Pyramids

Suppose that the producers at the base of an energy pyramid contain 330,000 kilocalories.
Calculate Using **Figure 5** as a guide, label how much energy would be available at each level of the pyramid based on the questions below.

330 kcal
Third-Level Consumers

3,300 kcal
Second-Level Consumers

33,000 kcal
First-Level Consumers

330,000 kcal
Producers

1. If mice ate all of the plants, how much energy would be available to them as first-level consumers?

2. If all of the mice were eaten by snakes, how much energy would the snakes receive?

3. If all of the snakes were eaten by the owl, how much energy would the owl receive?

4. **CHALLENGE** About how much energy would the owl use for its life processes or lose as heat? *297 kcal*

5. **CHALLENGE** How much energy would be stored in the owl's body? *33 kcal*

Lab zone Do the Lab Investigation *Ecosystem Food Chains.*

Assess Your Understanding

2a. Define A food (web/**chain**) is a series of events in which one organism eats another and obtains energy. A food (**web**/chain) consists of many overlapping food (webs/**chains**).

b. Compare and Contrast Why is a food web a more realistic way of portraying an ecosystem than a food chain?
Because most organisms are part of many overlapping food chains

c. Relate Cause and Effect Why are there usually fewer organisms at the top of an energy pyramid?
Since so much energy is lost from one level to the next level up, the energy available at the top level can only support a few organisms.

got it?

○ I get it! Now I know that energy moves through an ecosystem when *organisms eat other organisms.*

○ I need extra help with *See TE note.*

Go to **my science COACH** *online for help with this subject.*

637

Do the Math!

L1 Review with students the way energy moves through the levels of the energy pyramid. Some students may have difficulty with the last two questions. Point out that 10% of 330 is 33 and 330 − 33 = 297.

See *Math Skill and Problem-Solving Activities* for support.

Lab Resource: Lab Investigation **Lab zone**

L2 **ECOSYSTEM FOOD CHAINS** Students will observe food chains in a local ecosystem.

Evaluate

Assess Your Understanding

After students answer the questions, have them evaluate their understanding by completing the appropriate sentence.

RTI Response to Intervention

2a, b. If students need help distinguishing between food webs and food chains, **then** have them compare the food chain shown in **Figure 3** with the food web shown in **Figure 4**.

c. If students have trouble with energy pyramids, **then** refer them to **Figure 5** and ask how many snakes they think it takes to keep an owl fed and how many mice they think it takes to keep a snake fed.

my science COACH Have students go online for help in understanding energy flow in ecosystems.

Differentiated Instruction

L1 Visualize Energy Transfers To assist students needing help visualizing energy transfers in an energy pyramid, divide the class into groups of three. Distribute scissors and graph paper. The first student, the "producer," should cut a 10-by-10 block of squares from graph paper. The block represents the total amount of food energy stored in the producer. The "producer" should then cut a row of 10 squares from the block and pass it on to the second student, the "first-level consumer." That student should cut one square from the row and pass it to the third student, the "second-level consumer." Students will see that only a small portion of the original energy stored in the producer reaches the second-level consumer.

Name _____ Date _____ Class _____

 After the Inquiry Warm-Up

Energy Flow in Ecosystems

Inquiry Warm-Up, *Where Did Your Dinner Come From?*
In the Inquiry Warm-Up, you investigated where certain foods come from. Using what you learned from that activity, answer the questions below.

1. **DRAW CONCLUSIONS** What is a benefit of knowing the source of a certain food? Explain.

   _____

   _____

2. **MAKE GENERALIZATIONS** Look at the lists of a few of your fellow students. Which source of food was listed the most? Which source was listed the least?

   _____

   _____

3. **COMMUNICATE** Like macaroni, some foods come from multiple sources. Draw a Venn diagram showing the source(s) for the following foods: chicken salad, green peas, bacon, fish, popcorn, beef stew.

4. **INTERPRET DATA** Which foods in the diagram are in the multiple sources category?

   _____

Assess Your Understanding

Energy Flow in Ecosystems

What Are the Energy Roles in an Ecosystem?

1a. **DESCRIBE** An organism's energy role is determined by how it obtains

_____ and how it _____ with other

organisms.

b. **APPLY CONCEPTS** What is the main source of energy for all three

energy roles? Why? _____

_____

got it? ....

○ **I get it!** Now I know that the energy roles in an ecosystem are _____

_____

○ **I need extra help with** _____

How Does Energy Move Through an Ecosystem?

2a. **DEFINE** A food (web/chain) is a series of events in which one organism
eats another and obtains energy. A food (web/chain) consists of many
overlapping food (webs/chains).

b. **COMPARE AND CONTRAST** Why is a food web a more realistic way of
portraying an ecosystem than a food chain?

_____

_____

c. **RELATE CAUSE AND EFFECT** Why are there usually fewer organisms at
the top of an energy pyramid?

_____

_____

got it? ....

○ **I get it!** Now I know that energy moves through an ecosystem when _____

_____

○ **I need extra help with** _____

_____

Energy Flow in Ecosystems

What Are the Energy Roles in an Ecosystem?

An organism's energy role is determined by how it obtains energy and how it interacts with other organisms. **Each of the organisms in an ecosystem fills the energy role of producer, consumer, or decomposer.** Energy enters most ecosystems as sunlight. An organism that can make its own food is a **producer.** Producers are the source of all the food in an ecosystem. An organism that obtains energy by feeding on other organisms is a **consumer.** Consumers that eat only plants are **herbivores;** consumers that eat only animals are **carnivores;** consumers that eat both plants and animals are **omnivores.** A **scavenger** is a carnivore that feeds on the bodies of dead organisms. **Decomposers** break down wastes and dead organisms and return the raw materials to the ecosystem. Mushrooms and bacteria are common decomposers.

How Does Energy Move Through an Ecosystem?

Energy moves through an ecosystem when one organism eats another. A **food chain** is a series of events in which one organism eats another and obtains energy. A **food web** consists of many overlapping food chains in an ecosystem. Organisms may play more than one role in an ecosystem. Just as food chains overlap and connect, food webs interconnect also. When an organism in an ecosystem eats, it obtains energy. The organism uses some of this energy to move, grow, reproduce, and carry out other life activities. These activities produce heat, a form of energy, which is then released into the environment. When heat is released, the amount of energy that is available to the next consumer is reduced. A diagram called an **energy pyramid** shows the amount of energy that moves from one feeding level to another in a food web. **The most energy is available at the producer level of the pyramid. As energy moves up the pyramid, each level has less energy available than the level below.**

On a separate sheet of paper, explain the energy roles in an ecosystem.

Energy Flow in Ecosystems

Understanding Main Ideas

Answer the following questions on a separate sheet of paper.

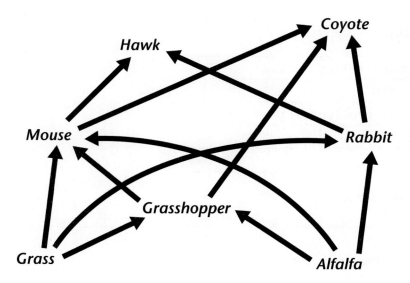

1. Which organism in the food web above is sometimes a first-level consumer and sometimes a second-level consumer? Explain.
2. Choose one food chain in the web. Name all the organisms in that chain. Start with the producer and end with the top-level consumer.
3. Draw an energy pyramid for the food chain you chose. Label the pyramid to tell how much food energy is available at each level.

Building Vocabulary

On a separate sheet of paper, write the term that fits each definition below.

4. Organisms that make their own food
5. Organisms that obtain energy by feeding on other organisms
6. Organisms that break down wastes and dead organisms and return the raw materials to the environment
7. Consumers that eat only animals
8. Consumers that eat only plants
9. Consumers that eat both plants and animals
10. Consumers that feed on the bodies of dead organisms

Energy Flow in Ecosystems

The open ocean, like all land ecosystems, has many food webs. The chart below provides a list of animals in a typical South Atlantic food web and their sources of food energy. Study the table and answer the questions that follow.

Food Webs in the Ocean

Organisms	Obtain food energy from…
Squid	shrimp, fish
Algae	make their own food by photosynthesis
Fishes	shrimp
Penguins	squid

1. Which organisms are the producers?

   _____

2. Which organism is a first-level consumer?

   _____

3. What makes the squid's role different from that of other consumers listed in the table?

   _____

   _____

4. In the space below, draw the ocean food web. Label each organism to identify its energy role in the ecosystem.

Lesson Quiz

Energy Flow in Ecosystems

If the statement is true, write *true*. If the statement is false, change the underlined word or words to make the statement true.

1. _____ A <u>food web</u> is a series of events in which one organism eats another and obtains energy.

2. _____ Each of the <u>organisms</u> in an ecosystem fills the energy role of producer, consumer, or decomposer.

3. _____ Organisms may play <u>only one role</u> in an ecosystem.

4. _____ An organism that obtains energy by feeding on other organisms is a <u>decomposer</u>.

5. _____ Energy enters most ecosystems as <u>sunlight</u>.

Fill in the blank to complete each statement.

6. An organism that can make its own food is a _____.

7. Mushrooms and bacteria are common _____.

8. _____ moves through an ecosystem when one organism eats another.

9. The most energy is available at the _____ level of the pyramid.

10. As energy moves up the pyramid, each level has _____ energy available than the level below.

Energy Flow in Ecosystems

Answer Key

After the Inquiry Warm-Up

1. Accept all reasonable responses. Students may say: Some people may become sick by or are allergic to certain foods and their ingredients. Knowing the source of a food would help them avoid discomfort or worse.

2. Accept all reasonable responses. Students may say: Animal/meat is listed the most, plant/vegetable is listed the least.

3. Sample: Students should draw a Venn diagram with at least two overlapping categories: Plant, Animal. In the Plant circle: green peas, popcorn; in the Animal circle: bacon and fish; and in the Plant/Animal overlap: chicken salad and beef stew.

4. Chicken salad and beef stew

Key Concept Summaries

An organism's energy role—producer, consumer, or decomposer—is determined by how it gets energy and interacts with other organisms. Energy enters most ecosystems as sunlight. Organisms that make their own food are producers. Organisms that get energy by feeding on other organisms are consumers. There are three types of consumers: herbivores eat only plants; carnivores eat only animals; omnivores eat both. Decomposers break down wastes and dead organisms and return the raw materials to the ecosystem.

Review and Reinforce

1. The mouse; it is a first-level consumer when it eats grass or alfalfa and a second-level consumer when it eats a grasshopper.

2. There are many different food chains in the web. Examples include grass ⟶ mouse ⟶ hawk; alfalfa ⟶ grasshopper ⟶ mouse ⟶ coyote; and grass ⟶ rabbit ⟶ hawk. All chains cited by students should start with grass or alfalfa and end with the hawk or coyote.

3. Students' diagrams should show the producer at the base and the top-level consumer at the apex. The levels should be labeled in 10-percent increments—producer, 100%; first-level consumer, 10%; second-level consumer, 1%; third-level consumer, 0.1%.

4. producers
5. consumers
6. decomposers
7. carnivores
8. herbivores
9. omnivores
10. scavengers

Enrich

1. algae
2. shrimp
3. The squid is a second-level consumer when it eats shrimp and a third-level consumer when it eats fish.
4. Students should identify algae as producers, shrimp as first-level consumers, and fishes and penguins as second-level consumers. Squid are first-level consumers and second-level consumers.

Lesson Quiz

1. food chain
2. true
3. more than one role
4. consumer
5. true
6. producer
7. decomposers
8. Energy
9. producer
10. less

Place the outside corner, the corner away from the dotted line, in the corner of your copy machine to copy onto letter-size paper.

Cycles of Matter

2 How do energy and matter move through ecosystems?

Blended Path
Active learning using Student Edition, Inquiry Path, and Digital Path

Lesson Pacing: 2–3 periods or 1–1½ blocks

🕐 **SHORT ON TIME?** To do this lesson in approximately half the time, do the Activate Prior Knowledge activity followed by a discussion of the Key Concepts to familiarize students with the lesson content. Use the Explore the Big Q to help students trace four cycles of matter. Have students do the Quick Labs. The rest of the lesson can be completed by students independently.

Preference Navigator, in the online Planning tools, allows you to customize *Interactive Science* to your own teaching style. You can also edit lesson plans by selecting the Lesson Planner option.

Digital Teacher's Edition allows you to access your Teacher's Edition and Resource materials online.

Lesson Vocabulary
- evaporation
- condensation
- precipitation
- nitrogen fixation

Content Refresher
Professional Development Note

Making Nutrients Available Ecosystem cycles are critical to providing organisms with basic building blocks needed for survival. One such building block is the element nitrogen. Nitrogen is needed for the formation of amino acids, which combine to form proteins. Some proteins are enzymes, which are catalysts for an organism's chemical reactions. Other proteins are the key components of many body tissues, such as muscle and skin. However, an organism cannot use all forms of nitrogen. In an ecosystem, those organisms that are part of the nitrogen cycle make it possible for nitrogen to be converted into forms other organisms can use.

LESSON OBJECTIVES

- Name and describe processes involved in the water cycle.
- Explain how carbon and oxygen are recycled.
- Define and describe the nitrogen cycle.

ENGAGE AND EXPLORE

To teach this lesson using a variety of resources, begin by reading **My Planet Diary** as a class. Have students share their opinions about using animals to save human lives. Then have students do the **Inquiry Warm-Up activity.** Students will investigate their part in the water cycle. Discuss the formation of evaporation of water vapor and students' part in the process. The **After the Inquiry Warm-Up worksheet** sets up a discussion about students' part in a water cycle. Have volunteers share their answers to number 4 about other cycles students may be a part of.

EXPLAIN AND ELABORATE

Teach Key Concepts by explaining the processes of evaporation, condensation, and precipitation in the water cycle.

Continue to **Teach Key Concepts** by explaining how, in an ecosystem, the processes by which carbon and oxygen are recycled are linked. Ask students to explain the roles producers, consumers, and decomposers play in these cycles. Then have students look at **Figure 2** and ask volunteers to share their answers. Students can then practice the lesson's inquiry skill in the **Apply It activity.**

Using **Figure 4, Teach Key Concepts** by asking students how free nitrogen in the air is mixed into compounds. Use the **Explore the Big Q activity** to relate carbon and oxygen, water, and nitrogen cycles and the food chain. Hand out the **Key Concept Summaries** as a review of each part of the lesson. Students can also use the online **Vocab Flash Cards** to review key terms.

EVALUATE

Have students take the **Lesson Quiz.** For an alternate assessment, see the **EXAM**VIEW® Assessment Suite, Progress Monitoring Assessments, or SuccessTracker™.

ⒺⓁⓁ Support

1 Content and Language
Compare the words *evaporation, condensation, precipitation,* and *fixation* in the vocabulary. Explain what the word parts signal. The *-ation* means a process. The word parts *evapor-, condens-, precipit-,* and *fix-* tell about the process; *evapor*—change to steam or vapor; *condens*—change to liquid; *precipit*—condense from a vapor; and *fix*—fasten or hold.

DIFFERENTIATED INSTRUCTION KEY
L1 Struggling Students or Special Needs
L2 On-Level Students **L3** Advanced Students

LESSON PLANNER 16.2

Lab zone **Inquiry Path** Hands-on learning in the Lab zone

ENGAGE AND EXPLORE

Teach this lesson with an emphasis on inquiry. Begin with the **Inquiry Warm-Up activity** in which students will explore evaporation and condensation. Discuss the processes and how they differ. Have students do the **After the Inquiry Warm-Up worksheet.** Talk about students' roles in a water cycle. Have volunteers share their answers to number 4 about other cycles students may be a part of.

EXPLAIN AND ELABORATE

Focus on the **Inquiry Skill** for the lesson. Point out that when you infer, you draw a conclusion by reasoning. What conclusion can be drawn from the results of activities in the **Inquiry Warm-Up activity?** *(You can be part of a water cycle of condensation and evaporation.)* Have students do the first **Quick Lab** and then share their observations about the elements of the water cycle.

Review *producer, consumer,* and *decomposer* before beginning the **Apply It activity.** Ask volunteers to share what they know about the carbon and oxygen cycles. The **Build Inquiry activity** allows students to participate in a minds-on activity about producers and consumers. Have students do the second **Quick Lab** to explore the role of producers in the carbon and oxygen cycles.

Give students an opportunity to role-play various organisms and materials of a nitrogen cycle in the last **Quick Lab.** Students can use the online **Vocab Flash Cards** to review key terms.

EVALUATE

Have students take the **Lesson Quiz.** For an alternate assessment, see the **EXAM**VIEW® Assessment Suite, Progress Monitoring Assessments, or SuccessTracker™.

Digital Path Online learning at my science online.com

ENGAGE AND EXPLORE

To teach this lesson using digital resources, begin by having students explore cycles of matter at **My Planet Diary** online. Have them access the Chapter Resources to find the **Unlock the Big Question activity.** There they can answer the questions and refine their responses as they continue through the lesson. You can re-assign the activity and have students submit their work so you can track their progress.

EXPLAIN AND ELABORATE

Students reading above, at, or below the lexile measure of this lesson can access basic content readings at their level at **My Reading Web.** Have students do the online **Interactive Art activity** to identify the processes of the water cycle. Have students do the first **Quick Lab** and then share their observations about the elements of the water cycle. Encourage students to use the online **Vocab Flash Cards** to preview key terms.

Review *producer, consumer,* and *decomposer* before assigning the online **Apply It activity.** Ask volunteers to share what they know about the carbon and oxygen cycles and have them submit their work to you. Have students do the second **Quick Lab** to explore the role of producers in the carbon and oxygen cycles.

Have students do the online **Interactive Art activity** to observe how energy and matter are cycled through an ecosystem. Have students do the **Quick Lab** to explore to understand the organisms and materials of a nitrogen cycle. The **Key Concept Summaries** online allow students to read a summary and see an image associated with each part of the lesson. Online remediation is available at **My Science Coach.**

EVALUATE

Have students take the **Lesson Quiz.** For an alternate assessment, see the **EXAM**VIEW® Assessment Suite, Progress Monitoring Assessments, or SuccessTracker™.

2 Frontload the Lesson

Preview the lesson visuals, labels, and captions. Ask students what they know about the words *evaporation, condensation, precipitation,* and *fixation.* Explain the specific meanings these words have in science.

3 Comprehensible Input

Have students study the visuals and their captions in **Figure 1, Figure 2,** and **Figure 4** to support the key concepts of the lesson.

4 Language Production

Pair or group students with varied language abilities to complete labs collaboratively for language practice. Have each student copy the completed written lab for personal reference.

5 Assess Understanding

Make true or false statements using lesson content and have students indicate if they agree or disagree with a thumbs up or thumbs down gesture to check whole-class comprehension.

LESSON 16.2

Cycles of Matter

Establish Learning Objectives

After this lesson, students will be able to:

🔑 Name and describe processes involved in the water cycle.

🔑 Explain how the carbon and oxygen cycles are related.

🔑 Define and describe the nitrogen cycle.

Engage ———————

Activate Prior Knowledge

MY PLANET DIARY Read *Canaries and Coal* with the class. Explain that in certain extreme locations, such as at very high altitudes or below ground, it is challenging for humans to get enough oxygen. Some students may find this passage upsetting. Point out that canaries are not used in this way in coal mines any longer. Ask: **What effect does fresh circulating oxygen have in an underground space like a coal mine?** *(It makes it possible for people to breathe.)*

BIG IDEAS OF SCIENCE REFERENCE LIBRARY 📖
Have students look up the following topic: Great Lakes.

Explore ———————

Lab Resource: Inquiry Warm-Up 🔺

L1 **ARE YOU PART OF A CYCLE?** Students will explore how they are part of the oxygen cycle.

LESSON

2 Cycles of Matter

🔑 **What Processes Are Involved in the Water Cycle?**

🔑 **How Are the Carbon and Oxygen Cycles Related?**

🔑 **How Does Nitrogen Cycle Through Ecosystems?**

my planet diary   DISASTER

Canaries and Coal

Have you ever stopped to listen to a bird sing? If you were a coal miner in the early 1900s, your life may have depended on it! Sometimes miners stumbled upon pockets of carbon monoxide, a toxic, odorless gas that makes it difficult for the body to get enough oxygen. Without fresh air circulating in the mineshafts, the miners would fall asleep and eventually die. To prevent this disaster from happening, canaries were used to monitor the air quality. A singing canary indicated that all was well. If the canary stopped singing and died, the miners knew that they needed to quickly leave the mine.

Answer the question below.
Do you think it was ethical, or fair, to use canaries this way? Explain.

Sample: Yes; I think it was ethical to use canaries to save human lives.

▶ PLANET DIARY Go to **Planet Diary** to learn more about cycles of matter.

 Lab zone Do the Inquiry Warm-Up *Are You Part of a Cycle?*

What Processes Are Involved in the Water Cycle?

Recycling is important for ecosystems because matter is limited. To understand how matter cycles through an ecosystem, you need to know a few terms that describe the structure of matter. Matter is made up of tiny particles called atoms. Two or more atoms that are joined and act as a unit make up a molecule. For example, a water molecule consists of two hydrogen atoms and one oxygen atom.

Water is essential for life. The water cycle is the continuous process by which water moves from Earth's surface to the atmosphere and back. 🔑 **The processes of evaporation, condensation, and precipitation make up the water cycle.**

638 Ecosystems and Biomes

SUPPORT ALL READERS

Lexile Measure = 980L   Lexile Word Count = 1292

Prior Exposure to Content: May be the first time students have encountered this topic

Academic Vocabulary: *infer, observe, sequence*

Science Vocabulary: *evaporation, condensation, precipitation*

Concept Level: May be difficult for students who struggle with abstract ideas

Preteach With: My Planet Diary "Canaries and Coal" and Figure 1 activity

Go to **My Reading Web** to access leveled readings that provide a foundation for the content.

my science online

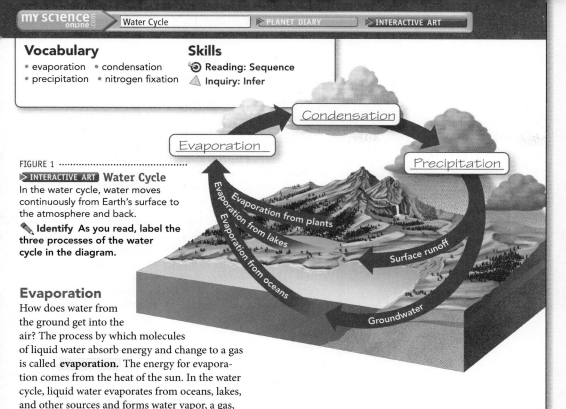

Vocabulary
- evaporation • condensation
- precipitation • nitrogen fixation

Skills
- Reading: Sequence
- Inquiry: Infer

FIGURE 1 ·················

▶ **INTERACTIVE ART** Water Cycle
In the water cycle, water moves continuously from Earth's surface to the atmosphere and back.

✎ **Identify** As you read, label the three processes of the water cycle in the diagram.

Evaporation
How does water from the ground get into the air? The process by which molecules of liquid water absorb energy and change to a gas is called **evaporation.** The energy for evaporation comes from the heat of the sun. In the water cycle, liquid water evaporates from oceans, lakes, and other sources and forms water vapor, a gas, in the atmosphere. Smaller amounts of water also evaporate from living things. Plants release water vapor from their leaves. You release liquid water in your wastes and water vapor when you exhale.

Condensation As water vapor rises higher in the atmosphere, it cools down. The cooled vapor then turns back into tiny drops of liquid water. The process by which a gas changes to a liquid is called **condensation.** The water droplets collect around dust particles and form clouds.

Precipitation As more water vapor condenses, the drops of water in the clouds grow larger. Eventually the heavy drops fall to Earth as **precipitation**—rain, snow, sleet, or hail. Precipitation may fall into oceans, lakes, or rivers. The precipitation that falls on land may soak into the soil and become groundwater, or run off the land, flowing back into a river or ocean.

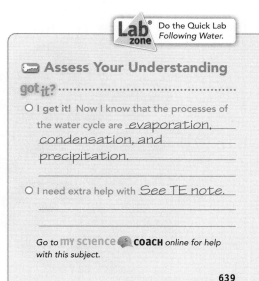

Lab zone Do the Quick Lab
Following Water.

🔑 **Assess Your Understanding**

got it? ·················

○ I get it! Now I know that the processes of the water cycle are _evaporation,_ _condensation, and_ _precipitation._

○ I need extra help with _See TE note._

_____

Go to **my science** ⑤ **coach** online for help with this subject.

639

Explain

Introduce Vocabulary

To help students understand the relationship among the terms *evaporation, condensation,* and *precipitation,* point out the suffix *-tion/-ation* and explain that in these three words it means "the process of."

Teach Key Concepts 🔑

You may want to make sure that students understand the meaning of the word *cycle* and ask them for examples. *(Seasons of the year, days of the week, plants growing from seeds)* Explain to students that several processes take place in the water cycle. Draw students' attention to **Figure 1.** Ask: **What is the function of the water cycle?** *(It moves water from Earth's surface to the atmosphere and back.)* **What are the three processes that move water between Earth's surface and the atmosphere?** *(Evaporation, condensation, precipitation)* Point out to students that the process in which water evaporates from plant leaves is a type of evaporation called transpiration. **Which process includes melted snow entering rivers?** *(Surface runoff)* **How can you tell from the figure that the water cycle is continuous?** *(All three processes happen over and over again.)*

Lab Resource: Quick Lab ⬛

L2 **FOLLOWING WATER** Students will make a solar still and observe elements of the water cycle.

Evaluate

Assess Your Understanding

Have students evaluate their understanding by completing the appropriate sentence.

⬛Ⓣ⬛ Response to Intervention

If students need help with the water cycle, **then** call on volunteers to describe steps in the water cycle while you diagram each of these steps on the board.

my science ⑤ **coach** Have students go online for help in understanding the water cycle.

My Planet Diary provides an opportunity for students to explore real-world connections to the carbon and oxygen cycles.

Interactive Art allows students to identify the processes of the water cycle.

my science online.com | Water Cycle

ⒺⓁⓁ Support

1 Content and Language
Ask students to identify the common suffix in *evaporation, condensation,* and *precipitation.* The suffix *-tion* means "the act or process of doing something."

2 Frontload the Lesson
To help students understand why it is called the *water cycle,* ask students to explain what a cycle is. Simplify **Figure 1** by drawing a water cycle

with two parts—liquid and gas (vapor)—and arrows that form a cycle going from one to another.

3 Comprehensible Input
Explain the Explore the Big Q image and caption, restating information as needed. Have students complete the **Figure 5** activity, allowing them to draw and write according to their language proficiency level.

Explain

Teach Key Concepts 🔑

Remind students that the carbon and oxygen cycles are linked and that producers and consumers play a part in both cycles. Review the basic processes of photosynthesis and respiration. Ask: **What is the role of producers in the carbon and oxygen cycles?** *(Producers take in carbon dioxide during photosynthesis and use it to make food in the form of carbon-containing molecules. They release oxygen as a product of photosynthesis.)* **How do consumers fit into the carbon and oxygen cycles?** *(Consumers take in carbon-containing molecules by eating producers; when they break these molecules down, they release carbon dioxide. Consumers use oxygen to get energy from the food they have eaten.)* **How will depriving a closed terrarium of sunlight affect the oxygen and carbon cycles of the plants and small animals inside?** *(Without sunlight, plants can't make food and won't release oxygen; consumers will have no food sources and insufficient oxygen and will not release carbon dioxide.)*

Teach With Visuals

Tell students to look at **Figure 2**. Ask: **What two cycles are illustrated in this diagram?** *(Carbon cycle, oxygen cycle)* **How are these two cycles represented in the diagram?** *(Violet arrows and lines illustrate the processes of the carbon cycle, and yellow arrow and lines illustrate the processes of the oxygen cycle.)* You may want to point out to students a key difference between the carbon and oxygen cycles illustrated in **Figure 2** and the water cycle in **Figure 1**. The water cycle involves physical changes as water changes state. The carbon and oxygen cycles involve the chemical changes of photosynthesis and cellular respiration.

Elaborate

Apply It!

L1 Review the definitions of *producer, consumer,* and *decomposer* before beginning the activity.

▲ **Infer** Remind students that when they infer, they use the information they are given as well as their prior knowledge to answer a question or draw a conclusion. Make sure students understand that a cow is a first-level consumer. Discuss with students how a cow obtains oxygen and carbon.

How Are the Carbon and Oxygen Cycles Related?

Carbon and oxygen are also necessary for life. Carbon is an essential building block in the bodies of living things. For example, carbon is a major component of bones and the proteins that build muscles. And most organisms use oxygen for their life processes. 🔑 **In ecosystems, the processes by which carbon and oxygen are recycled are linked. Producers, consumers, and decomposers all play roles in recycling carbon and oxygen.**

The Carbon Cycle Most producers take in carbon dioxide gas from the air during food-making or photosynthesis. They use carbon from the carbon dioxide to make food—carbon-containing molecules such as sugars and starches. As consumers eat producers, they take in the carbon-containing molecules. Both producers and consumers then break down the food to obtain energy. As the food is broken down, producers and consumers release carbon dioxide and water into the environment. When producers and consumers die, decomposers break down their remains and return carbon molecules to the soil. Some decomposers also release carbon dioxide into the air.

The Oxygen Cycle Look at **Figure 2**. Like carbon, oxygen cycles through ecosystems. Producers release oxygen as a result of photosynthesis. In fact, photosynthesis is responsible for most of the oxygen in Earth's atmosphere. Most organisms take in oxygen from the air or water and use it to carry out their life processes.

Human Impact Human activities also affect the levels of carbon and oxygen in the atmosphere. When humans burn oil and other plant-based fuels, carbon dioxide is released into the atmosphere. Carbon dioxide levels can also rise when humans clear forests for lumber, fuel, and farmland. Increasing levels of carbon dioxide are a major factor in global warming.

As you know, producers take in carbon dioxide during photosynthesis. When trees are removed from the ecosystem, there are fewer producers to absorb carbon dioxide. There is an even greater effect if trees are burned down to clear a forest. When trees are burned down, additional carbon dioxide is released during the burning process.

apply it!

Producers, consumers, and decomposers all play a role in recycling carbon and oxygen.

△ **Infer** On the lines below, describe how you think a cow eating grass is part of both the carbon and oxygen cycles.

Sample: The cow takes in oxygen from the air and carbon molecules from the grass. Carbon dioxide is released by the cow as a waste product.

Digital Lesson: Assign the *Apply It* activity online and have students submit their work to you.

Carbon and Oxygen Cycles

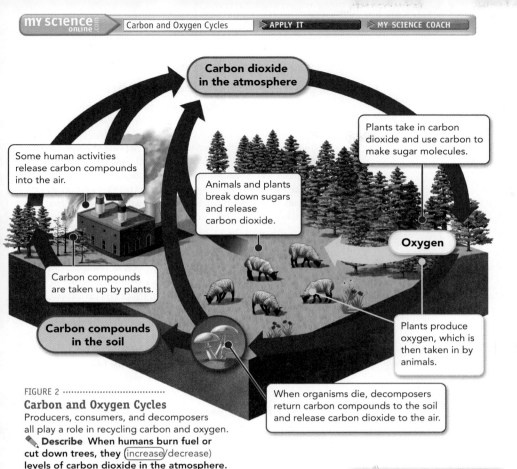

Carbon dioxide in the atmosphere

Some human activities release carbon compounds into the air.

Plants take in carbon dioxide and use carbon to make sugar molecules.

Animals and plants break down sugars and release carbon dioxide.

Carbon compounds are taken up by plants.

Oxygen

Carbon compounds in the soil

Plants produce oxygen, which is then taken in by animals.

When organisms die, decomposers return carbon compounds to the soil and release carbon dioxide to the air.

FIGURE 2 ·····································
Carbon and Oxygen Cycles
Producers, consumers, and decomposers all play a role in recycling carbon and oxygen.
✎ **Describe** When humans burn fuel or cut down trees, they (increase/decrease) levels of carbon dioxide in the atmosphere.

Lab zone Do the Quick Lab *Carbon and Oxygen Blues.*

⬌ Assess Your Understanding

1a. Identify Carbon and oxygen are both
<u>recycled</u> in an ecosystem.

b. Develop Hypotheses How might the death of all the producers in a community affect the carbon and oxygen cycles?

<u>The cycles would halt because</u>
<u>no oxygen or carbon would be</u>
<u>made available to consumers.</u>

got it?

○ **I get it!** Now I know that the carbon and oxygen cycles are related by <u>the roles</u>
<u>producers, consumers, and</u>
<u>decomposers play in</u>
<u>recycling them.</u>

○ **I need extra help with** <u>See TE note.</u>

Go to my science ⬤ coach *online for help with this subject.*

641

Build Inquiry **Lab** zone

L2 PREDICT CARBON AND OXYGEN CYCLING

Materials none

Time 10 minutes

Review the differing roles of producers and consumers in recycling and carbon and oxygen. Describe for students a sealed jar containing guppies, plants, algae, and snails. Provide a picture if possible. (If you provide a picture, make sure that the algae are not green. Green algae are classified as plants, not protists.)

Ask: **Which organisms in the jar are producers?** *(The plants and algae)* **What do the producers release when they conduct photosynthesis?** *(Oxygen)* **What happens to the oxygen?** *(It is taken in by the guppies and snails.)* **Where do the producers get the carbon dioxide they need?** *(It is released by the guppies and snails.)* **Would you predict that this cycle would go on indefinitely? Why or why not?** *(Yes; as long as the producers receive sunlight and the guppies and snails receive food, the carbon and oxygen will continue to cycle between the producers and the consumers.)*

Lab Resource: Quick Lab **Lab** zone

L2 CARBON AND OXYGEN BLUES Students will explore the role of producers in the carbon and oxygen cycles.

Evaluate ⎯⎯⎯⎯⎯⎯⎯

Assess Your Understanding

After students answer the questions, have them evaluate their understanding by completing the appropriate sentence.

R T I Response to Intervention

1. If students have trouble with the carbon and oxygen cycles, **then** help them trace the path of carbon and oxygen through the diagram that shows the two cycles.

my science ⬤ coach Have students go online for help in understanding the carbon and oxygen cycles.

LESSON 16.2

Differentiated Instruction

L3 Research Effects of Carbon Dioxide in the Atmosphere Challenge students to do research to learn more about how increasing carbon dioxide levels in the atmosphere relate to global climate change. Urge students to prepare a written report and to include a list of their reference sources.

L1 Two Cycles Some students may find it helpful to look at the carbon cycle and oxygen cycle as separate cycles.

Have students diagram the oxygen cycle and then the carbon cycle on separate sheets of paper. Then have students compare their diagrams to the combined cycle diagram in **Figure 2.** If students have previously studied photosynthesis and respiration, they can apply their understanding of these processes to trace how carbon and oxygen cycle through producers, consumers, and decomposers.

Explain

Teach Key Concepts 🔑

Explain to students that the nitrogen cycle shares some characteristics with other cycles of matter, such as the carbon and oxygen cycles. Ask: **In what three places is nitrogen found?** *(In the soil, in the air, and in living things)* **What is "free" nitrogen?** *(Nitrogen gas, which is not combined with other kinds of atoms)* Remind students that most organisms cannot utilize nitrogen gas. Ask: **By what process do bacteria turn nitrogen into a usable form?** *(Nitrogen fixation)* **What organisms return simple nitrogen compounds to the soil?** *(Decomposers)*

21st Century Learning

INFORMATION LITERACY The application of nitrogen fertilizers to crops and lawns has resulted in the leaching of nitrates into groundwater. The contaminated groundwater eventually flows into streams, rivers, and lakes, affecting numerous ecosystems. This contamination affects water and habitat quality, which eventually leads to changes in the plant and animal populations. Encourage students to research the dangers of fertilizer contamination and what is now being done to help solve this problem. For instance, many local municipalities have begun to pass laws restricting when fertilizer can be applied and how much fertilizer can be used. Students can present their findings to the class in a short presentation.

How Does Nitrogen Cycle Through Ecosystems?

Like carbon, nitrogen is one of the necessary building blocks that make up living things. For example, in addition to carbon, nitrogen is also an important component of proteins. 🔑 **In the nitrogen cycle, nitrogen moves from the air into the soil, into living things, and back into the air or soil.** Since the air around you is about 78 percent nitrogen gas, you might think that it would be easy for living things to obtain nitrogen. However, most organisms cannot use nitrogen gas. Nitrogen gas is called "free" nitrogen because it is not combined with other kinds of atoms.

Nitrogen Fixation Most organisms can use nitrogen only after it has been "fixed," or combined with other elements to form nitrogen-containing compounds. The process of changing free nitrogen into a usable form of nitrogen, as shown in **Figure 4,** is called **nitrogen fixation.** Most nitrogen fixation is performed by certain kinds of bacteria. These bacteria live in bumps called nodules (NAHJ oolz) on the roots of legumes. These plants include clover, beans, peas, alfalfa, peanuts, and some trees.

The relationship between the bacteria and the legumes is an example of mutualism. Both the bacteria and the plants benefit from this relationship: The bacteria feed on the plants' sugars, and the plants are supplied with nitrogen in a usable form.

Return of Nitrogen to the Environment
Once nitrogen is fixed, producers can use it to build proteins and other complex compounds. Nitrogen can cycle from the soil to producers and then to consumers many times. At some point, however, bacteria break down the nitrogen compounds completely. These bacteria then release free nitrogen back into the air, causing the cycle to continue.

FIGURE 3 ·······································

Growth in Nitrogen-Poor Soil
Pitcher plants can grow in nitrogen-poor soil because they obtain nitrogen by trapping insects in their tube-shaped leaves. The plants then digest the insects and use their nitrogen compounds.

✏ **Circle the correct word in each sentence.**

1. **Identify** If nitrogen in the soil isn't (fixed / free), then most organisms cannot use it.

2. **CHALLENGE** The relationship between the pitcher plant and the insects is an example of (competition / predation / symbiosis).

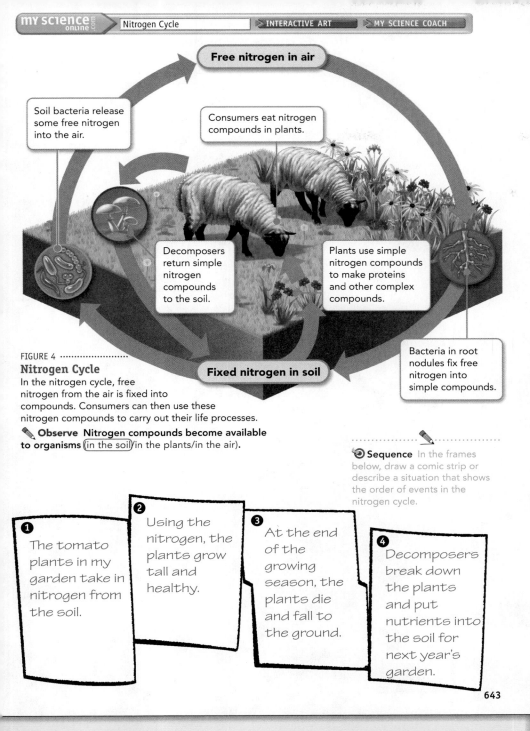

Free nitrogen in air

Soil bacteria release some free nitrogen into the air.

Consumers eat nitrogen compounds in plants.

Decomposers return simple nitrogen compounds to the soil.

Plants use simple nitrogen compounds to make proteins and other complex compounds.

Bacteria in root nodules fix free nitrogen into simple compounds.

Fixed nitrogen in soil

FIGURE 4 ·····················

Nitrogen Cycle
In the nitrogen cycle, free nitrogen from the air is fixed into compounds. Consumers can then use these nitrogen compounds to carry out their life processes.

✏ **Observe** Nitrogen compounds become available to organisms (in the soil/in the plants/in the air).

↩ **Sequence** In the frames below, draw a comic strip or describe a situation that shows the order of events in the nitrogen cycle.

❶ The tomato plants in my garden take in nitrogen from the soil.

❷ Using the nitrogen, the plants grow tall and healthy.

❸ At the end of the growing season, the plants die and fall to the ground.

❹ Decomposers break down the plants and put nutrients into the soil for next year's garden.

643

Teach With Visuals

Have students look at **Figure 4.** Ask: **Why is nitrogen essential for living things?** *(It is used to make proteins.)* **What kinds of organisms return nitrogen compounds to the soil?** *(Bacteria and other decomposers)*

↩ **Sequence** Explain that sequencing involves organizing events or steps in a process in their correct order. Students should use the information in **Figure 4** to help them determine the correct order of events in the nitrogen cycle.

21st Century Learning

L3 CRITICAL THINKING Ask students to review the cycles of matter they have seen in this lesson and look for similarities and differences in the way materials move through the ecosystem. Also ask students to compare the way living things use water, carbon, oxygen, and nitrogen. Encourage students to recognize that the elements in these cycles—carbon, nitrogen, oxygen, and hydrogen (from water) are essential elements necessary to the make-up of living things. Ask: **How does the nitrogen cycle differ from the carbon and oxygen cycles?** *(Nitrogen becomes available to organisms through the soil rather than being absorbed from the air.)*

Differentiated Instruction

L1 Illustrate Mutualism Have pairs of students create simple diagrams to show how the relationship between bacteria and legumes represents mutualism. Students' diagrams should include labels and a simple rendering of bacteria in a nodule on the roots of a legume. Students might use arrows as well as text descriptions to convey the fact that the bacteria feed on the plant's sugars and that the plant is supplied with usable nitrogen.

L3 Nitrogen in the Soil Challenge students to do research to learn about the important role that nitrogen plays in agriculture. Students might focus on their region or state as they gather information that shows how farmers' economic success is dependent on their soil having sufficient nitrogen.

Explain

Teach With Visuals

Tell students to look at **Figure 5.** Point out that there are different ways to represent the cycles and the food chain in the diagram. Explain that students may use different details and may configure a cycle or food chain differently from one another. Ask: **Which two animals in the illustration are essentially interchangeable, in terms of their function in cycles of matter and food chains?** *(Pig, rabbit)*

Remind students that the plants and fungi pictured play the same role as the animals in the carbon cycle. They break down carbon-containing molecules in food, releasing carbon into the air (as carbon dioxide) and into the soil.

Elaborate

Explore the Big Q ? UbD

Direct students' attention to the particular details—sky, clouds, precipitation, trees, grass, water, soil, plants and their roots, fish, snake, field mouse, rabbit, pig, mushrooms—that are included in **Figure 5.** Ask: **Which of the cycles involves the atmosphere?** *(All four)* **Which of the cycles involves the roots of plants?** *(Nitrogen)* **What is the only third-level consumer in the illustration?** *(Snake)*

21st Century Learning   DK

COMMUNICATION Have students read *Great Lakes* in the **Big Ideas of Science Reference Library** and create a poster using the Great Lakes watershed to illusrate the three processes of the water cycle.

Lab Resource: Quick Lab

L1 PLAYING NITROGEN CYCLE ROLES Students will explore the processes and relationships involved in the nitrogen cycle by role-playing various materials and organisms.

Cycles of Matter

EXPLORE THE BIG ?

How do energy and matter move through ecosystems?

FIGURE 5

> INTERACTIVE ART Energy and matter are constantly being cycled through an ecosystem. These cycles can occur at the same time.

Interpret Diagrams Using colored pencils, draw arrows to represent the following in the figure below: water cycle (blue), carbon cycle (purple), oxygen cycle (yellow), nitrogen cycle (orange), food chain (green). Label each cycle.

Carbon and oxygen cycle

Water cycle

Food chain

644 Ecosystems and Biomes

Interactive Art allows students to observe how energy and matter are cycled through an ecosystem.

my science online   Nitrogen Cycle

Nitrogen cycle

🗝 Assess Your Understanding

2a. Describe (Fixed/Free) nitrogen is not combined with other kinds of atoms.

b. Predict What might happen in a community if farmers did not plant legume crops?

Consumers and producers would not survive because they depend on the nodules on the roots of legumes to fix nitrogen. Fixed nitrogen is needed to make the compounds they need for life processes. The nitrogen cycle would stop.

c. ⓐANSWER How do energy and matter move through ecosystems?

Food webs move energy through an ecosystem. Cycles move matter such as water, carbon, oxygen, and nitrogen through an ecosystem.

got it?

○ I get it! Now I know that the nitrogen cycle moves nitrogen from the air into the soil, into living things, and back into the air or soil.

○ I need extra help with See TE note.

Go to **my science COACH** *online for help with this subject.*

645

Evaluate

Assess Your Understanding

After students answer the questions, have them evaluate their understanding by completing the appropriate sentence.

Answer the Big Q ❓ UbD

To help students focus on the Big Question, lead a class discussion about how energy and matter move through an ecosystem.

RTI Response to Intervention

2a, b. If students need help with the nitrogen cycle, **then** help them trace the movement of nitrogen through the ecosystem, especially the steps involving bacteria.

c. If students have trouble with cycles of matter, **then** have them review the illustrations of the cycles covered in this lesson.

my science 🕲 COACH Have students go online for help in understanding cycles of matter.

Differentiated Instruction

L1 Compare and Contrast Cycles
Have pairs or groups of students use Venn diagrams, drawings, or tables to compare and contrast the water, carbon, oxygen, and nitrogen cycles. Encourage students to review the figures in this lesson, comparing and contrasting both the individual steps in the processes and the overall functions of each cycle.

L3 Human Effects on Cycles of Matter Challenge students to write a composition in which they describe in detail how particular human activities affect the water, carbon, oxygen, or nitrogen cycle. Students may wish to research using the Internet before beginning their compositions.

Lab zone **After the Inquiry Warm-Up**

Cycles of Matter

Inquiry Warm-Up, *Are You Part of a Cycle?*
In the Inquiry Warm-Up, you investigated your part in the water cycle. Using what you learned from that activity, answer the questions below.

1. **RELATE CAUSE AND EFFECT** What process caused the water vapor to form on the mirror?

   _____

   _____

2. **OBSERVE** What happened to the water vapor on the mirror after a few moments?

   _____

   _____

3. **USE PRIOR KNOWLEDGE** What happens to the water vapor after it evaporates into the air?

   _____

   _____

4. **USE PRIOR KNOWLEDGE** Describe one other cycle of which you are a part.

   _____

   _____

Name _____ Date _____ Class _____

Cycles of Matter

What Processes Are Involved in the Water Cycle?

got$_{it}$? ....

○ **I get it!** Now I know that the processes of the water cycle are _____

_____

_____

○ **I need extra help with** _____

_____

How Are the Carbon and Oxygen Cycles Related?

1a. **IDENTIFY** Carbon and oxygen are both _____ in an ecosystem.

b. **DEVELOP HYPOTHESES** How might the death of all the producers in a community affect the carbon and oxygen cycles?

_____

_____

_____

got$_{it}$? ....

○ **I get it!** Now I know that the carbon and oxygen cycles are related by _____

_____

_____

○ **I need extra help with** _____

_____

Assess Your Understanding

Cycles of Matter

How Does Nitrogen Cycle Through Ecosystems?

2a. **DESCRIBE** (Fixed/Free) nitrogen is not combined with other kinds of atoms.

b. **PREDICT** What might happen in a community if farmers did not plant legume crops?

_____

_____

_____

_____

_____

c. **ANSWER** 🔵 How do energy and matter move through ecosystems?

_____

_____

_____

_____

_____

got it? ....

○ **I get it!** Now I know that the nitrogen cycle _____

_____

_____

○ **I need extra help with** _____

_____

Key Concept Summaries

Cycles of Matter

What Processes Are Involved in the Water Cycle?

The water cycle is the continuous process by which water moves from Earth's surface to the atmosphere and back. **The processes of evaporation, condensation, and precipitation make up the water cycle.** The process by which molecules of liquid water absorb energy and change to a gas is called **evaporation.** In the water cycle, liquid water evaporates from oceans, lakes, plants, and other living things and forms water vapor, a gas, in the atmosphere. As water vapor rises higher in the atmosphere, it cools and turns back into liquid water. The process by which a gas changes to a liquid is called **condensation.** As more water vapor condenses, drops of water fall to Earth as **precipitation**—rain, snow, sleet, or hail.

How Are the Carbon and Oxygen Cycles Related?

Carbon is an essential building block in the bodies of living things. Most organisms use oxygen for their life processes. **In ecosystems, the processes by which carbon and oxygen are recycled are linked.** **Producers, consumers, and decomposers all play roles in recycling carbon and oxygen.** Human activities also cause the levels of carbon dioxide in the atmosphere to rise.

How Does Nitrogen Cycle Through Ecosystems?

Nitrogen is one of the necessary building blocks that make up living things. **In the nitrogen cycle, nitrogen moves from the air into the soil, into living things, and back into the air.** The air around us is about 78 percent nitrogen gas, but most organisms cannot use nitrogen gas, or "free nitrogen." The process of changing free nitrogen into a usable form of nitrogen is called **nitrogen fixation.** This process is performed by some kinds of bacteria.

On a separate sheet of paper, explain the water cycle.

Cycles of Matter

Understanding Main Ideas

Answer the following questions on a separate sheet of paper.

1. What is the source of energy for the process of evaporation?
2. What happens to rainwater that falls on land?
3. How are oxygen and carbon cycled between plants and animals?
4. Why are nitrogen-fixing bacteria so important to other organisms?

Building Vocabulary

Answer the following question and identify labels in the spaces provided.

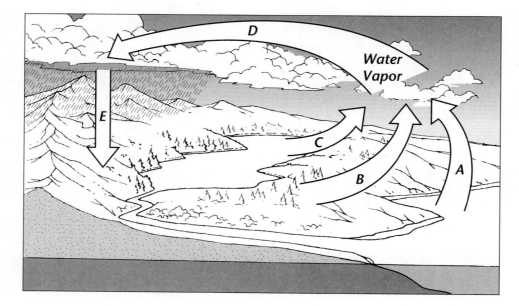

5. Which cycle is shown in the diagram above?

_____

Identify each process labeled in the diagram.

6. A _____

7. B _____

8. C _____

9. D _____

10. E _____

Cycles of Matter

Deepa wanted to study how oxygen and carbon dioxide move through ecosystems. To do this, she set up three jars to represent consumers, producers, and consumers and producers together. She tested the jars for the presence of oxygen and carbon dioxide. Deepa's procedure and results are shown below. Study this information and then use a separate sheet of paper to answer the questions.

Testing for Oxygen and Carbon Dioxide

Procedure

Bromthymol blue (BTB) is a chemical that turns yellow in the presences of carbon dioxide. In the presence of oxygen, BTB stays blue. Deepa put the same amount of BTB in the three jars, and varied the organisms she placed in each jar. In Jar A, she put two aquatic snails. In Jar B, she put two sprigs of Elodea, an aquatic plant. In Jar C, she put two snails and two sprigs of Elodea.

 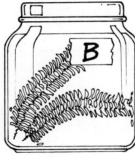 

Results

Deepa examined the jars every day for three days. These are the observations she recorded.

Analyze and Conclude

1. Why did the BTB solution in Jar A turn yellow?
2. Why did the BTB solution in Jar B stay blue?
3. Why did the BTB solution in Jar C stay blue?
4. Which jar showed what happens during the carbon and oxygen cycles in nature? Describe the process that occurred in that jar.

Jar	Observations
A	The BTB solution turned yellow.
B	The BTB solution stayed blue.
C	The BTB solution stayed blue.

Lesson Quiz

Cycles of Matter

Fill in the blank to complete each statement.

1. The processes of evaporation, condensation, and precipitation make up

   _____.

2. The process by which a gas changes to a liquid is called _____.

3. In ecosystems, producers, consumers, and decomposers are linked by their roles in

   recycling carbon and _____.

4. _____ is a major component of bones and the proteins that build
   muscles.

5. The process of changing free nitrogen into a usable form of nitrogen is called

   _____.

If the statement is true, write _true_. If the statement is false, change the underlined word or words to make the statement true.

6. _____ Condensation is the continuous process by which water moves
   from Earth's surface to the atmosphere and back.

7. _____ In the water cycle, liquid water evaporates from oceans, plants,
   and other living things and forms water vapor, a gas, which rises in the atmosphere,
   then cools and turns back to drops of liquid water.

8. _____ Most organisms take in nitrogen from the air or water and use
   it to carry out their life processes.

9. _____ In a(n) food web, nitrogen moves from the air into the soil, into
   living things, and back into the air.

10. _____ The air around us is about 78 percent nitrogen gas, but most
    organisms cannot use this "free nitrogen."

Cycles of Matter

Answer Key

After the Inquiry Warm-Up

1. condensation due to the temperature difference between the mirror and air coming out of your lungs

2. It evaporated into the air.

3. It condenses and falls to Earth as precipitation.

4. Accept all reasonable responses. Students may say: carbon cycle

Key Concept Summaries

The water cycle is the continuous process by which water moves from Earth's surface to the atmosphere and back through evaporation, condensation, and precipitation. In evaporation, molecules of liquid water absorb energy and change to water vapor, a gas, in the atmosphere. As water vapor rises higher, it cools and turns back into liquid water. This process, in which a gas changes to a liquid, is condensation. As more water vapor condenses, drops of water fall to Earth as precipitation—rain, snow, sleet, or hail.

Review and Reinforce

1. the sun

2. It soaks into the soil and becomes groundwater or runs off the land and flows into a river or ocean.

3. Plants take in carbon dioxide in the air, use the carbon to make their own food in photosynthesis, and release oxygen as a waste product. Animals take in oxygen in the air, use it in their life processes, and release carbon dioxide as a waste product.

4. Other organisms cannot use "free" nitrogen in the air. Nitrogen-fixing bacteria combine "free" nitrogen with other elements to form nitrogen-containing compounds that other organisms can use.

5. the water cycle

6. evaporation from oceans

7. evaporation from plants

8. evaporation from lakes

9. condensation

10. precipitation

Enrich

1. The change from blue to yellow indicated the addition of carbon dioxide, which was released by the snails.

2. No color change indicated that no carbon dioxide was added to the solution. Plants release oxygen, which would not change the solution's color.

3. The amount of oxygen released by the plants was equal to or greater than the amount of carbon dioxide released by the snails.

4. Jar C: The snails released carbon dioxide as a waste product; the plants used carbon dioxide to make their own food during photosynthesis and released oxygen as a waste product; the snails used oxygen dissolved in the water for their life processes.

Lesson Quiz

1. the water cycle

2. condensation

3. oxygen

4. Carbon

5. nitrogen fixation

6. the water cycle

7. true

8. oxygen

9. nitrogen cycle

10. true

Biomes

Lesson Pacing: 2–3 periods or 1–1½ blocks

🕐 **SHORT ON TIME?** To do this lesson in approximately half the time, do the Activate Prior Knowledge activity followed by a discussion of the Key Concept to familiarize students with the lesson content. Have students do the Quick Lab. The rest of the lesson can be completed by students independently.

Preference Navigator, in the online Planning tools, allows you to customize Interactive Science to your own teaching style. You can also edit lesson plans by selecting the Lesson Planner option.

Digital Teacher's Edition allows you to access your Teacher's Edition and Resource materials online.

my science online.com

Lesson Vocabulary

- biome • climate • desert • rain forest • emergent layer
- canopy • understory • grassland • savanna
- deciduous tree • boreal forest • coniferous tree • tundra
- permafrost

 ## Content Refresher

Climate and Biomes Although many factors determine the types of organisms that live in a biome, climate is especially important. The two main characteristics that determine the climate of an area are temperature and precipitation. In temperate and tropical regions, the various biomes are distinguished more by amounts of precipitation than by temperature. Temperate rain forests and temperate deserts experience very different amounts of precipitation, and therefore, they vary greatly in their physical conditions and species compositions. Both tundra and boreal forests have similar levels of yearly precipitation, but their temperatures, and therefore, their organisms, differ vastly.

LESSON OBJECTIVE

🔑 Name the six major biomes found on Earth.

Blended Path
Active learning using Student Edition, Inquiry Path, and Digital Path

ENGAGE AND EXPLORE

Teach this lesson using a variety of resources. Begin by reading **My Planet Diary** as a class. Have students share ideas about animals that live in their region whose habits change according to seasonal changes. Then have students do the **Inquiry Warm-Up activity.** Students will investigate the amount of rain that falls in four different regions. The **After the Inquiry Warm-Up worksheet** sets up a discussion about the amount of rain falling in different regions and its effect on organisms. Have volunteers share their graphs to number 4, a bar graph that includes the annual precipitation for their state.

EXPLAIN AND ELABORATE

Teach Key Concepts by explaining the terms *climate* and *biome* and how *climate* helps determine the six *biomes:* desert, rain forest, grassland, deciduous forest, boreal forest, and tundra. Continue to **Teach Key Concepts** by describing each of the biomes. Ask students to describe animal adaptations for each biome. **Lead a Discussion** about precipitation and temperature in desert biomes. **Lead a Discussion** about locations and climates of the two types of rain forests. Use the **Support the Big Q** to illustrate the amazing variety of consumers in the tropical rain forest. Discuss how the rain forest supports these consumers. **Lead a Discussion** about grassland, deciduous forest, boreal forest, and tundra biomes. Have students describe locations, climates, and animal adaptations in these biomes. **Lead a Discussion** about how mountains are not classified to one biome and offer unique ecosystems. Then have students practice the inquiry skill in the **Apply It activity.** Hand out the **Key Concept Summaries** as a review of the lesson. Students can also use the online **Vocab Flash Cards** to review key terms.

EVALUATE

Have students take the **Lesson Quiz.** For an alternate assessment, see the **EXAM**VIEW® Assessment Suite, Progress Monitoring Assessments, or SuccessTracker™.

E L L Support

1 Content and Language
Three of the more difficult vocabulary words—*boreal, coniferous,* and *deciduous*—have Latin roots. *Boreal* comes from a Latin word north or northwind, *coniferous* comes from a Latin word meaning cone bearing, and *deciduous* comes from a Latin word meaning to fall from or fall off.

DIFFERENTIATED INSTRUCTION KEY
L1 Struggling Students or Special Needs
L2 On-Level Students **L3** Advanced Students

LESSON PLANNER 16.3

 **Inquiry Path** Hands-on learning in the Lab zone

Digital Path Online learning at my science online.com

ENGAGE AND EXPLORE

To teach this lesson with an emphasis on inquiry, begin with the **Inquiry Warm-Up activity.** Students will investigate and compare rainfall amounts for different regions. Lead a discussion about how the regions differ. Have students do the **After the Inquiry Warm-Up worksheet.** Talk about student predictions in numbers 1 and 4. Have volunteers share their graphs for number 4, which include precipitation in their state.

EXPLAIN AND ELABORATE

Focus on the **Inquiry Skill** for the lesson. Point out that when you draw a conclusion, you make a judgment after considering information or data. What conclusion can be drawn from the graph in the **Inquiry Warm-Up activity?** *(Different regions receive different amounts of precipitation. These amounts can be arranged in order from least to greatest.)* Use the **Support the Big Q** illustrate how organisms interact in tropical rain forests. Have students **Build Inquiry** by reminding them that a habitat offers an organism the means to live, grow, and reproduce. **Build Inquiry** by having students illustrate how mountain habitats represent different biomes. Review the world maps noting the colors assigned to certain biomes before beginning the **Apply It activity.** Ask volunteers to share their descriptions. Have students do the **Quick Lab** to reinforce understanding of forest climates and share their results. Students can use the online **Vocab Flash Cards** to review key terms.

EVALUATE

Have students take the **Lesson Quiz.** For an alternate assessment, see the **EXAM**VIEW® Assessment Suite, Progress Monitoring Assessments, or SuccessTracker™.

ENGAGE AND EXPLORE

Teach this lesson using digital resources. Begin by having students explore biomes and animal adaptations at **My Planet Diary** online. Have them access the Chapter Resources to find the **Unlock the Big Question activity.** There they can answer the questions and refine their responses as they continue through the lesson. You can re-assign the activity and have students submit their work so you can track their progress.

EXPLAIN AND ELABORATE

Students reading above, at, or below the lexile measure of this lesson can access basic content readings at their level at **My Reading Web.** Have students use the online **Vocab Flash Cards** to preview key terms. Have students do the **Quick Lab** to reinforce understanding of forest climates and then ask students to share their results.

Have students do the online **Interactive Art activity** to recognize that mountains and ice are not part of any major biome. Assign the **Do the Math activity** online and have students submit their work to you. Review the world maps noting the colors assigned to certain biomes before assigning the online **Apply It activity.** Ask volunteers to share their descriptions. Have students submit their work to you. The **Key Concept Summaries** online allow students to read a summary and see an image associated with each part of the lesson. Online remediation is available at **My Science Coach.**

EVALUATE

Have students take the **Lesson Quiz.** For an alternate assessment, see the **EXAM**VIEW® Assessment Suite, Progress Monitoring Assessments, or SuccessTracker™.

2 Frontload the Lesson
Preview the lesson visuals, labels, and captions. Ask students to relate any real-world experiences of the six major biomes to the class.

3 Comprehensible Input
Have students study the visuals and their captions to support the key concepts of the lesson.

4 Language Production
Pair or group students with varied language abilities to complete labs collaboratively for language practice. Have each copy the completed written lab for personal reference.

5 Assess Understanding
Make true or false statements about each of the six major biomes and have students indicate if they agree or disagree by raising their right hands for agreement and left for disagreement to check whole-class comprehension.

646B

Biomes

Establish Learning Objective

After this lesson, students will be able to:

 Name the six major biomes found on Earth.

Engage

Activate Prior Knowledge

MY PLANET DIARY Read *That's Super Cool!* with the class. Point out that animals hibernate in other places besides the Arctic. Encourage students to think of examples of animals in your region that are not evident at certain times of year. Explain that animals' movements and habits may change according to seasonal changes. Ask: **Why might arctic ground squirrels hibernate for such long stretches of time?** *(To survive when food is scarce)*

BIG IDEAS OF SCIENCE REFERENCE LIBRARY Have students look up the following topics: Atacama Desert, Rainforest.

Explore

Lab Resource: Inquiry Warm-Up

L2 **HOW MUCH RAIN IS THAT?** Students will use data in a table to create a bar graph representing amounts of rainfall in four different biomes.

 What Are the Six Major Biomes?

MY PLANET DIARY

That's Super Cool!

Misconception: It is always fatal when body temperatures drop below freezing.

Fact: In the tundra, arctic ground squirrels hibernate up to eight months a year. During this time, a squirrel's body temperature drops below freezing! This is called supercooling and gives the squirrel the lowest body temperature of any mammal. Without waking, a squirrel will shiver for several hours every couple of weeks to increase its body temperature.

MISCONCEPTION

Answer the question below.
What do you think are the advantages of supercooling?

Sample: Supercooling allows an organism to use minimal energy during the winter so that it doesn't have to wake up and eat food.

> **PLANET DIARY** Go to **Planet Diary** to learn more about biomes.

 Do the Inquiry Warm-Up *How Much Rain Is That?*

What Are the Six Major Biomes?

Imagine that you are taking part in an around-the-world scientific expedition. On this expedition you will collect data on the typical climate and organisms of each of Earth's biomes. A **biome** is a group of ecosystems with similar climates and organisms.

The six major biomes are desert, rain forest, grassland, deciduous forest, boreal forest, and tundra. It is mostly the **climate**—the average annual temperature and amount of precipitation—in an area that determines its biome. Climate limits the species of plants that can grow in an area. In turn, the species of plants determine the kinds of animals that live there.

646 Ecosystems and Biomes

SUPPORT ALL READERS

Lexile Measure = 930L   Lexile Word Count = 2325

Prior Exposure to Content: Most students have encountered this topic in earlier grades

Academic Vocabulary: *compare, contrast, explain, interpret*

Science Vocabulary: *biome, climate*

Concept Level: Generally appropriate for most students in this grade

Preteach With: My Planet Diary "That's Super Cool!" and Figure 1 activity

Go to **My Reading Web** to access leveled readings that provide a foundation for the content.

my science online

Vocabulary
- biome
- climate
- desert
- rain forest
- emergent layer
- canopy
- understory
- grassland
- savanna
- deciduous tree
- boreal forest
- coniferous tree
- tundra
- permafrost

Skills
- ➔ Reading: Compare and Contrast
- ⚠ Inquiry: Draw Conclusions

Desert Biomes The first stop on your expedition is a desert. You step off the bus into the searing heat. A **desert** is an area that receives less than 25 centimeters of rain per year. Some of the driest deserts may not receive any precipitation in a year! Deserts often undergo large shifts in temperature during the course of a day. A scorching hot desert like the Namib Desert in Africa cools rapidly each night when the sun goes down. Other deserts, such as the Gobi in central Asia, have a yearly average temperature that is below freezing.

Organisms that live in the desert, like the fennec in **Figure 1**, must be adapted to little or no rain and to extreme temperatures. For example, the stem of a saguaro cactus has folds that are similar to the pleats in an accordion. The stem expands to store water when it is raining. Gila monsters can spend weeks at a time in their cool underground burrows. Many other desert animals are most active at night when the temperatures are cooler.

FIGURE 1 ·····························

Desert
Organisms must be adapted to live in the desert.

✎ **Complete these tasks.**

1. **CHALLENGE** How do you think the fennec's ears and fur are adaptations to the desert's extreme temperatures?

   Big ears get rid of extra heat; fur keeps it warm.

2. **List** Write five things you'll need to be well adapted to desert conditions. Pack carefully!

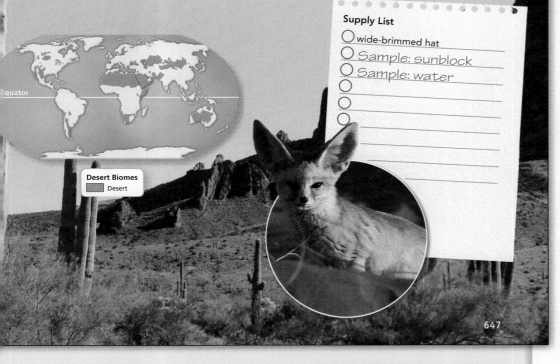

Supply List
- ○ wide-brimmed hat
- ○ Sample: sunblock
- ○ Sample: water
- ○
- ○
- ○

647

Explain

Introduce Vocabulary

Explain that *weather* is the condition outside at any particular time and place, whereas *climate* is the weather conditions of a place over a long period.

Teach Key Concepts 🔑

Explain to students that a group of ecosystems with similar climates and similar organisms makes up a biome. Ask: **What are the six major biomes on Earth?** (*Desert, rain forest, grassland, deciduous forest, boreal forest, tundra*) **In which biome do you live?** (*Students should indicate the local biome.*) **Which other biome have you ever been in?** (*Accept all reasonable responses.*) Invite students who have been in other biomes to describe the conditions in those biomes.

Lead a Discussion

DESCRIBE DESERT BIOMES Ask students who have visited a desert to describe it. Remind students that climate incorporates both temperature and precipitation. Indicate to students that the areas indicated on the map in **Figure 1** represent only hot and dry deserts. Ask: **What can you say about precipitation and evaporation in the desert?** (*Deserts receive less than 25 centimeters of precipitation each year; evaporation is greater than precipitation.*) **How might desert temperatures vary over a 24-hour day?** (*Deserts are hot during the day, but they can be cold at night.*)

Address Misconceptions

L1 DESERTS It is a common misconception that all deserts are hot. Several deserts, such as the Atacama Desert in South America and the Gobi Desert in Asia, are actually cold. Reinforce the idea that deserts are characterized by minimal precipitation, and not hot climates. Students may be surprised to learn that the biggest desert in the world is Antarctica. In fact, the majority of the world's desert area is cold and dry.

21st Century Learning

CREATIVITY Have students read *Atacama Desert* in the **Big Ideas of Science Reference Library** and create a humorous real estate brochure to try to attract settlers to the area.

My Planet Diary provides an opportunity for students to explore real-world connections to a tundra biome.

my science online.com | Biomes

LESSON 16.3

1 Content and Language
Write and define the word *adaptation*. Have students conduct a picture walk of the lesson and discuss how they would dress if they lived in each of the six biomes. Relate this idea to the fact that animals and plants must be adapted to the biomes in which they live.

2 Frontload the Lesson
List the six biomes on the board. Then have students conduct a picture walk of

the lesson, asking them to use detailed words to describe each biome based on the visual aids shown.

3 Comprehensible Input
Guide students back to the text to help them fill in the labels in **Figure 3**. Have students describe how the words *tallest, underneath,* and *below* help indicate the order of each of the tree layers.

Explain

Lead a Discussion

RAIN FORESTS Tell students that tropical and temperate rain forests share many traits but differ in location and temperatures. Display a world map or globe and help students locate these biomes. Students should refer to the biome map on this page. Ask: **Where are the world's tropical rain forests located?** *(All are located at or near the equator.)* **How do the location and climate of temperate rain forests differ from tropical rain forests?** *(Temperate rain forests are much farther north and much cooler.)* **How are temperate and tropical rain forests similar?** *(Both are humid, receive a lot of rain, and have a large variety of plant and animal species.)*

Compare and Contrast Explain that when you compare and contrast, you look for similarities and differences. Remind students that the qualities shared by both temperate and tropical rain forests belong in the overlapping section of the diagram.

Compare and Contrast As you read about temperate and tropical rain forests, fill in the Venn diagram.

Temperate

Huge trees
U.S. Pacific Northwest
Moderate temperature

Wet
Lots of plants
Lots of animals

Humid; tree layers
Hot temperature
Near equator

Tropical

FIGURE 2 ·······

Temperate Rain Forests
The sugar pine is the tallest kind of pine tree, reaching heights of 53 to 61 meters. It also produces the largest pine cones. A sugar pine cone can reach a length of 30 to 56 centimeters. The sugar pine cone shown here is actual size!

Identify What conditions do you think allow a tree to grow so tall?

Moderate temperatures
and the large amount
of rain the area
receives

Rain-Forest Biomes The second stop on your expedition is a rain forest. **Rain forests** are forests in which large amounts of rain fall year-round. This biome is living up to its name—it's pouring! After a short shower, the sun reappears. However, very little sunlight reaches the ground.

Plants are everywhere in the rain forest. Some plants, like the vines hanging from tree limbs, even grow on other plants! And animals are flying, creeping, and slithering all around you.

Temperate Rain Forests You may think that a rain forest is a warm, humid "jungle" in the tropics. But there is another type of rain forest. The Pacific Northwest of the United States receives more than 300 centimeters of rain a year. Huge trees grow there, including redwoods, cedars, and firs. Many ecologists refer to this ecosystem as a temperate rain forest. The term *temperate* means "having moderate temperatures."

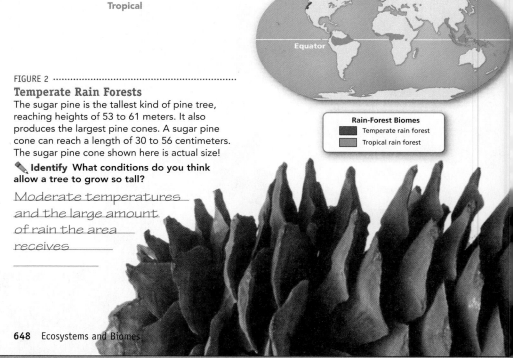

Equator

Rain-Forest Biomes
■ Temperate rain forest
■ Tropical rain forest

648 Ecosystems and Biomes

Professional Development Note — **Teacher to Teacher**

Survivor Project Students assume the roles of rescued plane crash survivors. Having survived in one of the six major biomes, their job is to record what they learned in a Survival Manual. Students begin with a description of an ecosystem in one of the biomes. Chapters in their manual include: vegetation, animals (predator/prey relationships, where survivors acted on the food web), type of shelter built (using available resources). One chapter describes how organisms interacted with each other and with the nonliving environment. Students conclude their publication with a description of the effect they had on the ecosystem.

✉ *Emily Compton*
Park Forest Middle School
Baton Rouge, LA

Tropical Rain Forests As you can see on the map, tropical rain forests are found in regions close to the equator. The climate is warm and humid all year long, and there is a lot of rain. Because of these climate conditions, an amazing variety of plants grow in tropical rain forests.

Trees in the rain forest form several distinct layers. The tallest layer of the rain forest which receives the most sunlight and can reach up to 70 meters, is the **emergent layer.** Underneath, trees up to 50 meters tall form a leafy roof called the **canopy.** Below the canopy, a layer of shorter trees and vines, around 15 meters high, form an **understory.** Understory plants grow well in the shade formed by the canopy. The forest floor is nearly dark, so only a few plants live there. Look at the tree layers in **Figure 3.**

The abundant plant life in tropical rain forests provides habitats for many species of animals. Ecologists estimate that millions of species of insects live in tropical rain forests. These insects serve as a source of food for many reptiles, birds, and mammals. Many of these animals, in turn, are food sources for other animals. Although tropical rain forests cover only a small part of the planet, they probably contain more species of plants and animals than all the other biomes combined.

Emergent layer

Canopy

Understory

Forest floor

FIGURE 3 ·······················
Tropical Rain Forests
On the edge of this tropical rain forest, an amazing variety of organisms can be found in the different layers.

✎ **Relate Text and Visuals** Based on your reading, label the four distinct layers of the tropical rain forest in the boxes above.

649

649

Support the Big Q ? UbD

CONSUMERS IN THE RAIN FOREST Discuss with students the abundance of animals in tropical rain forests. Ask: **What do many of the reptiles, birds, and mammals feed on in tropical rain forests?** *(Insects)* **What do you think the insects feed on?** *(Plants)* **Why does the tropical rain forest support so many species of animals?** *(There are many plant species that provide habitats for various animals and are the producers in a food chain.)*

21st Century Learning

CRITICAL THINKING Point out that the layers of trees found in a tropical rain forest demonstrate a series of causes and effects. Ask: **What causes the trees of the emergent layer to grow tallest?** *(They receive the most sun.)* **How does the presence of the trees in the emergent layer affect the trees below?** *(The emergent layer creates shade, which prevents trees below from growing as high as those in the top layer.)* **How does the presence of the trees in the canopy affect the trees below?** *(The canopy creates even more shade, which prevents trees below from growing as high as those in the top two layers.)* **How does the presence of the trees in the understory affect the trees and plants below?** *(The understory creates still more shade, which prevents vegetation below from growing very high.)*

Teach With Visuals

Have students look at **Figure 3.** Have students identify the layers of the rain forest shown. You may wish to have students add height information to their labels. Ask: **How much open space is there below the emergent layer?** *(Very little)* **How much open space is there below the canopy?** *(There is a large open space below the canopy and above the understory.)*

Differentiated Instruction

L1 Define Terms Relating to Tropical Rain Forests Have pairs of students work with a dictionary to find meanings for the terms *emergent* and *canopy.* Then have them break apart the compound word *understory* in order to analyze the two words that comprise it.

L3 Identify Main Ideas About Tropical Rain Forests Call on students to state the main idea of each paragraph about tropical rain forests.

L1 Compare Biomes Pair students to assist each other. Assign three headings: *Temperate rain forest, Tropical rain forest, Both,* and a list of words from these pages: *firs, rain, trees, equator, warm, cool.* Have students read the text and place the terms under the appropriate headings *(Temperate rain forest—firs, cool; Tropical rain forest—warm, equator; Both—rain, trees).*

Explain

Lead a Discussion

GRASSLANDS Describe grasslands as widely distributed ecosystems that have moderate climates and are dominated by grasses. Have students use a world map or globe to locate countries that have large areas of grasslands. Also have students locate prairie areas in the United States. Ask: **What parts of Earth do not have grasslands?** *(Land areas in the extremes of the Northern Hemisphere and of the Southern Hemisphere)* **Which is the only continent without a grasslands biome?** *(Antarctica)* **How do savannas differ from prairies?** *(Savannas are closer to the equator; they receive more rain.)*

Teach With Visuals

Tell students to look at **Figure 4.** Ask: **What typical features of grassland biomes are visible in Figure 4?** *(Tall grass, large grassland birds)* **What kinds of plants are not found in grasslands?** *(Trees)* **What characteristics do the three birds have in common?** *(They are large and have long legs.)*

A — Rhea, South America
B — Cassowary, Australia
C — Ostrich, Africa

FIGURE 4 ·······················

Grasslands
The rhea, cassowary, and ostrich are grassland birds that live on different continents.

✎ **Interpret Maps** On the world map, identify the continents in which these three birds are located. List three characteristics that these grassland birds all share.

Sample: long, slender necks; long legs; large bodies

_____

_____

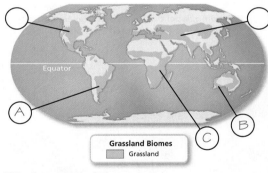

Equator

Grassland Biomes
☐ Grassland

Grassland Biomes The third stop on the expedition is a grassy plain called a prairie. Temperatures are more comfortable here than they were in the desert. The breeze carries the scent of soil warmed by the sun. This rich soil supports grasses as tall as you. Startled by your approach, sparrows dart into hiding places among the waving grass stems.

Although the prairie receives more rain than a desert, you may notice only a few scattered areas of trees and shrubs. Ecologists classify prairies, which are generally found in the middle latitudes, as grasslands. A **grassland** is an area that is populated mostly by grasses and other nonwoody plants. Most grasslands receive 25 to 75 centimeters of rain each year. Fires and droughts are common in this biome. Grasslands that are located closer to the equator than prairies are known as savannas. A **savanna** receives as much as 120 centimeters of rain each year. Scattered shrubs and small trees grow on savannas, along with grass.

Grasslands are home to many of the largest animals on Earth—herbivores such as elephants, bison, antelopes, zebras, giraffes, kangaroos, and rhinoceroses. Grazing by these large herbivores maintains the grasslands. Their grazing keeps young trees and bushes from sprouting and competing with the grass for water and sunlight. You can see some grassland birds in **Figure 4.**

650 Ecosystems and Biomes

Deciduous Forest Biomes Your trip to the fourth biome takes you to another forest. It is now late summer. Cool mornings here give way to warm days. Several members of the expedition are busy recording the numerous plant species. Others are looking through binoculars, trying to identify the songbirds.

You are now visiting a deciduous forest biome. Many of the trees in this forest are **deciduous trees** (dee sɪJ oo us), trees that shed their leaves and grow new ones each year. Oaks and maples are examples of deciduous trees. Deciduous forests receive enough rain to support the growth of trees and other plants, at least 50 centimeters of rain per year. Temperatures can vary greatly during the year. The growing season usually lasts five to six months.

The variety of plants in a deciduous forest creates many different habitats. Many species of birds live in different parts of the forest, eating the insects and fruits in their specific areas. Mammals such as chipmunks and skunks live in deciduous forests. In a North American deciduous forest you might also see wood thrushes and white-tailed deer.

If you were to return to this biome in the winter, you would not see much wildlife. Many of the bird species migrate, or fly great distances, to warmer areas. Some of the mammals hibernate, or enter a state of greatly reduced body activity similar to sleep. Look at **Figure 5**. During the winter months, animals that hibernate get energy from fat stored in their bodies.

FIGURE 5 ·······························

Deciduous Forest
Most of the trees in a deciduous forest have leaves that change color and drop to the forest floor each autumn. In the leaves, this dormouse hibernates through the winter.

✎ **Infer** Is hibernation an adaptation to life in a deciduous forest? Explain your answer.

Sample: Yes; hibernation is an adaptation because it allows organisms to survive the winter months.

did you know? ·······················

How far would you be willing to migrate? The bobolink has one of the longest songbird migration routes. The birds travel south from southern Canada and the northern United States to northern Argentina. This migration route is approximately 20,000 kilometers round trip!

Equator

Deciduous Forest Biomes
Deciduous forest

651

Lead a Discussion

DECIDUOUS FORESTS Tell students that deciduous forests experience seasonal changes to which organisms are adapted. Ask: **What is the climate like in a deciduous forest?** *(Temperatures vary greatly during the year; there is enough rainfall to support trees.)* **How are trees adapted to seasonal changes in this biome?** *(They shed their leaves and grow new ones each year.)* **How are animals adapted?** *(Many birds migrate in winter; some mammals hibernate.)* **How do the many animal species coexist in a deciduous forest?** *(The different plants create a mix of habitats within the forest.)*

Teach With Visuals

Tell students to look at **Figure 5**. Help students find the curled-up dormouse. Point out that this image is a close-up of the forest floor. If possible, show students photographs of deciduous trees from a field guide. Ask: **What plant materials can you see around the dormouse?** *(Pieces of leaves, ferns, and grass.)* Help students identify the green and greenish-yellow lichens growing nearby.

Elaborate ─────────────

Build Inquiry Lab zone

L2 **MAKE MODELS OF A DECIDUOUS FOREST**

Materials none

Time 20 minutes

Remind students that a habitat provides the things an organism needs to live, grow, and reproduce.

Ask: **Suppose you want to model a rotting-log habitat on the forest floor. What abiotic materials would you need?** *(Soil, a source of filtered light, water, a rotting log, dead leaves or other dead plant material)* **What organisms would you place in the model habitat?** *(Mosses, ferns, fungi, earthworms, sow bugs, crickets, salamanders or toads)*

Have students draw a model of a rotting-log habitat. Ask: **What other deciduous forest habitats can you name?** *(Bird roosts and squirrel nests in trees, chipmunk burrows, bear dens, deer grazing areas, and the like)*

Differentiated Instruction

L1 Review Geographical Terms and Names Have students review basic geographical terms and names in order to clarify the information shown in the two world maps. As necessary, help students understand terms such as *equator, hemisphere,* and *pole,* as well as the names and locations of the planet's seven continents.

L3 Research a Grasslands Bird Challenge students to do research on one or more of the grasslands birds shown in this section. Students can gather and organize information about a bird's habitat, diet, physical characteristics, predators, and life span.

Explain

Lead a Discussion

EXPLORE A COLD CLIMATE Tell students that boreal forests are found in northern locations that have cold climates. Ask: **Why is water availability a challenge in boreal forests?** *(Temperatures are low enough that water is frozen much of the year.)* **How do plants in boreal forests adapt to lack of water?** *(Coniferous trees have thick, waxy needles that prevent water loss.)* **Can you describe a boreal forest food chain?** *(Producers—seeds and bark of coniferous trees; first-level consumers—red squirrel, insects, birds, snowshoe hare, moose, beaver; second-level consumers—wolf, bear, lynx, great horned owl)*

Teach With Visuals

Have students examine the map of boreal forest biomes on this page. Ask: **Where are most boreal forests located?** *(Boreal forests are located in the Northern Hemisphere in a band at latitudes where the climate is too cold for deciduous forests.)* **Why are there no boreal forests in the Southern Hemisphere?** *(There are no large landmasses in the Southern Hemisphere at the appropriate latitude below the equator.)*

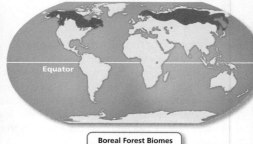

Boreal Forest Biomes
☐ Boreal forest

FIGURE 6 ···

Boreal Forest
🖉 This lynx and snowshoe hare are adapted to life in the boreal forest.

1. Infer Choose the best answer. The feet of each animal are an adaptation to its

○ food.   ○ climate.
○ predators.   ◉ all of the above

2. Explain Defend your answer.

Sample: Large feet allow each
animal to run across snow to
get food or escape predators.
The fur also keeps the feet
warm in cold climates.

652 Ecosystems and Biomes

Boreal Forest Biomes Now the expedition heads north to a colder biome, the boreal forest. The term *boreal* means "northern," and **boreal forests** are dense forests found in upper regions of the Northern Hemisphere. The expedition leaders claim they can identify a boreal forest by its smell. When you arrive, you catch a whiff of the spruce and fir trees that blanket the hillsides. Feeling the chilly early fall air, you pull a jacket and hat out of your bag.

Boreal Forest Plants Most of the trees in the boreal forest are **coniferous trees** (koh NIF ur us), trees that produce their seeds in cones and have leaves shaped like needles. The boreal forest is sometimes referred to by its Russian name, the *taiga* (TY guh). Winters in these forests are very cold. The snow can reach heights well over your head! Even so, the summers are rainy and warm enough to melt all the snow.

Tree species in the boreal forest are well adapted to the cold climate. Since water is frozen for much of the year, trees must have adaptations that prevent water loss. Coniferous trees, such as firs and hemlocks, all have thick, waxy needles that prevent water from evaporating.

Boreal Forest Animals Many of the animals of the boreal forest eat the seeds produced by the coniferous trees. These animals include red squirrels, insects, and birds such as finches. Some herbivores, such as moose and beavers, eat tree bark and new shoots. The variety of herbivores in the boreal forest supports many predators, including lynx, otters, and great horned owls. **Figure 6** shows an herbivore and its predator.

Tundra Biomes As you arrive at your last stop, the driving wind gives you an immediate feel for this biome. The **tundra** is extremely cold and dry. Expecting deep snow, many are surprised to learn that the tundra may receive no more precipitation than a desert.

Most of the soil in the tundra is frozen all year. This frozen soil is called **permafrost.** During the short summer, the top layer of soil thaws, but the underlying soil remains frozen. Because rainwater cannot soak into the permafrost, shallow ponds and marshy areas appear in the summer.

Tundra Plants Mosses, grasses, and dwarf forms of a few trees can be found in the tundra. Most of the plant growth takes place during the long days of the short summer season. North of the Arctic Circle, the sun does not set during midsummer.

Tundra Animals In summer, the insects are abundant. Insect-eating birds take advantage of the plentiful food by eating as much as they can. But when winter approaches, these birds migrate south. Mammals of the tundra include caribou, foxes, and wolves. The mammals that remain on the tundra during the winter grow thick fur coats. What can these animals find to eat on the tundra in winter? The caribou scrape snow away to find lichens. Wolves follow the caribou and look for weak members of the herd to prey upon.

FIGURE 7

Tundra
Although the ground is frozen for most of the year, mosses, grasses, and dwarf willow trees grow here.

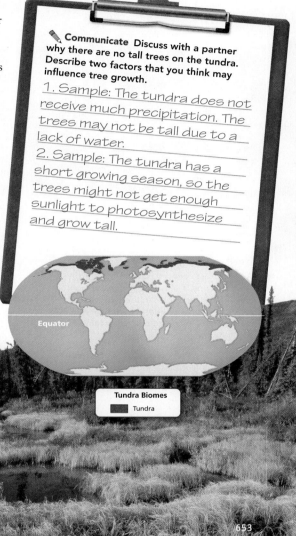

✎ **Communicate** Discuss with a partner why there are no tall trees on the tundra. Describe two factors that you think may influence tree growth.

1. Sample: The tundra does not receive much precipitation. The trees may not be tall due to a lack of water.

2. Sample: The tundra has a short growing season, so the trees might not get enough sunlight to photosynthesize and grow tall.

Equator

Tundra Biomes
◼ Tundra

653

Lead a Discussion

TUNDRA BIOMES Tell students that the term *tundra* comes from a Sami word meaning "marshy plain." Explain that the Sami are the indigenous people of northern Europe. Direct students' attention to **Figure 7.** Have them locate the tundra areas of northern Europe. Ask: **What does the land look like in this photograph of the tundra?** *(It is flat and marshy.)* **Do you think "marshy plain" is a good description of the tundra?** *(Students will probably indicate that the description seems apt, citing the flat land and the wet areas.)*

Elaborate

21st Century Learning

CRITICAL THINKING Explain that because the permafrost does not allow water to drain from the soil and because the low temperatures slow evaporation, the tundra's soil is constantly saturated with water, even though the area receives little precipitation. Ask: **Why are insects, such as mosquitoes, so common on the tundra in summer?** *(Many insects breed in the standing water that cannot sink into the permafrost.)*

Differentiated Instruction

L1 Permafrost Help students solidify their understanding of the word *permafrost* by pointing out the fact that the word combines *frost* with the root of the word *permanent*. Have students use a dictionary to find the definition of *permanent*. Then have them explain to a partner how this word contributes to the meaning of *permafrost.*

L3 Compare and Contrast Biomes Have students create a detailed compare/contrast table showing rainfall and temperature differences among the six major biomes. Encourage students to do additional research to present a fuller picture of conditions in each biome.

Explain

Lead a Discussion

HIGH-ALTITUDE HABITATS Explain that mountains and ice do not fit into one biome classification, but they have unique ecosystems. Ask: **Is the habitat at the bottom of a mountain the same as at the top?** *(No, the habitats change with altitude.)* **What countries or continents are covered with ice?** *(Antarctica; most of Greenland)* **Can ice sheets support organisms?** *(Yes)* **What are some examples?** *(Polar bears and leopard seals)*

Elaborate

Build Inquiry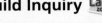

L1 **DRAW MOUNTAIN HABITATS**

Materials paper and pencils

Time 10 minutes

Have students illustrate mountain habitats representing different biomes. Divide students into small groups. Have each group draw a side-view diagram of a mountain and label it with the biome names given in the text: grassland at the base, deciduous forest next, then boreal forest, and finally tundra at the top.

Ask: **Why do the biomes vary at different locations on a mountain?** *(Climate becomes colder from the base of a mountain to its top.)* **From what you know about this mountain's biomes, does the top of the mountain receive much rain?** *(No, because it is tundra habitat, which is dry)*

Do the Math!

L1 Point out that this line graph makes it possible to see how the average temperature changes or remains the same over twelve months of time. In addition to allowing students to analyze average temperatures in two different locations, the graph also lets students compare and contrast the two locations. Ask students to identify the highest average temperature and the lowest average temperature for each location.

▲ **Draw Conclusions** Remind students that drawing a conclusion involves making a statement that sums up what they have learned about a topic or question.
See *Math Skill and Problem-Solving Activities* for support.

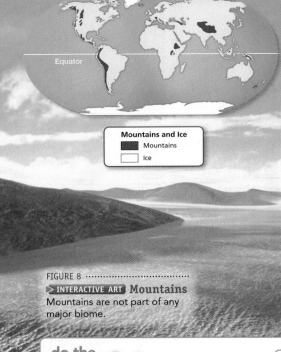

Equator

Mountains and Ice
- ■ Mountains
- □ Ice

FIGURE 8 ························
> **INTERACTIVE ART** **Mountains**
Mountains are not part of any major biome.

Mountains and Ice Some land areas are not classified as biomes. Recall that biomes are defined by abiotic factors such as climate and soil, and by biotic factors such as plant and animal life. Because the organisms that live in these areas vary, mountain ranges and land covered with thick ice sheets are not considered biomes.

The climate of a mountain changes from its base to its summit. If you were to hike all the way up a tall mountain, you would pass through a series of biomes. At the base, you might find grasslands. As you climbed, you might pass through deciduous forest and then boreal forest. As you neared the top, your surroundings would resemble the cold, dry tundra.

Other places are covered year-round with thick ice sheets. Most of Greenland and Antarctica fall into this category. Organisms that are adapted to life on ice include leopard seals and polar bears.

do the math!

Biome Climates

An ecologist collected climate data from two locations. The graph shows the monthly average temperatures in the two locations. The total yearly precipitation in Location A is 250 centimeters. In Location B, the total yearly precipitation is 14 centimeters.

❶ **Read Graphs** Provide a title for the graph. What variable is plotted on the horizontal axis? On the vertical axis?

Month; temperature

❷ **Interpret Data** Study the graph. How would you describe the temperature over the course of a year in Location A? In Location B?

Location A temperatures are steady; Location B temperatures rise and fall.

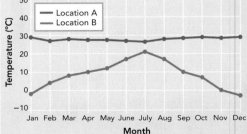

Average Monthly Temperatures

Temperature (°C)

— Location A
— Location B

Jan Feb Mar Apr May June July Aug Sep Oct Nov Dec
Month

❸ **Draw Conclusions** Given the precipitation and temperature data for these locations, in which biome would you expect each to be located?

Based on the temperatures and the amount of precipitation, Location A is a tropical rain forest and Location B is a desert.

Interactive Art allows students to recognize that mountains and ice are not part of any major biome.

Digital Lesson
- Assign the *Do the Math* activity online and have students submit their work to you.
- Assign the *Apply It* activity online and have students submit their work to you.

my science online.com ▶ **Biomes**

apply it!

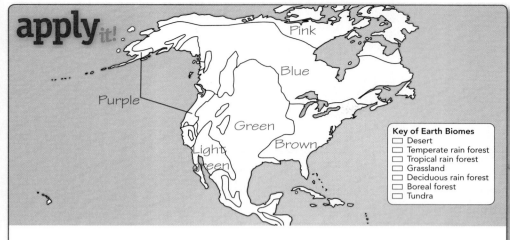

Key of Earth Biomes
- ☐ Desert
- ☐ Temperate rain forest
- ☐ Tropical rain forest
- ☐ Grassland
- ☐ Deciduous rain forest
- ☐ Boreal forest
- ☐ Tundra

❶ **Interpret Maps** Using the colors shown in the biome maps throughout this lesson, color in the key above. Use the key to color in the areas on the map of North America.

❷ **Draw Conclusions** Where are most of the boreal forests located? Why are there no boreal forests in the Southern Hemisphere?

Boreal forests are located far from the equator in cold climates. There are no boreal forests in the Southern Hemisphere because there is not enough land at the appropriate latitudes.

❸ **Describe** Mark the area in which you live with an *X* on the map. What is the climate like where you live? How do you think your climate affects which organisms live there?

Accept all reasonable answers.

_____

_____

_____

_____

_____

_____

Lab zone® Do the Quick Lab *Inferring Forest Climates.*

🔲 Assess Your Understanding

1a. Review *Temperature* and *precipitation* are the two main factors that determine an area's biome.

b. Infer What biome might you be in if you were standing on a bitterly cold, dry plain with only a few, short trees scattered around?
Tundra

got it? ·····················

○ **I get it!** Now I know that the six major biomes are *desert, rain forest, grassland, deciduous forest, boreal forest, and tundra.*

○ **I need extra help with** *See TE note.*

Go to **my science** 💬 **COACH** *online for help with this subject.*

655

Apply It!

🔲 Review each of the world maps shown in this lesson, noting the colors assigned to certain biomes before beginning the activity. Then have them use colored pencils to fill in the key and to color the map of North America using the same colors to signify specific biomes presented in the lesson.

🔺 **Draw Conclusions** As they draw conclusions, students must decide whether or not the data they collected supports their hypothesis.

Lab Resource: Quick Lab 🔲

🔲 **INFERRING FOREST CLIMATES** Using a globe, students will mark locations of deciduous and boreal forests.

Evaluate

Assess Your Understanding

After students answer the questions, have them evaluate their understanding by completing the appropriate sentence.

🔲🔲🔲 Response to Intervention

1a. If students have trouble naming factors that determine a biome, **then** ask volunteers to describe climate conditions in various biomes.

b. If students need help identifying a specific biome, **then** review with them the major biomes and eliminate those that do not fit the description.

my science 💬 **COACH** Have students go online for help in understanding biomes.

Differentiated Instruction

🔲 **Altitude and Latitude** Help students understand the changes in biomes going up a mountain by comparing an increase in altitude with an increase in latitude. The latitude of the equator is 0°. As they go "up" from the equator to the North Pole, they see the climate change from hot to cold. As they go up a mountain, they see similar changes.

🔲 **Identify Biome Distribution** Have students use biome maps and a world atlas or globe to locate biomes for a given continent. Provide each student or group an outline map of that continent. If possible, assign a different continent to each student or group. Students should refer to the map resources to sketch the locations of the various biomes found on their continent.

Lab zone **After the Inquiry Warm-Up**

Biomes

Inquiry Warm-Up, *How Much Rain Is That?*

In the Inquiry Warm-Up, you investigated rainfall amounts for different regions. Using what you learned from that activity, answer the questions below.

1. **PREDICT** Ignoring all other factors, will an organism that requires abundant moisture, such as an amphibian, survive better in the Mojave Desert or the Costa Rican rain forest? Explain.

   _____

   _____

2. **CALCULATE** How many more times precipitation fell in the Great Smoky Mountains than in the Mojave Desert?

   _____

3. **INFER** Obviously, if 350 centimeters of precipitation fell all at once, people wouldn't be able to live in or near the Costa Rican rain forest. Over what period of time were these precipitation measurements most likely taken—a day, a week, a year, or a century?

   _____

4. **GRAPH** Predict the amount of precipitation that falls each year in the state in which you live. Then using reference materials recommended by your teacher, check to see how close you came to the correct answer. Draw a simple bar graph that includes the four locations shown in the lab and your state, arranged from lowest to highest precipitation amounts.

Assess Your Understanding

Biomes

What Are the Six Major Biomes?

1a. **REVIEW** _____ and _____ are the two main factors that determine an area's biome.

b. **INFER** What biome might you be in if you were standing on a bitterly cold, dry plain with only a few, short trees scattered around?

_____

gotit**?** ···

○ **I get it!** Now I know that the six major biomes are _____

_____

_____

_____

○ **I need extra help with** _____

_____

Biomes

What Are the Six Major Biomes?

A **biome** is a group of ecosystems with similar climates and organisms. **The six major biomes are desert, rain forest, grassland, deciduous forest, boreal forest, and tundra.** It is mostly the **climate**—the average annual temperature and amount of precipitation—in an area that determines its biome. Climate limits the species of plants that can grow in an area. The species of plants determine the kinds of animals that live there.

A **desert** is an area that receives less than 25 centimeters of rain per year. Organisms that live in the desert must be adapted to little or no rain and to extreme temperatures. **Rain forests** are forests in which large amounts of rain fall year-round. The Pacific Northwest of the U.S. is home to a temperate rain forest, where over 300 centimeters of rain falls yearly. Tropical rain forests are found close to the equator. The climate is warm, and there is a lot of rain. Trees form several layers. The tallest layer of the rain forest that receives the most sunlight and can reach up to 70 meters, is the **emergent layer.** Underneath, trees up to 50 meters tall form a leafy roof called the **canopy.** Below the canopy, a layer of shorter trees and vines, around 15 meters high, form an **understory.** Although tropical rain forests cover only a small part of the planet, they probably contain more species of plants and animals than all other biomes combined. A **grassland** is an area that is populated mostly by grasses and other nonwoody plants. A prairie is a grassland in the middle latitudes that receives between 25 and 75 centimeters of rain yearly. Grasslands located closer to the equator are called savannas. A **savanna** receives as much as 120 centimeters of rain each year. Grasslands are home to many of the largest animals on Earth.

In a deciduous forest biome, many trees are **deciduous trees** that shed their leaves and grow new ones each year. Oaks and maples are examples of deciduous trees. Deciduous forests receive at least 50 centimeters of rain a year, and temperatures vary greatly. Many species of plants, birds, mammals, and insects live in different parts of the forest. The term *boreal* means "northern," and **boreal forests** are dense forests found in upper regions of the Northern Hemisphere. Most of the trees in the boreal forest are **coniferous trees,** trees that produce their seeds in cones and have leaves shaped like needles. Winters are cold and snowy, and summers are rainy and fairly warm. Many of the animals of the boreal forest eat seeds produced by coniferous trees. The sixth biome, the **tundra,** is extremely cold and dry. The tundra often receives the same amount of precipitation as a desert. The soil in the tundra that is frozen most of the year is called **permafrost.** Mosses, grasses, and dwarf forms of a few trees grow on the tundra, as well as insects, birds, and a few mammals live on the tundra.

On a separate sheet of paper, identify Earth's six major biomes and briefly describe each one.

Name _____ Date _____ Class _____

Biomes

Understanding Main Ideas
Answer the following questions on a separate sheet of paper.

1. How does climate affect the type of biome found in an area?
2. What are two adaptations that enable mammals to survive cold winters?
3. Why are tropical rain forests such rich habitats for many species of animals?
4. Why does a deciduous forest have a variety of habitats?

Building Vocabulary
Name each biome described in the table below.

	Biome	Climate and Organisms
5.		warm summers, cold winters; receives at least 50 cm of precipitation per year; trees shed their leaves and grow new ones each year
6.		hot in daytime, cool or cold at night; very dry; organisms are adapted to extreme temperatures and dry conditions
7.		warm, rainy summers; very cold winters with heavy snow; trees produce cones with seeds that are eaten by many animals
8.		warm temperatures do not vary much throughout the year; very wet and humid; greater variety of species than any other biome
9.		extremely cold winters, 10.warmer summers; windy; very dry; no trees, only low-growing plants
10.		receives between 25 and 75 centimeters of rain each year; populated by grasses and many large herbivores

Name _____ Date _____ Class _____

Biomes

The map below shows the six major biomes on Earth. Examine the map carefully. Then follow the instructions below.

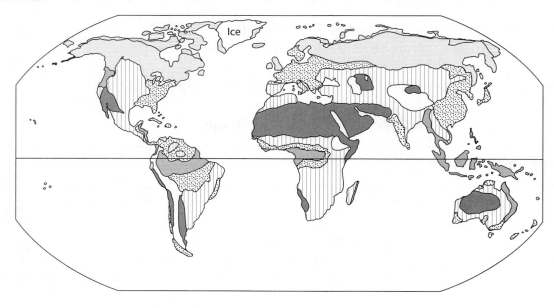

Key:

 _____

 _____

 _____

 _____

_____   _____

1. Label North America, South America, Europe, Asia, Africa, and Australia on the map.
2. Color each block in the key a different color.
3. Color the biomes on the map, using the same colors you used in the key.
4. Write the names of the biomes in the key.
5. Mark a red dot where you live. In which biome do you live?

_____

6. Locate the equator on the map. Which biome is most common along the equator?

_____

Lesson Quiz

Biomes

If the statement is true, write *true*. If the statement is false, change the underlined word or words to make the statement true.

1. _____ <u>A group of animals</u> limits the species of plants that can grow in an area.

2. _____ The Pacific Northwest is home to a <u>temperate rain forest</u>, where over 300 centimeters of rain falls yearly.

3. _____ Tropical rain forests cover a small part of the planet, yet they contain more species of plants and animals than <u>all other biomes combined</u>.

4. _____ <u>Rain forests</u> are home to many of the largest animals on Earth.

5. _____ In a <u>boreal forest biome</u>, many trees shed their leaves and grow new ones each year.

Fill in the blank to complete each statement.

6. A biome is a group of ecosystems with similar _____ and organisms.

7. Organisms that live in the _____ must be adapted to little or no rain and to extreme temperatures.

8. Prairies and savannas are two types of _____.

9. A _____ biome is a dense forest found in upper regions of the Northern Hemisphere.

10. Mosses, grasses, dwarf forms of a few trees, insects, birds, and a few mammals live on the _____ biome.

Biomes

Answer Key

After the Inquiry Warm-Up

1. Sample: Amphibians and other organisms that require abundant moisture, would do better in the rain forest than the desert, because there's more precipitation in the rain forest.

2. The Great Smoky Mountains get twelve (12) times as much precipitation as does the Mojave Desert.

3. a year

4. Sample: Bar graph with five bars. Your state should be positioned according to its precipitation amount relative to the other four locations.

Key Concepts Summaries

The six major biomes are desert, rain forest, grassland, deciduous forest, boreal forest, and tundra. A desert receives little rain, and organisms must be adapted to little rain and to extreme temperatures. Rain forests receive large amounts of rainfall year-round, and often contain several layers of tree growth. Tropical rain forests contain a huge number of plant and animal species. A grassland is an area of grasses and other nonwoody plants, as well as many large animals. A deciduous forest contains deciduous trees, which shed their leaves and grew new ones each year, as well as many species of plants, birds, mammals, and insects. A boreal forest is a dense forest of coniferous trees found in upper regions of the Northern Hemisphere. The tundra is extremely cold and dry, and its soil that stays frozen most of the year is called permafrost.

Review and Reinforce

1. It is mostly the climate conditions—temperature and precipitation—that determine the plants that grow in a region. The plants determine the animals, and both determine the ecosystems.

2. hibernation, thick fur

3. The number and variety of plants in a rain forest provide food for many different species.

4. It has a wide variety of plant life.

5. deciduous forest   6. desert

7. boreal forest   8. tropical rain forest

9. tundra   10. grassland

Enrich

1. Check that students have labeled the continents correctly.

2. Make sure students have coded each biome with the same color on both the key and the map.

3. Make sure students have coded each biome with the same color on both the key and the map.

4. Students should include the following biomes in their keys: tundra, rain forest, grassland, deciduous forest, boreal forest, desert.

5. Answers will depend on your location.

6. tropical rain forest

Lesson Quiz

1. Climate   2. true

3. true   4. Grasslands

5. deciduous forest biome   6. climates

7. desert   8. grasslands

9. boreal forest   10. tundra

Place the outside corner, the corner away from the dotted line, in the corner of your copy machine to copy onto letter-size paper.

Aquatic Ecosystems

 How do energy and matter move through ecosystems?

Lesson Pacing: 1–2 periods or $\frac{1}{2}$–1 block

⏱ **SHORT ON TIME?** To do this lesson in approximately half the time, do the Activate Prior Knowledge activity followed by a discussion of the Key Concept to familiarize students with the lesson content. Have students do the Quick Lab. The rest of the lesson can be completed by students independently.

> **Preference Navigator,** in the online Planning tools, allows you to customize Interactive Science to your own teaching style. You can also edit lesson plans by selecting the Lesson Planner option.
>
> **Digital Teacher's Edition** allows you to access your Teacher's Edition and Resource materials online.

Lesson Vocabulary

- estuary
- intertidal zone
- neritic zone

Content Refresher

Professional Development Note

Land and Sea Estuaries are marine ecosystems that serve as transitions between freshwater and saltwater habitats. They can include bays, marshes, sounds, mangrove forests, swamps, and other habitats. Because estuaries are linked to the ocean, they are tidal. They receive and trap large deposits of decaying plant matter from the adjacent land as currents move the materials toward the ocean. Thus, typical estuaries offer nutrient-rich soils that support a wide array of organisms. Estuaries provide a buffer between land and ocean. Estuaries absorb the impact of storms and floods, reducing potential damage to coastal communities. Estuaries also act as filters, containing river pollutants before they are released to the ocean.

LESSON OBJECTIVE

🔑 Name the two major types of aquatic ecosystems.

Blended Path
Active learning using Student Edition, Inquiry Path, and Digital Path

ENGAGE AND EXPLORE

Teach this lesson using a variety of resources. Begin by reading **My Planet Diary** as a class. Have students share ideas about real-world connections, such as Alvin, to aquatic ecosystems. Then have students do the **Inquiry Warm-Up activity.** Students will investigate how an organism's structure helps it survive in its habitat. The **After the Inquiry Warm-Up worksheet** sets up a comparison of students' structures and those of a fish. Have volunteers share and compare their answers to number 4 to identify the many structures of a fish.

EXPLAIN AND ELABORATE

Teach Key Concepts by explaining the terms intertidal and neritic. *Inter-* means between, so *intertidal* means between the highest high tide line and the lowest low tide line. *Neritic* may be derived from the Latin word for marine snails to describe their habitat and refer to the shallow water below the lowest low tide line that extends over the continental shelf. Continue to **Teach Key Concepts** by explaining that there are two major aquatic ecosystems. Ask students to name these ecosystems and tell how they differ. Use the **Support the Big Q** to distinguish among the living organisms in the intertidal and neritic zones and among the organisms in these two zones and the open ocean. **Lead a Discussion** to have students share their experiences with aquatic ecosystems, such as swimming or fishing. Then have students practice the inquiry skill in the **Apply It activity.** Hand out the **Key Concept Summaries** as a review of the lesson. Students can also use the online **Vocab Flash Cards** to review key terms.

EVALUATE

Have students take the **Lesson Quiz.** For an alternate assessment, see the **EXAM**VIEW® Assessment Suite, Progress Monitoring Assessments, or SuccessTracker™.

ⓔⓛⓛ Support

1 Content and Language

Explain that the word *estuary* means a place where the fresh water of a river or stream meets the salt water of an ocean. It is often found between fresh water ecosystems and marine ecosystems.

LESSON PLANNER 16.4

DIFFERENTIATED INSTRUCTION KEY
L1 Struggling Students or Special Needs
L2 On-Level Students **L3** Advanced Students

Lab zone Inquiry Path
Hands-on learning in the Lab zone

Digital Path
Online learning at **my science online**.com

ENGAGE AND EXPLORE

Teach this lesson with an emphasis on inquiry. Begin with the **Inquiry Warm-Up activity** in which students will investigate how an organism's structure helps it survive in its habitat. Lead a discussion about these structures. Have students do the **After the Inquiry Warm-Up worksheet.** Talk about student hand and speaking gestures. Have volunteers share their answers to number 4 about structures that help fish swim through the water.

EXPLAIN AND ELABORATE

Focus on the **Inquiry Skill** for the lesson. Point out that when you communicate, you share information. What might students communicate from the **Inquiry Warm-Up activity?** (*Information about fish structures and how they help fish in their habitats.*) Use the **Support the Big Q** to distinguish among the organisms in the intertidal and neritic zones and among the organisms in these two zones and the open ocean. Have students **Build Inquiry** by discussing what kind of organism a coral is and what a coral structure is. Review **Figure 2** before beginning the **Apply It activity.** Ask volunteers to name organisms likely to be found on the ocean floor. Have students do the **Quick Lab** to understand how oxygen dissolves. Students can use the online **Vocab Flash Cards** to review key terms.

EVALUATE

Have students take the **Lesson Quiz.** For an alternate assessment, see the **EXAM**VIEW® Assessment Suite, Progress Monitoring Assessments, or SuccessTracker™.

ENGAGE AND EXPLORE

To teach this lesson using digital resources, begin by having students explore aquatic ecosystems at **My Planet Diary** online. Have them access the Chapter Resources to find the **Unlock the Big Question activity.** There they can answer the questions and refine their responses as they continue through the lesson. You can re-assign the activity and have students submit their work so you can track their progress.

EXPLAIN AND ELABORATE

Students reading above, at, or below the lexile measure of this lesson can access basic content readings at their level at **My Reading Web.** Have students use the online **Vocab Flash Cards** to preview key terms. Have students do the **Quick Lab** on dissolved oxygen and then ask students to share their results. Review **Figure 2** before assigning the online **Apply It activity.** Ask volunteers to name organisms likely to be found on the ocean floor. Have students submit their work to you. The **Key Concept Summaries** online allow students to read a summary and see an image associated with each part of the lesson. Online remediation is available at **My Science Coach.**

EVALUATE

Have students take the **Lesson Quiz.** For an alternate assessment, see the **EXAM**VIEW® Assessment Suite, Progress Monitoring Assessments, or SuccessTracker™.

2 Frontload the Lesson

Preview the lesson visuals, labels, and captions. Ask students what they know about the words *marine* and *freshwater.* Explain the specific meanings these words have in science. Some students may have heard the word *marine* used to describe saltwater or ocean water.

3 Comprehensible Input

Have students study the visuals and their captions to support the key concepts of the lesson.

4 Language Production

Pair or group students with varied language abilities to present oral reports on additional plants and animals found in freshwater and marine ecosystems.

5 Assess Understanding

Have students take notes during oral presentations and then summarize the notes in concise paragraphs to check comprehension.

Lexile Measure = 960L

Aquatic Ecosystems

Establish Learning Objective

After this lesson, students will be able to:

 Name and describe the two major types of aquatic ecosystems.

Engage

Activate Prior Knowledge

MY PLANET DIARY Read *Underwater* Alvin with the class. Point out that the deepest and most remote regions of the ocean are all but impossible for scuba divers to explore. Ask: **What characteristics of an HOV make it an excellent way to explore the ocean floor?** (*Sample: An HOV can go deeper and farther than a scuba diver.*)

BIG IDEAS OF SCIENCE REFERENCE LIBRARY 📖
Have students look up the following topics: Bay of Fundy, Beaches, Deep Sea Vents, Everglades.

Explore

Lab Resource: Inquiry Warm-Up 🔬

L1 WHERE DOES IT LIVE? Students will look at photos and determine where the organisms that are depicted live.

🔑 What Are the Two Major Aquatic Ecosystems?

my planet diary   TECHNOLOGY

Underwater *Alvin*

Meet *Alvin*, an HOV (Human-Occupied Vehicle). Equipped with propulsion jets, cameras, and robotic arms, *Alvin* helps scientists gather data and discover ecosystems that exist deep in the ocean. Built in 1964, *Alvin* was one of the world's first deep-ocean submersibles and has made more than 4,500 dives. *Alvin* is credited with finding a lost hydrogen bomb, exploring the first known hydrothermal vents, and surveying the wreck of the *Titanic*.

Calculate Suppose that on each of the 4,500 dives *Alvin* has made, a new pilot and two new scientists were on board. How many scientists have seen the deep ocean through *Alvin's* windows? How many people, in total, traveled in *Alvin*?

<u>9,000 scientists;</u>
<u>13,500 people total</u>

▷ **PLANET DIARY** Go to **Planet Diary** to learn more about aquatic ecosystems.

 Lab zone Do the Inquiry Warm-Up *Where Does It Live?*

What Are the Two Major Aquatic Ecosystems?

Since almost three quarters of Earth's surface is covered with water, many living things make their homes in and near water. 🔑 **There are two types of aquatic, or water-based, ecosystems: freshwater ecosystems and marine (or saltwater) ecosystems.** All aquatic ecosystems are affected by the same abiotic, or nonliving, factors: sunlight, temperature, oxygen, and salt content. Sunlight is an important factor in aquatic ecosystems because it is necessary for photosynthesis in the water just as it is on land. Half of all oxygen produced on Earth comes from floating algae called phytoplankton. Because water absorbs sunlight, there is only enough light for photosynthesis to occur near the surface or in shallow water.

656 Ecosystems and Biomes

SUPPORT ALL READERS
Lexile Measure = 960L   Lexile Word Count = 864

Prior Exposure to Content: May be the first time students have encountered this topic

Academic Vocabulary: *classify, outline*

Science Vocabulary: *estuary, intertidal zone, neritic zone*

Concept Level: Generally appropriate for most students in this grade

Preteach With: My Planet Diary "Underwater *Alvin*" and Figure 2 activity

Go to **My Reading Web** to access leveled readings that provide a foundation for the content.

my science online.com ▷

Vocabulary
- estuary
- neritic zone
- intertidal zone

Skills
- ⟳ Reading: Outline
- △ Inquiry: Communicate

Freshwater Ecosystems No worldwide expedition would be complete without exploring Earth's waters. Even though most of Earth's surface is covered with water, only 3 percent of the volume is fresh water. Freshwater ecosystems include streams, rivers, ponds, and lakes. On this part of your expedition, you'll find that freshwater biomes provide habitats for a variety of organisms.

Streams and Rivers At the source of a mountain stream, the water flows slowly. Plants take root on the bottom, providing food for insects and homes for frogs. These consumers then provide food for larger consumers. Stream currents increase as streams come together to make larger streams, often called rivers. Animals here are adapted to strong currents. For example, trout have streamlined bodies to swim in the rushing water. As the current speeds up, it can become cloudy with sediment. Few plants or algae grow in this fast-moving water. Consumers such as snails feed on leaves and seeds that fall into the stream. At lower elevations, streams are warmer and often contain less oxygen, affecting the organisms that can live in them.

Ponds and Lakes Ponds and lakes are bodies of still, or standing, fresh water. Lakes are generally larger and deeper than ponds. Ponds are often shallow enough that sunlight can reach the bottom, allowing plants to grow there. In large ponds and most lakes, however, algae floating at the surface are the major producers. Many animals are adapted for life in still water. Dragonflies, snails, and frogs live along the shores of ponds. In the open water, sunfish feed on insects and algae close to the surface. Scavengers such as catfish live near the bottoms of ponds. Bacteria and other decomposers also feed on the remains of other organisms.

⟳ **Outline** As you read, make an outline on a separate sheet of paper that includes the different types of aquatic ecosystems. Use the red headings for the main ideas and the black headings for the supporting details.

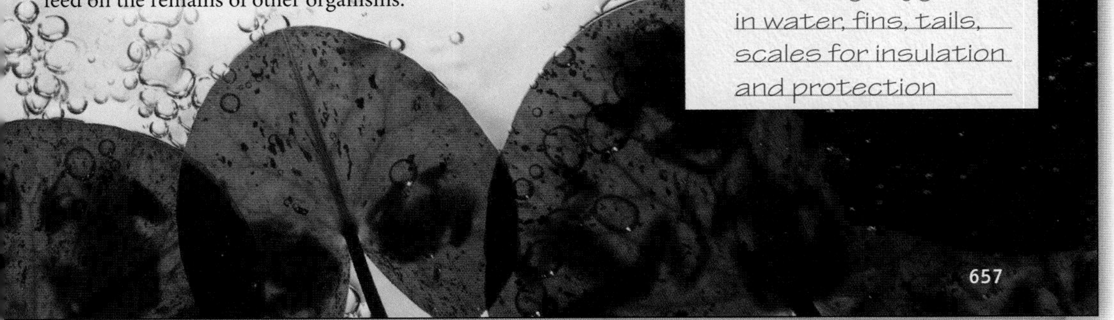

FIGURE 1
Freshwater Ecosystems
Water lilies live in ponds and lakes.
✎ Answer the questions.

1. **Identify** What are two abiotic factors that can affect water lilies?

Water temperature
and amount of
sunlight

2. **CHALLENGE** What adaptations do fish have that allow them to live in water?

Sample: gills for
breathing oxygen
in water, fins, tails,
scales for insulation
and protection

657

Explain

Introduce Vocabulary

Explain that the word *intertidal* combines a form of the word *tide* with a prefix (*inter*-) meaning "between." The intertidal zone of the ocean is the area between the waterline at high tide and at low tide.

Explain

Teach Key Concepts 🔑

Explain to students that water-based ecosystems are called aquatic ecosystems. Ask: **What two major categories are aquatic ecosystems divided into?** *(Freshwater ecosystems and saltwater, or marine, ecosystems)* The source of most freshwater on Earth is in glaciers and in water underground. In fact, 99% of liquid freshwater is found underground. Almost half of the world's lake water is saltwater, such as the Great Salt Lake of Utah. Saltwater lakes can be up to ten times saltier than the ocean. Point out that sunlight, temperature, oxygen, and salt content are factors that affect all aquatic ecosystems. Ask: **Why is sunlight important to aquatic ecosystems?** *(Sunlight is needed for photosynthesis.)* **Where does most photosynthesis take place?** *(Near the surface or in shallow water where there is light)* **What are two groups of freshwater ecosystems?** *(Flowing water and standing water)*

21st Century Learning

CRITICAL THINKING Help students compare and contrast types of aquatic ecosystems. Ask: **What are two examples of flowing water ecosystems?** *(Streams and rivers)* **How do these ecosystems differ?** *(Streams tend to be smaller and the water flows slowly near their source. Rivers tend to be wider, deeper, and faster-moving.)* **What are two examples of standing water ecosystems?** *(Ponds and lakes)* **How do these ecosystems differ?** *(Lakes are larger and deeper than ponds. Sunlight can reach the bottom of many ponds, but not lakes.)*

⟳ **Outline** Outlining helps organize information in a visual way that makes it easier to see the relationships between ideas. Make sure students follow the proper format for an outline.

My Planet Diary provides an opportunity for students to explore real-world connections to aquatic ecosystems.

my science online.com | Aquatic Ecosystems

ⓔ ⓛ ⓛ Support

1 Content and Language
Allow students to create entries for the vocabulary terms in their own science glossaries. Students should briefly define each word, draw a picture, and include the word in their native language if needed.

2 Frontload the Lesson
Have students name organisms they have seen in marine ecosystems, even at an aquarium. Have students

cooperatively discuss the habitats of these organisms.

3 Comprehensible Input
Have students suggest other marine organisms they have seen that are not shown in **Figure 2**. Ask students to hypothesize the depth at which the organism can be found.

Explain

Support the Big Q ? UbD

PRODUCERS IN THE OCEAN Ask students to look at the intertidal zone in **Figure 2.** Ask: **What difference do you see in what is living here compared to the other zones?** *(This zone has plants attached to the bottom and the others do not.)* Ask: **In which other zones do algae live?** *(Neritic zone and surface zone of the open ocean)* **Why are these organisms important to marine ecosystems?** *(They produce oxygen and are food for other organisms.)* Help students appreciate the importance of producers in the ocean by explaining that floating algae called phytoplankton produce half of Earth's oxygen.

Lead a Discussion

Invite students to share their knowledge of water-based ecosystems, which may have come from experiences such as swimming, fishing, boating, or observing from shore. Ask: **What aquatic ecosystems have you seen?** *(Students will likely name ponds, lakes; rivers, streams; bays, or open oceans.)* **What plants and animals did you observe?** *(Students will likely mention green algae, water lilies, marsh grasses, "seaweed," fish, frogs, turtles, waterfowl, or other birds.)* Encourage students who have seen different aquatic ecosystems to share differences and similarities between the ecosystems.

21st Century Learning

CRITICAL THINKING Discuss with students the differences and similarities among marine ecosystems in location, water depth, amount of salt in water, organisms, and sunlight. Ask: **How are an estuary and the intertidal zone different?** *(Different organisms live in them; the water in the intertidal zone is saltier than the water in an estuary; the estuary has few waves.)* **How are an estuary and the intertidal zone alike?** *(In both, the land is sometimes covered with water and at other times exposed to the air and sunlight.)*

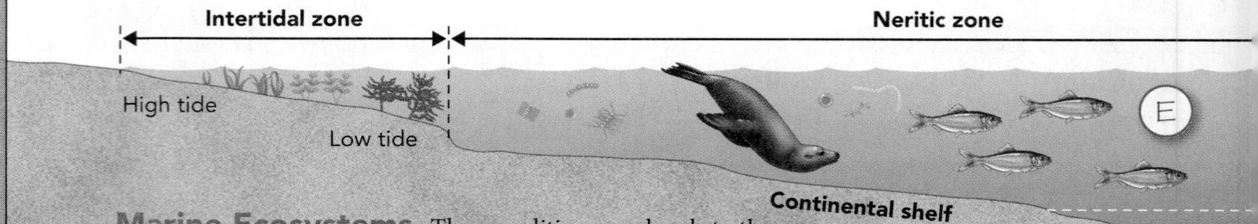

Intertidal zone   Neritic zone

High tide   Low tide   Continental shelf   E

Marine Ecosystems The expedition now heads to the coast to explore some marine biomes. On your way, you'll pass through an estuary. An estuary (ES choo ehr ee), is found where the fresh water of a river meets the salt water of an ocean. Algae and plants provide food and shelter for animals, including crabs and fish. Many animals use the calm waters of estuaries for breeding grounds. Last, you explore the different ocean zones as described in **Figure 2.**

Ocean Zones

Zone	Location	Inhabitants
Intertidal zone	Located on the shore between the highest high-tide line and the lowest low-tide line	Organisms must be able to survive pounding waves and the sudden changes in water levels and temperature that occur with high and low tides. For example, barnacles and sea stars cling to the rocks while clams and crabs burrow in the sand.
Neritic zone	Region of shallow water found below the low-tide line and extending over the continental shelf	Sunlight passes through shallow water, allowing photosynthesis to occur. Many living things, such as algae and schools of fish, live here. Coral reefs can also be found here in warmer waters.
Surface zone, open ocean	Located beyond the neritic zone and extending from the water's surface to about 200 meters deep	Sunlight penetrates this zone, allowing photosynthesis to occur in floating phytoplankton and other algae. Tuna, swordfish, and some whales depend on the algae for food.
Deep zone, open ocean	Located beneath the surface zone to the ocean floor	Little, if any, sunlight passes through. Animals feed on the remains of organisms that sink down. Organisms, like the giant squid and anglerfish, are adapted to life in the dark.

FIGURE 2 ·······
Marine Ecosystems
The ocean is home to a number of different ecosystems.

✎ **Classify** Using the clues, determine at which depth each organism belongs. In the circles in the ocean, write the letter for each organism in the correct zone.

C

D

Yellowfin Tuna
Found in open waters and has been known to eat squid

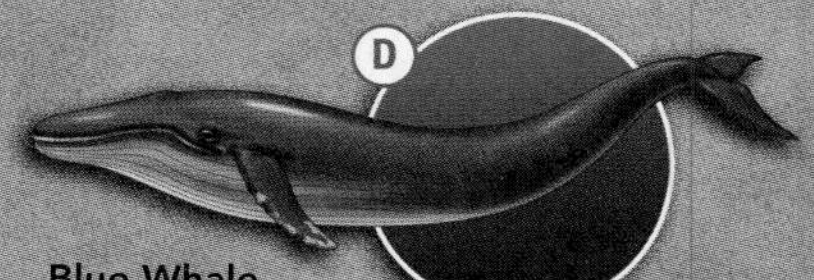

Blue Whale
Feeds on shrimplike creatures at depths of more than 100 meters during the day

A

Anglerfish
Females have a lighted lure to help them attract prey in the dark.

B

Tripod Fish
This fish has three elongated fins to help it stand.

E

Swordfish
Often seen jumping out of the water to stun smaller fish

658 Ecosystems and Biomes

Digital Lesson: Assign the *Apply It* activity online and have students submit their work to you.

my science online.com   **Aquatic Ecosystems**

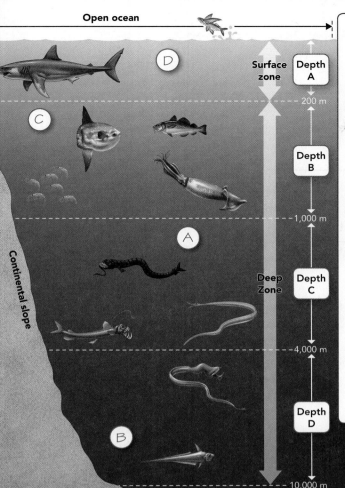

Open ocean

Surface zone

Depth A

— 200 m

Depth B

— 1,000 m

Deep Zone

Depth C

— 4,000 m

Depth D

— 10,000 m

Continental slope

apply it!

While on a deep sea exploration, you discover a new marine organism on the ocean floor.

△ **Communicate** Draw or describe the new organism below. Identify the structures and adaptations it has to live in the deep zone.

Sample: The organism is very small so it doesn't require much food. It is very strong to withstand the pressure of the water. Big eyes help it see in the dark.

Lab zone ▷ Do the Quick Lab *Dissolved Oxygen.*

🔑 Assess Your Understanding

1a. List The four abiotic factors that affect all aquatic ecosystems are

sunlight, temperature, oxygen, and salt content.

b. Make Generalizations Why is sunlight important to all aquatic ecosystems?

Sunlight is needed for producers to make food and oxygen.

got it?

○ **I get it!** Now I know that the two major types of aquatic ecosystems are *freshwater and marine.*

○ **I need extra help with** *See TE note.*

Go to **my science COACH** *online for help with this subject.*

659

Elaborate

Build Inquiry 🔬Lab

L1 INFER CORAL STRUCTURE

Materials coral

Time 10 minutes

Ask students if a coral is a plant or an animal (*Animal*) Provide samples of different types of coral for students to examine. Emphasize that these pieces of coral are not the animals, which are soft, but the structures they produced and left behind when they died.

Ask: **Where do you think the coral animals lived?** (*Inside the tiny holes*) **How do you think this hard structure helps coral animals survive?** (*It provides protection for the animals' soft bodies and also anchors them to the ocean floor.*)

Apply It!

L1 Review details listed in the Ocean Zones table and the Marine Ecosystems illustrations before beginning the activity. Make sure students understand that the new organism should have structures and adaptations that are appropriate for the deep zone of the open ocean. Point out that students might "borrow" one or more characteristics from several existing organisms in order to create a new kind of organism.

△ **Communicate** Tell students that including details will help them convey their ideas more clearly.

Lab Resource: Quick Lab 🔬Lab

L2 DISSOLVED OXYGEN Students will explore how oxygen is dissolved in water.

Evaluate

Assess Your Understanding

After students answer the questions, have them evaluate their understanding by completing the appropriate sentence.

RTI Response to Intervention

1a. If students have trouble listing factors that affect aquatic ecosystems, **then** call on volunteers to list factors that affect land ecosystems. Then ask students which of these factors affect aquatic ecosystems, and to add any additional factors.

b. If students need help with the importance of sunlight, **then** ask them which kinds of organisms require sunlight and why.

my science COACH Have students go online for help in understanding aquatic ecosystems.

Differentiated Instruction

L1 Draw the Ocean's Four Zones Have each student draw a diagram showing the ocean's four zones and label each zone without referring to the illustration in this section. Have students check their work when they have finished their diagrams. Students' diagrams might be displayed on a classroom or hallway bulletin board.

L3 Aquatic Photos Challenge students to find photographs of two

different aquatic ecosystems. Have them take notes on the similarities and differences between the ecosystems and the organisms that live in them. Students can then explain those characteristics to the class. Remind students of the factors to consider in comparing the ecosystems: salty water or fresh water, amount of available sunlight, still or moving water, types of organisms, and so on.

Name ______________________ Date __________ Class __________

Lab zone® After the Inquiry Warm-Up

Aquatic Ecosystems

Inquiry Warm-Up, *Where Does It Live?*
In the Inquiry Warm-Up, you investigated how an organism's structure helps it survive in its habitat. Using what you learned from that activity, answer the questions below.

1. **USE PRIOR KNOWLEDGE** Are their structures in your hand that help you survive? List at least two structures in your hand and their functions.

____

____

2. **USE PRIOR KNOWLEDGE** List all the structures of your body necessary in order for you to say a word.

____

____

3. **COMMUNICATE** Draw a simple diagram of a fish. Label as many different structures on the fish as you can.

4. **EXPLAIN** List all the structures of the fish that help it swim through water.

____

____

____

____

Place the outside corner, the corner away from the dotted line, in the corner of your copy machine to copy onto letter-size paper.

Assess Your Understanding

Aquatic Ecosystems

What Are the Two Major Aquatic Ecosystems?

1a. LIST The four abiotic factors that affect all aquatic ecosystems are

_____

b. MAKE GENERALIZATIONS Why is sunlight important to all aquatic ecosystems?

_____

gotit?..

○ **I get it!** Now I know that the two major types of aquatic ecosystems are _____

_____

○ **I need extra help with** _____

_____

Aquatic Ecosystems

What Are the Two Major Aquatic Ecosystems?

There are two types of aquatic, or water-based, ecosystems: freshwater ecosystems and marine (or saltwater) ecosystems. All aquatic ecosystems are affected by the same abiotic, or nonliving factors: sunlight, temperature, oxygen, and salt content.

Most of Earth's surface is covered with water, yet only 3 percent is fresh water. Freshwater ecosystems include streams, rivers, ponds, and lakes. Freshwater biomes provide habitats for a variety of organisms. Few plants or algae can grow in this fast-moving water. Slower moving water in rivers is warmer and contains less oxygen, so different organisms are adapted to life there. Plants take root on the river bottom, providing food for insects and homes for frogs. These consumers provide food for larger consumers. Ponds and lakes are bodies of still fresh water. Usually lakes are larger and deeper than ponds. In large ponds and most lakes, algae floating at the surface are major producers. Many animals are adapted for life in still water, such as dragonflies, snails, frogs, sunfish, and catfish. Bacteria and other decomposers also feed on the remains of other organisms.

An **estuary** is found where the fresh water a river meets the salt water of an ocean. Algae and plants provide food and shelter for animals, including crabs and fish. Many animals use the calm waters of estuaries for breeding grounds. Marine ecosystems have different ocean zones. There are four ocean zones. Located on the shore between the highest high-tide line and the lowest low-tide line, the **intertidal zone** is home to organisms, such as barnacles, clams, and crabs, that survive pounding waves and sudden changes in water levels and temperature, The **neritic zone** is a shallow water region found below the low-tide line and extending over the continental shelf. Living things, such as algae and fish, live here. The surface zone is open ocean located beyond the neritic zone and extending from the water's surface to a few hundred meters deep. Tuna, swordfish, and some whales feed on algae here. The deep zone is the deeper, darker water below the surface zone. Animals feed on the remains of organisms that sink down. Organisms, like the giant squid and anglerfish, are adapted to life in the dark.

On a separate sheet of paper, identify the categories into which freshwater ecosystems and marine ecosystems are divided.

Place the outside corner, the corner away from the dotted line, in the corner of your copy machine to copy onto letter-size paper.

Review and Reinforce

Aquatic Ecosystems

Understanding Main Ideas
Answer the following question in the spaces provided.

1. What are the four main types of freshwater ecosystems?

_____

_____

2. What conditions to organisms face in the intertidal zone?

_____

_____

_____

_____

3. Why is the neritic zone particularly rich in living things?

_____

_____

_____

Building Vocabulary
Fill in the blank to complete each statement.

4. The _____ zone is the point along the shoreline between the highest high-tide line and the lowest low-tide line.

5. The point where the fresh water of a river meets the salt water of the ocean is called a(n) _____.

6. The _____ zone is out in the open ocean where light penetrates only to a depth of a few hundred meters.

7. The _____ zone is a region of shallow water below the low-tide line that extends over the continental shelf.

8. The _____ zone is almost totally dark.

Enrich

Aquatic Ecosystems

A hydrothermal vent is a place very hot water from Earth's crust rises to the ocean floor and is released into the surrounding seawater through cracks in the ocean floor. Read the passage and then answer the questions on a separate sheet of paper.

Hydrothermal Vent Communities

There are many ecosystems within the marine environment including estuaries, the intertidal zone, and the open ocean. Within each of these ecosystems, life is rich and diverse. The open ocean can be divided into two main zones, the surface zone, where light penetrates water to a depth of a few hundred meters, and the deep zone, where there is little to no light. In the surface zone, algae are the producers, using light energy from the sun to undergo photosynthesis and produce glucose, an energy-rich compound. In the deepest areas of the ocean, where there is no light, photosynthesis cannot take place. Although vast areas of the deep-ocean floor are empty of life, one unique community of organisms exists in some of the deepest areas of the ocean, around hydrothermal vents.

At hydrothermal vents, the hot water is rich in minerals, including sulfur compounds. Certain types of bacteria can produce glucose from the sulfur compounds through a process called *chemosynthesis*. These bacteria are producers. Like algae in the surface zone that use light energy to produce glucose, the bacteria use the energy in the sulfur compounds to do the same.

These communities have been found as deep as 2.2 km below the ocean surface. The bacteria in a hydrothermal vent community can live on rocks that are heated to temperatures of 110°C from the water gushing out of cracks in the ocean floor. They coat the hot rocks and are grazed on by shrimp. The shrimp and other grazers are eaten by crabs and fishes.

1. What process do producers in the surface zone undergo to produce glucose?
2. What are hydrothermal vent communities?
3. Which organisms are the producers in a hydrothermal vent community? What process do these organisms undergo to produce glucose?
4. How can these bacteria produce glucose without light energy from the sun?
5. Predict what would happen if the hot, sulfur-containing water stopped entering the surrounding ocean water.

Name _____ Date _____ Class _____

Aquatic Ecosystems

Fill in the blank to complete each statement.

1. _____ ecosystems include streams, rivers, ponds, and lakes.

2. A(n) _____ is found where the fresh water of a river meets the salt water of an ocean.

3. Located on the shore, the _____ zone is home to organisms that can survive pounding waves and sudden changes in water levels and temperature.

4. There are two types of aquatic ecosystems: freshwater biomes and _____ biomes.

5. Organisms like the giant squid and anglerfish are adapted to life in the dark of the _____ zone.

If the statement is true, write *true*. If the statement is false, change the underlined word or words to make the statement true.

6. _____ All <u>aquatic ecosystems</u> are affected by the same nonliving factors: sunlight, temperature, oxygen, and salt content.

7. _____ Most of Earth's surface is covered with water, yet only <u>30 percent</u> is fresh water.

8. _____ Usually lakes are <u>smaller and shallower</u> than ponds.

9. _____ Tuna, swordfish, and some whales feed on algae in the <u>intertidal</u> zone.

10. _____ The <u>neritic zone</u> is a region of shallow water where many living things, such as algae and schools of fish, live.

Aquatic Ecosystems

Answer Key

After the Inquiry Warm-Up

1. Accept all reasonable responses. Students may say: Yes, fingers help to grip, nails for scratching or picking at something.

2. Accept all reasonable responses. Students may say: mouth, tongue, vocal cords, and lungs.

3. Sample: Simple line drawing of a fish with labeled structures, such as: eye, gills, fin, tail, etc.

4. Sample: Gills for breathing underwater, fins for turning and stability, tail for propulsion.

Key Concept Summaries

Freshwater ecosystems and marine ecosystems are the two types of aquatic ecosystems. Freshwater ecosystems include streams, rivers, ponds, and lakes. Streams tend to be fast-moving and cold, and rivers tend to be slower and warmer. Ponds and lakes are bodies of still fresh water. Usually lakes are larger and deeper than ponds. An estuary is found where the fresh water of a river meets the salt water of an ocean. The ocean is divided into four zones. The intertidal zone is located on the shore between the highest high-tide line and the lowest low-tide line. The neritic zone is shallow water found below the low-tide line and extending over the continental shelf.

The surface zone is open ocean located beyond the neritic zone and extending from the water's surface to a few hundred meters deep. The deep zone is the deeper, darker water below the surface zone.

Review and Reinforce

1. streams, rivers, ponds, lakes

2. They face pounding waves as well as sudden changes in water levels and temperature that occur with high and low tides.

3. It is rich in organisms because sunlight passes through its shallow water enabling photosynthesis to occur.

4. intertidal
5. estuary
6. surface
7. neritic
8. deep

Enrich

1. photosynthesis

2. communities of organisms that form near areas of the deep ocean floor where super-heated water that contains sulfur compounds is released into surrounding ocean water from Earth's crust

3. bacteria; chemosynthesis

4. Since sunlight does not penetrate to the deep-ocean floor, these bacteria use the energy in the sulfur compounds in place of light energy to produce glucose, a process called chemosynthesis.

5. The bacteria would not be able to undergo chemosynthesis without a source of energy and have to move to a new vent area or die. Since the bacteria are the producers supporting the entire community, the consumers would have to find another food source, move to a new vent, or die.

Lesson Quiz

1. Freshwater
2. estuary
3. intertidal
4. marine
5. deep
6. true
7. 3 percent
8. larger and deeper
9. surface
10. true

Place the outside corner, the corner away from the dotted line, in the corner of your copy machine to copy onto letter-size paper.

Biodiversity

How do energy and matter move through ecosystems?

Lesson Pacing: 1–2 periods or $\frac{1}{2}$–1 block

🕐 **SHORT ON TIME?** To do this lesson in approximately half the time, do the Activate Prior Knowledge activity. A discussion of the Key Concepts will familiarize students with the lesson content. Use the Explore the Big Q to help students understand how natural and human activities change ecosystems. Have students do the Quick Labs and the Virtual Lab online. The rest of the lesson can be completed by students independently.

Lesson Vocabulary

- biodiversity • keystone species • gene • extinction
- endangered species • threatened species
- habitat destruction • habitat fragmentation • poaching
- captive breeding

Content Refresher

Pollution by DDT Pesticides such as DDT can threaten biodiversity by endangering animal species. At one time, DDT was applied for crop protection and insect control. DDT killed vast numbers of insects quickly and offered protection for months. But it also created problems. DDT passed through food chains, with increasing concentrations at each level, a mechanism called biological magnification. One study found DDT concentrations increased more than 400 times from producer to top carnivore in the local food chain. Scientists also learned humans were accumulating it. DDT was banned from general use in the U.S. in the late 1970s.

LESSON OBJECTIVES

🔑 Explain the value of biodiversity.

🔑 Identify the factors that affect biodiversity.

🔑 Identify ways that human activity threatens and protects biodiversity.

ENGAGE AND EXPLORE

Teach this lesson using a variety of resources. Begin by reading **My Planet Diary** as a class. Have students share ideas about how they could protect and encourage wildlife. Then have students do the **Inquiry Warm-Up activity.** Students will investigate the biodiversity of different ecosystems. Discuss the differences in relation to the ecosystems temperatures. The **After the Inquiry Warm-Up worksheet** compares diversities in different ecosystems and asks students to make inferences. Have volunteers share their answers to question 4. If there are two different points of view, ask students to defend each point of view.

EXPLAIN AND ELABORATE

Teach Key Concepts by explaining the terms economic value and ecological value. Use **Figure 1** to discuss the wide diversity of insect species. **Lead a Discussion** about local biodiversity.

Continue to **Teach Key Concepts** by describing how climate area and diversity of niches affect the biodiversity of an ecosystem. Use **Figure 3** to estimate areas of circles, rectangles, and irregular figures. **Lead a Discussion** to remind students of what climate is and how it affects an ecosystem. Before beginning the **Apply It activity,** discuss how crops that lack a diverse gene pool may respond to changes.

Teach Key Concepts by asking students how they think people affect biodiversity both negatively and positively. Use the **Explore the Big Q** and **Figure 6** to have students understand the variety of life in a coral reef ecosystem. Use the **Answer the Big Q** to have students understand how natural and human activities change ecosystems over time.

Hand out the **Key Concept Summaries** as a review of each part of the lesson. Students can also use the online **Vocab Flash Cards** to review key terms.

EVALUATE

Have students take the **Lesson Quiz.** For an alternate assessment, see the **EXAM**VIEW® Test Bank CD-ROM powered by **EXAM**VIEW® Assessment Suite, Progress Monitoring Assessments, or SuccessTracker™.

🄴🄻🄻 Support

1 Content and Language

Have students make a vocabulary notebook for the vocabulary words in this lesson. Have students define the terms in their own words.

Lab zone Inquiry Path
Hands-on learning in the Lab zone

Digital Path
Online learning at **my science online**.com

ENGAGE AND EXPLORE

To teach this lesson with an emphasis on inquiry, begin with the **Inquiry Warm-Up activity.** Students will investigate various ecosystems and their biodiversity. Discuss with students what might lead to greater diversity in an ecosystem. Have students do the **After the Inquiry Warm-Up worksheet.** Talk about question 4. You might want students to list human activities beneficial and harmful to an ecosystem.

EXPLAIN AND ELABORATE

Focus on the **Inquiry Skill** for the lesson. Point out that when you infer, you use prior knowledge to make an inference. What inference could be made from the **Inquiry Warm-Up activity?** *(Wider variety of tree species can support a greater variety of organisms that depend of the trees for survival)* Have students do the **Quick Lab** to model keystone species using building blocks and then share their results.

Use **Build Inquiry** to help students identify factors that contribute to diversity. Review how lack of diversity may contribute to a plant's response to change before beginning the **Apply It activity.** Ask volunteers to give another example similar to Ireland's potato famine. Do the **Quick Lab** to reinforce understanding of the concept of gene pool.

Use the **Explore the Big Q** and **Figure 6** to help students understand the variety of life in a coral reef ecosystem. Use the **Answer the Big Q** to help students understand how natural and human activities change ecosystems. Have students do the **Quick Lab** so they can identify ways that humans affect biodiversity positively and negatively. Students can use the online **Vocab Flash Cards** to review key terms.

EVALUATE

Have students take the **Lesson Quiz.** For an alternate assessment, see the **EXAM**VIEW® Test Bank CD-ROM powered by **EXAM**VIEW® Assessment Suite, Progress Monitoring Assessments, or SuccessTracker™.

ENGAGE AND EXPLORE

Teach this lesson using digital resources, begin by having students learn more about diversity at **My Planet Diary** online. Have them access the Chapter Resources to find the **Unlock the Big Question activity.** There they can answer the questions and refine their responses as they continue through the lesson. You can re-assign the activity and have students submit their work so you can track their progress.

EXPLAIN AND ELABORATE

Students reading above, at, or below the lexile measure of this lesson can access basic content readings at their level at **My Reading Web.**

Have students use the online **Vocab Flash Cards** to preview key terms. Have students do the first **Quick Lab.** Ask students to share their results modeling keystone species.

Review the effects of a lack of diversity in gene pools before assigning the online **Apply It activity.** Ask volunteers to share their ideas for preventing famine. Have students submit their work to you. Have students do the **Quick Lab** to identify gene pools.

Use the **Virtual Lab** to **Explore the Big Q** and have students learn about the variety of life in a coral reef ecosystem. Use the **Answer the Big Q** to help students understand how natural and human activities change ecosystems. Have students do the **Quick Lab** to explore how humans protect and threaten biodiversity. The **Key Concept Summaries** online allow students to read a summary and see an image associated with each part of the lesson. Online remediation is available at **My Science Coach.**

EVALUATE

Have students take the **Lesson Quiz.** For an alternate assessment, see the **EXAM**VIEW® Test Bank CD-ROM powered by **EXAM**VIEW® Assessment Suite, Progress Monitoring Assessments, or SuccessTracker™.

2 Frontload the Lesson
Preview the lesson visuals, labels, and captions. Ask students what they know about *endangered* and *threatened species*. Explain the specific meanings these words have in science.

3 Comprehensible Input
Have students study the visuals and their captions to support the Key Concepts of the lesson.

4 Language Production
Pair or group students with varied language abilities to complete labs collaboratively for language practice. Have each student copy the completed written lab for personal reference.

5 Assess Understanding
Divide the class into small groups. Have each student identify a key concept from the lesson to discuss in his or her group. After the discussions, have students talk about the Key Concepts as a group.

Biodiversity

Establish Learning Objectives

After this lesson, students will be able to:

- 🔑 Explain the value of biodiversity.
- 🔑 Identify the factors that affect biodiversity.
- 🔑 Identify ways that human activity threatens and protects biodiversity.

Engage

Activate Prior Knowledge

MY PLANET DIARY Read *Max's Blog* with the class. Tell students that all the species in an ecosystem are connected to one another. Ask: **How are the brown bat, tree, and mosquito connected?** *(Sample: The tree helps provide habitat for the bat; the bat and mosquito are predator and prey)*

BIG IDEAS OF SCIENCE REFERENCE LIBRARY 📖 Have students look up the following topics: Biodiversity, Frozen Zoo, Insects.

Explore

Lab Resource: Inquiry Warm-Up 🧪

L1 HOW MUCH VARIETY IS THERE? Students will compare the variety of tree species in a tropical rain forest and deciduous forest.

Biodiversity

- 🔑 What Is Biodiversity's Value?
- 🔑 What Factors Affect Biodiversity?
- 🔑 How Do Humans Affect Biodiversity?

MY PLANET DIARY

BLOG

Posted by: Max

Location: Hagerstown, Maryland

I went to summer camp to learn about wildlife and how to protect it. One of the activities that I liked the most was making "bat boxes." These are wooden homes for brown bats, which often need places to nest. Making these houses is important, because without brown bats, there would be too many mosquitoes. I hope the bats like their new homes as much as I loved making them.

Communicate Discuss the question with a group of classmates. Then write your answers below.

How do you think helping the bats in an area helps other species nearby?

Sample: If there were not enough bats to eat bugs, there would be too many bugs. Too many bugs could also affect other species. Species that eat bats would also be in trouble.

▶ **PLANET DIARY** Go to **Planet Diary** to learn more about biodiversity.

 Do the Inquiry Warm-Up *How Much Variety Is There?*

What Is Biodiversity's Value?

No one knows exactly how many species live on Earth. As you can see in **Figure 1,** scientists have identified more than 1.6 million species so far. The number of different species in an area is called the area's **biodiversity.** It is difficult to estimate the total biodiversity on Earth because many areas have not been thoroughly studied.

660 Ecosystems and Biomes

SUPPORT ALL READERS

Lexile Measure = 950L   Lexile Word Count = 1698

Prior Exposure to Content: Many students may have misconceptions on this topic

Academic Vocabulary: *compare, contrast, infer*

Science Vocabulary: *biodiversity, keystone species, extinction*

Concept Level: Generally appropriate for most students in this grade

Preteach With: My Planet Diary "Max's Blog" and Figure 1 activity

Go to **My Reading Web** to access leveled readings that provide a foundation for the content.

my science online.com

Vocabulary
- biodiversity • keystone species • gene • extinction
- endangered species • threatened species
- habitat destruction • habitat fragmentation
- poaching • captive breeding

Skills
- 🔄 Reading: Compare and Contrast
- 🔺 Inquiry: Infer

There are many reasons why preserving biodiversity is important. One reason to preserve biodiversity is that wild organisms and ecosystems are a source of beauty and recreation. 🔑 **In addition, biodiversity has both economic value and ecological value within an ecosystem.**

Economic Value Many plants, animals, and other organisms are economically valuable for humans. These organisms provide people with food and supply raw materials for clothing, medicine, and other products. No one knows how many other useful species have not yet been identified. Ecosystems are economically valuable, too. Many companies now run wildlife tours to rain forests, savannas, mountains, and other places. This ecosystem tourism, or ecotourism, is an important source of jobs and money for such nations as Brazil, Costa Rica, and Kenya.

Ecological Value All the species in an ecosystem are connected to one another. Species may depend on each other for food and shelter. A change that affects one species can affect all the others.

Some species play a particularly important role in their ecosystems. A **keystone species** is a species that influences the survival of many other species in an ecosystem. Sea otters, as shown in **Figure 2,** are one example of a keystone species.

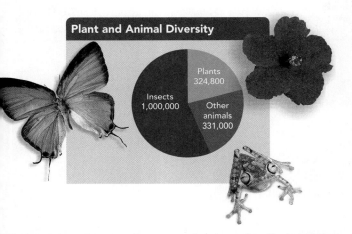

Plant and Animal Diversity

Insects 1,000,000

Plants 324,800

Other animals 331,000

FIGURE 1 ······························
Species Diversity
There are many more species of insects than plant or other animal species on Earth!

✏️ **Calculate** What percentage of species shown on the pie graph do insects represent? Round your answer to the nearest tenth.

60.4%

661

Explain

Introduce Vocabulary

Point out the term *poaching*. Students may already know this word as a way to cook eggs or snowboarding in a ski area where snowboarding is prohibited. Explain that in environmental science, *poaching* means illegally killing wildlife or removing wildlife from their habitats.

Teach Key Concepts 🔑

Explain to students that biodiversity can make the world more beautiful and provide opportunities to make money. Have students describe the different organisms in some of their favorite areas.

Ask: **How can entire ecosystems, such as rain forests and mountain ranges, be used to generate sources of money?** *(They can be used for ecotourism, which creates jobs and brings in money from people who visit the sites.)* **What might happen if the biodiversity of some of these ecosystems is disrupted?** *(Other species might die out; the area might not be as attractive to tourists)* **How might this affect the economy of the area?** *(Fewer people might visit the sites, resulting in loss of jobs and revenue.)*

Make Analogies

L1 KEYSTONE SPECIES Tell students that the term *keystone species* comes from the way a stone arch is built. Ask students if they have ever seen an arch where the stone at the center of the arch was larger than other stones. That is the keystone. If the keystone is removed, the arch will fall down. Ask: **What is a keystone species?** *(A species that influences the survival of many other species in an ecosystem)* **What would happen if the keystone species is removed from an ecosystem?** *(The ecosystem would be greatly changed.)*

Teach With Visuals

Point out to students that **Figure 1** shows known species. The number of species for bacteria, archaea, protists, and fungi are not included because their numbers are too uncertain. In addition, some organisms have not been classified or even discovered yet. Ask: **Do you think the number of species shown in Figure 1 are accurate?** *(No, new species may have been recently discovered or have yet to be classified.)*

My Planet Diary provides an opportunity for students to explore real-world connections to biodiversity.

ⒺⒽⒸ Support

1 Content and Language
Explain that the graph in **Figure 1** indicates the number of *species* that exist, as opposed to species *populations*.

2 Frontload the Lesson
Ask students to read aloud the red subheads, *Damaging Biodiversity* and *Protecting Biodiversity*. Ask students to predict which section will discuss the positive effects humans have on biodiversity, and which will discuss negative effects.

3 Comprehensible Input
Read aloud the captions in **Figure 2,** and then draw a cause and effect graphic organizer on the board. Reread the comic, asking students to identify the cause (sea otter population decreases) and effect (sea urchin population explodes).

Explain

Lead a Discussion

BIODIVERSITY Have students name organisms that thrive in the area where they live. Encourage students to consider a wide variety of organism types, including insects, worms, mosses, algae, plants, and bacteria, as well as mammals, birds, fish, reptiles, and amphibians. Ask: **Would you say that there is a great deal of diversity among the species living here?** *(Sample: Yes, especially if we consider plants, too.)*

Elaborate

Lab Resource: Quick Lab

L2 MODELING KEYSTONE SPECIES Students will use building blocks to model an analogy between an architectural keystone and a keystone species.

Evaluate

Assess Your Understanding

Have students evaluate their understanding by completing the appropriate sentence.

RTI Response to Intervention

If students cannot explain the importance of biodiversity, **then** have them locate and reread the boldface Key Concept statement and the sentences that precede it.

my science COACH Have students go online for help in understanding the importance of biodiversity.

FIGURE 2

Keystone Otters

Sea otters are a keystone species in the kelp forest ecosystem.

Describe Read the comic. In the empty panel, draw or explain what happened to the kelp forest when the otters returned. Write a caption for your panel.

In the 1800s, many otters were killed for their fur.

The sea otter is a keystone species in a kelp forest ecosystem.

Without otters preying on them, the population of kelp-eating sea urchins exploded, destroying kelp forests.

Under new laws that banned the hunting of sea otters, the sea otter population grew again.

Accept all reasonable drawings or explanations of a kelp forest.

The sea otters reduced the urchin population. The kelp forest recovered.

Lab zone — Do the Quick Lab *Modeling Keystone Species.*

Assess Your Understanding

got it?

O **I get it!** Now I know that biodiversity has *economic and ecological value within an ecosystem.*

O **I need extra help with** *See TE note.*

Go to **my science COACH** online for help with this subject.

662 Ecosystems and Biomes

What Factors Affect Biodiversity?

Biodiversity varies from place to place on Earth. **Factors that affect biodiversity in an ecosystem include climate, area, niche diversity, genetic diversity, and extinction.**

Climate The tropical rain forests of Latin America, southeast Asia, and central Africa are the most diverse ecosystems in the world. The reason for the great biodiversity in the tropics is not fully understood. Many scientists hypothesize that it has to do with climate. For example, tropical rain forests have fairly constant temperatures and large amounts of rainfall throughout the year. Many plants grow year-round. This continuous growing season means that food is always available for other organisms.

Area See **Figure 3.** Within an ecosystem, a large area will usually contain more species than a small area. For example, you would usually find more species in a 100-square-meter area than in a 10-square-meter area.

did you know?

Rain forests cover only about seven percent of the Earth's land surface. But they contain more than half of the world's species, including the chimpanzee!

FIGURE 3 ······
Park Size
A park manager has received three park plans. The dark green area represents the park.

✎ **Complete each task.**

1. **Identify** Circle the plan the manager should choose to support the most biodiversity.

2. **Calculate** Suppose that 15 square meters of the park could support seven species of large mammals. About how many species could the park you circled support?

933 species

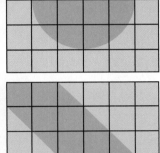

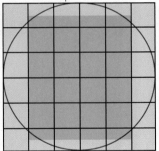

10 m
10 m

663

Explain ─────────

Teach Key Concepts 🗝

Explain that five main factors—climate, area, niche, genetic diversity, and extinction—affect the level of biodiversity in an ecosystem. Ask: **What kind of climate fosters biodiversity in an ecosystem?** *(A warm sunny climate with ample precipitation)* **Which probably has greater biodiversity, a 100-square-meter area of desert or a 10-square-meter area of desert?** *(A 100-square-meter area)* **Why?** *(The larger area of an ecosystem usually contains more species.)* **Why does a tropical rain forest have such a diverse ecosystem?** *(A tropical rain forest has a climate that allows many species to survive and supports many different niches.)*

Lead a Discussion

CLIMATE Remind students that climate is the typical weather pattern—precipitation and temperature—of an area over a long period of time. Ask: **Which area is more likely to have greater biodiversity, a tropical rain forest or an area closer to Earth's poles?** *(A rain forest)* **Why?** *(Plants in a rain forest can grow year-round, making food available all year to other organisms.)* **What might happen to the biodiversity of an area if its climate becomes colder?** *(Its biodiversity might decrease.)*

Teach With Visuals

Tell students to look at **Figure 3.** After students have examined the diagram, point out that it shows how the land area of a forest affects biodiversity. Explain that the diagram does not take into account the vegetation in the park. Ask: **How does a forest with trees of varying heights affect biodiversity?** *(Sample: A forest with trees of varying heights can support more bird species than a forest with trees of mostly the same height. Raptors can nest in the high trees. Birds that eat insects can forage at lower levels.)*

Differentiated Instruction

L3 Research Keystone Species Have students do research to find a keystone species in an area near their home. Remind students to follow prescribed guidelines for internet use. Students should be able to explain which species' survival are affected by the keystone species and how. Encourage students to find an image of the keystone species to share with the class.

L1 Apply Vocabulary Review the meanings of the terms *area* (space covered), *climate* (the typical weather pattern in an area over a long period), and *niche* (an organism's unique role in an ecosystem). Point out the red heads that contain each term. Have students work in pairs to read aloud and identify the main idea under each heading.

Explain

Lead a Discussion

DIVERSITY AND GENES Point out that members of the same species can vary; for example, dogs of the same breed can vary in color and size. Tell students that genes determine some of an organism's characteristics. Ask: **What is the gene pool of a species?** *(All the shared and differing genes among individuals in a species)*

21st Century Learning

INFORMATION LITERACY The greatest genetic diversity exists at the single-cell level. Archaea, which are similar to bacteria, possess genes in a circular form but lack a nucleus or organelles. They use sugar, hydrogen gas, and sunlight, among others, as sources of energy. Archaea can be found in harsh environments such as hot springs and salt lakes as well as oceans and marshlands. They play an important role in the carbon and nitrogen cycles. Some archaea are found in humans and aid in food digestion. Have students do research to get more information about archaea.

Teach With Visuals

Look at **Figure 4**. Ask: **Which of the animals pictured are extinct?** *(None, all are endangered.)* **How do endangered species differ from threatened species?** *(Endangered species are in danger of becoming extinct. Threatened species could become endangered in the near future.)* **Where are endangered species found?** *(On every continent and in every ocean)*

Address Misconceptions

L1 **NEWLY EXTINCT SPECIES** Some people believe that all extinct animals lived long ago and became extinct under mysterious circumstances. In fact, in the past few centuries, the rate of extinction of species has increased dramatically. Ask: **What has caused the extinction of some species in relatively recent times?** *(Sample: Human actions like hunting and habitat destruction)*

Elaborate

Apply It!

L1 Review information about genetic diversity before beginning the activity. Point out that any time a large area is used to grow a single crop, the risk of loss due to disease is greater than if a variety of crops are grown.

Niche Diversity Coral reefs are the second most diverse ecosystems in the world. Found only in shallow, warm waters, coral reefs are often called the rain forests of the sea. A coral reef supports many different niches. Recall that a niche is the role of an organism in its habitat, or how it makes its living. A coral reef enables a greater number of species to live in it than a more uniform habitat, such as a flat sandbar, does.

Genetic Diversity Diversity is very important within a species. The greatest genetic diversity exists among species of unicellular organisms. Organisms in a healthy population have diverse traits such as color and size. **Genes** are located within cells and carry the hereditary information that determines an organism's traits. Organisms inherit genes from their parents.

The organisms in one species share many genes. But each organism also has some genes that differ from those of other individuals. Both the shared genes and the genes that differ among individuals make up the total gene pool of that species. Species that lack a diverse gene pool are less able to adapt to and survive changes in the environment.

apply it!

New potato plants are created from pieces of the parent plant. So a potato crop has the same genetic makeup as the parent plant. In 1845, Ireland was struck by a potato famine. A rot-causing fungus destroyed potato crops, which were an important part of the Irish diet. Many people died of starvation, and many more left the country to find food.

❶ **Apply Concepts** How did a potato crop without a variety of different genes lead to the Irish potato famine of 1845?

Because the potato crop did not have a large variety of different genes, a fungus was able to destroy the whole crop.

❷ **CHALLENGE** What could farmers do to prevent another potato famine?

Sample: Farmers could increase the genetic diversity of their crops by planting different types of potatoes.

Digital Lesson: Assign the *Apply It* activity online and have students submit their work to you.

my science online | **Factors Affecting Biodiversity**

Green sea turtle ▲

Extinction of Species The disappearance of all members of a species from Earth is called **extinction.** Extinction is a natural process that occurs when organisms do not adapt to changes in their environment. In the last few centuries, the number of species becoming extinct has increased dramatically. Once a population drops below a certain level, the species may not recover. People have directly caused the extinction of many species through habitat destruction, hunting, or other actions.

Species in danger of becoming extinct in the near future are called **endangered species.** Species that could become endangered in the near future are called **threatened species.** Endangered and threatened species are found on every continent and in every ocean.

Blackburn's ▲
sphinx moth

FIGURE 4 ··········
Endangered Species
Large animals, like the green sea turtle, are the most publicized endangered species. Did you know insects and plants can also be endangered? ✎ **Infer** Why do you think some endangered species get more attention than others?

Sample: People know more about them due to media exposure. People may not know that insects and plants can be endangered.

Hawaiian alula ▲

Lab Do the Quick Lab
zone Grocery Gene Pool.

🖿 Assess Your Understanding

1a. Review A (smaller/larger) area will contain more species than a (smaller/larger) area.

b. Explain How is biodiversity related to niches?
The more niches, the greater the biodiversity.

c. 🔄 **Compare and Contrast** What is the difference between an endangered species and a threatened species?
A threatened species is not yet endangered but could be in the near future.

got **it**? ·······················

○ **I get it!** Now I know that the factors that affect biodiversity include climate, area, niche diversity, genetic diversity, and extinction.

○ **I need extra help with** See TE note.

Go to **my science ⬤ coach** *online for help with this subject.*

665

Build Inquiry **Lab zone**

L2 COMPARE BIODIVERSITY

Materials photographs of ecosystems

Time 15 minutes

Display pictures of different types of ecosystems. Have students analyze the pictures to determine the number and types of organisms shown.

Ask: **What are the abiotic, or nonliving, factors in this ecosystem?** (Sample: Air, light, water, temperature, soil) **Which ecosystems have the greatest biodiversity?** (Sample: The rain forest and coral reef) **What factors most likely contribute to the diversity?** (Climate, area, and diversity of niches)

Lab Resource: Quick Lab **Lab zone**

L1 GROCERY GENE POOL Students will infer whether a fruit or vegetable has a diverse gene pool, based on the variety of the fruit or vegetable available for sale.

△ **Infer** Remind students that they should use prior knowledge to help them make an inference about the attention different endangered species receive.

Evaluate ─────────

Assess Your Understanding

After students answer the questions, have them evaluate their understanding by completing the appropriate sentence.

RTI Response to Intervention

1a, b. If students have trouble explaining factors that affect biodiversity, **then** have them review the material under *Area* and *Niche Diversity*.

c. If students cannot contrast endangered species and threatened species, **then** have them review the two boldfaced terms and definitions.

my science ⬤ coach Have students go online for help in understanding factors that affect biodiversity.

Explain

Teach Key Concepts 🔑

Explain to students that humans can negatively or positively affect biodiversity. Ask: **What are four ways in which humans can negatively affect biodiversity?** *(Through habitat destruction, poaching, pollution, and introducing exotic species)* **How does habitat fragmentation contribute to extinction?** *(Sample: Clearing forests can expose trees to wind damage; animals may not be able to find enough resources in a smaller area.)* **What is the illegal removal of wildlife called?** *(Poaching)* **How can pollution contribute to species extinction?** *(Pollution can weaken organisms, kill them, or cause birth defects.)* **What are four positive ways in which humans can affect biodiversity?** *(Though captive breeding, laws and treaties, and habitat preservation)*

Make Analogies

L1 **HABITAT DESTRUCTION** To help students understand the concept of habitat destruction, compare an animal's habitat to a human's town or city. Ask: **What resources that you need to survive are provided, or can be purchased, in your town?** *(A place to live, food, water, clothing)* **Suppose you are out of town and your town is destroyed by a natural disaster, such as a hurricane, flood, earthquake, or volcanic eruption. Compare and contrast how this would affect you to how clearing a forest would affect a bear that lives there.** *(Like the bear after the forest is cleared, if my town were destroyed in a natural disaster, I would have no home—nowhere to sleep and no way to get the things I need to survive, such as food and water. Unlike the bear, I could move fairly easily to another place that would meet my basic needs.)*

How Do Humans Affect Biodiversity?

Humans interact with their surroundings every day. The many choices people make impact the environment and affect species. 🔑 **Biodiversity can be negatively or positively affected by the actions of humans.**

Damaging Biodiversity A natural event, such as a hurricane, can damage an ecosystem, wiping out populations or even entire species. Human activities can also threaten biodiversity and cause extinction. These activities include habitat destruction, poaching, pollution, and the introduction of exotic species.

FIGURE 5 ···

Habitat Fragmentation

Breaking habitats into pieces can have negative effects on the species that live there.

✎ **Interpret Diagrams** In the first diagram below, a road divides a habitat in two. On the second diagram, redraw the road so it divides the habitat's resources equally.

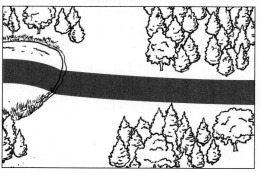

Habitat Destruction The major cause of extinction is **habitat destruction,** the loss of a natural habitat. Clearing forests or filling in wetlands changes those ecosystems. Breaking larger habitats into smaller, isolated pieces, or fragments, is called **habitat fragmentation.** See **Figure 5.** Some species may not survive such changes to their habitats.

Poaching The illegal killing or removal of wildlife from their habitats is called **poaching.** Some endangered species are valuable to poachers. Animals can be sold as pets or used to make jewelry, coats, belts, or shoes. Plants can be sold as houseplants or used to make medicines.

Pollution Some species are endangered because of pollution. Pollution may reach animals through the water they drink, the air they breathe, or the food they eat. Pollutants may kill or weaken organisms or cause birth defects.

Exotic Species Introducing exotic species into an ecosystem can threaten biodiversity. Exotic species can outcompete and damage native species. The gypsy moth was introduced into the United States in 1869 to increase silk production. Gypsy moth larvae have eaten the leaves off of millions of acres of trees in the northeastern United States.

Protecting Biodiversity Some people who preserve biodiversity focus on protecting individual endangered species. Others try to protect entire ecosystems. Three methods of protecting biodiversity are captive breeding, laws and treaties, and habitat preservation.

Captive Breeding **Captive breeding** is the mating of animals in zoos or on wildlife preserves. Scientists care for the young, and then release them into the wild. Much of the sandhill crane habitat in the United States has been destroyed. To help the population, some cranes have been taken into captivity. The young are raised and trained by volunteers to learn the correct behaviors, such as knowing how and where to migrate. They are then released into the wild.

✏️

➲ **Compare and Contrast**
The photos on top show young sandhill cranes being raised by their parents. The photos on the bottom show humans copying this process to increase the crane population. What is a possible disadvantage of the human approach?

Sample: The cranes could become used to people and endanger themselves by approaching people.

667

21st Century Learning

CRITICAL THINKING Have students look at the images of captive breeding. Ask: **How do you think scientists learned how to raise young cranes?** _(By observing cranes or other wading birds)_ **What interactions do you think occurred over time between scientists and cranes?** _(Sample: You could say that by "allowing" scientists to observe them, the cranes helped humans learn, and the humans used that knowledge to help the cranes and the ecosystem.)_

➲ **Compare and Contrast** Explain to students they should contrast the two processes to determine possible disadvantages of the human approach.

Teach With Visuals

Explain that the garment worn by the workers has a beak-like "glove" that resembles the head of a bird. The garment masks the body of the worker, allowing the worker to mimic an adult bird training the young birds.

Lead a Discussion

WILDLIFE PROTECTION CAREERS Discuss with students whether they think they might like to work as a scientist helping to protect biodiversity. Ask: **What kinds of scientists might be involved in protecting biodiversity?** _(Sample: Biologists, botanists)_ **What kinds of places might a scientist work where he or she could help protect biodiversity?** _(Sample: In a zoo, in a wildlife rehabilitation facility, with a wildlife protection agency such as the World Wildlife Fund)_ Have students write a job advertisement for a company that wants to hire a scientist to help protect biodiversity.

Differentiated Instruction

L1 **Compare and Contrast** Remind students that when you compare, you find similarities. When you contrast, you find differences. Students should think about how humans might affect the young cranes differently than actual parent cranes. Have students consider how a crane becoming used to people might negatively affect the animal in the future. Encourage students to answer the question using a graphic organizer, such as a Venn diagram.

L3 **Species Competition** Encourage students to research introduced species that compete with native species in the United States. Have students report on where competition is prevalent and describe the consequences to the native species. Example species include purple loosestrife, kudzu, leafy spurge, flathead catfish, sea lamprey, zebra mussel, gypsy moth, fire ant, brown tree snake, and starling.

LESSON 16.5

Explain

21st Century Learning

ACCOUNTABILITY Call on students to briefly explain the three ways of protecting biodiversity presented in the text. *(Help endangered or threatened species reproduce and survive through captive breeding, for example, mating of animals in zoos or wildlife preserves; pass laws and sign treaties to protect threatened and endangered species; preserve habitat by setting aside wildlife habitats as parks and refuges)*

Elaborate

Explore the Big Q ? UbD

Direct students' attention to **Figure 6.** Ask: **What species do you see in this ecosystem?** *(Samples: Orange fish, striped fish, larger fish, coral, and sea anemones)* **Which species do you think might be a keystone species? Why?** *(Sample: The coral and sponges might be keystone species because they provide living space for many of the other species in this ecosystem.)* **Coral can be damaged when it is touched or broken off for souvenirs by divers. How might diving affect the coral reef over time?** *(Sample: The coral reef may become smaller unless divers are careful not to damage the coral. Other populations of species will decrease if there is less living space available.)*

Make Connections

ECOSYSTEM DYNAMICS Introduce students to the term *ecosystem dynamics* and explain its meaning (the processes through which an ecosystem becomes self-sustaining and capable of recovery when external forces, such as damaging storms or volcanic eruptions, disrupt it.) Have students research and report on examples of natural and human-caused events that have had an effect on ecosystem dynamics. Assemble a list of the students' examples.

SPECIES SURVIVAL Remind students that disturbances to ecosystems may threaten the survival of some species and enhance the survival of others. Have a class discussion in which students compare and contrast the examples from the list generated in the Ecosystem Dynamics activity and suggest how each event may have affected various species in the ecosystems.

Life in a Coral Reef

How do natural and human activities change ecosystems?

FIGURE 6 ···

▶ **VIRTUAL LAB** This photo shows the diversity of the organisms in a coral reef ecosystem. The coral and sponges provide living space for algae and shelter for crabs, fishes, and other animals. Some fishes eat the algae.

✎ Predict Answer the questions in the boxes.

Suppose many more orange fish immigrate to this ecosystem, doubling the species' population. How might the increased numbers of orange fish impact other populations in the ecosystem? Explain.

Sample: The other fish populations might decrease because the food supply would be limited.

Laws and Treaties In the United States, the Endangered Species Act prohibits trade of products made from threatened or endangered species. This law also requires the development of plans to save endangered species. The Convention on International Trade in Endangered Species is an international treaty that lists more than 800 threatened and endangered species that cannot be traded for profit or other reasons anywhere in the world.

Habitat Preservation The most effective way to preserve biodiversity is to protect whole ecosystems. Protecting whole ecosystems saves endangered species, the species they depend upon, and those that depend upon them. Many countries have set aside wildlife habitats as parks and refuges. Today, there are about 7,000 nature parks, preserves, and refuges in the world.

668 Ecosystems and Biomes

Virtual Lab allows students to explore the impact humans have on biodiversity.

MY SCIENCE online.com ▷ **Human Impact on Biodiversity**

Make Connections

INVESTIGATING ECOSYSTEM DYNAMICS Divide the class into groups. Tell them that each group represents a research team that is investigating the relationships between ecosystem dynamics and human activity. Have each group pick a different ecosystem to study and develop a testable question to investigate. Next, have the groups create written plans to investigate their questions, including a description of the types of observations and data to be collected. Then have the groups exchange plans, analyze and critique the plans, and provide feedback.

Suppose people start to overfish this area. How might this change the ecosystem? Explain.

Sample: The fish species will decrease or may become extinct because of the over-fishing. The populations of the fishes' prey, such as algae, will increase as a result.

Suppose a tsunami, a huge ocean wave, were to hit this ecosystem, destroying much of the reef. Do you think the ecosystem would come back after the tsunami? Explain.

Sample: Yes. The organisms may be adapted to survive tsunamis. The sponges, coral, and algae may reproduce and increase their populations. Then the fish return when more shelter and food is available.

Lab zone® Do the Quick Lab *Humans and Biodiversity.*

🔑 Assess Your Understanding

2a. Define What is poaching?

Poaching is the illegal killing or removal of wildlife from their habitats.

b. How do natural and human activities change ecosystems?

Sample: They damage an eco-system, wipe out populations, and may cause species to become extinct.

got it? ···

○ **I get it!** Now I know that humans affect biodiversity *either positively or negatively, depending on their actions.*

○ **I need extra help with** *See TE note.*

Go to **my science COACH** *online for help with this subject.*

669

Lab Resource: Quick Lab

L2 HUMANS AND BIODIVERSITY Students will explore how humans both protect and threaten biodiversity.

Evaluate

Assess Your Understanding

After students answer the questions, have them evaluate their understanding by completing the appropriate sentence.

Answer the Big Q ? UbD

To help students focus on the Big Question, lead a class discussion about how natural and human activities change ecosystems over time.

RTI Response to Intervention

2a. If students need help defining poaching, **then** have them locate and reread the sentence in which the boldfaced term appears.

b. If students cannot describe how natural and human activities change ecosystems, **then** have them skim the blue questions throughout the chapter to locate sections that describe the effects of natural and human activities.

my science COACH Have students go online for help in understanding how humans affect biodiversity.

Differentiated Instruction

L1 Coral Reef Biodiversity Have students reread the caption for **Figure 6.** Before they work on the activity, have them draw a diagram to show the interactions of the populations in the coral reef ecosystem. Then have them work in pairs to answer the questions in **Figure 6.** Encourage them to use their diagrams when addressing each question's scenario.

L3 Human Impact Have students research the recent effects of human activities on coral reefs. Then have them make a poster to present their findings to the class. Students should include suggestions for how humans can help protect the coral reefs in their reports.

Lab®**zone** **After the Inquiry Warm-Up**

Biodiversity

Inquiry Warm-Up, *How Much Variety Is There?*
In the Inquiry Warm-Up, you investigated the biodiversity of various ecosystems. Using what you learned from that activity, answer the questions below.

1. **USE PRIOR KNOWLEDGE** Give a reason why you think a tropical rain forest would have greater diversity than a deciduous forest. Explain.

   _____

   _____

   _____

2. **INTERPRET DATA** Based solely on the results from the Inquiry Warm-Up, approximately how many times more types of trees exist in a tropical rain forest than a deciduous forest?

   _____

3. **INFER** What can you infer about the biodiversity of cold, polar regions relative to a tropical rain forest or a deciduous forest? Explain.

   _____

   _____

   _____

   _____

4. **DRAW CONCLUSIONS** Human activities can often drastically decrease the biodiversity of an area. In the context of the Inquiry Warm-Up, are such activities beneficial or harmful to an ecosystem? Explain.

   _____

   _____

   _____

Assess Your Understanding

Biodiversity

What Is Biodiversity's Value?

got it? ···

○ **I get it!** Now I know that biodiversity has _____

_____

○ **I need extra help with** _____

_____

What Factors Affect Biodiversity?

1a. **REVIEW** A (smaller/larger) area will contain more species than a (smaller/larger) area.

b. **EXPLAIN** How is biodiversity related to niches?

_____

_____

_____

c. **COMPARE AND CONTRAST** What is the difference between an endangered species and a threatened species?

_____

_____

_____

got it? ···

○ **I get it!** Now I know that the factors that affect biodiversity include _____

_____

○ **I need extra help with** _____

_____

Assess Your Understanding

Biodiversity

How Do Humans Affect Biodiversity?

2a. DEFINE What is poaching?

_____

_____

b. How do natural and human activities change ecosystems?

_____

_____

got it? ⋯⋯⋯⋯⋯⋯⋯⋯⋯⋯⋯⋯⋯⋯⋯⋯⋯⋯⋯⋯⋯⋯⋯⋯⋯

○ **I get it!** Now I know that humans affect biodiversity _____

_____

○ **I need extra help with** _____

_____

Key Concept Summaries

Biodiversity

What Is Biodiversity's Value?

The number of different species in an area is called the area's **biodiversity.** One reason to preserve biodiversity is that wild organisms and ecosystems are a source of beauty and recreation. **In addition, biodiversity has both economic value and ecological value within an ecosystem.** Many plants, animals and other organisms are economically valuable to humans. Also, all the species in an ecosystem are connected to one another. A **keystone species** is a species that influences the survival of many other species in an ecosystem.

What Factors Affect Biodiversity?

Factors that affect biodiversity in an ecosystem include climate, area, and diversity of niches. Tropical rain forests are the most diverse ecosystems in the world. Many scientists hypothesize that the reason for the great biodiversity in the tropics has to do with climate. Coral reefs are the second most diverse ecosystems. A coral reef supports many different niches.

Species need genetic diversity. Organisms in a healthy population have diverse traits such as color and size. **Genes** are located within cells and carry the hereditary information that determines an organism's traits. Species that lack a diverse gene pool are less able to adapt and survive changes in the environment.

The disappearance of all members of a species from Earth is called **extinction.** Species in danger of becoming extinct in the near future are called **endangered species.** Species that could become endangered in the near future are called **threatened species.**

How Do Humans Affect Biodiversity?

Biodiversity can be negatively or positively affected by the actions of humans. The major cause of extinction is **habitat destruction,** the loss of a natural habitat. Breaking larger habitats into smaller, isolated pieces is called **habitat fragmentation.** The illegal killing or removal of wildlife from their habitats is called **poaching.**

Three methods of protecting biodiversity are captive breeding, laws and treaties, and habitat preservation. **Captive breeding** is the mating of animals in zoos or wildlife preserves.

On a separate sheet of paper, explain the value of biodiversity and tell how humans can positively or negatively affect it.

Review and Reinforce

Biodiversity

Understanding Main Ideas

Answer the following questions in the spaces provided. Use a separate sheet of paper if you need more room.

1. What three factors affect the biodiversity of an ecosystem?

   _____

   _____

2. What is one reason coral reefs are such diverse ecosystems?

   _____

   _____

3. How does having a diverse gene pool help a species survive?

   _____

   _____

4. Name and describe three ways to protect the world's biodiversity.

   _____

   _____

Building Vocabulary

Write a definition for each of these terms on a separate sheet of paper.

5. keystone species

6. extinction

7. endangered species

8. habitat fragmentation

9. poaching

10. captive breeding

Enrich

Biodiversity

The table below lists the number of endangered species in the United States and worldwide in 2000. Study the data in the table. Then use a separate sheet of paper to answer the questions that follow the table.

Endangered Species

Category	United States	World
Mammals	53	301
Birds	74	227
Reptiles	16	74
Amphibians	6	14
Fishes	53	64
Snails	3	4
Clams	37	39
Crustaceans	8	8
Insects	11	12
Arachnids	3	3
Plants	179	180

1. Which category had the highest number of endangered species in 2000?

2. Which category of animals had the highest number of endangered species in the United States? Which had the highest number worldwide?

3. In which categories did the United States have all the endangered species?

4. How many endangered animal species were there in the United States in 2000? How many endangered animal species were there worldwide?

Lesson Quiz

Biodiversity

If the statement is true, write *true*. If the statement is false, change the underlined word or words to make the statement true.

1. _____ The major cause of extinction is <u>habitat fragmentation</u>.

2. _____ Species that could become endangered in the near future are called <u>extinct species</u>.

3. _____ The <u>Threatened Species Act</u> prohibits trade or products made from threatened or endangered species.

4. _____ Protecting <u>whole ecosystems</u> is the most effective way to preserve biodiversity.

Fill in the blank to complete each statement.

5. Biodiversity has both _____ and ecological value within an ecosystem.

6. The sea otter is a(n) _____ that influences the survival of many other species in its ecosystem.

7. Climate, area, and _____ affect biodiversity in an ecosystem.

8. _____ are the most diverse ecosystems in the world.

9. _____ are the second most diverse ecosystems in the world.

10. Scientists think people have directly caused the extinction of some species through habitat destruction, _____, or other actions.

Biodiversity

Answer Key

After the Inquiry Warm-Up

1. Sample: The tropics receive a greater amount of sunlight (being nearer to the equator) and are usually wetter and warmer on average than other climates. These factors help support a greater variety of plant and animal life all year around unlike yearly seasonal climate changes in other parts of the world further from the equator (i.e., Northern Hemisphere summers versus winters).

2. Approximately 2 times as many types of trees.

3. Sample: Since polar regions receive less sunlight than a tropical rain forest or a deciduous forest, I believe there should be less biodiversity near the Earth's poles.

4. Sample: A decrease in biodiversity of an area narrows the variety of organisms that the area can support, making the ecosystem more vulnerable to collapse, and in extreme cases, the extinctions of species.

Key Concept Summaries

Sample: Biodiversity has ecological and economic value. Humans can positively affect biodiversity through habitat preservation, treaties and laws, and captive breeding. Humans can negatively affect biodiversity through poaching, habitat fragmentation, and habitat destruction.

Review and Reinforce

1. area, climate, and niche diversity

2. Coral reefs provide many different niches for organisms, so more species can live there than in a more uniform ecosystem.

3. A species with a diverse gene pool is better able to adapt and survive changes in the environment.

4. Sample: Habitat preservation, setting aside entire ecosystems, can protects biodiversity

against the threat of habitat destruction. Captive breeding can protect biodiversity. It involves breeding and raising animals in zoos or wildlife preserves and then releasing the young animals into the wild. Laws and treaties can protect threatened and endangered species by, for example, forbidding people from trading them for profit.

5. a species that influences the survival of many other species in an ecosystem

6. the disappearance of all members of a species from Earth

7. species in danger of becoming extinct in the near future

8. breaking larger habitats into smaller, isolated pieces

9. the illegal killing or removal of wildlife from their habitats

10. the mating of animals in zoos or wildlife preserves for release into the wild

Enrich

1. plants

2. birds; mammals

3. crustaceans and arachnids

4. 264, 746

Lesson Quiz

1. habitat destruction
2. threatened species
3. Endangered Species Act
4. true
5. economic
6. keystone species
7. diversity of niches
8. Tropical rain forests
9. Coral reefs
10. hunting

Study Guide

Review the Big Q ? UbD

Have students complete the statement at the top of the page. These Key Concepts support their understanding of the chapter's Big Question. Have students return to the chapter opener question. What is different about how students view the image of the owl and the mouse now that they have completed the chapter? Thinking about this will help them prepare for the *Apply the Big Q* activity in the Review and Assessment.

Partner Review

Have partners review definitions of vocabulary terms by using the Study Guide to quiz each other. Students could read the Key Concept statements and leave out words for their partner to fill in, or change a statement so that it is false and then ask their partner to correct it.

Class Activity: Poster

Have students work in groups to create an illustrated, labeled poster that shows the six major biomes, the two major types of aquatic ecosystems, four cycles of matter, biodiversity, and energy flow through ecosystems. Encourage students to integrate these subjects in the poster as much as possible. For example, the water cycle could be shown as part of the illustration for a biome such as deciduous forest or grassland or rain forest. Students should include an explanation of how the lesson's title relates to the Big Idea, as
well as key terms and concepts. Urge students to use the following questions to help them organize their ideas:

- What are the energy roles in an ecosystem?
- How does energy move through an ecosystem?
- What processes are involved in the water cycle?
- How are the carbon and oxygen cycles related?
- How does nitrogen cycle through ecosystems?
- What are the six major biomes?
- What are the two major aquatic ecosystems?
- What is biodiversity's value?
- What factors affect biodiversity?
- How do humans affect biodiversity?

My Science Coach allows students to complete the *Practice Test* online.

The Big Question allows students to complete the *Apply the Big Q* activity about how energy and matter cycle through an ecosystem.

Vocab Flash Cards offer a way to review the chapter vocabulary words.

my science online.com `Ecosystems and Biomes`

---

16 Study Guide

Producers, <u>consumers</u>, and <u>decomposers</u> help to cycle energy through ecosystems.

LESSON 1 Energy Flow in Ecosystems

🔑 Each of the organisms in an ecosystem fills the energy role of producer, consumer, or decomposer.

🔑 Energy moves through an ecosystem when one organism eats another.

🔑 The most energy is available at the producer level of the pyramid. As energy moves up the pyramid, each level has less energy available than the level below.

Vocabulary
- producer • consumer • herbivore • carnivore
- omnivore • scavenger • decomposer • food chain • food web • energy pyramid

LESSON 2 Cycles of Matter

🔑 The processes of evaporation, condensation, and precipitation make up the water cycle.

🔑 The processes by which carbon and oxygen are recycled are linked. Producers, consumers, and decomposers play roles in recycling both.

🔑 Nitrogen moves from the air into the soil, into living things, and back into the air or soil.

Vocabulary
- evaporation • condensation
- precipitation • nitrogen fixation

LESSON 3 Biomes

🔑 The six major biomes are desert, rain forest, grassland, deciduous forest, boreal forest, and tundra.

Vocabulary
- biome • climate • desert • rain forest
- emergent layer • canopy • understory
- grassland • savanna • deciduous tree
- boreal forest • coniferous tree • tundra
- permafrost

LESSON 4 Aquatic Ecosystems

🔑 There are two types of aquatic, or water-based, ecosystems: freshwater ecosystems and marine (or saltwater) ecosystems.

Vocabulary
- estuary
- intertidal zone
- neritic zone

LESSON 5 Biodiversity

🔑 Biodiversity has both economic value and ecological value within an ecosystem.

🔑 Factors that affect biodiversity in an ecosystem include climate, area, niche diversity, genetic diversity, and extinction.

🔑 Biodiversity can be negatively or positively affected by the actions of humans.

Vocabulary
- biodiversity • keystone species • gene
- extinction • endangered species
- threatened species • habitat destruction • habitat fragmentation • poaching • captive breeding

---

E L L Support

4 Language Production

Divide the class into small groups with one student acting as recorder. Ask the Big Question and give students time to think about answers. Then have members of the groups share responses with one another, and have their responses written down by the recorder.

Beginning
LOW/HIGH Allow students to answer with single words or short phrases.

Intermediate
LOW/HIGH Have students draft sentences to answer the Big Question.

Advanced
LOW/HIGH Have students assist by acting as the recorder in each group.

Review and Assessment

LESSON 1 Energy Flow in Ecosystems

1. A diagram that shows how much energy is available at each feeding level in an ecosystem is a(n)

  a. food web.   **b.** food chain.

  c. water cycle.   **(d.)** energy pyramid.

2. A(n) <u>herbivore</u> is a consumer that eats only plants.

3. Interpret Diagrams Which organisms in the illustration are producers? Consumers?

<u>Producers: the</u>
<u>plants;</u>
<u>consumers: the</u>
<u>fish and snails</u>

4. Compare and Contrast How are food chains and food webs different?

<u>A food chain shows only one</u>
<u>possible path of energy flow,</u>
<u>while a food web shows many</u>
<u>food chains.</u>

5. **Write About It** Think about your own food web. Name the producers and consumers that make up your diet.

<u>Sample: The main producers in</u>
<u>my diet are wheat, rice, broccoli,</u>
<u>tomatoes, corn, and squash.</u>
<u>Chickens, cows, and fish are</u>
<u>consumers in my diet.</u>
<u>See TE rubric.</u>

LESSON 2 Cycles of Matter

6. When drops of water in a cloud become heavy enough, they fall to Earth as

  a. permafrost.   **b.** evaporation.

  (c.) precipitation.   **d.** condensation.

7. Evaporation, condensation, and precipitation are the three main processes in the

<u>water cycle.</u>

8. Infer Which process is responsible for the droplets visible on the glass below? Explain.

<u>Condensation;</u>
<u>water vapor</u>
<u>in the air</u>
<u>condenses on</u>
<u>the glass.</u>

9. Classify Which group of organisms is the source of oxygen in the oxygen cycle? Explain.

<u>Producers; they release oxygen</u>
<u>as a result of photosynthesis.</u>

10. Make Generalizations Describe the roles of producers and consumers in the carbon cycle.

<u>Producers use carbon dioxide</u>
<u>to produce food (carbon</u>
<u>compounds) via photosynthe-</u>
<u>sis. Consumers break down</u>
<u>food and release carbon dioxide</u>
<u>as a waste product.</u>

11. Draw Conclusions What would happen if all the nitrogen-fixing bacteria disappeared?

<u>Free nitrogen from the air would</u>
<u>not be changed into a form</u>
<u>that other organisms could use</u>
<u>and organisms would die.</u>

671

Review and Assessment

Assess Understanding

Have students complete the answers to the Review and Assessment questions. Have a class discussion about what students find confusing. Write Key Concepts on the board to reinforce knowledge.

RTI Response to Intervention

3. If students have trouble identifying producers and consumers, **then** remind students that the words' non-scientific meanings provide clues about the role of each type of organism: a producer "makes" and "assembles" while a consumer "eats" or "devours."

11. If students cannot explain the importance of nitrogen-fixing bacteria, **then** review with them the nitrogen cycle as shown in **Figure 4** in the lesson.

Alternate Assessment

L1 **DESIGN A SCREEN SAVER** Have students design and produce a series of images—illustrations, diagrams, or other graphic devices—to appear as a screen-saver loop on an idle computer display. Each image should convey key ideas and terms having to do with energy flow, cycles of matter, biomes, and aquatic ecosystems. Challenge students to create each image so that its information can be absorbed in 15 or 20 seconds, before it is replaced by another image.

Write About It Assess student's writing using this rubric.

SCORING RUBRIC	SCORE 4	SCORE 3	SCORE 2	SCORE 1
Identify producers and consumers in diet	Names producers and consumers accurately	Names some producers and some consumers accurately	Inaccurately names producers and consumers	Does not name producers and consumers
Relate personal diet to food web	Recognizes place in food web and applies this knowledge with clarity and detail	Recognizes place in food web, but omits details about the web	Struggles to recognize place in food web and applies knowledge in general way	Does not recognize place in food web

Review and Assessment, Cont.

RTI Response to Intervention

13. If students cannot explain what a biome is, **then** have them scan the text in Lesson 3 for the highlighted term and review the definition.

16. If students have trouble identifying the neritic zone, **then** review with them the information on the table in **Figure 2**.

19. If students cannot explain what extinction means, **then** have them look for the highlighted term and review the definition.

Apply the Big Q ? UbD

TRANSFER Students should be able to demonstrate understanding of how energy and matter move through ecosystems by answering this question. See the scoring rubric below.

Connect to the Big Idea ? UbD

BIG IDEA Living things interact with their environment.

Send students back to the Big Ideas of Science at the beginning of their student edition. Have them read what they wrote about interactions of living things and their environment before they started the chapter. Lead a class discussion about how their thoughts have changed. If all chapters have been completed, have students fill in the bottom section for the Big Idea.

L3 WRITING IN SCIENCE Ask students to write a voice-over narration for a science video explaining how the cycles that occur in ecosystems show how living things interact on Earth.

CHAPTER
16 Review and Assessment

LESSON 3 Biomes

12. Little precipitation and extreme temperatures are main characteristics of which biome?

(a.) desert   **b.** grassland

c. boreal forest   **d.** deciduous forest

13. A _biome_ is a group of ecosystems with similar climates and organisms.

14. Compare and Contrast How are the tundra and desert similar? How are they different?

Sample: Both biomes have similar rainfall amounts. They have different latitudes, with the tundra much farther north. The desert is much hotter than the tundra.

LESSON 4 Aquatic Ecosystems

15. In which ocean zone would you find barnacles, sea stars, and other organisms tightly attached to rocks?

a. neritic zone   (b.) intertidal zone

c. estuary ecosystem   **d.** freshwater ecosystem

16. Coral reefs are found in the shallow, sunny waters of the _neritic zone._

17. Compare and Contrast How are a pond and lake similar? How do they differ?

Ponds and lakes are both freshwater ecosystems. In both cases, floating algae are major producers. Ponds are smaller and shallower than lakes, so sunlight may reach the bottom.

672 Ecosystems and Biomes

LESSON 5 Biodiversity

18. The most effective way to preserve biodiversity is through

a. captive breeding

b. habitat destruction

(c.) habitat preservation

d. habitat fragmentation

19. _Extinction_ occurs when all members of a species disappear from Earth.

20. Predict How could the extinction of a species today affect your life in 20 years?

Sample: It could affect the larger ecosystem and other species. Those species might have been used for medicines or other products.

APPLY ? How do energy and matter cycle through ecosystems?

21. Many acres of the Amazon rain forest have been destroyed to create farmland. Describe how the amount of energy in the food web for this area might be affected. How might the carbon and oxygen cycle also be affected?

Sample: If the vegetation is destroyed, then there will be fewer producers. Without producers to capture and use energy, there will be less energy in the food web for the consumers. Fewer producers means there will be fewer organisms to absorb carbon dioxide and release oxygen into the environment. See TE rubric.

? How do energy and matter cycle through ecosystems?
Assess student's response using this rubric.

SCORING RUBRIC	SCORE 4	SCORE 3	SCORE 2	SCORE 1
Describe how energy might be affected	Describes specific effects on producers and consumers	Describes effects but doesn't name energy roles	Describes effects with inaccuracies about energy	Does not describe effects on food web
Describe how carbon and oxygen cycle might be affected	Describes specific effects on carbon and oxygen cycling	Describes effects without details to carbon and oxygen cycles	Describes effects with inaccuracies on carbon and oxygen cycles	Does not describe effects on carbon and oxygen cycles

Standardized Test Prep

Multiple Choice

Circle the letter of the best answer.

1. At which level of this energy pyramid is the *least* energy available?

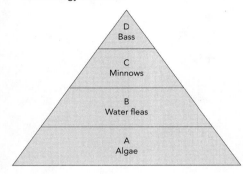

D
Bass

C
Minnows

B
Water fleas

A
Algae

A Level A   B Level B
C Level C   Ⓓ Level D

2. You are in an area in Maryland where the fresh water of the Chesapeake Bay meets the Atlantic Ocean. Which of the following terms describes where you are?

A tundra   Ⓑ estuary
C neritic zone   D intertidal zone

3. Which pair of terms could apply to the same organism?

A carnivore and producer
Ⓑ consumer and carnivore
C scavenger and herbivore
D producer and omnivore

4. Which of the following terms describes a species that is in danger of becoming extinct in the near future?

A captive species
B keystone species
Ⓒ endangered species
D threatened species

5. Which of the following human activities has a positive impact on Earth's ecosystems?

A habitat fragmentation
B urban growth
Ⓒ soil monitoring
D landfill development

Constructed Response

Use the diagram below and your knowledge of science to help you answer Question 6. Write your answer on a separate piece of paper.

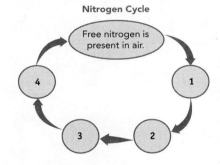

Nitrogen Cycle

Free nitrogen is present in air.

4

1

3

2

6. Describe each numbered part of the cycle shown in the diagram above.
See TE note.

Standardized Test Prep

Test-Taking Skills

INTERPRETING DIAGRAMS Tell students that when they answer questions such as Question 1, which include diagrams, they should read all of the text in the diagram carefully. Students should make sure that they understand the meaning of shapes, and all other visual elements of the diagram. One way to approach the answer is to eliminate those answer choices that are not supported by the diagram.

Constructed Response

6. 1) Bacteria fix nitrogen in the soil; 2) Nitrogen moves from soil to producers; 3) Consumers get nitrogen from producers; 4) Decomposers return nitrogen to soil.

Additional Assessment Resources

Chapter Test
EXAMVIEW® Assessment Suite
Performance Assessment
Progress Monitoring Assessments
SuccessTracker™

CHAPTER 16

ELL Support

5 Assess Understanding
Have ELLs complete the Alternative Assessment. Provide guidelines on the information that it must cover, and a rubric for assessment.

Beginning
LOW/HIGH Allow students to create screen savers with visuals and images only.

Intermediate
LOW/HIGH Have students incorporate vocabulary terms in their screen savers.

Advanced
LOW/HIGH Have students use more extended language to explain any diagrams they use in their screen savers.

Remediate If students have trouble with...

QUESTION	SEE LESSON	STANDARDS
1	1	
2	4, 5	
3	1	
4	5	
5	5	
6	2	

Science Matters

Everyday Science

Have students read *A Lake Can't Last Forever.* Explain that *eutrophication* comes from the Greek *eutrophos* and means "well nourished." Eutrophication is a normal part of the flow of energy and matter through a freshwater ecosystem. Ask: **Under normal circumstances, how does organic matter enter a lake and get broken down into nutrients?** *(Sample: Leaves, branches, and plants fall into the water; aquatic plants and animals die. Bacteria decompose the plant and animal matter, releasing nutrients into the water that are then used by producers, such as algae, to make food.)*

An increase in the level of organic matter entering an ecosystem, which is usually the result of human activity, can cause serious imbalances. Ask: **How is eutrophication affected by human activities?** *(Sample: Pollution increases the amount of nutrients in the water.)* **How does the increased level of nutrients contribute to the death of a lake?** *(Sample: As bacteria decompose more dead matter, algae blooms can form since there are more nutrients in the water. This clouds the water and reduces sunlight entering the water, resulting in the death of more plant and animal life. Gradually, the lake will fill in and become a forest over time.)*

A Lake Can't Last forever

Much like living things, lakes change over time and even have life spans. Scientists call this change "lake succession". One way this occurs is through eutrophication.

Eutrophication refers to the addition of nutrients to bodies of water. It occurs naturally, but human activity can speed up the process. Nutrients—especially phosphorus and nitrogen—are necessary for algae and plants to grow in lakes. However, too many nutrients, such as those from fertilizers and sewage, can lead to excessive algae growth or "blooms."

These blooms often kill plant and animal life by upsetting the oxygen and carbon dioxide cycles. Decomposers, such as bacteria, feed off the algae, using up dissolved oxygen in the water in the process. This limits the amount and kinds of aquatic life that can live there.

Over many years, a lake becomes shallower when it fills with dying plant and animal matter. Material also builds up from outside the lake. The lake becomes a marsh that, over time, turns into dry land.

Research It With your classmates, analyze a body of water to determine its ability to support life. To study biotic factors, obtain and identify samples of organisms. Find information about how to count the kinds and numbers of invertebrates to judge pollution levels. Then look at abiotic factors. Use thermometers, probeware, and water chemistry kits to determine temperature, dissolved oxygen, and pH levels. Research information about how these factors affect the survival of organisms. Compile findings in a table and graph data. Pass records on to future classes to interpret and predict changes over time.

Quick Facts

The Arbor Day Foundation runs a program called Tree City USA®. This program encourages, supports, and recognizes community forestry programs. Any city, town, or community can become a Tree City as long as it has a Tree Board or Department, a Tree Care Ordinance, a Community Forestry Program, and an Arbor Day Observance and Proclamation. Over 3,000 communities participate in the Tree City USA program and some receive money from the government for developing their forestry programs. Have students do an Internet search to determine whether your community is a Tree City. If so, find out how you and your students can help out. If not, research what is needed for your community to become a Tree City.

Trees: Environmental Factories

Some of the most important members of your community don't volunteer. They consume huge amounts of water and they make a mess. Despite these drawbacks, these long-standing community members do their share. Who are these individuals? They're trees!

Keeping it clean: Trees remove pollutants from the air. Some researchers have calculated the value of the environmental cleaning services that trees provide. One study valued the air-cleaning service that trees in the Chicago area provide at more than $9 million every year.

Keeping it cool: Trees provide shade and lower air temperature by the process of transpiration. Pollutants, like ozone and smog, form more easily when air temperatures are high, so by keeping the air cool, trees also keep it clean.

Acting locally and globally: Trees help fight global environmental problems such as climate change. Trees remove carbon dioxide from the air and store the carbon as they grow. Experts estimate that urban trees in the United States remove more than 700 million tons of carbon from the air every year.

Helping the local economy: Trees are also good for business. One study found that shoppers spend more money in urban areas where trees are planted than they do in similar areas that don't have trees!

Research It Examine a topographical map of the area where you live. Compare it to an aerial photograph from a library or local archive. Identify areas with a lot of trees, and areas that you think could benefit from more trees. Create a proposal to plant trees in one of the areas you identified. What kinds of trees will you plant? What do those trees need in order to grow well?

Schools, clubs, and civic groups all over the United States volunteer to plant trees in their communities. ▶

Science and Society

Have students read *Trees: Environmental Factories*. Point out that trees provide many benefits to a community. The benefits shown are mostly from trees in urban areas. In the suburbs, trees are often planted at the edges of property. Along streets, this can create a beautiful shady path for drivers. In backyards, trees can provide privacy and mark the border between neighboring properties. They can also provide fun places for a parent to hang a swing for their child to play on.

In rural communities, trees can provide an economic benefit. Many fruits grow on trees. Farmers harvest these fruits and sell them at local farmer's markets. In wooded areas, trees provide habitats for animals. Wooded areas are also nice places for a fun day of exercise or hiking. Have students volunteer ways they think the trees in their community benefit them.

If possible, have students compare a current or recent aerial photograph to an older photograph. Ask them what they notice about the change in the number of trees and suggest possible reasons for that change.

Ask: Why might a community choose to plant trees near a factory or a heavily traveled highway? *(Sample: Factories and cars that travel on highways create a lot of pollution and trees help eliminate pollution from the air.)* **Why would a community choose to plant trees in a local park?** *(Sample: Trees provide shade, providing a cool place for people to relax on a sunny day.)*

675

this is your book

you can write in it

676

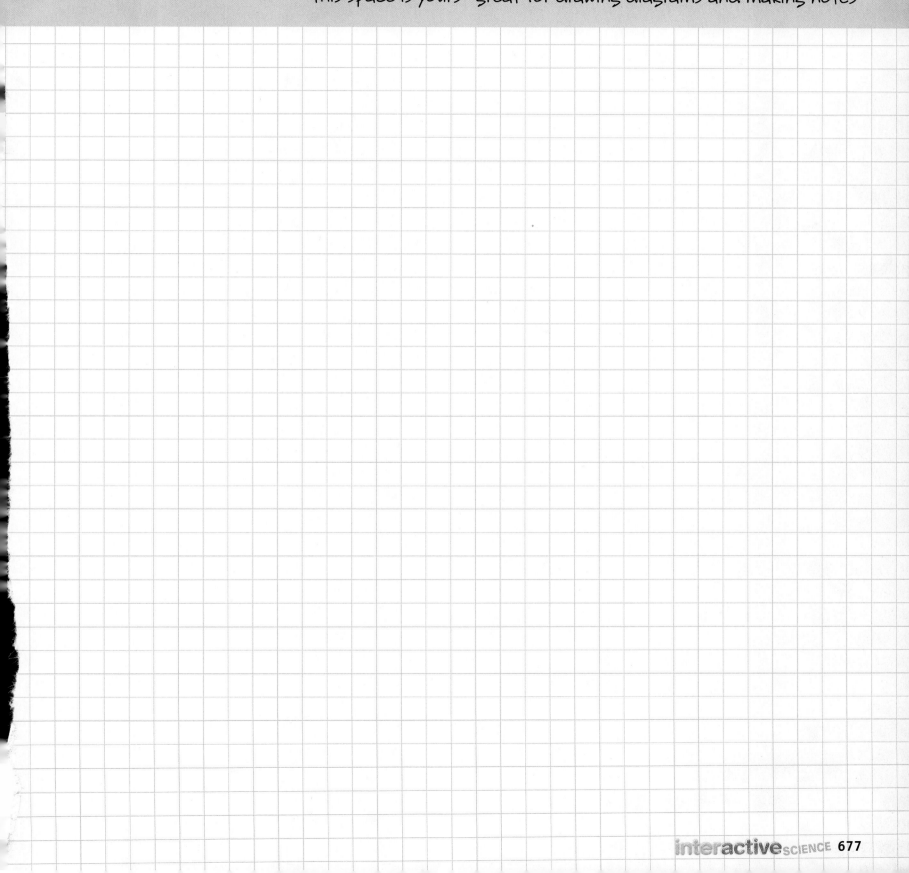

this is your book

you can write in it